# SLASH-AND-BURN AGRICULTURE

# Slash-and-Burn Agriculture

## THE SEARCH FOR ALTERNATIVES

*Edited by Cheryl A. Palm, Stephen A. Vosti,*
*Pedro A. Sanchez, and Polly J. Ericksen*

*A Collaborative Publication by the Alternatives to Slash and Burn Consortium,*
*the World Agroforestry Centre, The Earth Institute at Columbia University,*
*and the University of California, Davis*

COLUMBIA UNIVERSITY PRESS    NEW YORK

Columbia University Press

Publishers Since 1893

New York    Chichester, West Sussex

Copyright © 2005 Columbia University Press

Part opening art: Part 1, Yurimaguas, Peru. (Photo by Pedro Sanchez.) Part 2, Nkolbisson, Cameroon. (Photo by Pedro Sanchez.) Part 3, Krui Sumatra, Indonesia. (Photo by Pedro Sanchez.) Part 4, Manaus, Brazil. (Photo by Erick Fernandes.) Part 5, New slash-and-burn field in Pedro Peixoto, Acre, Brazil. (Photo by Pedro Sanchez.)

Library of Congress Cataloging-in-Publication Data

   Slash-and-burn agriculture : the search for alternatives / edited by Cheryl A. Palm ... [et al.].
      p. cm.
   A collaborative publication by the Alternatives to Slash and Burn consortium, and others.
   Includes bibliographical references (p.    ) and index.
   ISBN 0–231–13450–9 (cloth : alk. paper) — ISBN 0–231–13451–7 (pbk. : alk. paper)
   1. Alternatives to Slash-and-Burn (Programme)—Congresses. 2. Shifting cultivation—Tropics—Congresses. 3. Shifting cultivation—Environmental aspects—Tropics—Congresses. 4. Deforestation—Control—Tropics—Congresses. I. Palm, C. A. (Cheryl Ann) II. Alternatives to Slash-and-Burn (Programme)
S602.87.S63 2005

631.5′818—dc22

# Contents

# Foreword

This remarkable volume addresses the sustainable management of tropical forests with unstinting sophistication, moving the analysis beyond clichés to the true complexities of the challenge. The world's tropical forests, in Latin America, Africa, and Asia, are being cut down, at enormous costs to local and global biodiversity and ecosystem services. The carbon released by tropical deforestation is a significant factor in the overall increase in atmospheric greenhouse gases. Yet the "best bets" to deal with the challenge of tropical deforestation remain far from obvious. The studies collected here offer new conceptual tools and a rich compendium of empirical analyses that will be needed to formulate a set of viable responses to this major global challenge.

The traditional interpretation of tropical deforestation has usually proceeded in something like the following way. A rising population of smallholder farmers at the forest margin—the boundary between farm and forest—leads to deforestation as forests are cut to make room for new farms. At the same time, existing farmland is abandoned because of land degradation, soil erosion, and soil nutrient depletion. The loss of existing farmland is exacerbated by the pressure of shortened fallows, caused by the rise of population densities. In this traditional view, the best way to slow or stop deforestation would be to raise productivity on existing farms in a sustainable manner—for example, through the systematic replenishment of soil nutrients, so that pressures to expand into new lands can be eased.

There are of course important aspects of truth in this conventional view, but as the studies in this volume make clear, the situation is far more complex. Natural population growth on the forest margin is not the only, or even the key, driver of deforestation. Population growth often results from in-migration of settlers, rather than from the natural population increase among existing residents. Ironically, in such circumstances, intensification of agricultural techniques, even in a sustainable manner, can increase rather than decrease the rate of deforestation, by raising the profitability of farming and thereby inducing the in-migration of settlers to the forest margin. There may be a strong case for improving the productivity of agricultural practices, but that step alone may not solve the problem of deforestation.

Moreover, population increases of smallholders, whether by natural population increase or by in-migration, are just part of the overall story. Land clearing results not only from the expansion of land for crop production, but also from cattle ranching, commercial logging, and other extractive activities. Since deforestation for such purposes is often highly profitable for private actors, even if it is socially costly (e.g., due to the loss of biodiversity, or the increase of carbon emissions), deforestation will not be stopped merely through the introduction of sustainable agronomic practices. Policies will be needed that explicitly aim to tilt the incentives toward forest conservation. It may be advisable, for example, to compensate landowners for the conservation of nonmarketed ecosystem services such as conserved habitats and sequestered carbon.

Some economists stop at that point, saying that all that is needed is to "get the prices right," by putting market prices on ecosystem services. This book explains why that insight, valuable as it might be, only touches the surface of the practical issues. Lurking beneath the idea of setting prices for ecosystem services are measurement and conceptual problems of enormous scientific complexity. Identifying and valuing nonmarket ecosystem services require the very best of ecological, soil, and farming sciences, indeed just what the essays in this volume provide.

How much carbon, for example, is actually sequestered by various land use systems? How does the soil carbon change over time under particular agronomic practices, and how can the soil carbon best be measured and monitored? How can we measure "biodiversity" and "habitat" in a practical manner, in order to promote the conservation of biodiversity in a managed ecosystem? What indicators should be used reliably to link observed land use patterns to economic incentives such as payments for carbon or habitat preservation?

The ASB studies in this volume offer a uniquely informed and up-to-date treatment of these challenging issues, and many more issues as well. The essays combine rigorous science, new conceptual and empirical tools, and thoughtful policy analysis. Moreover, the studies describe these issues in a remarkable range of settings, in all three affected continents and for a wide variety of land use systems. The introduction and concluding essays are masterful in setting out the issues, as well as identifying the practical and policy uncertainties not yet solved by the ASB project. In short, this book is a landmark on the path to sustainable development.

*Jeffrey D. Sachs*
*Jeffrey D. Sachs is Director of the Earth Institute at Columbia University and Special Advisor to U.N. Secretary General Kofi Annan.*

# Preface

At the start of the twenty-first century an area of humid tropical forest about the size of Nicaragua, New York State, or Greece (130,000 km²) is destroyed every year. Tropical deforestation remains a major worldwide concern because it threatens the high plant and animal biodiversity these forests contain, the large carbon stocks stored in them, and the many ecosystem services they provide. Small-scale farmers practicing slash-and-burn agriculture clear forests to produce food and make a living for their families. To escape poverty, these families often have few options other than to continue clearing tropical forests. Striking an equitable balance between the legitimate interests of these rural households and the equally legitimate global concerns over the environmental consequences of tropical deforestation is one of the major challenges of the coming decades.

The Alternatives to Slash and Burn (ASB) consortium was established in 1992 by a group of concerned national and international research institutions and nongovernment organizations in response to recommendations in the Rio Earth Summit's Agenda 21 to halt destructive forms of shifting cultivation by addressing the underlying social and ecological causes and to reduce damage to forests by promoting sustainable management at the forest margins. At that time, there was much understanding of how slash-and-burn agriculture was performed, but knowledge of its global environmental consequences was sketchy, and what was known about the socioeconomic factors driving slash-and-burn agriculture was not particularly useful to policymakers seeking to reduce deforestation and improve human welfare. Moreover, there were few cross-country studies and almost no cross-disciplinary research efforts involving agricultural scientists, environmental scientists, and social scientists to draw on for scientific or policy guidance.

The ASB consortium—eventually comprising more than forty organizations spread across the humid tropical belt—met this challenge by identifying more sustainable land use practices and enabling policies that help conserve environmental functions of the tropical forest margins while increasing household income and food security for millions of poor people. After initial support from the Global Environment Facility, ASB became a systemwide program of the Consultative Group on International Agricultural Research in 1994 and has since been supported by its members and by the participating national research institutions in Brazil, Cameroon, Indonesia, Peru, Philippines, and Thailand. The ASB consortium changed the way scientists and policymakers work together to tackle major global challenges.

This book is a synthesis of the first decade of ASB's work, written by a team of seventy-nine soil scientists, economists, ecologists, anthropologists, and foresters encompassing twenty-six nationalities. Forty-one of them are national scientists affiliated with government research institutes, universities, and nongovernment organizations of eight tropical countries, and twenty-six others are affiliated with international agricultural research centers. This synthesis is organized in five sections. The first chapter introduces slash-and-burn activities and the overall research framework used by ASB, including its tradeoff matrix. The second section focuses on the different environmental, agronomic, and socioeconomic dimensions of deforestation and tropical agriculture, including chapters on carbon dynamics, greenhouse gas emissions, above-ground and below-ground biodiversity, agronomic sustainability, and the effects of macroeconomic policy on land and forest use. The third section focuses on specific best-bet alternatives to slash-and-burn, including community forest management, jungle rubber, shade coffee, and reclamation of degraded grasslands and pastures. The fourth section describes the perspectives of the main countries involved—Brazil, Indonesia, Cameroon, Peru, and Thailand—regarding the environmental, economic, and social importance of slash-and-burn agriculture at the local, regional, and national levels and the contribution of ASB to addressing key research and capacity-strengthening issues. The final section compares the different sites and assesses the tradeoffs between the environmental, agronomic, and economic costs and benefits of alternative uses of forests and cleared land and identifies the roles of science and policy action in effecting known tradeoffs today and improving the terms of these tradeoffs in the future.

The editors held ASB leadership positions while working at the Tropical Soil Biology and Fertility Programme (Palm), the World Agroforestry Centre (Sanchez and Ericksen), and the International Food Policy Research Institute and the University of California, Davis (Vosti), in the past decade. All editors want to acknowledge the vision of Nyle Brady, who brought the idea to reality; the assistance of the ASB global coordination office at the World Agroforestry Centre in Nairobi, particularly Joyce Kasyoki for her hard work and institutional memory; the copyediting work of Sherri Mickelson; and the formatting by Rafael Flor. The editors also thank Anthony Juo of Texas A&M University for his review of the early versions of several chapters. We would also like to thank the Australian Centre for International Agricultural Research for funding that supported the production of this book and the symposium that launched the chapters for this book at the American Society of Agronomy meetings in Salt Lake City and the United States

Agency for International Development for funds that assisted in the editing of this book.

Cheryl A. Palm, Pedro A. Sanchez, Polly J. Ericksen
*The Earth Institute at Columbia University*

Stephen A. Vosti
*University of California, Davis*

January 2004

# Contributors

Julio Alegre    Senior Soil Scientist, World Agroforestry Centre–Peru; Centro Internacional de la Papa, Apartado 5969, Lima, Peru; e-mail: j.alegre@cgiar.org

Henrique J. B. de Araújo    Forest Engineer, Research Scientist at the Agroforestry Research Center of Acre; Caixa Postal 392, Rio Branco–AC, Brazil, CEP 6990080; e-mail: henrique@cpafac.embrapa.br

Manuel Arca    Research Director, INIA; Av. La Universidad s/no; La Molina, Lima 12, Apartado 2791, Peru; e-mail: marcab@fenix.inia.gob.pe

Luis Arévalo    Research Officer, World Agroforestry Centre–Peru; Km. 4.2 Carretera Federico Basadre, Pucallpa–Ucayali, Peru; e-mail: l.arevalo@cgiar.org

David E. Bignell    Professor of Zoology, School of Biological Science; Queen Mary, University of London, Mile End Road, London, UK, E1 4NS; e-mail: D.Bignell@qmul.ac.uk

Evaldo M. Bráz    Forest Engineer, Research Scientist at the National Forest Research Center-Embrapa Floresta, Curitiba–PR, Brazil; e-mail: evaldo@cnpf.embrapa.br

David F. R. P. Burslem    Senior Lecturer, University of Aberdeen, School of Biological Sciences; Cruickshank Building, St. Machar Drive, Aberdeen AB24 3UU, Scotland, UK; e-mail: d.burslem@abdn.ac.uk

Chantal L. Carpentier    Program Manager, Environment, Economy, and Trade, North American Commission for Environmental Cooperation; 393 St-Jacques O., Suite 200, Montreal, Quebec, Canada H2Y 2A7; e-mail: clcarpentier@ccemtl.org

Carlos E. Castilla    Soil and Water Management Program, CENIPALMA; Calle 21, no. 42C-47, Bogota, Colombia; e-mail: cecastilla@unipacifico.edu.co

Andrea Cattaneo    Economist, Resource Economics Division, Economic Research Service, USDA; 1800 M Street, NW, Washington, DC 20036; e-mail: cattaneo@ers.usda.gov

Simon Chater    Director, Green Ink Publishing Services Ltd.; Hawson Farm, Buckfastleigh, Devon, UK; e-mail: s.chater@cgnet.com

Divonzil G. Cordeiro    Soil Scientist, Embrapa–Acre; BR-364, KM 14, Caixa Postal 381, CEP: 69 908–970, Rio Branco, Acre, Brazil; e-mail: matell@mdnet.com.br

Chimere Diaw    Scientist, CIFOR, IITA Humid Forest Ecoregional Centre; B.P. 2008 (Messa), Yaoundé, Cameroon; e-mail: c.diaw@cgiar.org

Luc Dibog    Soil Macrobiologist (Termites), Institute of Agricultural Research for Development, IRAD; P.O. Box 2067, Yaoundé, Cameroon; e-mail: lucdibog@yahoo.com, luc.dibog@caramail.com

Polly J. Ericksen    Research Fellow, International Research Institute for Climate Prediction, The Earth Institute at Columbia University; 61 Route 9W, P.O. Box 1000, Palisades, NY 10960, USA; e-mail: ericksen@iri.columbia.edu, p.ericksen@cgiar.org

Achmad M. Fagi    ASB National Facilitator, Indonesian Center for Food Crops Research and Development (ICFORD); Jl. Merdeka No. 147, Bogor 16111, Indonesia; e-mail: crifc@indo.net.id

Helmut J. Geist    Executive Director, Land-Use & Cover Change Project, LUCC International Project Office (IPO); University of Louvain, 3 Place Louis Pasteur, B-1348 Louvain-la-Neuve, Belgium; e-mail: geist@geog.ucl.ac.be

Andrew N. Gillison    Director, Center for Biodiversity Management; P.O. Box 120, Yungaburra, Queensland 4872, Australia; e-mail: andy.gillison@austarnet.com.au

James Gockowski    Agricultural Economist, IITA–Humid Forest Station; B.P. 2008, Yaoundé, Cameroon; e-mail: j.gockowski@cgiar.org

Kurniatun Hairiah    Professor of Soil Biology and Root Ecology, Brawijaya University; Jl. Veteran, Malang 65145, Indonesia; e-mail: soilub@malang.wasantara.net.id

Stefan Hauser    Soil Physicist/Agronomist IITA Humid Forest Station; B.P. 2008, Yaoundé, Cameroon; e-mail: s.hauser@cgiar.org

Sinung Hendratno    Socioeconomic Researcher, Pusat Penelitian Karet Sembawa, Balai Penelitian Sembawa; Jl. Raya Palembang-Sekayu Km 29, Kotak Pos 1127, Palembang, Sumatra, Selatan 300031, Indonesia; e-mail: irri-sbw@mdp.co.id

Shiou Pin Huang    Professor, Departamento de Filopatalogia, Universidade de Brasilia; CEPP 7099–970, Brasilia, DF, Brazil; e-mail: huang@guarany.cpd.unb.br

Shigehiro Ishizuka    Senior Scientist, Forest and Forest Product Research Institute (FFPRI); 7 Hitsujigaoka, Toyohira-ku, Sapporo, Hokkaido 062-8516, Japan; e-mail: ishiz03@ffpri.affrc.go.jp

David Kaimowitz    Director General, Center for International Forestry Research (CIFOR), Jalan CIFOR; P.O. Box 6596, JKPWB, Jakarta 10065, Indonesia

Joyce Kasyoki    Programme Administrator, ASB; World Agroforestry Centre, UN Avenue, Gigiri, P.O. Box 30677, 00100 GPO, Nairobi, Kenya; e-mail: j.kasyoki@cgiar.org

Jean Kotto-Same    Soil Scientist, Institut de la Recherche Agricole pour le Développement (IRAD); B.P. 2067, Yaoundé, Cameroon; e-mail: jkottosame@yahoo.fr

Ricardo Labarta    Research Assistant Economist, World Agroforestry Centre–Peru; Km. 4.2 Carretera Federico Basadre, Pucallpa–Ucayali, Peru; e-mail: r.labarta@cgiar.org

Eric F. Lambin    Professor, Department of Geography, University of Louvain; 3 Place Pasteur, B-1348 Louvain-la-Neuve, Belgium; e-mail: lambin@geog.ucl.ac.be

Jessa Lewis    Consultant; 8268 Sugarman Drive, La Jolla, CA 92037, USA; e-mail: jessa.lewis@stanfordalumni.org

Fátima Moreira    Soil Microbiologist, Dep. de Ciencia do Solo, Universidade Federal de Lavras; CEP 37200–000, Lavras, Minas Gerais, Brazil; e-mail: fmoreira@esal.ufla.br

Appolinaire Moukam    Deceased; Soil Scientist, Institut de la Recherche Agricole pour le Développement, IRAD, Yaoundé, Cameroon

Daniel Murdiyarso    Professor, Department of Geophysics and Meteorology, Bogor Agricultural University; Jl. Raya Pajajaran, Bogor, 16143, Indonesia; e-mail: d.murdiyarso@icsea.org

Ousseynou Ndoye    Regional Coordinator; Center for International Forestry Research (CIFOR), Regional Office for Central and West Africa; c/o IITA-HFC, B.P. 2008, Yaoundé, Cameroon; e-mail: o.ndoye@cgiar.org

Rosaline Njomgang    Soil Chemist, Institut de la Recherche Agricole pour le
Développement (IRAD); B.P. 2067, Yaoundé, Cameroon; e-mail: j.tonye@camnet.cm

Dieudonné Nwaga    Soil Microbiologist, University of Yaoundé, Plant Biology Department;
P.O. Box 812, Yaoundé, Cameroon; e-mail: j.tonye@camnet.cm

Marcus V. N. d'Oliveira    Forestry Scientist, Embrapa Acre; BR-364 km 14, CEP 69.901–
180, Caixa Postal 321, Rio Branco, Acre, Brazil; e-mail: mvno@cpafac.embrapa.br

Cheryl A. Palm    Senior Research Scientist, The Earth Institute at Columbia University; 167
Monell, Lamont–Doherty Earth Observatory, 61 Route 9W, P.O. Box 1000, Palisades,
NY 10960, USA; e-mail: cpalm@iri.columbia.edu

Soetjipto Partohardjono    Principal Researcher, Indonesian Center for Food Crops Research
and Development (ICFORD); Jl. Merdeka No. 147, Bogor 16111, Indonesia; e-mail:
crifc@indo.net.id

William J. Parton    Senior Research Scientist, Natural Resource Ecology Laboratory,
Colorado State University; Fort Collins, CO 80523, USA; e-mail: billp@nrel.colostate.
edu

Djuber Pasaribu    Researcher, Indonesian Center for Food Crops Research and Development
(ICFORD); Jl. Merdeka 147, Bogor 16111, Indonesia; e-mail: crifc1@indo.net.id,
crifc3@indo.net.id

Beto Pashanasi    Lecturer, Universidad Nacional de la Amazonia Peruana, Yurimaguas, Peru;
e-mail: l.arevalo@cgiar.org

Eliane Guimarães Pereira    Environmental Engineer, Soil and Plant Nutrition, Universidade
Federal de Itajubá, Av. BPS, 1303, Pinheirinho, Itajubá, Minas Gerais, 37500-903,
Brazil; e-mail: elianegp@unifei.edu.br

Komon Pragtong    Division of Silvicultural Research and Botany, National Park, Wildlife
and Plant Conservation Department, Ministry of Natural Resources and Environment;
Paholyothin Rd., Jatujak, Bangkok, 10900, Thailand

Pornchai Preechapanya    Division of Watershed Conservation and Management, National
Park, Wildlife and Plant Conservation Department, Ministry of Natural Resources and
Environment Station; 130/1 M4 Don Keaw, Mae Rim, Chiang Mai 50180, Thailand;
e-mail: pcpc@loxinfo.co.th, pornchaiP@icraf-cm.org

Pratiknyo Purnomosidhi    Associate Research Officer, World Agroforestry Centre–
Kotabumi; P.O. Box 167, Kotabumi 34500, Lampung, Indonesia; e-mail:
icrafktb@lampung.wasantara.net.id

Subekti Rahayu    Data Technician, World Agroforestry Centre–Indonesia; Jl. Cifor, Situ
Gede, Sindang Barang, Bogor, Indonesia; e-mail: S.Rahayu@cgiar.org

Auberto Ricse    Forestry Scientist, INIA, Agrarian Systems for Mountains Programme; Km.
4 Carretera Federico Basadre, Pucallpa–Ucayali, Peru; e-mail: eepuc@terra.com.pe

Vanda Rodrigues    Soil Scientist, Embrapa–Rondônia; BR-364km, 5, 5, Caixa Postal 406,
CEP 78900, Porto Velho, Rondônia, Brazil; e-mail: vanda@ronet.com.br

Nu Nu San    Postdoctoral Researcher, University of West Virginia; 450 Medical Center Dr.,
Apt. B302, Morgantown, WV 26505, USA

Pedro A. Sanchez    Director of Tropical Agriculture, The Earth Institute at Columbia
University; 2G Lamont Hall, Lamont–Doherty Earth Observatory, 61 Route 9W, P.O.
Box 1000, Palisades, NY 10964, USA; e-mail: sanchez@iri.columbia.edu

Syukur M. Sitompul    Professor, Agronomy Department, Faculty of Agriculture, Brawijaya
University; Jl. Veteran Malang, Jawa Timur 65145, Indonesia; e-mail: smtom@malang.
wasantara.net.id

Carmen Sotelo-Montes    Forester, World Agroforestry Centre–Peru; Av. La Molina 1895, La Molina, Lima 12, Peru; e-mail: c.sotelo@cgiar.org

Fred Stolle    Lab de Télédetection, Université Catholique Louvain (UCL); Place Louis Pasteur 3, B 1348 Louvain-la-Neuve, Belgium; e-mail: stolle@geog.ucl.ac.be

William D. Sunderlin    Program Leader Forest, Society, and Policy Program, Center for International Forestry Research (CIFOR); Situ Gede, Sindangbarang, Bogor Barat 16680, Indonesia; e-mail: w.sunderli@cgiar.org

Plodprasop Suraswadi    Director General, Royal Forestry Department; 61 Paholythin Road, Chatujak, Bangkok 10900, Thailand; e-mail: chahut@forest.go.th

Francis-Xavier Susilo    Lecturer, Department of Plant Protection, Faculty of Agriculture, Universitas Lampung; Gedung Bioteknologi Pertanian, Lantai 2 Universitas Lampung, Jalan Sumantri Brojonegoro No. 1, Bandar Lampung, 35145, Indonesia; e-mail: fxsusilo@telkom.net fxsusilo2000@yahoo.com

Michael D. Swaine    Senior Lecturer, Department of Plant and Soil Science, Aberdeen University; Aberdeen AB24, United Kingdom; e-mail: m.swaine@abdn.ac.uk

Michael J. Swift    Consultant, IRD Centre de Montpellier; 911 Avenue Agropolis, B.P. 64501, 34394 Montpellier Cedex 5, France; e-mail: swift@mpl.ird.fr, swiftmj@yahoo.co.uk

David E. Thomas    Senior Policy Analyst, World Agroforestry Centre–Chiang Mai; P.O. Box 267 CMU Post Office, Chiang Mai 50202, Thailand; e-mail: Thomas2@loxinfo.co.th

Téophile Tiki-Manga    Agronomist, Institut de la Recherche Agricole pour le Développement (IRAD); B.P. 2067, Yaoundé, Cameroon; e-mail: j.tonye@camnet.cm

Thomas P. Tomich    Principal Economist and Global Coordinator ASB Programme; World Agroforestry Centre, UN Avenue, Gigiri, P.O. Box 30677, 00100 GPO, Nairobi, Kenya; e-mail: t.tomich@cgiar.org

Jerome Tondoh    Soil Microbiologist, Laboratoire d'Ecologie des Sols Tropicaux; 32 Avenue Varagnat, 93 143 Bondy Cedex, France; e-mail: yazi@bondy.orstom.fr

Jean Tonyé    ASB National Coordinator and Director, Farming Systems, IRAD; P.O. Box 2067, Yaoundé, Cameroon; e-mail: j.tonye@camnet.cm

Zac Tschondeau    Senior Scientist, World Agroforestry Centre, Cameroon; B.P. 2067, Yaoundé, Cameroon; e-mail: Z.Tchoundjeu@cgiar.org

Haruo Tsuruta    Senior Scientist, National Institute of Agro-Environmental Sciences (NIAES); 3-1-1 Kan-Nondai, Tsukuba, Ibaraki 305, Japan; e-mail: tsuruta@niaes.affrc.go.jp

Judson F. Valentim    Pasture Researcher, Embrapa–Acre; KM-14, BR-364, Caixa Postal 392, 69.801–180 Rio Branco–Acre, Brazil; e-mail: judson@cpafac.embrapa.br

Meine van Noordwijk    Regional Coordinator for Southeast Asia, World Agroforestry Centre, Indonesia; P.O. Box 161, Bogor 16001, Indonesia; e-mail: m.van-noordwijk@cgiar.org

Héctor Vidaurre    Forester, World Agroforestry Centre–Peru; Centro Internacional de la Papa, Apartado 5969, Lima, Peru

Stephen A. Vosti    Adjunct Assistant Professor, Department of Agricultural and Resource Economics; Center for Natural Resources Policy Analysis, University of California–Davis, Davis, CA 95616, USA; e-mail: vosti@primal.ucdavis.edu

John C. Weber    Senior Forest Geneticist, World Agroforestry Centre, Peru; 2224 NW 11th Street, Corvallis, OR 97330, USA; e-mail: JohnCRWeber@aol.com

Stephan Weise    Vegetation Management Team Leader and ASB Regional Coordinator, IITA Humid Forest Station; B.P. 2008, Yaoundé, Cameroon; e-mail: s.weise@cgiar.org

Horst Weyerhaeuser   Senior Natural Resource Management Researcher, World Agroforestry Centre/Chiang Mai; P.O. Box 267 CMU Post Office, Chiang Mai 50202, Thailand; e-mail: horst@loxinfo.co.th

Douglas White   Senior Research Fellow, Agricultural and Environmental Economist, Centro Internacional de Agricultura Tropical (CIAT), Centro Eco-Regional–INIA; A.P. 558, Pucallpa, Peru; e-mail: d.white@cgiar.org

Gede Wibawa   Head of Research Bureau, Research Institute for Estate Crops GAPKINDO; Jl. Salak 1, Bogor 16151, Indonesia; e-mail: G.Wibawa@cgiar.org

Julie Witcover   Graduate Student, University of California–Davis; 1429 H St. #1, Davis, CA 95616, USA; e-mail: witcover@primal.ucdavis.edu

Paul L. Woomer   Visiting Scientist, Sacred Africa; P.O. Box 79, Village Market, Nairobi, Kenya; e-mail: plwoomer@africaonline.co.ke, format@nbnct.co.kc, plwoomer@nbnet.co.ke

David Yanggen   Agricultural and Natural Resource Economist, Centro Internacional de la Papa; Apartado 1558, Lima 12, Peru; e-mail: d.yanggen@cgiar.org

Louis Zapfack   Botanist, Senior Lecturer, University of Yaoundé I, Faculty of Sciences, Department of Plant Biology; P.O. Box 812, Yaoundé, Cameroon; e-mail: lzapfack@uycdc.uninet.cm

# Acronyms and Abbreviations

| | |
|---|---|
| AARD | Agency for Agricultural Research and Development |
| AC | Acre State, Brazil |
| ACIAR | Australian Centre for International Agricultural Research |
| AGBD | above-ground biodiversity |
| AMF | arbuscular mycorrhizal fungi |
| AMR | mean annual mortality |
| ANOVA | analysis of variance |
| ANU | Australian National University |
| ASB | Alternatives to Slash and Burn Agriculture |
| ASC | active soil carbon |
| BAPPENAS | Badan Perencanaan Pembangunan Nasional |
| BASA | Banco da Amazônia S.A. |
| BC | benefit:cost ratios |
| BD | bulk density |
| BGBD | below-ground biodiversity |
| BPS | Biro Pusat Statistik |
| CABI | CAB International |
| CAP_PRD | improved productivity of capital |
| CATIE | Centro Agronómico Tropical de Investigación y Enseñanza |
| CBD | Convention on Biological Diversity |
| CDM | Clean Development Mechanism |
| CEB | Casa do Estudante do Brasil |
| CENFOR | Center for Forestry Research |
| CGE | computable general equilibrium |
| CGIAR | Consultative Group on International Agricultural Research |
| CIAT | Centro Internacional de Agricultura Tropical |
| CIFOR | Center for International Forestry Research |
| CIRAD | Centre de Cooperation Internationale en Recherche Agronomique pour le Développement |
| CMU | Chiang Mai University |
| CODESU | Consorcio para el Desarrollo Sostenible de Ucayali |
| CPAF | Centro de Pesquisa Agroflorestal |
| CPAF/AC | Centro de Pesquisa Agroflorestal do Acre |
| CPATU | Centro de Pesquisa Agroflorestal da Amazônia Oriental |

| | |
|---|---|
| CRFC | Center for Research on Food Crops |
| CSIRO | Commonwealth Scientific and Industrial Research Organization |
| DANIDA | Danish Agency for Development Assistance |
| DF | Distrito Federal |
| DGE | Directorate General of Estate |
| Ditjenbun | Direktorat Jenderal Perkebunan |
| EMATER | Empresa de Assistência Técnica e Extensão Rural |
| Embrapa | Empresa Brasileira de Pesquisa Agropecuária |
| EPTD | Environment and Production Technology Division |
| ESALQ | Escola Superior de Agricultura "Luiza de Queiroz" |
| FAEALQ | Fundação de Estudos Agrários Luiz de Aueiroz |
| FaleBEM | Farm Level Bioeconomic Model |
| FAO | Food and Agriculture Organization |
| FCCC | Framework Convention on Climate Change |
| fcFA | Central African franc |
| FFTC | Food and Fertilizer Technology Center |
| FGV | Fundação Getulio Vargas |
| FNMA | National Environmental Fund |
| FUNTAC | State Technological Foundation of Acre |
| GDP | gross domestic product |
| GEF | Global Environment Facility |
| GHG | greenhouse gas |
| GIS | geographic information system |
| GMS | Greater Mekong Subregion |
| GPS | global positioning system |
| GTCE | Global Change in Terrestrial Ecosystems |
| HDI | Human Development Index |
| HMSO | Her Majesty's Stationery Office |
| HTI | *hutan tanaman industri* (industrial timber estate) |
| IBAMA | Brazilian Institute for the Environment and Natural Resources |
| IBGE | Instituto Brasileiro de Geografia e Estatística |
| IBMA | Instituto Brasileiro do Meio Ambiente e dos Recursos Naturais Renováveis |
| IBSRAM | International Board for Soil Research and Management |
| ICFORD | Indonesian Center for Food Crops Research and Development |
| ICRAF | World Agroforestry Centre |
| IDB | InterAmerican Development Bank |
| IDESP | Instituto de Estudos Econômicos, Sociais e Políticos |
| IFAD | International Fund for Agricultural Development |
| IFDC | International Fertilizer Development Center |
| IFPRI | International Food Policy Research Institute |
| IGES | Institute for Global Environmental Strategies |
| IIAP | Institutio de Investigación de la Amazonía Peruana |
| IICA | Instituto Interamericano de Cooperación para la Agricultura |
| IIED | International Institute for Environment and Development |
| IITA | International Institute for Tropical Agriculture |

| | |
|---|---|
| IMAC | Instituto de Meio Ambiente do Acre |
| INCRA | Instituto Nacional de Colonização e Reforma Agrária |
| INEI | Instituto Nacional de Esatadística e Informática |
| INIA | Instituto Nacional de Investigación Agraria |
| INIFAP | Instituto Nacional de Investigación Agrícola, Pecuaria y Forestal |
| INPE | Instituto Nacional de Pesquisas Espaciais |
| INRM | integrated natural resource management |
| IPCC | Intergovernmental Panel on Climate Change |
| IPEA | Instituto de Pesquisa Econômica Aplicada |
| IRAD | Institut de Recherche Agricole pour le Développement |
| IRD | Institut de Recherche pour le Développement |
| IRR | internal rates of return |
| ITTO | International Tropical Timber Organization |
| IUCN | International Union for the Conservation of Nature and Natural Resources |
| IUFRO | International Union of Forest Research Organizations |
| JICA | Japanese International Cooperation Agency |
| JIRCAS | Japan International Research Center for Agricultural Sciences |
| KDTI | Dawasan Dengan Tijuana Istimewa (Zone with Distinct Purpose) |
| LAB_PRD | improved productivity of labor |
| LANDSAV | improvements in labor and capital productivity that increases the overall productivity of land |
| LF | long fallow |
| LN | natural logarithm |
| LP | linear programming |
| LUS | land use system |
| LUT | land use type |
| MAB | Man and the Biosphere |
| m a.s.l. | meters above sea level |
| MDS | multidimensional scaling |
| MMSEA | mountainous mainland Southeast Asia |
| MPN | most probable number per unit of soil volume |
| MPS | mean particle size |
| NDTR | nutrient depletion time range |
| NGO | nongovernment organization |
| NIES | National Institute for Environmental Studies |
| NNE | net nutrient export |
| NPV | net present value |
| NRC | National Research Council |
| NTFP | nontimber forest product |
| OM | soil organic matter content |
| PAM | Policy Analysis Matrix |
| PAR | photosynthetically active radiation |
| PC | colonization project |
| PCARRD | Philippine Council for Agriculture, Forestry, and Natural Resources Research |
| PESACRE | Grupo de Pesquisa e Extensão em Sistemas Agroflorestais do Acre |

| | |
|---|---|
| PFA | plant functional attribute |
| PFC | plant functional complexity |
| PFT | plant functional type |
| PLP | participatory land use planning |
| PPP | purchasing power parity |
| PROCITROPICOS | Programa Cooperativo de Investigación y Transferencia de Tecnología para los Trópicos Suramericanos |
| PROSEFOR | Proyecto de Semillas Forestales |
| PSP | permanent sample plot |
| QFRI | Queensland Forestry Research Institute |
| RAP | Rapid Assessment Program |
| RBA | rapid biodiversity assessment |
| RFD | Royal Forestry Department |
| RNRV | relative nutrient replacement value |
| RO | Rondônia |
| SAM | social accounting matrix |
| SAREC | Sciences d'Anticipation Reconnaissance Evaluation Contrôle |
| SC | shifting cultivation |
| SE | soil exposure |
| SECTMA | Secretaria de Ciência, Tecnologia e Meio Ambiente do Acre |
| SF | short fallow |
| SIF | Sociedade de Investigações Florestais |
| SIFRECA | Sistema de Informações de Fretes para Cargas Agrícolas |
| SOBER | Sociedade Brasileira de Economia Rural |
| SOM | soil organic matter |
| SPI | Servico de Produção de Informação |
| SUDAM | Superintendência de Desenvolvimento da Amazônia |
| SUFRAMA | Superintendência da Zona Franca de Manaus |
| TAC | Technical Advisory Committee |
| TDRI | Thailand Development Research Institute |
| TFP | total factor productivity |
| TSBF | Tropical Soil Biology and Fertility Programme |
| UCA | Universidad Centro Americana |
| UCA/SAREC | Universidad Centro Americana/Science d'Anticipation Reconnaissance Evaluation Contrôle |
| UEPAE | Unidade de Execução de Pesquisa de Âmbito Estadual |
| UNDP | United Nations Development Program |
| UNEP | United Nations Environment Programme |
| USAID | United States Agency for International Development |
| USDA-ARS | United States Department of Agriculture, Agricultural Research Service |
| USGS | United States Geological Survey |
| WFPS | water-filled pore space |
| WRI | World Resources Institute |
| WWF | World Wildlife Fund |
| ZEE | Zoneamento Ecológico Econômico |

# I. THE PROBLEM AND APPROACH

# 1   Alternatives to Slash and Burn

## CHALLENGE AND APPROACHES OF AN INTERNATIONAL CONSORTIUM

Pedro A. Sanchez and Cheryl A. Palm
> *The Earth Institute at Columbia University  New York, New York*

Stephen A. Vosti
> *University of California and Center of Natural Resource Policy Analysis  Davis, California*

Thomas P. Tomich and Joyce Kasyoki
> *World Agroforestry Centre  Nairobi, Kenya*

## THE CHALLENGE

The world has lost about half of its forests to agriculture and other uses, and 78 percent of what remains is heavily altered, bearing little resemblance to the original forests (Bryant et al. 1997). About 72 percent of the original 1450 million ha of tropical forests have been converted to other uses (Myers 1991; FAO 1997). Deforestation rates for the humid tropics were estimated to be 6.9 million ha/yr at the end of the 1970s (Lanly 1982) and doubled to 14.8 million ha/yr by 1991 (Myers 1993). More recent studies indicate that deforestation rates decreased by about 10 percent in the 1990s (Durst 2000). These values are fraught with methodological problems. Achard et al. (2002) asserted that previous methods overestimated tropical deforestation rates by as much as 25 percent. Brazil, the country with the largest area of tropical forests, reports that deforestation rates in the Brazilian Amazon increased by as much as 40 percent from 2001 to 2002 (INPE 2003). Despite these limitations, it is obvious that tropical deforestation and subsequent ecosystem degradation continue at alarming rates. They remain a major worldwide concern because of the high levels of plant and animal biodiversity these forests contain, the large carbon (C) stocks stored in them, and the many other ecosystem services tropical forests provide (Myers 1993; Laurance et al. 1997).

Small-scale farmers often are viewed as the primary agents of deforestation (Hauck 1974), accounting for as much as 96 percent of forest losses (Amelung and Diehl 1992). Myers (1994) reported that the aggregate actions of small-scale farmers resulted in greater deforestation than the activities of large-scale operations and accounted for about 70 percent of the deforestation in Africa, 50 percent in Asia, and 30 percent in Latin America. Although the predominant role played by small-scale farmers has come into question (Geist and Lambin 2002; chapter 18, this volume), they are often part of the deforestation process.

Small-scale farmers practicing slash-and-burn agriculture clear forests to produce food and make a living for their families. They often have few options other than to continue clearing tropical forests because of the benefits and profits derived from deforestation. In many cases, these farmers are marginalized from society and government support programs, and often they are migrants escaping from poverty and inequities elsewhere in the country. Any efforts to arrest deforestation must consider this group; in the absence of alternatives they will continue to clear forest to meet their needs for food and income.

Early approaches to conserve tropical forests were done at the exclusion of small-scale farmers that depend on the forest for their livelihoods (FAO Staff, 1957). These "fence off the forest" approaches often increased conflicts between conservation and development efforts and ignored the causes of deforestation. The importance of agricultural development for reducing poverty of the small-scale farmers and the economic development of developing countries is increasingly recognized. Therefore the development and promotion of agricultural systems that reduce poverty must be integrated with strategies to conserve tropical forests and the biodiversity and carbon they house (McNeely and Scherr 2003). The challenges are to identify alternative systems that meet farmers' needs and that can reduce pressure to clear more forest or minimize the impacts on biodiversity and other global environmental resources. The Alternatives to Slash and Burn (ASB) consortium was created to address this challenge.

This chapter introduces the ASB Program, an international consortium of researchers and extension groups that was established specifically to investigate the causes and consequences of deforestation by small-scale farmers and to identify land use systems that enhance both local livelihoods and the environment and the policies and other changes needed to support them. It begins with a description and distinction of shifting cultivation and slash-and-burn practices and continues with a summary of land use intensification pathways in the tropics. This is followed by the objectives, benchmark site locations, broad methods, and activities of the ASB consortium. The subsequent chapters of the book describe in detail the methods and results of the past 10 years of this interdisciplinary, multi-institutional effort and include suggestions for implementation of the findings.

## LAND USE AT THE TROPICAL FOREST MARGINS

Almost all tropical forests are cleared by similar methods that start with slashing the forest with chainsaws, axes, and machetes and burning the felled vegetation after it has dried. In this sense, slash-and-burn is simply a land-clearing technique. The subsequent land use pathway that follows land clearing differs depending on the different groups of people involved—indigenous forest dwellers, small-scale farmers, and large-scale private operators—and the intended use of the land, including the various types of shifting cultivation, agroforestry, logging, cattle ranching, and commercial tree plantations. There is much confusion in the literature regarding the use of the terms *shifting cultivation* and *slash-and-burn agriculture;* the following sections distinguish between the different land use pathways that follow the clearing of tropical forests.

## SHIFTING CULTIVATION OR SLASH-AND-BURN AGRICULTURE?

Shifting cultivation is probably the oldest farming system (Nye and Greenland 1960) and is remarkably similar throughout the humid tropics. Farmers slash and burn a hectare or so of primary or tall secondary forest, grow food crops in polyculture for 1 to 3 years, and abandon the land to secondary forest fallow regrowth for 20 to 40 years, then repeat the cycle. This traditional shifting cultivation with short cropping periods and long secondary forest fallow periods is now rare, practiced primarily by indigenous communities disconnected from the national economy. It is socially and environmentally sustainable (Thrupp et al. 1997), albeit at low levels of agricultural productivity and human population densities of less than thirty people per square kilometer (Boserup 1965). Shifting cultivation is known by a variety of terms, referring mostly to cleared fields: *swidden* (Old English), *rai* (Sweden), *milpa, conuco, roza* (Latin America), *shamba, chitemene* (Africa), *jhum* (India), *kaingin* (Philippines), *ladang* (Indonesia and Malaysia), and many others. Fallows are commonly called bush fallow and *jachere* in Africa; *barbecho, capoeira,* and *purma* in Latin America; and *belukar* and other terms in Indonesia. The concept of fallows in the tropics differs from that used in the temperate zone, where the term *fallow* normally means leaving the soil bare (Sanchez 1999). The vegetative fallow phase restores carbon and nutrient stocks in the biomass, improves soil physical properties, and suppresses weeds (Nye and Greenland 1960; Sanchez 1976; Szott and Palm 1986).

When human population pressures exceed a critical density that varies with agroecological zones and inherent soil fertility, traditional shifting cultivation is replaced by a variety of other agricultural practices that still involve clearing by slash-and-burn methods. We suggest that the loosely used terminology be specified as follows: *shifting cultivation* refers to the traditional long-fallow rotational system, and *slash-and-burn agriculture* refers to other farming systems characterized by slash-and-burn clearing, short-term fallows, or no fallows at all. These systems include the shortened fallow–food crop systems and the establishment of tree-based systems such as complex agroforests, simple agroforests, or monoculture tree crop plantations such as oil palm (*Elaeis guineensis* Jacquin), coffee (*Coffea* spp.), rubber (*Hevea brasiliensis* [Willd. ex A. Juss.] Muell.-Arg.), or pulp and timber species. Slash-and-burn is also the means of establishing pastures that are found throughout the humid forest zone of Latin America. These slash-and-burn systems differ from shifting agriculture in that the crops are interplanted with pastures or tree seedlings, or in some cases the cropping period is omitted. Many of the systems are still rotational to some degree, with occasional slash-and-burn clearing when the productivity of the system declines.

## LAND USE INTENSIFICATION PATHWAYS

The pathway of agricultural intensification depends to some extent on the biophysical environment but is modified by the demographic composition and pressures, production technologies, and natural resource management practices, infrastructure, institutions, and policy environment present at the time. The usual pathway begins with the reduction of the fallow period to less than 10 years and more commonly less than 5 years. These short fallows are incapable of accumulating sufficient nutrient stocks in the biomass and suppressing weeds by shading. Unlike shifting cultivation, where soil erosion is seldom a problem, slash-and-burn systems have less vegetative cover and often exposed, compacted soils that increase water runoff and soil erosion rates (Lal et al. 1986). This change in vegetation and soil structure may lead to changes in the hydrologic cycle, with negative consequences downstream (Bruijnzeel 1990; Tinker et al., 1996). The combined effects of shortened fallows result in systems with declining productivity, depending more and more on less and less fallow biomass. In some cases, the systems reach a point at which the trees are replaced by other, highly degraded systems such as *Imperata cylindrica* (L.) Beauv grasslands in Southeast Asia and West Africa (Garrity 1997) and degraded pastures in Latin America (Serrão and Homma 1993). This pathway of land use intensification, land degradation, and the resulting losses of carbon stocks, nutrients, and biodiversity is depicted in the left-hand, declining curve in figure 1.1, line *a*. It is important to remember that those and other ecosystem services have been traded for private benefits, including food, feed, fiber, and cash.

With further increases in population density come increased access to markets and decreased access to forest products. A point may be reached when land degradation begins to be reversed with changes in land tenure institutions that facilitate investments in improved land management. This process was recognized by Boserup (1965) and is sometimes called induced institutional innovation (Hayami and Ruttan 1985). Land rehabilitation usually is accomplished by replenishing lost plant nutrients; using improved crop germplasm, agronomic practices, and soil conservation methods; introducing livestock; and planting more trees.

Farmers will invest in improved land management and care for the environment when they have reasonably secure land or tree tenure and if it is profitable compared with other investment options within the context of household constraints and individual time preferences and attitudes toward risk. Examples of soil and land rehabilitation with increasing population pressure are well documented as "more people, less erosion" (Tiffen et al. 1996) and "more people, more trees" (Sanchez et al. 1998). They are accompanied by increasing productivity and profitability. Ecosystem stocks

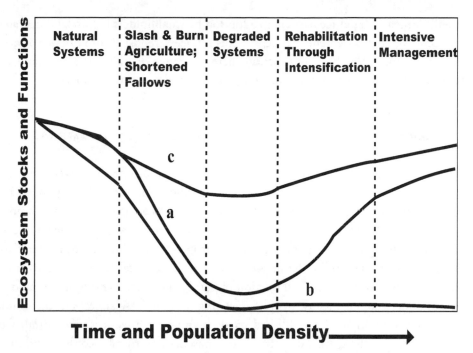

*Figure 1.1* Land use intensification pathways and changes in stocks of natural capital such as carbon and nutrient stocks, biodiversity, and other ecosystem services, with time and increasing population density in the tropics (Sanchez et al. 1998). Line *a* represents the usual pattern of land degradation and eventual rehabilitation when the proper policies and institutions are in place, line *b* represents the continued state of degradation that can occur in the absence of appropriate policies and institutions, and line *c* represents the desired course where there is little degradation of the resource base yet improved livelihoods are achieved.

of carbon and nutrients increase and other ecosystems services also return, the level of which depends on the previous state of degradation and on the type of land use system that is established. Livelihoods may continue to improve as more and more valuable economic products are obtained from the system. The tradeoffs between the environmental services and profitability are lower than those in the degraded state. This is the right-hand side of figure 1.1, line *a*. In some cases, the policy environment does not provide incentives to rehabilitate these degrading lands (line *b* in figure 1.1), and the challenge is to find policy tools that will provide those incentives.

Alternative land use intensification pathways that do not first involve severe land degradation (line *c* in figure 1.1) do exist in the form of the complex agroforests that have been developed by indigenous communities (Padoch and de Jong, 1987; Michon and de Foresta 1996; Duguma et al., 2001). The challenge is, first, to identify and understand barriers to adoption of other systems by smallholders when such systems are superior alternatives in terms of their environmental impacts and sustainability as well as their profitability, food security, riskiness, and other measures of acceptability to smallholders. When such superior win–win alternatives exist, the next challenge is to identify means to reduce barriers to adoption by smallholders before land degradation occurs to such an extent that ecosystems services are lost. More often, however, there is no single "best bet," but instead there is a range of tradeoffs across land use alternatives regarding environmental and agricultural development objectives.

## WHO ARE THE SMALL-SCALE SLASH-AND-BURN FARMERS?

The number of people who depend on shifting cultivation for their livelihoods has for decades been estimated at about 250 to 300 million (Hauck 1974; Myers, 1994). Recent georeferenced population and farming system data suggest that the numbers are an order of magnitude lower. Dixon et al. (2001) report that 37 million people, or 2 percent of the agricultural population of the tropics, practice some form of shifting cultivation in about 1 billion ha or 22 percent of the tropical land area. This is the area of influence, but only a small fraction of that is under actual cropping or fallows. These numbers do not include people practicing more intense systems in the humid tropics that were originally established by slash-and-burn practices. The number of people involved in these other crop-based, tree-based, or pasture-based slash-and-burn systems is several times that of shifting cultivators (Dixon et al. 2001).

Deforestation by slash-and-burn farmers is a response to underlying root causes. Population growth is naturally viewed as a main driver of deforestation, and economic growth often is viewed in the same vein. But no direct relationship between deforestation and population growth or economic growth has been found. Myers (1991) noted that whereas the population of forested tropical countries increased by 15 to 35 percent in the 1980s, deforestation expanded by 90 percent during the same period. The recent analysis by Geist and Lambin (2002) shows that in-migration to the forest margins is a much larger factor in deforestation than high internal population growth. Brown and Pearce (1994) obtained inconclusive results when attempting to relate gross domestic product (GDP) growth rates, foreign debt, and population growth with deforestation in tropical countries. Rudel and Roper (1997) found that in tropical countries with large forested areas, deforestation increases with increasing GDP, whereas in countries with mainly forest fragments, increasing GDP decreases deforestation.

Whereas traditional, indigenous people practice shifting cultivation, many (in some cases most) of the people practicing slash-and-burn agriculture are migrants from other parts of their country who seek a better life at the forest margins. In some countries, large numbers of migrants to the forest margins come as part of government-sponsored colonization programs aimed at transmigrating poor people from densely populated areas to the forest frontier, particularly in Brazil and Indonesia (Hecht and Cockburn 1989; Kartasubrata 1991). Others are spontaneous migrants who, acting independently with little or no government support, follow the opening of roads and logging trails. Planned and spontaneous migrations of poor people from crowded regions such as Java, the Andes, and northeastern and southern Brazil have undeniably contributed to deforestation. Opening of roads into primary forests such as the Belém-Brasília, Transamazônica, and São Paulo–Rio Branco in Brazil, the Carretera Marginal de la Selva and the Federico Basadre in Peru, and the Trans-Sumatra and Trans-Gabon highways have provided access to forests to both small-scale farmers and commercial interests.

Many of these migrants are unfamiliar with the humid tropics, are largely unaware of the knowledge-intensive practices of indigenous shifting cultivators, and attempt to establish cropping systems that work where they came from (Moran 1981). People in these situations usually lack alternative employment opportunities; have limited access to markets, credit, and information; and often are politically marginalized. These people are a major focus of the ASB consortium.

## THE ASB CONSORTIUM

The ASB consortium is an international group of researchers, extension workers, and nongovernment organizations (NGOs) established in February 1992 to investigate the causes and consequences of deforestation by small-scale farmers and to identify land use systems that enhance local livelihoods and the environment and the policies and other changes needed to support them. The ASB focuses on areas with high rates of deforestation where rapid increases in population density caused primarily by in-migration result in conversion of natural forests and where the environment–livelihood tradeoffs are large. The ASB does not focus on shifting cultivation, but in some locations where it did occur, it was included in the comparative analysis. Similarly, larger-scale slash-and-burn operations also were included in some of the comparisons.

### STATE OF KNOWLEDGE

A literature review undertaken in 1992 showed much process-based understanding of agricultural practices, empirical understanding of global environmental processes and social processes, some policy research, and almost no multidisciplinary research (Sanchez and Bandy 1992; Bandy et al. 1993; Sanchez and Hailu 1996). The biophysical processes of shifting cultivation and slash-and-burn systems have been well understood through decades of long-term, place-based research (Nye and Greenland 1960; Jurion and Henry 1969; Sanchez 1976; Juo and Lal 1977; Seubert et al. 1977; Serrão et al. 1979; MacIntosh et al. 1981; Toky and Ramakrishnan 1981; Sanchez et al. 1983, 1987; Ramakrishnan 1984, 1987; Smyth and Bastos 1984; Von Uexkull 1984; Alegre and Cassel 1986, 1996; Sanchez and Benites 1987; Wade et al. 1988; Kang et al. 1990; Cerri et al. 1991; Palm and Sanchez 1991; Smyth and Cassel 1995; Juo and Manu 1996; Palm et al. 1996).

The environmental consequences of slash-and-burn and tropical deforestation on greenhouse gas emissions have been modeled or estimated with limited data on the rates of deforestation, the carbon stored in the forests, and subsequent land use systems (Houghton et al. 2000). Much data have been gathered on the effects of tropical deforestation on above-ground biodiversity (Whitmore and Sayer 1992; Heywood 1995) and watershed hydrology (Bruijnzeel 1990; Tinker et al. 1996), but with limited specificity to slash-and-burn agriculture. There were only a few studies on below-ground biodiversity (Lavelle and Pashanasi 1989).

The anthropological aspects of shifting cultivation have been described extensively (Conklin 1954, 1963; Cowgill 1962; Padoch and de Jong 1987; Thrupp et al. 1997), with more recent studies focusing on migrants practicing slash-and-burn agriculture (Moran 1981; Colfer et al. 1988; Rhoades and Bidegaray 1987; Fujisaka et al. 1991). There have been several studies about the economics and policies of deforestation and slash-and-burn practices, focused primarily on Brazil (Mahar 1988; Binswanger 1991; Brown and Pearce 1994; Mahar and Schneider 1994).

What this incomplete literature review showed was an almost total absence of multidisciplinary work. Social and biophysical scientists have seldom worked together on slash-and-burn issues. There was no tradition of joint research and collaboration between economic groups and the environmental community dealing with this issue (Repetto and Gillis 1988), or between the agricultural, economic, and environmental communities. The ASB consortium was established to link the diverse research disciplines and the development community to address jointly the problems of deforestation, unsustainable land use, and rural poverty at the humid forest margins.

## INCEPTION

A United Nations Development Programme (UNDP)–sponsored workshop was held in Porto Velho, Rondônia, Brazil, on February 16–21, 1992, attended by twenty-six environmental policymakers and research leaders from eight tropical countries, five NGOs, six international agricultural research centers, three regional research organizations, and six donor agencies (ASB 1992). Participants concluded that a global effort was needed because the problem and impacts were global and that cross-site comparisons of causes and solutions could provide insights not possible from isolated studies. The participants created the ASB consortium, set the broad basis for collaboration, selected three initial benchmark sites, and formed a governing body to guide the intricate linkages and processes.

Two key recommendations of the Rio Earth Summit that was held later in 1992 provided international legitimacy to the ASB consortium. They appear in chapter 11, "Combating Deforestation," of Agenda 21, as follows (Keating 1993):

> *Limit and aim to halt destructive shifting cultivation by addressing the underlying social and ecological causes.*
> *Reduce damage to forests by promoting sustainable management of areas adjacent to the forests.*

## GOAL, HYPOTHESIS, AND OBJECTIVES

The overall goals of the ASB consortium are to help reduce the rate of deforestation caused by slash-and-burn agriculture, rehabilitate degraded lands created by slash-and-burn, and improve the well-being of slash-and-burn farmers by providing economically and ecologically viable alternative land use practices.

The underlying hypothesis at the inception of ASB was that intensification of agricultural systems on already cleared lands and rehabilitation of degraded lands at the humid forest margins would reduce deforestation. Although this hypothesis has since been shown to be too simplistic because the underlying behavioral assumptions were wrong (Angelsen and Kaimowitz 2001), it provided a framework around which the program focused its initial research objectives and activities:

- *Site characterization.* Assess the principal socioeconomic and biophysical processes leading to deforestation, including government policy and decision-making patterns of farmers practicing slash-and-burn.
- *Environmental and agronomic sustainability studies.* Quantify the contribution of slash-and-burn agriculture and alternative land use practices to global, regional, and local environmental changes such as climate change, biodiversity loss, and land degradation.
- *Socioeconomic studies and tradeoff analysis.* Integrated assessment of land use alternatives to identify appropriate technologies and develop improved production systems that are economically feasible, socially acceptable, and environmentally sound alternatives to current slash-and-burn systems or to understand tradeoffs between land use alternatives.
- *Policy research and implementation.* Identify policy options and institutional reforms that can facilitate the adoption of the improved systems and the balancing of tradeoffs to attain a more desirable mix of outcomes and discourage further deforestation.

Succinctly stated, are there alternative land use systems to slash-and-burn that reduce deforestation, poverty, and global environmental changes such as greenhouse gas emissions and biodiversity loss? What are the type and magnitude of the environmental and livelihood tradeoffs for these different systems? And, based on that tradeoff analysis, how can the systems be influenced to attain better outcomes for a range of stakeholders, including farmers?

The slash-and-burn topic is complex, involving multiple agents, land use objectives, and driving forces (Tomich et al. 1998b). In addition, slash-and-burn is carried out in a diverse array of biophysical, socioeconomic, and policy environments. To address the objectives of the ASB consortium requires an understanding of the influence of these multiple factors and environments on the economic viability, sustainability, and environmental impacts of the alternatives. From the outset ASB determined four key features to assist in this complex task: a cross-disciplinary approach combining biophysical and behavioral sciences, the participation of diverse kinds of institutions, work based at benchmark sites, and common methods to be used at all sites. The benchmark sites and standard protocols are introduced in this chapter, and the details of the methods, their application, and results are presented in subsequent chapters in the book.

## CROSS-DISCIPLINARY RESEARCH AND DEVELOPMENT FRAMEWORK

The ASB developed a conceptual framework in which the land use system adopted by farmers depends on farm households' objectives; their natural, human, social, technical, and financial resources; and the biophysical, social, economic, and political constraints to the use of these resources. The effects of these land use systems for alleviating poverty, conserving resources, and reducing deforestation were then assessed along with the impacts of current and alternative policies (Palm et al. 1995; ASB 1996). An integrated natural resource management (INRM) research framework that was later developed by the international agricultural research centers (figure 1.2; CIFOR 2000; Izac and Sanchez 2001) was based largely on the ASB experience. The various steps

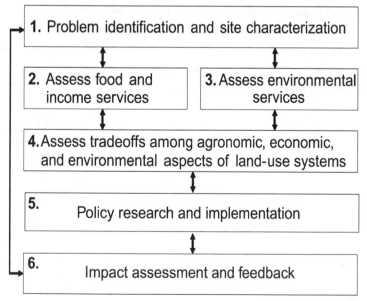

*Figure 1.2* The research and development framework used by ASB (modified from ASB 1996; CIFOR 2000; Izac and Sanchez 2001).

in the research process of problem identification, assessment of food and income services, assessment of ecosystem services, tradeoff analysis, policy research and implementation, and impact analysis are discussed in the following sections.

## DIVERSE INSTITUTIONS

In 2001 the ASB consortium was composed of seven national agricultural research systems, four other national agencies, seven international agricultural research centers, twenty universities and advanced research institutions, and five local and national NGOs, many of them represented in this volume. The ASB researchers have organized themselves in an evolving collection of multidisciplinary thematic working groups, including site characterization, biodiversity (above- and below-ground), climate change, agronomic sustainability, sustainable land use mosaics, farmer concerns, policy and institutional issues, synthesis and linkages, and training and capacity building. A Global Steering Group provides governance to the consortium. It meets yearly and sets overall policy, funding strategy, and reporting. A global coordinator with a small global team of two to three staff facilitates operations (Swift and Bandy 1995).

## BENCHMARK SITES

A network of benchmark sites was identified to represent large, active areas of deforestation caused by slash-and-burn practices. The sites that were selected provide a range of biophysical and socioeconomic conditions under which slash-and-burn occurs and include a land use intensity gradient from traditional shifting cultivation to intensive continuous cropping and degraded lands. Benchmark sites were also selected based on sufficient infrastructure to conduct the research and development activities. Each benchmark site covers a large area and has a national research station as its physical base, but the bulk of the work is done locally with researchers, NGOs, extension services, farmers, and policymakers.

### Latin America

Two areas were selected in the Amazon Basin; they represent areas that have experienced rapid deforestation as a result of government colonization programs (western Amazon Brazilian benchmark site) and other areas of lower population density and poor infrastructure where population densities are increasing through spontaneous migration from the overcrowded urban and Andean areas (Peruvian benchmark site). The site in the western Brazilian Amazon encompasses two colonization projects, Pedro Peixoto, Acre and Theobroma, Rondônia, and areas along the BR-362 highway (see details and map in chapter 12 this volume). Settlements are all under government sponsorship, with migrants assigned 50- to 100-ha plots, and currently undergoing rapid development. The site headquarters is the Empresa Brasileira de Pesquisa Agropecuária (Embrapa)–Acre research center, near Rio Branco. The Peruvian benchmark area focuses on Pucallpa and Yurimaguas in the Ucayali and Loreto regions of the Selva Baja (see details in chapter 15, this volume). The site is managed from the Center for Forestry Research (CENFOR) of the Instituto Nacional de Investigación Agraria (INIA), working in close cooperation with Consorcio para el Desarrollo Sostenible de Ucayali (CODESU), a group of NGOs, the Ucayali Regional Government, the Instituto de Investigación de la Amazonía Peruana (IIAP), and INIA's Yurimaguas Experiment Station.

A third area in Latin America represents the humid and subhumid forests of the Atlantic Coast of Central America and Mexico where encroaching urban areas and slash-and-burn has reduced the extent of the northernmost extension of tropical forests. The benchmark area in the Yucatan in southeast Mexico was managed by Instituto Nacional de Investigación Agrícola, Pecuaria y Forestal (INIFAP).

## Africa

A site in Cameroon represents the equatorial Congo Basin rainforest of Congo–Kinshasa, Congo–Brazzaville, Equatorial Guinea, Gabon, Central African Republic, and Cameroon, where there is low but increasing population density and largely indigenous slash-and-burn agriculture. The site includes a north–south gradient, from rapid, spontaneous colonization around Yaoundé at the north, though an intermediate situation at M'Balmayo, to very low population density at Ebolowa in the southern end, close to the Gabon–Equatorial Guinea border (see details and map in chapter 14, this volume). Site headquarters are at the Institut de Recherche Agricole pour le Développement (IRAD) at Nkolbisson, near Yaoundé, with strong support from the IITA Humid Forest Centre.

## Southeast Asia

Sites in Southeast Asia represent three quite different forest ecosystems. The Sumatran benchmark area in Indonesia represents the equatorial rainforests of the Indonesian and Malaysian archipelago. Located in Jambi and Lampung provinces, it covers a broad gradient from primary forests in the Jambi area to degraded *Imperata* grasslands in Lampung Province, including both indigenous farmers and colonization projects as well as large-scale plantations and logging companies (see details and maps in chapter 13, this volume). The site is managed from the Central Research Institute for Food Crops (CRIFC) of the Agency for Agricultural Research and Development (AARD) in Bogor, Java. A benchmark area in the Philippines represents the monsoonal forests, where only forest remnants exist on steep mountain slopes and degraded grasslands dominate the landscape. The sites in Claveria and Lantapan in Northern Mindanao, Philippines, are operated by the Philippine Council for Agriculture, Forestry, and Natural Resources Research (PCARRD) together with a number of other organizations. A benchmark area in the Ma Chaem watershed near Chiang Mai, Thailand, represents the extensive area of subtropical hill forests of mainland mountain Southeast Asia found in Thailand, Myanmar, Laos, Vietnam, and southern China. The site was chosen to extend ASB research into higher-elevation areas with broad ranges of slope conditions where issues of land use management often overlap with issues of watershed management. Chapter 16 provides additional details. The benchmark site is managed by Thailand's Royal Forest Department in close collaboration with Chiang Mai University.

All benchmark sites fall within the tropical and subtropical moist broadleaf forest biome (WWF 2001). To indicate how much the benchmark sites represent other areas in the tropics, regional similarity classes were developed from a set of key physical, environmental determinants of plant growth. The DOMAIN potential mapping procedure developed by Carpenter et al. (1993) was used to generate the map shown in figure 1.3 of matching climate surface values for each of 108 sample locations in ASB's benchmark sites in Brazil, Indonesia, and Cameroon. The various similarity classes indicate the degree to which the ASB sites can be extrapolated over a global surface using the same climate variables.

Initial ASB research was concentrated in the Brazil, Cameroon, and Indonesian benchmark sites, and these three thus serve as the focus for much of this book, although much progress has also been made in Thailand and Peru, the results of which are presented in chapters 15 and 16.

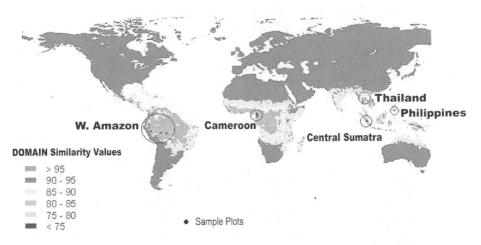

*Figure 1.3* Map indicating the location and global environmental representativeness of the ASB sites in western Amazon, Indonesia, Thailand, Philippines, and Cameroon. The DOMAIN similarity values are based on elevation, potential evapotranspiration, total annual precipitation, precipitation in the driest month, precipitation range, minimum average monthly temperature, and maximum average monthly temperature (Gillison 2000).

## RESEARCH THEMES AND METHODS

The ASB integrates a range of geographic sites, spatial and temporal scales, disciplines, and partner institutions. To implement the various steps of the interdisciplinary INRM research framework at the various sites demanded a minimum, common research approach for making cross-site comparisons. Standardized methods were developed for identifying problems and characterizing sites (figure 1.2, step 1), quantifying the environmental, agronomic, and socioeconomic parameters of the different land use alternatives (steps 2 and 3), assessing the economic and environmental tradeoffs (step 4), and researching and implementing policies (step 5). The various methods are described in detail in this section.

### CHARACTERIZING SITES

The first phase of ASB research involved characterizing the benchmark sites. The purpose of the characterization was to describe the biophysical, socioeconomic, and policy settings of the sites, define the extent and process of slash-and-burn agriculture in forming land use patterns, investigate the driving forces for slash-and-burn, develop typologies of slash-and-burn land use systems that exist across the ASB sites, establish a baseline of information for future impact assessments, and provide regional and global extrapolation domains for research results. The results were used to identify research priorities and develop research protocols for the subsequent steps.

Guidelines were developed for characterizing the rates of forest conversion; dominant land use systems; and the biophysical, socioeconomic, and policy environments in which they are found at the regional, benchmark, community, and farm and household scales (Palm et al. 1995). Within each benchmark site there are numerous communities that represent a range of demographic conditions and land use histories that result in different local land use patterns. The characterization process also included detailed interviews to establish the problems, opportunities, constraints, and resources at the community and farm or household scales, the responses to which were important for identifying factors that affect decision making and driving forces of land use and for establishing research agendas for finding sustainable alternatives to slash-and-burn. Remote sensing and geographic information system (GIS) techniques were used to assess rates of deforestation and land use patterns at the sites.

Site characterization results for the first three benchmark sites are documented by Ávila (1994) for Brazil, Ambassa-Kiki and Tiki Manga (1997) for Cameroon, and Gintings et al. (1995) and van Noordwijk et al. (1995) for Indonesia. Information is also presented in benchmark site reports (Tomich et al. 1998a; Kotto-Same et al. 2000; Lewis et al., 2002). A comparison of some of the key biophysical and socioeconomic conditions shows the broad range encompassed by benchmark sites (table 1.1).

Table 1.1 Selected Site Characterization Parameters for the ASB Benchmark Areas

| Characterization Parameter | Western Amazon, Brazil | Southern Cameroon | Sumatran Lowlands, Indonesia | Selva Baja of Peru | Ma Chaem, North Thailand |
|---|---|---|---|---|---|
| Rainfall (mm/yr) | 1700–2400 | 1400–1900 | 2500–3000 | 1500–2200 | 1200–1500 |
| Latitude | 7–12°S | 2–4°N | 0–6°S | 6–12°S | 20°N |
| Months dry season (<100 mm) | June–September | July–August; October–February | June–August | June–August | November–April |
| Dominant original vegetation | Tropical moist forest; semideciduous forest | Tropical moist forest; semideciduous forest | Tropical moist forest | Tropical moist forest | Tropical semideciduous montane forest |
| Predominant soils (U.S. Soil Taxonomy) | Paleudults, hapludox | Kandiudults | Hapludox, kandiudox, kandiudults, dystrudepts | Paleudults, paleaqualfs | Haplustults, dystrustepts |
| Population density (people/km²) | 3–5 | 4–200 | 2–175 | 1–9 | 20 |
| Farm size (ha/household) | 15–250[a] | 5–30 | 2–10 | 2–50 | 2.4–16 |
| Agricultural wage (US $/d)[b] | 6.25 | 1.21 | 1.67 | 2.5 | 1.45, 1.75[c] |

[a]Indicates small-scale farms as initially defined for Brazil.
[b]Wage rates are from 1996–1997.
[c]For women and men, respectively.
Source: Modified from Tomich et al. (1998b).

Comparable activities and approaches for Mexico and the Philippines are presented in Haggar et al. (2001) and Mercado et al. (2001), respectively.

## Meta–Land Use Systems

A set of meta–land use systems was identified from the site characterization process that aggregates the broad range of specific land use systems found in the diverse benchmark sites (ASB 1996). Such systems were initially identified as "best-bet" and "worst-bet" alternative systems for specific benchmark sites (Tomich et al. 1998b). Meta–land use systems include forests, complex agroforests, simple agroforests, crop–fallow rotations, continuous food crops, and pastures and grasslands (table 1.2). This array of land uses covers a gradient often used by biophysical scientists to describe varying levels of disturbance of forest for agriculture (Ruthenberg 1980; NRC 1993). General descriptions of these meta–land use systems and some specific examples are given here.

### Forests
Undisturbed or so-called primary forests are rare in and around the benchmark sites. Disturbed forests, with some degree of logging, are dominant, with the intensity of logging low in Cameroon, where a few trees are harvested per hectare, intermediate in Brazil and Peru, and high in Indonesia and Thailand. Extractive reserves, where nontimber forest products are harvested, are perhaps best known in the Amazon, where Brazil nuts or castanha (*Bertholletia excelsa* Humb. & Bonpl.) and rubber are harvested from naturally occurring trees, but at all sites some amount of nontimber forest products is harvested from forests of the different categories. The concept of sustainably managed community-based forests is being developed at the Brazil benchmark site by Embrapa (chapter 8, this volume). Community-protected secondary forests are found in the Thailand site (chapter 16, this volume) and in Sumatra, Indonesia.

### Complex Agroforests
Complex agroforests contain a wide variety of economic plant species and usually have a rotation time greater than 20 years. The complex agroforests of Indonesia are indigenous systems established over generations by local peoples living at the margins of tropical rainforests in Sumatra, Borneo, and other islands (Torquebiau 1984; Foresta and Michon 1994). Primary or old secondary forests are slashed and burned, food crops, citrus, and robusta coffee (*Coffea canephora* Pierre ex Froehner) are planted along with several trees species, and natural regeneration of forest species is allowed. The trees eventually shade out the crops, occupy different strata, and produce high-value products such as fruits, resins, medicines, and commercially valuable timber. Main economic tree species include damar (*Shorea javanica* Koord. & Valeton), durian *(Durio zibethinus* Murray), duku (*Lansium domesticum* Corr.), and rubber. In the case of rubber, production declines after 20 or 30 years, and the slash-and-burn cycle typically begins again; some of the other tree species, notably damar, can have much

Table 1.2 Meta–Land Use Systems and Candidate Best-Bet Alternative Systems (with Some Worst Bets) at Each ASB Benchmark Site

| Meta–Land Use System | Brazil | Cameroon | Indonesia | Peru | Thailand |
|---|---|---|---|---|---|
| Forests | Natural forests<br>Logged forests<br>Extractive reserves<br>Community-managed forests | Natural forests<br>Logged forests<br>Community-managed forests | Natural forests<br>Logged forests<br>Community-managed forests | Natural forests<br>Logged forests<br>Extractive reserves | Natural forests<br>Logged forests<br>Community-protected forests |
| Complex agroforests | None | Cocoa agroforests (jungle cocoa) | Rubber agroforests (jungle rubber) | Bora system | Tea agroforests (jungle tea)<br>Fruit orchards |
| Simple agroforests and intensive tree crops | Multistrata agroforests (cupuaçú + pupunha + castanha)<br>Coffee + rubber<br>Coffee + fast-growing timber<br>Coffee monoculture | Oil palm plantations | Oil palm plantations<br>Rubber monoculture plantations<br>Pulpwood plantations | Peach palm<br>Bolaina<br>Capirona | |
| Food crop-fallow systems | Annual food crop, 3-yr fallowAnnual food crop, 2-yr legume fallow | Melon and mixed food crop, 15-yr fallow<br>Mixed food crop, 4-yr bush fallow<br>Mixed food crop, 4-yr *Chromolaena* fallow | Upland rice, 10-yr bush fallow<br>Mixed food crops, 5-yr bush fallow<br>Cassava, 2-yr *Imperata* fallow | Upland rice, cassava, short fallows | Upland rice, barley, ginger, short fallows |
| Continuous food crops | None | None | Cassava | | Cabbages |
| Pasture and grasslands | Degraded pasturesImproved pastures | None | *Imperata* grasslands | Degraded pasturesImproved pastures | *Imperata* grasslands |

longer cycles. Alternatively, agroforests can be managed with gap replanting that eliminates the need for subsequent slash-and-burn cycles. In either case, such agroforests, composed of hundreds of small plots managed by individual families, occupy large contiguous areas in Sumatra and can be mistaken for forests to the untrained eye. Biophysical scientists have documented the high productivity and ecosystem services provided by these agroforests (Michon and de Foresta 1996; Michon 1997). Plant diversity in the mature complex agroforests is on the order of 300 species/ha, which approximates that of adjacent undisturbed forests (420 plant species/ha). The richness of bird species in mature agroforests is approximately 50 percent that of the original rainforest, and almost all mammal species are present in the agroforest (Foresta and Michon 1994). The villagers in Krui, Lampung Province, who make a living from these complex agroforests, have an obviously higher standard of living than those neighbors who grow only food crops (Bouamrane 1996).

Complex agroforests based on cacao (*Theobroma cacao* [Linn.]) as the major cash crop have been developed in humid forest margins of West Africa over the past century (Duguma et al. 2001; chapter 14, this volume). Jungle tea (*Camellia sinensis* [L.] Kuntze) complex agroforests occur in North Thailand, where the naturally occurring tea trees are left when the forest is cleared and fruit trees are interplanted (chapter 16, this volume). Jungle rubber is a complex agroforest occupying 3 million ha where most of the rubber is produced in Indonesia (chapter 9, this volume). Indigenous Bora communities of the Peruvian Amazon establish complex agroforests by interplanting trees in upland rice and cassava crops (Padoch and de Jong 1987). Economic trees include peach palm (*Bactris gasipaes* Kunth) for fruits and heart of palm, *Inga* spp. for fruits and firewood, arazá (*Eugenia stipitata* McVaugh) for fruit, and timber trees such as mahogany (*Swietenia macrophylla* King) and tornillo (*Cedrelinga cataeniformis* Ducke).

### Simple Agroforestry Systems and Intensive Tree Crop Systems

Simple agroforestry systems usually contain fewer than five economic plant species, whereas tree crop plantations include only one. Both systems may include a leguminous crop cover. These systems are common in many parts of the humid tropics, particularly where infrastructure is well developed. Nevertheless, most of these start with slash-and-burn, in some cases followed by food crops interplanted with tree seedlings. Intensive tree crop systems include the classic monoculture plantations such as oil palm and rubber, timber plantations such as pine (*Pinus* spp.), *Eucalyptus* spp., and cypress (*Cupressus* spp.), and fast-growing pulpwood plantations such as *Acacia mangium* and albizia (*Paraserianthes falcataria* [L.] I. Nielsen). These systems can be vast and run by corporations or run by individual smallholder farmers.

Simple agroforestry systems have less plant diversity than complex agroforests, higher levels of management are needed, and the regeneration of forest species is restricted. Included in this category are shade coffee, cacao, and coconut plantations found throughout the humid tropics and the peach palm–based systems in Latin America. A slightly more diverse system based on peach palm, Brazil nut (*Bertholletia excelsa*), and cupuaçú (*Theobroma grandiflorum* [Willd. ex Spreng.] Schum) has been developed at the western Brazilian Amazon site (chapter 12, this volume).

### Food Crop–Fallow Rotations

Traditional shifting cultivation with long-term fallows was only found in the southern reaches of the Cameroon benchmark site and is absent in or disappearing from the other sites. Fallows of 10 years or less are more common at the other sites and include either natural secondary forest fallows or managed fallows (Sanchez 1999). In the northern parts of the Cameroon benchmark site, shortening of the fallow period has resulted in the invasion and dominance of the bush *Chromolaena odorata* (L.) R.M. King and H. Robinson, a member of the Asteraceae family.

Improved or managed fallows, where trees are planted into the fallow, are now being tried in some of the benchmark sites. The planted trees often are nitrogen-fixing legumes that restore soil fertility more rapidly and include *Inga edulis* Mart. in Brazil and Peru or *Calliandra calothyrsus* Meissner in Cameroon. Deliberately planted fallows of *Tithonia diversifolia* (Hemsl.) Gray, another Asteraceae, are commonly found in the uplands of Southeast Asia, practiced by indigenous communities (Cairns and Garrity 1999). Improved fallows using leguminous cover crops kept in the field for less than 2 years occur in Peru and include kudzu (*Pueraria phaseoloides* [Roxb.] *Benth*) (Sanchez and Benites 1987), *Mucuna* spp., and *Centrosema macrocarpum* Benth. (Palm et al. 2002a).

### Continuous Food Crop Production

Continuous cropping is found in valley bottoms as irrigated paddy rice (*Oryza sativa* L.) in Indonesia, Peru, and Thailand, but because it is so well established and is rarely associated with slash-and-burn and deforestation it was not included in the analysis by ASB (except in Thailand). In Cameroon and Thailand, intensive horticulture with high rates of use of mineral fertilizers and pesticides forms an important option near the large urban centers of Yaoundé and Chiang Mai. Cassava is grown continuously in the Lampung area of the Indonesian benchmark site, particularly on transmigration settlement sites, and often eventually degrades through invasion by *Imperata cylindrica* into landscape patches or large grasslands.

### Pastures and Grassland Systems

Pastures for beef production dominate the deforested landscape in the Brazilian and Peruvian benchmark sites. These include traditional, extensive pasture systems that degrade within a decade or so, as well as more intensive grazing systems with improved grass species (*Brachiaria humidicola* [Rendle] Schweick; *B. brizantha* [Hochst.] Stapf) often mixed with pasture legumes such as *Pueraria phaseoloides, Desmodium ovalifolium* Wall, *Arachis pintoi Krap. & Greg.,* and others (Serrão et al. 1979; Serrão and Toledo, 1990). The pasture species are tolerant to aluminum toxicity and are normally planted into a preceding crop of upland rice or maize (*Zea mays* L.). In parts of Brazil, these pastures are rejuvenated by burning, plowing, and fertilizing a maize crop to which pastures are replanted.

Extensive areas of *Imperata cylindrica* grasslands occur throughout Southeast Asia and parts of West Africa. This species is known as alang-alang in Indonesia and cogon in the Philippines. These grasslands are dominant in the Lampung area of the Indonesian benchmark site (Garrity 1997; chapter 11, this volume). This coarse, unpalatable grass invades areas where the fallow cycle has been shortened and is basically a degraded system. It is difficult to eradicate and is maintained by frequent fires. Fortunately *Imperata cylindrica* grasslands do not occur in Latin America, where less invasive *Imperata* species exist and pose no major problems.

These meta–land use categories were used to set up land use intensity transects or chronosequences (see chapter 2, this volume) at several locations in each benchmark site where environmental, agronomic, and socioeconomic factors were evaluated by standard protocols. Whenever and wherever possible the different measurements were all taken from the same plot, farm, or location in the landscape. Natural forest was considered the point of departure for all land uses, and grasslands, short-fallow cultivation systems, and pastures were included as the other endpoint, representing degraded conditions. The specific environmental, agronomic, and socioeconomic measurements are described in the sections that follow.

## Quantifying Environmental, Agronomic, and Socioeconomic Parameters

### Climate Change

Tropical deforestation and land use change contribute as much as 25 percent of the annual flux of carbon dioxide ($CO_2$) to the atmosphere (IPCC 2001), yet there is still much debate on this issue because of uncertainties in biomass estimates, rates of deforestation, and land use change sequences (chapter 2, this volume). Changes in carbon stocks and the associated sources or sinks of atmospheric $CO_2$ and fluxes of nitrous oxide ($N_2O$) and methane ($CH_4$), the three most important greenhouse gases, were measured in the different land use systems at the Brazil, Cameroon, Indonesia, and Peru benchmark sites. Whereas most previous studies have focused on measurements in the forest and grassland or continuous cropping systems—in other words, the extremes—the dataset from ASB, described in chapter 2, included measurements from many of the tree-based systems that often dominate the landscape in the humid tropics (Wood et al. 2000).

Carbon stocks in the above- and below-ground vegetation and in the top 20 cm of the soil were estimated by a combination of allometric equations (for converting tree diameters into biomass) and destructive harvest. The concept of the average amount of carbon stored in each of the land use systems during the time course of the rotations, or time-averaged carbon, was used for comparing land use systems with different rotations times. The standardized methods for sampling are presented in Woomer et al. (2000) and Woomer and Palm (1998), and those for calculating time-averaged carbon are presented in chapter 2. Results are presented in Woomer et al. (2000), Palm et al. (2002b), and chapter 2.

Estimating $N_2O$ and $CH_4$ fluxes entails intensive, long-term sampling. This was not possible at most of the ASB sites. To obtain some estimates for annual fluxes and seasonal patterns for the different land use systems, $N_2O$ and $CH_4$ fluxes were measured monthly over the course of 2 years in the Indonesia and Peruvian benchmark sites using static chamber techniques. The sampling protocol and results are detailed in chapter 3 and in Ishizuka et al. (2002) and Palm et al. (2002a).

## Biodiversity

Tropical forests contain two-thirds of the estimated 250,000 world's terrestrial plant species, 90 percent of world's insects, and many bird species (Osborne 2000), making tropical deforestation a primary cause of global biodiversity loss (Heywood 1995; Stork 1997). The extent of biodiversity loss associated with different land use systems has seldom been considered, although many traditional land management strategies have supported biodiversity maintenance (McNeely et al. 1995; McNeely and Scherr 2003). Diversity of the above-ground vegetation and below-ground biota were measured in the range of land use systems at the benchmark sites to address these issues.

Above-ground plant diversity was measured as the number of plant species occurring in transects in each land use type but also according to plant functional types (PFTs) (Gillison and Carpenter 1997). Assessing plant diversity in the tropics is time-consuming and difficult, necessitating expertise in tropical plant identification and classification. The functional analysis uses a combination of adaptive morphologic or functional features (leaf size class, leaf inclination class, leaf form and type) and enables rapid characterization by people with minimal training. It includes measures of site physical features, vegetation structure, species composition, and PFTs (Gillison 2001, 2002). Results from the benchmark sites are found in Gillison (2000) and in chapter 4.

Assessing diversity of below-ground biota is even more complex than above-ground vegetation, partly because many of the species have never been identified but also because sampling strategies that capture the spatial heterogeneity of the different types of biota have not been developed. The ASB below-ground biodiversity group designed a prototype sampling strategy and focused on assessing the biodiversity of certain functional groups of soil biota including macrofauna (earthworms, ants, and termites), nematodes, arbuscular mycorrhizal fungi, and rhizobial microsymbionts. Methods and results are presented in Swift and Bignell (2001) and in chapter 5.

## Agronomic Sustainability

The majority of soils in the humid tropics are acid and have low native fertility (Sanchez 1976). Crops planted after slash-and-burn benefit from the nutrients in the ash, but rapid nutrient depletion takes place with successive nutrient removal in crop harvests, nutrient leaching, runoff and erosion promoted by high rainfall, and rapid decomposition of soil organic matter after burning. Soil physical properties also degrade with exposure caused by removal of the protective vegetation, and weeds invade fields, both of which contribute to declining crop yields (Sanchez et al. 1987; Juo and Manu, 1996). The long vegetative fallow characteristic of traditional shifting cultivation restores soil physical properties, accumulates carbon and nutrients in the fallow biomass, and eradicates weed populations. But as fallows shorten, their ability to perform these functions diminishes. The sustainability of the different land use systems depends on the ability to maintain these vital ecosystem functions. A set of measurements that could indicate the sustainability of the systems was developed and includes soil structure and biological activity, nutrient balances and replacement costs, and weeds, pests, and diseases. These criteria were assessed for the different land use systems and then, based on expert judgment, translated into scales indicating the relative degree of difficulty farmers would face in solving the problem (chapter 6, this volume).

## Household Economic and Social Concerns

Regardless of the global environmental benefits or agronomic sustainability of a land use system, farmers cannot be expected to adopt it unless it contributes more to meeting household objectives, does not entail excessive risks, and is compatible with the social and cultural norms of the community. The promotion of systems with greater environmental benefits must specifically consider the profitability, labor needs, food security, and equity issues associated with them, as well as the institutions needed.

Methods to assess these objectives, their social and institutional needs, and the ability of farm households and communities to meet these needs were developed by the ASB consortium (Tomich et al. 1998a; Vosti et al. 2000) and used to assess the alternative land uses within and across sites. Key parameters included profitability (measured in terms of economic returns to land and labor), labor and capital needs for establishing and maintaining land use systems, the potential contribution of given land use systems to meet household food security needs, and market and nonmarket institutional needs of specific land use systems. Detailed results of these studies for Brazil, Cameroon, and Indonesia are found in Vosti et al. (2001), Gockowski et al. (2001), and Tomich et al. (2001) and are summarized in chapter 17.

## Analyzing Tradeoffs: The ASB Matrix

Land use at the humid forest margins is perceived by three general sets of beneficiaries. The global community is interested in saving tropical forests, increasing carbon sequestration, reducing greenhouse gas emissions, and preserving plant and animal biodiversity. Small-scale farmers are interested in household food security, property rights, the profitability of their farms, and the institutions that support their goals. National policymakers occupy intermediate positions and can be the key actors. In 1996, ASB researchers developed a framework known as the ASB matrix to help evaluate the local, national, and global impacts of the alternative land use systems and guide their decisions (table 1.3; Tomich et al. 1998b).

The evaluation criteria include the environmental, agronomic, and socioeconomic impacts, previously described, for each of the land use options. The matrix puts together the food and income functions with ecological functions (production, human welfare, and environmental impacts) of each system, indicating the potential tradeoffs between the perspectives and interests of different stakeholders. This framework is intended for use in selecting from among the land use alternatives. The challenge is for the multiple stakeholders to weigh tradeoffs between their varied objectives. The notion of best-bet alternatives was introduced to indicate the systems that provide the combination of environmental services, poverty level, and economic growth that is most acceptable to society in the production (private) and environmental (global) functions. Some advantages and limitations of the matrix are discussed in Vosti et al. (2000) and Tomich et al. (1998b). The filled-in tradeoff matrices from the Brazil, Cameroon, and Indonesia benchmark sites are reported in chapter 18.

The analysis of the resulting tradeoff matrix must be done with full participation of the various stakeholders and is crucial for achieving a common understanding of the different viewpoints, vested interests, and potential conflicts associated with the different choices. An example of the types of tradeoffs is that between the carbon stored in different land use systems and the private profitability realized from them. This tradeoff at the Cameroon benchmark site is shown in chapter 18. There is no win–win alternative system that combines maximum carbon stocks with maximum farmer profitability. There is a lose–lose or worst-bet alternative: food crops followed by short fallows. But there are two medium-carbon systems that have high levels of farmer profitability: cacao–fruit tree complex agroforests and small-scale oil palm plantations. These are the best-bet alternatives for minimizing the tradeoffs between carbon sequestration and farmer profitability, and one can envision how policies or programs could be established to promote these systems to replace the other systems with low carbon and low profits (chapters 14 and 18, this volume).

## RESEARCHING AND IMPLEMENTING POLICIES

Once the diverse stakeholders have decided which land use systems provide the desired combination of production, human welfare, and environmental services, such as the example just described, it is necessary to search for policy instruments that can balance these tradeoffs and that will lead to a broad-based adoption of those desired systems. Typically, there are few (if any) proven policy or institutional mechanisms to address these environment–development tradeoffs. ASB has been involved with various part-

Table 1.3 ASB Matrix Comparing the Environmental, Agronomic, Socioeconomic, and Policy Aspects of the Alternative Land Use Systems

| Meta–Land Use Systems | Global Environmental Concerns | | Agronomic Sustainability | Smallholders' Socioeconomic Concerns | | Policy and Institutional Issues |
|---|---|---|---|---|---|---|
| | Carbon Sequestration (above-ground time-averaged; Mt/ha) | Biodiversity (above-ground plant species per plot) | Plot-Level Production Sustainability (overall rating) | Potential Profitability (returns to land, US $/ha) | Employment (average labor input; d/ha/yr) | Production Incentives at Private Prices (returns to labor; US $/d) |
| Forests | | | | | | |
| Complex agroforests | | | | | | |
| Simple agroforests; intensive tree crops | | | | | | |
| Crop–fallow rotations | | | | | | |
| Continuous annual crops | | | | | | |
| Grasslands, pastures | | | | | | |

Source: Modified from ASB (1996).

ners in policy research at different levels, some of which are described in chapter 7 for national and international policy arenas and chapters 10, 17, and 18 and the various country chapters in part IV for the national and local policy levels.

## ASSESSING IMPACT AND PROVIDING FEEDBACK

The last step in the ASB research and development framework is the assessment of the impacts of the options thus devised (figure 1.2). Although implementation of the various land use alternatives that have been identified as best bets is still in progress, in its first decade of existence the ASB consortium has had impacts on scientific methods and improved datasets, national research institutions, global forums concerned with poverty, the environment, and deforestation in the tropics, and policymakers. At the national scale, impacts are described for the benchmark sites in their respective chapters in this publication (chapter 12 for Brazil, chapter 13 for Indonesia, chapter 14 for Cameroon, chapter 15 for Peru, and chapter 16 for Thailand) and globally in chapter 18. A summary follows.

### Impact on Science

Perhaps the greatest impact on science has been the research process and framework designed and implemented by ASB. The research framework established the basis for integrated natural resource management research of the CGIAR centers (CIFOR 2000). The ASB matrix and tradeoff analysis provides a way to tackle complex problems and reconcile the interests of different stakeholders. ASB has also shown how the disciplinary strengths in climate change, biodiversity, agronomy, policy reform, and adoption can be used in a balanced and positive way, with combined, mutually accepted standard methods.

Other scientific contributions relate to improved methods of data collection and analysis and include improved equations for estimating carbon in young and regrowing trees, where the original equations overestimated carbon by as much as 100 percent (Ketterings et al. 2001; chapter 2, this volume); refinement of the concept of time-averaged carbon for comparing carbon stored in land use systems with different rotation times (van Noordwijk et al. 1998); validation of the use of plant functional attributes for above-ground biodiversity assessment (chapter 4, this volume); methods for assessing below-ground soil biodiversity by the use of functional groups (Swift and Bignell 2001); and the identification of agronomic sustainability indicators (chapter 6, this volume) which is a major advance in the concept of soil quality.

The ASB has enriched the scientific literature substantially, particularly with articles written by national colleagues in international journals, with almost 450 publications by the end of 2003.

## Impact on National Institutions

The country chapters in part IV of this volume identify many of the effects of the ASB consortium on the collaborating national institutes including implementing the cross-disciplinary research approach, moving much of the work away from experiment stations to farmer fields and communities, and developing meaningful dialogues with policymakers. In addition, the "south–south" exchange between scientists and policymakers visiting the ASB sites has spurred the imagination of many, resulting in the direct transfer of knowledge generated at one site to another. Such visits and workshops, along with the publication efforts, have "internationalized" many national partners, but this is an area in which a great deal of potential for impact remains to be tapped.

## Impact on Policymakers

Substantive and long-term interactions have developed between ASB researchers and national policymakers, based on the solid scientific foundation ASB brings to the discussions. Chapter 18 and the country chapters in part IV describe much of this policy research.

At the national level, work with the Indonesian Ministry of Forestry resulted in a presidential decree that recognized the property rights of the people managing the complex agroforests on government lands in Sumatra (Fay et al. 1998). ASB has also worked with the Indonesian government to address the devastating forest fires associated with El Niño events. Suggestions include selective restrictions on burning during El Niño events, monitoring and penalizing large companies that misuse fire to clear land, recognizing long-standing land claims to help minimize conflicts over land allocation, reducing or eliminating policies that depress timber prices, and encouraging people who clear land to sell excess wood rather than burn it. At the regional level ASB scientists have promoted enabling policies to support community-based forest management plots with the government of the State of Acre in Brazil and to provide credits for on-farm reforestation with the Ucayali regional government in Peru.

## Impacts on Global Organizations and Forums

ASB is now a systemwide program of the CGIAR and an NGO accredited by the Global Environment Facility. The ASB network of well-characterized benchmark sites in the world's tropical moist forests has attracted the attention of other groups concerned with the issues of poverty, the environment, and deforestation at the forest margins. This includes the World Bank, the Asian Development Bank, the International Fund for Agricultural Development (IFAD), many bilateral donors, the Intergovernmental Panel on Climate Change (IPCC), the Millennium Ecosystem Assessment, the Rainforest Challenge Partnership, and many others. Many of the approaches and results are being mainstreamed as new projects emerge. The methods for assessing carbon stocks and the improved estimates from the ASB assessment have been recognized and used by the IPCC (Paustian et al. 1997; IPCC 2001).

### External Reviews

The ASB consortium has been periodically evaluated by external teams (Eswaran 1995; Hansen et al. 1997; Technical Advisory Committee [TAC] 2000). The review by the Scientific and Technical Advisory Panel of the Global Environment Facility considered ASB "exceptional and pioneering in its design, coverage, methodology, organization and scope for transferability and replicability" (Hansen et al. 1997:1). According to TAC (2000:xxi), "the Alternatives to Slash and Burn Programme has gone further than others in relating its research sites to the whole area over which the problem occurs, and in scaling up to the global level in its findings on tradeoffs. This is very helpful for the global debate on sustainability issues." These positive reviews should be balanced with the real limitations of the ASB consortium, including recurring funding shortfalls and the communication challenge of keeping culturally diverse partners informed across the tropical belt.

### The Way Forward

The first decade of the consortium was evaluated in 1999 at a conference in Chiang Mai on environmental services and land use change. Details of the findings and recommendations are found in van Noordwijk et al. (2001b), Tomich et al. (2004), and chapter 18, this volume. Two of the major gaps that were identified included the assessment of hydrologic, ecological, and other environmental services at the watershed or community scale and methods for the various stakeholders to develop workable responses and monitor the impacts of ongoing change.

A range of flexible tools will be identified and developed for communities, local government agencies, NGO activists, research managers, policymakers, and other officials. Diverse stakeholders can then better explore their options to influence the individual choices that really determine the rate and pattern of land use change (van Noordwijk et al. 2001b).

## CONCLUSION

The ASB consortium has contributed scientifically and from a policy perspective to addressing the issues of poverty and deforestation in the humid tropics and has complied with the two Agenda 21 recommendations that formed the reason for its existence: "Limit and aim to halt destructive shifting cultivation by addressing the underlying social and ecological causes" and "Reduce damage to forests by promoting sustainable management of areas adjacent to the forests." But tropical deforestation remains at alarming levels, and so do the poverty and harsh living conditions of most forest margins dwellers. The challenge has been partially met, and the response requires continuous hard work across the research–development continuum throughout the humid tropics. Latin American, African, and Asian scientists have learned how to work together and have experienced first hand the benefits of cross-disciplinary and interinstitutional collaboration, working with international scientists, farming communities, government policymakers, and leaders of international institutions, and are equipped with the methods and partners to meet this continuing challenge.

## References

Achard, F., H.D. Eva, H.-J. Stilbig, P. Mayaus, J. Gallego, T. Richards, et al. 2002. Determination of deforestation rates of the world's humid tropical forests. Science (Washington, DC) 297:999–1002.

Alegre, J.C., and D.K. Cassel. 1986. Effect of land-clearing methods and postclearing management on aggregate stability and organic carbon content of a soil in the humid tropics. Soil Sci. 142:289–295.

Alegre, J.C., and D.K. Cassel. 1996. Dynamics of soil physical properties under alternative systems to slash-and-burn. Agric. Ecosyst. Environ. 58:39–48.

Ambassa-Kiki, R., and T. Tiki Manga. 1997. Biophysical and socioeconomic characterization of the humid forest zone of Cameroon. Inst. de Recherche Agricole pour le Développement (IRAD), Yaoundé, Cameroon.

Amelung, T., and M. Diehl. 1992. Deforestation of tropical rain forests: Economic causes and impact on development. Kieler Studien no. 241. Inst. für Weltwirtschaft, Kiel, Germany.

Angelsen, A., and D. Kaimowitz (eds.). 2001. Agricultural technologies and tropical deforestation. CAB Int., Wallingford, UK.

ASB (Alternatives to Slash and Burn). 1992. Alternatives to slash and burn. Program brief. 28 Feb. 1992. ICRAF, Nairobi.

ASB (Alternatives to Slash and Burn). 1996. Report of the meeting of the 5th global steering group. 3–6 Oct. 1996. ICRAF, Nairobi.

Ávila, M. 1994. Alternatives to slash-and-burn in South America: Report of research site selection in Acre and Rondônia states of Amazon Region of Brazil. Alternatives to Slash-and-Burn Agriculture Programme. Conducted from 31 Aug. to 15 Sept. 1992. ICRAF, Nairobi.

Bandy, D.E., D.P. Garrity, and P.A. Sanchez. 1993. The world wide problem of slash and burn agriculture. Agrofor. Today 5(3):2–6.

Binswanger, H.P. 1991. Brazilian policies that encourage deforestation in the Amazon. World Dev. 19(7):821–829.

Boserup, E. 1965. The conditions of agricultural growth: The economics of agrarian change under population pressure. Aldine, Chicago.

Bouamrane, M. 1996. The season of gold: Putting a value on harvests from Indonesian agroforests. Agrofor. Today 8 (1):8–10.

Brown, K., and D.W. Pearce (eds.). 1994. The causes of tropical deforestation: The economic and statistical analysis of factors giving rise to the loss of tropical forests. UCL Press, London.

Bruijnzeel, L.A. 1990. Hydrology of moist tropical forests and effects of conversion: A state of knowledge review. UNESCO, Free Univ. of Amsterdam.

Bryant, D., D. Nielsen, and L. Tangley. 1997. The last frontier forests: Ecosystems & economies on the edge. World Resources Inst., Washington, DC.

Cairns, M., and D.P. Garrity. 1999. Improving shifting cultivation in Southeast Asia by building on indigenous fallow management strategies. Agrofor. Syst. 47:37–48.

Carpenter, G., A.N. Gillison, and J. Winter. 1993. DOMAIN: A flexible modeling procedure for mapping potential distributions of plants and animals. Biodiversity Conserv. 2:667–680.

Cerri, C.C., B. Volkoff, and F. Andreaux. 1991. Nature and behavior of organic matter in soils under natural forest, and after deforestation, burning and cultivation near Manaus. Forest Ecol. Manage. 38:247–257.

CIFOR (Center for International Forestry Research). 2000. Integrated natural resource management research in the CGIAR. CIFOR, Bogor, Indonesia.

Colfer, C.J.P., D.W. Gill, and F. Agus. 1988. An indigenous agricultural model from West Sumatra: A source of scientific insight. Agric. Syst. 26:191–209.

Conklin, H.C. 1954. An ethno ecological approach to shifting cultivation. Trans. New York Acad. Sci. II 17(2):133–142.

Conklin, H.C. 1963. The study of shifting cultivation. Studies and monographs, VI. Union Panamericana, Washington, DC.

Cowgill, U.M. 1962. An anthropological study of the southern Maya lowlands. Am. Anthropologist 64:273–286.

Dixon, J., A. Gulliver, and D. Gibbon. 2001. Farming systems and poverty. Improving farmers' livelihoods in a changing world. FAO, Rome.

Duguma, B., J. Gockowski, and J. Bekala. 2001. Smallholder cacao (*Theobroma cacao* Linn.) cultivation in agroforestry systems of West and Central Africa: Challenges and opportunities. Agrofor. Syst. 51 (3):177–188.

Durst, P. 2000. Forest news. Tigerpaper 27(3 July–Sept. 2000).

Eswaran, H. 1995. External evaluation of the project Alternatives to Slash-and-Burn. UNDP, New York.

FAO (Food and Agriculture Organization). 1997. State of the world's forests. FAO, Rome.

FAO (Food and Agriculture Organization) Staff. 1957. Shifting cultivation. Trop. Agric. (Trinidad) 34:159–164.

Fay, C., H. de Foresta, M. Sarait, and T.P. Tomich. 1998. A policy breakthrough for Indonesian farmers in the Krui damar agroforests. Agrofor. Today 10 (2):25–26.

Foresta, H. de, and G. Michon. 1994. Agroforests in Indonesia: Where ecology and economy meet. Agrofor. Today 6:12–14.

Fujisaka, S., G. Kirk, J.A. Litsinger, K. Moody, N. Hosen, A. Yusef, et al. 1991. Wild pigs, poor soils, and upland rice: a diagnostic survey of Sitiung, Sumatra, Indonesia. IRRI Res. Paper Ser. IRRI, Manila.

Garrity, D.P. (ed.). 1997. Agroforestry innovations for Imperata grassland rehabilitation. Kluwer Academic Publ., Dordrecht, The Netherlands.

Geist, H.J., and E.F. Lambin. 2002. Proximate causes and underlying driving forces of tropical deforestation. BioScience 52(2):143–149.

Gillison, A.N. (coord.). 2000. Above-ground biodiversity assessment working group summary report 1996–98. Impact of different land uses on biodiversity and social indicators. Alternatives to Slash and Burn Project, ICRAF, Nairobi.

Gillison, A.N. 2001. A field manual for rapid vegetation classification and survey for general purposes (including instructions for the use of a rapid survey proforma and VegClass computer software). CIFOR, Bogor, Indonesia. (CD-ROM and hard copy.)

Gillison, A. 2002. A generic, computer-assisted method for rapid vegetation classification and survey: Tropical and temperate case studies. Conserv. Ecol. 6:3. Available at http://www.consecol.org/vol6/iss2/art3 (verified 7 Dec. 2003).

Gillison, A.N., and G. Carpenter. 1997. A plant functional attribute set and grammar for dynamic vegetation description and analysis. Functional Ecol. 11:775–783.

Gintings, A.N., S. Partohardjono, T. Sukandi, S. Sukmana, K. Suradisastra, P. Cooper, et al. 1995. Site selection for alternatives to slash-and-burn in Indonesia: Report of a site-selection exercise in Kalimantan and Sumatra, 18–27 Aug. 1992. ICRAF, Nairobi.

Gockowski, J., B. Nkamleu, and J. Wendt. 2001. Implications of resource use intensification for the environment and sustainable technology systems in the central African rainforest. pp. 197–217. *In* D. Lee and C. Barrett (eds.) Tradeoffs or synergies? Agricultural intensification, economic development and the environment. CAB Int., Wallingford, UK.

Haggar, J., A. Ayala, B. Diaz, and C.U. Reyes. 2001. Participatory design of agroforestry systems: Developing farmer participatory research methods in Mexico. Develop. Practice 11(4):417–424.

Hansen, S., M.H. Allegretti, R.D. Fall, and M.N. Salleh. 1997. Alternatives to slash and burn agriculture. STAP Selective Rev. Rep. of GLO/95/g32 (Phase 1). Scientific and Technical Advisory Panel, Global Environment Facility, Oslo.

Hauck F.W. 1974. Shifting cultivation and soil conservation in Africa. FAO Soils Bull. 24: 1–4.

Hayami, Y., and V.W. Ruttan. 1985. Agricultural development: An international perspective, 2nd ed. Johns Hopkins Univ. Press, Baltimore.

Hecht, S.B., and A. Cockburn. 1989. The fate of the forest: Developers, destroyers, and defenders of the Amazon. Versco, London.

Heywood, V.H. 1995. Global biodiversity assessment. Cambridge Univ. Press, Cambridge.

Houghton, R.A., D.L. Skole, C.A. Nobre, J.L. Hackler, K.T. Lawrence, and W.H. Chomentowski. 2000. Annual fluxes of carbon from deforestation and regrowth in the Brazilian Amazon. Nature (London) 403:301–304.

INPE (Instituto Nacional de Pesquisas Espaciais). 2003. Monitoramento da floresta amazônica brasileira por satellite: Projeto PRODES. Available at www.obt.inpe.br/prodes.html.

IPCC (Intergovernmental Panel on Climate Change). 2001. Climate change 2001: The scientific basis. J.T. Houghton, Y. Ding, .D.J. Griggs, M. Nogues, P.J. van der Linden, K. Dai, et al. (eds.). Cambridge Univ. Press, Cambridge.

Ishizuka, S., H. Tsuruta, and D. Murdiyarso. 2002. An intensive field study on $CO_2$, $CH_4$, and $N_2O$ emissions from soils at four land-use types in Sumatra, Indonesia. Global Biogeochem. Cycles 16:1049–1059.

Izac, A.-M. N., and P.A. Sanchez. 2001. Towards a natural resource management paradigm for international agriculture: The example of agroforestry research. Agric. Syst. 69:5–25.

Juo, A.S.R., and R. Lal. 1977. The effect of fallows and continuous cultivation on the chemical and physical properties of an alfisol in western Nigeria. Plant Soil 47:567–584.

Juo, A.S.R., and A. Manu. 1996. Chemical dynamics in slash-and-burn agriculture. Agric. Ecosyst. Environ. 58:49–60.

Jurion, F., and J. Henry. 1969. Can primitive farming be modernized? INEAC Series. Inst. Natl. pour l'Etude Agron. du Congo, Brussels.

Kang, B.T., L. Reynolds, and A.N. Attra-Krah. 1990. Alley farming. Adv. Agron. 43:315–339.

Kartasubrata, J. 1991. Deforestation and sustainable land use development in Indonesia. Bogor Agric. Univ., Indonesia.

Keating, M. 1993. The Earth Summit's agenda for change. A plain language version of Agenda 21 and the other Rio Agreements. Center for Our Common Future, Geneva, Switzerland.

Ketterings, Q.M., R. Coe, M. van Noordwijk, Y. Ambagau, and C.A. Palm. 2001. Reducing uncertainty in the use of allometric biomass equations for predicting above-ground tree biomass in mixed secondary forests. Forest Ecol. Manage. 146:201–211.

Kotto-Same, J., A. Moukam, R. Njomgang, T. Tiki-Manga, J. Tonye, C. Diaw, et al. (eds.). 2000. Alternatives to Slash-and-Burn in Cameroon. Summary report and synthesis of phase II. ASB Programme, ICRAF, Nairobi.

Lal, R., P.A. Sanchez, and R.W. Cummings, Jr. (eds.). 1986. Land clearing and development in the tropics. Balkema, Rotterdam.

Lanly, J.-P. 1982. Tropical forest resources. FAO, Rome, Italy.

Laurance, W.F., S.G. Laurance, L.V. Ferreira, J.M. Rankin-de Merona, C. Gascon, and T.E. Lovejoy. 1997. Biomass collapse in Amazonian forest fragments. Science (Washington, DC) 278:1117–1118.

Lavelle, P., and B. Pashanasi. 1989. Soil macrofauna and land management in Peruvian Amazonia (Yurimaguas, Loreto). Pedobiologia 33:283–291.

Lewis, J., S. Vosti, J. Witcover, P.J. Ericksen, R. Guevara, and T.P. Tomich (eds.). 2002. Alternatives to Slash-and-Burn (ASB) in Brazil: Summary report and synthesis of phase II. November 2002. World Agroforestry Center (ICRAF), Nairobi.

MacIntosh, J.L., I.G. Ismail, S. Effendi, and M. Sudjadi. 1981. Cropping systems to preserve fertility of red-yellow Podzolic soils in Indonesia. Int. Symp. on Distribution, Characterization and Utilization of Problem Soils. TARC, Tsukuba, Japan.

Mahar, D. 1988. Government policies and deforestation in Brazil, Amazon Region. World Bank Environment Dep. Working Paper No. 7. World Bank, Washington, DC.

Mahar, D., and R. Schneider. 1994. Incentives for tropical deforestation: Some examples from Latin America. In K. Brown and D.W. Pearce (eds.) The causes of tropical deforestation. UCL Press, London.

McNeely, J.A., M. Gadgil, C. Leveque, C. Padoch, and K. Redford. 1995. Human influences on biodiversity. pp. 711–821. In V.H. Heywood (ed.) Global biodiversity assessment. Cambridge Univ. Press, Cambridge.

McNeely, J.A., and S.J. Scherr. 2003. Ecoagriculture: Strategies to feed the world and save biodiversity. Island Press, Washington, DC.

Mercado, A.R., Jr., M. Patindol, and D.P. Garrity. 2001. The landcare experience in the Philippines: Technical and institutional innovations for conservation farming. Develop. Practice (11) 4:495–509.

Michon, G. 1997. Indigenous gardens: Re-inventing the forest. pp. 88–89. In T. Whitten and J. Whitten (eds.) The Indonesian heritage, vol. Plants. Grollier, Singapore.

Michon, G., and H. de Foresta. 1996. Agroforests as an alternative to pure plantations for the domestication and commercialization of NTFPS. pp. 160–175. *In* R.R.B. Leakey, A.T. Temu, M. Melnyk, and P. Vantomme (eds.) Domestication and commercialization of non-timber forest products for agroforestry. Non-wood forest products 9. FAO, Rome.

Moran, E.F. 1981. Developing the Amazon. Indiana Univ. Press, Bloomington.

Myers, N. 1991. Tropical forests: Present status and future outlook. Climatic Change 19:3–32.

Myers, N. 1993. Tropical forests: The main deforestation fronts. Environ. Conserv. 20 (1):9–16.

Myers N. 1994. Tropical deforestation: Rates and patterns. *In* K. Brown and D.W. Pearce (eds.). The causes of tropical deforestation. UCL Press, London.

NRC (National Research Council). 1993. Sustainable agriculture and the environment in the humid tropics. National Academy Press, Washington, DC.

Nye, P.H., and D.J. Greenland. 1960. The soil under shifting cultivation. Technical Communications 51. Commonw. Bureau of Soils, Harpenden, UK.

Osborne, P.L. 2000. Tropical ecosystems and ecological concepts. Cambridge Univ. Press, Cambridge.

Padoch, C., and W. de Jong. 1987. Traditional agroforestry practices of native and Ribereño farmers in the lowland Peruvian Amazon. pp. 179–194. *In* H.L. Gholz (ed.) Agroforestry: Realities, possibilities and potentials. Martinus Nijhoff, Dordrecht, The Netherlands.

Palm, C.A., J.C. Alegre, L. Arevalo, P.K. Mutuo, A.R. Mosier, and R. Coe. 2002a. Nitrous oxide and methane fluxes in six different land use systems in the Peruvian Amazon. Global Biogeochem. Cycles 16:1073.

Palm, C.A., A.M. Izac, and S. Vosti. 1995. ASB procedural guidelines for characterization. ICRAF, Nairobi.

Palm, C.A., and P.A. Sanchez. 1991. Nitrogen release from the leaves of some tropical legumes as affected by their lignin and polyphenolic contents. Soil Biol. Biochem. 23:83–88.

Palm, C.A., M.J. Swift, and P.L. Woomer. 1996. Biological dynamics in slash-and-burn agriculture. Agric. Ecosyst. Environ. 58:61–74.

Palm, C.A., P.L. Woomer, J. Alegre, C. Castilla, K. Cordeiro, K. Hairiah, et al. 2002b. Carbon sequestration and trace gas emissions in slash-and-burn and alternative land uses in the tropics. Alternatives to Slash-and-Burn Phase II Final Rep. ICRAF, Nairobi.

Paustian, K., O. Andrian, H.H. Janzen, R. Lal, P. Smith, G. Tian, et al. 1997. Agricultural soils as a sink to mitigate $CO_2$ emissions. Soil Use Manage. 13:230–244.

Ramakrishnan, P.S. 1984. The science behind rotation bush fallow agricultural system (jhum). Proceedings Indian Academy of Sciences. Plant Sci. 93(3):79–400.

Ramakrishnan, P.S. 1987. Shifting agriculture and rainforest ecosystem management. Biol. Int. 15:17–18.

Repetto, R., and M. Gillis (eds.). 1988. Public policies and the misuse of forest resources. Cambridge Univ. Press, Cambridge.

Rhoades, R.E., and P. Bidegaray. 1987. The farmers of Yurimaguas: Land use and cropping strategies in the Peruvian jungle. Int. Potato Center, Lima, Peru.

Rudel, T., and J. Roper. 1997. The paths to rain forest destruction: Cross-national patterns of tropical deforestation, 1975–1990. World Develop. 25:53–65.

Ruthenberg, H. 1980. Farming systems in the tropics. Clarendon Press, Oxford.

Sanchez, P.A. 1976. Properties and management of soils in the tropics. Wiley, New York.

Sanchez, P.A. 1999. Improved fallows come of age in the tropics. Agrofor. Syst. 47:3–12.

Sanchez, P.A., and D.E. Bandy. 1992. Alternative to slash and burn: A pragmatic approach to mitigate tropical deforestation. Ann. Acad. Bras. Ciên. 64:7–33.

Sanchez, P.A., and J.R. Benites. 1987. Low-input cropping for acid soils of the humid tropics. Science (Washington, DC) 238:1521–1527.

Sanchez, P.A., and M. Hailu (eds.). 1996. Special issue on alternatives to slash and burn agriculture. Agric. Ecosyst. Environ. 58:1–86.

Sanchez, P.A., A.J. Simons, and F.J. Place. 1998. More people, more trees: The future of trees is on farm in Africa. p. 48. *In* 1998 Agronomy abstracts. ASA, Madison, WI.

Sanchez, P.A., E.R. Stoner, and E. Pushparajah (eds.). 1987. Management of acid tropical soils for sustainable agriculture (Yurimaguas–Brasília Workshop). IBSRAM Proceedings No. 2. IBSRAM, Bangkok.

Sanchez, P.A., J.H. Villachica, and D.E. Bandy. 1983. Soil fertility dynamics after clearing a tropical rainforest in Peru. Soil Sci. Soc. Am. J. 47:1171–1178.

Serrão, E.A.S., I.C. Falesi, J.B. Veiga, and J.F. Texeira. 1979. Productivity of cultivated pastures in low fertility soils of the Amazon of Brazil. pp. 195–226. *In* P.A. Sanchez and L.E. Tergas (eds.) Pastures production in acid soils of the tropics. CIAT, Cali, Colombia.

Serrão, E.A.S., and A.K.O. Homma. 1993. Country profiles: Brazil. pp. 263–351. *In* Sustainable agriculture and the environment in the humid tropics. Natl. Res. Council, National Academy Press, Washington, DC.

Serrão, E.A.S., and J.M. Toledo. 1990. The search for sustainability in Amazonian pastures, pp. 195–214, In A.B. Anderson, ed. Alternatives to deforestation. Columbia Univ. Press, New York.

Seubert, C.E., P.A. Sanchez, and C. Valverde. 1977. Effects of land clearing methods and soils properties of an ultisol and crop performance in the Amazon jungle of Peru. Trop. Agric. 54:307–321.

Smyth, T.J., and J.B. Bastos. 1984. Alteraçoes na fertilidade em um latossolo amarelo álico pela queima da vegetaçao. Rev. Bras. de Ciênc. Solo 8:127–132.

Smyth, T.J., and D.K. Cassel. 1995. Synthesis of long-term soil management research on ultisols and oxisols in the Amazon. *In* R. Lal and B.A. Stewart (eds.) Soil management: Experimental basis for sustainability and environmental quality. Lewis Publ., Boca Raton, FL.

Stork, N.E. 1997. Measuring biodiversity and its decline. pp. 41–68. *In* M.L. Reaka-Kudla, D.E. Wilson, and E.O. Wilson (eds.) Biodiversity II. John Henry Press, Washington, DC.

Swift, M.J., and D.E. Bandy. 1995. Alternatives to slash-and-burn: Project management by consortium. ICRAF, Nairobi.

Swift, M., and D. Bignell. 2001. Standard methods for the assessment of soil biodiversity and land-use practice. ASB Lecture Note 6B. ICRAF, South East Asian Regional Res. Programme, Bogor, Indonesia.

Szott, L.T., and C.A. Palm. 1986. Soil and vegetation dynamics in shifting cultivation fallows. pp. 360–379. *In* First Symp. on the Humid Tropics. Vol. 1. Embrapa, Belem, Pará, Brazil.

TAC (Technical Advisory Committee). 2000. First review of systemwide programmes with an ecoregional approach. p. xxi. TAC, of the Consultative Group on International Agricultural Research. FAO, Rome.

Thrupp, L.A., S.B. Hecht, and J.O. Browder. 1997. The diversity and dynamics of shifting cultivation: Myths, realities, and policy implications. World Resources Inst., Washington, DC.

Tiffen, M., M. Mortimore, and F. Gichuki. 1994. More people, less erosion: Environmental recovery in Kenya. Wiley, New York.

Tinker, P.B., J.S.I. Ingram, and S. Struwe. 1996. Effects of slash-and-burn agriculture and deforestation on climate change. Agric. Ecosyst. Environ. 58:13–22.

Toky, O.P., and P.S. Ramakrishnan. 1981. Cropping and yields in agricultural systems of the north eastern hill region of India. Agro Ecosyst. 7:11–25.

Tomich, T.P., M. van Noordwijk, S. Budidarsono, A. Gillison, T. Kusumanto, D. Murdiyarso, et al. 1998a. Alternatives to Slash-and-Burn in Indonesia. Summary report and synthesis of phase II. ASB, ICRAF, Nairobi.

Tomich, T.P., M. van Noordwijk, S. Budidarsono, A. Gillison, T. Kusumanto, D. Murdiyarso, et al. 2001. Agricultural intensification, deforestation and the environment: Assessing tradeoffs in Sumatra, Indonesia. pp. 221–244. *In* D. Lee and C. Barrett (eds.) Tradeoffs or synergies? Agricultural intensification, economic development and the environment. CAB Int., Wallingford, UK.

Tomich, T.P., M. van Noordwijk, and D.E. Thomas. 2004. Environmental services and land use change in Southeast Asia: From recognition to regulation or reward? Agric. Ecosyst. Environ. In press.

Tomich, T.P., M. van Noordwijk, S.A. Vosti, and J. Witcover. 1998b. Agricultural development with rainforest conservation: Methods for seeking best bet alternatives to slash-and-burn, with applications to Brazil and Indonesia. Agric. Econ. 19(1–2):159–174.

Torquebiau, E. 1984. Man-made dipterocarp forest in Sumatra. Agroforestry Systems 2:103–128.

van Noordwijk, M., K. Hairiah, P.L. Woomer, and D. Murdiyarso. 1998. Criteria and indicators of forest soils used for slash-and-burn agriculture and alternative land uses in Indonesia. pp. 137–153. The contributions of soil science to the development and implementation of criteria and indicators of sustainable forest management. SSSA Spec. Publ. 53. SSSA, Madison, WI.

van Noordwijk, M., T.P. Tomich, and B. Verbist. 2001a. Negotiation support models for integrated natural resource management in tropical forest margins. Conserv. Ecol. 5(2). Available at http://www.consecol.org/vol5/iss2/art21.

van Noordwijk, M., T.P. Tomich, R. Winahyu, D. Murdiyarso, S. Suyanto, S. Partoharjono, et al. (eds.). 1995. Alternatives to Slash-and-Burn in Indonesia: Summary report of phase 1. ASB–Indonesia Rep. No. 4. ASB–Indonesia Consortium and ICRAF, Bogor, Indonesia.

van Noordwijk, M., S.E. Williams, and B. Verbist (eds.). 2001b. Toward integrated natural resource management in forest margins of the humid tropics: Local action and global concerns. ASB Lecture Notes 1–12. ICRAF, Bogor, Indonesia. Available at http://www.icraf.cgiar.org/sea/Training/Materials/ASB-TM/ASB-ICRAFSEA-LN.htm.

Von Uexkull, J.R. 1984. Managing acrisols in the humid tropics. Food and Fertilizer Technol. Center (FFTC) Book Ser. 27:382–397. FFTC, Taipei, Taiwan.

Vosti, S.A., J. Witcover, C.L. Carpenter, S.J.M. de Oliveira, and J.C. dos Santos. 2001. Intensifying small-scale agriculture in the western Brazilian Amazon: Issues, implications and implementation. pp. 245–266. *In* D. Lee and C. Barrett (eds.) Tradeoffs or synergies? Agricultural intensification, economic development and the environment. CAB Int., Wallingford, UK.

Vosti, S.A., J. Witcover, J. Gockowski, T.P. Tomich, C.L. Carpentier, M.D. Faminow, et al. 2000. Working Group on Economic and Social Indicators: Report on methods for the ASB matrix. Alternatives to Slash-and-Burn Agriculture Research Programme, August 2000. World Agroforestry Center (ICRAF), Nairobi.

Wade, M.K., D.W. Gill, H. Subagjo, M. Sudjadi, and P.A. Sanchez. 1988. Overcoming soil fertility constraints in a transmigration area of Indonesia. TropSoils Bull. 88–01. North Carolina State Univ., Raleigh.

Whitmore T., and J. Sayer (eds.). 1992. Tropical deforestation and species extinction. Chapman & Hall, London.

Wood, S., K. Sebastian, and S.J. Scherr. 2000. Pilot analysis of global ecosystems: Agroecosystems. IFPRI and WRI, Washington, DC.

Woomer, P.L., and C.A. Palm. 1998. An approach to estimating system carbon stocks in tropical forests and associated land uses. Commonw. For. Rev. 77:181–190.

Woomer, P.L., C.A. Palm, J. Alegre, C. Castilla, D.G. Cordeiro, K. Hairiah, et al. 2000. Slash-and-burn effects on carbon stocks in the humid tropics. pp. 99–115. *In* R. Lal, J.M. Kimble, and B.A. Stewart (eds.) Global climate change and tropical ecosystems. Advances in soil science. CRC Press, Boca Raton, FL.

WWF (World Wildlife Fund). 2001. Terrestrial ecoregions database (unpublished data and readme file). Washington, DC: WWF-US.

# II. THEMATIC RESEARCH

# 2 Carbon Losses and Sequestration After Land Use Change in the Humid Tropics

Cheryl A. Palm
*The Earth Institute at Columbia University  Palisades, New York*
Meine van Noordwijk
*World Agroforestry Centre, Indonesia  Bogor, Indonesia*
Paul L. Woomer
*Sacred Africa  Nairobi, Kenya*
Julio C. Alegre
*World Agroforestry Centre, Peru  Pucallpa, Peru*
Luis Arévalo
*World Agroforestry Centre, Peru  Pucallpa, Peru*
Carlos E. Castilla
*Cenipalma, Bogatá, Colombia*
Divonzil G. Cordeiro
*Embrapa, Acre  Rio Branco, Acre, Brazil*
Kurniatun Hairiah
*Brawijaya University  Malang, Indonesia*
Jean Kotto-Same
*Institut de Recherche Agricole pour le Développement  Yaoundé, Cameroon*
Appolinaire Moukam
*Deceased*
William J. Parton
*Colorado State University  Fort Collins, Colorado*
Auberto Ricse
*Instituto Nacional de Investigacion Agraria  Pucallpa, Peru*
Vanda Rodrigues
*Embrapa, Rondonia  Porto Velho*
Syukur M. Sitompul
*Brawijaya University  Malang, Indonesia*

The role of tropical forests in the global carbon (C) cycle has been debated over the past 20 years, as several estimates of the flux of carbon dioxide ($CO_2$) from tropical deforestation have been proposed (Houghton et al. 1987; Detwiler and Hall 1988; Brown et al. 1993). Current estimates indicate that land use change in the tropics released 1.7 (0.6–2.5) Gt C/yr, compared with $5.4 \pm 0.3$ Gt C/yr from fossil fuel emissions (IPCC 2001). This flux has been attributed primarily to deforestation in the tropical zone, with Asia and Latin America accounting for more than 80 percent of the flux (Houghton 1997). However, a recent analysis of the net carbon flux from the Brazilian Amazon suggests that carbon sources created by deforestation are offset by carbon sinks from the undisturbed forest and regrowing secondary vegetation (Houghton et al. 2000). As noted by DeFries et al. (1999), reducing the uncertainty of estimates of $CO_2$ emissions caused by land use change is key to balancing the global carbon budget. Much of the uncertainty in the values of $CO_2$ flux from the tropics is a result of inadequate estimates for rates of different land use transitions, the biomass of the vegetation that is cleared, the rates of regrowth, and levels of biomass recovery of the subsequent land use systems. In particular there is little information on the carbon stored and the potential to sequester carbon in many of the land use systems of the humid tropics other than for continuous cropping and pasture systems, both of which have low carbon storage potential. However, there is significant tree cover on deforested, agricultural, and abandoned land in the rainfed, or humid, tropics (Fearnside and Guimaraes 1996; Houghton et al. 2000; Silver et al. 2000; Wood et al. 2000) that could provide a potentially large sink for carbon.

One of the primary objectives of the Alternatives to Slash and Burn (ASB) program was to improve information on the carbon stored in the biomass of the vegetation and soils during the various stages of the land use systems established after deforestation in the humid tropics. Changes in carbon stocks associated with the different land use systems combined with details on the time course of these changes during the land use rotation are necessary to estimate the net carbon losses and sequestration potential associated with these different land use conversions.

## METHODS

### FIELD SAMPLING

Above-ground (live trees and understory, dead vegetation, litter layer) and below-ground (roots and soil to 20-cm depth) carbon stocks were measured in forests or other land uses established after slash-and-burn clearing in the benchmark sites in Brazil (Pedro Peixoto and Theobroma), Cameroon (Yaoundé, M'Balmayo, and Ebolowa), and Indonesia (Lampung and Jambi). The land uses sampled at each site together made up a time course, or chronosequence, of land use change. In this type of sampling, called type II studies by Sanchez et al. (1985), the time courses of changes in carbon stocks for different land use scenarios are reconstructed by sampling areas of known but different ages. The preferred sampling method, a type I study, in which the changes in carbon stocks are followed in a single plot through time, is impractical because of the long-term nature of these studies. In type II studies, in which space substitutes for time, care must be taken to sample areas in a chronosequence that have similar soil texture; if not, then differences in carbon stocks that are attributed to land use change might actually be a result of differences in site characteristics that affect carbon storage (Sanchez et al. 1985).

At each location in the benchmark sites, one or two land use chronosequences were sampled. Each chronosequence included the meta–land use systems (chapter 1, this volume) appropriate for each benchmark site. Natural or selectively logged forests served as reference points for baseline data on initial carbon stocks for each chronosequence. The land use sequence was then represented by areas that had recently been slashed, burned, and cropped combined with areas that included various stages of the crop and fallow cycles; various ages of lands subsequently planted to pastures, agroforests, or tree plantations; or stages of cropland and pasture degradation. The management practices, age, and time course, including rotation time of each land use system sampled, were obtained by interviewing the farmers. The land use systems that were evaluated for carbon stocks in each of the benchmark sites are summarized in table 2.1.

Above-ground and below-ground carbon stocks were measured for each land use within the chronosequences according to standardized methods described in Woomer and Palm (1998) and Woomer et al. (2000). Briefly, tree biomass was determined by measuring diameter at breast height (dbh) for all trees with dbh greater than 2.5 cm in five 4- by 25-m quadrats. Diameter was converted to tree biomass by use of the allometric equations for tropical moist forest trees in Brown et al. (1989) or FAO (1997).

Understory biomass was determined by destructively harvesting and drying all vegetation less than 2.5 cm dbh within two 1-m² quadrats placed in each tree quadrat. The biomass of the litter layer was determined by removing all surface litter from a 0.5- by 0.5-m quadrat placed in each understory plot. Roots were excavated and soil carbon assessed in a minimum of four 0.2- by 0.2-m quadrats, for the 0- to 0.2-m and 0.2- to 0.5-m soil depths, for each land use per chronosequence. Vegetation, root, and litter biomass were all converted to carbon multiplying by a factor of 0.45. As discussed later, root data were ignored because of their variability.

## CALCULATING TIME-AVERAGED ABOVE-GROUND CARBON STOCKS AND NET CARBON LOSS OR SEQUESTRATION

The carbon stocks of the different land use systems at the ASB sites are presented in Kotto-Same et al. (1997), Fujisaka et al. (1998), and Tomich et al. (1998) and summarized in Woomer et al. (2000). In this chapter, that information was used to calculate the above-ground time-averaged carbon for the different land use systems. The carbon loss or sequestration potential of a land use system is determined not by the maximum carbon stock of the system or the stocks at any one point in time but, rather, by the average carbon stored in that land use system during its rotation time

*Table 2.1* Details of the Major Components and Management of the Different Land Use Systems Evaluated for Above-Ground Time-Averaged Carbon for the Different A S B Benchmark Areas

---

**Brazil**

---

*Pastures:* both extensive and intensive (grass–legume mixtures)

*Simple agroforests* (single tree crop systems): monoculture coffee plantations (1000 plants/ha), assuming a 7-yr establishment phase plus 5 more years of production for a total rotation time of 12 yr

*Simple agroforestry systems* (includes three systems: coffee [*Coffea canephora* Pierre ex Froehner] + rubber [*Hevea brasiliensis* (Willd. ex A. Juss.) Muell.-Arg.], coffee + bandarra (*Schizolobium amazonicum* Huber ex Ducke); and cupuaçú [*Theobroma grandiflorum* (Willd. ex Spreng.) Schum] + pupunha (*Bactris gasipaes* Kunth) + castanha [*Bertholletia excelsa* Humb. & Bonpl.]), with an establishment phase of 12 yr and rotation time of 20 yr

*Crop–short fallow systems:* annual crop–fallow cycles with 3 yr of cropping and 5 yr of natural bush fallow

*Crop–short improved fallow systems:* annual crop–improved tree fallow with inga (*Inga edulis* Mart.) or senna (*Senna reticulata* [Willd.] H. Irwin and Barneby) cycles with 3 yr of cropping and 5 yr of fallow

---

**Cameroon**

---

*Crop*–Chromolaena *fallow systems:* 2 yr of annual cropping followed by 4 yr of *Chromolaena odorata* (L.) R.M. King and H. Robinson fallow

*Crop–short fallow system:* 2 yr of cropping followed by 9 yr of secondary forest fallow

*Crop–long fallow system:* 2 yr of cropping followed by 23 yr of secondary forest fallow

*Complex agroforests:* 2 yr of cropping followed by establishment of *Theobroma cacao* (jungle cacao) with a 25-yr establishment phase and 40-yr rotation

*Complex agroforests:* a permanent, nonrotational cacao system established through gap and understory plantings of cacao

*Simple agroforests (single tree crop system):* 1 yr of cropping followed by establishment of an oil palm plantation with 146 trees/ha with a 7-yr establishment phase and a 25-yr rotation

---

**Indonesia**

---

*Complex agroforests:* 2 yr of annual cropping followed by establishment of a rubber plantation (jungle rubber) with a 25-yr establishment phase and 30-yr rotation time

*Complex agroforests:* a nonrotational, permanent rubber agroforestry system established through understory and gap plantings

*Simple agroforests (intensive tree crop systems):* establishment of an industrial oil palm plantation with 120 trees/ha and an establishment phase of 7 yr and rotation time of 25 yr

*Simple agroforests (single tree crop system):* establishment of an industrial timber plantation of a single fast-growing tree (*Paraserianthes falcataria, Eucalyptus* sp., *Acacia mangium*) with a rotation time of 8 yr

*Crop–fallow rotation:* 7 yr of cassava followed by 3 yr of *Imperata cylindrica* (L.) Beauv grassland

(ICRAF 1996). This quantity is referred to here as the time-averaged carbon stock and is similar to the average carbon storage method described in the Intergovernmental Panel on Climate Change (IPCC) Special Report on Land Use, Land-Use Change and Forestry (Watson et al. 2000). The time-averaged carbon takes into account the dynamics of systems that include tree regrowth and harvesting and allows the comparison of land use systems that have different tree growth and harvesting rotation times and patterns.

The time-averaged carbon stock depends on the carbon accumulation rates, the maximum and minimum carbon stored in the system during a full rotation, the time it takes to reach maximum carbon, and the rotation time of the system (figure 2.1). Carbon accumulation rates ($I_c$), in tons of carbon per hectare per year, for above-ground vegetation regrowth were calculated as the carbon stock value of the sampled vegetation (Cs) divided by the age ($T_s$) of the vegetation (ICRAF 1996). Average carbon accumulation rates were obtained for each land use system in each country from the individual rates for the replicate chronosequences. It is assumed that the carbon increase rates ($I_c$) are linear throughout the time period of vegetation regrowth after clearing ($T_f$). This appears to hold at least for the first 20 years (Brown and Lugo 1990; Fearnside and Guimaraes 1996). The maximum carbon stored in fallows (Cm) at the time of clearing ($T_f$) is calculated as $Cm = I_c \times T_f$. The time-averaged carbon stock for a crop–fallow system that has negligible carbon stored in a short cropping phase is essentially the carbon stored in the fallow vegetation at the time of reclearing (Cm) divided by 2, or the carbon accumulation rate ($I_c$) times the years of fallow ($T_f$) divided by 2 (figure 2.1a). For tree crop plantations or some agroforestry systems, however, the maximum carbon stock ($C_{max}$) may be reached at a time ($T_{max}$) before the end of the rotation ($T_r$). As an example, a coffee (*Coffea* spp.) plantation may reach the maximum carbon stock in 7 years (establishment phase), but production continues for an additional 5 years (production phase), giving a rotation time ($T_r$) of 12 years, at which time the plantation is cut and reestablished. The time-averaged carbon stock for such land use systems is determined as the weighted average of the time-averaged carbon stocks for the different phases of the rotation (figure 2.1b).

Details of the sites sampled, including location, land use categories, and age since clearing and the above-ground and soil carbon stocks used for calculating time-averaged carbon can be found in Palm et al. (2002).

Differences in above-ground carbon stocks between the forest and the above-ground time-averaged carbon of the different land use systems were used to calculate the loss of carbon with the alternative slash-and-burn systems. Likewise the potential for different land use systems to sequester carbon relative to other systems was determined by pairwise comparisons of their time-averaged carbon.

## BELOW-GROUND CARBON

The time-averaged comparison just described was calculated only for the above-ground carbon stocks because the root and soil data were extremely variable and consistent

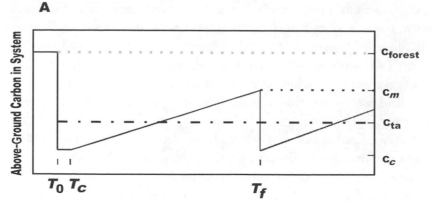

**A**

Carbon accumulation rate = $I_c = (C_m - C_c) / (T_f - T_c)$, or if $T_c$ and $C_c$ are small, then
$$I_c = C_m / T_f$$

Time-averaged carbon = $(I_c * T_f) / 2$, assuming $T_c$ and $C_c$ are small

$C_m$ = Carbon in fallow at time of clearing
$C_c$ = Carbon in crop, assumed to be negligible
$C_{ta}$ = Time-averaged carbon
$T_f$ = Time (years) in fallow phase
$T_c$ = Time in crop phase, assumed short compared with $T_f$

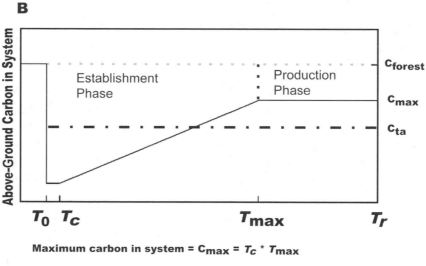

**B**

Maximum carbon in system = $C_{max} = T_c * T_{max}$

Time-averaged carbon in system = $LUCS_{ta}$

= Weighted mean ($C_{ta}$ establishment and production phases)

$C_{ta}$ establishment phase = $C_{estab} = (I_c * T_{max}) / 2$
$C_{ta}$ production phase = $C_{prod} = C_{max}$
= $[(C_{estab} * T_{max}) + (C_{prod} * [T_r - T_{max}])] / T_r$

$T_r$ = Time of rotation

*Figure 2.1* Schematic of the changes in carbon stocks and means for calculating time-averaged carbon stocks after forest clearing and establishment of (**a**) crop–fallow systems and (**b**) tree plantations.

time trends did not emerge that are needed for such calculations. The root data in particular were not useful in making comparisons between land use systems because few significant differences emerged between land use systems.

The soil data were also variable within chronosequences, partially because of textural differences in the soils of the chronosequence sampled at each site, despite attempts to sample similar soils. To account for the variability caused by differences in soil texture within a site, the soil carbon data were normalized using equation 2.1, developed by van Noordwijk et al. (1997) for estimating the soil carbon equilibrium values:

$$\text{Calculated forest soil C} - C_{ref} - \exp(1.333 + 0.00994 \times \% \text{ clay} + 0.00699 \times \% \text{ silt} - 0.156 \times pH_{KCl}). \tag{2.1}$$

The equation was derived with soil carbon data from Sumatra to estimate equilibrium topsoil carbon values for undisturbed forest systems. This $C_{ref}$ value referred to the carbon content of the topsoil as identified in the soil survey data, with a variable depth but generally between 0–5 and 0–10 cm. Another equation developed by van Noordwijk et al. (2000) provides a means for standardizing soil carbon according to variable sampling depths. Equation 2.2, developed from soil data from Jambi Province, Indonesia, shows a relationship between soil carbon content and soil depth in the top 100 cm:

$$\% C = 8.38 \, Z^{-0.58} (R^2 = 0.86), \tag{2.2}$$

where $Z$ is the midpoint of the soil-sampling depth.

By integrating this equation over the sampling depth, we obtain a correction factor:

$$C_{ref}(Z_2) = C_{ref}(Z_1) \times (Z_2/Z_1)^{-0.58}, \tag{2.3}$$

where $Z_2$ and $Z_1$ are the midpoint of the sampling depth of a specific sample and the sampling depth, 7 cm, that was used to establish the initial $C_{ref}$ equation, respectively.

The calculated $C_{ref}$ values, corrected for texture and sampling depth, for each land use per site were then compared with the actual carbon measured ($C_{act}$) to give a relative carbon value ($C_{rel}$) = $C_{act}/C_{ref}$. The $C_{rel}$ values indicated the soil carbon in the land use system relative to that expected from a forest system on a similar soil type. The $C_{rel}$ of a forest soil should be 1 if the equation is appropriate for that location and the sampling depth is similar to that used in deriving the equation. The $C_{rel}$ of soils from the different land use systems was then used to estimate the gain or loss of soil carbon relative to that of the forest, with a $C_{rel}$ less than 1 indicating a loss of soil carbon.

An approximation of a time-averaged carbon for the soil over the rotation could then be calculated in a manner similar to that for above-ground carbon. The time-

Table 2.2 Average Above-Ground Carbon Stocks (standard deviation) and Age of the Land Use Systems Sampled at the A S B Benchmark Areas and the Calculated Carbon Accumulation Rates, Maximum Carbon Stock, and Land Use System Time-Averaged Carbon Stock

| Meta–Land Use Systems | Country and Specific Land Use | Replicates | Average Carbon Stock of Sample Plots, in t C/ha (SD) | Average Age of Sample Plots, in yr (SD) | Carbon Accumulation Rate, 100 t C/ha/yr (SD) | Age at Maximum Carbon (yr) | Rotation Time of Land Use System (yr) | Maximum Carbon Stock (t C/ha)[a] | Time-Averaged Above-Ground Carbon of Land Use System (t C/ha)[b] |
|---|---|---|---|---|---|---|---|---|---|
| Undisturbed forest | Indonesia | 2 | 306 (99) | >100 | NA | NA | NA | 306 (207–405) | 306 (207–405) |
| Managed and logged forests | Brazil | 4 | 148 (19) | ? | NA | NA | NA | 148 (129–149) | 148 (129–149) |
|  | Cameroon | 5 | 228 (27) | ? | NA | NA | NA | 228 (221–255) | 228 (221–255) |
|  | Indonesia | 4 | 93.2 (41.3) | ? | NA | NA | NA | 93.2 (51.9–134) | 93.2 (51.9–134) |
| Crop–fallow rotations | Shifting cultivation, 23-yr fallow | 7 | 131 (37) | 18.5 (4.2) | 7.26 (2.02) | 25 | 25 | 167 (120–213) | 77.0 (60.2–107) |
|  | Bush fallow, 9.5 yr | 5 | 64.1(18.8) | 9.6 (0.9) | 6.68 (1.76) | 9 | 11 | 56.2 (44.3–76.0) | 28.1 (22.1–38.1) |
|  | Chromolaena fallow, 4 yr | 6 | 5.78 (2.76) | 2 | 2.89 (1.38) | 4 | 6 | 11.6 (6.04–17.1) | 4.52 (2.6–6.38) |

Cameroon

| | | | | | | | | | |
|---|---|---|---|---|---|---|---|---|---|
| Brazil | Short fallow, 5 yr | 3 | 15.4 (9.43) | 4 (4.0) | 3.91 (1.66) | 5 | 8 | 19.6 (1.2–28.4) | 6.86 (4.27–9.61) |
| | Improved fallow, 5 yr | | 13.7 (2.51) | 2 (0) | 6.86 (1.26) | 5 | 8 | 34.3 (28.0–40.6) | 11.5 (9.50–13.4) |
| Complex agroforests | | | | | | | | | |
| Cameroon | Cacao | 5 | 88.7 (31.6) | NA | NA | NA | NA | 88.7 (57.2–120) | 88.7 (57.2–120) |
| Indonesia | Rubber | 4 | 89.2 (39.8) | NA | NA | NA | NA | 89.2 (49.4–129) | 89.2 (49.4–129) |
| Cameroon | Cacao | 5 | 88.7 (31.6) | 25 (0) | 3.55 (1.26) | 25 | 40 | 88.7 (57.2–120) | 61 (40–83) |
| Indonesia | Rubber | 4 | 89.2 (39.8) | 30 | 3.57 (1.59) | 25 | 30 | 89.2 (49.4–129) | 46.2 (28.9–75.2) |
| Simple agroforests and intensive tree crops | | | | | | | | | |
| Brazil | Coffee monoculture | 3 | 15.0 (2.66) | 8 (2.31) | 2.14 (0.38) | 7 | 12 | 15.0 | 11.0 (8.73–12.5) |
| Brazil | Multistrata system | 3 | 70.5 (24.3) | 10 (5.2) | 7.26 (1.63) | 12 | 20 | 87.1 (67.6–106.7) | 61.2 (47.5–74.7) |
| Cameroon | Oil palm | 1 | 42.2 | 15 | 6.03 | 7 | 25 | 42.2 | 36.4 |
| Indonesia | Pulp trees | 2 | 22.0 (1.91) | 2.5 (2.1) | 9.29 (3.39) | 8 | 8 | 74.3 (47.2–101) | 37.2 (23.6–50.7) |
| Grasslands and crops | | | | | | | | | |
| Brazil | Extensive pastures | 4 | 5.70 (3.43) | 11 (1.0) | — | — | 8 | — | 2.85 |
| Brazil | Intensive pastures | 3 | 6.04 (1.91) | 10 (3.6) | — | — | 8 | — | 3.06 |
| Indonesia | Cassava–Imperata | 11 | 2.05 (0.98) | — | — | — | 10 | 1.97 | <2 |

[a]The range is given in parentheses and was determined by multiplying the age at maximum carbon by ± 1 $SD$ of the carbon accumulation rate.

[b]The range was obtained by inserting the range in values for the maximum carbon into the equations for calculating $C_{ta}$.

averaged calculations for soil carbon are complicated by the pattern of carbon loss and recovery for soil, which shows a time lag relative to that of the recovery of vegetation. There is typically a loss of 10 to 40 percent of the topsoil carbon the first 2 to 5 years after clearing of forests or fallows, with the percentage loss depending on several factors that influence the amount of organic materials returned to the soil. After the loss phase, there is recovery of soil carbon to a level depending on the land use management and rotation times (Szott and Palm 1986; Sommer et al. 2000). For purposes of this study, because there was insufficient detail of the pattern and time course of soil carbon for the different land use systems, the time-averaged topsoil carbon was assumed to simply be that at the end of the rotation indicated in table 2.2. These estimates do not include the temporary loss of soil carbon after fallow clearing and thus would be slight overestimates.

## Modeling Carbon Dynamics with Land Use Change

Obtaining more accurate values of carbon stocks, rates of carbon accumulation, and the time course of changes in carbon stocks in tropical land use systems is essential for improving our understanding of the role of tropical land use in the global carbon budget. Yet obtaining this information is extremely time consuming and costly. Once sufficient data have been collected, they can be used to parameterize and validate models that simulate changes in carbon with land use change. Version 4.0 of the CENTURY model is well suited for the purposes of simulating carbon changes with land use in the ASB program because it includes the growth of trees and crops and the complex management practices used in tropical agroecosystems (Metherell et al. 1993). The CENTURY model is a generic plant–soil ecosystem model that has been used to simulate carbon, nitrogen, and phosphorus dynamics of natural and managed ecosystems. Once tested and validated for the different soils, climates, crops and trees of the ASB benchmark sites, the CENTURY model can be used to explore the productivity and carbon losses and sequestration potential of land use alternatives beyond the time frame possible from direct field experimentation and for additional land use systems.

Soil, climate, and land use management data, including clearing and burning, crop type, and sequencing, were used to simulate the pulpwood plantations and cassava–*Imperata* land uses in Indonesia (Sitompul et al. 1996) and conversion from traditional slash-and-burn to tree-based systems in Cameroon (Woomer et al. 2000).

## RESULTS AND DISCUSSION

### Time-Averaged Above-Ground Carbon

The above-ground carbon stocks in the forest systems differed between sites; the highest, with more than 300 t C/ha, was reported for the natural or undisturbed forests of Indonesia (table 2.2). There were no measurements of natural undisturbed forests at the other sites because they were not found near the study areas. The decreasing above-ground carbon in the managed or logged forests, from a high of 228 t C/ha in Cameroon to a low of 93 t C/ha in Indonesia, reflected varying extraction intensities from a few boles per hectare by the local farmers in Cameroon and Brazil to large-scale extraction by commercial loggers in Indonesia. The values for above-ground carbon in selectively logged forests in Indonesia and Brazil are similar to values reported by FAO (1997). The average value for Brazilian forests fell into the lower estimates used by Houghton et al. (2000) for calculating net $CO_2$ fluxes from the area. The values for the logged forest of Cameroon and the undisturbed forest of Indonesia were higher than the few values reported by FAO (1997). Increasing the FAO values by 20 to 30 percent to account for understory vegetation, trees with dbh less than 10 cm, and the litter layer (Sandra Brown, pers. comm. 1998) may account for the tendency of higher biomass values obtained with the ASB method.

Slash-and-burn clearing generally is from logged or secondary forests and not undisturbed forests (Fujisaka et al. 1998), so the current carbon losses from slash-and-burn would be lower than if undisturbed forests were cleared. The carbon of logged forests therefore was used as reference point with which other systems were compared. The least intensive of the land use systems, the permanent cacao or rubber agroforests of Cameroon and Indonesia, had maximum and time-averaged carbon stocks of 90 t C/ha, or 40 to 100 percent of the logged forests, respectively. There was a further drop to about 50 t C/ha time-averaged carbon for the rotational, complex cacao and rubber agroforests of Cameroon and Indonesia, representing 22 and 54 percent of the carbon of the logged forests, respectively. The time-averaged carbon of the other rotational, more intensively managed tree-based systems depends on a variety of factors, including planting densities, rotation time, and management factors. The values ranged from a high of 60 t C/ha for the multistrata fruit tree complex agroforests in Brazil to a low of 11 t C/ha in monoculture coffee plantations. The time-averaged carbon of an oil palm plantation in Cameroon was about half that of the cacao complex agroforestry system.

The more intensively managed tree plantation systems do not necessarily have lower time-averaged carbon stocks than the simple agroforestry systems such as the coffee- and oil palm–based ones. As an example, the *Acacia mangium* Willd. or *Paraserianthes falcataria* (L.) I. Nielsen (now called *Falcataria moluccana* [Miq.] Barneby and Grimes) pulp plantations in Indonesia attained a lower maximum carbon stock (74 t C/ha) than complex rubber agroforests (90 t C/ha), but the faster carbon accumulation rates of almost 9 t C/ha/yr compared with 3.5 t C/ha/yr result in similar time-averaged carbon stocks of 40 t C/ha. This emphasizes the importance of regrowth rates and rotation times in time-averaged carbon stocks.

The time-averaged carbon stock of the traditional, long-fallow shifting cultivation still practiced in parts of Cameroon was almost 80 t C/ha. Intensifying the cropping system by shortening the fallow period in Cameroon reduced time-averaged carbon stocks to 28 and 5 t C/ha for systems with 9- and 4-year fallows, respectively. In Brazil, the time-averaged carbon stock of the 5-year natural fallow was 7 t C/ha (5 percent of the forest); the value increased to only 12 t C/ha for improved fallows planted with *Inga* or *Senna* trees but with similar rotation times.

Eventual conversion of deforested land to pastures or continuous cropping systems reduced time-averaged carbon stocks to only about 3 t C/ha, 2 percent that of the logged forest. The average rotation time of a pasture is 8 to 10 years before reestablishment. Intensifying pastures through management or introduction of legumes increased the above-ground carbon by less than 1 C/ha above the traditional pasture systems. Similarly, the cassava–*Imperata* systems in Indonesia had time-averaged carbon stocks of only 2 t C/ha.

Above-ground carbon accumulation rates differed between the meta–land use system categories (table 2.2). Rates were highest, up to 9.3 t C/ha/yr, in the intensive tree crop systems and simple agroforests. The exception to this was coffee monocultures, which had a low accumulation rate of 2.1 t C/ha/yr, a result of the low planting density and intensive pruning. Crop–fallow successions had lower carbon accumulation rates, averaging 3 t C/ha/yr and 7 t C/ha/yr for the short- and long-term natural secondary fallows, respectively. The improved tree fallows in Brazil had a higher carbon accumulation rate of 7 t C/ha/yr, compared with 4 t C/ha/yr for the natural tree fallow of the same rotation time. The chromolaena (*Chromolaena odorata* [L.] R.M. King and H. Robinson) fallow in Cameroon had the lowest accumulation rate, probably because of arrested succession caused by the aggressive cover of the low-biomass chromolaena plants. The complex cacao and rubber agroforestry systems had carbon accumulation rates about half that of the natural fallows, probably from selective slashing and thinning of understory vegetation to reduce competition with the tree cash crops.

There are few data with which to compare the ASB carbon stock and regrowth rates of the fallows, tree crop plantations, and agroforestry systems. Houghton et al. (1993) reported time-averaged carbon values of 50 to 100 t C/ha for agroforestry systems and plantations. These values, in general, are higher than those measured in the ASB systems.

The regrowth rates of the natural fallows estimated for the ASB systems are in the upper range reported in other studies (Uhl et al. 1988; Szott et al. 1994; Fearnside and Guimaraes 1996; Houghton et al. 2000; Silver et al. 2000). The lower regrowth rates are generally found after pasture, rather than crop, abandonment (Uhl et al. 1988; Fearnside and Guimaraes 1996); most of the ASB fallow systems followed cropping, which could partly explain the high regrowth rates.

The ASB dataset allows comparisons of carbon stocks and time-averaged carbon values between meta–land use systems and between sites. Some caution must be taken regarding the precision and accuracy of these estimates. There are several steps in which errors can affect the estimates, including the plot size used for estimating biomass of large trees (Brown et al. 1995), the allometric equations used for estimating tree biomass (Ketterings et al. 2001), an insufficient number of replicates for some of the land use systems, and inaccurate ages of plots and rotation times. The carbon estimates for some of the tree plantations and agroforestry systems were obtained from only two replicates, and the ages at which maximum biomass is attained and rotation times for some of the land use systems were sometimes informed guesses. Further sampling and time course delineation may improve estimates of carbon stocks and time-averaged carbon in some of these tree-based systems.

One of the factors that could introduce the largest errors in carbon stock estimates is the choice of allometric equations used for estimating tree biomass. The equation used for estimating tree biomass for the ASB sites was developed primarily from old age forest stands and for trees with diameters greater than 10 or even 25 cm (Brown et al. 1989). Most of the nonforest, tree-based systems in the ASB site were younger than 20 years, and the majority of trees had diameters less than 25 cm. New allometric equations have since been developed from young secondary forests and fallows in Indonesia (Ketterings et al. 2001) that result in biomass estimates half those obtained from the equation of Brown et al. (1989). The main factors influencing the tree biomass were the height of the trees and the wood density. Several other recent studies have shown a wide range in allometric equations for both primary and secondary forests in the humid tropics of Brazil (Alves et al. 1997; Araújo et al. 1999; Nelson et al. 1999). Such a wide range in carbon estimates for trees stresses the difficulty in assessing vegetation biomass. It does, at least, set an upper (Brown et al. 1989) and lower limit (Ketterings et al. 2001) to these estimates. Further testing and application of the new allometric equations will assist in reducing the uncertainty in carbon stocks and fluxes particularly for the younger fallow and tree-based systems.

## BELOW-GROUND CARBON

As mentioned previously, the root biomass data were extremely variable and did not indicate differences between the land use systems. Apparently the excavation method used did not adequately sample large roots, so the values for roots in forests and other tree-based systems were underestimates. These data are not included in the results and will not be discussed. A means for estimating roots through the time course of regrowth of tree-based systems could be to use the root-to-shoot ratios of 0.42 for 5-year regrowth and 0.20 for 20-year secondary regrowth obtained by Fearnside and Guimaraes (1996). Basically this would show that including roots from tree-based systems would magnify the differences in carbon stocks between the land use systems already reported for above-ground vegetation. The case of pasture systems may be quite different, as discussed later in this chapter.

The baseline topsoil (0–20 cm) carbon stocks in the forest systems ranged from 45 to 50 t C/ha in Indonesia and Cameroon and were 35 t C/ha in the Brazil forest sites (table 2.3). Values for the logged forests in Indonesia did not differ from those of the undisturbed forest sites. The baseline values for the ASB sites are on the low end compared with the range of 46 to 69 t C/ha reported by Detwiler (1986), assuming that 45 percent of the carbon in a 1-m profile reported in his study is located in the top 20 cm (Moraes et al. 1995). The values for the soils sampled at the benchmark sites in Brazil are exceptionally low when compared with the range reported by Moraes et al. (1995) for undisturbed forests in the Amazon.

The soil carbon stocks for the other land use systems did not reflect the expected trends, with some land use systems having higher topsoil carbon than the forest systems (table 2.3). Generally, land use systems on soils with higher clay content had higher soil carbon, indicating that attempts at selecting land use systems on soils of similar texture within a chronosequence were unsuccessful. The wide range in soil carbon losses results from variation in the length of time since clearing, the type of land use, the soil type, and topsoil erosion. To correct for the differences in soil texture, the $C_{rel}$ values of the different land use systems were used to indicate relative changes in soil carbon (table 2.3).

*Table 2.3* Actual Soil Carbon Values and Values Corrected According to Soil Texture (equation 1, van Noordwijk et al. 1997a) and Soil Sampling Depth (van Noordwijk et al. 2000) and the Soil Carbon Stocks Measured for the Forest Systems and Corrected for the Land Use Systems Sampled at A S B Sites

| Country and Land Use (sampling depth, cm) | $C_{actual}$ (g/kg) | $C_{land\ use}/C_{forest}$ (uncorrected) | $C_{reference}$ (g/kg) | $C_{relative} = C_{actual}/C_{reference}$ | Average Soil Carbon Stock,[a,b] t C/ha (*SD*) |
|---|---|---|---|---|---|
| **Brazil (0–20)** | | | | | |
| Forest | 1.78 | 1.00 | 1.82 | 0.98 | 35 (1.3) |
| Agroforestry | 1.52 | 0.85 | 1.91 | 0.80 | 28[c] |
| Fallow | 0.96 | 0.54 | 1.52 | 0.63 | 22[c] |
| Pasture | 1.12 | 0.63 | 1.54 | 0.73 | 26[c] |
| Crop | 1.70 | 0.96 | 1.95 | 0.87 | 30[c] |
| **Cameroon (0–20)** | | | | | |
| Forest | 1.56 | 1.00 | 1.62 | 0.97 | 45 (8.5) |
| Jungle cacao | 1.47 | 0.94 | 1.43 | 1.03 | 46[c] |
| Fallow (8 yr) | 1.72 | 1.10 | 1.65 | 1.04 | 47[c] |
| Fallow (2 yr) | 1.49 | 0.96 | 2.30 | 0.65 | 39[c] |
| Crop | 1.62 | 1.04 | 1.53 | 1.06 | 48[c] |
| **Indonesia (0–5)** | | | | | |
| Forest | 1.01 | 1.00 | 1.00 | 1.01 | 48 (7.6) |
| Logged forest | 1.21 | 1.20 | 1.09 | 1.11 | 49 (3.8) |
| Jungle rubber | 1.91 | 1.89 | 1.59 | 1.20 | 54[c] |
| Pulpwood plantation | 1.12 | 1.11 | 1.11 | 1.01 | 49[c] |
| Rubber plantation | 1.54 | 1.52 | 1.90 | 0.81 | 39[c] |
| Cassava | 1.09 | 1.08 | 1.64 | 0.66 | 32[c] |
| *Imperata* | 0.76 | 0.75 | 1.59 | 0.48 | 23[c] |

[a]Values for the forest systems are the measured values of soil carbon stocks of forest systems at the different A S B sites.

[b]Calculated as the forest soil carbon stock $\times$ $C_{reference}$.

[c]Indicates estimated time-averaged carbon for the topsoil.

The $C_{rel}$ values for the forest systems in Brazil, Cameroon, and Indonesia were remarkably close to 1.0 (table 2.3), indicating that the equation for normalizing soil carbon for texture and sampling depth that was developed from soils in Indonesia applies well to other humid tropical forest sites. The $C_{rel}$ index shows there was little or no change in soil carbon for most the land use systems considered in Cameroon, except for the 2-year fallows, which had 35 percent less soil carbon (table 2.3). This drop is indicative of the changes that occur the first 2 to 5 years after forest or fallow clearing, followed by a recovery of soil carbon as the fallow period increases. The lack of change in topsoil carbon in the other systems is consistent with the low land use intensity of this benchmark area. In contrast to Cameroon, topsoil carbon losses of 11 to 53 percent were found in the more intensive pastures and croplands in Brazil and degraded grasslands and continuous cropping in Indonesia. In general, the tree-based plantations and agroforestry systems lost less than 20 percent of the topsoil carbon, and the complex rubber and cacao agroforests had levels of soil carbon similar to the forests.

The relative soil carbon losses as calculated for the different land use systems are similar to those reported by Detwiler (1986) in a review of soil carbon changes with land use change in the humid tropics. Improved pasture management from the ASB sites in Brazil did not show an increase in the topsoil carbon compared with the traditional or degraded pastures, at least to levels that would be significant for carbon sequestration. Fisher et al. (1994) found substantial amounts of carbon in the roots and subsoil of improved pastures in the drier, subhumid savanna areas of Brazil. Subsoil carbon and roots were not measured in the ASB plots, so there may actually be some storage through improved pastures, although Nepstad et al. (1994) and Trumbore et al. (1995) found dramatic decreases in occurrence of deep roots on conversion of forest to pasture in the seasonal zone of the eastern Brazilian Amazon. Sommer et al. (2000) found that the biomass of deep roots and root patterns with depth were similar under forests and young secondary vegetation but substantially less under intensive plantations. These differences in root profiles were accompanied by decreases of 25 to 50 percent carbon in the topsoil in the plantations and a reduction in carbon throughout the profile. These findings indicate that there are also large losses of soil carbon at depth with the conversion of forest to other systems without deep rooting. More root and subsoil carbon measurements are needed on a variety of land use systems in different soil and climate regimes in the tropics to verify these findings.

## MODELING CHANGES IN CARBON STOCKS WITH CHANGES IN LAND USE

CENTURY model simulations of the *Paraserianthes* pulpwood plantations and cassava–*Imperata* systems in Indonesia agreed with the vegetation carbon stocks measured in the field for the tree plantation and the cassava–*Imperata* systems (figure 2.2) (Sitompul et al. 1996). However, the biomass carbon simulated for the primary

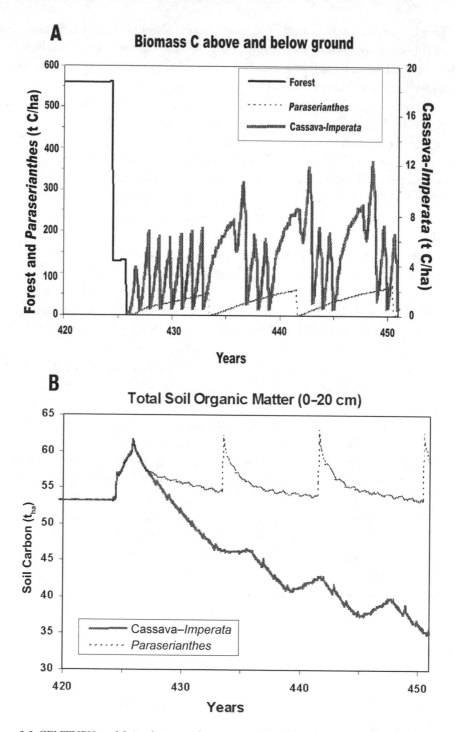

*Figure 2.2* CENTURY model simulations and measured values of (**a**) biomass and (**b**) soil carbon changes on conversion of forest to *Paraserianthes* tree plantations or cassava–*Imperata* systems. Note the different *y*-axes for estimating carbon values in *Paraserianthes* and *Imperata* systems (Sitompul et al. 1996).

forest is high by about 25 percent, indicating there may be a need for further model parameterization and validation for the Indonesia site. The simulated topsoil soil carbon (figure 2.2) shows that the tree plantation maintains a steady-state level similar to that of the forest; the blips are a result of the slash that is added and decomposes after tree harvest. Field measurements also indicate little or no drop in soil carbon in the plantations (table 2.3). However, the cassava–*Imperata* simulation shows a dramatic and continuing decline in soil carbon, declining by 40 percent in 20 years, similar to that from field measurements.

The simulations reported for Cameroon of the current traditional slash-and-burn agriculture with a declining fallow phase and two alternative systems indicated a slight overestimation of total system carbon (Woomer et al. 2000). The model simulated 350 t C/ha in the undisturbed forest, compared with a measured total system carbon of 280 t C/ha for logged forests and 270 t/ha system carbon for a 20-year fallow compared with 210 t C/ha measured in those systems. Use of the model to simulate traditional slash-and-burn agriculture and an alternative land use that included soil conservation and retention of some of the larger trees showed increases in carbon stocks compared with that of the traditional system, but the system carbon still declined with decreasing fallow length but at a slower rate. These comparisons of measured and simulated changes in carbon stocks with several land use systems found in the humid tropics show that, with some minor adjustments, CENTURY Version 4.0 will be useful for extrapolating and predicting carbon changes for a variety of alternative land use systems.

## CONCLUSION

Carbon losses and potential carbon sequestration associated with the various land use transitions can be estimated by combining information on the above-ground time-averaged carbon and the relative soil carbon values for the different land use systems (table 2.4, figure 2.3). In table 2.4 a net loss of carbon from the vegetation is considered a flux to the atmosphere and is indicated by a positive sign (+) with the values in the table. Likewise, a net sink of carbon into the vegetation is indicated by a negative sign (−).

The carbon losses from converting the natural forests to logged forests ranges from a low of 80, in the case of Cameroon, to a high of 200 t C/ha for Indonesia, assuming the carbon stock of the natural forests in all countries are similar to that of Indonesia. There is little if any carbon loss from the topsoil (table 2.3). Further losses from conversion of logged forests to other tree-based systems range from 40 to 190 t C/ha above ground and 6 to 12 t C/ha from the soil. Eventual conversion of logged forest to continuous cropping or pasture systems results in a net loss of 90 to 200 t C/ha from the vegetation and 12 to 27 t C/ha from the topsoil. It is important to note that these losses would be larger if roots were included in the calculations.

*Table 2.4* Carbon Sequestered (–t C/ha) or Lost (+) from Above-Ground Vegetation by Converting from One Land Use System (column) to Another Land Use System (row)

| Indonesia | Primary Forest | Logged Forest | Jungle Rubber (permanent) | Jungle Rubber (rotational) | Oil Palm | Pulpwood Plantation | Crop–*Imperata* |
|---|---|---|---|---|---|---|---|
| Time-averaged C (t C/ha¹) | 306 | 93 | 89 | 46 | 54 | 37 | 2 |
| Logged forest | 213 | NA | –4 | –47 | –39 | –56 | –91 |
| Jungle rubber (permanent) | 217 | 4 | NA | –43 | –35 | –52 | –87 |
| Jungle rubber (rotation) | 260 | 47 | –43 | NA | 8 | –9 | –44 |
| Oil palm | 252 | 39 | –35 | –8 | NA | –17 | –52 |
| Pulp plantation | 269 | 56 | –52 | 9 | 17 | NA | –35 |
| Crop–*Imperata* | 304 | 91 | –87 | 44 | 52 | 35 | NA |

| Cameroon | Logged Forest | Shifting Cultivation (long fallow) | Jungle Cacao (permanent) | Jungle Cacao (rotational) | Oil Palm | Crop–Bush Fallow | Crop–*Chromalaena* Fallow |
|---|---|---|---|---|---|---|---|
| Time-averaged C (t C/ha¹) | 228 | 77 | 89 | 61 | 36 | 38 | 6 |
| Forest | NA | –151 | –139 | –167 | –192 | –190 | –222 |
| Shifting cultivation | 151 | NA | 12 | –16 | –41 | –39 | –71 |

| | | | | | | |
|---|---|---|---|---|---|---|
| Jungle cacao (permanent) | 139 | -12 | NA | -28 | -53 | -51 | -83 |
| Jungle cacao (rotational) | 167 | 16 | 28 | NA | -25 | -23 | -55 |
| Oil palm | 192 | 41 | 53 | 25 | NA | 2 | -30 |
| Crop–bush fallow | 190 | 39 | 51 | 23 | -2 | NA | -32 |
| Crop–*Chromolaena* | 222 | 71 | 83 | 55 | 30 | 32 | NA |

| Brazil | Logged Forest | Multistrata Agroforest | Coffee Plantation | Crop–Improved Fallow | Crop–Natural Fallow | Pasture |
|---|---|---|---|---|---|---|
| Time-averaged C (t C/ha⁻¹) | 148 | 61 | 11 | 11 | 7 | 3 |
| Forest | NA | -87 | -137 | -137 | -141 | -145 |
| Multistrata agroforestry | 87 | NA | -50 | -50 | -54 | -58 |
| Coffee | 137 | 50 | NA | 0 | -4 | -8 |
| Crop–improved fallow | 137 | 50 | 0 | NA | -4 | -4 |
| Crop–fallow | 141 | 54 | 0 | NA | NA | -8 |
| Pasture | 145 | 58 | 8 | 8 | 4 | NA |

Values are determined by subtracting the time-averaged carbon value for the system in the row from that of the time-averaged value of the system in the column (e.g., Indonesia, primary forest (306) to oil palm (54) = 306 – 54 = + 252 t C lost to atmosphere).

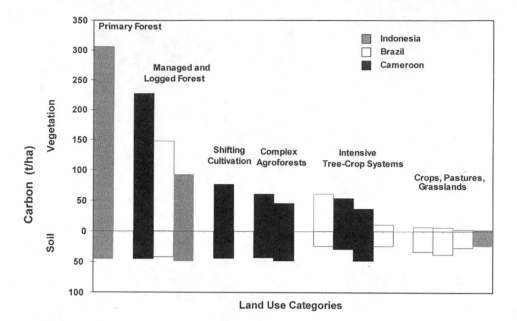

*Figure 2.3* Above-ground time-averaged and topsoil (0–20 cm) carbon of the meta–land use systems for the three benchmark sites.

If croplands and pastures were taken as the endpoint, in terms of carbon stocks resulting from the conversion of tropical forests, then rehabilitation through conversion to tree-based systems would result in carbon sequestration. The amount of carbon that could be sequestered above ground would range from 5 t C/ha for coffee plantations to 60 t C/ha for more complex agroforestry systems over a 20- to 25-year period (table 2.4); 5 to 25 t C/ha could be sequestered in the topsoil (table 2.4). Silver et al. (2000) reported soil carbon sequestration rates of 1.3 t C/ha/yr for the first 20 years after reforestation or abandonment of agricultural lands or pastures in the tropics. Such rates would result in soil carbon sequestration values at the upper end of those estimated here for conversion of croplands to complex agroforestry systems over a 20-year time span. Overall our results indicate that the potential for carbon sequestration in the humid tropics is much greater above ground than in the topsoil, as was also shown by Sommer et al. (2000).

The total carbon sequestered through the establishment of tree-based systems depends on the areas of degraded grasslands, pastures, or croplands available for conversion. Estimates of such areas in the humid tropics range from 300 million to 1 billion ha (Grainger 1988; Houghton et al. 1993). In addition to the major environmental benefits that could be gained from converting degraded lands to tree-based systems, many of these systems also provide net profit to the individual farmers (see chapter 17, this volume). Yet these conversions are not occurring on a broad scale. Reason for farmers not choosing to rehabilitate these degraded lands systems could be lack of planting materials, lack of funds to purchase inputs, and the long lag between establishing the trees and realizing profits. Other obstacles include policy issues, such as land tenure and tree rights, and lack of infrastructure for input and output markets. The Clean Development Mechanism (CDM) of the Kyoto Protocol (UNFCCC 1997) may eventually provide a means of overcoming some of these obstacles. If land use change and forestry are eventually included under the CDM, this would allow industrialized nations to meet some of their greenhouse gas reductions via carbon offset projects that provide farmers with the inputs or policy changes needed to establish these profitable, tree-based systems that sequester carbon.

## ACKNOWLEDGMENTS

The work reported here was made possible through grants to the Alternatives to Slash and Burn Program of the Consultative Group on International Agricultural Research from the Global Environment Facility and the Danish International Development Agency. In addition, each of the collaborating institutions contributed substantially in terms of staff, facilities, operations, and enthusiasm.

### REFERENCES

Alves, D.S., J.S. Soares, S. Amaral, E.M.K. Mello, S.A.S. Almeida, O.F. da Silva, et al. 1997. Biomass of primary and secondary vegetation in Rondônia, western Brazilian Amazon. Climate Change Biol. 3:451–461.

Araújo, T.M., N. Higuchi, and J.A. Carvalho Jr. 1999. Comparison of formulae for biomass content determination in a tropical rain forest site in the state of Pará, Brazil. For. Ecol. Manage. 117:43–52.

Brown, I.F., L.A. Martinelli, W.W. Thomas, M.Z. Moreira, C.A. Ferreira, and R.A. Victoria. 1995. Uncertainty in the biomass of Amazonian forests: An example from Rondônia, Brazil. For. Ecol. Manage. 75:175–189.

Brown, S., A.J.R. Gillespie, and A.E. Lugo. 1989. Biomass estimation methods for tropical forests with applications to forest inventory data. For. Sci. 35:881–902.

Brown, S., C.A.S. Hall, W. Knabe, J. Raich, M.C. Trexler, and P. Woomer. 1993. Tropical forests: Their past, present and potential future role in the terrestrial carbon budget. Water, Air, Soil Pollut. 70:71–94.

Brown, S., and A.E. Lugo. 1990. Tropical secondary forests. J. Trop. Ecol. 6:1–32.

DeFries, R.S., C.B. Field, I. Fung, G.J. Collatz, and L. Bounoua. 1999. Combining satellite data and biogeochemical models to estimate global effects of human-induced land cover change on carbon emissions and primary productivity. Global Biogeochem. Cycles 13:803–815.

Detwiler, R.P. 1986. Land use change and the global carbon cycle: The role of tropical soil. Biogeochemistry 2:67–93.

Detwiler, R.P., and C.A.S. Hall. 1988. Tropical forests and the carbon cycle. Science (Washington, DC) 239:42–47.

FAO (Food and Agriculture Organization). 1997. Estimating biomass and biomass change of tropical forests: A primer. FAO Forestry Paper 134. FAO, Rome, Italy.

Fearnside, P.M., and W.M. Guimaraes. 1996. Carbon uptake by secondary forests in Brazilian Amazonia. For. Ecol. Manage. 80:35–46.

Fisher, M.J., I.M. Rao, M.A. Ayarza, C.E. Lascano, J.I. Sanz, R.J. Thomas, et al. 1994. Carbon storage by introduced deep-rooted grasses in the South American savannas. Nature (London) 371:236–238.

Fujisaka, S., C. Castilla, G. Escobar, V. Rodrigues, E.J. Veneklaas, R.J. Thomas, et al. 1998. The effects of forest conversion on annual crops and pastures: Estimates of carbon emissions and plant species loss in a Brazilian Amazon colony. Agric. Ecosyst. Environ. 69:17–26.

Grainger, A. 1988. Estimating areas of degraded tropical lands requiring replenishment of forest cover. Int. Tree Crops J. 5:31–61.

Houghton, R.A. 1997. Terrestrial carbon storage: Global lessons from Amazonian research. Ciencia Cultura 49:58–72.

Houghton, R.A., R.D. Boone, J.R. Fruci, J.E. Hobbie, J.M. Melillo, C.A. Palm, et al. 1987. The flux of carbon from terrestrial ecosystems to the atmosphere in 1980 due to changes in land use: Geographic distribution of the global flux. Tellus 39B:122–139.

Houghton, R.A., D.L. Skole, C.A. Nobre, J.L. Hackler, K.T. Lawrence, and W.H. Chomentowski. 2000. Annual fluxes of carbon from deforestation and regrowth in the Brazilian Amazon. Nature (London) 403:301–304.

Houghton, R.A., J.D. Unruh, and P.A. Lefebvre. 1993. Current land cover in the tropics and its potential for sequestering carbon. Global Biogeochem. Cycles 7:305–320.

ICRAF (International Center for Research in Agroforestry). 1996. Carbon balance of shifting cultivation and fallow rotation systems. pp. 107–109. *In* International Centre for Research in Agroforestry, Annual Report 1996. ICRAF, Nairobi.

IPCC (Intergovernmental Panel on Climate Change). 2001. Climate change 2001: The scientific basis. J.T. Houghton, Y. Ding, .D.J. Griggs, M. Nogues, P.J. van der Linden, K. Dai, et al. (eds.). Cambridge Univ. Press, Cambridge.

Ketterings, Q.M., R. Coe, M. van Noordwijk, Y. Ambagau, and C.A. Palm. 2001. Reducing uncertainty in the use of allometric biomass equations for predicting above-ground tree biomass in mixed secondary forests. Forest Ecol. Manage. 146:201–211.

Kotto-Same, J., Woomer, P.L., A. Moukam, and L. Zapfack. 1997. Carbon dynamics in slash and burn agriculture and land use alternatives of the humid forest zone of Cameroon. Agric. Ecosyst. Environ. 65:245–256.

Metherell, A.K., L.A. Harding, C.V. Cole, and W.J. Parton. 1993. CENTURY: Soil organic matter model environment. Agroecosystem Version 4. Great Plains System Research Unit Tech. Rep. no. 4. USDA-ARS, Fort Collins, CO.

Moraes, J.L., C.C. Cerri, J.M. Melillo, D. Kicklighter, C. Neill, D.L. Skole, et al. 1995. Soil carbon stocks of the Brazilian Amazon Basin. Soil Sci. Soc. Am. J. 59:244–247.

Nelson, B.W., R. Mesquita, J.L.G. Pereira, S.G.A. de Souza, G.T. Batista, and L.B. Couto. 1999. Allometric regressions for improved estimate of secondary forest biomass in the central Amazon. For. Ecol. Manage. 117:149–167.

Nepstad, D.C., C.R. de Carvalho, E.A. Davidson, P.H. Jipp, P.A. Lefebvre, G.H. Negreiros, et al. 1994. The role of deep roots in the hydrological cycles of Amazonian forests and pastures. Nature (London) 372:666–669.

Palm, C.A., P.L. Woomer, J. Alegre, C. Castilla, K. Cordeiro, K. Hairiah, et al. 2002. Carbon sequestration and trace gas emissions in slash-and-burn and alternative land uses in the tropics. Alternatives to Slash-and-Burn Phase II Final Rep. ICRAF, Nairobi.

Sanchez, P.A., C.A. Palm, L.T. Szott, C.B. Davey, and C.E. Russell. 1985. Trees as soil improvers in the humid tropics? pp. 331–332. *In* M.G.C. Cannell and J.E. Jackson (eds.) Trees as crop plants. Inst. of Terrestrial Ecol., Huntington, UK.

Silver, W.L., R. Ostertag, and A.E. Lugo. 2000. The potential for carbon sequestration through reforestation of abandoned tropical agricultural and pasture lands. Restoration Ecol. 8:394–407.

Sitompul, S.M., K. Hairiah, M. van Noorwijk, and P.L. Woomer. 1996. Organic matter dynamics after conversion of forests to food crop or sugarcane: Predictions of the CENTURY model. Agrivita 19:198–205.

Sommer, R., M. Denich, and P.L.G. Vlek. 2000. Carbon storage and root penetration in deep soils under small-farmer land-use systems in the eastern Amazon region, Brazil. Plant Soil 219:231–241.

Szott, L.T., and C.A. Palm. 1986. Soil and vegetation dynamics in shifting cultivation fallows. pp. 360–379. *In* First Symp. on the Humid Tropics. Vol. 1. Embrapa, Belem, Pará, Brazil.

Szott, L.T., C.A. Palm, and C.B. Davey. 1994. Biomass and litter accumulation under managed and natural tropical fallows. For. Ecol. Manage. 67:177–190.

Tomich, T.P., M. van Noordwijk, S. Budidarsono, A. Gillison, T. Kusumanto, D. Murdiyarso, et al. 1998. Alternatives to Slash-and-Burn in Indonesia. Summary report and synthesis of phase II. ASB, ICRAF, Nairobi.

Trumbore, S.E., E.A. Davidson, P.B. de Camargo, D.C. Nepstad, and L.A. Martinelli. 1995. Belowground cycling of carbon in forests and pastures of eastern Amazonia. Global Biogeochem. Cycles 9:515–528.

Uhl, C., R. Buschbacher, and E.A.S. Serrao. 1988. Abandoned pastures in eastern Amazonia. I. Patterns of plant succession. J. Ecol. 76:663–681.

UNFCCC (United Nations Framework Convention on Climate Change). 1997. Kyoto Protocol to the United Nations Framework Convention on Climate Change. FCCC/CP/1997/7/Add 1.

van Noordwijk, M., C. Cerri, P.L. Woomer, K. Nugroho, and M. Bernoux. 1997. Soil carbon dynamics in the humid tropical forest zone. Geoderma 79:187–225. Available at http://www.iges.or.jp/cc/napiid/PDF/2_LULUCF2.pdf.

van Noordwijk, M., K. Hairiah, and S.M. Sitompul. 2000. Reducing uncertainties in the assessment at national scale of C stock impacts of land use change. pp. 151–163. *In* D.B. Magcale-Macandog (ed.) Proceedings of the IGES/NIES Workshop on GHG Inventories for Asia–Pacific Region. IGES, Hayama, Japan.

Watson, R.T., I.R. Noble, B. Bolin, N.H. Ravindranath, D.J. Verardo, and D.J. Doken (eds.). 2000. Land use, land-use change and forestry. Intergovernmental Panel on Climate Change. Cambridge Univ. Press, Cambridge.

Wood, S., K. Sebastian, and S.J. Scherr. 2000. Pilot analysis of global ecosystems: Agroecosystems. IFPRI and WRI, Washington, DC.

Woomer, P.L., and C.A. Palm. 1998. An approach to estimating system carbon stocks in tropical forests and associated land uses. Commonw. For. Rev. 77:181–190.

Woomer, P.L., C.A. Palm, J. Alegre, C. Castilla, D.G. Cordeiro, K. Hairiah, et al. 2000. Slash-and-burn effects on carbon stocks in the humid tropics. pp. 99–115. *In* R. Lal, J.M. Kimble, and B.A. Stewart (eds.) Global climate change and tropical ecosystems. Advances in soil science. CRC Press, Boca Raton, FL.

# 3 Greenhouse Gas Fluxes in Slash and Burn and Alternative Land Use Practices in Sumatra, Indonesia

Daniel Murdiyarso
   *Bogor Agricultural University  Bogor, Indonesia*
Haruo Tsuruta
   *National Institute of Agro-environmental Sciences  Tsukuba, Japan*
Shigehiro Ishizuka
   *Forestry and Forest Products Research Institute  Sapporo, Japan*
Kurniatun Hairiah
   *Brawijaya University  Malang, Indonesia*
Cheryl A. Palm
   *The Earth Institute at Columbia University  Palisades, New York*

Tropical deforestation and land use change occur rapidly and on a large scale in the Alternatives to Slash and Burn (ASB) program benchmark sites because natural resource–based development has traditionally been the main pathway to establish new arable land and to gain revenues. When this land use change occurs on a large scale, it results in significant environmental consequences, including changes in biogeochemical cycles. Sources and sinks of carbon and other nutrients are altered with the changing land cover and land use practices. In some cases the land use change is promoted by government policies, often for the expansion of agricultural lands to meet the needs for food, fiber, and settlement. A better understanding of the environmental consequences of land use changes from natural forests to managed ecosystems is needed to support successful policy interventions that involve tradeoffs between global climate change, which is associated with greenhouse gas (GHG) emissions and the sustainability of the systems to support the local needs (Sanchez et al. 1994).

Globally, land use, land use change, and forestry activities in the last decade have annually contributed around 1.7 Gt, or 25 percent of the total carbon dioxide ($CO_2$) emissions of 8.0 Gt, and a resulting net emission of 2.9 Gt (IPCC 2001). Meanwhile, the global net methane ($CH_4$) emission is only 0.022 Gt (IPCC 2001). However, $CH_4$ has a radiative forcing or heat trapping capacity twenty-one times as large as that of $CO_2$. Tropical deforestation has been well documented to substantially contribute in the global net increase in nitrous oxide ($N_2O$) concentration. The current annual global $N_2O$ emission is 0.004 Gt, 25 percent of which comes from land use–related activities, mainly in the tropics (IPCC 2001). Such a small emission has become significant because the radiative forcing of $N_2O$ is 310 times larger than that of $CO_2$ (Watson et al. 2000).

The effect of land use change on GHG fluxes from soils is associated with the changes in biophysical and chemical properties of the soils caused by changes in land cover and management. Soil water content controls $CH_4$ uptake through porosity-dependent parameters that affect gas transport mechanisms, namely air permeability and gas diffusivity. Low permeability, which is related to soil structure, prevents methane-containing air from being consumed by microorganisms near and below the soil surface (Ball et al. 1997). Long-term measurements in temperate soils carried out by Castro et al. (1995) indicated that when water-filled pore space (WFPS) increased to a range of 60 to 100, $CH_4$ uptake decreased significantly. Forest soils absorbed $CH_4$, whereas pasture soils, which had poor drainage, generally produced $CH_4$ (Lessard et al. 1993). Rates of $CH_4$ uptake substantially increased from 5–15 µg/m²/hr to 100–150 µg/m²/hr after land use was changed from arable agriculture to woodland in northern Europe (Prieme et al. 1997). In the humid tropics conversion of tropical forest soils to agriculture, in general, reduces the consumption of $CH_4$ (Keller et al. 1990; Mosier and Delgado 1997), and pasture systems can become a net source of $CH_4$ (Keller and Reiners 1994; Steudler et al. 1996).

Soil microbiological activities are also affected by soil moisture and bulk density because the activity of $CH_4$-consuming bacteria is less in anaerobic and compacted soils. Soil compaction experimentally reduced $CH_4$ uptake by at least half (Hansen et al. 1993). As concluded by Dobbie and Smith (1996), $CH_4$ uptake is controlled partly by diffusion and partly by biological processes. Data from a variety of temperate and tropical native and managed ecosystems confirm that the activity of soil microbial processes responsible for $CH_4$ production and consumption can be roughly predicted from soil WFPS (Del Grosso et al. 2000).

Land management can also change soil chemical properties that affect trace gas fluxes. Many studies show that $CH_4$ uptake can be suppressed in systems that receive high nitrogen inputs (Steudler et al. 1989; Keller et al. 1990; Hansen et al. 1993; Hutsch et al. 1993, 1994; Hutsch 1996; Mosier and Delgado 1997). In compacted soils, nitrogen fertilization could reduce $CH_4$ uptake up to 78 percent (Hansen et al. 1993).

There is a substantial amount of information regarding $N_2O$ emissions from tropical soils, mainly from Latin America (Keller 1986; Luizao et al. 1989; Vitousek et al. 1989; Piccolo et al. 1994; Neill et al. 1995; Veldkamp and Keller 1997). Tropical soils are believed to be the major natural source of $N_2O$. Deforestation results in a large flux of $N_2O$ from soils that may be as much as three times that of an intact forest ecosystem (Luizao et al. 1989). The increased gaseous release is associated with rapid nitrogen mineralization and nitrification as a result of the deforestation process. This occurs at a time when there is low plant demand for nitrogen, and excess mineral nitrogen builds up in the soil and is susceptible to loss (Vitousek and Reiners 1975). This large flux of $N_2O$ apparently is temporary and can last from a few months to a few years. Otherwise natural systems generally have higher fluxes than converted, unfertilized systems. Fertilized cropping systems in the humid and subhumid tropics can have $N_2O$ fluxes as much as ten times that of the natural systems depending on the rates and timing of application of nitrogenous fertilizers (Davidson et al. 1996; Erickson and Keller 1997; Veldkamp and Keller 1997; Matson et al. 1998).

Nitrous oxides are formed via nitrification and denitrification, the former being an aerobic and the later an anaerobic process. Fluxes in the humid tropics are positively correlated with some measure of nitrogen availability and with WFPS (Verchot et al. 1999; Davidson et al. 2000). Nitrification is the primary source of nitrogen gas below 60 percent WFPS, the dominant form of gas being NO rather than $N_2O$; above 60 percent WFPS denitrification dominates and $N_2O$ becomes the dominant form of gas, and $N_2$ dominates at even higher WFPS (Davidson et al. 2000). Although flooded rice (*Oryza sativa* L.) cultivation is not considered an important source of $N_2O$ because of the complete reduction to $N_2$ under more complete anaerobic conditions, $N_2O$ formation may be significant in flooded rice cultivation with alternate irrigation and drainage cycles (Granli and Bøkman 1994; Cai et al. 1997; Tsuruta et al. 1997; Xu et al. 1997; Suratno et al. 1998).

Most studies on trace gas emissions from the humid tropics have been from natural forests and pasture systems, and much of that has been done in Latin America. One objective of the global ASB Program has been to quantify the consequences of land use change on emissions of trace gases, primarily $CH_4$ and $N_2O$, at the benchmark sites across the humid tropics. These benchmark sites encompass a broad range of land use systems and can therefore greatly expand information for the humid tropics. A protocol for measurements was developed and used for comparisons of regions and land use systems. This chapter summarizes the analysis of $CH_4$ and $N_2O$ flux measurements from soils under alternative land use practices in Sumatra, Indonesia, and compares the results obtained in another study at the ASB benchmark site in Yurimaguas, Peru (Palm et al. 2002). By comparing the two benchmark sites we hope to better understand and document the effects of land use intensification in the tropics on GHG emissions.

## MATERIALS AND METHODS

### STUDY SITE

In ASB's Sumatran sites, Jambi and Lampung Provinces, landscapes are dominated by tree-based agriculture. Changes in natural vegetation are associated with the conversion of tropical forests to provide land for settlement, agriculture, and large-scale plantations. Many smallholder farmers (mainly local inhabitants) practice tree-based agriculture, using annual crops while new plantations are becoming established or old trees are regenerating. Very often they use fire, which is considered the cheapest and easiest way to clear.

A general survey of trace gas emissions was carried out in three districts in Jambi Province, and intensive monthly samplings were set up at the area of Pasir Mayang Research Station in the lowland of Jambi Province. The detailed biophysical characteristics of the area were described by Murdiyarso and Wasrin (1995). The average monthly rainfall during the experimental period in the wet season (October–March) was 250 mm, or twice as much as the average monthly rainfall of the dry season (April–September). Ultisols were the major soil type of the sampling sites; general soil properties are shown in table 3.1.

## Sampling Protocol

A standard gas sampling protocol was used in the field throughout the study. The same protocol was also used in Peru. A closed sampling chamber with a diameter of 30 cm and height of around 12 cm was used. Gas samples were collected from the chamber by means of a syringe and then transferred to evacuated glass vials. Sampling intervals from the closed chamber of 0, 10, 20, and 40 minutes were adopted to determine the flux rates. Gas chromatography techniques were used to determine the concentration of the gases.

*Table 3.1* Properties of Soils Under Each Land Use Type at Pasir Mayang, Sumatra

| Land-Use Type | Depth (cm) | pH (H$_2$O) | Total C (mg/g) | Total N (mg/g) | C/N | Bulk Density (Mg/m$^3$) | Microbial Biomass (μg C/g) |
|---|---|---|---|---|---|---|---|
| P1 | 0–10 | 4.2 | 30 | 1.9 | 16.2 | 1.12 | 554 |
|  | 10–20 | 4.7 | 19 | 1.6 | 11.5 | 1.22 | 262 |
|  | 20–30 | 4.9 | 19 | 1.6 | 11.5 | 1.16 | 199 |
| L1 | 0–10 | 4.8 | 35 | 2.4 | 14.5 | 0.81 | 471 |
|  | 10–20 | 4.3 | 25 | 2.0 | 12.5 | 1.26 | 316 |
|  | 20–30 | 4.4 | 23 | 1.9 | 12.2 | 1.35 | 274 |
| L2 | 0–10 | 4.0 | 45 | 6.5 | 6.9 | 0.88 | 449 |
|  | 10–20 | 4.1 | 23 | 1.7 | 13.3 | 1.19 | 512 |
|  | 20–30 | 4.4 | 10 | 0.8 | 11.5 | 1.17 | 85 |
| Op | 0–10 | 4.0 | 36 | 3.0 | 12.0 | 1.20 | 374 |
|  | 10–15 | 4.3 | 36 | 3.0 | 12.0 | 1.17 | 278 |
| R | 0–10 | 4.7 | 16 | 1.2 | 13.0 | 0.98 | 322 |
|  | 10–20 | 4.6 | 11 | 0.9 | 13.4 | 1.03 | 255 |
|  | 20–30 | 4.5 | 9 | 0.8 | 13.4 | 1.06 | 153 |

P1, primary forest; L1 and L2, logged-over forest; Op, open land; R, rubber agroforest.
*Source:* Ishizuka et al. (2002).

## COMPONENTS OF STUDY

Trace gas emissions were evaluated first through a sampling survey of trace gases along a land use intensity gradient in Jambi. That study was followed by more intensive monthly sampling in one area of Jambi to investigate seasonality of gas fluxes in a few selected land use types. An additional study compared fluxes from cores incubated in the laboratory with the average annual fluxes measured in the field and with those obtained in the field the same day the core was sampled.

### General Survey

To explore the spatial variability of $CH_4$ and $N_2O$ fluxes, a general survey was carried out covering fifteen sites and representing five land uses across a land use intensity gradient in the lowlands of Jambi Province in July–August 1996, the dry season. The five land use types, representing a land use intensity gradient, included primary forest, logged-over forest, rubber agroforests, field crops of cassava (*Manihot esculenta* Crantz), and degraded *Imperata cylindrica* (L.) Beauv grasslands. The intensity of land management depends on the land productivity and availability of labor and is usually highest in areas of high population density. The samples were collected only one time, with three replicates for each land use type. The results were then used to select land use types for the intensive study that followed. The fluxes were also compared with those measured in another land use intensity gradient in Yurimaguas, Peru (Palm et al. 2002).

### Intensive Study

To monitor seasonal variation of $CH_4$, $N_2O$, and $CO_2$ fluxes, monthly samplings were carried out beginning in September 1997 for 1 year. The samples were taken from fixed points in each of the selected land use types. The monthly sampling was carried out around the same dates and at the same time of the day for each land use. Three replicates were collected for each land use.

Four land use types were monitored: a primary forest, logged-over forest, newly open or deforested area, and a rubber plantation. The primary forest (P1 and P2, 1°05.164′S, 102°05.702′E) was a 200-ha old-growth forest that had not been affected by human activities for more than 50 years. P1 was located on a 15° slope, whereas P2 was on a flat top of the hill. Two plots of logged-over forests had been selectively logged in 1977 and consisted of tall trees with evenly distributed diameters. The first logged-over forest (L1, 1°3.810′S, 102°9.754′E) was slashed in September 1997. The slashed material less than 50 cm in diameter was dried on site and burned in March

1998, before a rubber plantation was established by a large-scale operator. The second logged-over forest (L2, 1°5.235′S, 102°6.586′E) was located near the primary forest and was not disturbed by human activities during this experimental period. The deforested site (Op, 1°3.660′S, 102°9.681′E) was clear-cut and burned in August 1996, followed by the establishment of a plantation of *Gmelina arborea* Roxb. (India), a fast-growing tree species. The height of planted trees was about 4 m in October 1997. The rubber agroforest site (R, 1°5.648′S, 102°7.207′E) was a 5-year-old rubber plantation managed by a smallholder and was occasionally intercropped with annual crops, a practice commonly observed in Sumatra. Neither fertilizer nor herbicides were applied to control the commonly found weed, alang-alang grass (*Imperata*).

Soil samples were collected from each land use type at three depths of 0–10, 10–20, and 20–30 cm to determine their physical and chemical properties. The sampling was carried out once in the wet and once in the dry season.

## Incubation Experiment

A laboratory incubation of soil cores was established to evaluate the potential of assessing GHG emissions from the soils through laboratory methods (Ishizuka et al. 2000). Soil core samples were collected at P1, L1, L2, Op, and R in September 1997 using core sampler with a diameter and height of 5 cm from the depth of 0–5 cm, 10–15 cm, and 20–25 cm. Triplicate samples were collected from each depth. The incubations were set up within 14 days of soil core collection. For each sample, an intact soil core was set into an incubation jar with a volume of $0.5 \times 10^{-3} m^3$. The jars were equipped with a butyl rubber stopper for gas sampling. The soils were incubated at 25°C, and soil moisture was maintained at the levels similar to those of the different soils on the day they were collected from the field.

Gas fluxes were determined from sampling of the headspace of the incubation jars over a 24-hour period. The gas concentrations of $CO_2$ and $N_2O$ increased linearly, and the emission rates were calculated by linear regression. The $CH_4$ concentration decreased according to first-order kinetics, and the following equation was used for calculating emission rates:

$$C t = C_0 e^{-kt},$$

where $Ct$ $(m^3/m^3)$ is the $CH_4$ concentration at time $t$ (hours), $C_0$ $(m^3/m^3)$ is the $CH_4$ concentration of the headspace at the beginning, and $k$ is the reaction rate coefficient. The uptake potential rate was defined by $kC_0$ (namely, $C_0$ was approximately 1.8 $\mu g/m^3/m^3$).

The GHG uptake and release from the core samples were compared with the average of seasonal fluxes from the field and fluxes obtained from field measurement taken on the same day the cores were taken.

## Soil Gas Concentration Profile

Soil gas profiles were developed by collecting gas samples at 5- or 10-cm depth intervals, up to a depth of 50 cm, where possible. Samples were collected by inserting stainless steel tubes (outer diameter of 3 mm and inner diameter of 1 mm) into the soil. Samples were taken with a syringe and stored in evacuated vials and later analyzed by gas chromatography. The samples were collected in January 1997 at P1, L1, and Op and in October 1998 at L1 after slashing and burning.

## RESULTS AND DISCUSSION

### GENERAL SURVEY OF FLUXES FROM ALTERNATIVE LAND USES

The one-time measurements of $CH_4$ fluxes from the land use survey in Jambi showed that land use intensification reduced the soil sink strength (figure 3.1). The $CH_4$ consumption ranged from a high of 30 and 36 µg $CH_4 \bullet C/m^2/hr$ in the primary and

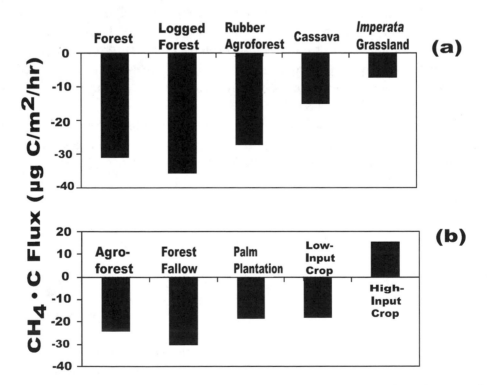

*Figure 3.1* Mean methane ($CH_4$) fluxes from alternative land uses in (a) Jambi, Indonesia, and (b) Yurimaguas, Peru (adapted from Palm et al. 2002).

logged forests, respectively, to a low of 7.3 μg $CH_4$•C/m²/hr in the degraded grass-land. These fluxes are within the range reported elsewhere in the humid tropics. In Yurimaguas, the range of $CH_4$ uptake ranged from a high of 30 μg $CH_4$•C/m²/hr in the shifting cultivation forest fallow to a net $CH_4$ release in the high-input cropping system of 15.2 μg $CH_4$•C/m²/hr (Palm et al. 2002). The $CH_4$ consumption rates of the soil in the tree-based systems and low-input cropping system in Yurimaguas were slightly lower than those of the forest fallow and were similar to the fluxes in Jambi. The decrease in $CH_4$ uptake or sink strength at both sites indicates that soil proper-ties that determine $CH_4$ uptake were affected. In Yurimaguas the $CH_4$ sink strength decreased with increasing bulk density and WFPS. Also, the net efflux of $CH_4$ from the high-input cropping system in Yurimaguas is similar to previous findings that nitrogen fertilization can suppress $CH_4$ uptake (Keller et al. 1990; Keller and Reiners 1994; Steudler et al. 1996; Mosier and Delgado 1997). Although in this case the net efflux probably is more related to soil compaction and high WFPS, leading to anaero-bic conditions that favor $CH_4$ production (Palm et al. 2002), others have reported net $CH_4$ production in pastures in the humid tropics during the rainy season (Keller and Reiners 1994; Steudler et al. 1996).

The $N_2O$ flux in Jambi ranged between 2 and 12 μg $N_2O$•N/m²/hr. The flux from the *Imperata* grassland was the lowest, and the highest was found in the rubber agroforest (figure 3.2). Therefore the fluxes were not directly related to land use inten-sity, with the managed systems having fluxes both higher and lower than those in the primary and logged forests. Fluxes in Yurimaguas were similar to those in Jambi and ranged from 6 to 14 μg $N_2O$•N/m²/hr in the unfertilized systems but almost doubled to 27 μg $N_2O$•N/m²/hr in the nitrogen-fertilized high-input cropping system (Palm et al. 2002). Others have noted that managed but unfertilized systems had lower fluxes than forest systems; this follows a brief increase in flux after deforestation (Davidson et al. 2000).

## LAND USE INTENSITY AND SEASONAL FLUXES IN JAMBI

The average $CH_4$ uptake shown in figure 3.3a followed a similar pattern with respect to land use intensity to that observed in the general survey (figure 3.1), the $CH_4$ sink strength was substantially lower under managed systems. The highest uptake level was in the primary forest (P1), followed by the undisturbed logged forest (L2) and the 5-year-old rubber agroforest (R), then the site that had been slashed and burned 1 year previously (Op), and finally the logged forest that had been slashed in 1997, when the measurements began (L1). The low uptake in both the Op and L1 sites probably was caused by compaction from the slashing. Also, when L1 was logged in 1994, heavy equipment was used to drag the logs. The bulk density of L1 below the surface (10–30 cm) ranged between 1.3 and 1.4 Mg/m³ and was higher than in the other land uses; diffusion would be less, causing less $CH_4$ to be absorbed. Methane consumption rates were slightly higher when the land was replanted (Op and R).

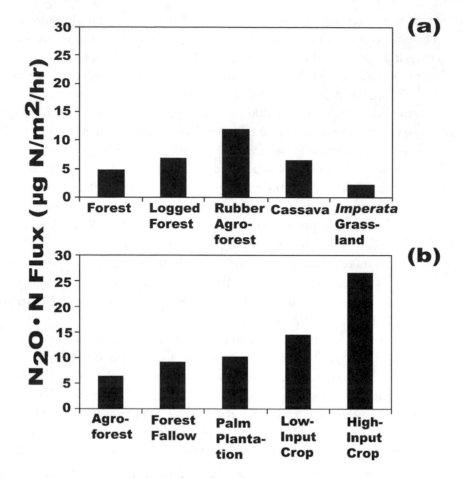

*Figure 3.2* Mean nitrous oxide (N$_2$O) fluxes from alternative land uses in (a) Jambi, Indonesia, and (b) Yurimaguas, Peru (adapted from Palm et al. 2002).

In general, differences in CH$_4$ flux seasonally were not large (figure 3.4a). Other studies have reported that CH$_4$ consumption rates during the dry season were twice those during the wet season (Keller and Reiners 1994; Steudler et al. 1996). Only in the primary forest in Jambi does there appear to be higher CH$_4$ consumption during the dry season, when gas diffusion would be at a maximum.

The average N$_2$O fluxes were highest, 15 μg N$_2$O/m$^2$/hr, in the logged forest (L1) that had been slashed in September 1997 (figure 3.3b). The site that had been deforested the previous year (Op) had fluxes only slightly higher than those of the forest and rubber agroforests. These trends are consistent with others that have found temporary increases in N$_2$O fluxes after deforestation (Keller et al. 1993, 1997; Davidson et al. 2001). This increase often is associated with higher soil temperatures and increased decomposition rates.

There was also a further temporary increase in N$_2$O flux from L1 to around 40 μg N$_2$O/m$^2$/hr in March 1998 (figure 3.4b). This increase corresponded with the rainy season and also followed the burn in March 1998. Fluxes in the other systems

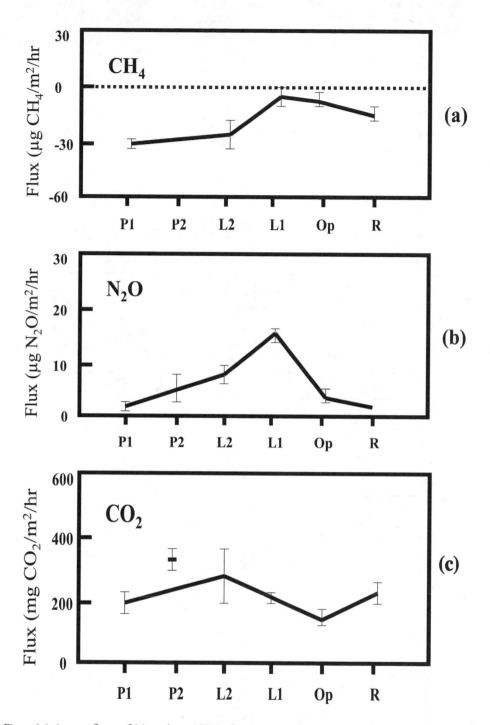

*Figure 3.3* Average fluxes of (a) methane ($CH_4$), (b) nitrous oxide ($N_2O$), and (c) carbon dioxide ($CO_2$) from different land uses: primary forest (P1 and P2), logged-over forest (L1 and L2), newly planted open land (Op), and rubber agroforest (R). The data were an average of the first 6 months of measurements before clear-felling of the logged-over forest (L1).

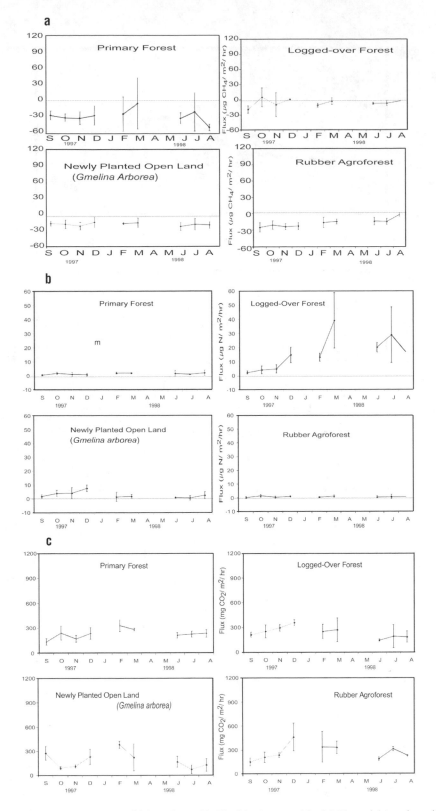

*Figure 3.4* Seasonal variation of (**a**) methane ($CH_4$), (**b**) nitrous oxide ($N_2O$), and (**c**) carbon dioxide ($CO_2$) fluxes from primary forest, logged-over forest, newly planted open land, and rubber agroforest in Jambi.

remained low (less than 5 μg $N_2O/m^2/hr$) and did not show such marked increases with the rains. The $N_2O$ fluxes often are 50 to 80 percent higher during the rainy season (Keller and Reiners 1994; Verchot et al. 1999). The higher $N_2O$ fluxes in the recently deforested lands (L1 and Op) are correlated with higher nitrification rates in the soil surface (0–10 cm) (table 3.2; R = .746). However, this conclusion needs further clarification because nitrification data are not available from all systems in both the dry and wet seasons. The overall low $N_2O$ emission rates in this study were related to the low levels of nitrate and low rates of nitrification that are often associated with infertile and acidic soil properties. Similarly low levels of nitrate and nitrification were measured in the systems in Yurimaguas, and $N_2O$ fluxes were significantly correlated to nitrification rates and WFPS (Palm et al. 2002).

The average fluxes of $CO_2$ from soils show a slight variation between land use types (figure 3.3c) compared with seasonal variation (figure 3.4c), except for the lower flux from the deforested system (Op); this lower flux probably was caused by the absence of surface litter and hence lower decomposition rates compared with the other areas. With such a low variation, a rate of 300 mg $CO_2/m^2/hr$ may be taken as an average across land use types.

*Table 3.2* Soil Inorganic Nitrogen Content and Rate of Nitrogen Mineralization in the Different Land Use Systems During the Dry and Wet Seasons

| Land Use Type | Depth (cm) | NH$_4$ (μg/g) | NO$_3$ (μg/g) | Nitrification (μg/g/d) | Nitrogen Mineralization (μg/g/d) |
|---|---|---|---|---|---|
| **Dry Season (September 1997)** | | | | | |
| P1 | 0–10 | 17.9 | 4.9 | 0.03 | 0.80 |
| | 10–20 | ND | ND | ND | ND |
| | 20–30 | ND | ND | ND | ND |
| L2 | 0–10 | 15.0 | 12.7 | 0.07 | 0.76 |
| | 10–20 | 7.6 | 8.3 | 0.13 | 0.69 |
| | 20–30 | 6.4 | 4.6 | 0.09 | 0.56 |
| R | 0–10 | 4.3 | 2.8 | 0.14 | 0.39 |
| | 10–20 | 4.8 | 3.0 | 0.24 | 0.35 |
| | 20–30 | 5.0 | 2.7 | 0.17 | 0.28 |
| **Wet Season (January 1998)** | | | | | |
| P1 | 0–10 | 8.6 | 6.6 | 0.15 | 0.94 |
| | 10–20 | 5.0 | 0.8 | 0.04 | 0.47 |
| | 20–30 | 4.7 | 1.3 | 0.04 | 0.52 |
| L1 | 0–10 | 5.5 | 9.4 | 0.45 | 0.83 |
| | 10–20 | 3.2 | 2.0 | 0.11 | 0.48 |
| | 20–30 | 3.5 | 2.4 | 0.19 | 0.43 |
| Op | 0–10 | 4.2 | 13.6 | 0.35 | 0.55 |
| | 10–15 | 5.5 | 10.9 | 0.32 | 0.28 |

P1, primary forest; ND, not determined; L1 and L2, logged-over forest; R, rubber agroforest; Op, open land.
*Source:* Ishizuka et al. (2002).

In contrast to methane and nitrous oxide, there was seasonal variation in $CO_2$ emissions from all land use types (figure 3.4c). High rates of around 450 mg $CO_2$/ $m^2$/hr usually were reached in the wet season (December 1997–February 1998). In general the lowest rates, closer to 100 mg $CO_2$/$m^2$/hr, were measured in the dry season (June or July), with the lowest in Op at around 50 mg $CO_2$/$m^2$/hr (July 1998).

## INCUBATION EXPERIMENTS

Methane flux rates from core samples incubated in the laboratory were plotted against the seasonal average fluxes obtained from the monthly field measurements in September 1997 to August 1998 (figure 3.5a, *top*) and against the flux rates from the field measurements taken on the same day the core samples were collected (figure 3.5a, *bottom*). These data indicate that results obtained from the core incubations explained 60 percent of the variation obtained from both the average of the monthly field measurements and the field samples collected during core sampling. For $CH_4$ there is no difference in using either monthly average data or one-time sample data. However, the 40 percent unexplained variation suggests a need for more soil core samples collected in more locations and seasons to incorporate more spatial and temporal variations.

A higher correlation was obtained for $N_2O$ fluxes between the laboratory incubations and same-day field samples ($R^2 = .73$, figure 3.5b, *bottom*). The correlation with the monthly average, however, was quite poor ($R^2 = .39$). The outlier that explains the low correlation is from L1, which for the average includes measurements from both before and after the burn, whereas the core sample was collected before the burn. As shown in figure 3.4b, $N_2O$ fluxes were affected by the burn in March 1998, but there was less effect on the other gases.

High coefficients of determination were obtained when $CO_2$ fluxes from the laboratory incubation experiments were related with both averaged monthly data ($R^2 = .97$) and the one-time field sample ($R^2 = .78$). Again, the outlier is L1, which was more than 600 µg $CO_2$/$m^2$/hr from field data during core sampling (figure 3.5c, *bottom*) but less than 400 µg $CO_2$/$m^2$/hr from the monthly average (figure 3.5c, *top*). This difference may be explained by the fact that organic inputs, and hence decomposition, were still high before L1 was burned.

Overall it could be concluded that laboratory incubation of soil cores can explain much of the spatial and temporal variability of gas fluxes when there is no change in system management during the sampling period. More core samples would be needed to incorporate temporal variations caused by changes in land management.

## GHG CONCENTRATION IN SOIL PROFILE

In general, the concentration of $CH_4$ decreased with depth in the soil profile, whereas $N_2O$ and $CO_2$ concentrations increased with depth (figure 3.6). The profiles reflect

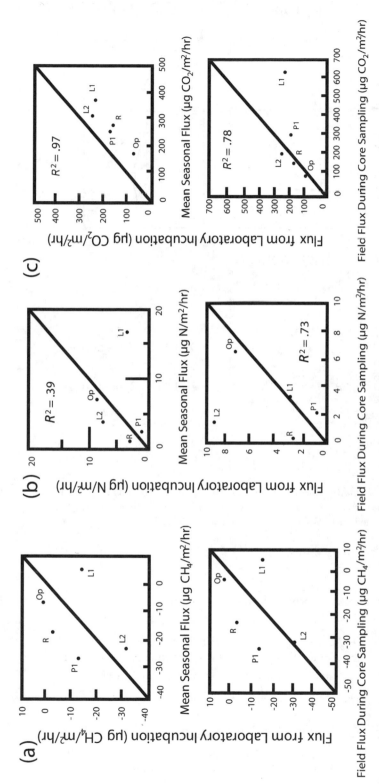

*Figure 3.5* Comparisons of (a) methane ($CH_4$), (b) nitrous oxide ($N_2O$), and (c) carbon dioxide ($CO_2$) fluxes obtained from laboratory incubations of soil cores with (*top*) the average monthly flux from field measurements and (*bottom*) fluxes obtained from field measurement taken on the same day the cores were taken. L1 and L2, logged-over forest; Op, newly planted open land; P1, primary forest; R, rubber agroforest.

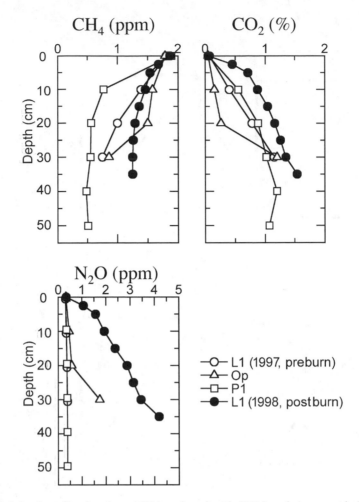

*Figure 3.6* Soil depth profile of methane ($CH_4$), carbon dioxide ($CO_2$), and nitrous oxide ($N_2O$) concentrations under logged-over forest (L1), newly opened area (Op), and primary forest (P1). L1 was slashed in September 1997 and burned in March 1998 (Ishizuka et al. 2002).

the biological processes of production and consumption of the different gases. They also suggest that the gas diffusion occurred throughout the profile. The $CO_2$ and $N_2O$ are produced throughout the profile but only diffuse from the soil surface. On the other hand, $CH_4$ shows net consumption in the profile: As it enters from the atmosphere it is consumed, and concentrations decrease. From an applied perspective, to maintain the $CH_4$ sink strength of the soil it would be necessary to allow gas diffusion at the soil surface.

Concentration of $N_2O$ in the soil before burning did not markedly change with depth. After the burn of L1, however, there was a significant increase in $N_2O$ concentrations at all depths in the soil, and the concentrations increased more with depth. These higher $N_2O$ concentrations in the soil after the burn in L1 were matched by higher fluxes of $N_2O$ from L1 (figure 3.4b).

# CONCLUSION

GHG fluxes from soils in Jambi, Sumatra, and Yurimaguas, Peru, are associated with land management. Tropical deforestation has caused the weakening of the $CH_4$ sink strength of tropical soils and an increase of $N_2O$ fluxes in some of the systems in Sumatra. The trend for decreased methane sink strength was confirmed in the Peruvian Amazon, although decreasing $N_2O$ fluxes with increasing land use intensity were found there, as long as nitrogen fertilizers were not applied.

Globally, the current $CH_4$ emission is around 600 Tg/yr, and only 30 Tg is absorbed by soil (IPCC 2001). This means that the role of land use change accounts for only 5 percent of the total $CH_4$ uptake. Forest soils in Europe are estimated to oxidize 0.6 Tg $CH_4$/yr and the corresponding agricultural land 0.23 Tg $CH_4$/yr (Dobbie and Smith 1996). Tropical forest soils could play important roles in sequestering $CH_4$ through proper land management while addressing the tradeoffs that meet the national and local objectives.

When the net global warming potentials of the combined $CO_2$, $CH_4$, and $N_2O$ fluxes from deforestation and land use change are considered together, the trace gas fluxes of $CH_4$ and $N_2O$ are basically irrelevant when compared with the $CO_2$ fluxes resulting from deforestation (Tomich et al. 1998; Palm et al. 2004). The amount of carbon released from the soil is also far smaller than that emitted from the removal of above- and below-ground biomass during deforestation or land use changes. In the landscape of Jambi Province, for example, we estimate that as much as 8 t C/ha/yr was released through land use and land cover change over a 25-year period; at the same time only 0.8 t C/ha/yr was released from the soil. Therefore the deforestation process itself provides the largest source of GHGs to the atmosphere, primarily as $CO_2$ from the burn, the amount depending on the land use system established (see chapter 2, this volume). The subsequent losses of carbon from the soil have minor impacts in terms of global consequences but can be of local significance in terms of soil fertility and sustainability (see chapter 6, this volume).

# ACKNOWLEDGMENTS

D. Murdiyarso, K. Hairiah, and C. Palm would like to thank the ASB Program, which has channeled the Global Environment Facility and United Nations Development Program funding, and the Australian Centre for International Agricultural Research for financial support. The involvement of Haruo Tsuruta and Shigehiro Ishizuka was made possible by the support of the Japan Environmental Agency.

## References

Ball, B.C., K.E. Dobbie, J.P. Parker, and K.A. Smith. 1997. The influence of gas transport and porosity on methane oxidation in soils. J. Geophys. Res. 102(D19):23, 301–323.

Cai, Z., G. Xing, X. Yan, H. Xu, H. Tsuruta, K. Yagi, et al. 1997. Methane and nitrous oxide emissions from rice paddy as affected by nitrogen fertilizers and water management. Plant Soil 196:7–14.

Castro, M.S., P.A. Steudler, and J.M. Melillo. 1995. Factors controlling atmospheric methane consumption by temperate forest soils. Global Biogeochem. Cycles 9(1):1–10.

Davidson, E.A., M.M.C. Bustamente, and A. de Siqueira Pinto. 2001. Emissions of nitrous oxide from soils of native and exotic ecosystems of the Amazon and Cerrado regions of Brazil. *In* Optimizing nitrogen management in food and energy production and environmental protection: Proceedings of the 2nd International Nitrogen Conference on Science and Policy. The Scientific World 1(S2):312–319.

Davidson, E.A., M. Keller, H.E. Erickson, L.V. Verchot, and E. Veldkamp. 2000. Testing a conceptual model of soil emissions of nitrous and nitric oxide. BioScience 50:667–680.

Davidson, E.A., P.A. Matson, and P.D. Brooks. 1996. Nitrous oxide emission controls and inorganic nitrogen dynamics in fertilized tropical agricultural soils. Soil Sci. Soc. Am. J. 60:1145–1152.

Del Grosso, S.J., W.J. Parton, A.R. Mosier, D.S. Ojioma, C.S. Potter, W. Borken, et al. 2000. General $CH_4$ oxidation model and comparisons of $CH_4$ oxidation in natural and managed systems. Global Biogeochem. Cycles 14:999–1019.

Dobbie, K.E., and K.A. Smith. 1996. Comparison of $CH_4$ oxidation rates in woodland, arable, and set aside soils. Soil Biol. Biochem. 28(10):1357–1365.

Erickson, H.E., and M. Keller. 1997. Tropical land use change and soil emissions of nitrogen oxides. Soil Use Manage. 13:278–287.

Granli, T., and O.C. Bøkman. 1994. Nitrous oxide from agriculture. Norw. J. Agric. Sci. Suppl. 12:34–40.

Hansen, S., J.E. Maechlum, and L.R. Bakken. 1993. $N_2O$ and $CH_4$ fluxes in soils influenced by fertilization and tractor traffic. Soil Biol. Biochem. 25:621–630.

Hutsch, B.W. 1996. Methane oxidation in soils of two long-term fertilization experiments in Germany. Soil Biol. Biochem. 28:773–782.

Hutsch, B.W., C.P. Webster, and D.S. Powlson. 1993. Long-term effects of nitrogen fertilization on methane oxidation in soil of the Broadbalk wheat experiment. Soil Biol. Biochem. 25:1307–1315.

Hutsch, B.W., C.P. Webster, and D.S. Powlson. 1994. Methane oxidation in soils as affected by land use, soil pH and N fertilization. Soil Biol. Biochem. 26:1613–1622.

IPCC (Intergovernmental Panel on Climate Change). 2001. Climate change 2001: The scientific basis. J.T. Houghton, Y. Ding, .D.J. Griggs, M. Nogues, P.J. van der Linden, K. Dai, et al. (eds.). Cambridge Univ. Press, Cambridge.

Ishizuka, S., T. Sakata, and K. Ishizuka. 2000. Methane oxidation in Japanese forest soils. Soil Biol. Biochem. 32:769–777.

Ishizuka, S., H. Tsuruta, and D. Murdiyarso. 2002. An intensive field study on $CO_2$, $CH_4$, and $N_2O$ emissions from soils at four land-use types in Sumatra, Indonesia. Global Biogeochem. Cycles 16:1049–1059.

Keller, M. 1986. Emissions of $N_2O$, $CH_4$ and $CO_2$ from tropical forest soils. J. Geophys. Res. 91:11791–11802.

Keller, M., J. Mellilo, and W.A. de Mello. 1997. Trace gas emissions from ecosystems of the Amazon Basin. Cienc. Cult. 49:87–97.

Keller, M., M.E. Mitre, and R.F. Stallard. 1990. Consumption of atmospheric methane in soils of central Panama: Effects of agricultural development. Global Biogeochem. Cycles 4:21–27.

Keller, M., and W.A. Reiners. 1994. Soil–atmosphere exchange of nitrous oxide, nitric oxide and methane under secondary succession of pasture to forest in the Atlantic lowlands of Costa Rica. Global Biogeochem. Cycles 8(4):399–409.

Keller, M., E. Veldkamp, A.M. Wietz, and W.A. Reiners. 1993. Effect of pasture age on soil trace-gas emission from a deforested area of Costa Rica. Nature (London) 365:244–246.

Lessard, R., P. Rochette, E. Topp, E. Pattey, R.L. Desjardins, and G. Beaumont. 1993. Methane and carbon dioxide fluxes from poorly drained adjacent cultivated and forest sites. Can. J. Soil Sci. 73(2):139–146.

Luizao, F., P. Matson, G. Livingston, R. Luizao, and P. Vitousek. 1989. Nitrous oxide flux following tropical land clearing. Global Biogeochem. Cycles 3(3):281–285.

Matson, P.A., R. Naylor, and I. Ortiz-Monasterio. 1998. Integration of environmental, agronomic, and economic aspects of fertilizer management. Science (Washington, DC) 280:12–115.

Mosier, A.R., and J.A. Delgado. 1997. Methane and nitrous oxide fluxes in grasslands in western Puerto Rico. Chemosphere 35:2059–2082.

Murdiyarso, D., and U.R. Wasrin. 1995. Estimating land use change and carbon release from tropical forests conversion using remote sensing technique. J. Biogeogr. 22:715–721.

Neill, C., M.C. Piccolo, P.A. Steudler, J.M. Melillo, B.J. Feigl, and C.C. Cerri. 1995. Nitrogen dynamics in soils of forests and active pastures in the western Brazilian Amazon Basin. Soil Biol. Biochem. 27:1167–1175.

Palm, C.A., J.C. Alegre, L. Arevalo, P.K. Mutuo, A.R. Mosier, and R. Coe. 2002. Nitrous oxide and methane fluxes in six different land use systems in the Peruvian Amazon. Global Biogeochem. Cycles 16:1073.

Palm, C.A., T. Tomich, M. van Noordwijk, S. Vosti, J. Gockowski, J. Alegre, and L. Verchot. 2004. Mitigating GHG emissions in the humid tropics: Case studies from the Alternatives to Slash and Burn Program (ASB). Environment, Development and Sustainability 6:145–162.

Piccolo, M.C., C. Neill, and C.C. Cerri. 1994. Net nitrogen mineralization and net nitrification along a tropical forest-to-pasture chronosequence. Plant Soil 162:61–70.

Prieme, A., S. Christensen, K.E. Dobbie, and P.A. Smith. 1997. Slow increase in rate of methane oxidation in soils with time following land-use change from arable agriculture to woodland. Soil Biol. Biochem. 29(8):1269–1273.

Sanchez, P.A., P.L. Woomer, and C.A. Palm. 1994. Agroforestry approaches for rehabilitating degraded lands after tropical deforestation. pp. 108–119. *In* Rehabilitation of degraded forest lands in the tropics. JIRCAS Int. Symp. Ser. no. 1. JIRCAS, Tsukuba, Japan.

Steudler, P.A., R.D. Bowden, J.M. Mellilo, and J.D. Aber. 1989. Influence of nitrogen fertilization on methane uptake in temperate forest soils. Nature (London) 341:314–315.

Steudler, P.A., J.M. Melillo, B.J. Feigl, C. Neill, M.C. Piccolo, and C.C. Cerri. 1996. Consequences of forest-to-pasture conversion on $CH_4$ fluxes in the Brazilian Amazon Basin. J. Geophys. Res. 101(D13):18, 547–554.

Suratno, W., D. Murdiyarso, F.G. Suratmo, I. Anas, M.S. Saeni, and A. Rambe. 1998. Nitrous oxide flux from irrigated rice fields in West Java. Environ. Pollut. 102(S1):159–166.

Tomich, T.P., M. van Noordwijk, S. Budidarsono, A. Gillison, T. Kusumanto, D. Murdiyarso, et al. 1998. Alternatives to Slash-and-Burn in Indonesia. Summary report and synthesis of phase II. ASB, ICRAF, Nairobi.

Tsuruta, H., K. Kanda, and T. Hirose. 1997. Nitrous oxide emission from rice paddy fields. Nutr. Cycling Agroecosyst. 49:51–58.

Veldkamp, E., and M. Keller. 1997. Nitrogen oxide emissions from a banana plantation in the humid tropics. J. Geophys. Res. 102:15889–15898.

Verchot, L.V., E.A. Davidson, J.H. Cattânio, I.L. Ackerman, H.E. Erickson, and M. Keller. 1999. Land use change and biogeochemical controls of nitrogen oxide emissions from soils in eastern Amazonia. Global Biogeochem. Cycles 13:31–46.

Vitousek, P., P. Matson, and C. Volkmann. 1989. Nitrous oxide flux from dry tropical forests. J. Geophys. Res. 102:15889–15898.

Vitousek, P.M., and W.A. Reiners. 1975. Ecosystem succession and nutrient retention: A hypothesis. BioScience 25:376–381.

Watson, R.T., I.R. Noble, B. Bolin, N.H. Ravindranath, D.J. Verardo, and D.J. Doken (eds.). 2000. Land use, land-use change and forestry. Intergovernmental Panel on Climate Change. Cambridge Univ. Press, Cambridge.

Xu, H., G. Xing, Z. Cai, and H. Tsuruta. 1997. Nitrous oxide emissions from three rice paddy fields in China. Nutr. Cycling Agroecosyst. 49:23–28.

# 4 The Potential Role of Above-Ground Biodiversity Indicators in Assessing Best-Bet Alternatives to Slash and Burn

Andrew N. Gillison
*Center for Biodiversity Management Yungaburra, Queensland, Australia*

Improvements in agricultural productivity usually are counterproductive to maintaining or enhancing indigenous biodiversity. Habitat loss, the main factor associated with biodiversity decline, increases with intensive, permanent, large-area cropping systems. Biodiversity continues to be reduced globally, partly because it is consistently undervalued and partly because of the lack of sufficient incentives for its retention and maintenance (UNEP/CBD 2002). Major contributing factors are the extraordinarily high biotic complexity in tropical forested lands and difficulties in devising and implementing cost-efficient methods for biodiversity survey and evaluation. Few published data demonstrate significant links between biodiversity and ecosystem dynamics in a way that can be used to attach a meaningful value to biodiversity or to provide related landscape-based indicators of profitability.

Against this background Alternatives to Slash and Burn (ASB) has sought readily observable field indicators that can be used to assess the status of nutrient dynamics and help forecast the impact of a specified land use on biodiversity and net primary productivity. To be acceptable to management, methods of biodiversity assessment must be cost-effective and easy to implement. Although a truly generic means of rapid biodiversity assessment remains elusive, surveys using newly developed protocols along comparable, putative land use intensity gradients in different global ecoregions have generated improved baseline datasets that provide new insights into response couplings between biodiversity and land use condition (Gillison and Liswanti 1999; Gillison 2000a). This is a significant point of entry into exploring the next important step: the biodiversity–profitability dynamic. Apart from local and regional needs, a global challenge for developing generic assessment methods is to facilitate the comparison of vegetation response to environmental change between different continents where environment and plant adaptation may be similar but where species differ. In this way lessons learned in one region may be translated to another, thereby improving the information feedback loop to farmers and enhancing international dialogue on alternatives to slash-and-burn. For management and planning to be effective, assessment techniques should be readily transferable and should deliver interpretable results with tangible, practical outcomes.

The ASB ecoregional studies to date conclude that managers and planners should be better empowered to assess their existing resources to improve management practices. This strategy should provide a more acceptable, rational, and scientific basis for adapting management to meet unpredicted changes in the physical environment caused by events such as El Niño extremes, war, change in governments, or price shocks in global and regional markets. This chapter discusses the need to improve the efficiency of existing vegetation survey and classification methods and the ways in which these methods can be integrated with multitaxon surveys to identify, calibrate, and test appropriate biodiversity indicators. Finally, case studies from tropical, lowland rainforest environments illustrate ways in which policymakers and managers can use the outcomes from these procedures in selecting more attractive alternatives to slash-and-burn.

The need to conserve biodiversity is reflected in the mission of the international Convention on Biological Diversity (CBD), which highlights a demand for improved methods of assessing biodiversity and an understanding of the nexus between biodiversity and socioeconomic incentives (UNEP/CBD 2002). Despite the clear need to develop a science-based, practical framework for biodiversity conservation, there is as yet no operational definition for biodiversity. As Weitzman (1995:21) points out, the implementation of any plan to preserve biodiversity is hampered by the lack of an operational framework: "We need a more-or-less consistent and useable measure of the value of biodiversity that can tell us how to trade off one form of diversity against another." Miller and Lanou (1995) maintain that the issue of attaching a value to biodiversity is governed largely by the interaction between human society and biodiversity. This implies that there should be a demonstrable, dynamic link between biodiversity and productivity for human needs (UNEP/CBD 2002). And although the World Bank (1995) has made a case for integrating biodiversity concerns into national decision making, the mechanisms for achieving this remain elusive. In Indonesia, as in many other developing countries, the government recognizes that a lack of scientific and management expertise is a serious impediment to biodiversity conservation (Government of Indonesia 1993). This constraint is further aggravated by the current policies of property rights on public lands and waters and the failure to use much of the financial returns from the use of the country's natural living resources (e.g., via logging) to support biodiversity conservation (Barber et al. 1995; see also chapter 13, this volume). These concerns highlight the need not only for a working definition of biodiversity but also for a cost-efficient, generic, science-based tool for its assessment. Both should aim to provide practical outcomes for government and corporate policy planners and managers involved in natural resource management.

# BIODIVERSITY INDICATORS

## THE NEED

One of the tenets of rapid biodiversity assessment (RBA) is that for practical purposes there should be readily observable indicators or surrogates of more complex plant and animal assemblages. Whether this is a pious hope or a genuine possibility is a continuing source of debate (Cranston and Hillman 1992; Reid et al. 1993; Pearson 1995; Howard et al. 1996; Lawton et al. 1998). For example, there may be questionable theoretical support for targeting so-called keystone or flagship species (Tanner et al. 1994; Williams 2002). It can be argued that without a clear understanding of multidimensional, causal relationships or trophic webs, simple, linear correlations between singular, ecosystem variables such as woody plant basal area and primates may lead to incorrect forecasts of land use impact. On the other hand, comparative estimates of ecosystem variables such as soil nutrients, soil structure, plant species richness, and richness of plant and animal functional types can provide important insights into ecosystem behavior and biodiversity when examined along key environmental gradients (Gillison 1981; Gillison and Brewer 1985; Wessels et al. 1998).

An in-depth study of biodiversity conservation in Ugandan forests led Howard et al. (1996, 1997) to conclude that although the value of indicators and their ability to provide an accurate assessment of biodiversity within a particular site remain debatable, practical factors compel their use. Thus much importance is placed on selecting appropriate indicator groups for which selection criteria involve ease of sampling and availability of resources (Howard et al. 1996, 1997). In similar vein, Miller et al. (1995) argue for reduced, manageable attribute sets that can be used to convey more complex information such as the status of key pollinators and seed dispersers that may not be available at the time of survey. In the absence of experimental data, an inescapable outcome is that demonstrating indicator efficiency entails, at the very least, calibration from intensive baseline studies of taxa and functional types at a comprehensive range of spatial, temporal, and environmental scales. But because traditional survey methods attract high logistic costs, such studies are almost nonexistent in complex tropical environments. And depending on environmental context and the variables used, surveys may demonstrate conflicting, correlative trends between biotic and abiotic variables. For example, a multitaxon baseline study of Sumatran rainforests (Gillison et al. 1996), showed that whereas plant biodiversity increased with elevation from 500 to 900 m above sea level, the converse was true for insects and birds. Although such confounding effects can be accommodated in part by appropriate regression models and site stratification, predictive models of biodiversity based on environmental correlates such as elevation must be evaluated carefully before being adopted by managers. It follows that environmental context and scale are critical in designing field studies of biodiversity and interpreting the results (see also He et al. 1994). This chapter briefly discusses the relative merits of certain forms of biodiversity indicators in a specific environmental context. These include Linnean species, functional types, diversity indexes, and measurable elements of vegetation structure.

## SPECIES

Despite recent advances in the use of alternative indicators, the species remains the most widely used currency for biodiversity assessment. Other species-based approaches may use higher taxa such as families or genera (Prance 1995) or a measure of phylogenetic distance that includes taxic richness or genealogical relationships embodied in taxonomic classifications, typically by weighting the relative number of species per genus, genera per family, and so on (Vane-Wright et al. 1991; Williams et al. 1992; Faith 1995). In complex, tropical lowland forests, however, species identification can be difficult, costly, and time-consuming. For this and other ecological reasons there is growing concern that as long as the species remains the preferred indicator, there will be little progress in biodiversity assessment (cf. Wulff 1943; Heywood and Baste 1995). When used in isolation from other, more dynamic descriptors of organism behavior and performance, species richness and abundance can seriously misinform and distort biodiversity assessment. Parity in richness alone between sites does not guarantee equivalence in either genetic composition or genetically determined, adaptive response to environment. Yet from a conservation management perspective, response characterization of individuals to environmental impact should form an important benchmark for assessing biodiversity and the degree to which biodiversity is affected by external factors such as disturbance and habitat modification. Therefore there is a clear need for other biotic descriptors that offer a reasonable alternative or complement to the use of species in biodiversity assessment.

## FUNCTIONAL TYPES

Partly through increasing dissatisfaction with species as sole indicators, an emerging school of thought now holds that biodiversity or other forms of ecological assessment should include functional aspects of individuals as well as species (Box 1981; Gillison 1981, 1988; Nix and Gillison 1985; Cowling et al. 1994a, 1994b; Huston 1994; Collins and Benning 1996; Martinez 1996; Woodward et al. 1996). Diaz (1998:18) regards functional types (FTs) as "sets of organisms showing similar responses to environmental conditions and having similar effects on the dominant ecosystem processes" (see also Cramer et al. 1999). This is an extension of an earlier definition by Shugart (1997:20), who used plant functional types (PFTs) " to connote species or groups of species that have similar responses to a suite of environmental conditions." Varying definitions of FTs are most commonly associated with guilds (organisms that share the same resources) (Gillison 1981; Bahr 1982; Huston 1994; Gillison and Carpenter

1997; Gitay and Noble 1997; Mooney 1997; Shugart 1997; Smith 1997; Smith et al. 1997). But as Martinez (1996:115–116) asserts, "The functional aspects of biodiversity are a broad and vague concept that needs substantial added specification in order to become scientifically more useful." According to Cramer (1997), the task of screening all the world's species for FTS is impossible, and for a global model, a breakdown of the world's vegetation can be achieved only based on major physiognomic or otherwise recognizable features. Such views are rapidly changing; Cramer et al. (1999) now argue that PFTS may be considered a necessary and appropriate simplification of species diversity, with the added advantage that ecosystem types often correspond naturally with PFT assemblages.

Gillison (1981) devised a method of assembling plant functional attributes (PFAS) into a functional modus or PFT and demonstrated correlations between PFTS or modi and landscape disturbance patterns. A formal, generic approach for characterizing vascular plants as PFTS from combinations of a basic set of thirty-five PFAS was developed by Gillison and Carpenter (1997:Appendix). Whereas species identification, especially in complex tropical forests, demands botanical expertise that is often unavailable, PFTS can be applied by observers with limited botanical and ecological experience.

## PLANT FUNCTIONAL TYPES

As described by Gillison and Carpenter (1997), PFTS or functional modi are combinations of essentially adaptive morphologic or functional attributes (e.g., leaf size class, leaf inclination class, leaf form and type [distribution of chlorophyll tissue]) coupled with a modified Raunkiaerean life form and the type of above-ground rooting system. The PFTS are derived according to a specific grammar or rule set from a minimum set of thirty-five functional attributes. An individual with microphyll-sized, vertically inclined, dorsiventral leaves supported by a phanerophyte life form would be a PFT expressed as MI-VE-DO-PH. Although they tend to be indicative for a species, they are independent of species in that more than one species can occur in one PFT and more than one PFT in a species. The PFTS allow the recording of genetically determined, adaptive responses of plant individuals that can reveal intraspecific as well as interspecific response to environment (e.g., land use) in a way that is not usually contained in a species name. Because they are generic, they have a singular advantage in that they can be used to record and compare datasets derived from geographically remote regions where, for example, adaptive responses and environments may be similar but where species differ.

Functional characteristics can be used to compare adaptive properties between individuals and sets of individuals independently of species, for example, where taxa may be geographically disjunct but where individuals possess similar adaptations to environment. In a comparative study of methods of characterizing site productivity and growth patterns in North Queensland rainforests (Vanclay et al. 1996), the PFT-based approach was more efficient in estimating site productivity potential for commercial tree species than traditional methods of site characterization based on species and vegetation structure. Consistently high correlations have been demonstrated between total numbers of species and total numbers of unique PFT plots across a wide range of environments (Gillison et al. 1996; see also Baskin 1994). The implications from these studies are that for surveys where taxonomic expertise is lacking, PFTs can be used to predict species richness with a high degree of confidence should this be needed. This may also benefit rapid assessment of plant biodiversity and improve correlations between plant and animal biodiversity (cf. Gillison et al. 1996). A field technique (the VegClass procedure, Gillison 2001, 2002) embodying this approach and designed specifically for rapid survey is now available for use by observers with minimal training. This technique enables rapid characterization of site physical features, vegetation structure, species composition, and PFTs and is supported by a training manual and a software package that facilitates data compilation and analysis (Gillison 2002).

## DIVERSITY MEASURES AND INDEXES

Plant species richness (the number of species per unit area) can be a useful descriptor of animal habitat but does not in itself reflect evenness or dominance of species, as do the frequently used diversity indexes of Shannon-Wiener and Simpson (Magurran 1988). Despite the widespread application of these complex indexes, ecologists rarely agree about their interpretive value. For this reason, species richness is still the most commonly applied diversity index in biodiversity studies, although the search for more ecologically meaningful indexes continues (Cousins 1991; Majer and Beeston 1996). Most diversity indexes are based on species abundance (number of individuals per species) and at best are usually regarded as a species-based stand attribute with potentially low ecological information. Generating such indexes entails time-consuming counts of individuals, which is rarely cost-effective, especially in rapid surveys of complex, tropical forested landscapes. To circumvent this problem, Gillison et al. (1999; see also Gillison 2000a) developed a method for calculating Shannon-Wiener, Simpson's, and Fisher's alpha diversity indexes based primarily on PFT data. Unlike several other approaches (e.g., Martinez 1996), this has the advantage that in rapid survey it is the number of species per PFT rather than numbers of individuals (abundance) per species that is counted in each plot. Using PFTs alone, a measure of plant functional complexity (PFC) developed by the same authors can be computed as a functional numeric distance between PFT assemblages derived from a table of weighted transformation values between specific PFAS (Gillison and Carpenter 1997; Gillison 2000a). The PFC value can be used to discriminate between two plots where species and PFT richness are similar but where PFT composition varies. Such discrimination is potentially useful in discriminating between successional sequences in forest types or between widely differing vegetation types such as mediterranean heaths and tropical forests with similar PFT and species richness. Under such circumstances measures such as PFC can add useful information to biodiversity assessment.

## VEGETATION STRUCTURE

Vegetation classification and survey methods typically combine broad structural variables with seasonality (e.g., evergreenness, deciduousness) and a list of dominant species or higher taxa, as in "Very tall evergreen Dipterocarp forest." Although this may be relevant for geographic purposes, it is inappropriate for management at a 1:50,000 mapping scale. In addition, structurally similar interregional vegetation types rarely contain the same plant species. Although vegetation structure may be used to predict animal habitat within a region, sites with similar vegetation structure in widely separated ecoregions are not necessarily ecologically equivalent. Where enhanced sensitivity is needed to discriminate between biodiversity patterns within and between regions, additional attributes such as PFTs can provide the necessary value-added discriminants.

## THE LANDSCAPE AS A SAMPLING FRAMEWORK FOR BIODIVERSITY INDICATORS

Given that plant and animal taxa and FTs tend to be distributed throughout a variety of land use mosaics, the landscape matrix seems to be a logical framework for studying biodiversity (cf. Forman and Godron 1986; Franklin 1993). This is the underlying concept for survey design and data collection across all the ASB ecoregional benchmark sites. Because landscape disturbance is a critical determinant of biodiversity (Petraitis et al. 1989; van der Maarel 1993; Phillips et al., 1994), factors such as agriculture, shifting cultivation, and forest fragmentation should be considered in survey design (Grime 1979; Bierregard et al. 1992; Sayer and Wegge 1992; Margules and Gaston 1994; Brooker and Margules 1996; Margules and Pressey 2000). For this reason ASB ecoregional sites are located as far as possible along representative, successional gradients of land use and vegetation types, from pristine rainforest and logged-over forest to plantations and degraded grasslands. These successional or so-called land use intensity transects have been generally called chronosequences in ASB (chapter 2, this volume).

Within landscapes, the issue of plot size selection continues to be argued among plant ecologists. Although plot size may vary typically from 1 to 50 ha (Dallmeier 1992; Condit 1995), some studies show that for characterizing plant diversity, useful information can be recorded from complex, humid tropical forest plots as small as 50 by 2 m (Parker and Bailey 1991; Parker and Carr 1992; Parker et al. 1993) or 40 by 5 m (Gillison et al. 1996). At landscape mosaic scale, efficiency in biodiversity survey usually is improved through the application of many small plots rather than a few large plots (cf. Keel et al. 1992). Whereas large (e.g., 50-ha plots) tend to focus only on tree species and mask important fine-scale habitat variability, a 40- by 5-m plot, or multiples of them, can be used to record all vascular plant species and positioned to target organisms with restricted or specific environmental ranges (e.g., streambanks, ridge crests, and forest margins). Environmental variability at this typically complex scale demands cost-effective survey techniques (cf. Margules and Haila 1996) where cost efficiency is governed by the nature of the variables being recorded as well as management scale and purpose. In selecting best-bet options for sustainably managing biodiversity and productivity, a manager or planner needs access to a variety of management procedures with forecastable outcomes across a variety of landscape facets. For this reason, the largely stochastic nature of landscape biodiversity dynamics requires that samples should include the widest possible environmental range of taxa and functional types. This may include a variety of land use types (LUTs) ranging from largely unaltered to highly modified forests, home gardens, and intensive agricultural plots to degraded grasslands. Within a region or subregion other factors such as climate (temperature, light, moisture), drainage, and soil gradients also play a significant role in survey design.

## METHODS

### FIELD STUDIES

Ecoregional land use intensity gradients were investigated in Brazil, Cameroon, and Indonesia. These contained LUTs, also called meta–land use systems in ASB, and lowland, forested landscape mosaics that are common in many tropical developing countries. The study was implemented at two levels: The first compared broad-scale, plant-based biodiversity patterns across similar LUTs in the three ecoregions using a standardized survey protocol. At a second and much more detailed level, the Indonesian ecoregion was subjected to an intensive biophysical, multitaxon (plant and animal) biodiversity baseline study. Sites in the three benchmark areas included sixteen in Jambi Province, Central Sumatra, mainly on ultisols but ranging across intact and logged-over rainforests, rubber plantations, jungle rubber, softwood timber plantations, agricultural subsistence gardens, and farmed *Imperata* grassland (cassava and other crops) to degraded *Imperata* grassland (table 4.1). In Brazil, twenty-five sites were located along a similarly putative but more widely distributed land use intensity gradient mainly in the western Amazon Basin (Rondônia–Acre). These ranged from logged-over rainforest on acid soils of moderate to poor fertility (ultisols) through coffee (*Coffea canephora* Pierre ex. Fröhner L.), cacao (*Theobroma cacao* L.), and rubber plantations in various combinations with other agricultural and agroforestry crops, to newly established subsistence gardens. To include a more comprehensive gradient of soil features, other sites were added to include short-stature, closed forests (campinharana) on leached sands (spodosols) north of Manaus and shrubby heaths on lithosolic sandstone soils (psamments), an oil palm plantation on a latosol (oxisol), and a semi-closed woodland savanna (cerradão) on an oxisol near Brasília (table 4.2). In Cameroon in humid tropical West Africa, twenty-one sites were located primarily along a regional, rainfall seasonality gradient from rainforest in the south at Awae, Akok, and Mbalmayo, extending north through Yaoundé to include sub-Sahelian savanna

Table 4.1 Site Physical Environment and Vegetation Features in Jambi Province, Indonesia

| Site Number | Location | Latitude (DMS) | Longitude (DMS) | Elevation (m) | Land Use Type | Mean Canopy Height (m) | Crown Cover (%) | Mean Basal Area, All Woody Plants (m²/ha) | PFTs | Plant Species | Species per PFT |
|---|---|---|---|---|---|---|---|---|---|---|---|
| BS01 | Pasir Mayang | 01-04-47 S | 102-06-02 E | 76 | Intact rainforest (outside BIOTROP permanent plot) | 21 | 75 | 27.33 | 35 | 102 | 2.91 |
| BS02 | Pasir Mayang | 01-04-45 S | 102-05-53 E | 60 | Intact rainforest (BIOTROP permanent plot) | 20 | 65 | 32.67 | 35 | 101 | 2.89 |
| BS03 | Pasir Mayang | 01-04-43 S | 102-05-55 E | 85 | Logged over 1984 (old log ramp secondary forest) | 10 | 35 | 13.33 | 24 | 50 | 2.08 |
| BS04 | Pasir Mayang | 01-04-53 S | 102-06-09 E | 60 | Logged over 1979–1980 (secondary forest) | 24 | 80 | 32.67 | 39 | 108 | 2.77 |
| BS05 | Pasir Mayang | 01-04-56 S | 102-06-05 E | 75 | Logged over 1983 (secondary forest) | 28 | 70 | 27.33 | 38 | 111 | 2.92 |
| BS06 | Pasir Mayang | 01-04-59 S | 102-06-43 E | 65 | Paraserianthes falcataria plantation 1993–1994 | 6 | 40 | 6.00 | 28 | 43 | 1.54 |
| BS07 | Pasir Mayang | 01-03-09 S | 102-08-10 E | 55 | Paraserianthes falcataria | 16 | 30 | 8.00 | 33 | 46 | 1.39 |

*Table 4.1* (Continued)

| Site Number | Location | Latitude (DMS) | Longitude (DMS) | Elevation (m) | Land Use Type | Mean Canopy Height (m) | Crown Cover (%) | Mean Basal Area, All Woody Plants (m²/ha) | PFTs | Plant Species | Species per PFT |
|---|---|---|---|---|---|---|---|---|---|---|---|
| BS08 | Pasir Mayang | 01-05-25 S | 102-07-05 E | 53 | Rubber monoculture plantation (8 yr) | 11 | 65 | 14.67 | 37 | 66 | 1.78 |
| BS09 | Pasir Mayang | 01-05-27 S | 102-06-56 E | 53 | Rubber monoculture plantation (8 yr) | 12 | 70 | 15.33 | 30 | 54 | 1.80 |
| BS10 | Pancuran Gading | 01-10-12 S | 102-06-50 E | 30 | Jungle rubber (15–38 yr) | 14 | 50 | 18.00 | 47 | 112 | 2.38 |
| BS11 | Pancuran Gading | 01-10-13 S | 102-06-46 E | 30 | Jungle rubber (15–38 yr) | 14 | 50 | 20.67 | 41 | 97 | 2.37 |
| BS12 | Kuamang Kuning | 01-35-58 S | 102-21-11 E | 40 | Tall *Imperata* grassland | 1 | 90 | 0.01 | 10 | 11 | 1.10 |
| BS13 | Kuamang Kuning | 01-35-56 S | 102-21-12 E | 40 | Short *Imperata* grassland | 1 | 90 | 0.01 | 5 | 7 | 1.40 |
| BS14 | Kuamang Kuning | 01-36-05 S | 102-21-22 E | 48 | Cassava plantation | 1.8 | 50 | 0.10 | 12 | 15 | 1.25 |
| BS15 | Kuamang Kuning | 01-36-00 S | 102-21-21 E | 48 | Cassava plantation | 1.8 | 40 | 0.10 | 13 | 19 | 1.46 |
| BS16 | Pancuran Gading | 01-10-13 S | 102-06-58 E | 30 | *Chromolaena, Clibadium* 4-yr fallow | 2 | 95 | 0.10 | 32 | 43 | 1.34 |

DMS, degrees, minutes, and seconds; PFT, plant functional type; BS, Bina Samaktha plots now referred to as SUM (Sumatra) sites; BIOTROP, Southeast Asian Regional Centre for Tropical Biology.

Table 4.2 Site Physical Environment and Vegetation Features in Brazil

| Site Number | Location | Latitude (DMS) | Longitude (DMS) | Elevation (m) | Land Use Type | Mean Canopy Height (m) | Crown Cover (%) | Mean Basal Area, All Woody Plants (m²/ha) | PFTs | Plant Species | Species per PFT |
|---|---|---|---|---|---|---|---|---|---|---|---|
| BRA01 | Ji Parana, Rondônia | 10-55-23 S | 61-57-25 W | 230 | Agroforestry plot, rubber and coffee, 12 yr old | 8 | 45 | 8.67 | 13 | 16 | 1.23 |
| BRA02 | Ji Parana, Rondônia | 10-55-23 S | 61-57-25 W | 230 | Agroforestry plot, rubber and coffee, 12 yr old | 8 | 45 | 8.00 | 13 | 15 | 1.15 |
| BRA03 | Ji Parana, Rondônia | 10-55-14 S | 61-58-27 W | 225 | Brachyaria pasture, natural forest cleared 20 yr ago | 0.8 | 95 | 0.03 | 10 | 12 | 1.20 |
| BRA04 | Ji Parana, Rondônia | 10-55-14 S | 61-58-27 W | 225 | Brachyaria pasture, natural forest cleared 20 yr ago | 0.8 | 95 | 0.03 | 9 | 14 | 1.56 |
| BRA05 | Ji Parana, Rondônia | 10-58-30 S | 62-00-58 W | 265 | Schizolobium (bandarra) & Coffea robusta plantation | 22 | 30 | 7.33 | 19 | 27 | 1.42 |
| BRA06 | Ji Parana, Rondônia | 10-58-30 S | 62-00-58 W | 265 | Schizolobium (bandarra) and Coffea robusta plantation | 21 | 40 | 7.33 | 19 | 27 | 1.42 |

Table 4.2 (Continued)

| Site Number | Location | Latitude (DMS) | Longitude (DMS) | Elevation (m) | Land Use Type | Mean Canopy Height (m) | Crown Cover (%) | Mean Basal Area, All Woody Plants (m²/ha) | PFTs | Plant Species | Species per PFT |
|---|---|---|---|---|---|---|---|---|---|---|---|
| BRA07 | Theobroma, Rondônia | 10-06-18 S | 62-11-40 W | 230 | Capoéira–cassava plantation (after slash-and-burn) | 2.2 | 15 | 0.50 | 29 | 34 | 1.17 |
| BRA08 | Theobroma, Rondônia | 10-06-12 S | 62-11-40 W | 230 | Inga edulis plantation | 5 | 90 | 8.67 | 21 | 32 | 1.52 |
| BRA09 | Theobroma, Rondônia | 10-06-12 S | 62-11-40 W | 230 | Capoéira–Cassia siamea plantation | 4.5 | 95 | 7.00 | 17 | 21 | 1.24 |
| BRA10 | Theobroma, Rondônia | 10-06-40 S | 62-11-58 W | 242 | Rubber and coffee plantation with mixed fruit trees | 8 | 15 | 5.00 | 15 | 17 | 1.13 |
| BRA11 | Theobroma, Rondônia | 10-06-40 S | 62-11-58 W | 240 | Rubber and coffee plantation with mixed fruit trees | 8 | 10 | 3.33 | 15 | 16 | 1.07 |
| BRA12 | Theobroma, Rondônia | 10-13-03 S | 62-23-49 W | 252 | Secondary rainforest | 22 | 85 | 18.00 | 39 | 79 | 2.03 |
| BRA13 | Reca, Rondônia | 09-46-48 S | 66-37-44 W | 287 | Mixed agroforestry plantation: cupuaçú, Bactris, and Brazil nut | 12 | 40 | 13.33 | 33 | 50 | 1.52 |
| BRA14 | Reca, Rondônia | 09-46-48 S | 66-37-44 W | 287 | Mixed agroforestry plantation: cupuaçú, Bactris, and Brazil nut | 12 | 40 | 11.33 | 33 | 47 | 1.42 |
| BRA15 | Reca, Rondônia | 09-46-48 S | 66-37-43 W | 232 | New subsistence garden, slash-and-burn, Bactris | 0.4 | 10 | 0.01 | 20 | 26 | 1.30 |
| BRA16 | Reca, Rondônia | 09-46-48 S | 66-37-43 W | 232 | New subsistence garden, slash-and-burn, Bactris | 0.4 | 10 | 1.00 | 20 | 23 | 1.15 |
| BRA17 | Pedro Peixoto, Acre | 10-01-13 S | 67-09-39 W | 270 | Moderately disturbed rainforest, grazed | 26 | 90 | 22.33 | 44 | 80 | 1.82 |

| BRA18 | Pedro Peixoto, Acre | 10-01-13 S | 67-09-39 W | 295 | Secondary forest: capoéira (3–4 yr after maize garden) | 12 | 95 | 16.00 | 32 | 63 | 1.97 |
|---|---|---|---|---|---|---|---|---|---|---|---|
| BRA19 | Pedro Peixoto, Acre | 10-01-13 S | 67-09-39 W | 295 | Secondary forest: capoéira (3–4 yr after maize garden) | 12 | 95 | 11.67 | 43 | 82 | 1.91 |
| BRA20 | Pedro Peixoto, Acre | 10-01-03 S | 67-09-27 W | 316 | >10-yr-old *Brachiaria brizantha* pasture | 0.2 | 95 | 0.01 | 12 | 18 | 1.50 |
| BRA21 | Pedro Peixoto, Acre | 10-01-03 S | 67-09-27 W | 316 | >10-yr-old *Brachiaria brizantha* pasture | 0.2 | 95 | 0.10 | 10 | 14 | 1.40 |
| BRA22 | Jardin do Botanica | — | — | 100 | Low, semievergreen vine thicket, woodland, some bromeliads | 4.50 | 70 | 13.33 | 36 | 90 | 2.50 |
| BRA23 | Presidente Figueiredo Igarape do lajes | 01-59-39 S | 60-01-34 W | 130 | Shrubby heath, moderately disturbed | 2.50 | 80 | 2.67 | 28 | 36 | 1.29 |
| BRA24 | Reserva Biologica de Campina | 02-35-21 S | 60-01-55 W | 120 | Campinharana (intact forest on white sand) | 0 | 80 | 18.67 | 25 | 44 | 1.76 |
| BRA25 | Embrapa Acre | 02-53-34 S | 59-58-21 W | 120 | 15- to 18-yr oil palm (*Elaeis guineensis*) plantation | 7.50 | 35 | 20.00 | 21 | 24 | 1.14 |

DMS, degrees, minutes, and seconds; PFT, plant functional type; BRA, Brazil.

Table 4.3 Site Physical Environment and Vegetation Features in Cameroon

| Site no. | Location | Latitude (DMS) | Longitude (DMS) | Elevation (m) | Land Use Type | Mean Canopy Height (m) | Crown Cover (%) | Mean Basal Area, All Woody Plants (m²/ha) | PFTs | Plant Species | Species per PFT |
|---|---|---|---|---|---|---|---|---|---|---|---|
| CAM01 | Awae Village | 03-36-05 N | 11-36-15 E | 657 | Secondary forest, heavily disturbed | 20.00 | 70 | 18.00 | 43 | 103 | 2.40 |
| CAM02 | Awae | 03-36-05 N | 11-36-15 E | 657 | 2-yr Chromolaena fallow | 2.50 | 95 | 2.00 | 37 | 61 | 1.65 |
| CAM03 | Awae | 03-36-05 N | 11-36-15 E | 657 | New garden with groundnut and cassava | 0.40 | 5 | 0.50 | 19 | 20 | 1.05 |
| CAM04 | Awae | 03-36-05 N | 11-36-15 E | 657 | 8- to 10-yr Chromolaena fallow | 3.50 | 95 | 4.67 | 35 | 54 | 1.54 |
| CAM05 | Nkol-fulu | 03-55-31 N | 11-35-49 E | 696 | Secondary forest, heavily disturbed | 12.00 | 95 | 7.33 | 33 | 50 | 1.52 |
| CAM06 | Nkol-fulu Mefou and Afamba Department | 03-55-31 N | 11-35-49 E | 696 | 4-yr Chromolaena fallow | 2.60 | 95 | 2.17 | 22 | 30 | 1.36 |
| CAM07 | Nkol-fulu Mefou and Afamba Department | 03-55-41 N | 11-35-49 E | 696 | New cultivation, egusi melon | 0.40 | 30 | 4.67 | 12 | 14 | 1.17 |
| CAM08 | Mengomo (Ebolowa Station) | 02-34-45 N | 07-02-05 E | 554 | Secondary forest, heavily disturbed | 18.00 | 70 | 20.67 | 42 | 93 | 2.21 |

| CAM09 | Mengomo (Ebolowa Station) | 02-34-37 N | 11-01-29 E | 576 | 2-yr *Chromolaena* fallow | 2.50 | 95 | 0.50 | 47 | 76 | 1.62 |
|---|---|---|---|---|---|---|---|---|---|---|---|
| CAM10 | Mengomo (Ebolowa Station) | 02-34-37 N | 11-01-29 E | 576 | >45-yr-old jungle *Cacao* | 12.00 | 75 | 17.33 | 47 | 80 | 1.70 |
| CAM11 | Akok (Ebolowa Station) | 02-42-19 N | 11-16-09 E | 554 | 2-yr *Chromolaena* fallow | 2.30 | 95 | 1.50 | 50 | 71 | 1.42 |
| CAM12 | Akok | 02-42-27 N | 11-16-30 E | 554 | 1-yr garden | 2.00 | 90 | 1.00 | 55 | 78 | 1.42 |
| CAM13 | Akok (Ebolowa Station) | 02-43-08 N | 11-17-05 E | 585 | 4-yr *Chromolaena* fallow | 3.50 | 95 | 1.00 | 66 | 100 | 1.52 |
| CAM14 | Akok | 02-43-12 N | 11-16-58 E | 585 | 2-yr *Chromolaena* fallow | 2.50 | 95 | 1.00 | 44 | 61 | 1.39 |
| CAM15 | Akok (Ebolowa Station) | 02-42-45 N | 11-16-42 E | 559 | >30-yr *Cacao* plantation | 18.00 | 75 | 20.00 | 43 | 63 | 1.47 |
| CAM16 | Bafia (20 km after Bafia) | 04-48-58 N | 11-10-27 E | 560 | 1-yr cassava field | 2.50 | 50 | 2.00 | 37 | 51 | 1.38 |
| CAM17 | Makam III–Batoum II | 05-02-40 N | 10-42-04 E | 977 | Humid savanna | 3.00 | 70 | 2.00 | 41 | 47 | 1.15 |
| CAM18 | Nkometou II | 04-04-51 N | 11-33-17 E | 596 | 1-yr *Chromolaena* fallow | 1.80 | 98 | 0.20 | 29 | 45 | 1.55 |
| CAM19 | Near Bafia | 04-48-56 N | 11-10-25 E | 640 | Shrub savanna | 4.00 | 8 | 0.67 | 18 | 25 | 1.39 |
| CAM20 | Nkolitam | 03-28-21 N | 11-29-25 E | 600 | *Raffia* palm swamp | 18.00 | 90 | 14.00 | 29 | 57 | 1.97 |
| CAM21 | Akok "Enuzam" | 02-42-45 N | 11-16-45 E | 550 | Old secondary forest | 20.00 | 85 | 26.00 | 41 | 57 | 1.39 |

DMS, degrees, minutes, and seconds; PFT, plant functional type; CAM, Cameroon.

sites (Makham III), with the soils in the southern zone being primarily ultisols. Along this gradient LUTs ranged from closed, logged, and community-managed rainforest, through cacao plantations and agricultural subsistence gardens with varying fallow systems, to cassava and maize in farmed savanna, to nonagricultural woodland savanna (table 4.3).

Within each ecoregional gradient, sites were located according to the gradient-based or gradient-oriented transect (gradsect) method of Gillison and Brewer (1985). With gradsects, sites are located according to a hierarchical nesting of presumed key physical environmental determinants such as climate, elevation, parent rock type, soil, vegetation type, and land use. Because the distribution of plants and animals is determined mainly by environmental gradients, the gradsect approach offers a means of sampling such variation. In most cases where the intent is to maximize information about environmental variability and species distribution in the area, the method is logistically much more efficient than surveys based on purely random or purely systematic grid designs (Gillison and Brewer, 1985) and is finding increasing application in regional surveys (Austin and Heyligers 1989, 1991; Sorrells and Glenn 1991; Green and Gunarwadena 1993; USGS 2001; FAO 2002). In addition, the sampling of environmental gradients rather than discrete, non–gradient-oriented samples tends to enhance efficiency of extrapolative spatial models by ensuring a more comprehensive coverage of environmental range. Although the method was originally designed and evaluated for vegetation survey, more recent, comparative assessments indicate that the gradsect approach also performs more efficiently for fauna than many other survey procedures (Wessels et al. 1998).

At each location, a standardized vegetation survey method (modified from Gillison 1988 and updated in part by Gillison and Carpenter 1997; Gillison 2002) was used to record a minimum set of biophysical characteristics (table 4.4) and determine the species and PFT for each plant (see appendix). In each case, the data were recorded along a 40- by 5-m strip transect located along the prevailing topographic contour. In the Sumatran site an intensive, multitaxon baseline study was undertaken across all land use types by a group of animal and plant specialists. Above- and below-ground biodiversity was assessed (large and small mammals, birds, insects, soil macrofauna, and vascular plants) in addition to soil physicochemical variables and above-ground carbon. The vegetation transect was the focal point for all other specialist studies (details of methods are available in Gillison 2000a).

## Data Analysis

Data were compiled using a laptop computer and a recently developed software package, VegClass (Gillison 2001), that facilitates compilation of PFTs according to the rule set of Gillison and Carpenter (1997). The Windows-based software provides a means of recording all field data according to a standardized format. These include all site physical and vegetational features listed in table 4.4. In addition, the VegClass

*Table 4.4* List of Data Variables Recorded for Each 40- by 5-m Plot

| Site Feature | Descriptor | Data Type |
|---|---|---|
| Location reference | Location | Alphanumeric |
| | Date (dd-mm-yr) | Alphanumeric |
| | Plot number (unique) | Alphanumeric |
| | Country | Text |
| Observer(s) | Observer(s) by name | Text |
| Physical | Latitude (deg.min.sec., GPS) | Alphanumeric |
| | Longitude (deg.min.sec., GPS) | Alphanumeric |
| | Elevation (m a.s.l., aneroid and GPS) | Numeric |
| | Aspect (compass degrees, perpendicular to plot) | Numeric |
| | Slope percentage (perpendicular to plot) | Numeric |
| | Soil depth (cm) | Numeric |
| | Soil type (U.S. soil taxonomy) | Text |
| | Parent rock type | Text |
| | Litter depth (cm) | Numeric |
| | Terrain position | Text |
| Site history | General description and land use or landscape context | Text |
| Vegetation structure | Vegetation type | Text |
| | Mean canopy height (m) | Numeric |
| | Crown cover percentage (total) | Numeric |
| | Crown cover percentage (woody) | Numeric |
| | Crown cover percentage (nonwoody) | Numeric |
| | Cover abundance (Domin) of bryophytes | Numeric |
| | Cover abundance of woody plants <1.5 m tall | Numeric |
| | Basal area (mean of 3, m²/ha) | Numeric |
| | Furcation index (mean and coefficient of variation % of 20) | Numeric |
| | Profile sketch of 40- by 5-m plot (scannable) | Digital image |
| Plant taxa | Family | Text[a] |
| | Genus | Text[a] |
| | Species | Text[a] |
| | Botanical authority | Text[a] |
| | If exotic (binary, presence–absence)[b] | Numeric |
| PFT | Plant functional elements combined according to published rule set | Text[a] |
| Quadrat listing | Unique taxa and PFTs per quadrat (for each of 8 [5- by 5-m] quadrats)[b] | Numeric |
| Photograph | Hard copy and digital image[b] | Digital and hard copy image |

GPS, global positioning system; PFT, plant functional type.

[a]Summary of presence–absence by site for numerical analyses.

[b]Not available for all sites.

software facilitates on-demand data summaries and graphs of desired combinations of variables within and between plots that can be exported to industry-standard spreadsheet and relational database software. For data recorded for each contiguous 5- by 5-m quadrat within the 40- by 5-m transect, graphs of cumulative species and PFT totals per unit area can be generated to allow the subjective inspection of asymptotic curves as an indicator of sample efficiency for a specific vegetation type or LUT (Gillison 2002). If needed, the sampling procedure can be used to discriminate between successional stages of vegetation independently of species. And because it contains adaptive morphological (PFT) as well as taxonomic attributes, VegClass exhibits a higher sensitivity to changes in environment than more traditional classification methods. The same software was used to calculate PFT-based, Shannon-Wiener, Simpson's, and Fisher's alpha indexes as well as PFC.

The most efficient vegetation correlates of animal distribution acquired from an intensive multitaxon survey in Central Sumatra were obtained by linear regression (Pearson product moment) between all attribute values using the Minitab (version 13.32) software package. The most efficient plant-based predictors of animal taxa overall were plant species richness, PFT richness, species richness:PFT richness ratio, mean canopy height, and basal area of all woody plants. Using a method of multidimensional scaling (MDS) of these variables (Belbin 1992) based on a Gower metric similarity measure, the two best eigenvector solutions were extracted for each ecoregional dataset. These vectors were then plotted as a two-dimensional display of relative site distribution. With this procedure, the raw data variables can be back-correlated against each vector axis to determine their relative contribution to overall pattern should this be needed. The data from all ecoregional sites were then pooled and the MDS procedure repeated to display the relative distribution for the entire dataset.

As an additional exploratory measure, for each ecoregional dataset, the same MDS procedure was used to extract the best single eigenvector. The single eigenvalues thus acquired were standardized and ranked on a 1–10 scale for each site in order to identify any biodiversity-related trend according to an intuitive ranking of land use intensity gradients. For Brazil this was restricted to twenty-one sites in the Rondônia–Acre region of the western Amazon Basin to focus on a more constrained pattern of land use. These ranked values were used as an integrated vegetation index (V-index) (Gillison 2000a). The V-index is used here as an additional, potentially useful predictor for biodiversity; high values indicate more complex vegetation structure and richness in species and PFTs. For this reason V-index values were included in the correlative analyses of the Sumatran multitaxon baseline study.

## RESULTS AND DISCUSSION

In the Sumatran sites, richness in both plant species and PFTs, mean canopy height, basal area, and cover abundance of understory woody plants were the most efficient predictors of fauna (table 4.5). Among the better indicators there is a clear tendency

*Table 4.5* Linear Correlations[a] Between Richness of Plant Species, PFTs and Their Ratios, and Various Animal Taxa and Above-Ground Plant Carbon

| Faunal Groups | Plant Species | PFT | Species per PFT | PFC | V-Index | Shannon | Simpson | F-Alpha | Mean Canopy Height (m) | Basal Area (m²/ha) | Crown Cover (%) | WPlts | FI |
|---|---|---|---|---|---|---|---|---|---|---|---|---|---|
| **Ground-Dwelling Arthropods** | | | | | | | | | | | | | |
| Termite abundance | 0.844 | 0.732 | 0.944 | 0.654 | 0.810 | 0.687 | -0.643 | -0.656 | 0.832 | 0.872 | 0.384 | 0.748 | -0.767 |
| | 0.017 | 0.061 | 0.001 | 0.111 | 0.096 | 0.088 | 0.119 | 0.109 | 0.080 | 0.054 | 0.524 | 0.053 | 0.130 |
| Termite species | 0.849 | 0.705 | 0.976 | 0.564 | 0.811 | 0.650 | -0.630 | 0.564 | 0.900 | 0.869 | 0.481 | 0.773 | -0.813 |
| | 0.016 | 0.077 | 0.000 | 0.187 | 0.096 | 0.114 | 0.122 | 0.187 | 0.038 | 0.056 | 0.412 | 0.041 | 0.094 |
| **Canopy Arthropods** | | | | | | | | | | | | | |
| Acari | 0.190 | -0.232 | 0.443 | -0.465 | 0.328 | -0.662 | 0.624 | -0.648 | 0.356 | 0.427 | 0.154 | 0.622 | -0.704 |
| | 0.576 | 0.493 | 0.172 | 0.150 | 0.325 | 0.027 | 0.040 | 0.031 | 0.283 | 0.190 | 0.651 | 0.041 | 0.016 |
| Blattodea | 0.124 | -0.014 | 0.204 | -0.061 | 0.086 | -0.452 | 0.563 | -0.456 | -0.010 | 0.075 | -0.287 | 0.554 | -0.060 |
| | 0.716 | 0.966 | 0.548 | 0.858 | 0.801 | 0.162 | 0.071 | 0.158 | 0.977 | 0.827 | 0.392 | 0.077 | 0.861 |
| Coleoptera | 0.312 | 0.458 | 0.127 | 0.481 | 0.166 | 0.075 | 0.231 | -0.093 | 0.016 | 0.111 | -0.026 | 0.453 | 0.416 |
| | 0.350 | 0.156 | 0.709 | 0.134 | 0.625 | 0.826 | 0.494 | 0.785 | 0.963 | 0.746 | 0.940 | 0.162 | 0.203 |
| Collembola | 0.643 | 0.089 | 0.882 | -0.130 | 0.776 | -0.374 | 0.402 | -0.720 | 0.799 | 0.768 | 0.567 | 0.729 | -0.739 |
| | 0.033 | 0.795 | 0.000 | 0.703 | 0.005 | 0.258 | 0.221 | 0.013 | 0.003 | 0.006 | 0.069 | 0.011 | 0.009 |
| Diptera | 0.038 | 0.404 | -0.197 | 0.350 | -0.035 | 0.279 | 0.002 | 0.261 | -0.066 | 0.077 | 0.179 | -0.158 | 0.453 |
| | 0.912 | 0.217 | 0.562 | 0.291 | 0.918 | 0.406 | 0.995 | 0.438 | 0.847 | 0.821 | 0.597 | 0.644 | 0.161 |
| Formicidae | 0.274 | 0.370 | 0.142 | 0.426 | 0.121 | 0.082 | 0.145 | -0.054 | -0.040 | 0.030 | -0.235 | 0.576 | 0.234 |
| | 0.415 | 0.262 | 0.676 | 0.191 | 0.723 | 0.810 | 0.671 | 0.875 | 0.906 | 0.929 | 0.487 | 0.064 | 0.489 |
| Formicidae, total | 0.371 | 0.572 | -0.052 | 0.829 | 0.069 | 0.713 | -0.724 | -0.045 | -0.177 | -0.158 | -0.391 | 0.005 | 0.522 |
| | 0.538 | 0.313 | 0.933 | 0.021 | 0.912 | 0.072 | 0.066 | 0.924 | 0.776 | 0.799 | 0.524 | 0.993 | 0.366 |
| Hemiptera | 0.098 | 0.229 | -0.026 | 0.254 | 0.005 | 0.073 | -0.032 | 0.161 | -0.039 | -0.061 | -0.495 | 0.507 | -0.245 |
| | 0.774 | 0.499 | 0.920 | 0.454 | 0.988 | 0.832 | 0.925 | 0.637 | 0.910 | 0.858 | 0.121 | 0.111 | 0.469 |
| Hymenoptera | 0.302 | 0.446 | 0.129 | 0.426 | 0.169 | 0.068 | 0.194 | -0.063 | 0.061 | -0.075 | -0.105 | 0.560 | 0.207 |
| | 0.367 | 0.169 | 0.705 | 0.192 | 0.619 | 0.843 | 0.567 | 0.854 | 0.858 | 0.827 | 0.759 | 0.074 | 0.541 |

Table 4.5 (Continued)

| Faunal Groups | Plant Species | PFT | Species per PFT | PFC | V-Index | Shannon | Simpson | F-Alpha | Mean Canopy Height (m) | Basal Area (m²/ha) | Crown Cover (%) | WPlts | FI |
|---|---|---|---|---|---|---|---|---|---|---|---|---|---|
| **Canopy Arthropods** | | | | | | | | | | | | | |
| Isoptera (canopy) | 0.417 | 0.140 | 0.496 | 0.192 | 0.519 | -0.134 | 0.132 | -0.308 | 0.652 | 0.444 | 0.289 | 0.076 | -0.409 |
|  | 0.203 | 0.681 | 0.121 | 0.571 | 0.102 | 0.695 | 0.698 | 0.337 | 0.030 | 0.171 | 0.389 | 0.824 | 0.212 |
| Neuroptera | -0.038 | -0.267 | 0.172 | -0.323 | 0.161 | -0.509 | 0.527 | -0.443 | 0.279 | 0.271 | 0.464 | -0.313 | -0.212 |
|  | 0.911 | 0.428 | 0.613 | 0.333 | 0.636 | 0.110 | 0.096 | 0.172 | 0.406 | 0.419 | 0.151 | 0.349 | 0.532 |
| Orthoptera | 0.545 | 0.378 | 0.528 | 0.395 | 0.467 | -0.223 | 0.432 | -0.531 | 0.380 | 0.345 | -0.025 | 0.709 | -0.154 |
|  | 0.083 | 0.252 | 0.095 | 0.229 | 0.147 | 0.509 | 0.185 | 0.093 | 0.249 | 0.298 | 0.942 | 0.014 | 0.651 |
| Psocoptera | 0.398 | 0.148 | 0.457 | 0.019 | 0.451 | -0.457 | 0.019 | -0.562 | 0.458 | 0.471 | 0.353 | 0.535 | -0.019 |
|  | 0.225 | 0.664 | 0.157 | 0.956 | 0.164 | 0.158 | 0.956 | 0.072 | 0.157 | 0.144 | 0.287 | 0.090 | 0.956 |
| Spiders | 0.186 | 0.307 | 0.050 | 0.298 | 0.097 | -0.066 | 0.307 | -0.042 | 0.011 | 0.074 | -0.162 | 0.484 | 0.184 |
|  | 0.584 | 0.359 | 0.884 | 0.374 | 0.776 | 0.847 | 0.358 | 0.903 | 0.973 | 0.829 | 0.635 | 0.131 | 0.588 |
| Thysanoptera | 0.470 | 0.756 | 0.138 | 0.693 | 0.244 | 0.426 | -0.099 | 0.061 | 0.066 | 0.124 | 0.020 | 0.416 | 0.352 |
|  | 0.144 | 0.007 | 0.685 | 0.018 | 0.470 | 0.191 | 0.772 | 0.859 | 0.847 | 0.717 | 0.954 | 0.203 | 0.289 |
| Insects, total | 0.593 | 0.487 | 0.526 | 0.529 | 0.515 | 0.002 | 0.261 | -0.287 | 0.395 | 0.422 | 0.078 | 0.667 | -0.036 |
|  | 0.055 | 0.129 | 0.096 | 0.094 | 0.105 | 0.995 | 0.438 | 0.392 | 0.229 | 0.196 | 0.819 | 0.025 | 0.916 |
| Insects, unidentified | 0.771 | 0.418 | 0.839 | 0.439 | 0.820 | -0.101 | 0.294 | -0.483 | 0.773 | 0.774 | 0.429 | 0.545 | -0.406 |
|  | 0.005 | 0.201 | 0.001 | 0.177 | 0.002 | 0.768 | 0.380 | 0.133 | 0.005 | 0.005 | 0.188 | 0.083 | 0.216 |
| Bird spp., total | 0.599 | 0.347 | 0.704 | 0.306 | 0.661 | 0.157 | -0.157 | -0.370 | 0.726 | 0.625 | 0.291 | 0.442 | -0.244 |
|  | 0.040 | 0.269 | 0.011 | 0.334 | 0.019 | 0.627 | 0.627 | 0.237 | 0.008 | 0.024 | 0.447 | 0.150 | 0.445 |
| Above-ground carbon[b] | 0.796 | 0.558 | 0.909 | 0.484 | 0.771 | 0.383 | -0.295 | -0.380 | 0.792 | 0.730 | 0.626 | 0.382 | -0.535 |
|  | 0.000 | 0.025 | 0.000 | 0.057 | 0.005 | 0.143 | 0.268 | 0.147 | 0.004 | 0.011 | 0.039 | 0.145 | 0.090 |

PFT, plant functional type; PFC, plant functional complexity; V-index, vegetation index; Shannon, Shannon-Wiener diversity index for PFTs; Simpson, Simpson's diversity index for PFTs; F-Alpha, Fisher's alpha diversity index for PFTs; WPlts, cover abundance of woody plants <1.5 m tall; FI, mean furcation index canopy trees.

[a] Correlation *r* value on first line. Probability value on second line.

[b] Above-ground carbon data from Hairiah and van Noordwijk (2000).

for the species:PFT ratio rather than species or PFT richness alone to improve prediction for above-ground carbon and for certain animal groups such as birds, collembolans, and termites. There is no clear ecological reason as to why this ratio should be a better predictor. However, one can speculate that higher ratios in the later and more complex successional stages of forest development reflect less available above-ground ecological niche space for larger (more readily measurable) organisms where more species are represented by fewer PFTs.

When the general pattern of plant and animal taxonomic distribution along the LUTs is examined, it is evident that the highest biodiversity richness occurs in certain pristine forest types and in the more disturbed jungle rubber. This may be explained partly by the nature of the available ecological niches in both. The jungle rubber plots have both higher species and PFT richness than the older growth forests but a lower species:PFT ratio. Whereas the former has allowed the development of cryptic terrestrial and arboreal habitats over a longer time frame, the younger and more dynamic jungle rubber displays a much wider variety of ecological niches and canopy gap openings where the fragmentary nature of the stand is maintained mainly by frequent disturbance from humans and to a much lesser extent by large mammals such as elephants and tapirs. This is consistent with the intermediate disturbance hypothesis, which states that highest species richness will occur in zones of intermediate disturbance rather than in old growth.

Although the high correlations for many variables do not in themselves provide a valid argument for identifying cause and effect, in this study the traditional hypothesis that richness begets richness is consistent with forest successional trends and the coevolution of increasingly complex food webs and abundance of autotrophs and heterotrophs including detritivores. The distribution of plant cellulose, as represented by mean canopy height, basal area, and above-ground carbon, along a land use intensity gradient corresponds closely with species and abundance of ground-dwelling termites, and this may be explained in part by termite feeding habits (see also Bignell et al. 2000; Jones et al. 2002).

In surveys of tropical forested landscapes, meaningful correlates between plants and birds can be difficult to achieve (Jepson and Djarwadi 2000; Beehler et al. 2001), and in temperate regions investigations using plant functional groups to predict bird distribution can be inconclusive (cf. Abernethy et al. 1996). This study may be the first of its kind to reveal the potential of a newer suite of plant-based variables to predict bird species richness across a range of LUTs in tropical, forested landscapes. Table 4.5 reveals highly significant correlations between bird species richness, plant species richness, species:PFT richness ratio, mean canopy height, basal area, and V-index. When bird species richness is correlated with the ratio of mean canopy height to furcation index (FI) of canopy woody plants (indicative of branching density) the correlation $r$ value increases to 0.792 ($p = .006$), indicating that bird species richness may be a function of both canopy height and "branchiness." A regression of bird species richness against combined mean canopy height and FI gave a significant $R^2$ of 53.2

Table 4.6 Plant-Based Linear Correlates[a] with Soil Physicochemical Attributes[b]

| | pH–H$_2$O | pH–KCl | Organic C (%) | N_tot, % | K | Na | Mg | Al | ECEC | AL_sat | Bulk Density |
|---|---|---|---|---|---|---|---|---|---|---|---|
| Mean canopy height | -0.719 | -0.828 | 0.486 | 0.386 | 0.005 | -0.205 | -0.370 | 0.632 | 0.441 | 0.558 | -0.770 |
| | 0.002 | 0.000 | 0.056 | 0.140 | 0.984 | 0.446 | 0.159 | 0.009 | 0.087 | 0.025 | 0.000 |
| Basal area (m²/ha) | -0.684 | -0.780 | 0.503 | 0.395 | 0.048 | -0.198 | -0.347 | 0.684 | 0.491 | 0.595 | -0.784 |
| | 0.004 | 0.000 | 0.047 | 0.130 | 0.859 | 0.462 | 0.188 | 0.003 | 0.053 | 0.015 | 0.000 |
| Crown cover (%) | 0.215 | 0.125 | 0.092 | 0.095 | -0.063 | 0.076 | 0.278 | -0.057 | -0.107 | -0.089 | -0.120 |
| | 0.424 | 0.644 | 0.737 | 0.728 | 0.818 | 0.779 | 0.298 | 0.833 | 0.694 | 0.743 | 0.659 |
| WPlts | -0.285 | -0.206 | 0.502 | 0.376 | 0.475 | 0.381 | 0.300 | 0.296 | 0.512 | 0.137 | -0.627 |
| | 0.284 | 0.445 | 0.048 | 0.151 | 0.063 | 0.146 | 0.259 | 0.265 | 0.043 | 0.614 | 0.009 |
| Cover abundance of bryophytes | -0.593 | -0.777 | 0.459 | 0.526 | 0.097 | -0.164 | -0.300 | 0.697 | 0.584 | 0.527 | -0.743 |
| | 0.016 | 0.000 | 0.074 | 0.037 | 0.720 | 0.545 | 0.260 | 0.003 | 0.018 | 0.036 | 0.001 |
| FI | 0.172 | 0.293 | -0.144 | -0.026 | 0.093 | 0.175 | 0.180 | -0.123 | -0.094 | -0.074 | 0.291 |
| | 0.525 | 0.270 | 0.594 | 0.925 | 0.732 | 0.516 | 0.504 | 0.651 | 0.728 | 0.786 | 0.274 |
| PFT | -0.402 | -0.471 | 0.878 | 0.742 | 0.609 | 0.393 | 0.097 | 0.643 | 0.880 | 0.279 | -0.890 |
| | 0.123 | 0.066 | 0.000 | 0.001 | 0.012 | 0.132 | 0.720 | 0.007 | 0.000 | 0.295 | 0.000 |

| | | | | | | | | | | |
|---|---|---|---|---|---|---|---|---|---|---|
| Total plant species | -0.550 | -0.653 | 0.716 | 0.550 | 0.329 | 0.104 | -0.225 | 0.587 | 0.650 | 0.484 | -0.868 |
| | 0.027 | 0.006 | 0.002 | 0.027 | 0.214 | 0.700 | 0.403 | 0.303 | 0.006 | 0.058 | 0.000 |
| Species per PFT | -0.683 | -0.745 | 0.405 | 0.278 | -0.012 | -0.196 | -0.463 | 0.516 | 0.353 | 0.602 | -0.742 |
| | 0.004 | 0.001 | 0.120 | 0.298 | 0.966 | 0.466 | 0.071 | 0.011 | 0.180 | 0.014 | 0.001 |
| V-index | 0.664 | 0.755 | -0.611 | -0.477 | -0.174 | 0.056 | 0.291 | -0.588 | -0.575 | -0.544 | 0.852 |
| | 0.005 | 0.001 | 0.012 | 0.061 | 0.520 | 0.838 | 0.274 | 0.003 | 0.020 | 0.029 | 0.000 |
| PFC | -0.283 | -0.387 | 0.855 | 0.722 | 0.714 | 0.503 | 0.084 | 0.589 | 0.865 | 0.208 | -0.843 |
| | 0.288 | 0.162 | 0.000 | 0.002 | 0.002 | 0.047 | 0.757 | 0.016 | 0.000 | 0.444 | 0.000 |
| Shannon | 0.352 | 0.231 | -0.507 | -0.496 | -0.545 | -0.327 | -0.348 | -0.366 | -0.732 | -0.049 | 0.615 |
| | 0.181 | 0.390 | 0.045 | 0.051 | 0.029 | 0.217 | 0.186 | 0.163 | 0.001 | 0.858 | 0.011 |
| Simpson | -0.367 | -0.309 | 0.722 | 0.661 | 0.647 | 0.445 | 0.327 | 0.479 | 0.866 | 0.100 | -0.767 |
| | 0.162 | 0.244 | 0.002 | 0.005 | 0.007 | 0.084 | 0.216 | 0.060 | 0.000 | 0.712 | 0.001 |
| F-alpha | 0.488 | 0.542 | 0.240 | 0.174 | 0.585 | 0.633 | 0.876 | -0.348 | 0.290 | -0.651 | -0.018 |
| | 0.055 | 0.030 | 0.370 | 0.519 | 0.017 | 0.009 | 0.000 | 0.287 | 0.276 | 0.006 | 0.946 |

N_tot, total nitrogen; ECEC, effective cation exchange capacity; Al_sat, aluminum saturation; WPlts, cover abundance of woody plants <1.5 m tall; Bryo, cover abundance of bryophytes; FI, mean furcation index of canopy trees; PFT, plant functional types; V-index, vegetation index; PFC, plant functional complexity; Shannon, Shannon-Wiener diversity index for PFTs; Simpson, Simpson's diversity index for PFTs; F-alpha, Fisher's alpha diversity index for PFTs.

[a]Linear correlation $r$ value on first line of each cell, probability value on second line.

[b]Soil analytical data from Hairiah and van Noordwijk (2000).

percent. This potential has been demonstrated in a similar, independent ASB study in northern Thailand (Gillison and Liswanti 1999).

Table 4.6 outlines correlations between plant-based variables and a range of soil physicochemical variables; only the most statistically significant are listed. These include highly significant correlations between certain soil variables such as bulk density, pH, organic carbon, total nitrogen and aluminum, species and PFT richness, vegetation structure, and V-index. There is no immediate explanation as to why these soil attributes correspond more closely than others with both plant species and PFT richness. Land use practices also confound speculation about the biodiversity–soil nutrient dynamic. In Jambi, Sumatra, for example, total soil nitrogen is highest in monoculture rubber plantations (added artificial fertilizer), with only moderate species and PFT richness, and in the (unfertilized) jungle rubber plots (plots 10 and 11, table 4.1) that are richest in plant taxa and PFTs. Among the soil variables, bulk density corresponds most closely with species and PFT richness. Although diversity indexes are rarely accepted without question as biodiversity indicators, in the present study each of the PFT-based, Shannon-Wiener, Simpson's, and Fisher's alpha values is significantly correlated with a variety of key soil variables (table 4.6). The reasons underlying this correlative pattern warrant study if cause-and-effect relationships are to be better understood.

Evidence of plant morphological adaptation such as PFAs (and by association PFTs) to varying soil nutrient conditions is widely documented along gradients of salinity, pH, total and available nitrogen, phosphorus, and potassium and in certain extreme soil and parent rock mineral complexes such as limestone and serpentinites. These are characterized among well-documented plant assemblages such as "calcicolous" or "serpentinite" flora. Despite clear trends between PFTs and the nutrient and physical substrate, physiological explanations for these phenomena usually are extraordinarily complex (Larcher 1975) and are likely to be further confounded by soil–climate interaction. Apart from the correlates revealed here for humid, lowland tropical forested lands, in boreal forests pH and soil organic matter content are considered to be among the best soil-related predictors of biodiversity (Koptsik et al. 2001). Nevertheless, the Sumatran study suggests that, for this area at least, despite a lack of evidence for cause and effect, the utility of plants as indicators of biodiversity and related soil nutrient availability (and hence potential agricultural productivity) is clearly enhanced by the use of species richness, PFT richness, and their ratios both individually and in combination. When combined with vegetation structural predictors of animal distribution (such as mean canopy height and basal area) these plant-based attributes become potentially powerful indicators of animal habitat. Whereas terrestrial animal diversity is governed largely by plants, in the study area, plant-based diversity in turn can be shown to vary predictably with soil nutrients as well as pH and bulk density across all LUTs. The Sumatran study does not aim to provide generic soil-based indicators of biodiversity or to elucidate soil–plant dynamics. But it has produced a readily testable hypothesis that certain soil variables are distributed in a predictable way with certain key plant and animal assemblages. If this model can be shown to hold, it will have positive implications for adaptive management.

Multidimensional scaling of sites in Indonesia, Cameroon, and Brazil using the plant-based variables listed in tables 4.1, 4.2, and 4.3 (with the exception of crown cover percentage) reveal tight clustering of complex agroforests adjacent to intact forest. In Indonesia these are represented by jungle rubber (figure 4.1), in Cameroon by both jungle and mixed *Cacao* plantations (figure 4.2), and in Brazil by complex agroforests containing cupuaçú, coffee, *Bactris* palm, and Brazil nut (*Bertholletia excelsa* Humb. & Bonpl.) (figure 4.3). These clusters represent best-bet agroforestry scenarios in each country. The ordinations (figures 4.1, 4.2, and 4.3) that compare similar LUTs in Brazil, Cameroon, and Indonesia reveal consistent trends between plant-based biodiversity in complex agroforests and jungle rubber and *Cacao* along land use intensity gradients. These are clearly evident when examined in the context of gradient extremes between degraded or highly simplified grasslands (including improved pastures) and intact forest. When the datasets from each ecoregion are combined and the MDS repeated (figure 4.4), a central zone for best bets is indicated, with the separation between agroforests reflected mainly by regional differences in species richness and with Sumatra and Cameroon indicating higher forest species and PFT richness than the Brazilian sites sampled in this study.

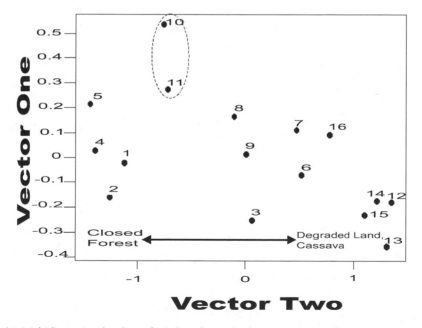

*Figure 4.1* Multidimensional scaling of 16 plots along a land use intensity gradient in Sumatra. Dashed lines indicate area of best-bet alternatives to slash-and-burn (in this case jungle rubber). See table 4.1 for plot details and context of land use types.

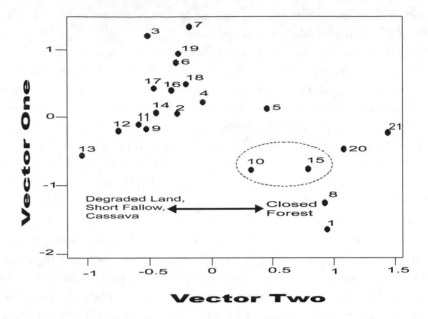

*Figure 4.2* Multidimensional scaling of 21 plots along a land use intensity gradient in Cameroon. Dashed lines indicate area of best-bet alternatives to slash-and-burn (in this case periodically tended *Cacao* plantation and jungle *Cacao*). See table 4.3 for plot details and land use types.

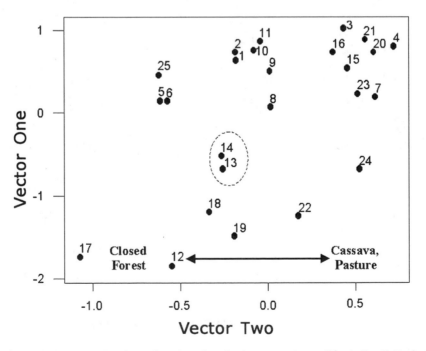

*Figure 4.3* Multidimensional scaling of 25 plots along land use intensity gradient in Brazil. Dashed lines indicate area of best-bet alternatives to slash-and-burn (in this case periodically tended, mixed agroforestry plantation: cupuaçú, *Bactris,* and Brazil nut). See table 4.2 for plot details and context of land use types.

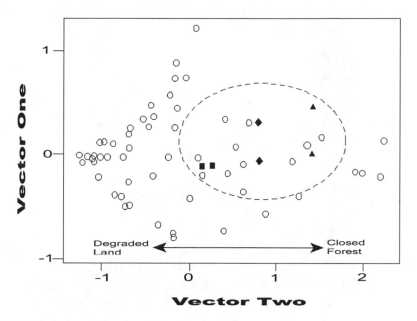

*Figure 4.4* Multidimensional scaling of site data from all three ecoregions showing relative positioning of relative best-bet agroforests in Sumatra *(solid triangles)*, Cameroon *(solid diamonds)*, and Brazil *(solid squares)*.

The V-index values for each ecoregion (figures 4.5, 4.6, and 4.7) reflect patterns of vegetation complexity that correspond with an intuitive assessment of land use intensity and, in the case of Sumatra, with patterns of plant and animal biodiversity. As expected, across all ecoregions, similar values for low-productivity land use such as cassava (*Manihot exculenta* Crantz) and degraded grassland are evident at the lowest index values, with highest values recorded for older-growth and secondary forests. The V-indexes are not designed to produce generic values for LUTs but rather a relative within-region index that may be potentially useful in regional planning. It is of interest nonetheless that the two most similar land use gradients (Sumatra and Cameroon) present similar V-index values for best-bet jungle rubber (Jambi sites 10 and 11, with V-indexes of 7.9 and 7.6, respectively) and jungle cacao and 30-year-old plantation cacao (Cameroon sites 10 and 15, with V-indexes of 7.0 and 7.7, respectively). The Brazilian mixed agroforest plots 13 and 14 have V-indexes of 6.4 and 6.0, respectively with higher values of 7.8 occurring in Capoéira secondary forest (forest that has reinvaded abandoned pasture land). The lower values for the Brazilian agroforests may reflect age since establishment (7–8 years) where V-indexes can be expected to increase with time but also the more intensively managed nature of the Brazilian systems. Although the V-index is an integrated measure of vegetation complexity (species, PFTs, and structure) rather than biodiversity, the high correlations between V-indexes and animal groups, especially birds (table 4.5), suggests it may have a useful role in biodiversity assessment.

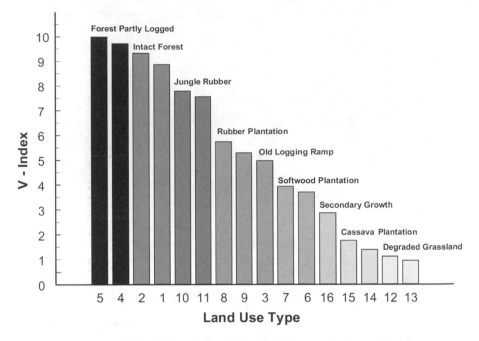

*Figure 4.5* Land use types in Jambi, central Sumatra, ranked by vegetation index (V-index).

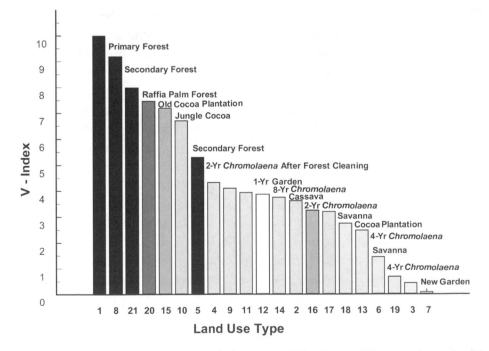

*Figure 4.6* Land use types in Cameroon (Mbalmayo and Makam), ranked by vegetation index (V-index).

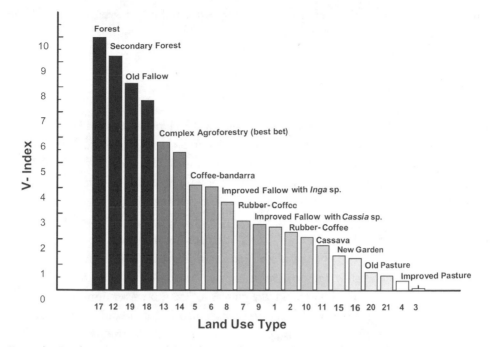

*Figure 4.7* Land use types in Brazil (Rondônia and Acre), ranked by vegetation index (V-index).

Despite the improvements in plant-based biodiversity indicators recorded here, generalizations from these lowland studies must be made with due care because other preliminary studies (Gillison et al. 1996) indicate that similar predictive relationships may not hold in highland tropical environments. More robust predictive models therefore will require similarly calibrated surveys but within a wider array of ecoregional variation. Results emerging from parallel ASB studies in Thailand and South Sumatra (Gillison 2000b, 2000c) on the impacts of differing tenurial systems in coffee and oil palm management systems also support the concept that complex agroforests provide the best options for long-term management, despite the fact that short-term profit is greatest where capital exists to promote permanent, intensive farming systems.

There is increasing evidence that biodiversity, at least in certain circumstances (cf. those described by Tilman and Downing 1994), contributes to ecosystem stability and productivity, although this is not without debate (Hector et al. 1999; Huston et al. 2000; Loreau et al. 2001). In the present study, apparent links between agricultural productivity and profitability suggest that apart from fertilizer-enhanced, permanent, intensive cropping systems in which biodiversity is greatly reduced and short-term profitability increased, higher biodiversity is associated with higher soil nutrients and site productivity under longer fallows and under complex agroforests. Therefore a key challenge is to identify the principal biophysical and socioeconomic drivers of biodiversity and related profitability. Current ASB activities are pursuing this goal, seeking how best to identify and calibrate indicators that can be used directly in a policy analysis matrix and in the formulation of appropriate policy interventions needed to sustain both economic growth and biological diversity.

## CONCLUSION

The present studies demonstrate highly significant correlations between key plant and animal species, functional groups, vegetation structure, above-ground carbon, and key soil variables. These represent improvements on biodiversity predictors so far evaluated in other lowland, tropical, forested landscapes under slash-and-burn. Although a clearer understanding of the soil–plant–land use dynamic is needed to better manage ecosystem productivity, the study reveals potentially useful links between land use type and biodiversity. As shown in this and other studies in tropical forests, elements of vegetation structure can be used as a primary indicator of site productivity potential and biodiversity, and they can be significantly enhanced by the addition of readily observable plant functional types and key plant species. A best-bet option for managers of forested and agroforested lands is to maintain a mosaic of land cover types with a focus on complex agroforests rather than intensive monocropping. This strategy seeks to maximize the availability of ecological niches and thus biodiversity while sustaining an adequate soil nutrient base. Not only is this likely to enhance biodiversity, but it may also serve as an added buffer to unexpected variation in environmental and socioeconomic change. Incentives for adopting best-bet alternatives will be made more attractive to all stakeholders if these outcomes can be used to demonstrate more specific links between biodiversity and profitability.

### APPENDIX

*Plant Functional Attributes and Elements Used in the Plant Functional Type Grammar*

| Attribute | Element | Description |
| --- | --- | --- |
| *Photosynthetic Envelope* | | |
| Leaf size | nr | No repeating leaf units |
| | pi | Picophyll ($<2$ mm$^2$) |
| | le | Leptophyll (2–25 mm$^2$) |
| | na | Nanophyll (25–225 mm$^2$) |
| | mi | Microphyll (225–2025 mm$^2$) |
| | no | Notophyll (2025–4500 mm$^2$) |
| | me | Mesophyll (4500–18,200 mm$^2$) |
| | pl | Platyphyll (18,200–36,400 mm$^2$) |
| | ma | Macrophyll (36,400–18 $\times$ 10$^4$ mm$^2$) |
| | mg | Megaphyll ($>18 \times 10^4$ mm$^2$) |
| Leaf inclination | ve | Vertical ($>30°$ above horizontal) |
| | la | Lateral ($\pm30°$ to horizontal) |
| | pe | Pendulous ($>30°$ below horizontal) |
| | co | Composite |

| Chlorotype | do | Dorsiventral |
| | is | Isobilateral or isocentric |
| | de | Deciduous |
| | ct | Cortic (photosynthetic stem) |
| | ac | Achlorophyllous (without chlorophyll) |
| Morphotype | ro | Rosulate or rosette |
| | so | Solid 3-dimensional |
| | su | Succulent |
| | pv | Parallel-veined |
| | fi | Filicoid (fern; Pteridophytes) |
| | ca | Carnivorous (e.g., *Nepenthes*) |

### *Supporting Vascular Structure*

| Life form | ph | Phanerotype |
| | ch | Chamaephyte |
| | hc | Hemicryptophyte |
| | cr | Cryptophyte |
| | th | Therophyte |
| | li | Liane |
| Root type | ad | Adventitious |
| | ae | Aerating (e.g., pneumatophore) |
| | ep | Epiphytic |
| | hy | Hydrophytic |
| | pa | Parasitic |

## REFERENCES

Abernethy, V.J., D.I. McCracken, A. Adam, I. Downie, G.N. Foster, R.W. Furness, et al. 1996. Functional analysis of plant–invertebrate–bird biodiversity on Scottish agricultural land. pp. 51–59. *In* I.A. Simpson and P. Dennis (eds.) The spatial dynamics of biodiversity. International Association for Landscape Ecology, Aberdeen.

Austin, M.P., and P.C. Heyligers. 1989. Vegetation survey design for conservation: Gradsect sampling of forests in north-eastern New South Wales. Biol. Conserv. 50:13–32.

Austin, M.P., and P.C. Heyligers. 1991. New approaches to vegetation survey design: Gradsect sampling. pp. 31–37. *In* C.R. Margules and M.P. Austin (eds.) Nature conservation: Cost effective survey and data analysis. CSIRO, Australia.

Bahr, L.M. 1982. Functional taxonomy: An immodest proposal. Ecol. Model. 15:211–233.

Barber, C.V., S. Afiff, and A. Purnomo. 1995. Tiger by the tail? Reorienting biodiversity conservation and development in Indonesia. World Resources Inst., Washington, DC.

Baskin, Y. 1994. Ecosystem function of biodiversity. BioScience 44:657–660.

Beehler, B.M., J.P. Angle, D. Gibbs, M. Hedemark, and D. Kuro. 2001. A field survey of resident birds of Southern New Ireland. pp. 61–66. *In* B.M. Beehler and L.E. Alonso (eds.) Southern New Ireland, Papua New Guinea; A biodiversity assessment. RAP Bull. of Biological Assessment. Conserv. Int., Washington, DC.

Belbin, L. 1992. PATN pattern analysis package: Technical reference. CSIRO Div. Wildlife and Ecology, Canberra.

Bierregaard, R.O.J., T.E. Lovejoy, V. Kapos, A.A. dos Santos, and R.W. Hutchings. 1992. The biological dynamics of tropical rain forest fragments. BioScience 42:859–866.

Bignell, D.E., E. Widodo, F.X. Susilo, and H. Suryo. 2000. Soil macrofauna: Ground-dwelling ants, termites, other macroarthropods and earthworms. pp. 91–127. *In* A.N. Gillison (coord.) Above-ground Biodiversity Assessment Working Group summary report 1996–99. Impact of different land uses on biodiversity. Alternatives to Slash and Burn Project. ICRAF, Nairobi.

Box, E.O. 1981. Macroclimate and plant forms: An introduction to predictive modelling. Junk, The Hague.

Brooker, M.G., and C.R. Margules. 1996. The relative conservation value of remnant patches of native vegetation in the wheatbelt of Western Australia: I. Plant diversity. Pac. Conserv. Biol. 2:268–278.

Collins, S.L., and T.L. Benning. 1996. Spatial and temporal patterns in functional diversity. pp. 253–280. *In* K.J. Gaston (ed.) Biodiversity: A biology of numbers and difference. Blackwell Science, Oxford.

Condit, R. 1995. Research in large, long-term tropical forest plots. Trends Ecol. Evol. 10:18–22.

Cousins, S.H. 1991. Species diversity measurement: Choosing the right index. Trends Ecol. Evol. 6:190–192.

Cowling, R.M., K.J. Esler, G.F. Midgley, and M.A. Honig. 1994a. Plant functional diversity, species diversity and climate in arid and semi-arid southern Africa. J. Arid Environ. 27:141–158.

Cowling, R.M., P.J. Mustart, H. Laurie, and M.B. Richards. 1994b. Species diversity: Functional diversity and functional redundancy in fynbos communities. Suid-Afrikaanse Tydskrif vir Wetenskap 90:333–337.

Cramer, W. 1997. Using plant functional types in a global vegetation model. pp. 271–288. *In* T.M. Smith, H.H. Shugart, and F.I. Woodward (eds.) Plant functional types: Their relevance to ecosystem properties and global change. Cambridge Univ. Press, Cambridge.

Cramer, W., H.H. Shugart, I.R. Noble, F.I. Woodward, H. Bugmann, A. Bondeau, et al. 1999. Ecosystem composition and structure. pp. 190–228. *In* B.H. Walker, W.L. Steffen, J. Canadell, and J.S.I. Ingram (eds.) The terrestrial biosphere and global change. Int. Geosphere–Biosphere Programme Book Ser. no. 4. Cambridge Univ. Press, Cambridge.

Cranston, P., and T. Hillman. 1992. Rapid assessment of biodiversity using "biological diversity technicians." Aust. Biol. 5:144–154.

Dallmeier, F. 1992. Long-term monitoring of biological diversity in tropical forest areas: Methods for establishment and inventory of permanent plots. MAB Digest 11. UNESCO, Paris.

Diaz, S. 1998. The effects of global change on functional group diversity. pp. 18. *In* E. Huber-Sannwald and V. Wolters (eds.) Effects of global change on biodiversity and ecological complexity. GTCE Int. Office, Canberra, Australia.

Faith, D. 1995. Phylogenetic pattern and the quantification of organismal biodiversity. pp. 45–58. *In* D.L. Hawksworth (ed.) Biodiversity measurement and estimation. Chapman & Hall in association with the Royal Society, London.

FAO (Food and Agriculture Organization). 2002. Designing a biometric inventory for NWFPs in non-wood forest products 13. Resource assessment of non-wood forest products. Available at http://www.fao.org/DOCREP/004/Y1457E/Y1457e10.htm (verified 7 Dec. 2003).

Forman, R.T.T., and M. Godron. 1986. Landscape ecology. Wiley, New York.

Franklin, J.R. 1993. Preserving biodiversity: Species, ecosystems, or landscapes? Ecol. Appl. 3:202–205.

Gillison, A.N. 1981. Towards a functional vegetation classification. pp. 30–41. *In* A.N. Gillison and D.J. Anderson (eds.) Vegetation classification in Australia. CSIRO and Australian Natl. Univ. Press, Canberra.

Gillison, A.N. 1988. A plant functional proforma for dynamic vegetation studies and natural resource surveys. Tech. Mem. 88/3. CSIRO Div. Water Resources, Canberra.

Gillison, A.N. (coord.). 2000a. Above-ground biodiversity assessment working group summary report 1996–98. Impact of different land uses on biodiversity and social indicators. Alternatives to Slash and Burn Project, ICRAF, Nairobi.

Gillison, A.N. 2000b. Rapid vegetation survey. pp. 25–38. *In* A.N. Gillison (coord.) Above-ground biodiversity assessment working group summary report 1996–99. Impact of different land uses on biodiversity and social indicators. Alternatives to Slash and Burn Project, ICRAF, Nairobi.

Gillison, A.N. 2000c. Summary and overview. pp. 19–24. *In* A.N. Gillison (coord.) Above-ground biodiversity assessment working group summary report 1996–99. Impact of different land uses on biodiversity and social indicators. Alternatives to Slash and Burn Project, ICRAF, Nairobi.

Gillison, A.N. 2001. A field manual for rapid vegetation classification and survey for general purposes (including instructions for the use of a rapid survey proforma and VegClass computer software). CIFOR, Bogor, Indonesia. (CD-ROM and hard copy.)

Gillison, A. 2002. A generic, computer-assisted method for rapid vegetation classification and survey: Tropical and temperate case studies. Conserv. Ecol. 6:3. Available at http://www.consecol.org/vol6/iss2/art3 (verified 7 Dec. 2003).

Gillison, A.N., and K.R.W. Brewer. 1985. The use of gradient directed transects or gradsects in natural resource surveys. J. Environ. Manage. 20:103–127.

Gillison, A.N., and G. Carpenter. 1997. A plant functional attribute set and grammar for dynamic vegetation description and analysis. Functional Ecol. 11:775–783.

Gillison, A.N., G. Carpenter, and M.R. Thomas. 1999. Plant functional diversity and complexity: Two new complementary measures of species diversity. Unpublished data.

Gillison, A.N., and N. Liswanti. 1999. Biodiversity and productivity assessment for sustainable agroforest ecosystems. Mae Chaem, Northern Thailand: Preliminary report. Part D. *In* A.N. Gillison (coord.) Above-Ground Biodiversity Assessment Working Group summary report 1996–99. Impact on biodiversity of different land uses. Alternatives to Slash and Burn Project, ICRAF, Nairobi.

Gillison, A.N., N. Liswanti, and I. Arief-Rachman. 1996. Rapid ecological assessment, Kerinci Seblat National Park Buffer Zone, Central Sumatra: Report for plant ecology. CIFOR Working Paper No. 14, Bogor, Indonesia.

Gitay, H., and I.R. Noble. 1997. What are functional groups and how should we seek them? pp. 3–19. *In* T.M. Smith, H.H. Shugart, and F.I. Woodward (eds.) Plant functional types: Their relevance to ecosystem properties and global change. Cambridge Univ. Press, Cambridge.

Government of Indonesia: State Ministry of Environment. 1993. Indonesian national strategy on the management of biological diversity. Gov. of Indonesia, Jakarta.

Green, M.J.B., and E.R.N. Gunarwadena. 1993. Conservation evaluation of some natural forest in Sri Lanka. UNDP, FAO, and IUCN unpublished report.

Grime, P.J. 1979. Plant strategies and vegetation processes. Wiley, Chichester, UK.

Hairiah, K., and M. van Noordwijk. 2000. Soil properties and carbon stocks. pp. 143–154. *In* A.N. Gillison (coord.) An intensive biodiversity baseline study in Jambi province, Central Sumatra, Indonesia. Above-ground Biodiversity Assessment Working Group summary report 1996–99. Impact of different land uses on biodiversity. Alternatives to Slash and Burn Project, ICRAF, Nairobi.

He, F., P. Legendre, and C. Bellehumeur. 1994. Diversity pattern and spatial scale: A study of a tropical rain forest of Malaysia. Environ. Ecol. Stat. 1:265–286.

Hector, A., B. Schmid, and C. Beierkuhnlein. 1999. Plant diversity and productivity experiments in European grasslands. Science (Washington, DC) 286:1123–1127.

Heywood, V.H., and I. Baste. 1995. Introduction. *In* V. Heywood (ed.) and R.T. Watson (chair) Global biodiversity assessment. United Nations Environ. Programme, Kenya; Cambridge Univ. Press, Cambridge.

Howard, P., T. Davenport, and M. Baltzer (eds.). 1996. Rwenzori Mountains National Park, Biodiversity Report. Rep. No. 2. Republic of Uganda Forest Dep., Kampala.

Howard, P., T. Davenport, and F. Kigeny. 1997. Planning conservation areas in Uganda's natural forests. Oryx 31:253–262.

Huston, M.A. 1994. Biological diversity: The coexistence of species in changing landscapes. Cambridge Univ. Press, Cambridge.

Huston, M.A., L.W. Aarssen, M.P. Austin, B.S. Cade, J.D. Fridley, E. Garnier, et al. 2000. No consistent effect of biodiversity on productivity. Science (Washington, DC) 289:1255a. (Includes reply by Hector et al.)

Jepson, P., and Djarwadi. 2000. Birds. pp. 41–53. *In* A.N. Gillison (coord.) Above-ground Biodiversity Assessment Working Group summary report 1996–99. Impact of different land uses on biodiversity and social indicators. Alternatives to Slash and Burn Project, ICRAF, Nairobi.

Jones, D.T., F.-X. Susilo, D.E. Bignell, H. Suryo, A.N. Gillison, and P.E. Eggleton. 2002. Termite assemblage collapse along a land-use intensification gradient in lowland central Sumatra, Indonesia. J. Appl. Ecol. 40:380–391.

Keel, S., A.H. Gentry, and L. Spinzi. 1992. Using vegetation analysis to facilitate the selection of conservation sites in Eastern Paraguay. Conserv. Biol. 7:66–75.

Koptsik, G.N., S.V. Koptsik, and S.Y. Livantsova. 2001. Assessment of soil quality for biodiversity conservation in boreal forest ecosystems. pp. 627–634. *In* D.E. Stott, R.H. Mohtar, and G.C. Steinhardt (eds.) Sustaining the global farm. Purdue Univ. and USDA-ARS National Soil Erosion Res. Lab., Purdue Univ., West Lafayette, IN.

Larcher, W. 1975. Physiological plant ecology. Springer-Verlag, Berlin.

Lawton, J.H., D.E. Bignell, B. Bolton, G.F. Bloemers, P. Eggleton, P.M. Hammond, et al. 1998. Biodiversity inventories, indicator taxa and effects of habitat modification in tropical forest. Nature (London) 391:72–76.

Loreau, M., S. Naeem, P. Inchausti, J. Bengtsson, J.P. Grime, A. Hector, et al. 2001. Biodiversity and ecosystem functioning: Current knowledge and future challenges. Science (Washington, DC) 294:804–808.

Magurran, A.E. 1988. Ecological diversity and its measurement. Croom Helm, London.

Majer, J.D., and G. Beeston. 1996. The biodiversity integrity index: An illustration using ants in Western Australia. Conserv. Biol. 10:64–73.

Margules, C.R., and K.J. Gaston. 1994. Biodiversity and agriculture. Science (Washington, DC) 265:457.

Margules, C.R., and Y. Haila. 1996. Survey research in conservation biology. Ecography 19:323–331.

Margules, C.R., and R.L. Pressey. 2000. Systematic conservation planning. Nature (London) 405:243–253.

Martinez, N.D. 1996. Defining and measuring functional aspects of biodiversity. pp. 114–148. *In* K.J. Gaston (ed.) Biodiversity: A biology of numbers and difference. Blackwell Science, Oxford.

Miller, K., M.H. Allegretti, N. Johnson, and B. Jonsson. 1995. Measures for conservation of biodiversity and sustainable use of its components. pp. 915–1061. *In* V. Heywood (ed.) and R.T. Watson (chair) Global biodiversity assessment. United Nations Environ. Programme, Kenya; Cambridge Univ. Press, Cambridge.

Miller, K.R., and S. Lanou. 1995. National biodiversity planning: Guidelines from early experience worldwide. World Resources Inst., Washington, DC.

Mooney, H.A. 1997. Ecosystem function of biodiversity. pp. 341–354. *In* T.M. Smith (ed.) Plant functional types: Their relevance to ecosystem properties and global change. Cambridge Univ. Press, Cambridge.

Nix, H., and A.N. Gillison. 1985. Towards an operational framework for habitat and wildlife management. pp. 39–45. *In* J. Kikkawa (ed.) Wildlife management in the forests and forestry-controlled lands in the tropics and the southern hemisphere. IUFRO SI 08. Wildlife and Its Habitats. Int. Union of For. Res. Organizations, Austria and the Univ. of Queensland, St. Lucia.

Parker, T.A. III, and B. Bailey (eds.). 1991. A biological assessment of the Alto Madidi region and adjacent areas of northwest Bolivia. RAP Working Paper. no. 1. Conserv. Int., Washington, DC.

Parker, T.A. III, and J.L. Carr. 1992. Status of forest remnants in the Cordillera de la Costa and adjacent areas of southwestern Ecuador. Conserv. Int., Rapid Assessment Program. RAP Working Paper No. 2. Conserv. Int., Washington, DC.

Parker, T.A., A.H. Gentry, R.B. Foster, L.H. Emmons, and J.V. Remsen Jr. 1993. The lowland dry forests of Santa Cruz, Bolivia: A global conservation priority. Rapid Assessment Program, Conserv. Int. and Fundacion Amigos de la Naturaleza. RAP Working Paper No. 4. Conserv. Int., Washington, DC.

Pearson, D.L. 1995. Selecting indicator taxa for the quantitative assessment of biodiversity. pp. 75–79. *In* D.L. Hawksworth (ed.) Biodiversity measurement and estimation. Chapman & Hall in association with the Royal Soc., London.

Petraitis, P.S., R.E. Latham, and R.A. Niesenbaum. 1989. The maintenance of species diversity by disturbance. Quart. Rev. Biol. 64:393–418.

Phillips, O.L., P. Hall, A.H. Gentry, S.A. Sawyer, and R. Vásquez. 1994. Dynamics and species richness of tropical rain forests. Proc. Natl. Acad. Sci. USA 91:2805–2809.

Prance, G. 1995. A comparison of the efficacy of higher taxa and species numbers in the assessment of the biodiversity in the neotropics. pp. 89–99. *In* D.L. Hawksworth (ed.) Biodiversity measurement and estimation. Chapman & Hall in association with the Royal Soc., London.

Reid, W.V., J.A. McNeely, D.B. Tunstall, D.A. Bryant, and M. Winograd. 1993. Biodiversity indicators for policy makers. World Resources Inst., Washington, DC.

Sayer, J.A., and P. Wegge. 1992. Biological conservation issues in forest management. pp. 1–4. *In* J.M. Blockhus, M. Dillenbeck, J.A. Sayer, and P. Wegge (eds.) Conserving biological diversity in managed forests. The IUCN Forest Conservation Programme, IUCN/ITTO, Gland, Switzerland.

Shugart, H.H. 1997. Plant and ecosystem functional types. pp. 20–43. *In* T.M. Smith, H.H. Shugart, and F.I. Woodward (eds.) Plant functional types: Their relevance to ecosystem properties and global change. Cambridge Univ. Press, Cambridge.

Smith, T.M. 1997. Examining the consequences of classifying species into functional types: A simulation model analysis. pp. 319–340. *In* T.M. Smith, H.H. Shugart, and F.I. Woodward (eds.) Plant functional types: Their relevance to ecosystem properties and global change. Cambridge Univ. Press, Cambridge.

Smith, T.M., H.H. Shugart, and F.I. Woodward. 1997. Preface. *In* T.M. Smith, H.H. Shugart, and F.I. Woodward (eds.) Plant functional types: Their relevance to ecosystem properties and global change. Cambridge Univ. Press, Cambridge.

Sorrells, L., and S. Glenn. 1991. Review of sampling techniques used in studies of grassland plant communities. Proc. Oklahoma Acad. Sci. 71:43–45.

Tanner, J.E., T.P. Hughes, and J.H. Connell. 1994. Species coexistence, keystone species, and succession: A sensitivity analysis. Ecology 75:2204–2219.

Tilman, D., and J.A. Downing. 1994. Biodiversity and stability in grasslands. Nature (London) 367:363–366.

USGS (United States Geological Survey). 2001. National Parks Service Vegetation Mapping Program, 2001. Available at http://www.biology.usgs.gov/npsveg/badl/sect3.html.

UNEP/CBD (United Nations Environment Programme/Convention on Biological Diversity). 2002. Report of the Seventh Meeting of the Subsidiary Body on Scientific Technical and Technological Advice. UNEP/CBD/COP/6/4, 7 Dec. 2001.

Vanclay, J.K., A.N. Gillison, and R.J. Keenan. 1996. Using plant functional attributes to quantify site productivity and growth patterns in mixed forests. For. Ecol. Manage. 94:149–163.

van der Maarel, E. 1993. Some remarks on disturbance and its relations to diversity and stability. J. Vegetation Sci. 4:733–736.

Vane-Wright, R.I., C.J. Humphries, and P.H. Williams. 1991. What to protect? Systematics and the agony of choice. Biol. Conserv. 55:235–254.

Weitzman, M.L. 1995. Diversity functions. pp. 21–43. *In* C. Perrings (ed.) Biodiversity loss. Cambridge Univ. Press, Cambridge.

Wessels, K.J., A.S. Van Jaarsveld, J.D. Grimbeek, and M.J. Van der Linde. 1998. An evaluation of the gradsect biological survey method. Biol. Conserv. 7:1093–1121.

Williams, P. 2002. Measuring biodiversity: Complex problems and a simple solution. The Natural History Museum. Available at http://www.nhm.ac.uk/science/projects/world-map/index.html.

Williams, P.H., C.J. Humphries, and R.I. Vane-Wright. 1992. Measuring biodiversity: Taxonomic relatedness for conservation priorities. Aust. Syst. Bot. 4:665–680.

Woodward, F.I., T.M. Smith, and H.H. Shugart. 1996. Defining plant functional types: The end view. pp. 355–359. *In* T.M. Smith, H.H. Shugart, and F.I. Woodward (eds.) Plant functional types: Their relevance to ecosystem properties and global change. Cambridge Univ. Press, Cambridge.

World Bank. 1995. Mainstreaming biodiversity in development: A World Bank assistance strategy for implementing the convention on biological diversity. p. 29 (Annexes I–IV). Environ. Dep. Paper no. 29. Biodiversity Ser. World Bank, Washington, DC.

Wulff, E.V. 1943. An introduction to historical plant geography. A new series of plant science books, vol. X. Chronica Botanica, Waltham, MA.

# 5 Below-Ground Biodiversity Assessment

DEVELOPING A KEY FUNCTIONAL GROUP
APPROACH IN BEST-BET ALTERNATIVES
TO SLASH AND BURN

David E. Bignell
> *Queen Mary, University of London  London, England*

Jerome Tondoh
> *Université d'Abobo-Adjame  Abidjan, Côte d'Ivoire*

Luc Dibog
> *Institut de Recherche Agricole pour le Développement  Yaoundé, Cameroon*

Shiou Pin Huang
> *Universidade de Brasília  Brasília, DF, Brazil*

Fátima Moreira
> *Universidade Federal de Lavras  Lavras Minas Gerais, Brazil*

Dieudonné Nwaga
> *Université de Yaoundé  Yaoundé, Cameroon*

Beto Pashanasi
> *Universidad Nacional de la Amazonia Peruana  Yurimaguas, Peru*

Eliane Guimarães Pereira
> *Universidade Federal de Itajubá  Itajubá, Minas Gerais, Brazil*

Francis-Xavier Susilo
> *University of Lampung  Sumatra, Indonesia*

Michael J. Swift
> *Tropical Soil Biology and Fertility Institute of CIAT  Nairobi, Kenya*

## THE IMPORTANCE OF BELOW-GROUND BIODIVERSITY

Plants make up most of the living biomass in terrestrial systems, are the basis of food webs, and are thus the primary determinants of ecosystem structure and function. As members of the below-ground biotic community, plants share the soil environment with a suite of other organisms ranging from large animals to bacteria. The latter community also helps to shape the ecosystem because soil biological processes play a vital role in maintaining ecosystem functions (Hole 1981; Lavelle 1996; Brussaard et al. 1997; Lavelle et al. 1997;

van Breemen and Finzi 1998). The most important of these functions are thought to be as follows:

- *Decomposition of organic matter.* This is carried out largely by bacteria and fungi but greatly facilitated by soil animals such as mites, millipedes, earthworms, and termites, which shred residues and disperse microbial propagules. Collectively, such animals are known as litter transformers. The organic carbon released can be mineralized as $CO_2$ or $CH_4$ or incorporated into various kinds of soil organic matter, which vary in their stability and longevity but are generally in equilibrium with the inflows and outflows of carbon from the system.

- *Nutrient cycling.* This is closely associated with organic decomposition and includes transformations of nitrogen, phosphorus, sulfur, and other essential elements as well as carbon. Although microorganisms mediate most of these transformations, grazing by micropredators (protozoa and nematodes) can be rate-limiting. Larger animals may enhance some transformations by providing niches for microbial growth within their guts, excrements, or nests. Specific fungi (mycorrhiza) and root-nodulating bacteria may form mutualistic associations with plant roots, which improve nutrient acquisition. Some soil bacteria are chemolithotrophic, that is, involved in elemental transformations without direct dependence on organic matter as a food source, but may nonetheless be affected indirectly by such factors as water content, soil stability, porosity, and carbon content, which the other biota control.

- *Bioturbation.* Plant roots, earthworms, termites, ants, and some other soil macrofauna are physically active in the soil, forming channels, pores, aggregates, and mounds or moving particles from one horizon to another, in ways that affect and determine physical structure and the distribution of organic materials. Such soil ecosystem engineers (*sensu* Stork and Eggleton 1992; Jones et al. 1994) thereby create and modify microhabitats for other smaller organisms and determine soil properties such as aeration, drainage, aggregate stability, and water-holding capacity. In addition, the macrofauna produce feces, which are organomineral complexes, stable over periods of months or more (Lavelle et al. 1997).

- *Suppression of soilborne diseases and pests.* It is widely assumed that reduced species diversity renders agroecosystems vulnerable to harmful soil organisms by reducing overall antagonisms. Critical interactions influencing population stabilities may be those between micropredators and the bacteria and fungi on which they feed.

- *Environmental service functions.* Examples are biodiversity conservation (allowing the replacement of functionally important species that are temporarily lost), watershed protection from the preservation of soil structure (especially constancy of stream flow and water quality), mitigation of greenhouse gas emissions (carbon sequestration into long-term pools of complex organic matter by fungi and eubacteria, and methane oxidation by archaea), and bioremediation after specific pollution events (metabolism of pesticides by eubacteria and sequestration of heavy metals by a variety of organisms).

In this chapter, we define *functional group* as an assemblage of species, of any taxonomic affiliation and living at whatever spatial scale, whose collective impact in a soil ecosystem is one of the aforementioned generic ecosystem functions, with the assumption that all five functions must be manifested in any soil that has sustainable fertility and structural stability. There is limited knowledge of the extent to which the biota below ground and the functions its species perform depend on the biota above ground, and vice versa. This limits predictions of the effects of land use change on ecosystem processes and the evaluation of specific scenarios such as climate change, agricultural intensification, and pollution. Furthermore, the question remains as to what relationship exists between species diversity, functional diversity (the number of functional groups), functional composition (the nature of functional groups), and the occurrence and intensity of ecological processes. The question of possible links between species diversity and ecosystem stability is topical in ecology (Naeem et al. 1994; Tilman and Downing 1994; Gaston 1996; Lawton 1996; Lawton et al. 1996, 1998). However, in soil systems the poor state of taxonomy and the lack of agreed or adequate methods for extracting and enumerating many groups have driven both theoretical treatments and practical fieldwork to the use of the functional group concept as an indispensable aid to assessing the role of the biota in maintaining ecosystem processes.

The minimum number of functional groups, and species within functional groups, to ensure soil resilience against natural and anthropogenic stresses is not precisely known. Circumstantial evidence and intuition suggest that stress and disturbance (defined as the removal or disruption by humans of functionally significant components of the natural forest ecosystem) affecting functional groups that are composed of few species are the most likely to cause loss or reduction of ecosystem services. To the best of our knowledge this holds for shredders of organic matter, nitrifying and denitrifying bacteria, bacteria involved with single–carbon atom compound and hydrogen transformations, iron and sulfur chemolithotrophs, mycorrhizal fungi, and bioturbators.

Ecological impacts by plants that affect soil include vegetation cover determining soil climate, root penetration and water extraction affecting soil structure, and nutrient supply to soil organisms, which is derived from a variety of litters and plant exudates, including photosynthate transferred directly to microsymbionts (Swift and Anderson 1993; Angers and Caron 1998). The reverse relationship, that is, the impacts of soil organisms on plants, includes formation and stabilization of soil structure, texturing, and horizonation (Wilson and Agnew 1992; Lavelle et al. 1997; Angers and Caron 1998); nutritional provision (Douglas 1995); and modifications of microbial growth conditions (Visser 1985). To these extents, above-ground diversity and below-ground diversity are linked and mutually dependent, but whereas above-ground changes are visible and documented, changes in soil communities are commonly overlooked, not only because they may be invisible but also because there is no common standard for survey and assessment (Wolters et al. 2000).

Intensification of agriculture, defined here as a reduction in the period in fallow to period in crop ratio, can lead to fundamental transformation of vegetation cover or to gradual alterations of existing land use without obvious botanical change (Scholes and van Breemen 1997). The goal of maximizing crop yield rapidly overrides all other factors controlling plant community structure, so the morphological impacts of plants on the soil community (i.e., microclimate) are immediately altered, with subsequent changes in resource provision to soil biota as litter and exudates. There is therefore ample justification for studying below-ground biodiversity in the context of any program addressing the sustained improvement of agricultural productivity (Swift and Anderson 1993).

Alternatives to Slash and Burn (ASB) is a global program designed to identify optimal schemes for tropical forest-based subsistence agriculture that are consistent with alleviating poverty, providing increased food security, enhancing environmental resilience, and conserving biodiversity (Kenyatta 1997). A part of the program specifically addresses biodiversity issues, both above and below ground, with four main activities:

- Improving rapid assessment tools for biodiversity
- Developing a biodiversity assessment database and models
- Devising techniques for restoring or conserving native biodiversity
- Building capacity of biodiversity assessment expertise

The ASB aims to answer the question, What is the effect of land use change on biodiversity, and what are the implications for ecosystem services and resilience and for agricultural productivity? Here we report on what has been achieved with below-ground biodiversity, concentrating on the development of a rapid assessment method, the organization of results into a biodiversity assessment database, and the establishment of basic trends that may implicate soil biota in the maintenance of good soil function. Our work mainly encompasses development of rapid assessment tools for biodiversity and a biodiversity assessment database and models.

## ASB WORKING HYPOTHESES

The ASB Soil Biodiversity Network operates under the following series of linked hypotheses, which our field sampling was designed to test:

a. Agricultural intensification (as we define it) results in a reduction of soil biodiversity.
b. Reduction in soil biodiversity leads to a loss of ecosystem function detrimental to sustained productivity.
c. Above-ground and below-ground biodiversity are interdependent across scales of resolution from individual plant communities to the landscape.
d. Agricultural diversification promotes soil biodiversity and enhances sustained productivity.
e. Sustainable agricultural production in tropical forest margins is significantly improved by enhancement of soil biodiversity.

Hypotheses (a), (c), and (d) can be answered from the data generated by below-ground biodiversity sampling discussed in this chapter. Hypothesis (b) is best considered in the context of all ASB data (i.e., the global synthesis), whereas hypothesis (e) is to be addressed in later work programs within and following ASB.

## APPROACH AND METHODS

### LAND USE SYSTEMS SAMPLED

A list of land uses sampled for below-ground biodiversity is given in table 5.1. In most cases, the same sites were also sampled for above-ground biodiversity and emissions of greenhouse gases (see chapters 2–4, this volume). Because of inevitable differences in crop types, traditional practices, biogeography, socioeconomic development, and national science capacities, equal sampling regimes could not be imposed in all four countries. Nevertheless, it was possible to group the seventy-six sites investigated into nine primary land uses along an intensification gradient, which forms the basic level of analysis reported here. Where appropriate to assist clarity, we have consolidated land uses into four generic categories: forest, agroforest, fallow vegetation, and crops. Differences within land uses and land covers, such as age of fallow, type of agroforest, and the mixture of food crops, were deliberately included to embrace the full spectrum of practices typical of particular regions and remain an implicit part of the database, but they will be examined elsewhere.

### TARGET ORGANISMS AND FUNCTIONAL GROUPS

Because the taxonomic diversity of soil biota is very high and many species are undescribed (Eggleton et al. 1996; Lavelle et al. 1997; Lawton et al. 1998; Hooper et al.

*Table 5.1* Land-Use Systems Sampled for Below-Ground Biodiversity by ASB, Showing Number of Sites for Each Country

| Land Use System | Brazil | Cameroon | Indonesia | Peru | Total |
|---|---|---|---|---|---|
| Primary forest | — | 1 | 2 | 2 | 5 |
| Logged-over forest | 3 | — | 5 | 1 | 9 |
| Secondary forest | — | 2 | 1 | 3 | 6 |
| Fallows (by age) | 3 | 2 | — | 4 | 9 |
| Tree plantation (by type) | — | — | 2 | 2 | 4 |
| Pasture | 3 | — | — | 3 | 6 |
| Agroforestry (by type) | 3 | 1 | 10 | 2 | 16 |
| Crop field (by type) | 3 | 2 | 5 | 5 | 15 |
| *Imperata* grassland | — | — | 6 | — | 6 |
| Total | 15 | 8 | 31 | 22 | 76 |

2000), selection of representative organisms to sample is essential before fieldwork can be attempted. In addition, there is no single method available for addressing soil biodiversity, so it is necessary to adopt a subset of protocols that can be accommodated in a single field campaign, within the resources available. We selected seven target taxa (table 5.2) on the basis of their diverse functional significance to soil fertility and overall ease of sampling simultaneously, across a range of land use types. These groups and some of their important functional group affiliations are described here:

- Earthworms, which influence both soil porosity and nutrient relations through channeling and ingestion of mineral and organic matter. Earthworms can be divided into further functional categories: epigeic (living and feeding on the surface), anecic (living below ground but feeding on the surface), and endogeic (living and feeding below ground).
- Termites and ants, which influence soil porosity and texture through tunneling, soil ingestion and transport, and gallery construction and nutrient cycles through transport, shredding, and digestion of organic matter. Ants can be further classified by feeding habits: carnivores, generalists, seed collectors, and honeydew feeders. Termites are heuristically divided into grass-feeders, wood-feeders, wood- and soil-feeders, and soil-feeders (Bignell and Eggleton 2000), but other trophic functional classifications are possible, based on gut content analysis (Donovan et al. 2001)
- Other macrofauna, which for our purposes includes woodlice, millipedes, and some types of insect larvae that act as litter transformers, with an important shredding action on dead plant tissue. Their predators (centipedes, larger arachnids, some other types of insect) usually are sampled at the same time when pitfall traps are used and can be included in enumerations. These other macrofauna may be considered together with termites and ants (sampled separately), as "all macroarthropods." *All macrofauna* means all macroarthropods, together with earthworms.
- Nematodes, which influence turnover of carbon and nutrients in their roles as root grazers, fungivores, bacterivores, omnivores, and predators; occupy existing small pore spaces, in which they depend on water films; and usually have very high generic and species richness. Nematodes can be given a functional classification as bacterivores, fungivores, plant parasites, omnivores, and predators (Yeates et al. 1993).
- Mycorrhizae, which associate with plant roots, improve nutrient and water use, and reduce attacks by plant pathogens.
- Root-nodulating bacteria, which transform $N_2$ into forms available for plant growth.
- Overall microbial biomass, which is an indirect measure of the total decomposition and nutrient recycling community of a soil. It is contributed by fungi, protists, and bacteria (including archaea and actinomycetes).

Functional distinctions are essentially idiosyncratic for any given taxon but helpful in data analysis. Two obvious exclusions from the taxa investigated are mesofauna (principally mites, other small arachnids, and collembolans) and protists. The exclu-

*Table 5.2* Biotic Groups Addressed by Below-Ground Sampling During A S B Campaigns in Four Countries

| Biotic Group | Datasets Obtained, by Country | | | |
| --- | --- | --- | --- | --- |
| | Brazil | Cameroon | Indonesia | Peru |
| All macrofauna | Abundance, biomass | Abundance, biomass | Abundance, biomass, functional group diversity[a] | Abundance, biomass |
| Termites | Abundance, biomass | Abundance, biomass, α-diversity | Abundance, biomass, α-diversity[a] | Abundance, biomass |
| Ants | Abundance, biomass | Abundance, biomass | Abundance, biomass, α-diversity[a] | Abundance, biomass |
| Earthworms | Abundance, biomass | Abundance, biomass | Abundance, biomass, trophic group diversity[a] | Abundance, biomass, α-diversity |
| **Nematodes** | | | | |
| Generic | Abundance, diversity indices | — | Abundance | — |
| Trophic group | Abundance, trophic dominance | — | Abundance | — |
| **Mycorrhizae (arbuscular mycorrhizal fungi)[b]** | | | | |
| Generic | — | Diversity after trapping | Percentage in sample | Percentage in sample |
| Spore counts | Quantitative | Quantitative, morphotype diversity | Quantitative | Quantitative |
| Root infection | — | Percentage examined | — | Percentage examined |
| **Root-Nodulating Bacteria** | | | | |
| Generic | Diversity from explant | Diversity from capture | Diversity from capture | — |
| Strain | Limited diversity data | — | — | — |
| Symbiotic efficiency | Quantitative[c] | Quantitative[c] | — | — |
| MPN | Quantitative | Quantitative | Quantitative | — |
| Microbial biomass (as carbon) | Quantitative[d] | Quantitative[d] | Quantitative[d] | — |

α-diversity, species richness; MPN, most probable number per unit of soil volume.
[a]Not all sites.
[b]Unless otherwise specified, *quantitative* indicates number per unit of soil volume.
[c]Either shoot dry weight or nodule dry weight after capture.
[d]Weight per gram of dry soil.

sion arises from the lack of adequate taxonomic expertise and, in the case of protists, a real lack of practical sampling methods rather than ignorance of their important role in soil systems.

Table 5.2 shows the types of data obtained for these seven broad taxonomic groups in four countries. Although the ASB campaign addresses biodiversity, resolution at the species or strain level ($\alpha$-diversity) was not achieved in every case. In diverse groups, such as, Brazilian nematodes, which were distributed in 159 genera (S. Huang, pers. comm. 1999), and termites, where morphospecies are commonly used (Dibog 1998; Eggleton et al. 1999), generic diversity and morphospecies diversity are assumed to be adequate surrogates.

Additionally, it is usually possible to add to basic data on abundance and biomass by allocating specimens or whole taxonomic units to broad functional groups. This is illustrated by the three groups of earthworms described earlier, a classification that can also be applied to the "all macrofauna" category. For microsymbionts, raw data on propagule abundance or inoculum potential in soil samples are less meaningful without some measure of efficiency or suitability for mutualism. In best practice, therefore, microsymbiont diversity should be assessed after capture or trapping by candidate host plants, although some information and taxonomic allocation can be made from spore morphotypes.

To an extent, the biology of particular groups dictates the nature of the diversity measurement; for example, abundance is not the same concept for macrofauna and root-nodulating bacteria because the former are enumerated as living individuals of whatever condition and the latter are numbered as nodule-forming units (i.e., on the basis of viability as a symbiont). However, sampling methods also impose their own constraints, particularly within the ASB remit of applying rapid assessment techniques simultaneously across the entire taxonomic spectrum of soil biota. Lawton et al. (1998) make the point that sampling effort and taxonomic difficulty in biodiversity measurement both increase with decreasing size of the organisms concerned. The concept is neatly illustrated by the present study: Whereas macrofauna are sampled by simple capture, nematodes first must be extracted and microsymbionts must be either extracted and then multiplied or isolate, captured, and cultured. Available time and resources therefore limit diversity data much more at the lower end of the size scale. With bacteria, the task of determining diversity is daunting: Torsvik et al. (1996) estimate that 1 g of soil could contain $10^8$ to $10^{10}$ different strains. We argue that it is therefore acceptable to add crude surrogates, such as percentage root infection and total microbial carbon. In the absence of taxonomic expertise and resources, abundance and biomass data at the site level, without specific diversity indexes, are also useful in addressing ASB objectives.

A full dataset to meet all ASB objectives for characterizing below-ground biodiversity would comprise the following:

- *Diversity* (or taxonomic richness) at the strain, species, genus, and higher taxonomic level for target taxa

- *Abundance* in mean individuals or colony-forming units per square meter (transformation as $[\log_{10} x + 1]$ with 95 percent confidence interval is helpful; see Eggleton et al. 1996)
- *Biomass* in grams per square meter (normally on a wet weight basis, with log transformation)
- *Taxonomic community composition* as a percentage per taxon (based on relative abundance and relative biomass)
- *Functional community composition* as a percentage per functional group (based on relative abundance or relative biomass) or ± basis
- *Diversity indexes* combining species richness and relative abundance (see Southwood 1978)

## The Field Transect

The methods used to sample soil biotas, the original Tropical Soil Biology and Fertility (TSBF) Programme protocols, and our current recommendations of best sampling practice are summarized in table 5.3. A full discussion of sampling is beyond the scope of this chapter (for a fuller consideration, see Swift and Bignell 2001), but our approaches should be seen as an evolution of methods from the basic field transect recommendation for macrofauna made by Anderson and Ingram (1993). The main premises are to have rapid assessment (this roughly means completing field sampling of any one site in 1 or 2 days) and to be able to address all the biotic groups targeted at the same time and in the same place. This is the rationale of the short transect, which also has the advantage of fitting into the small plots of fallow and food crops that typify tropical subsistence agriculture. In larger plots a transect can, in theory, examine whether proximity to the plot boundary (i.e., to the forest margin) influences below-ground biodiversity.

The main additions to the original TSBF protocol are an increase in the length of the transect from 25 to 40 m, increases in the number of monoliths (for macrofauna assessment) and cores taken (for nematodes and microsymbionts) within the transect, and extra sampling for termites and other macrofauna outside (but adjacent to) the transect (Jones and Eggleton 2000). The modifications are intended to increase the accuracy of biodiversity assessment by achieving resolution at both the species and the functional group level but also to mitigate the variability of data from short transects for groups with typically patchy distributions. There are two key issues: For quantitative sampling, how much replication is necessary to assess the true variance in the abundances of soil biota? For qualitative sampling, how much of a given habitat must be investigated to sample its inherent diversity adequately (this means identifying all the functional groups present)? Although it is easy to design theoretical sampling that is statistically sound, it is much more difficult to devise procedures that can be applied across diverse taxa, within strict time limits and limited budgets, and often in remote locations.

*Table 5.3* Methods Used for Below-Ground Biodiversity Sampling by A S B : Theory and Practice

| Suggested and Adopted | Sampling Plot | Macrofauna | Nematodes | Mycorrhiza | Root-Nodulating Bacteria | Microbial Biomass |
|---|---|---|---|---|---|---|
| TSBF recommendations, ca. 1993 | 25- by 4-m transect | 5–10 monoliths | 5 cores, bulked | 5 composite cores at 1-m separation | 5 composite cores at 1-m separation and nodule dissection | TSBF fumigation and extraction |
| **Brazil** | | | | | | |
| Adopted | 25- by 4-m transect | 5 monoliths | 10 composite cores (2) | 3 composite cores (6) | 20 cores, bulked | 4 composite cores (5) with fumigation and extraction |
| [Additionally] | — | — | — | — | [Nodule inspection] | — |
| **Cameroon** | | | | | | |
| Adopted | 40 by 5 m transect | 5 monoliths | — | 8 composite cores (20) | Same soil | Same soil with fumigation and extraction |
| [Additionally] | [Adjacent 100-m termite transect] | [10 pitfalls] | — | [Root inspection] | [Root inspection] | — |

| | | | | | |
|---|---|---|---|---|---|
| Indonesia Adopted | 40- by 5-m transect | 5 or 9 monoliths | — | — | 1 core in each of 3 subplots | Same soil with fumigation and extraction |
| [Additionally] | [Adjacent 100-m termite transect] | [10 pitfalls] | — | — | — | — |
| Peru Adopted | 25- by 25-m plot | 10 or 20 monoliths in 1 or 3 transects per plot | — | — | — | — |
| Best practice (per transect) | 40- by 5-m transect; 3 transects per site and 100-m termite transect | 10 monoliths of 25 by 25 by 10 cm and 10 pitfalls | 3–5 composite cores (20) at ca. 4-m intervals, using zigzag sampling pattern | 3–5 composite cores (20) at 4- or 5-m intervals | 3–5 composite cores (20) at 4- or 5-m intervals | Amato and Ladd (1988) fumigation and extraction |

Unless otherwise specified, monoliths are 25 by 25 by 30 (depth) cm and cores are 1 to 7 cm diameter to 20 cm depth. *Bulked* means all samples thoroughly mixed together. *Composite* means mixing samples from a defined portion of the transect, such as two cores from each 1-m subsection. Number of samples mixed, where specified, is given in parentheses. One transect is used per site, although this may be divided into subplots. Unless otherwise indicated, all sampling is within the transect; "[additionally]" indicates sampling added on local initiative.

TSBF, Tropical Soil Biology and Fertility Programme.

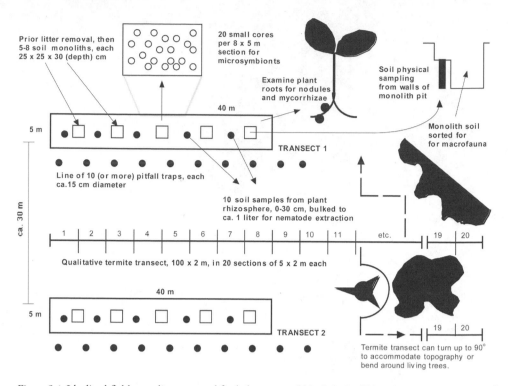

*Figure 5.1* Idealized field sampling protocol for below-ground biodiversity. Two quantitative transects of 40 by 5 m and one qualitative transect of 100 by 2 m are recommended per plot.

Figure 5.1 illustrates our concept of best sampling practice but is not intended to be prescriptive. Although we recognize that two transects should be deployed per plot, almost all the actual sampling we report has used only one. Sampling should take place under the most stable conditions available, toward the end of the rainy season and at the maximum biomass of crops (before senescence). To avoid unintended disturbance, we recommend sampling in the order pitfalls, then cores or roots, then monoliths, then termite transect. In practice, no more than twelve people can be involved without mutual interference and excessive trampling of a site.

## ILLUSTRATIVE RESULTS

### DEMONSTRATING BIODIVERSITY CHANGE IN RELATION TO LAND USE

Taxonomic groups showed significant differences in below-ground biodiversity between different land uses (table 5.4), but the trends differ between countries and between taxa. For example, overall macrofaunal diversity across seven land uses in Jambi Province, Sumatra, Indonesia, varied from more than seventy species or morphospecies per

*Table 5.4* Summary of Answers to Key ASB Questions and Comments on Functional Implications

| ASB Question | Affirmative Evidence | Qualifying Comments | Functional Implications |
|---|---|---|---|
| 1. Does LUS change affect BGBD? | Macrofauna, termites, nematodes, mycorrhizaRoot-nodulating bacteria | Not all countries or sites. | Sustainability or renewal of soil fertility may be compromised. |
| 2. Does agricultural intensification reduce BGBD or affect community composition? | Macrofauna, termites (reduction and community change); nematodes (community change); cf. mycorrhizae (increase and community change) | Not all countries or sites. Trends different within macrofauna (termites vs. earthworms) and between macrofauna and smaller biota.[a] | Management systems and site histories may be influential. |
| 3. Does agricultural diversification promote or sustain BGBD? | Macrofauna, termites | Agroforestry retains macrofaunal diversity in three countries, but trend is opposite for smaller biota. | Canopy cover promotes the large biota, but agroforestry is variable in its nature and effects. |
| 4. Is extreme disturbance highly damaging to BGBD? | Macrofauna, termites | Loss of canopy reduces some macrofauna, but others are unaffected.No consistent evidence for smaller biota. | Soil ecosystem engineers may be more vulnerable. |
| 5. Is BGBD linked to AGBD or production? | Termites | Link to woody basal areas and plant functional modi. | Termites are good indicators of niche diversity. |
|  | Root-nodulating bacteria | Link to shoot dry weight. | High soil abundance may promote plant production. |
| 6. Is BGBD influenced by proximity to forest? | Macrofauna, termites | New crop fields and small crop fields are more forest-like. Intermediate disturbance favors ants and earthworms. | Short fallow rotations are damaging to soil biotas. |
| 7. Are there effects on abundance and biomass independent of BGBD? | Macrofauna | Earthworms promoted at intermediate disturbance without great diversity. | Soil biotas are robust, except at extremes of disturbance. |
|  | Microbial biomass | Diminishes with agricultural intensification. |  |

LUS, land use system; BGBD, below-ground biodiversity; AGBD, above-ground biodiversity.

[a] *Smaller biota* means nematodes, mycorrhiza, and root-nodulating bacteria.

transect in jungle rubber, to fewer than ten in a degraded cassava (*Manihot esculenta* Crantz) garden site, with intermediate diversity in other sites including pristine forest and tree plantations (figure 5.2). In Cameroon, an average macrofaunal diversity of sixty units was associated with the *Chromolaena odorata* (L.) King & H.E. Robins fallows characteristic of low-input indigenous agriculture, compared with forty in mature forests and slightly lower levels (i.e., less than forty) in agroforest and crop fields. However, there were fewer variations across land uses in Peru (eighteen to twenty-six taxa), Brazil (ten to twelve taxa), and a site sequence in the Lampung region of Sumatra (fourteen to nineteen taxa), suggesting that land management impact on diversity in these systems is low, or perhaps that they are in a more depauperate state overall.

For Cameroon macrofauna, the expression of data as the Shannon-Weaver diversity index (which combines species richness and relative abundance) reveals a somewhat different pattern than $\alpha$-diversity alone: the highest Shannon-Weaver value $(2.69 \pm 0.43)$ was associated with agroforest, as was the highest $\alpha$-diversity, but the lowest $(1.01 \pm 0.35)$ was for primary forest, which had intermediate $\alpha$-diversity. Fallows were still high (2.40, 2.47), but two crop fields were also significantly different from

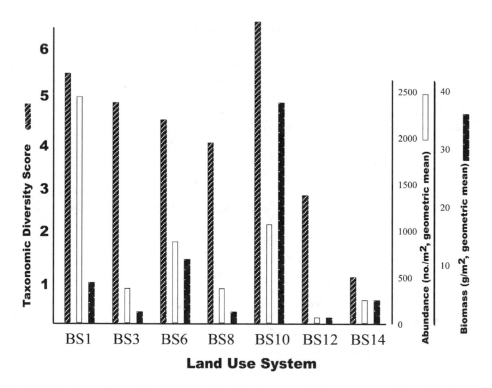

*Figure 5.2* Summary of macrofaunal biodiversity, abundance, and biomass across a forest disturbance gradient *(left to right)* in Jambi Province, Sumatra, Indonesia. Land uses are as follows: BS1, primary forest; BS3, logged-over forest; BS6, silviculture plantation; BS8, rubber plantation; BS10, jungle rubber agroforestry; BS12, alang-alang (*Imperata cylindrica* [L.] Raisch) degraded grassland; BS14, cassava garden. Taxonomic diversity score = ant species + termite species + earthworm species + other groups at ordinal level.

one another (1.59 vs. 2.81). This difference between the two assessments (species richness and diversity index) illustrates the high information content inherent in the data but also the need for multivariate analysis to achieve resolution at all spatial scales.

A different approach for looking at effects of land use can be taken by focusing on single taxa, which can be identified to species level (termites, ants, and earthworms in the present work). For example, about one-half of the macrofaunal diversity in the Jambi sequence (figure 5.2) is attributable to termites. There were thirty species in primary forest, compared with ten in rubber (*Hevea brasiliensis* [Willd. ex A. Juss.] Muell.-Arg.) plantation and twenty-one in jungle rubber (a form of agroforest). Ants have the opposite dynamic, rising from sixteen species in primary forest to twenty-four in tree plantation and peaking at thirty-three in jungle rubber. The combination of ant and termite dynamics gives a more complete picture of biodiversity changes than either taxon alone and is all the more remarkable considering that ant abundance and biomass are not significantly different across the whole gradient (see comments on abundance and biomass determinations later in this chapter). Earthworm diversity is generally low in tropical forest systems, but biomass contributions can be extremely large.

Table 5.5 summarizes the data obtained for nematodes in Brazil. The different diversity values of generic richness, Shannon's and Simpson's indexes, are consistent with each other in showing that the lowest diversities are associated with pasture and food crop fields and the highest with fallow and agroforest. Nematode abundance, on the other hand, is lowest in agroforest and food crop fields and highest in pasture. The abundance of root-nodulating bacteria is lowest in agroforest and highest in pasture (table 5.6).

Data for mycorrhizal diversity are few and are insufficient to permit statistical analysis, but in Cameroon there is some suggestion of a decline in richness from forest to other land uses. However, there is also a difference between diversity estimated from the spores in soil and that resulting from bioassay. Arbuscular mycorrhizal fungi cannot be cultured in vitro, so diversity assessment depends heavily on morphology. Counts of arbuscular mycorrhizal spores in soils in Brazil and Indonesia showed higher abundance in crop fields and grasslands than in other land uses. However, diversity data for Indonesia showed that richness varied only from twelve to fifteen species across the sites (not tabulated), so the changes with land use may not be extremely relevant. Diversity data are not yet available for rhizobia, but estimates of symbiont efficiency (the diversity of host plants nodulated, arguably a reasonable substitute) do not show distinctions between land uses.

## Demonstrating Functional Group Change in Relation to Land Use

We argued earlier that functional groups can substitute for species (or strains) in organisms whose taxonomy is difficult, but they also provide relevant additional information

*Table 5.5* Assessment of Nematode Communities in Five Land Use Systems of Amazonal Forest Margins

| Parameter | Disturbed Forest | Fallow | Agroforestry System | Pasture | Annual Crop |
|---|---|---|---|---|---|
| **Abundance** | | | | | |
| Number $\times$ $10^{-6}$/m$^3$ | 1.7145 ab[a] | 1.5966 ab | 1.2985 b | 2.4012 a | 1.2258 b |
| **Diversity** | | | | | |
| Generic richness | 7.305 ab | 8.126 a | 8.24 a | 5.819 c | 6.821 bc |
| Simpson's index | 6.6912 bc | 10.7709 a | 8.7127 ab | 5.7554 c | 6.0437 c |
| Shannon's index | 1.012 b | 1.177 a | 1.132 a | 0.9337 b | 0.9606 b |
| **Trophic Function** | | | | | |
| Trophic diversity | 2.004 d | 2.978 a | 2.847 ab | 2.171 cd | 2.559 bc |
| Trophic dominance | 0.5279 a | 0.3583 c | 0.3918 c | 0.4902 ab | 0.4182 bc |
| Plant parasites (%) | 69.65 a | 43.72 c | 53.14 b | 65.28 a | 53.72 b |
| Bacterial feeders (%) | 10.6 d | 24.22 a | 17.66 bc | 13.63 cd | 22.93 ab |
| **Decomposition Pathway** | | | | | |
| Fungivores and bacterivores | 0.9761 a | 0.2148 b | 0.7929 ab | 0.6469 ab | 0.5789 ab |
| (Fungivores + bacterivores)/ plant parasites | 0.1638 d | 0.7609 a | 0.4264 bc | 0.2256 cd | 0.5420 b |
| **Soil Disturbance Level** | | | | | |
| Maturity index[b] | 3.406 a | 3.303 ab | 3.317 ab | 3.065 bc | 2.929 c |
| Plant parasitic index | 3.178 d | 3.566 bc | 3.801 ab | 3.994 a | 3.444 cd |

[a]Different letters in horizontal level indicate difference at Tukey's test ($p < .05$).
[b]Lower values indicate more disturbed environments (Bongers 1990; Freckman and Ettema 1993).


about ecosystem function. The Brazilian nematode dataset (table 5.5) shows that the reduction in generic richness and associated diversity indexes in pasture and food crop fields, relative to forest, is not reflected to the same extent by the indexes of trophic diversity, trophic dominance, and the abundance (percentage total) of plant-feeding and bacterial-feeding groups. This can be interpreted as support for the conclusion that the fauna remains functionally robust over the range of land uses, land covers, and disturbances surveyed, with functional diversity being retained despite the reduction in generic richness. Fallow is noticeably different in functional composition, with more bacterial feeders. However, the maturity index points to the food crop field as the most disturbed land use. This index broadly assesses the balance between colonizers (species with high rates of reproduction and tolerant of disturbance) and persisters (typically with long life cycles and low rates of reproduction). On the basis of all these assessments, three tree-based systems (secondary forest, agroforest, and fallow) can be distinguished from two nontree systems (pasture and food crop field).

Table 5.6 Trends in the Diversity of Mycorrhizal Fungi in Cameroon and in the Abundance of Root-Nodulating Bacteria in Brazil, in Both Cases Across Disturbance Gradients from Forest to Food Crop Field and Pasture[a]

| Cameroon | | | Brazil | | | |
|---|---|---|---|---|---|---|
| Land Use and Site | Mycorrhizal Diversity by Morphotype[b] | | Land Use and Site | Abundance of Root-Nodulating Bacteria | | Nodulation Efficiency |
| | From Field Soil | After Trapping[c] | | MPN[d] (cells per g soil) | 95% Confidence Interval | as Siratro Shoot Dry Matter (mg)[e] |
| **Primary Forest** | | | | | | |
| Akokas | 5 | 10 | — | — | — | — |
| **Secondary Forest** | | | **Disturbed Forest** | | | |
| Akokas | 6 | 5 | Theobroma | 210 | 73–604 | 25.34 bcde |
| Nkolfoulou | 8 | 6 | Pedro Peixoto | 1,684 | 585–4,856 | 19.32 efg |
| | | | RECA | 346 | 120–998 | 22.25 cdef |
| **Fallow** | | | **Fallow** | | | |
| Akokas | 3 | 6 | Theobroma 2 | 10,123 | 3,511–29,184 | 20.60 def |
| Nkolfoulou | 4 | 6 | Pedro Peixoto | 3,735 | 1,296–10,768 | 15.67 fg |
| | | | Theobroma 1 | 147 | 51–425 | 28.20 abcd |
| **Agroforest** | | | **Agroforest** | | | |
| Awae | 5 | 6 | RECA | 61 | 21–177 | 32.18 ab |
| | | | Jí-Paraná 2 | 251 | 87–724 | 23.50 bcde |
| | | | Jí-Paraná 1 | 15 | 5–42 | — |
| **Food Crop Field** | | | **Food Crop Field** | | | |
| Akokas | 5 | 9 | Theobroma | 2,112 | 732–6,088 | 29.85 abc |
| Awae | 1 | 8 | Theobroma | 297 | 103–856 | 23.65 bcde |
| | | | Pedro Peixoto | 224 | 78–647 | 27.12 abcd |
| | | | **Pasture** | | | |
| | | | Pedro Peixoto | <20,000 | | 35.47 a |
| | | | Jí-Paraná | 10,123 | 3,511–20,184 | 22.27 cdef |
| | | | Theobroma | 166 | 58–480 | 29.10 abcd |
| **Total different morphotypes** | 17 | 22 | — | — | — | — |

RECA, Reflorestamento Econômico Consorciado Adensado.

[a]Note that the two gradients are not exactly equivalent.

[b]Identified to generic level from Morton and Benny (1990) and Schenck and Peres (1990).

[c]Using *Vigna unguiculata* (L.) Walp and *Pennisetum americanum* (L.) Leeke as host plants.

[d]From siratro cultured in sterile Jensen's solution, inoculated with serial soil dilutions. MPN, most probable number (method in Woomer et al. 1990).

[e]Means with the same letter are not significantly different (Duncan 5%).

Similar functional distinctions can be recognized in macrofaunal groups (between feeding groups) and between root-nodulating bacteria (between promiscuous and host-specific strains). As an example, the changes in termite diversity observed across the Jambi, Indonesia, land use sequence (figure 5.2) consist largely of losses of soil-feeding species, whereas wood-feeding and grass-foraging species are less affected. Taken together with abundance and biomass data, this might permit the conclusion that termite-mediated wood and litter decomposition would be unchanged under light and moderate disturbance, but the soil-conditioning role, normally the prerogative of soil feeders, might be compromised. Soil-feeding termites are known to be very sensitive to canopy reduction, and in the same land use sequence it can be shown that termite species richness and relative abundance are both highly significantly correlated with botanical species richness, canopy cover and woody plant basal area (A. N. Gillison et al., unpublished data 2002).

Functional group classifications usually are taxon-specific. However, some simple categorizations can be applied more generally. Figure 5.3 shows the relative change in functional group abundance for macrofauna across the Jambi land use sequence, using the epigeic, anecic, and endogeic classification first established for earthworms (Lavelle et al. 1997). The broad trend here is the loss of anecic and endogeic species as disturbance intensifies (jungle rubber is a possible exception). These are the organisms responsible for soil conditioning (rather than decomposition per se). The result

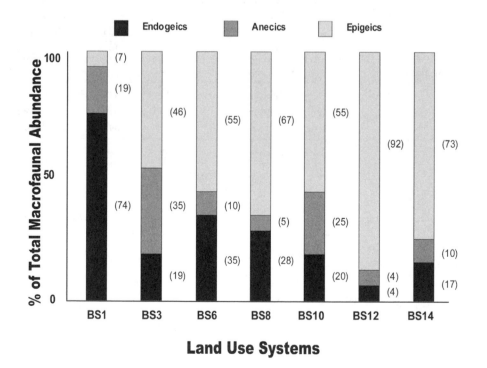

*Figure 5.3* Proportion (by abundance) of macrofaunal functional groups across a forest disturbance gradient *(left to right)* in Jambi Province, Sumatra, Indonesia. For land uses, see figure 5.2.

therefore underscores the conclusions reached from termite diversity and shows that functional diversity can be more useful in demonstrating significant changes in the below-ground community than trends of abundance and biomass.

## ABUNDANCE AND BIOMASS IN RELATION TO LAND USE

Abundance and biomass are problematic parameters for soil biotas because of high variance and the impracticality of sampling at high replication (see Eggleton et al. 1996; Swift and Bignell 2001). Unsurprisingly, species richness and functional group diversity often provide a distinction between land uses more readily, and with much less effort (Eggleton and Bignell 1995; Jones and Eggleton 2000). Nevertheless, the delivery of any given role or process in an ecosystem must be related to the abundance or biomass of the organisms responsible, and therefore these quantities cannot be ignored. As an example, figure 5.2 shows that trends in the total abundance and biomass of macrofauna across the Jambi land use sequence are different from and less clear-cut than those of taxonomic diversity. The notable peaks associated with tree plantation (BS6) and jungle rubber (BS10) are contributed largely by earthworms, although their diversities are hardly rich and exceed those of other sites by only one or two. In the same land use sequence, there are no significant differences for ant abundance and biomass. With termites, post hoc comparisons by Mann–Whitney show that the pristine primary forest site has significantly higher abundance and biomass than any of the others, but otherwise there are few differences between land uses, except for the degraded *Imperata* grassland, which has few termites and is depauperate. These results further emphasize the value of the functional group concept in achieving resolution between different agroecosystems.

Data on microbial biomass in the Brazilian land use sequence show that the secondary forest had significantly greater microbial carbon than pasture and agroforest. In Indonesia (Lampung sites), secondary forest had significantly more microbial carbon than all other sites, followed by agroforest, which was significantly greater than tree plantation and *Imperata* grassland, both of which were significantly greater than food crop fields. Therefore there is some agreement between data for different microbial groups and data for microbial biomass, at least to the extent of suggesting that agroforest and food crop field land uses may be impoverished compared with fallow, if not with forest.

## CONCLUSION

Assessment of the value of the work completed to date turns on three issues: Have we answered the ASB questions in whole or in part? Are we justified in our selection of taxa or functional groups? Have we learned from our experience by changing our methods and improving our skills?

The ASB below-ground biodiversity working hypotheses have been reworked into questions, which are presented in table 5.4. Some answers can be offered to at least some of those questions from the results presented earlier. An obvious criticism is that too many examples of links between land use and below-ground biodiversity are drawn from the macrofauna, which are the easiest group to sample. This does not invalidate evidence from macrofauna but does point to the need for improved methods with other groups that mediate different functions in the ecosystem. The observation that trends across land use sequences and along disturbance gradients differ between taxonomic groups self-evidently justifies extending biodiversity surveys to microfauna and microsymbionts. Because of the large numbers of individuals, in different functional groups, that can be extracted from a small number of soil samples, the potential for data accumulation from nematodes, given adequate taxonomic expertise, is impressive and should have good predictive value for ecosystem processes. In work with termites and nematodes, taxonomic resolution can be obtained at the genus or species level, and it is also possible to make functional group allocations from the morphology of each specimen. Better discrimination between land uses is then possible because the balance of functional groups, as well as species or generic diversity, can be assessed at the same time. Despite this, there is no evidence that any one taxonomic group can serve as a surrogate for others. Existing evidence points to the opposite conclusion. For example, in Cameroon Lawton et al. (1998) found that each of five unrelated animal groups (birds, beetles, ants, termites, and nematodes) showed its own pattern of diversity change across the same disturbance gradient (forest through tree plantation to cleared ground) and that the changes in one group did not predict changes in others.

The main addition to our protocol since the project began has been the 100-m termite transect. This places substantial demands on resources (20 work-hours for sampling, up to 300 work-hours for taxonomy; see Lawton et al. 1998) but provides high resolution and has the additional advantage that specimens can be allocated to functional groups directly from taxonomic affiliation (Jones and Eggleton 2000). Other improvements, tabulated under best sampling practice (table 5.3), address replication issues: increasing the number of monoliths per transect from five to eight or ten and avoiding or reducing the bulking of cores for nematodes and microsymbionts. Such modifications are easy to recommend but carry large resource implications. Similarly, the move toward molecular methods in characterizing root-nodulating bacteria (Bruijn et al. 1997) necessarily restricts the number of laboratories able to undertake such work in the short term.

Table 5.7 summarizes the difficulties attached to work with particular groups. Inevitably, although sampling expertise can be readily taught and disseminated, taxonomic bottlenecks are the main obstacles to assembling good datasets (see Eggleton and Bignell 1995; Lawton et al. 1998). Termites, earthworms, nematodes, mycorrhizal fungi, and rhizobia can all be cited as groups whose taxonomy is moderately difficult or difficult. However, these are also the groups where species or strain-level resolution is valuable in distinguishing between land uses.

*Table 5.7* Comparative Merits and Difficulties of the Biotic Groups Selected

| Group | Main Processes Mediated | Ease of Sampling (S) and Taxonomic Processing (T) | Resolution of Diversity Needed | Indicator Value |
|---|---|---|---|---|
| All macrofauna | Litter transformers and macropredators | Easy (S), easy (T) | Generally to ordinal level | Moderate |
| Termites | Decomposition and bioturbation → soil structure and quality | Moderate (S), difficult (T) | Species level | Good |
| Ants | | Easy (S), easy (T) | Species level | Moderate |
| Earthworms | | Difficult (S), moderate (T) | Species level | Good |
| Nematodes | Micropredators | Difficult (S), difficult (T) | Generic level | Good |
| Mycorrhiza | Nutrient acquisition | Moderate (S), moderate (T) | Species or spore morphotype | Moderate |
| Root-nodulating bacteria | Nitrogen fixation | Moderate (S), difficult (T) | Genus or strain | Good |
| Microbial biomass | Primary transformations | Easy (S), difficult (T) | — | Low |

A final question concerns the scaling of sampling. Is the assessment of below-ground biodiversity consistent from sampling point to plot and from plot to land use? To some extent this question returns the argument to the issues of replication of sampling and the variance of data. Are we justified in drawing conclusions about regional land uses from spot sampling in a few sites, albeit well-documented ones? Data on soil macrofauna from Indonesia, where replication of sampling arguably has been more extensive than elsewhere, suggests that for any given land use, average taxon diversity is consistently greater at the sampling location level (i.e., mean of taxa sampled over all locations) than the sampling point level (i.e., mean of all sampling points in all locations). This is as expected, given that a few samples will be highly taxon-rich whereas the majority will have lower diversity and, consequently, the maximum diversity found at any single point will be greater than the average of locations. However, the magnitudes of both these difference are consistent across five land uses from mature forest to degraded *Imperata* grassland (van Noordwijk 1999). This suggests that despite their inadequacies, our sampling methods are giving real information on the links between land management and soil biodiversity.

REFERENCES

Amato, M., and J.N. Ladd. 1988. Assay for microbial biomass based on ninhydrin-reactive nitrogen in extracts of fumigated soils. Soil Biol. Biochem. 20:107–114.
Anderson, J.M., and J.S.I. Ingram. 1993. Tropical soil biology and fertility: A handbook of methods, 2nd ed. CAB Int., Wallingford, UK.

Angers, D.A., and J. Caron. 1998. Plant-induced changes in soil structure: Processes and feed-backs. Biogeochemistry 42:55–72.

Bignell, D.E., and P. Eggleton. 2000. Termites in ecosystems. pp. 363–387. *In* T. Abe, D.E. Bignell, and M. Higashi (eds.) Termites: Evolution, sociality, symbioses, ecology. Kluwer Academic Publ., Dordrecht, The Netherlands.

Bongers, T. 1990. The maturity index: An ecological measure of environmental disturbance based on nematode species composition. Oecologia 83:14–19.

Bruijn, F.J. de, M.E. Davey, B. McSpadden-Gardener, A. Millcamps, J.L.W. Rademaker, D. Ragatz, et al. 1997. Molecular approaches in microbial ecology to assess genomic diversity and stress-induced gene expression in plant-associated diazotrophs. pp. 571–576. *In* C. Elmerich, A. Kondorosi, and W.E. Newton (eds.) Biological nitrogen fixation for the 21st century. Kluwer Academic Publ., Dordrecht, The Netherlands.

Brussaard, L., V. Behan-Pelletier, D. Bignell, V. Brown, W. Didden, P. Folgarait, et al. 1997. Biodiversity and ecosystem functioning in soil. Ambio 26:563–570.

Dibog, L. 1998. Biodiversity and ecology of termites (Isoptera) in a humid tropical forest, southern Cameroon. Ph.D. thesis, Univ. of London, London.

Donovan, S.E., P. Eggleton, and D.E. Bignell. 2001. Gut content analysis and a new feeding group classification of termites (Isoptera). Ecol. Entomol. 26:356–366.

Douglas, A.E. 1995. The ecology of symbiotic microorganisms. Adv. Ecol. Res. 26:69–103.

Eggleton, P., and D.E. Bignell. 1995. Monitoring the response of tropical insects to changes in the environment: Troubles with termites. pp. 473–497. *In* R. Harrington and N.E. Stork (eds.) Insects in a changing environment. Academic Press, London.

Eggleton, P., D.E. Bignell, W.A. Sands, N.A. Mawdsley, J.H. Lawton, T.G. Wood, et al. 1996. The diversity, abundance and biomass of termites under differing levels of disturbance in the Mbalmayo Forest Reserve, Southern Cameroon. Phil. Trans. R. Soc. Lond. Ser. B 351:51–68.

Eggleton, P., R. Homathevi, D.T. Jones, J. MacDonald, D. Jeeva, R.G. Davies, et al. 1999. Termite assemblages, forest disturbance, and greenhouse gas fluxes in Sabah, East Malaysia. Phil. Trans. R. Soc. Lond. Ser. B 354:1791–1802.

Freckman, D.W., and C.H. Ettema. 1993. Assessing nematode communities in agroecosystems of various human intervention. Agric. Ecosyst. Environ. 45:239–261.

Gaston, K.J. 1996. Biodiversity. Blackwell, Oxford.

Hole, F.D. 1981. Effects of animals on soil. Geoderma 25:75–112.

Hooper, D., J.M. Dangerfield, L. Brussaard, D.H. Wall, D.A. Wardle, D.E. Bignell, et al. 2000. Interactions between above and belowground biodiversity in terrestrial ecosystems: Patterns, mechanisms and feedbacks. BioScience 50:1049–1061.

Jones, C.G., J.H. Lawton, and M. Schachak. 1994. Organisms as ecosystem engineers. Oikos 69:373–386.

Jones, D.T., and P. Eggleton. 2000. Sampling termite species assemblages in tropical forests: Testing a rapid biodiversity assessment protocol. J. Appl. Ecol. 37:191–203.

Kenyatta, K. (ed.). 1997. Alternatives to slash-and-burn. Report of the 6th annual review meeting. ICRAF, Nairobi.

Lavelle, P. 1996. Diversity of soil fauna and ecosystem function. Biol. Int. 33:3–16.

Lavelle, P., D.E. Bignell, M. Lepage, V. Volters, P. Roger, P. Ineson, et al. 1997. Soil function in a changing world: The role of invertebrate ecosystem engineers. Eur. J. Soil Biol. 33:159–193.

Lawton, J.H. 1996. The role of species in ecosystems: Aspects of ecological complexity and biological diversity. pp. 215–228. *In* T. Abe, S.A. Levin, and M. Higashi (eds.) Biodiversity, an ecological perspective. Springer, New York.

Lawton, J.H., D.E. Bignell, G.F. Bloemers, P. Eggleton, and M.E. Hodda. 1996. Carbon flux and diversity of nematodes and termites in Cameroon forest soils. Biodiversity Conserv. 5:261–273.

Lawton, J.H., D.E. Bignell, B. Bolton, G.F. Bloemers, P. Eggleton, P.M. Hammond, et al. 1998. Biodiversity inventories, indicator taxa and effects of habitat modification in tropical forest. Nature (London) 391:72–76.

Morton, J.B., and G.L. Benny. 1990. A new order, Glomales, two new suborders, Glominae and Gigasporinae, and two new families, Acaulosporaceae and Gigasporinae with an emanclation Glomoceae. Mycataxon 37:471–491.

Naeem, S., L.J. Thompson, S.P. Lawler, J.H. Lawton, and R.M. Woodfin. 1994. Declining biodiversity can alter the performance of ecosystems. Nature (London) 368:734–737.

Schenck, N.C., and Y. Peres. 1990. Manual for the identification of VA mycorrhizal fungi, 3rd ed. Synergistic Publ., Gainesville, FL.

Scholes, R.J., and N. van Breemen. 1997. The effects of global change on tropical ecosystems. Geoderma 79:9–24.

Southwood, T.R.E. 1978. Ecological methods with particular reference to the study of insect populations, 2nd ed. Chapman & Hall, London.

Stork, N.E., and P. Eggleton. 1992. Invertebrates as determinants and indicators of soil quality. Am. J. Alt. Agric. 7:23–32.

Swift, M.J., and J.M. Anderson. 1993. Biodiversity and ecosystem function in agricultural systems. pp. 15–42. *In* E.D. Schulze and H.A. Mooney (eds.) Biodiversity and ecosystem function. Springer-Verlag, Berlin.

Swift, M., and D. Bignell. 2001. Standard methods for the assessment of soil biodiversity and land-use practice. ASB Lecture Note 6B. ICRAF, South East Asian Regional Res. Programme, Bogor, Indonesia.

Tilman, D., and J.A. Downing. 1994. Biodiversity and stability in grasslands. Nature (London) 367:363–366.

Torsvik, V., R. Sørheim, and J. Goksøyr. 1996. Total bacterial diversity in soil and sediment communities: A review. J. Indust. Microbiol. 17:170–178.

van Breemen, N., and A.C. Finzi. 1998. Plant–soil interactions: Ecological aspects and evolutionary implications. Biogeochemistry 42:1–19.

van Noordwijk, M. 1999. Evolution of land-use types in Indonesia and selection of Lampung (Tulang Bawang) and Jambi (Batang Hari) transects. pp. 161–175. *In* A. Gafur, F.X. Susilo, M. Utomo, and M. van Noordwijk (eds.) Proceedings of the Workshop Management of Agrobiodiversity for Sustainable Land Use and Global Environmental Benefits, Bogor, Indonesia, 19–20 Aug. 1999. Agency for Agric. Res. and Develop., Ministry of Agric. and Univ. of Lampung, Indonesia.

Visser, S. 1985. Role of the soil invertebrates in determining the composition of soil microbial communities. pp. 297–317. *In* A.H. Fitter, D. Atkinson, D.J. Read, and M.B. Usher (eds.) Ecological interactions in soil. Blackwell, Oxford.

Wilson, J.B., and A.D.Q. Agnew. 1992. Positive-feedback switches in plant communities. Adv. Ecol. Res. 23:263–336.

Wolters, V., W. Silver, D.C. Coleman, P. Lavelle, P. Van der Putten, D.H. de Ruiter, et al. 2000. Global change effects on above- and below-ground diversity in terrestrial ecosystems: Interactions and implications for ecosystem functioning. BioScience 50:1089–1098.

Woomer, P., J. Bennet, and R. Yost. 1990. Agroclimatology and modelling: Overcoming the inflexibility of most-probable-number procedures. Agron. J. 82:349–353.

Yeates, G.W., T. Bongers, R.G.M. de Goede, D.W. Freckman, and S.S. Georgieva. 1993. Feeding habits in soil nematode families and genera: An outline for soil ecologists. J. Nematol. 25:315–331.

# 6 Sustainability of Tropical Land Use Systems After Forest Conversion

Kurniatun Hairiah
   *Brawijaya University  Malang, Indonesia*
Meine van Noordwijk
   *ICRAF, Indonesia  Bogor, Indonesia*
Stephan Weise
   *IITA Humid Forest Station  Yaoundé, Cameroon*

Farmer decision making involves the weighing of many options, including those off farm and off site, and includes the possibility of migrating elsewhere. Of particular interest to natural resource management research is the balance between decisions for activities in the rural landscape that invest, plant, care, and conserve and those that exploit, harvest, and market the resources. When exploitation and harvesting dominate, the resources are likely to degrade, but the returns to labor and short-term profitability may be high. When conservation, planting and other types of investment dominate, the resources may recover from past exploitation but may not meet current livelihood demands. Finding a balance between these aspects within the landscape depends very much on the interactions between actors and stakeholders. Sustainability issues will play a role in farmers' decisions only if they are made aware of the problems and have other options.

Where a secure system of land tenure exists, the precept that "a man should always aim to hand over his farm to his son in at least as good a condition as he inherited it from his father" (Russell 1977) has been a major factor in promoting sustainable land management. Although the details may vary in different parts of the world (daughters may inherit farms, from either their mother or their father), the message remains clear: We have borrowed the resources from future generations and are supposed to return them intact.

There are many definitions of sustainability (table 6.1). Shifting cultivation systems can be sustainable if the fallow length is sufficient to undo the loss of productivity that occurs during a cropping period. If one looks at the cropping period in isolation the system appears to degrade, but when crop-

*Table 6.1* Definitions of Sustainable Agricultural Systems

| Definitions | Source |
| --- | --- |
| The successful management of resources for agriculture to satisfy changing human needs while maintaining or enhancing the quality of the environment and conserving natural resources. | FAO (1989) |
| A system that maintains an acceptable and increasing level of productivity that satisfies prevailing needs and is continuously adapted to meet the future needs for increasing the carrying capacity of the resource base and other worthwhile human needs. | Okigbo (1991) |
| A system in which the farmer continuously increases productivity at levels that are economically viable, ecologically sound, and culturally acceptable through the efficient management of resources and orchestration of inputs in numbers, quantities, qualities, sequences, and timing, with minimum damage to the environment and human life. | Okigbo (1991) |
| A system that involves the management and conservation of the natural resource base and the orientation of technological and institutional change in such a manner as to ensure the attainment and continued satisfaction of human needs for present and future generations. Such sustainable development conserves land, water, plant, and animal genetic resources and is economically viable and socially acceptable. | FAO (1991) |
| A cropping system is not sustainable unless the annual output shows a nondeclining trend and is resistant, in terms of yield stability, to normal fluctuations of stress and disturbance. | Spencer and Swift (1992) |
| A sustainable land management system is one that does not degrade the soil or significantly contaminate the environment while providing necessary support to human life. | Greenland (1994) |

*Source:* Greenland (1994).

ping and fallow periods are combined the basic resources are maintained from one cycle to the next and allow continued exploitation. This example may illustrate some of the considerations necessary for an assessment of sustainability:

• Sustainability of a larger system (crop and fallow) may be maintained even if a subsystem (the cropping period) is nonsustainable.
• Sustainability of a human livelihood system can be maintained even if specific activities are not sustainable as long as a sufficient array of options is maintained.

Whenever a specific form of land use runs into problems with one of the resources on which it depends, there may be alternative solutions that maintain the overall functioning of the system. These solutions may be more costly, but the fact that they exist means that sustainability assessments really depend on the boundary conditions that we set for such potential adaptations.

In general, however, it is easier to define what is nonsustainable than it is to say what is sustainable. Any system that does not maintain all essential parts of the resource base is nonsustainable, so finding one violation of the resource conservation rule is enough to characterize the system as a whole as nonsustainable. We can confirm that a system is sustainable only if we know the fate of all parts of the resource base and the degree to which they are essential; this is not a trivial task by any means. Sustainability at any level of complexity (from sustainability of cropping systems to that of human livelihoods) can be based on the sustainability of its components, possible adaptations, or the adaptive response of the key actors at each level in finding and fitting in new components (figure 6.1).

Sustainable livelihood options do not necessitate sustainable cropping systems or crops if there are enough potential alternatives. Existing sustainability indicators

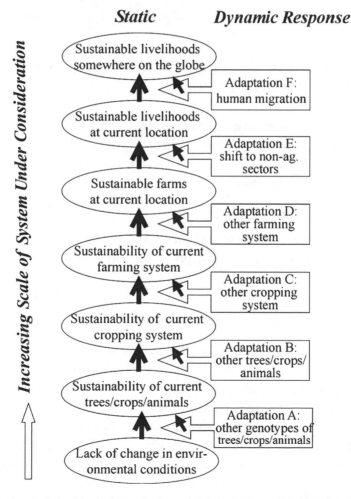

*Figure 6.1* At any single level in the hierarchy from abiotic resources to global livelihoods, sustainability can be defined either as the persistence of the underlying level (the resource base) or as the availability of options (allowing the manager to be resourceful or agile in making adaptations).

appear to focus on persistence, ignoring adaptation and change. Yet options for change are not the same everywhere, so they should be taken into account as well.

If we combine a persistence view of sustainability with the options for dynamic change (figure 6.1), we see that sustainability at one scale does not extend to the scales above or below. Changes in the resource base and options for future change can affect sustainability at higher levels in the hierarchy, even if persistence criteria for the current system are met. Conversely, lack of sustainability at any level can be compensated for to achieve sustainability at a higher level in the hierarchy if options for adaptation are maintained. Therefore we have to be explicit in the system boundaries before we can measure, quantify, or assess sustainability.

In the context of our integrated assessment of land use options for the humid tropics, we will discuss the following:

- Assessments of sustainability of land use practices at plot level
- Assessments of sustainable agricultural livelihood systems at landscape scale

## ASSESSMENTS OF SUSTAINABILITY OF LAND USE PRACTICES AT PLOT LEVEL

Sustainability of a range of land use systems that follow forest conversion can be assessed if we first specify the threats to persistence (figure 6.2). Four ways by which continued farming degrades its own resource base to a level that impairs future productive use of the land are as follows:

A. Not maintaining soil of sufficient structure
B. Not balancing the budget of nutrient exports and imports
C. Letting pest, weed, and disease problems reach unmanageable proportions
D. Not maintaining essential soil biota, such as mycorrhizal fungi and *Rhizobium*

Any of these problems can become such a constraint to continued farming that land may have to be abandoned, at least temporarily. Therefore the most serious category of problems determines the overall sustainability.

Other threats to continued farming that may dominate discussions of agricultural sustainability, especially in developed countries, are threats to water quality and quantity (E), air quality (F), and biodiversity (G) (figure 6.2). If there are serious negative effects on these factors, then outside stakeholders may take measures to stop the land use practice in its current form. Another threat is producing products of insufficient quality to meet consumers' expectations (H).

Categories A to D are essentially agronomic in nature; categories E to H depend on the perceptions and responses of consumers and other outside stakeholders, so

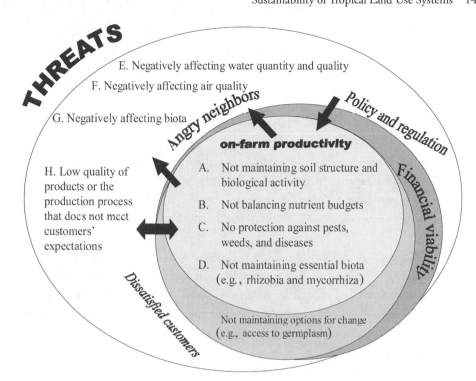

*Figure 6.2* Threats to agricultural sustainability: The inner circle is essentially agronomic and the outer circle is more focused on environment and market issues (van Noordwijk and Cadisch 2002).

they necessitate very different methods of investigation. They affect farming through government or local regulations and financial incentives. Other threats to continued farming are based on the lack of financial viability of a farm, changes in prices for the products, and a lack of options for change.

For each category of threats, numerous indicators can be developed at two levels:

• Easily observable phenomena that can be used in rapid qualitative assessments
• Real measurable parameters for which standardized protocols and interpretation schemes (which include specific threshold values) can be made

Qualitative field-level indicators may be sufficient for monitoring on-site changes by (forest) farmers or other land users. To them, the presence of a surface litter layer and clear forest streams may be enough to indicate that the system they work with is sustainable. Yet such simple indicators are not sufficient for legally binding commitments. The latter require rigorous, quantifiable indicators, but even with such procedures, the interpretation of data may not be unequivocal because absolute reference values are lacking for many of the parameters. For example, a debate on how often landslides occur in "natural forest" landscapes can cast doubt on any data on sediment loads of rivers after forest conversion.

No agricultural land use can consistently yield harvests of produce without management efforts being invested in maintaining the system. Therefore, all judgments of sustainability must be made in the context of a specified management regime and farmer efforts to overcome obstacles. For each indicator a tentative threshold has to be identified, which allows a final judgment to be expressed, for example, in terms of three categories:

0: No major problems beyond the range that normal farm management can address.

–0.5: Additional effort will be needed to address these issues, which may affect the profitability of the land use system but may otherwise be within the range of farmers' management options.

–1: Problems may be beyond farmers' ability to resolve.

In the Alternatives to Slash-and-Burn (ASB) project, a set of criteria and indicators was developed that can be measured easily, often using data already collected as part of the integrated survey of biodiversity, carbon stocks, and greenhouse gas emissions. Details of the various criteria that were used are presented in the following sections. After that, the values and results obtained in the assessments in Indonesia, Cameroon, and Brazil are discussed.

Criteria for evaluating the impacts of land use on former forest soils (table 6.2) can be grouped by soil function, focusing on the sustainability of land use practices and on externalities or effects on environmental functions of forest soils. However, the measurables for these various functions show a high degree of overlap. Many of them are linked with the maintenance of surface mulch and soil organic matter.

## CRITERION A: SOIL STRUCTURE AND BIOLOGICAL ACTIVITY

The following indicators can be used.

### A1: Soil Compaction

Soil compaction is measured from soil bulk density (dry weight per unit volume, $g/cm^3$) in the topsoil relative to that of a forest soil of the same texture. Isolated, individual measurements of soil bulk densities are difficult to interpret because soils of differing texture have different inherent bulk densities such that values that are high and unsustainable for one soil type may not be for another. By using a "pedotransfer" function we can estimate the normal bulk density ($BD_{ref}$) of a soil of the same texture, and we can use the ratio $BD/BD_{ref}$ as an indicator of change from the reference situation. Values above 1 indicate compaction, values below 1 a structure that is better than average (in the reference set). Wösten et al. (1995, 1998) derived such a pedotransfer function for a large set of soils from the temperate region that are under agricultural use:

*Table 6.2* Criteria and Indicators for Evaluating Sustainability of Plot-Level Land Use on Previous Forest Soils in the A S B Project

| Criteria | Indicators (qualitative) | Measurable Parameters (quantitative) |
| --- | --- | --- |
| **I. Maintain on-site productivity** | | |
| A. Maintain soil as a matrix of reasonable structure, allowing root growth and buffering water between supply (as precipitation) and demand (for transpiration) | Erosion: absence of gullies, presence of riparian filter strips and other sedimentation zones, soil cover by surface litter or understory vegetation Compaction: use of penetrometer Soil structure: spade test, root pattern Soil cover and absence of gullies as indicators of infiltration; absence of surface sealing and crusting | Net soil loss = internal soil loss − internal sedimentation. Percentage soil cover, integrated over the year (or over annual rainfall). Bulk density of topsoil. Soil macroporosity and $H_2O$ infiltration rates. Water infiltration vs. runoff. Soil water retention. Effective rooting depth. |
| B. Maintain the nutrient balance: buffer nutrients between supply from inside and outside the system and demands for uptake | Annual exports of phosphorus and cations as fraction of total and available stock Annual exports of nitrogen minus inputs from biological $N_2$ fixation as fraction of total nitrogen content of the soil Financial value of net nutrient exports as fraction of potential replacement costs in fertilizer | Changes in stocks of plant available nutrients. Changes in mineralization potential or size of organic matter pools. Carbon saturation deficit. Limiting-nutrient trials. |
| C. Keep pest, weed, and disease problems within a manageable range | Absence of major diseases and weeds | Rate of increase of pest incidence. Change in composition and quantity of weed flora. |
| D. Maintain essential soil biota, such as mycorrhizal fungi and *Rhizobium,* and ecosystem engineers | Sporocarps (mushrooms) for ectomycorrhizal species Signs of ecosystem engineers among the soil fauna: earthworms, termites | Spore counts for vesicular arbuscular mycorrhiza. Mycorrhizal infection and nodulation in roots in the field and in trap crops in the lab. For details see chapter 5. |
| **II. Externalities: Don't make the neighbors angry** | | |
| E. Provide a regular supply of high-quality water | Stream flow response time after rain storms; downstream areas free of floods and droughts Turbidity of streams | Stream flow amounts and variability. Sediment load of streams. Absence of agrochemicals in water. |

*Table 6.2* (Continued)

| Criteria | Indicators (qualitative) | Measurable Parameters (quantitative) |
| --- | --- | --- |
| **II. Externalities: Don't make the neighbors angry** | | |
| F. Air filter: mitigate net emission of greenhouse gases | Above-ground carbon stocks in biomass and necromass | Soil carbon stocks relative to soil carbon saturation deficit. Net emissions of $NO_2$ and $CH_4$. |
| G. Maintain biodiversity reservoirs: allow recolonization of depleted neighboring landscape units and germplasm collection for ex situ exploitation | Diversity of above-ground vegetation, based on diversity of plant functional attributes | Diversity of plant species. Diversity of soil biota in selected indicator groups. |
| **III. Keep the consumers happy** | | |
| H. Maintain a product quality that consumers want to buy | Actual consumer response | Criteria based on the consumer's perception of quality. These may involve positive attributes (e.g., taste, nutritional value), lack of negative attributes (e.g., no chemical residues or genetically modified components), or lack of production process (social and environmental concerns). |

For soils with Clay% + Silt% < 50 percent the following equation is used:

$$BD_{ref} = 1/[-1.984 + 0.01841 \times OM + 0.032 + 0.00003576 \times (Clay\% + Silt\%)^2 + 67.5/MPS + 0.424 \times \ln(MPS)],$$

where OM is the soil organic matter content ($=1.7 \times C_{org}$) and MPS is the mean particle size of the sand fraction, with a default value of 290 μm.

For soils with Clay% + Silt% > 50 percent the following equation is used:

$$BD_{ref} + 1/[0.603 + 0.003975 \times Clay\% + 0.00207 \times OM^2 + 0.01781 \times \ln(OM)].$$

Although these equations were based on agricultural soils in temperate regions, they have been used here to approximate bulk density values for soils from differing land uses and with differing texture. This pedotransfer refers to soil under normal agricultural use rather than under forest, so we expect $BD/BD_{ref}$ values to be below 1 for forest conditions.

## A2: Soil Carbon Saturation

Soil organic matter is considered to be a key characteristic in judging the sustainability of land use systems. Yet total soil organic matter content is not a very sensitive indicator because it changes slowly under different management regimes and often has a high spatial variability linked to variability in soil texture, pH, and elevation.

Current methods for inventory of soil organic matter are based on an estimate of the soil carbon stored under natural vegetation and relative changes caused by aspects of human land use, including soil tillage, drainage, and a reduction in organic inputs compared against the natural vegetation. The difference between current and potential carbon storage can then be expressed as a carbon saturation deficit (van Noordwijk et al. 1997, 1998). We can now calculate a carbon saturation deficit on the basis of the difference between the actual soil carbon content and amount that would be expected for a forest soil with a long history of large litter inputs for the same type of soil.

$$C_{satDeficit} = (C_{ref} - C_{org})/C_{ref} = 1 - C_{org}/C_{ref},$$

where $C_{org}/C_{ref}$ = soil organic carbon content relative to that for forest soils of the same texture and pH, and $C_{ref}$ = a reference soil carbon level representative of forest soil.

More details on the basis for the equations and values for the carbon saturation deficit can be found in chapter 2. If the value of the $C_{org}/C_{ref}$ ratio is 1, this means the soil is similar to that of a forest and basically carbon saturated, and values less than 1 indicate a carbon deficit relative to the forest soil.

## A3: Active Soil Carbon

Microbial biomass forms only 1 to 4 percent of the total carbon content of a soil, but it is the most active fraction because nearly all transformations in the soil depend on microbial activity. Numerous indicators have been identified for comparing the size of this microbial pool or some other fraction or activity of the labile soil carbon in different land use types in a given area relative to the natural forest on an equivalent soil type.

• Microbial biomass is generally estimated by comparing the amount of carbon or nitrogen that is released into the soil after a chloroform fumigation that (supposedly) kills all microbes. It is measured through incubation or extraction methods. Microbial biomass estimates derived in this way often correlate well with soil nitrogen mineralization rates and crop yields and therefore are an indication of soil microbial activity and fertility. Soil microbiologists generally prefer other methods that target specific groups of soil microbes or have a stricter separation of live and dead fractions of the biomass, but for a first assessment the overall microbial biomass measurement still has value.

• Soil respiration or nitrogen mineralization (during lab incubation) can be used as an indication of the biological activity of the soil.

• Dry weight of the light fraction of soil organic matter represents recent inputs of organic matter as food for soil biota. This fraction can be obtained using a separation technique based on liquids of different densities, called the size–density fractionation procedure (Sitompul et al. 2000).

• It is becoming apparent that individual measures of microbial biomass or light fraction may not reflect the active or labile fraction of soil organic matter (SOM) because both fractions contain labile carbon. Chemical oxidation approaches such as that described by Blair et al. (1997) may be a more integrative measure of labile soil carbon.

The use of these parameters is valid when they are judged against the values obtained for natural forest sites. Yet there are still no critical values below which one can say the system is no longer sustainable.

## A4: Soil Exposure

Soil exposure (SE) to the direct impact of raindrops and the sun, if frequent or for long periods of time, can lead to deterioration of soil structure. Therefore, a soil cover such as a surface litter layer or green leaves of plants growing close to the ground can protect the soil. Tree canopies alone do not count, however, because the energy of the splash impact of drips from the leaves can exceed that of rainfall.

Several indicators were developed to reflect both the percentage of time that a soil is exposed and the length of the cycle. The soil cover index integrates the information of both soil exposure and open time into one indicator. The indicators include the following:

Soil exposure = 100 × number of months of low (less than 75 percent) soil cover/length of system cycle in months, that is, proportion of the length of the whole cycle that the soil has a low cover

Time between clearing events, that is, the frequency of the removal of a protective canopy cover = total length of system cycle (in years)

Soil cover index = length of system cycle in months – soil exposure time in months

## CRITERION B: NUTRIENT BALANCE

Three indicators were developed to judge whether the nutrient balance is (or could potentially be) maintained in a cropping system.

## B1: Net Nutrient Export

Net nutrient export (NNE) can be calculated as the total nutrients contained in all harvested products (which are removed from a field) minus the amount of nutrients added in the form of fertilizer inputs for nitrogen, phosphorus, and potassium, in kilograms per hectare per year. The value does not include the nutrients that are recycled in the system such as litterfall or prunings, crop residues, or manures. High net exports indicate the likelihood of depletion of the resource base; high net surpluses, on the other hand, may indicate excessive fertilizer use and risks of pollution of ground and surface water. Nutrient imports can also include dinitrogen ($N_2$) fixation from legumes in the system.

## B2: Nutrient Depletion Time Range

Nutrient depletion time range (NDTR) represents the theoretical length of time (number of years) it would take for nutrient stocks to be depleted to zero (if current trends are extrapolated linearly). In any system, if nutrient stocks in soil and vegetation are large relative to net nutrient exports, nutrient offtake can be part of a wise natural resource management strategy. If exports are large relative to stocks, however, one can expect that yields will decline in the near future unless nutrient inputs are increased.

Two types of estimates were used for nutrient stocks in the system:

- The directly available nutrient pool in the soil
- The total nutrient content of soil plus vegetation (including less accessible pools in the soil)

Neither estimate is directly satisfactory, however, because measures of the available nutrient pool include arbitrary fractions and there is wide variation between plants in ability to access nonavailable nutrient sources. Because nutrient stocks depend on the soil type and vegetation cover, one cannot directly assign an NDTR value to a land use system. As an example from the peneplain of Sumatra, the inherently more fertile soils closer to rivers with a higher clay and silt content will have larger nutrient stocks than the sandier soils of the rest of the lowland peneplain. Thus, figures obtained may be accurate only within an order of magnitude.

## B3: The Relative Nutrient Replacement Value

The relative nutrient replacement value (RNRV) relates the export of nutrients in harvested products to the costs of putting them back into the agroecosystem in the form of chemical fertilizer. This assessment is based on the harvested products rather than the full production system.

## Criterion C: Crop Protection from Weeds, Pests, and Diseases

For criterion C, two indicators have been proposed, both based on expert opinion rather than direct measurements:

### C1: Potential for Weed Problems

Weed problems become a major constraint in the system unless addressed by additional labor or technical input.

### C2: Potential for Pest or Disease Problems

Pest or disease problems become a major constraint in the system unless addressed by additional labor or technical input.

## Criterion D: Maintenance of Essential Soil Biota

The relationship of different groups of soil biota to certain soil and ecosystem functions is discussed in chapter 5. Certain functional groups such as macrofauna (ants, termites, earthworms), nematodes, and plant microsymbionts have been identified as key to the maintenance of certain soil and ecosystem processes, but no critical values have been set.

## CASE STUDIES: RESULTS FROM ASB INDONESIA (SUMATRA), CAMEROON, AND BRAZIL

### Criterion A: Soil Structure and Biological Activity

Data collected from the Lampung and Jambi benchmark sites in Indonesia (table 6.3) show that there is a clear difference in mean bulk density between undisturbed forests and land under a cassava–*Imperata* cycle, with intermediate degrees of compaction under agroforests and other tree-based production systems. Serious localized soil compaction was clear in logged-over forest where tracks and logging ramps were compacted beyond easy recovery. It is easy to compact a soil, but in systems without soil tillage it can take a long time before the soil recovers. Soil compaction can affect water infiltration, root growth, and greenhouse gas emissions but probably stayed below critical levels in all cases observed.

*Table 6.3* Measured Soil Fertility Indicators for the Integrated Biodiversity Survey in Lampung and Jambi, A S B Benchmark Area (September – November 1996)

| | $BD/BD_{ref}$, 2–7 cm | $C_{org}/C_{ref}$, 0–5 cm | Light Organic Matter, 0–5 cm (g/kg) | Bacterial Population/ $C_{org}$ | Bacterial Population/ $(C_{ref}/C_{org})$ | Soil Respiration (mg $CO_2$/ kg/d) |
|---|---|---|---|---|---|---|
| Forest | 0.85 | 0.91 | 3.22 | 13.5 | 37 | 12.9 |
| **Relative to Forest** | | | | | | |
| Agroforest | 0.99 | 0.75 | 0.77 | 1.48 | 1.43 | 0.91 |
| Regrowing trees | 1.21 | 0.73 | 0.81 | 1.78 | 1.69 | 0.84 |
| Cassava | 1.14 | 0.52 | 0.35 | 1.56 | 1.51 | 0.59 |
| *Imperata* | 1.26 | 0.66 | 0.58 | 1.59 | 1.62 | 0.80 |

Soil samples were taken at the surface layer (0 – 5 cm only), except for bulk density (B D ), at 2–7 cm. See text for indicator descriptions.

The carbon saturation ($C_{org}/C_{ref}$) data show that no land use systems fully maintain the soil organic matter levels in the topsoil of a natural forest, as is shown by the values of $C_{org}/C_{ref}$ of less than 1.0. Declines greater than 25 percent were found only for the cassava–*Imperata* land use type, with the greatest reductions of almost 50 percent measured in cassava fields. The low current value of carbon saturation may have resulted partly from reclamation history and current land use (bulldozer land clearing can remove part of the topsoil to outside the field boundaries). The frequent fires and soil tillage, together with low organic inputs through cassava litterfall (0.6 Mg/ha/yr compared with 12 Mg/ha/yr in secondary forest), are the likely causes.

These same land uses, except for cassava, had a high respiration rate, but when estimates of total microbial population size are scaled by soil organic matter content or carbon saturation, the active fraction of the total soil organic matter pool in forests appears to have been lowest. On the basis of this evidence and other data in the soil biodiversity survey (see chapter 5, this volume) we conclude that there is no lack of active soil biota in any of the land uses for the basic functions of nutrient cycling and decomposition, and *Imperata* grasslands are not depleted ecosystems from a soil biological perspective, even though their soil organic capital has been reduced.

The indicator of soil cover (A4) requires inferences over the lifespan of the system rather than point measurements. Figure 6.3 shows that the nature of soil cover can shift from dead wood and leaf litter in forests to covers dominated by green biomass in a *Chromolaena* fallow. Bare soil is rarely exposed in the landscapes of the peneplains. In all land use systems with a slash-and-burn land-clearing event, soil may be exposed for about 6 months per cycle (or 2 percent of the time for a rubber system with a 25-year cycle). The only land use system in which soil exposure may be an issue is the cassava–*Imperata* cycle, where soil may be exposed during the first 3 months of a cassava crop and for about 1 month per year in all cases when the *Imperata* fallow is burned. Com-

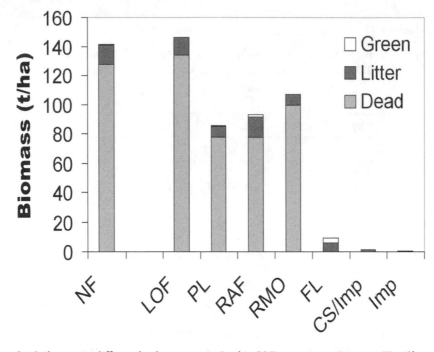

*Figure 6.3* Soil cover in different land use types in Jambi. CS/Imp, cassava–*Imperata;* FL, *Chromolaena* fallow; Imp, *Imperata;* LOF, logged-over forest; NF, natural forest; PL, timber plantation (Paraserianthes); RAF, rubber agroforest; RMO, rubber monoculture.

bined, this may lead to about 10 percent of the time with incomplete soil cover, when the soil is vulnerable to the direct impact of rain and sun.

In the case of Cameroon (table 6.4), the systems have the soil exposed from 7 (long fallow) to 20 percent (short fallow) of the cycle, with intermediate values for the other systems. However, these values do not adequately reflect the fact that these exposure events occur much less often in some of the systems, resulting in soil cover indexes six and two times higher than those of the short and long fallow systems, respectively. Therefore the combined soil cover index probably is much more useful when such different systems are compared.

To summarize all the soil measurements, sustainability ratings were assigned to the different land use types on the basis of criterion A (maintenance of soil structure and biological activity) (table 6.5). The measurements were translated into a qualitative value within the range of 0 to –1, where –1 = problems beyond those that farmers can solve, 0 = no major problems, and –0.5 = problems within the range of farmer management. For numerous land use systems the overall rating is thus –0.5. Only the cassava–*Imperata* system has questionable sustainability according to several criteria.

**Table 6.4** Soil Exposure, Time Between Clearing Events, and Soil Cover Index in Different Land Use Systems in the Cameroon Benchmark Area

| Land Use Systems | Soil Exposure (% of cycle length) | Time Between Clearing Events (yr) | Soil Cover Index (mo) |
|---|---|---|---|
| SF: food intercrop | 19.4 | 6 | 58 |
| LF: food intercrop | 7.3 | 16 | 178 |
| SF: intensive cocoa with or without fruit | 11.1 | 30 | 320 |
| FOR: extensive cocoa with or without fruit | 10.8 | 30 | 321 |
| SF: oil palm | 16.7 | 30 | 300 |
| FOR: oil palm | 17.5 | 30 | 297 |
| Community-based forest management | 0.0 | 100 | 360 |

SF, short fallow; LF, long fallow; FOR, derived from forest.
*Source:* Kotto-Same et al. (2000).

**Table 6.5** Overall Assessment of Severity of Sustainability Problems of Various Land Use Systems for the Peneplain of Sumatra

| Land Use System | A1 | A2 | A3 | A4 | B1 | B2 | B3 | C1 | C2 | Overall | Main Issues |
|---|---|---|---|---|---|---|---|---|---|---|---|
| Natural forest | 0 | 0 | 0 | 0 | 0 | 0 | 0 | 0 | 0 | 0 | |
| Community-based forest management | 0 | 0 | 0 | 0 | 0 | 0 | 0 | 0 | 0 | 0 | |
| Commercial logging | −0.5 | 0 | 0 | 0 | 0 | 0 | 0 | 0 | 0 | −0.5 | C |
| Rubber agroforests | 0 | 0 | 0 | 0 | 0 | 0 | 0 | 0 | 0 | −0.5 | |
| Rubber agroforests with selected planting material | 0 | 0 | 0 | 0 | −0.5 | −0.5 | 0 | 0 | −0.5 | −0.5 | C, K, W, P |
| Rubber monoculture | 0 | 0 | 0 | 0 | 0 | 0 | 0 | −0.5 | −0.5 | −0.5 | W, P |
| Oil palm monoculture | 0 | 0 | 0 | 0 | 0 | 0 | −0.5 | 0 | 0 | −0.5 | Fert |
| Upland rice–bush fallow rotation | 0 | 0 | 0 | 0 | 0 | −0.5 | −0.5 | 0 | −0.5 | −0.5 | Fert, P |
| Cassava–*Imperata* rotation | −0.5 | −0.5 | 0 | −0.5 | −0.5 | −0.5 | −1 | −0.5 | 0 | −1 | C, Fert, W |

C, soil compaction; K, potassium balance; W, weeds; P, pests and diseases; Fert, price of fertilizer.
0, no problem; −0.5, problem that probably can be overcome by the farmer, −1, problem probably out of reach of farmers' solutions.

## CRITERION B: NUTRIENT BALANCE (INDONESIA)

At yield levels of 15, 2, 10, and 0.7 Mg/ha/yr for cassava, upland rice, oil palm, and rubber, respectively, the expected annual nutrient removals with harvested products can be derived from table 6.6 to be highest for cassava (40 kg N/ha/yr, 5 kg P/ha/yr, 60 kg K/ha/yr), followed by oil palm (30 kg N/ha/yr, 5 kg P/ha/yr, 40 kg K/ha/yr), and lowest for rubber (4 kg N/ha/yr, 1 kg P/ha/yr and 3 kg K/ha/yr).

Many farmers in the benchmark area appear to use no fertilizer at all in the cassava–*Imperata* cycle. For such no-input versions the nutrient balance is clearly negative. A clear tradeoff may exist for this land use type between sustainability and profitability.

The nutrient depletion estimates showed that the nutrient for which the most rapid depletion may occur is potassium. If only the directly available pool is considered, depletion within a 25-year time frame may occur for the rubber systems and

*Table 6.6* Relative Nutrient Replacement Value for Main Products of Various Land Use Systems

**A.**

| | Nutrient Removal (g/kg product) | | | Nutrient Replacement Value (Rp/kg) (*a*) | Farmgate Value of Product (Rp/kg) (*b*) | Relative Nutrient Replacement Value (*a*/*b*) |
|---|---|---|---|---|---|---|
| | N | P | K | | | |
| NTFPs, rotan | 2 | 0.20 | 1 | 10 | 20,000 | <0.001 |
| NTFPs, petai and jengkol | 5 | 0.50 | 5 | 24 | 500 | 0.05 |
| NTFPs, durian | 3 | 0.30 | 6 | 28 | 1,000 | 0.03 |
| NTFPs, others | | | | | | <0.001 |
| Timber | 2.5 | 0.25 | 1.5 | 13 | 108 | 0.12 |
| Rubber (latex) | 6.3 | 1.20 | 4.4 | 42 | 2,000 | 0.02 |
| Oil palm (bunches) | 2.9 | 0.55 | 3.9 | 25 | 60 | 0.41 |
| Rice | 11.8 | 2.90 | 2.7 | 70 | 400 | 0.17 |
| Cassava | 2.8 | 0.36 | 3.9 | 22 | 50 | 0.44 |

**B. Data Needed for Calculating Nutrient Replacement Values**

| | N | P | K |
|---|---|---|---|
| Replacement price per nutrient exported, Rp/g [$x/(y \times z \times 1000)$] (*a*) | 2.3 | 12.0 | 2.9 |
| Fertilizer price, Rp/kg ($x$) | 260 | 480 | 400 |
| Proportion of nutrient in fertilizer ($y$) | 0.45 | 0.2 | 0.46 |
| Nutrient recovery[a] by crops or products (above) ($z$) | 0.25 | 0.2 | 0.3 |

Rupiah prices before July 1997, US $1 = 2300 Rp.

NTFPs, nontimber forest products.

[a]See text.

*Source:* Modified and extended from van Noordwijk et al. (1997a).

shifting cultivation as well as cassava production. If total stocks are considered (at least part of "nonavailable" potassium can be accessed by plants), the time frame to depletion becomes several decades at least. For nitrogen, no problems are to be expected for the land uses described here according to this calculation. However, these calculations are based on total soil nitrogen, and only 2 to 4 percent of that is mineralized and therefore available in any year. Also, the calculations do not include nutrient losses other than in harvested products, and substantial nitrogen losses, up to 80 percent of the nitrogen in the vegetation, occur during slash-and-burn clearing of forest lands and by leaching during subsequent periods of low nitrogen demand by the vegetation relative to the nitrogen supply from mineralization. A more refined estimate would have to include the full spectrum of processes incorporated in the Century model (Palm et al. 2002) and goes beyond the current sustainability assessment.

In the calculations for relative nutrient replacement values in table 6.6, the amounts of fertilizer needed to replace the nutrients exported in the harvested products are corrected for (long-term) nutrient recovery. It was assumed that only 25 percent of nitrogen, 20 percent of phosphorus, and 30 percent of potassium fertilizers that were applied were actually recovered (taken up) by the products or crops. Thus, for every gram of nitrogen exported in a harvested product, 4 g of nitrogen had been applied in the form of nitrogenous fertilizer. The $N_2$-fixing trees petai (*Parkia speciosa*) and jengkol (*Pithecellobium jiringa*) included in the nontimber forest products (NTFPs) scenario were assumed to derive two-thirds of their nitrogen from the atmosphere. The nutrient replacement value (*a* in table 6.6A) is calculated as the weight of each nutrient removed, multiplied by the replacement cost per nutrient (in table 6.6B), then totaled for nitrogen, phosphorus, and potassium (neglecting other nutrients).

Most relative nutrient replacement (RNRV) values are below 10 percent, and this indicates that nutrient replenishment would be within reach of farmers if, when, and where actual nutrient responses of the crop make fertilizer use necessary. For rice, the value is around 15 percent, and this indicates a range in which details of fertilizer use (and the various assumptions on efficiency made here) will be important for farmers' decisions on fertilizer use.

For oil palm and cassava the RNRV values are around 45 percent, indicating that fertilizer costs would be a major part of the farm budget if farmers had to balance the nutrient budgets. The high RNRV values for both products are caused by their low price (at the farmgate) per kilogram of product. For oil palm, marketing of fruits instead of bunches could reduce the nutrient exports and hence the RNRV. For cassava only a shift in farmgate prices of the product or of fertilizers could make fertilizer use more attractive.

To summarize all measurements, sustainability ratings were assigned to the different land use types on the basis of criterion B, maintaining nutrient balance (table 6.5). Only the cassava–*Imperata* rotation appears to be unsustainable in all the nutrient indexes and cannot be solved in most cases because of the current costs of fertilizers. Therefore it will be interesting to observe the economic and environmental trajectory of this land use system.

## Criterion C: Crop Protection from Weeds, Pests, and Diseases (Indonesia)

Weed problems are related mostly to *Imperata* (table 6.7), which is hard to control without herbicides that are often too expensive for smallholder food production or plowing (van Noordwijk et al. 1996a). In rubber-based agroforestry systems, damage by pigs and monkeys in newly planted fields can be a serious obstacle when clonal planting material is used because it is more expensive than the traditional planting stocks (Williams et al. 2001), whereas in the existing system, substantial tree losses are tolerated by planting low-cost seedlings at high densities. The natural secondary forest regrowth in rubber agroforests is probably less problematic as a "weed" than the grass or fern vegetation that develops under attempts at weed control.

## Synthesis of Sustainability Indicators for Sumatra

When all indicators are combined (table 6.5) we conclude that

• Most land use systems considered have one or more aspects that need attention, but most of these stay within the range of problems that are solvable at farm level.
• The cassava–*Imperata* cycle has numerous problems associated with it, and one of these (maintaining a nutrient balance) is so serious that it probably cannot be resolved at the farm level within the current constraints.

## An Overall Assessment for Cameroon

The overall assessment of agronomic sustainability for Cameroon is based on the information presented in table 6.8.

### Soil Structure

A significant decline in soil structure over time is observed in intensively managed, short fallow, annual food crop systems. This decline is related to the frequent disturbance of the fallow vegetation, which is reflected in the longer soil exposure and soil cover index in this system (table 6.4). Fire used for getting rid of the slashed vegetation and the soil tillage accompanying planting operations may also contribute to this decline. With shortening fallows, the fallow vegetation itself shifts to thickets often dominated by *Chromolaena* or grasses. Alternative planted fallow systems that fix nitrogen and contribute to the stabilization of the soil organic matter pool may

Table 6.7 Cross-Site Comparison of Assessments of Agronomic Sustainability

| | Soil Structure | | | Nutrient Balance | | | Crop Protection | | |
| --- | --- | --- | --- | --- | --- | --- | --- | --- | --- |
| | Brazil | Cameroon | Indonesia | Brazil | Cameroon | Indonesia | Brazil | Cameroon | Indonesia |
| Forest extraction | 0 | 0 | -0.5 | 0 | 0 | 0 | 0 | 0 | 0 |
| Multistrata agroforestry systems | 0–0.5 | 0–0.5 | 0 | -0.5–1 | -0.5–1 | -0.5 | 0–0.5 | -1 | -0.5 |
| Simple tree crop systems | -0.5 | 0–1 | 0 | -0.5 | -0.5 | 0–0.5 | -0.5 | -0.5 | 0–0.5 |
| Crop–fallow systems | 0–0.5 | -0.5–1 | 0 | 0–0.5 | 0–1 | 0 | -0.5–1 | 0–1 | 0 |
| Continuous annual cropping systems | — | — | -0.5 | — | — | -0.5 | — | — | -0.5 |
| Pastures | 0–1 | — | — | -0.5 | — | — | -0.5–1 | — | — |

*Table 6.8* Overall Sustainability Assessment of Soil Structure, Nutrient Balance, and Crop Protection Status in Different Land Use Systems in the Cameroon Benchmark Area

| Land Use Systems | Soil Structure | Nutrient Balance | Crop Protection |
|---|---|---|---|
| SF: food intercrop | −1 | −1 | −1 |
| LF: food intercrop | −0.5 | 0 | 0 |
| SF: intensive cocoa with fruit | 0 | −1 | −1 |
| SF: intensive cocoa without fruit | 0 | −1 | −1 |
| FOR: extensive cocoa with fruit | −0.5 | −0.5 | −1 |
| FOR: extensive cocoa without fruit | −0.5 | −0.5 | −1 |
| SF: oil palm | 0 | −0.5 | −0.5 |
| FOR: oil palm | −1 | −0.5 | −0.5 |
| Community-based forest | 0 | 0 | 0 |

SF, short fallow, LF, long fallow, FOR, derived from forest.
Scores: 0, no problem; −0.5, problem that probably can be overcome by the farmer; −1, problem probably out of reach of farmers' solutions.
*Source:* Kotto-Same et al. (2000).

reduce this potential problem. Converting the short fallow land into a perennial crop system would also help to protect the soil better than annual cropping systems because of their reduced disturbance and exposure. In contrast, a deterioration of soil structure is expected when perennial crop systems are planted into fields newly cleared from forest. This is associated with the initial exposure of the soil and the regular traffic associated with the management of the systems. However, there is greater concern about soil compaction in oil palm systems than in cocoa systems because of the slower canopy closure at establishment in the former and the more regular traffic needed for harvesting bunches.

## Nutrient Balance

The systems that cause most concern in terms of overexploitation of nutrients are the intensive perennial cocoa and oil palm systems. The potassium lost in the oil palm systems is compensated for by fertilizer use; however, no fertilizer is applied in the intensive cocoa system. The extensive cocoa system is of somewhat less concern because the yield levels are significantly lower. Fertilizer use can alleviate most of these concerns, and farmers are willing to use them if the institutional and financial environments are conducive. Although the nutrient exports from the short fallow and food crop system are moderate, we must assume that the nutrient stocks are already low in a system where the fallow period is only 4 years. Given that short fallows often are planted to subsistence crops with little cash return, the probability of farmers using external inputs is very low. Only the association of higher-value annual food and horticultural crops, such as tomato, with these systems would enable the use of fertilizers. Nitrogen could be supplied by the planting of N$_2$-fixing fallow species. Finally, no nutrient problems are expected in the long fallow and community forest systems.

## Crop Protection

Major weed, pest, and disease complexes can develop in recurrent short fallow systems. The lack of longer fallows that allow trees to shade out the arable weeds, including *Chromolaena,* result in greater weed pressure and the emergence of weeds that are more difficult to manage manually (e.g., *Sida* spp. and grasses). Intensive weed management associated with a prior high-value crop (e.g., tomato) may reduce the weed pressure in subsequent subsistence food crops. Short fallows also allow volunteer crops to survive during the fallow phase, facilitating carry-over of pests and diseases into the next cropping period (e.g., the African root and tuber scale in cassava). Breeding crops for resistance associated with appropriate integrated pest management practices can reduce crop loss. The cocoa systems also face a major challenge in terms of pest and disease problems. If not treated, black pod disease can reduce yields up to 80 percent, and mirids can kill trees. Managing these entails a concerted control effort at the farm and community levels, with significant inputs of pesticides, unless integrated tree management options are further developed and adopted. Weeds are a threat only during the establishment of all perennial systems.

## Overall Agronomic Sustainability

The most sustainable systems appear to be the long fallow and the community forest systems. The next sustainable is the establishment of oil palm systems on land previously under short fallows. All other systems have important agronomic constraints associated with them or lead to possible deterioration of the resource base. As indicated earlier, there are potential solutions, but the financial and institutional environment must be conducive.

## COMPARISON OF SUSTAINABILITY INDEXES ACROSS LAND USE SYSTEM TYPES AND BENCHMARK SITES

Table 6.7 provides an overview of the assessment of three components of agronomic sustainability—soil structure, nutrient balance, and crop protection—for the Indonesia, Cameroon, and Brazil benchmark sites. If commercial logging is excluded, all sites reported that forest extraction was the most sustainable system. The main issues of concern in multistrata agroforests relate to crop protection problems, such as pod rot in cocoa in Cameroon, and potentially negative nutrient balances depending on the specific systems assessed. The nutrient balance problem is greatest in the Brazilian multistrata agroforestry systems based on fruits, which have a net negative nitrogen balance of −109 kg N/ha/yr, whereas the values for the complex rubber agroforests in Indonesia are generally low (e.g., −5 kg/ha/yr) because they are based on latex harvest. Simple tree crop systems often are linked with problems of soil structure, besides crop protection concerns. However, these plantation systems often receive fertilizers and therefore exhibit less negative nutrient balances. Crop–fallow systems vary greatly in their effect on agronomic sustainability. The long fallow systems with low cropping intensity in Indonesia and Cameroon (traditional slash-and-burn shifting agriculture systems) are sustainable, but unimproved short fallow systems with intensified cropping, as in Cameroon, can have a detrimental effect on soil structure, nutrient balance, and crop health. Planted fallow systems with herbaceous and tree legumes can improve soil structural and nitrogen balance concerns. Continuous annual cropping, as with cassava in Indonesia, is problematic at all levels. Pastures, particularly with improved management practices, tend to have a medium level of impact on the natural resource base, although impacts on global environmental issues (biodiversity and greenhouse gas emissions) may be large (see chapter 4, this volume; Palm et al. 2004).

## SUSTAINABILITY ASSESSMENTS OF AGRICULTURAL LIVELIHOOD SYSTEMS AT THE LANDSCAPE SCALE

### FARMER PERCEPTIONS OF SUSTAINABILITY

As part of the characterization process at the ASB sites, farmers were asked for their views on the threats and constraints to various land use options. This is essentially an assessment at farm level and includes elements other than the plot-level sustainability discussed so far. Several problems in four types of cropping systems (sawah–lowland rice, upland food crops, sugar cane, and tree crop–based systems) that were identified by farmers in North Lampung are presented in figure 6.4.

Four common problems were reported for all the systems: soil fertility, drought, fire, and the weed *Imperata cylindrica*. The upland food crop system was perceived to have the greatest amount of problems of the four cropping systems.

### MAINTAINING OPTIONS FOR LAND USE CHANGE

The final criterion for sustainability is the possibility of continuing to farm on a given piece of land, keeping all threats at manageable levels. However, continued farming may depend on the ability to change and develop a farm in new directions. Whereas certain land use practices, such as cultivation of very efficient nutrient scavengers such as cassava, may meet the criterion of persistence for a period of, say, 20 years, this

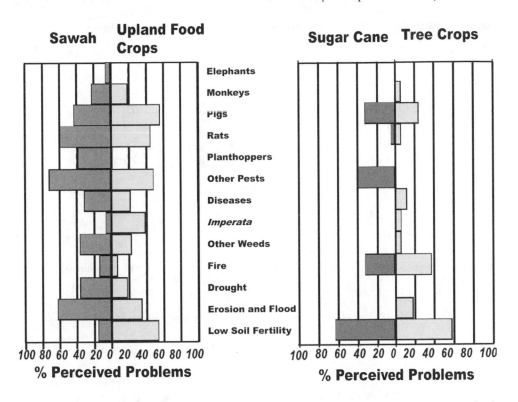

*Figure 6.4* Problems identified by farmers in the ASB North Lampung benchmark area (van Noordwijk et al. 1996b).

practice is likely to reduce the number of future options because the soil depletion it induces will necessitate substantial reinvestment in soil nutrient stocks before other crops can be grown. The criteria used in the previous sections apply to the field-level land uses per se, because they are measurable, whereas a full land use transition matrix can be assessed only by other means. Such adaptive capacity research has to specify the range of options available and the way these options themselves change in time and differ between stakeholders. It is unlikely that land uses will remain unchanged over more than one (or a few) human generations, so it may be interesting to evaluate which options are kept open with a given land use system (table 6.9).

Natural forest can be used as the starting point for all land use types, but in a strict sense it can originate only from forests; community-managed forests, some logging techniques, and extensive rubber agroforests can lead to a return of a vegetation close to that of natural forests. At the other end of the spectrum, the cassava–*Imperata* cycle can be started after any land use system but forms a dead end because it cannot maintain its own productivity, and substantial efforts and expense for nutrient replenishment and *Imperata* control (Friday et al. 1999) are needed to return to other more profitable and sustainable land use types. The various tree crop systems appear to be freely convertible into each other, but extensive rubber agroforests change in character

*Table 6.9* Land Use Transformations That Are Feasible in a 20- to 50-Year Period

| Land Use System | 1 | 2 | 3 | 4 | 5 | 6 | 7 | 8 | 9 | Comment |
|---|---|---|---|---|---|---|---|---|---|---|
| 1. Natural forest | X | X | X | X | X | X | X | X | X | Universal starting point |
| 2. Community-based forest management | ? | X | X | X | X | X | X | X | X | |
| 3. Commercial logging | ? | X | X | X | X | X | X | X | X | |
| 4. Rubber agroforests | ? | X | ? | X | X | X | X | X | X | |
| 5. Rubber agroforests with clonal planting material | | ? | ? | X | X | X | X | X | X | |
| 6. Rubber monoculture | | | | | X | X | X | X | X | |
| 7. Oil palm monoculture | | | | | X | X | X | X | X | |
| 8. Upland rice–bush fallow rotation | | X | | X | X | X | X | X | X | |
| 9. Cassava–*Imperata* rotation | | | | ? | ? | ? | | | ? | Self-incompatible, a dead end |

Crosses indicate where transitions from one land use system to another are possible. See text for discussion of "?" cases.

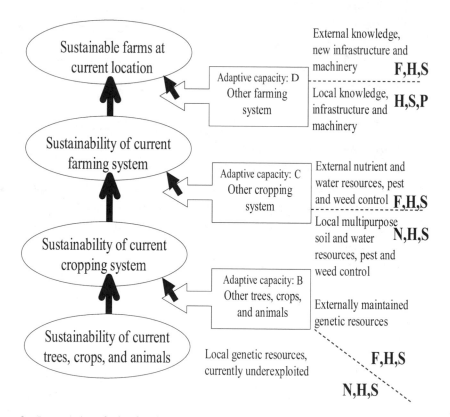

*Figure 6.5* Resource base for local and externally acquired new components that can be incorporated into fanning systems during an adaptation process (five types of capital: F, financial; H, human; N, natural; P, build up or infrastructural; S, social).

once the seedbank of original natural vegetation is depleted and the site is far from the natural vegetation, thus decreasing the possibility of seed dispersal. Table 6.9 strengthens the conclusion that the cassava–*Imperata* system is the most problematic of the land use systems considered here.

The resource base for adaptive capacity (resilience) can be viewed in light of the five types of capital described in Carney (1998): natural resource, human, social, physical, and financial capital. Adaptation of agroecosystems can be based on two mechanisms, one internal and one external to the current system. Agroecosystems, especially those rich in natural resource capital (agrodiversity and biological resources), can adapt by increasing the use of currently underexploited local resources or on the basis of new technology and resources (new crops, new cultivars, new management practices, new external inputs), depending on their financial, human and social capital. An indication of the types of capital needed for the various adaptive capacity aspects is given in figure 6.5. Agricultural research has supported a drive toward the simplification of agroecosystems. This drive results at least in part from the fact that research is less effective in dealing with more complex systems even if they would be superior (Vandermeer et al. 1998). Access to the fruits of this increasingly commercialized research depends on financial and social capital and is less likely in the less endowed parts of the world.

Adaptive capacity based on resources in the current landscape becomes more likely with an increasing choice of new components and resources in more complex agroecosystems, although we are not yet able to quantify how much complexity is needed for how much resilience (Vandermeer et al. 1998).

## CONCLUSION

Our search for indicators and thresholds of agronomic sustainability has yielded numerous yardsticks that can be used to assess land use options at plot level. Production of bulk products of low value per unit biomass (such as the cassava in our example) is likely to cause nutrient depletion of the soil because the nutrient replacement costs by fertilizer use probably will exceed the value of the products. Systems relying on products with a high value per unit biomass, such as many tree products, are likely to be more sustainable because farmers will be (financially) able to maintain the nutrient balance. Systems with low soil exposure times, such as long fallow and perennial tree crops, reduce chances of soil compaction and the subsequent erosion and runoff problems that compromise sustainability.

For the broader issue of farming sustainability, however, we do not yet have a satisfactory set of indicators. Options for future change should be an essential part of the assessment, as should the interactions of farms with feedback loops through society, the economy, and government policies, which may have overriding influences on sustainable land use.

## REFERENCES

Blair, G.J., R.D.B. Lefroy, B.P. Singh, and A.R. Till. 1997. pp. 273–281. *In* G. Cadisch and K.E. Giller (eds.) Driven by nature: Plant litter quality and decomposition. CAB Int., Wallingford, UK.

Carney, D. 1998. Implementing the sustainable rural livelihoods approach. pp. 3–23. *In* Sustainable rural livelihoods: What contribution can we make? Dep. for Int. Develop., London.

FAO (Food and Agriculture Organization). 1989. Sustainable agricultural production: Implications for international agricultural research. Res. and Tech. Paper 4. FAO, Rome, Italy.

FAO (Food and Agriculture Organization). 1991. The den Bosch declaration and agenda for action on sustainable agriculture and rural development. Rep. of the Conf. FAO, Rome, Italy.

Friday, K.S., M.E. Drilling, and D. Garrity. 1999. Imperata grassland rehabilitation using agroforestry and assisted natural regeneration. ICRAF, Southeast Asian Regional Research Programme, Bogor, Indonesia. Also in PDF format: http://www.icraf.cgiar.org/sea/ICRAFPubsList/Bookstore/.

Greenland, D.J. 1994. Soil science and sustainable land management. pp. 1–15. *In* J.K. Syers and D.L. Rimmer (eds.) Soil science and sustainable land management in the tropics. CAB Int., Wallingford, UK.

Kotto-Same, J., A. Moukam, R. Njomgang, T. Tiki-Manga, J. Tonye, C. Diaw, et al. (eds.). 2000. Alternatives to Slash-and-Burn in Cameroon. Summary report and synthesis of phase II. ASB Programme, ICRAF, Nairobi.

Okigbo, B.N. 1991. Development of sustainable agricultural systems in Africa. Distinguished African Scientist Lecture Ser. 1. IITA, Ibadan, Nigeria.

Palm, C.A., T. Tomich, M. van Noordwijk, S. Vosti, J. Gockowski, J. Alegre, and L. Verchot. 2004. Mitigating GHG emissions in the humid tropics: Case studies from the Alternatives to Slash and Burn Program (ASB). Environment, Development and Sustainability 6:145–162.

Palm, C.A., P.L. Woomer, J. Alegre, C. Castilla, K. Cordeiro, K. Hairiah, et al. 2002. Carbon sequestration and trace gas emissions in slash-and-burn and alternative land uses in the tropics. Alternatives to Slash-and-Burn Phase II Final Rep. ICRAF, Nairobi.

Russell, E.J. 1977. Foreword. *In* D.J. Greenland and R. Lal (eds.) Soil conservation and management in the humid tropics. Wiley, Chichester, UK.

Sitompul, S.M., K. Hairiah, G. Cadisch, and M. van Noordwijk. 2000. Dynamics of density fractions of macro-organic matter after forest conversion to sugarcane and woodlots, accounted for in a modified Century model. Neth. J. Agric. Sci. 48:61–73.

Spencer, D.S.C., and M.J. Swift. 1992. Sustainable agriculture: Definition and measurement. *In* K. Mulongoy, M. Gueye, and D.S.C. Spencer (eds.) Biological nitrogen fixation and sustainability of tropical agriculture. Wiley, Chichester, UK.

Vandermeer, J., M. van Noordwijk, C. Ong, J. Anderson, and Y. Perfecto. 1998. Global change and multi-species agroecosystems: Concepts and issues. Agric. Ecosyst. Environ. 67:1–22.

van Noordwijk, M., and G. Cadisch. 2002. Access and excess problems in plant nutrition. Plant Soil 247:25–39.

van Noordwijk, M., C. Cerri, P.L. Woomer, K. Nugroho, and M. Bernoux. 1997. Soil carbon dynamics in the humid tropical forest zone. Geoderma 79:187–225. Available at http://www.iges.or.jp/cc/napiid/PDF/2_LULUCF2.pdf.

van Noordwijk, M., K. Hairiah, S. Partoharjono, R.V. Labios, and D.P. Garrity. 1996a. Food-crop based production systems as sustainable alternatives for *Imperata* grasslands? Agrofor. Syst. 36:55–82.

van Noordwijk, M., K. Hairiah, P.L. Woomer, and D. Murdiyarso. 1998. Criteria and indicators of forest soils used for slash-and-burn agriculture and alternative land uses in Indonesia. pp. 137–153. The contributions of soil science to the development and implementation of criteria and indicators of sustainable forest management. SSSA Spec. Publ. 53. SSSA, Madison, WI.

van Noordwijk, M., B. Lusiana, S. Suyanto, and T.P. Tomich. 1996b. Soil and other constraints to agricultural production with or without trees in the North Lampung benchmark area of the "Alternatives to Slash and Burn" project. Agrivita 19:136–145.

Williams, S.E., M. van Noordwijk, E. Penot, J.R. Healey, F.L. Sinclair, and G. Wibawa. 2001. On-farm evaluation of the establishment of clonal rubber in multistrata agroforests in Jambi, Indonesia. Agrofor. Syst. 53:227–237.

Wösten, J.H.M., P.A. Finke, and M.J.W. Jansen. 1995. Comparison of class and continuous pedotransfer functions to generate soil hydraulic characteristics. Geoderma 66:227–237.

Wösten, J.H.M., A. Lilly, A. Nemes, and C. Le Bas. 1998. Using existing soil data to derive hydraulic parameters for simulation models and in land use planning, SC-DLO, Agricultural Res. Dep., Winand Staring Centre for Integrated Land, Soil and Water Res., Wageningen, the Netherlands.

# 7  The Forest for the Trees

## The Effects of Macroeconomic Factors on Deforestation in Brazil and Indonesia

Andrea Cattaneo
> Resource Economics Division  Economic Research Service,
> USDA  Washington, DC

Nu Nu San
> College of Agriculture, Forestry & Consumer Science  West Virginia
> University, Morgantown, West Virginia

Since colonial times, the settlement of new frontiers has been undertaken to open access to land and other types of natural resources. In this chapter, we take the approach adopted by Findlay (1995) in which frontier movement is described as the process of incorporating a periphery into an economic center through a network of trade, investment, and migration. Adopting this perspective, the recent Indonesian and Brazilian cases of forest frontier expansion have many commonalities but also interesting distinguishing features. We assume that relative product prices, factor availability, and transportation costs are the main economic factors affecting the movement of a frontier.

In Brazil, macroeconomic policies, credit and fiscal subsidies to agriculture, and technological change in agriculture have all acted as push factors in the migration process to remote areas that are, to this date, still sparsely populated (2.7 inhabitants per square kilometer). In this respect, the Indonesian case is very different, with the island of Java having an average population density of 799 inhabitants per square kilometer and Sumatra having 77 inhabitants per square kilometer. This difference between the Latin American and the Southeast Asian situations is bound to have repercussions, through labor availability, on the adoption and impact of the technologies proposed in the Alternatives to Slash and Burn (ASB) matrices developed for the two regions. In Brazil, regional development policies have attracted economic resources to the Amazon through the expansion of the road network, colonization programs, and fiscal incentives to agropastoral projects (Binswanger 1991). The Sumatran case shares some of these characteristics: Annual population growth rate here has been the highest in Indonesia (3.1

percent annually) and is linked to the government transmigration program that has so far resettled 220,000 families (ca. 1 million people) to Sumatra. The land allocated to transmigrants is well mapped and totals 6 percent of Sumatra's land surface.

Continuing the comparison, if we assume that there are two interconnected components to deforestation, namely logging and land clearing for agricultural purposes, it is interesting to note that in Sumatra commercial logging concessions started in the 1970s and reached their peak in the 1980s. Of the total area of Sumatra, 30 percent is under active or passive logging concession today. In Brazil, deforestation is considered to be driven by land clearing for agricultural purposes with much of the timber extracted as a byproduct of land clearing (Mahar 1989). This may be an oversimplification, given the heterogeneity in productive activities in the Amazon; in fact, it has been estimated that logging has accounted for approximately 10 percent of total deforestation in the state of Pará (Watrin and Rocha 1994). Because of its selective nature, logging in the Amazon rarely leads to complete land clearing, but it appears to increase deforestation by facilitating access to forested areas for farmers (Uhl and Vieira 1989; Burgess 1993). Even so, one can safely state that logging, as a component of deforestation, is less predominant in the Amazon than in Sumatra.

High transportation costs between the Amazon and the rest of the country, leading to high agricultural input costs and limiting interregional trade, also affect deforestation rates. This is confirmed by Pfaff (1997), in which greater distance from markets south of the Amazon leads to less deforestation. Transportation costs are less likely to limit Sumatran development because almost all areas are within 20 km of a river and 50 km of a road.

The potential drivers of deforestation in both Brazil and Sumatra occur at different geographic scales, are linked to economic processes guided by different macroeconomic policies, and are conditioned by region-specific factors such as labor supply, technology, and land tenure regimes. Computable general equilibrium models generally are used to capture fundamental differences in factor endowments and economic structure and to assess the effects of changes in exogenous shocks (e.g., changes in exchange rates) on land use and deforestation.

The next section clarifies the modeling strategy considered appropriate for the problem at hand, describes the database, and presents the results of devaluation simulations. Later in this chapter we present the results of an in-depth analysis of Brazil to determine the relative importance of different drivers of deforestation. The chapter concludes with an overview of results and a discussion of their policy implications.

## MODEL CHARACTERISTICS

Thiele (1994) and Wiebelt (1994) model deforestation in Indonesia and Brazil, respectively, using computable general equilibrium (CGE) models and consider deforestation to be driven by forest harvesting for logging purposes, following optimal intertemporal management practices (which assume replanting). The limitation of this approach to deforestation in both countries is that in reality logging is more similar to an extractive process than a managed forest operation. Second, in the Amazon deforestation is driven mostly by clearing for agricultural purposes.

Our approach in both the Brazil and Indonesia models is centered on the role of land as a factor of production. Land is endowed with different characteristics that affect the profitability of agricultural activities. Economic agents know this and use these characteristics, among other things, to determine product mix and production technology on particular types of land. To better describe this approach, it is useful to define some terms and concepts. In both models, land is differentiated into land types on the basis of land cover. For example, there are three land types in Brazil: forested land, arable land, and grassland or pasture. There are two ways to switch from one land type to another. The first (important in Brazil but less so in Sumatra and hence not included in the Sumatra model) is via the biophysical process of land transformation brought about by certain agricultural activities. An example is the transformation of arable land cultivated for upland rice (*Oryza sativa* L.) into grassland or pasture by the extraction of soil nutrients. Land transformation processes were modeled as first-order stationary Markov processes, with land use entering as an exogenous variable (Van Loock et al. 1973; Baker 1989).

Second, land conversion describes a transition between two land types brought about intentionally by economic agents as an investment. Examples of land conversion included in the models are as follows: In the Brazilian case, farmers clear forest to obtain arable land; in the Sumatran case, land can be converted from secondary forest to arable land.

The modeling approaches taken in the Sumatran and Brazilian case studies were also different in several other respects. First, the geographic level of aggregation in the two cases was different. In Brazil, a multiregional approach was adopted in which the Brazilian Amazon was one of four Brazilian macroregions modeled. For Indonesia, instead of modeling the whole country and including a Sumatra component, a stand-alone regional model of Sumatra was developed. Second, because of model size and data constraints, the level of detail incorporated in the two models was quite different. The Brazil model had a simpler sectoral and factor disaggregation than the Sumatra model.

In both cases we modeled deforestation processes as realistically as possible. In the Brazil case, the model adopted builds on the approach introduced by Persson and Munasinghe (1995) for a study of Costa Rica. They include logging and squatter sectors and therefore markets for logs and cleared land. We extend their approach to include land degradation as a feedback mechanism into the deforestation process. For the Sumatra case, deforestation is computed as the sum of the land under logging and the expansion of the sectors that are known to drive deforestation for agricultural purposes (we did not include explicitly a squatter deforestation sector). A comprehensive review of CGE model applications to deforestation can be found in Kaimowitz and Angelsen (1998).

## Representation of Production: Brazil

The production activities considered in the Brazil model are presented in table 7.1, along with the factors used in production and the commodities produced by these activities.

For Brazil, agricultural production is disaggregated by region (Amazon, center-west, northeast, and rest of Brazil), activities (annuals, perennials, animal production, forest products, and other agriculture), and scale of operation (smallholder, large farm enterprise). Regional agricultural producers sell their products to a national commodity market. All factors used by agriculture are region-specific. Agricultural technologies are specified as two-level production functions, with the first level representing an agricultural activity's use of primary factors of production and intermediate inputs in producing output that is transformed and the second level divided into commodities according to smooth, concave transformation frontiers. Each agricultural activity produces several agricultural commodities. This specification of production allows farmers to consider certain agricultural commodities as substitutes, and others as complements, in the production process.

*Table 7.1* Production Activities, Commodities, and Factors of Production in the Brazil Model

| Production Activities | Commodities Produced | Factors of Production |
|---|---|---|
| Annual crop production | Corn, rice, bean, manioc, sugar, soy, horticultural goods, and other annual crops | Arable land, unskilled rural labor, skilled rural labor, agricultural capital |
| Perennial tree crop production | Coffee, cacao, other perennial tree crops | Arable land, unskilled rural labor, skilled rural labor, agricultural capital |
| Animal products | Milk, livestock, poultry | Grassland, unskilled rural labor, skilled rural labor, agricultural capital |
| Forest products | Nontimber tree products, timber, and deforested land for agricultural purposes | Forest land, unskilled rural labor, skilled rural labor, agricultural capital |
| Other agriculture | Other agriculture | Arable land, unskilled rural labor, skilled rural labor, agricultural capital |
| Food processing | Food processing | Urban skilled labor, urban unskilled labor, urban capital |
| Mining and oil | Mining and oil | |
| Industry | Industry | |
| Construction | Construction | |
| Trade and transportation services | Trade and transportation services | |

Product mix and technology choice decisions are responsive to changes in relative prices (via own-price elasticities, which measure the percentage change in supply of a good associated with a change in its price) and are conditioned by technological constraints in transforming agricultural output from one commodity to another (via substitution elasticities, which measure the change in production of one commodity when the amount produced of another commodity changes). Values for substitution elasticities were obtained through expert interviews of researchers from the International Food Policy Research Institute (IFPRI) and Empresa Brasiliera de Pesquisa Agropecuária (Embrapa). Degrees of cross-commodity substitution are summarized in table 7.2.

Given that deforestation for agricultural purposes appears to be important in the Brazilian Amazon, a regional deforestation sector was introduced in the model. The

*Table 7.2* Cross-Commodity Substitution Possibilities in the Brazil Model

| Commodity Category | Commodity 1 | Commodity 2 | Degree of Substitutability |
|---|---|---|---|
| Annual crops | Corn | Rice, bean | Low |
| | Corn | Manioc | Low–medium |
| | Corn | Sugar, soy, horticulture, other annuals | Medium–high |
| | Rice | Bean | Low |
| | Rice | Manioc | Low–medium |
| | Rice | Sugar, soy, horticulture, other annuals | Medium–high |
| | Beans | Manioc | Low–medium |
| | Beans | Sugar, soy, horticulture, other annuals | Medium–high |
| | Manioc | Sugar, soy, horticulture, other annuals | Medium |
| | Sugar | Soy, horticulture, other annuals | High |
| | Horticultural products | Other annual crops | Medium–high |
| Perennials tree crops | Coffee | Cacao | High |
| | Coffee | Other perennials | Medium |
| | Cacao | Other perennials | Medium–high |
| Animal products | Livestock | Milk | Medium |
| | Poultry | Livestock, milk | Medium–high |
| Forest products | Deforested land (agriculture) | Timber | Low–medium |
| | Deforested land (agriculture) | Nontimber tree products | High |
| | Nontimber tree products | Timber | High |

*Source:* International Food Policy Research Institute and Embrapa expert interviews.

price for arable land produced by this sector, $P_{ar}$, is determined by the demand for agricultural land. In an infinite horizon framework, the flow return from an asset divided by the asset price must be equal to the rate of interest in the steady state. Deforesters, being the suppliers of arable land, are faced with this price, and the amount of land that will be deforested depends on $P_{ar}$ and on the deforesters' profit-maximizing behavior and technology. The behavior of agents carrying out the land clearing can be differentiated according to whether forest is an open-access resource or whether property rights governing the use of the forest resource are well defined and enforced. In this chapter, forests are considered an open-access resource, so the returns from standing forest are not included in calculating the profits of deforesters. By assuming an infinite planning horizon when using arable land, we allow agents to acquire full property rights through deforestation.

We assume that deforesters provide agricultural land to be sold to whatever agricultural entity is expanding its cultivated area and that logging, though not directly causing deforestation, is a complementary activity to land clearing (the price of lumber therefore indirectly affects deforestation rates). We also assume that reductions in soil productivity caused by annual crop production and cattle (*Bos taurus*) grazing add substantially to pressure to clear forests.

## REPRESENTATION OF PRODUCTION: SUMATRA

The production activities included in the Sumatra model, along with the commodities being produced by these activities and the specification of factor types, are presented in table 7.3. The emphasis in this case was on disaggregating the regional economy to capture all the sectoral linkages. Unlike in the approach taken for Brazil, each activity produces one commodity, allowing a more detailed description of the links between factor use and commodities produced but not permitting any representation of complementarity (or substitutability) in the production of different commodities between activities, as was done for Brazil.

Among the factors, labor is divided into ten categories according to location (urban or rural), skill level (skilled or unskilled), and employment relationship (hired or family). There are five land types, categorized according to the activities with which they are associated. Secondary forest sustains complex agroforestry systems; perennial land is used for monoculture rubber, oil palm, coffee, and other tree crop plantations; arable land permits the planting of annual crops; grassland sustains grazing; and aquaculture land is used only for fish or shrimp farming.

An important structural characteristic of production captured in model disaggregation is the distinction between smallholder and estate production of rubber and oil palm. This distinction is important because production techniques and land types used by smallholders and estate farms differ greatly.

*Table 7.3* Production Activities, Commodities, and Factors of Production in the Sumatra Model

| Production Activity | Commodities Produced | Factors of Production |
|---|---|---|
| Rice | Rice | **Labor** |
| Cassava | Cassava | |
| Soybean | Soybean | Rural agriculture, paid |
| Maize | Maize | Urban agriculture, paid |
| Horticulture | Horticulture | Rural agriculture, unpaid |
| Other food crop | Other food crop | Urban agriculture, unpaid |
| Estate rubber | Rubber | Rural production, machinery |
| Smallholder agroforestry rubber | Rubber | operator |
| Estate oil palm | Oil palm | Urban production, machinery |
| Smallholder oil palm | Oil palm | operator |
| Sugar cane | Sugar cane | Rural clerical and services |
| Coffee | Coffee | Urban clerical and service |
| Other estate crop | Other estate crop | Rural professional |
| Livestock | Livestock | Urban professional |
| Forestry | Forestry | |
| Fishery | Fishery | **Land** |
| | | Secondary forest |
| **Nonagriculture** | **Nonagriculture** | Perennial crop |
| | | Grass |
| Food processing | Food processing | Arable |
| Mining | Mining | Aquaculture |
| Other manufacturing | Other manufacturing | |
| Wood processing | Wood processing | **Capital** |
| Chemical and rubber | Chemical and rubber | |
| Services | Services | Food crop |
| Construction | Construction | Tree crop |
| Trade and transportation | Trade and transportation | Livestock |
| | | Forestry |
| | | Nonagriculture |

## MACROECONOMIC SHOCKS: CRISIS AND STRUCTURAL ADJUSTMENT

Beginning in August 1997, Indonesia suffered one of the greatest real exchange rate devaluations in recent economic history. In January 1999, Brazil followed suit when the widespread rumor that states might default on their debt to the Brazilian federal government sent foreign investors fleeing. Having to choose between making a stand for its overvalued currency or deciding not to intervene, the Brazilian government opted not to intervene and floated the exchange rate. The effect was an 80 percent nominal devaluation.

In this section we briefly review the mechanisms though which a devaluation can affect land use and deforestation, set out some basic assumptions regarding consumer, investor, and government behavior in the event of a devaluation, and present the results of model simulations of devaluations ranging from 5 to 40 percent. Where welfare effects are identified, they are reported.

The effects of a large devaluation reverberate through an economic system by affecting relative prices. On the supply side, prices of export goods rise relative to those of nontraded goods sold domestically (e.g., services and construction). This prompts production shifts toward sectors that produce goods with a high export share. On the demand side, the rise in price of imported goods leads to a greater demand for domestic substitutes for the imported goods. Given enough microeconomic detail in the CGE model, it is possible to follow the reverberations of a macroeconomic shock throughout the economy, for example, to regional agricultural production sectors and logging.

The basic assumption is that the macroeconomic shock is transmitted through the price system to reach a new equilibrium in all markets; however, other assumptions must be made at the macroeconomic level for the price transmission mechanism to be complete. First, one has to specify the behavior of macroeconomic aggregates, such as the country's savings rate, which affects aggregate levels of consumption and investment. Second, one has to specify the mobility of factors of production, such as capital and labor, across sectors and regions. We will refer to the set of assumptions as macroeconomic closure rules.

Among the different possible specifications for savings and investment behavior, we define balanced adjustment to be a balanced contraction of demand under a financial crisis scenario associated with a flexible savings rate (government consumption and investment spending as fixed shares of total demand) and capital flight as the extreme case in which both the government and consumers do not respond to a crisis but maintain fixed savings rates, and the capital flight resulting from the crisis occurs completely on the investment side of demand. Regarding factor mobility, scenarios are distinguished by the time horizon of the adjustment process devaluation as either short run (this assumes that wages are rigid, so excess supply in the labor market is possible; we assume that in the short run migration of labor and capital between regions is not possible) or long run (which assumes wages are flexible and that interregional migration of factors is unobstructed).

Combining the closure rule assumptions listed earlier, we obtain four possible scenarios: balanced adjustment in the short run and in the long run and capital flight in the short run and in the long run. Because the mechanisms underlying equilibrium in the labor and capital markets are complex and the relationship between factor migration and differences in factor wages is uncertain, the results are presented as a range of possible outcomes. Where in this range of outcomes an economy will actually reestablish equilibrium depends on the speed of adjustment of factor markets, among other things. Where appropriate, brackets containing the results attributable to changes in critical model parameter values are included. In particular, we identify upper and lower boundaries in deforestation rates to highlight the wide range of parameter-specific outcomes that can occur.

## DEVALUATIONS IN BRAZIL

In what follows we present the results for logging activities (table 7.4) and deforestation for agricultural purposes in the Amazon (figure 7.1) of model simulations of a range of devaluations under different model closure rules. Note that deforestation for agricultural purposes and logging react differently to devaluations, and the reaction depends on closure rules.

Logging in the Amazon (table 7.4) increases uniformly with the degree of devaluation in all simulations, with the capital flight scenario leading to slightly greater increases in logging than the balanced contraction scenario. This increase in logging arises from a substantial increase in the exports of processed wood products. From a policy standpoint, the only option to avoid this increase would be to place an export tax on processed wood products.

Deforestation to clear agricultural land (figure 7.1) is very sensitive to the aggregate behavior of the national economy and hence to model assumptions regarding aggregate responses to devaluation. The balanced contraction scenario, with a balanced reduction of private consumption, government demand, and investment, would lead to a reduction in deforestation that would be substantial in the short run, but the effect would be attenuated in the long run. The capital flight scenario, where government expenditures and household savings rates are left unchanged (meaning investment must decrease drastically), would lead, in the short run, to a small increase in deforestation for low levels of devaluation and a small decrease for higher levels. In the long run under the capital flight scenario, a substantial increase in deforestation rates would occur. Even with the uncertainty underlying the adjustment of factor markets to devaluation, the differences in these results underscore the importance of taking macroeconomic policy into account when analyzing deforestation: The types of policies adopted to address the shock are as important as the shock itself in understanding deforestation rates. For example, a 40 percent devaluation causes, in the long run, either a 12 percent increase or a 12 percent decrease in deforestation depending on policy variables; in absolute terms, this represents a difference of approximately 5000 km$^2$ in the amount of forest cleared.

The mechanism underlying the decrease in deforestation for the balanced contraction scenario is linked to the performance of Amazon agriculture relative to agri-

*Table 7.4* Effects of Devaluation on Logging in the Amazon, by Model Scenario

| Model Scenario Assumptions | | | Devaluation (%) | | | |
|---|---|---|---|---|---|---|
| | | | 10 | 20 | 30 | 40 |
| Percentage change in logging | Balanced contraction | Short run | 3.9 | 8.0 | 12.3 | 17.0 |
| | | Long run | 4.4 | 8.8 | 13.4 | 18.3 |
| | Capital flight | Short run | 4.5 | 9.4 | 14.8 | 21.1 |
| | | Long run | 4.9 | 10.0 | 15.4 | 21.3 |

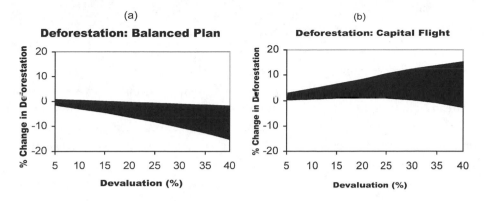

*Figure 7.1* Effects of devaluation on deforestation in the Amazon, by model scenario: (a) balanced plan, (b) capital flight.

culture in the three other regions of Brazil. A devaluation usually is thought to favor agriculture because it produces exportable goods; therefore one would expect that the incentive to deforest for agricultural purposes would increase with the devaluation. This does not occur in the balanced contraction scenario for two reasons:

• The Amazon has a smaller share of its agricultural production allocated to exports; although agriculture as a whole does expand, Amazon agriculture reaps little benefit from the devaluation relative to the other regions of Brazil that produce a larger share of exportable agricultural products.

• Because the Amazon produces primarily for the domestic market, the contraction in private consumption affects Amazon agricultural production more than production in the other regions.

In the capital flight scenario, the main component of demand to be adversely affected is investment. This has two important implications: Demand for agricultural products is not as affected as in the balanced contraction case, and sectors producing investment goods (construction and industry) undergo a dramatic contraction, especially the sectors producing nontraded goods. The combined effect of these changes is to increase deforestation because although the Amazon is still less favored than other regions in producing exportable agricultural goods, agriculture as a whole performs better than in the balanced contraction scenario and, furthermore, the contraction in industry and construction leads to an increase in unemployment. This leads to a larger migrant pool of displaced workers who move into agriculture and thereby affect the movement of the agricultural frontier in the Amazon. That said, it is important to note that the effect on deforestation is extremely dependent on the migration flows; for example, a 30 percent devaluation combined with restricted urban–rural labor flows generates a decrease in deforestation of –5 percent, whereas the same devaluation in a scenario permitting urban–rural labor flows generates a 35 percent increase in the deforestation rate.

## DEVALUATIONS IN INDONESIA

The first step in determining the impact of a devaluation on the Sumatran economy was to simulate the impact of the shock on the Indonesian economy as a whole using an already available CGE model for Indonesia. The devaluation results for Sumatra were then attained by imposing the commodity prices obtained from the national model as exogenous border prices for the Sumatran economy (conceptually similar to the world prices faced by sovereign countries).

The findings are less varied than in the Brazilian case, perhaps because of the absence in the models of feedback from Sumatra to the rest of the Indonesian economy. The change in deforestation rates, represented as the total increase in land under

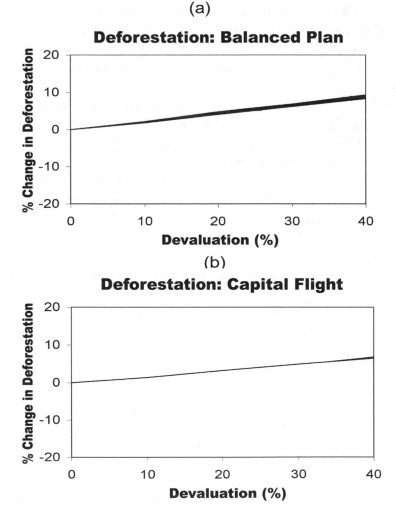

*Figure 7.2* Effects of devaluation on deforestation in Sumatra, by model scenario: (a) balanced plan, (b) capital flight.

logging and estate farming, is presented for the different macroeconomic scenarios in figure 7.2. The area bounded by the short-run and long-run results is very small, implying that they are very similar to each other for both the balanced plan and the capital flight scenario. The reason for this narrow response range is the high population density in Sumatra; labor is not a binding constraint for deforestation and can actually substitute for other factors of production that are fixed in the short run.

In the capital flight scenario, deforestation is slightly lower because capital flight causes investment to fall. This leads to a slower growth in the logging sector that provides an output that serves as an input to construction, which is an important component of investment demand. Overall, the impact of devaluation on deforestation in Sumatra is comparable, in terms of percentage change, to the highest levels obtained in the Brazilian case.

# THE EFFECTS OF CHANGES IN SOCIOECONOMIC CHARACTERISTICS ON DEFORESTATION IN BRAZIL

This section reports the results of the Brazil model simulations run to examine the effects on Amazonian deforestation of government investments in infrastructure, changes in land tenure regimes, and policy-induced changes in agricultural technology.

## LINKS BETWEEN IMPROVEMENTS IN TRANSPORTATION INFRASTRUCTURE AND DEFORESTATION

Large investments in transportation infrastructure are once again under way in the Brazilian Amazon. For example, a road through the Amazon to the Pacific is under construction in Acre, and a recently completed port facility in Rondônia has dramatically reduced transport costs for soybean (*Glycine max* [L.] Merr.) and other products of the region. On the eastern side of the Brazilian Amazon, the "center-north multimodal transportation corridor," including southeastern Pará, eastern Mato Grosso, and southern Maranhão will reduce the transportation costs of grains with investments in roads, railways, and waterways. The incentives that shape current deforestation rates and land use patterns in the area therefore may shift.

To assess the effects of these and other infrastructure investments, we assume that costs are reduced uniformly for all agricultural products of the Amazon. In all cases, a reduction in costs for transportation between the Amazon and the rest of Brazil increases deforestation rates (figure 7.3a). For small decreases in transport costs, one can ignore the uncertainty surrounding the elasticity of the response of the national commodity market to increased agricultural products from the Amazon. For large decreases in costs, though, it is important to know how the agricultural commodity markets react to such a shock. Because data to estimate such elasticities are not available, the results provided here are based on sensitivity analysis: Simulations were

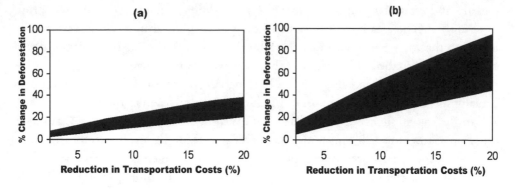

*Figure 7.3* The effects of reduced transportation costs in the Amazon on deforestation (**a**) when deforestation and logging are complements in production and (**b**) when logging and deforestation are substitutes in production.

performed with values for these elasticities of between 1 and 12. Because similar agricultural products produced in different regions are generally good substitutes for one another, this range should bracket the true but unknown elasticity values. Model results indicate that a 20 percent reduction in transportation costs for all agricultural products from the Amazon causes an increase in deforestation in the range of 21 to 39 percent (figure 7.3a).

Therefore deforestation rates can be expected to increase as transportation costs in the region decline. However, the extent of increase in deforestation was found to depend on the degree of complementarity in production between logging and deforestation activities. In the base run (figure 7.3a) the two activities were assumed to be complementary (elasticity of transformation 0.3). If instead it is assumed that producers view these activities as substitutes (elasticity of transformation 2.0), in effect decoupling them in their productive decisions and reacting based only on their relative financial returns, the deforestation rate after the reduction in transportation costs increases dramatically (figure 7.3b). This is because the reduction in the gap between farmgate and market prices benefits agriculturalists more than loggers, so in the base simulation deforesters are constrained by their complementarity with a product for which costs are not decreasing. If this forced complementarity is removed, which would be the case if deforesters decided to burn the logs instead of marketing them, which they often do, increased returns to Amazon agriculture would translate into dramatic increases in deforestation.

In general, as agricultural production in the Amazon becomes more profitable, the price of arable land increases, thereby increasing the incentive to deforest. But this induced deforestation (the environmental implications of which are reported elsewhere in this publication) can have welfare implications. The increase in profitability leads, in the long run (with mobile agricultural labor and capital), to a 6 to 23 percent increase in production by smallholders and a 3 to 9 percent increase in production by large farms. However, welfare effects at the national level are very limited (rural households at the national level gain only 0.5 to 0.9 percent in real income). This is because the increase in Amazon production, except for the share that is exported, replaces previous production from other regions; therefore, the positive regional welfare impact on Amazon development is offset by the negative welfare impact on other agricultural areas of Brazil.

The reduction in transportation costs scenario highlights how changes exogenous to the land use systems can dramatically affect deforestation by affecting the profitability of a single agricultural activity or, as in this case, the agricultural sector as a whole. Furthermore, the dampening effect of the complementary relationship between logging and land clearing for agricultural purposes stresses the importance of the wider context (of which a land use system is a component). The promotion of a specific land use alternative (e.g., one or more elements of the ASB matrix) may lead to unexpected results if the substitution and complementarity relationships it has with other productive activities have not been considered.

## LAND TENURE REGIMES AND DEFORESTATION IN THE AMAZON

The economic literature linking deforestation to tenure regimes has adopted either a partial equilibrium approach (Mendelsohn 1994) or an econometric approach based on the explanatory power of measures of tenure security using cross-country data (Deacon 1994, 1999; Alston et al. 1996). The approach adopted here is similar to Mendelsohn's partial equilibrium description, but the context in our case is one of general equilibrium. Whereas in the partial equilibrium setting deforesters had the choice between sustainable forest uses and a destructive agricultural process with decaying physical output, in a general equilibrium framework, deforesters have an array of additional choices ranging from wage labor on large farms to migrating to urban areas to simply cultivating the already-cleared land.

The assumptions made in simulating changes in tenure regimes must be laid out. We assume in this chapter that deforestation is done exclusively to clear land for agriculture and that by doing so farmers acquire informal property rights to unclaimed land. The impact of a change in tenure regimes is simulated by making informal property rights less secure through eviction. This change can be represented in one of two ways: as an increase in the discount rate equal to the probability of eviction (Mendelsohn 1994) or as a decrease in the expected time of residence on the plot before eviction. In the analysis that follows, the latter option is adopted (see the appendix for details).

The results (figure 7.4) show the change in deforestation rate as a function of the expected time to eviction. The shaded area represents the range of discount rates (15 to 50 percent) believed to bracket the true discount rate of farmers in the Amazon. The lower boundary of the region occurs when the discount rate is 15 percent and shows a slow decrease in the deforestation rates that occur as a result of reducing the expected time of residence on the plot from 22 to 14 years (−18 percent) and a marked

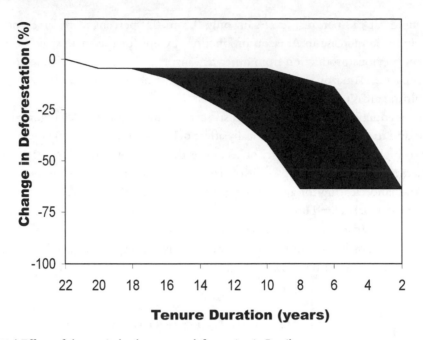

*Figure 7.4* Effects of changes in land tenure on deforestation in Brazil.

decrease from there on (–27 percent for 12 years). The deforestation rate levels off at around 37 percent of its original value when the expected time of residence is reduced to 8 years.

The leveling off occurs because as the risk of being evicted increases it becomes more convenient to deforest previously tenured forest land rather than unclaimed land. A switch in behavior occurs from deforesting as capitalization on property right acquisition (even if unsecured) to deforesting solely for the value added that comes from agricultural activities. An optimal deforestation rate (given the 1994–1996 average) would be around 7400 km²/yr. This value, though far from arresting deforestation, is still much lower than the current trend, suggesting that the mode of tenure acquisition and its enforcement should be top priority issues. On the other hand, if the discount rate is higher than 15 percent, the leveling off will be reached for expected times lower than 8 years (the upper boundary, using a discount rate of 50 percent, reaches the leveling-off value at 2 years).

The assumption that all current deforestation occurs on unclaimed land may cause the results to overemphasize the impact of regulating tenure. If a share of the deforestation is already occurring on tenured land, then this will raise the floor in the deforestation rate because this component will not be affected by changing tenure regimes. Because by construction we begin from an equilibrium point, we can neither validate nor contradict the hypotheses that tenure leads to more deforestation (Vosti et al. 2002) or to less deforestation (Deacon 1999). All this analysis can say is that relative to the 1995 base structure of the economy, assumed as an equilibrium, if unclaimed land is being deforested, then increasing the probability of eviction will decrease the deforestation rate to the point where it is profitable to clear only previously tenured land. In this respect, the results contradict the partial equilibrium results of Mendelsohn (1994), who stated that the possibility of eviction leads to destructive land uses.

The relevance of simulating the tenure regime modification is that it highlights how institutional issues may have to be pursued outside the domain of land use systems to reduce deforestation in certain areas of the tropics. It also reminds us that if a specific land use system is to be promoted, changes in tenure regimes could drastically alter its appeal to farmers. For example, with the possibility of eviction, few farmers will adopt technology involving perennial tree crops because the time gap between planting and fruit bearing can be beyond the expected presence on the farm of any one occupant.

## TECHNOLOGICAL CHANGE IN AMAZONIAN AGRICULTURE

At the level of land use systems or specific production activities, much research has been done on technological change in agriculture in the Amazon. Different farming and cattle-raising systems have been analyzed (Serrão and Homma, 1993; Mattos and Uhl 1994; Almeida and Uhl 1995; Toniolo and Uhl 1995), paying particular attention to characteristics such as profitability, credit requirements, agronomic sustainability, and other factors that can influence adoption. We address the issue of technological change at the sectoral level and examine the effects of different types and degrees of technological change within and across broad geographic regions. Technological change is assumed to be exogenous to farmers but not to policymakers, and although the values of key parameters examined here represent a reasonable range of technology options, they are not based on case studies.

We simulate technological change in the production of annual crops, perennial tree crops, and animal products and distinguish between smallholder and larger-scale production systems. Different degrees and types of technological change are analyzed for each activity. Our reference simulation incrementally increases total factor productivity (TFP) by 70 percent equally across all factors of productions, a process known as disembodied technological change. Other simulations replicate these incremental levels of overall productivity increase but spread increases unevenly across factors of production, a process known as embodied technological change. In these cases, the extent of specific factor productivity increase is inversely proportional to that factor's value share in production. Comparisons across simulations of the different types of technological change are presented in the form of a TFP index (see the note to figure 7.5 for details of this index).

Table 7.5 shows the different types of technological change examined in the simulations. Because it is difficult to imagine innovations at the Amazon-wide level that are purely labor improving or capital improving, results represent a range of possibilities

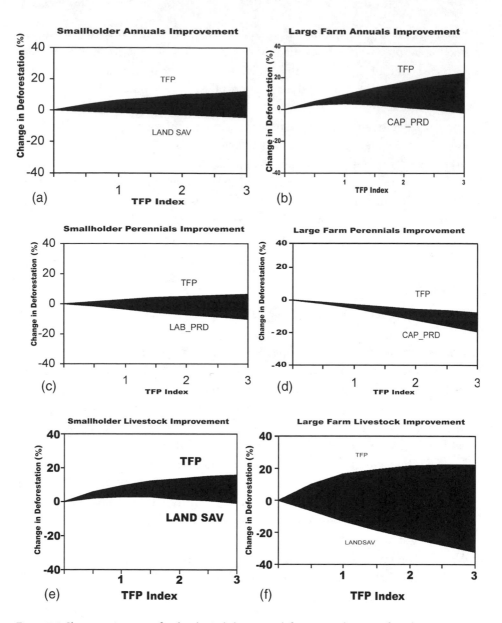

*Figure 7.5* Short-run impacts of technological change on deforestation, by type of productivity improvement and scale of operation. CAP_PRD, improved productivity of capital; LAB_PRD, improved productivity of labor; LAND SAV, improvements in labor and capital productivity that increase the overall productivity of land. The TFP index associated with technical change embodied in factor *f* is defined as TFP index = Δproductivity*f* (factor share).

*Table 7.5* Types of Technological Change

| Name | Comments | Acronym |
|---|---|---|
| Total factor productivity increase | Disembodied technological change: Improvements spread across all factors evenly. | TFP |
| Labor productivity increase | Improved labor productivity: Returns to labor increase. | LAB_PRD |
| Capital productivity increase | Improved capital productivity: Returns to capital increase. | CAP_PRD |
| Labor and capital productivity increase (land saving) | Replicates land intensification: Less land is needed to produce a unit of output. | LAND SAV |

covering all four types of technological change and their combinations. We will not discuss in detail all the possible combinations of technological change; rather we will describe for each activity the innovations that lead to the best- and worst-case scenarios in terms of deforestation rates.

We carry out simulations for the short run (can be interpreted as 1 to 2 years), in which agricultural labor and capital are confined to their regions, and for the long run (5 to 8 years) by allowing these factors to migrate interregionally.

## SHORT-RUN EFFECTS ON DEFORESTATION OF IMPROVING TECHNOLOGIES

Figure 7.5 presents the results over the short run of different types and degrees of product-specific technological change on deforestation for small-scale and large-scale production systems. The upper bound of each figure represents the results of balanced cross-factor productivity increases (TFP) for different production systems (annual crops, perennial tree crops, and livestock); the lower bounds of each figure represent the results of simulations that allowed some factors to benefit more than others from productivity gains and that were most forest-saving.

Increasing the productivity of annual crop production causes an increase in the deforestation rates of both smallholders and large farm enterprises, but especially the latter, which shift resources away from livestock into annual crops on their own farms and also force smallholders out of annual crops and into cattle production. Balanced technological change (the upper-bound, TFP cases in figure 7.5a and 7.5b) increases deforestation on large farms by more than 20 percent for high productivity gains (high TFP index readings). The lower boundaries of the shaded area in these figures represent types of technological change that are least disruptive to forests: for smallholders, land-saving technological change causes the least amount of forest loss; for large farms capital-intensive technological change actually reduced deforestation by attracting resources away from capital-intensive livestock.

Increasing productivity of perennial tree crop production in the short run generally reduces deforestation (figure 7.5d). Any technical change in production of perennials embodied in capital or labor has the effect of decreasing the demand for arable land, thereby allowing arable land to be used as pasture (lowering the price of pasture). The underlying cause of this shift is that perennials make intensive use of labor and capital per hectare cultivated (compared with annual crop production). This implies that as resources are drawn to perennials there will be less overall demand for arable land. A second reason for the decrease in deforestation is that perennials, as opposed to annuals, do not transform arable land to grassland. Therefore, there is a stock effect whereby the amount of available arable land increases, tending to reduce the demand for deforestation. Smallholders and large farms react differently to different types of technological change in perennials: Smallholders adopt innovations that are labor intensive, whereas large farms prefer capital-intensive changes. Thus, in figure 7.5c and 7.5d the lower boundaries of the shaded areas represent, respectively, labor-intensive innovation for smallholders and capital-intensive change for large farms.

The case of smallholders experiencing balanced technological change (figure 7.5c) appears to be the only exception to the decrease in deforestation associated with productivity gains in perennials. This occurs because the reduction in demand for arable land is offset by the increase in land productivity associated with a TFP improvement, which in turn raises the return to arable land. In practical terms, technological improvements in perennials will always have some positive spillover to land values. In any case, as long as the improvement in the productivity of land does not exceed the improvement in the productivity of the other factors, deforestation will decrease in the short run.

There is an expectation that improved pasture management and cattle production techniques in the Amazon will reduce deforestation by making more profitable and productive use of existing grasslands (Mattos and Uhl 1994; Arima and Uhl 1997). The model results presented in figure 7.5e and 7.5f suggest that the effects on deforestation depend on the type of technological change and the scale of operation. Almost all forms of technological change on small-scale farms increase deforestation; balanced TFP changes sharply increase deforestation rates, whereas no change in deforestation is evident in the land-saving scenario (figure 7.5e). The increase in deforestation rates can be traced back to the transfer of smallholder resources from annuals and perennials into livestock activities that use more land per unit value of output. Even arable land is converted to pasture as the livestock sector becomes more profitable. This is the least-cost solution in the short run; in fact, with a TFP index of 3, smallholder demand for arable land is reduced by 43 to 53 percent in all scenarios except the TFP case.

Technological improvement in cattle production systems operated by large farms appears to have great potential to reduce deforestation rates, especially if it is of the land-saving form (figure 7.5f). The difference vis-à-vis smallholders is that large farms already have large shares of their resources allocated to cattle production. By adopting new land-saving techniques, large farms reallocate resources between cattle and pasture management activities, reducing their land needs. When this is combined with arable land being used in part for pasture and reductions in the value of grassland caused by excess supply, the incentives to deforest decrease. Only the balanced productivity gains scenario (TFP) causes an increase in deforestation.

## LONG-RUN EFFECTS ON DEFORESTATION OF IMPROVING TECHNOLOGIES

Figure 7.6 presents the results over the long run of different types and degrees of product-specific technological change on deforestation for small-scale and large-scale production systems. The format of presentation of figure 7.6 is the same as that of figure 7.5.

Extending (to 5 years or more) the time horizon of analysis by allowing complete intersectoral and especially interregional migration of labor and capital generally causes all forms of technological change in agriculture to cause more deforestation than comparable short-term results. For example, technological improvements in annual crop production in the long run lead to higher deforestation rates than in the short-run case, especially for large farms (compare figure 7.5a with figure 7.6a and figure 7.5b with figure 7.6b). The basic tenet is that with all factors mobile land becomes the scarce factor. This implies that the returns to arable land are higher than in the short-run case, creating incentives to deforest.

Productivity gains in perennial tree crop production remain more likely to save forest than gains in other activities (figure 7.6c and 7.6d). For smallholders, the labor-intensive innovations save the most because producing more perennials leaves less labor for annual and cattle production activities. The underlying process is unchanged, but with migration there is no surplus arable land to be used as pasture; in fact, arable land increases in value. However, deforestation is still reduced by the dampening effect of lower returns to pasture land arising from factors shifting toward the production of perennials (which uses arable land). This dampening effect is also present in the TFP and the more capital-intensive scenarios, but it is not enough to offset the prospect of higher returns from arable land, so deforestation increases in the long run if smallholders adopt these types of innovations.

Increasing by whatever means the productivity of perennial tree crop production is a safe bet to reduce deforestation on large farms. The upper boundary in figure 7.6d is given by the capital-intensive innovation, which was also found to reduce deforestation in the short run. The lower boundary is now given by labor-intensive technological change scenario. The reason for this reversal is that in the short run labor is scarce and capital is abundant for large farms, so capital-intensive technological change is preferred by large farms. However, perennials are very labor intensive and therefore in the long run (i.e., when labor availability is no longer an issue) large farms favor labor-intensive innovations. In each case, the preferred option is the one that leads to the greatest expansion of perennials and a decrease in deforestation.

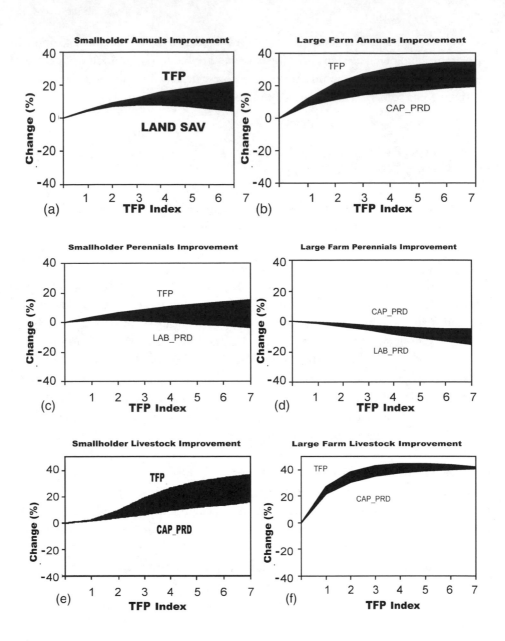

*Figure 7.6* Long-run impacts of technological change on deforestation, by type of productivity improvement and scale of operation. (See figure 7.5 for abbreviations.)

The expectation or hope that improved cattle and pasture management techniques in the Amazon can reduce deforestation rates is supported only by some short-run scenarios. This short-run perspective does not take into consideration the long-term effects of a more profitable cattle-ranching sector in the Amazon. In the long run (figure 7.6e and 7.6f), as resources are allowed to flow from other regions to the Amazon, the increased demand for pasture is met by increased deforestation. In all of the long-run scenarios, improving livestock productivity by any means will substantially increase deforestation. The increase in deforestation rates is particularly strong if the adoption of technological change in the livestock sector is carried out by the large farms (figure 7.6f). The reason for this dramatic increase is that, in the case of large farm adoption, returns to pasture land increase substantially and the price of arable land increases. The increased price of arable land comes about because production of annuals leads to land degradation and subsequent use of the land as pasture; therefore, as keeping the land in pasture becomes more attractive, the demand for arable land increases in expectation that it will be used as pasture in the future. In fact, in all the long-run scenarios, production of annual crops increases alongside that of livestock (although at a lower rate). Perennial tree crop production, also pursued on arable land but not a cause of land degradation, does not expand and in some cases actually declined.

Summarizing the results of technological change scenarios, the best option for reducing deforestation is to promote technological change in perennial tree crop production. This option has the added benefit of increasing smallholder incomes relative to those of large-farm enterprises. However, from a purely revenue-driven perspective, cattle production is the best alternative for both small and large farms. This result is problematic because any form of technological improvement in livestock will lead to higher deforestation rates in the long run. Improvements in annual crop production are possible in some parts of the Amazon and would yield returns roughly equivalent to those of improvements in perennial systems, but the former probably would cause higher deforestation rates than the latter.

## CONCLUSION

This chapter used economy-wide models of Brazil and Sumatra, Indonesia, to examine the effects of major currency devaluations on deforestation rates and then explored in detail the effects of infrastructure improvements and technological change in agriculture on deforestation in the Brazilian Amazon.

A major devaluation of the exchange rate can have an impact on deforestation that is similar in magnitude to that of technological change, but the direction of the effect of devaluations on deforestation cannot be known a priori. In the Sumatran case, devaluation leads unequivocally to higher deforestation rates because of the higher profitability of products exported by the agriculture and forest sectors. In the Brazil case, by contrast, policies adopted to address a major devaluation are as important as the shock itself in determining the direction of effect on deforestation rates: In the long run, a 40 percent devaluation causes either a 12 percent increase or a 12 percent decrease in deforestation rates, depending on the policy response. Consequently, understanding the processes that lead to these different outcomes is important when evaluating the vulnerability of specific land use systems to such macroeconomic shocks; systems producing exportable commodities are least vulnerable. However, the overall performance of agriculture in specific regions can also powerfully influence farmers' choices of land use systems and production technologies.

In the Brazilian Amazon, where transportation costs for agricultural products are much higher than the national average, improving transportation infrastructure will lead to substantial increases in deforestation rates. That said, assessing the effects of reduced transportation costs on the use of cleared land will be more challenging; different products have different transportation costs per unit value, so across-the-board reductions in transportation costs can alter product mix and choice of production technique. The link between logging and deforestation solely for agricultural purposes also affects the impact of a reduction in transportation costs on deforestation rates, as does the potential for the national economy to absorb products produced in the Amazon.

Regarding regional policy, regulating and enforcing land tenure is the best option to reduce deforestation, assuming that current deforestation is in large part occurring at the hands of untenured deforesters who acquire tenure in the process. Regulating tenure far surpasses the impacts of any form of technological change in agriculture. Unfortunately, new tenure regimes are difficult to develop, implement, and enforce in a region the size of the Brazilian Amazon. However, this result supports initiatives that aim to create buffer zones with integrated participatory management, create clear property rights in these buffer zones, and discourage any encroachment into protected areas.

Most forms of productivity-enhancing technological change in the Amazon were found to increase deforestation rates, especially over the long run, when interregional flows of capital and labor migrated to the Amazon to take advantage of productivity gains. Improvements in cattle production systems were likely to cause the largest increases in long-run deforestation rates, especially if large-scale ranchers adopted improved technologies. These systems remained the most lucrative even after technological advances in alternative systems were taken into account.

Technological improvement in perennial tree crop production systems was the only case that led to reductions in deforestation; increased productivity and profitability of this labor-intense product could draw labor and capital away from extensive alternative systems, especially if adopted by large farms.

The striking difference in the effects on deforestation rates of technology change between the short run and the long run highlights the importance of interregional flows of labor and capital in determining the expansion of the agricultural frontier. This distinction is very important in evaluating the benefits of alternative land use systems: A given system may be expected to reduce deforestation because it is land saving or because it diverts labor away from deforesting and activities that make extensive use of land; however, if this system is successful it may attract resources (labor or capital) from other regions and ultimately accelerate expansion of the agricultural frontier. Finally, the asset portfolios of agriculturalists mattered greatly in determining the links between technological change and deforestation; the behavior of smallholders often was quite different from that of large farms.

Unless deforestation is driven by subsistence needs in isolated areas, the transmission mechanisms from nonfrontier regions to the agricultural frontier are many and intertwined. Understanding these mechanisms is important in predicting the impact of policy changes and technological innovations on deforestation, something partial equilibrium analyses are not well equipped to do.

## ACKNOWLEDGMENTS

The authors wish to thank Steve Vosti, Sherman Robinson, Hans Löfgren, and seminar participants at the International Food Policy Research Institute (IFPRI), and participants at the Center for International Forestry Research workshop, "Technological Change in Agriculture and Deforestation," held in Costa Rica in March 1999. We are also indebted to Eustaquio Reis and all the staff at the Instituto de Pesquisa Econômica Aplicada for making this research possible and for their comments. This research was supported by IFPRI and Danish International Development Assistance through its contribution to the ASB Programme. The authors thank the two reviewers, Polly Ericksen and Steve Vosti, for providing helpful comments and suggestions on earlier drafts.

## APPENDIX: DATABASES AND KEY MODEL ASSUMPTIONS

### BRAZIL

The data used in this model were drawn from Cattaneo (2002). The original sources used to construct the social accounting matrix were the 1995 Input–Output (IO) table for Brazil (IBGE 1997a), and the national accounts data (IBGE 1997b). These source were integrated with the agricultural census data for 1995–1996 (IBGE 1998) to yield a regionalized representation of agricultural activities. Household data were obtained from the national accounts and the household income and expenditure surveys. Total labor, land, and capital value added were allocated across the agricultural activities based on the agricultural census. Labor was disaggregated into agricultural and nonagricultural labor and further differentiated as skilled or unskilled. Gross profits in agriculture were allocated in part to land based on the return to land being used by the activity (FGV 1998) and the remaining part to capital.

Regional marketing margins were estimated by calculating the average distance to the closest market and using the ratio of these values relative to the industrial South to multiply the trade and transportation coefficients of each agricultural sector as obtained from transportation cost surveys (SIFRECA 1998).

Deforestation (in hectares) in 1995 was assumed to equal average deforestation between 1994 and 1996. The coefficients for deforestation technology were obtained from Vosti et al. (2002). Estimates of timber production were obtained from the agricultural census. The economic rent to timber was based on a technological specification proposed by Stone (1998). Elasticities of substitution between production factors for industry were taken from Najberg et al. (1995). For agriculture, the substitution elasticity between land and capital was set at 0.4 for smallholders and 0.8 for large farms. These values are judgment-based estimates, assuming large farms can substitute more easily between factors. The substitution elasticities in the production process of agricultural commodities were obtained through expert interviews. Arable land is assumed to sustain annual production for 4 years before being transformed into pasture or grassland. Livestock can be sustained for 8 years on pasture or grassland before degrading land completely. This implies that, on average, 25 percent of arable land in annuals and 12.5 percent of pastureland in livestock is transformed through biophysical processes.

We note two limitations in the data and model formulation. Because of the uncertainty surrounding the elasticities, the results of the simulations are meant to clarify the sign and order of magnitude of impacts of regime shifts and should not be interpreted as precise quantitative measures. For this reason, the results are presented as a range of possible outcomes given the range of possible parameters. Second, this chapter compares the impacts of policy shocks in a comparative static framework; the dynamics of adjustment processes are not considerations.

## SUMATRA

The Sumatra model is based on Indonesia's 1990 intraregional IO table (BAPPNAS and JICA 1995) and on Indonesia's 1990 national social accounting matrix (BPS 1994). Complementary data allowed further disaggregation. For example, provincial crop production data for Sumatra for 1993 were used to disaggregate agricultural production. The 1993 population survey data were used to calculate factor payments to households. Disaggregated household consumption data were derived from the Sumatra household expenditure survey. For each household type, savings were calculated as a residual of income minus expenditures. Regional government revenue was derived from BPS (1996, 1997). Regional government savings were calculated as a residual of revenues minus expenses. A cross-entropy approach was used to balance the social accounting matrix (Robinson et al. 1998). The Sumatra model also adopted a comparative static framework.

# REFERENCES

Almeida, O.T. de, and C. Uhl. 1995. Developing a quantitative framework for sustainable resource-use planning in the Brazilian Amazon. World Dev. 23(10):1745–1764.

Alston, L.J., G.D. Libecap, and R. Schneider. 1996. The determinants and impacts of property rights: Land titles on the Brazilian frontier. J. Law Econ. Organiz. 12(2):25–61.

Arima, E.Y., and C. Uhl. 1997. Ranching in the Brazilian Amazon in a national context: Economics, policy, and practice. Soc. Nat. Res. 10:433–451.

Baker, W.L. 1989. A review of models of landscape change. Landscape Ecol. 2(2):111–133.

BAPPNAS (Badan Perencanaan Pembangunan Nasional) and JICA (Japanese International Cooperation Agency). 1995. Intra-regional Input–Output Table, Indonesia, 1990. BAPPNAS, Jakarta.

Binswanger, H.P. 1991. Brazilian policies that encourage deforestation in the Amazon. World Dev. 19(7):821–829.

BPS (Biro Pusat Statistik). 1994. Sistem neraca social ekonomi, Indonesia, 1990. Jilid I & II. Biro Pusat Statistik, Jakarta.

BPS (Biro Pusat Statistik). 1996. Financial statistics of the first level local government, 1990/1991–1993/1994. Biro Pusat Statistik, Jakarta.

BPS (Biro Pusat Statistik). 1997. General government accounts of Indonesia, 1989–1994. Biro Pusat Statistik, Jakarta.

Burgess, J.C. 1993. Timber production, timber trade, and tropical deforestation. Ambio 22(2–3):136–143.

Cattaneo, A. 2002. Rainforest or income growth in the Brazilian Amazon? The effects of institutional failures, missing markets, and technological change. Res. Rep., IFPRI, Washington, DC.

Deacon, R. 1994. Deforestation and the rule of law in a cross-section of countries. Land Econ. 70:414–430.

Deacon, R. 1999. Deforestation and ownership: Evidence from historical accounts and contemporary data. Land Econ. 75(3):341–359.

Findlay, R. 1995. Factor proportions, trade, and growth. The Ohlin Lectures no. 5. MIT Press, Cambridge, MA.

FGV (Fundação Getulio Vargas). 1998. Preços de terra (ARIES online database: www.fgv.br/cgi-win/aries.exe). FGV, Rio de Janeiro.

IBGE (Instituto Brasileiro de Geografia e Estatistica). 1997a. Matriz de insumo-produto Brasil 1995. IBGE, Rio de Janeiro.

IBGE (Instituto Brasileiro de Geografia e Estatistica). 1997b. Sistema de contas nacionais Brasil 1990–1995/96. IBGE, Rio de Janeiro.

IBGE (Instituto Brasileiro de Geografia e Estatistica). 1998. Censo agropecuário 1995/1996. IBGE, Rio de Janeiro.

Kaimowitz, D., and A. Angelsen. 1998. Economic models of tropical deforestation: A review. CIFOR, Bogor, Indonesia.

Mahar, D. 1989. Government policies and deforestation in Brazil's Amazon region. Environment Department Working Paper no. 7. World Bank, Washington, DC.

Mattos, M.M., and C. Uhl. 1994. Economic and ecological perspectives on ranching in the eastern Amazon. World Dev. 22(2):145–158.

Mendelsohn, R. 1994. Property rights and tropical deforestation. Oxford Econ. Pap. 46:750–756.

Najberg, S., F. Rigolon, and S. Vieira. 1995. Modelo de equilibrio geral computavel como instrumento de politica economica: Uma analise de cambio e tarifas. Texto para Discussão no. 30. Banco Nacional de Desenvolvimento Economico e Social, Rio de Janeiro.

Persson, A., and M. Munasinghe. 1995. Natural resource management and economy-wide policies in Costa Rica: A computable general equilibrium (CGE) modeling approach. World Bank Econ. Rev. 9(2):259–285.

Pfaff, A.S. 1997. What drives deforestation in the Brazilian Amazon? Evidence from satellite and socioeconomic data. Policy Research Working Paper no. 1772. World Bank, Washington, DC.

Robinson, S., A. Cattaneo, and M. El-Said. 1998. Estimating a social accounting matrix using cross entropy methods. Trade and Macroeconomics Div. Discussion Pap. no. 33. IFPRI, Washington, DC.

Serrão, E.A.S., and A.K.O. Homma. 1993. Country profiles: Brazil. pp. 263–351. *In* Sustainable agriculture and the environment in the humid tropics. Natl. Res. Council, National Academy Press, Washington, DC.

SIFRECA (Sistema de Informações de Fretes para Cargas Agrícolas). 1998. Sistema de Informações de Fretes para Cargas Agrícolas: Soja (9/97). Escola Superior de Agricultura "Luiz de Queiroz," Piracicaba–SP, Brazil.

Stone, S.W. 1998. Evolution of the timber industry along an aging frontier: The case of Paragominas (1990–95). World Dev. 26(3):433–448.

Thiele, R. 1994. How to manage tropical forests more sustainably: The case of Indonesia. Intereconomics 29:184–193.

Toniolo, A., and C. Uhl. 1995. Economic and ecological perspectives on agriculture in the eastern Amazon. World Dev. 23(6):959–973.

Uhl, C., and I.C.G. Vieira. 1989. Ecological impacts of selective logging in the Brazilian Amazon: A case study from the Paragominas region in the state of Pará. Biotropica 21:98–106.

Van Loock, H.J., W.L. Hafley, and R.A. King. 1973. Estimation of agriculture–forestry transition matrices from aerial photographs. South. J. Agric. Econ. (Dec.):147–153.

Vosti, S.A., J. Witcover, and C.L. Carpentier. 2002. Agricultural intensification by smallholders in the western Brazilian Amazon: From deforestation to sustainable use. IFPRI Res. Rep. 130. IFPRI, Washington, DC. Available at http://www.ifpri.org/pubs/pubs.htm#rreport (verified 7 Dec. 2003).

Watrin, O.S., and A.M.A. Rocha. 1994. Levantamento da vegetacão natural e do usu da terra no municipio de Paragominas (PA) utilizando imagens TM/LANDSAT. Boletim de Pesquisa 124. Brazilian Enterprise for Agricultural Research: Center for Agric. Res. 6 for the Humid Tropics, Belem, Pará, Brazil.

Wiebelt, M. 1994. Protecting Brazil's tropical forests: A CGE analysis of macroeconomic, sectoral and regional policies. Kieler Arbeitspapiere no. 638. Kiel Inst. of World Econ., Kiel, Germany.

# III. SITE-SPECIFIC ALTERNATIVES TO SLASH-AND-BURN AGRICULTURE

# 8 Sustainable Forest Management for Smallholder Farmers in the Brazilian Amazon

Marcus V. N. d'Oliveira
  *Embrapa–CPAF–Acre  Rio Branco, Brazil*
Michael D. Swaine and David F. R. P. Burslem
  *Aberdeen University  Aberdeen, United Kingdom*
Evaldo M. Bráz and Henrique J. B. de Araújo
  *Embrapa–CPAF–Acre  Rio Branco, Brazil*

The conventional forest management system in effect for the Brazilian Amazon is not widely applied because of political and technical constraints (Hummel 1995). On the technical side, there is a lack of appropriately trained foresters with the necessary skills. On the political side, a legal document (Forest Management Project) approved by the federal authority (Brazilian Institute for the Environment and Natural Resources [IBAMA]) is required to practice forest management. Acquiring this document can be a complex and lengthy process. In addition, the existing forest management system requires substantial investment, which is worthwhile only for large areas of forest. By contrast, most properties in the settlement projects have forest reserves areas of only 30 to 50 ha. The 20- to 30-year felling cycles discourage owners from implementing forest management. Forest conversion yields large volumes of timber, whereas managed forest produces less timber with higher costs. Timber from both practices competes in the same market, with the result that timber prices are low. In addition, policy for the Amazon was originally focused on agricultural systems, especially cattle (*Bos taurus* L.) ranching, and effectively encouraged forest clearance. The net result is that smallholders are more likely to convert their forest area to nonforest use. A change in the dominant paradigm governing forest management is needed if the small producers, such as colonists and rubber tappers, are to become involved. This change is needed to allow the implementation of techniques and levels of intervention appropriate to the scale of the production and the availability of investment capital for smallholders.

According to the forest code, 50 percent of the area of properties with less than 100 ha must be preserved as a legal forest reserve in the Brazilian Amazon. The only legal commercial uses of this land are extractivism and sustainable forest management. Despite the government's efforts to control land use, some of those forest reserve areas have already been converted to traditional shifting cultivation and pastures. In 1994, 40 percent of the area was deforested on farms sampled in Colonization Project (PC) Peixoto and Theobroma in Rondônia state, representing a mean deforestation rate of natural forest of 2.4 ha/yr per farm (Witcover et al. 1994). Assuming the same deforestation rate in 1999 as in 1994, the farmers in these settlement projects are reaching the 50 percent limit that they can legally slash and burn. It is likely that they will not stop, or even reduce, the deforestation rate on their properties unless they can find an economic and ecologically sound use for their forests.

Riverine populations of the flooded areas (*várzeas*) of the Amazon Basin have been harvesting timber for generations. In Amazonas state, the production of timber by riverine populations represents a significant proportion of total wood production (Santos 1986; Bruce 1989; Oliveira 1992). The harvesting intensity is low because only a few species are used and because of the high-diameter felling limit, making the practice as a whole environmentally sound (Oliveira 1992). This practice is also found in the *terra firme* (upland) forest but varies in intensity according to access and market proximity. The sustainability of the system is determined by the farmers' capacity to extract wood and the opportunity that they have to sell it because of the absence of rules and control. In these systems, timber extraction is a seasonal activity and integrated with hunting, fishing, nontimber product extractivism, and subsistence agriculture.

The existence of these traditional forest exploitation methods is proof of the ability of local people in the Amazon to implement sustainable forest management activities. However, the practice has not yet been formalized as a silvicultural system and documented sufficiently to allow its application in a systematic way. The forest management model proposed here is a formalization of these traditional methods and was designed for small farmers to generate a new source of family income. An additional aim is to maintain the structure and biodiversity of the legal forest reserves, conferring more value on forest than alternative forest uses (Dickinson et al. 1996), thereby increasing their importance for conservation. Formalization helps to reduce ad hoc changes in the method when external conditions change, such as drops in the price of extractivist products, economic recession, or third-party greed. In the absence of formal procedures, short-term changes in economic circumstances undermine the long-term perspective needed for sustainable forest production by small producers and may lead to fluctuations in harvesting rates and damaging impacts on the forest.

The ecological basis for this sustainable forest management system, the components of the management system, and their application in a pilot project on smallholder farms in the PC Pedro Peixoto in Acre state in the western Brazilian Amazon are described in this chapter. Preliminary results from the pilot project on tree growth, mortality, and recruitment after an initial harvesting are also discussed.

# RATIONALE AND ECOLOGICAL BASIS FOR THE FOREST MANAGEMENT SYSTEM

The proposed forest management system is based on low-intensity harvesting, low-impact disturbance, and short rotation cycles, which combined may alter the subsequent vegetation dynamics and composition compared with conventional forestry practices. Selective logging creates disturbances and canopy openings similar to those of natural tree falls that stimulate the growth of trees in advanced regeneration stages (Uhl et al. 1990). In contrast, conventional mechanized forest exploitation methods create significant simultaneous gaps (Johns et al. 1996). In addition, because mechanized logging operations usually are not planned, forest damage is greater, with the opening of unnecessary skid trails and excessive skidder maneuvering (Uhl and Vieira 1988; Oliveira and Bráz 1995; Johns et al. 1996). Large gaps may take longer to recover than small gaps because succession starts at the pioneer phase. Pioneer plants establish and grow rapidly, thus reducing the growth rate of desirable commercial species through competition. This pioneer effect imposes a longer cutting cycle and reduces yield. On the other hand, if the impacts of logging are distributed over time, a lower number of gaps will be created at the same time, and it is likely that the contribution of pioneer species to the natural regeneration will be lower.

Many factors affect decisions about the harvesting cycle length and intensity. The final choice is a balance of factors including financial needs, species composition, and site characteristics. Harvesting at low intensities but shorter intervals allows seed production and regeneration because most of the reproductively mature trees are retained in the residual stand. This is in contrast to long-rotation production systems in which entire populations of adult trees can be removed at harvesting. Retaining seed trees between harvesting events helps to maintain the genetic diversity of populations over time, particularly for species with intermittent reproduction and buffers the population against the possibility of stochastic disturbance events eliminating smaller size classes (Primack 1995). Shorter cutting cycles can also allow better biological control than longer cycles because diseased or infested trees can be cut more often. It is also easier to salvage dead trees if the smaller trees are marketable.

On the other hand, polycyclic silvicultural systems have been criticized for the damage they cause to the soil and residual trees because of the need to return to the forest at short intervals (Dawkins and Philip 1998). This damage can be minimized by reusing old logging roads and skid trails and through better-planned and -controlled logging operations (Silva et al. 1989; Bráz and Oliveira 1995). The use of mechanized logging in short-cycle systems probably is limited for both technical and economic reasons.

In summary, the proposed system is based on the hypothesis that low-impact disturbance at short intervals, combined with silvicultural treatments, will create gaps of different ages and permit the maintenance of a forest with a structure and biodiversity similar to those of the original natural forest. However, the longer-term ecological factors that are needed to ensure forest recovery of short-cycle systems must be balanced with the need for a minimum harvest volume intensity to make the activity economically viable.

## METHODS

### SITE DESCRIPTION

The PC Pedro Peixoto was created in 1977 in an original area of 408,000 ha that was later reduced to 378,395 ha. It includes the municipal districts of Rio Branco, Senador Guiomar, and Placido de Castro and is planned for settlement by 3000 families (Cavalcanti 1994). The forest management pilot project is located in two trails on the road BR-363, 80 and 90 km from Rio Branco and involved eleven farms with 80 ha each. Because the forest management area represents 50 percent of the properties, each farm has about 40 ha for forest management.

The nearest meteorological station to the area is the Centro de Pesquisa Agroflorestal do Acre (CPAF/AC) meteorological station at 160 m altitude, 9°58′22″S, 67°48′40″W. The climate is classified as Awi (Koppen) with an annual precipitation of 1890 mm/yr and an average temperature of 25°C (all data from Embrapa–CPAF–Acre 1996a, 1996b).

### COMPONENTS OF THE MANAGEMENT SYSTEM

The formalized systematic application of the forest management practices used by small farmers in the Brazilian Amazon entails the implementation of techniques for evaluating the production capacity of the forest (inventory), planning exploitation activities, and monitoring (Bráz and Oliveira 1996). The management system serves both harvesting and silvicultural treatments (Hendrison 1990). The basic components and operations of the proposed management system and the specifics of how they were applied in PC Pedro Peixoto are described in this section. Also refer to figure 12.6a in this volume.

#### Forest Inventory

A forest inventory is conducted 1 to 2 years before the first harvesting to characterize the structure and species composition of the forest and evaluate the potential for wood production.

A forest inventory was conducted in the managed forest areas of the PC Pedro Peixoto, the inventory was distributed among the 440 ha of the eleven farms, each with legal forest reserves of 40 ha. The inventory was performed using a systematic sampling design, with 10- by 100-m plots distributed along ten lines. There were twenty plots for each area, totaling 214 samples and a total sampled area of 21.4 ha, 4.87 percent of the total area. Later these lines were used as access routes for implementing all activities of the management plan.

All plants larger than 10 cm dbh were measured and identified. The natural regeneration (plants taller than 1.5 m and less than 10 cm dbh) were sampled in 10- by 10-m subplots located in the first 10 m of each plot. The species were identified by vernacular names by the Acre State Technological Foundation (FUNTAC), *mateiros* (local people with great experience in field identification of species), and herbarium work.

In 2000, Empresa Brasileira de Pesquisa Agropecuária (Embrapa) performed an inventory of the whole forest area of PC Pedro Peixoto (150,000 ha). This inventory will be used for future forest management planning in this site.

## Forest Management Compartments

Compartments are established within the forest area that will delimit the areas for the harvesting intervals according to commercial timber volume and cutting cycle length.

In the case of the Pedro Peixoto, the decision on cutting cycle length must be based on the small forest areas, the short time to execute all operations, the limited labor availability, and the use of animal traction for extraction. The small size of the felling area prevents the creation of many compartments and eliminates the possibility of using long cycles (at least when annual incomes are desired). For small properties the cutting cycle may be shortened so that it equals the number of annual felling compartments to create an annual income that allows the owner to pay taxes and forest management costs (Leuschner 1992).

Figure 8.1 provides a layout of a typical farm in Pedro Peixoto and includes ten compartments, measuring 100 by 400 m, in the forest reserve that will be harvested during the 10-year rotation. The compartments are harvested sequentially, with only one compartment harvested per year.

## Prospective Forest Inventory

A prospective forest inventory is performed in each targeted compartment 1 year before harvesting to allow planning of exploitation activities, defining the trees to be treated, logged, or preserved. The resulting map can include other information such as topographic features, the location of skid trails, and preservation areas.

All trees larger than 50 cm dbh are measured, identified, and plotted on a map. Usually only commercial species are measured in such inventories, but considering the small size of the plots in the Pedro Peixoto farms, all trees were mapped. This allows

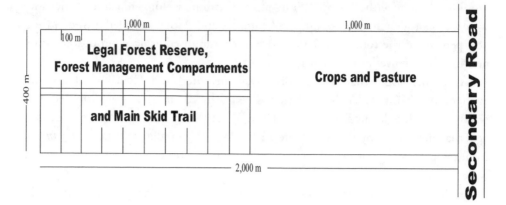

*Figure 8.1* Layout of a typical farm in the Pedro Peixoto colonization project, showing the distribution of the agricultural land (crops and pastures) and the legal forest reserve. The forest reserve area shows the forest management compartments based on a 10-yr rotation.

future decisions about which trees might be included in silvicultural treatments. In addition, the list of commercial species is changing rapidly, and recording all trees on prospective inventories helps to locate the commercial stems at future harvests.

Skid trails are planned on the basis of the prospective forest inventory. For this system, a main skid trail 1.5 m wide crosses the middle of the compartment, perpendicular to the direction of the nearest secondary road (figure 8.1). This trail is opened from the first to the tenth compartment at a rate of 100 m (the width of the compartment) per year.

Some silvicultural treatments can also be applied at this time. The only silvicultural treatment currently incorporated into the management system is climber cutting. Climbers often bind trees together, and when one is felled others come down; cutting climbers sufficiently ahead of time may significantly reduce damage (Fox 1968; Liew 1973). Because of the low harvesting impact (no more than two trees per hectare) of this system, treatments such as protective tree marking (Chai and Udarbe 1977) are not necessary, and the residual trees will be protected using the prospective inventory information (i.e., map of trees) and the practice of directional felling.

## Determination of Felling Rate

Species are selected and the felling rate determined on the basis of species diameter distribution, growth rate, and seed dispersal based on information obtained in the prospective forest inventory. The annual harvesting rate for Pedro Peixoto was determined on the basis of a minimum felling cycle of 10 years and harvesting intensity of 5 to 10 m³ of timber per hectare. This recommendation is based on a conservative yield estimate of 1 m³/ha/yr (Silva et al. 1996). The low yield predictions are based, in part, on the low level of silvicultural intervention that will be used, although it has been shown that usable timber volume can be increased silviculturally up to 5 m³/ha/yr (Miller 1981; Silva et al. 1996). An additional harvesting rule will be applied whereby a maximum of one-third of the total commercial volume (stems of commercial species greater than 50 cm dbh) is taken. A similar harvesting rate was used in Osa Peninsula, Costa Rica, where all trees larger than 60 cm dbh were felled in three cycles of 10 years (Howard 1993). This rule guarantees that there will be at least three rotations of the management system. Predicted yields may increase in the future after the growth studies on permanent plots.

## Selective Logging Operation

Logging is then conducted. Trees are directionally felled, when possible, to facilitate their transport and minimize damage to the forest. The logs are converted in the forest by chainsaw or one-person sawmills into planks, boards, or other products according to the characteristics of the timber and market demand. This phase is the most expensive and labor-intensive component of the entire system. Three different studies were conducted to determine the effectiveness and costs of the different phases of logging. These studies are described later in this section.

In upland forests, such as at Pedro Peixoto, it is also necessary to saw the logs so that animal traction can be used to skid them from the forest to the secondary roads. First the planks are carried to the main skid trail with the use of a zorra (an implement used regionally to skid planks), and then the planks are moved by wagon from the main skid trail to the secondary road. Haulage by animals has the advantage of generating less soil compaction and modification, and less damage to residual trees, than mechanical skidding equipment (Dykstra and Heinrich 1992; Ocaña-Vidal 1990; FAO 1995).

## Artificial Regeneration

Desirable species are planted in the felling gaps and on skid trails after logging. One of the challenges of forest management is to promote the regeneration of species with high economic value, maintain their populations, and preserve their genetic variability. The regeneration of some desirable species is difficult to achieve without intervention (Evans 1986). This difficulty is characteristic of several species that are under strong exploitation pressure in tropical forests (e.g., *Swietenia* spp. in South America, *Khaya* and some *Entandrophragma* spp. in West Africa).

The implementation of artificial regeneration is strongly limited by economic factors and the heavy demand for labor (Thang 1980). Therefore, its adoption can be enforced only by the force of law (presupposing an effective policing) in very favorable economic conditions (e.g., financing, subsidies, fiscal incentives, or elevated return rates) or only at small or medium management scales (Ramos and del Amo 1992). The most common technique is enrichment planting (Ramos and del Amo 1992), but in practice the application of these techniques has not been effective in Amazon because growth and survival has been low (Verissimo et al. 1995).

The artificial regeneration technique proposed for Pedro Peixoto pilot project is to establish species such as *Swietenia macrophylla* King, *Torresia acreana* Ducke, *Ceiba pentandra* (L.) Gaertn., *Bertholletia excelsa* Humb. & Bonpl., and *Cedrela odorata* L. in gaps and skidding trails immediately after forest exploitation, using the planting techniques proposed by Oliveira (2000). The planting will be carried out using a spacing of around 5 by 5 m. Before planting, manual cleaning of the areas must be executed. The farmers plant seedlings about 30 cm in height at the end of the dry season between October and December. No cleanings or other silvicultural treatments are needed after planting.


## Forest Monitoring

Monitoring of the forest responses to forest management is achieved through the study of the forest dynamics (growth, ingrowth, recruitment, damage, and mortality) in the permanent sample plots (PSPs) that were established during the prospective forest inventory. Forest dynamics are monitored in the PSPs 1 year before harvesting and then 1, 3, 5, and 10 years after logging to estimate logging damage and stocking of the residual stand.

In the PC Peixoto management areas, tree growth, recruitment, mortality, and species richness and diversity were monitored in five permanent PSPs for 3 years, with measurements starting before logging and repeated 1 and 2 years after logging. The PSPs were installed in five different management areas, two on the Nabor Junior trail 400 m apart and three on the Granada trail (the first two 400 m from each other and the third one about 800 m from the second). The distance between the two trails is 10 km. Each PSP is a square 1-ha plot, divided into 100 subplots each of 100 m$^2$ (10 by 10 m). All trees larger than 20 cm dbh were tagged, identified, and measured. In twenty randomly selected subplots in each PSP, all trees larger than 5 cm dbh were also tagged, identified, and measured.

Tree crown exposure was assessed following the same classification as Silva et al. (1996): full overhead light, when the complete crown received direct sunlight; some overhead light, when the crown receives some direct sunlight; and shaded, when the crown does not receive direct sunlight.

Species groups were assigned to the following categories: pioneer species that included both short-lived pioneers and large pioneers, shade-tolerant species divided between understory trees and canopy trees, and commercial species that included all species that have been sold in Rio Branco market by the farmers.

Species richness was defined as the total number of species on plots (Kent and Coker 1992) and diversity was expressed using Fisher's α. This index was chosen because it is stable with changes in sample sizes and can be used to predict the number of species in larger samples (Condit et al. 1996).

Mean annual mortality rates (AMRs) were calculated using the formula of Sheil et al. (1995): $AMR = 1 - (N_1/N_0)^{1/t}$, where $N_0$ and $N_1$ are population counts at the beginning and end of the measurement interval, $t$.

Recruitment rate includes all plants that attained the minimum measurement diameter of 5 cm dbh. Recruitment rate was standardized by dividing the total number of recruits in one census by the number of adults in the previous census, then dividing by the census interval (Condit et al. 1996).

Growth rates were calculated using the formula $(dbh_2 - dbh_1)/t$, where $dbh_1$ and $dbh_2$ are diameters at the beginning and end of measurement interval $t$, respectively. Differences in growth rates were tested statistically using Tukey's test after one-way analysis of variance (ANOVA) for species groups and crown exposure. Where there was evidence that the residuals were not normally distributed, the data were transformed using the Box Cox transformation (Minitab 12.23).

## Growth of Residual Trees

Growth of the residual trees and artificial regeneration of desirable species are assisted by removing badly formed or undesirable trees 5 years after logging.

## FOREST EXPLOITATION EXPERIMENTS

### Tree Felling and Conversion of Logs to Planks

A study was conducted to determine the time needed for each phase of the logging operation (tree felling, cutting the log, and converting the logs to planks). The efficiency of the conversion to planks was determined as the final volume of planks relative to the initial volume of logs. The study took place in two managed areas, one off the Nabor Junior secondary road and the other off the Granada secondary road. The data were collected during four logging events, using trees of *Guarea pterorachis* Harms, *Hymenolobium excelsum* Ducke, and *Dipteryx odorata* (Aubl.) Willd. from 45 to 97 cm dbh. A total of twenty-eight logs, each 2.2 m long, were processed by a team of three men.

### Plank Skidding

In this study, the time needed for the different steps in the skidding cycle were measured: the travel (unloaded) from the edge of the secondary road to the felling gap in the forest, loading of the planks, the time to travel back (loaded) to the secondary road, and the unloading of the planks. The time needed to rest the animals was considered wasted time. This study was carried out in two managed areas, both off the Granada secondary road. The data were collected in five skidding events and forty skidding cycles, where planks of four species were being skidded (*Couratari macrosperma* A.S. Smith, *Dipteryx odorata* (Aubl.) Willd., *Protium apiculatum* Swartz, and *Peltogyne* sp.). The skidding distances varied from 200 to 1400 m, and the planks were loaded onto a zorra. The skidding was performed with two teams of two men working with an ox on each team. The oxen used for skidding the planks were two individuals of the Melore breed of age 5 and 8 years and weighing around 500 kg.

## Forest Management Costs and Economic Analysis

Costs were estimated on the basis of the minimum salary offered in Brazil in 1997 of US$100 per month, a working day of 6 hours, a 5-day working week, and a team of three people for all activities except the skidding of the planks, where the team consisted of only two men. The depreciation of the chainsaw was calculated as 25 percent per year and the useful life of the oxen 10 years. The harvesting and conversion of the logs to planks was performed with a Stihl 051 chainsaw.

## RESULTS AND DISCUSSION

### FOREST INVENTORY

The vegetation is predominantly evergreen tropical forest with some deciduous species that included *Tabebuia serratifolia* (Vahl) Nichols., *Ceiba pentandra* (L.) Gaertn., and *Cedrela odorata* L. Structure varied from open (low-stature forest with a dense understory and high occurrence of lianas and palm trees) to dense (taller forest with greater standing timber volume and no dense understory). The structure depended on the drainage and topographic status of the site.

In total, 307 species were identified, from 185 genera and 54 families. The most common family was the Caesalpinaceae, with eighteen genera and twenty-three species sampled. The distribution of the species across the area was very irregular, with some species common (e.g., *Protium apiculatum* Swartz) and other rare species sampled only once in all 214 samples (e.g., *Macrolobium acaceifolium* Benth.).

The forest had an average of 375 trees/ha (trees larger than 10 cm dbh), an average basal area of 22 m$^2$/ha, and total volume of 180 m$^3$/ha. The volume of trees below commercial size of 50 cm dbh was 107.4 m$^3$/ha, and the volume of trees of commercial size was 73.1 m$^3$/ha (table 8.1).

The forest contained a high volume of commercial species, (46.5 m$^3$/ha above 10 cm dbh). This volume is composed of hardwood species used in construction, such as *Dipteryx odorata* (Aubl.) Willd. and *Hymenaea courbaril* L., and species with an inter-

*Table 8.1* Results of the Forest Inventory at Pedro Peixoto Colonization Project Showing Mean Values of Tree Density, Basal Area, Volume, and Standard Deviation (SD) and 95% Confidence Interval for Estimates of Total Volume

| | |
|---|---|
| Average number of trees (dbh > 10 cm)/ha | 375.4 |
| Basal area | 22.0 m²/ha |
| Total volume of timber (dbh > 10 cm) | 180.4 m³/ha |
| Standing volume (dbh > 50 cm) | 73.1 m³/ha |
| Standing volume (dbh 10–50 cm) | 107.4 m³/ha |
| Volume confidence interval ($p > .05$) | |
| Minimum | 171.0 m³/ha |
| Maximum | 189.7 m³/ha |
| *SD* | 71.6 |
| *SE* (%) | 4.8 |

mediate commercial value, such as *Aspidosperma vargasii* A.D.C., *Protium apiculatum* Swartz, and *Peltogyne* sp. However, highly desirable species such as *Cedrela odorata* L. and *Torresia acreana* Ducke were present but with low commercial volume.

The volume of commercial timber in the study site is around 20 to 30 m³/ha. Although the conventional forest management system in the Amazon uses a harvesting rate of 30 to 60 m³/ha on a 30-year cycle, it does not usually exceed 30 m³/ha (Johns et al. 1996). Thus, the outcome in terms of yield will be equivalent to the standard rotation of 25 to 30 years established by IBAMA for mechanized management. The annual felling rate should not fall below 5 m³/ha/cycle; otherwise, harvesting is likely to be uneconomic, returning less than the minimum salary practiced in Brazil around US$100.

Some species were very common in the natural regeneration such as *Trinorea publifora* (Benth.) Sprang & Sandwith, but others were rare, such as *Chrysophyllum* spp. Some species were recorded only in the regeneration and not in the adult population (e.g., *Piper hispidinervum* C.D.C.) because they have a low maximum size or are shrubs. Almost all commercial species were found in the regeneration. Some of the species not present in the inventory samples (e.g., *Torresia acreana* Ducke) were later sampled in the natural regeneration areas of the felling gaps study.

## MONITORING PERMANENT SAMPLE PLOTS

### Mean Diameter Growth Rate

During the study period, diameter increment varied from 2 cm/yr (e.g., *Jaracatea spinosa* Aubl.) to 0.1 cm/yr and even less for some understory species (e.g., *Quaribea guianensis*). The pioneer and shade-tolerant species groups showed significant differences in mean relative growth (table 8.2). The large difference in the mean diameter increment of canopy species and understory species indicates that even after group-

*Table 8.2* Annual Diameter Increment (mean and *SE*) for Species Groups of the Trees in the Five Permanent Sample Plots in Pedro Peixoto

| Group | Growth Rate[a] (cm/yr) | SE |
|---|---|---|
| Short-lived pioneer species | 0.63a | 0.25 |
| Big pioneer species | 0.57ab | 0.29 |
| All pioneer species group | 0.61a | 0.25 |
| Canopy species | 0.29b | 0.03 |
| Understory species | 0.21b | 0.03 |
| All tolerant species group | 0.26b | 0.28 |
| All trees | 0.28 | 0.04 |

[a]Means followed by the same letter are not significantly different (Tukey test, $p < .05$).

ing into shade-tolerant and pioneer species, there are still species with very different growth patterns in the groups.

Crown exposure had a strong influence on diameter increment, independent of ecological grouping. On the PSPs, the variation in mean diameter increment resulting from crown exposure was from 0.47 cm/yr (trees with full overhead sunlight) to 0.19 cm/yr (shaded trees). Trees that only received some direct sunlight had a mean growth rate of 0.34 cm/yr (table 8.3).

Diameter increment was not affected by diameter class when analyzed within crown exposure classes. The expectation that diameter increment increases with tree size may exist because most of the slow-growing trees die when they are small and because the big tree class includes no understory species (Swaine et al. 1987).

*Table 8.3* Mean Annual Diameter Increment by Diameter Class and Crown Illumination on the Permanent Sample Plots at Pedro Peixoto

| Diameter Class | Full Overhead Light | | Some Overhead Light | | Shaded | |
|---|---|---|---|---|---|---|
| | Growth Rate (cm/yr) | SE | Growth Rate (cm/yr) | SE | Growth Rate (cm/yr) | SE |
| 5–10 | 0.42 | 0.05 | 0.29 | 0.06 | 0.20 | 0.02 |
| 10–19.9 | 0.57 | 0.11 | 0.43 | 0.04 | 0.21 | 0.01 |
| 20–29.9 | 0.38 | 0.03 | 0.32 | 0.02 | 0.25 | 0.02 |
| 30–39.9 | 0.50 | 0.05 | 0.30 | 0.02 | 0.32 | 0.04 |
| 40–49.9 | 0.40 | 0.06 | 0.37 | 0.05 | 0.36 | 0.10 |
| 50–59.9 | 0.55 | 0.07 | 0.34 | 0.01 | 0.22 | 0.08 |
| >60.0 | 0.45 | 0.04 | — | — | — | — |
| Average for all plants[a] | 0.46a | 0.18 | 0.34b | 0.06 | 0.20c | 0.03 |

[a]Means followed by different letters are significantly different (Tukey test, $p < .05$)

The annual diameter increments recorded here were similar to other values obtained in tropical forests (e.g. Okali and Ola-Adams 1988; Chiew and Garcia 1989; Rai 1989; Silva et al. 1996), showing an average of 0.27 cm/yr for the plants measured on all PSPS in the period (CPAF/AC and PC Peixoto).

The effect of crown exposure on the growth rate of trees is well known and has been reported before (e.g., Silva et al. 1989; Silva and Whitmore 1990). However, the results presented in this work demonstrate that a large increase (of up to 100 percent) in the mean annual diameter increment can be expected after a change of the crown exposure of a tree (table 8.3). This finding provides strong support for the application of silvicultural treatments in the region.

## Stand Basal Area Increment

The total stand basal area in the PSPS before logging was 24.28 m²/ha, and that of the commercial species was 5.96 m²/ha. The logging of the areas caused a reduction in these to 22.93 and 4.89 m²/ha, respectively. Two years after logging the mean total stand basal area was 23.12 m²/ha, with 5.33 m²/ha for the commercial species. These changes represent a mean annual increment of 0.09 m²/ha/yr (0.76 m³/ha/yr) for the total stand basal area and 0.13 m²/ha/yr (1.06 m³/ha/yr) for the commercial species.

The greater volume increment of the commercial species (1.06 m³/ha/yr) in the PSPS at PC Pedro Peixoto compared with the total volume increment (0.76 m³/ha/yr) can be interpreted as an increase in the population of the commercial species in the total volume in the forest. This might be an affect of directional felling, which aimed to reduce the environmental impact of logging and the protection of residual trees of commercial and potential species. The volume increment of commercial species was compatible with the logging intensity and cycle length proposed.

## Mortality and Recruitment Rates

Tree mortality immediately after logging was 3.7 percent and 2 years after was 3.2 percent per year. The average for the period was 3.0 percent per year. A peak in the mortality was observed from 1998 to 1999 (4.0 percent), which might have been influenced by the El Niño event that year because 1 year after logging the mortality was only 2.2 (figure 8.2).

High recruitment rates of thirty-six plants per hectare per year in the first 2 years after logging were found in the pilot project. This rate is high partly because it included all trees above 5 cm dbh. Because recruitment considered only trees larger than 5 cm dbh, the time of the study was insufficient to include the cohort of trees that germinated immediately after the logging. Thus, an increase in the recruitment rates in those areas may be expected in the next few years.

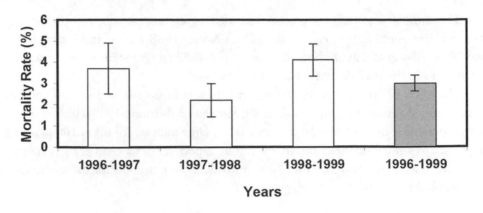

*Figure 8.2* Mortality of trees >5 cm dbh in the five permanent sample plots immediately after logging (1996–1997), 1 yr (1997–1998), and 2 yr (1998–1999) after logging, and the mean rate *(gray bar)* for the 2 yr after logging (1996–1999). Lines indicate *SD*.

## Damage by Timber Exploitation and Natural Causes

In this study, logging damage for all trees was estimated from the basal area of trees that fell or had their crowns destroyed in or around felling gaps (Oliveira and Bráz 1995). Therefore, it includes even the trees that fell as a result of natural causes (e.g., high winds and storms); logging operations were considered responsible by increasing the tree's crown exposure.

The damage caused by the low-impact forest management logging operations (*sensu* Oliveira and Bráz 1995) affected 1.21 m²/ha or 5.1 percent of the stand basal area 1 year after logging. The damage caused by natural causes (e.g., wind and storms) in the same period was 1.02 m²/ha, or 4.3 percent of the stand basal area (figure 8.3). The canopy opening caused by the harvesting was minimized by the low harvest intensity (two trees per hectare) and the use of oxen to skid the planks. The damage caused by logging was greater in the first years after logging, probably because of the death of damaged trees. Two years after logging there were still some effect of the logging, but the damage to the forest from natural causes was higher. The damage produced by natural causes showed a tendency to increase after the harvesting, from 0.61 m²/ha 1 year before to 1.61 m²/ha 2 years after logging (figure 8.3). The increased damage can be associated with the logging impact but was probably also associated with the fact that 1998 was an El Niño year, with more frequent and stronger storms in the area.

## Species Richness and Diversity

Two years after logging the number of species was lower in the managed area than before harvesting (235 and 259, respectively). The density of stems of commercial species larger than 5 cm dbh was similar before and 2 years after logging and therefore

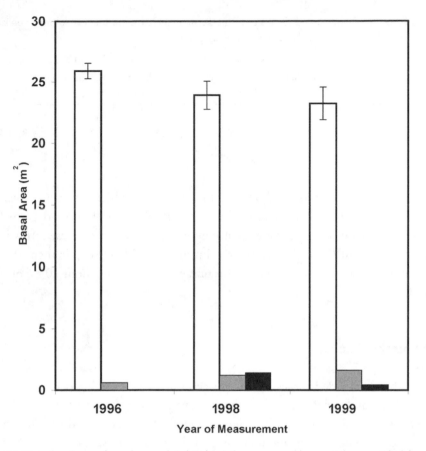

*Figure 8.3* Mean basal area of nondamaged *(white bars)*, damage caused by natural causes *(dark bars)*, and damage caused by logging *(light bars)*, before logging (1996), 1 yr (1998), and 2 yr (1999) after logging. Lines indicate *SE*.

apparently was not affected by a harvesting intensity of one or two trees per hectare. Fisher's index varied from around 84 before harvesting to 81 after logging (table 8.4). The variation in species richness and diversity before and after logging was too low to be considered significant. It is possible that diversity will increase above that before management started because opportunities for invasion by pioneer species increases with canopy opening.

## FOREST EXPLOITATION EXPERIMENTS: PRELIMINARY RESULTS

### Tree Felling and Conversion of Logs to Planks

The efficiency of conversion (in volume terms) of logs to planks was between 61 and 41 percent for the biggest and smallest trees, respectively, with an average of around 50 percent. The total time to convert 1 m³ was 5.1 work-hours. For a 6-hour work day,

*Table 8.4* Species Richness and Diversity in the Permanent Sample Plots of Colonization Project Pedro Peixoto Before and 2 Years After Logging

| | Total Number of Stems | Number of Stems of Commercial Species | Total Number of Species | Number of Commercial Species | Fisher's α Based on All Species |
|---|---|---|---|---|---|
| Before logging | 1737 | 265 | 259 | 35 | 84.3 |
| Two years after logging | 1390 | 225 | 235 | 32 | 81.1 |

a team of three people produced 3.6 m³ of sawn timber, which represents a very low productivity even when compared with that of a small sawmill (around 10 m³/day). On the other hand, because the annual potential production of these farms is only about 40 m³ (10 m³/ha × 4 ha/yr), the maximum annual labor requirement therefore is only about 18 work-days to convert this unsawn timber into about 20 m³ of planks (table 8.5).

## Skidding the Planks

The number of skidded pieces varied between one to four per ox per trip according to their shape and weight. The load therefore varied from around 0.19 m³ (*Dipteryx odorata* [Aubl.] Willd.) to 0.39 m³ (*Couratari macrosperma* A. S. Smith), with an average of 0.28 m³. The loading and unloading of the zorra also were strongly affected by the shape and specific weight of the wood. The pace of the oxen was approximately 4 km/hr and was kept constant even when the skidding distance increased from 200 to 1200 m. However, when the distance increased to 1400 m the time needed to load and unload the zorra was not long enough to rest the animals for continuous operation. The total volume skidded in 1 day by a team of two men and one ox varied according to skidding distance, from 1.14 m³ (skidding distance 1400 m) to 3.36 m³ (skidding distance 250 m) (table 8.6).

*Table 8.5* Work-Hours Needed to Complete Each of the Phases Involved in Felling Trees and Converting the Timber into Planks

| Phase | Time for the Complete Tree (work-hours, mean [SD]) | Time for 1 m³ (work-hours, mean [SD]) |
|---|---|---|
| Cutting the tree | 0.5 (0.20) | 0.1 |
| Cutting the logs | 1.0 (0.07) | 0.2 |
| Converting logs to planks | 23.0 (0.80) | 3.5 |
| Chainsaw maintenance | 6.0 (0.88) | 0.9 |
| Wasted time | 1.8 (0.32) | 0.4 |
| Total time | 32.3 (1.97) | 5.1 |

*Table 8.6* Breakdown of the Performance and Volumes Skidded by Two Teams of Two Men with One Ox per Team over Three Skidding Distances (200, 1200, and 1400 m) in the Managed Forest of the Pedro Peixoto Colonization Project

| Performance and Volume | Mean | SD | Mean | SD | Mean | SD |
|---|---|---|---|---|---|---|
| Skidding Distance (m) | 200 | | 1200 | | 1400 | |
| Effective work day average (work-hours) | 13.7 | | 11.00 | | 12.3 | |
| Total wasted time per day (work-hours)[a] | 0.5 | | 1.0 | | 2.0 | |
| Average time for complete cycle (work-hours) | 1.1 | 0.19 | 1.7 | 0.13 | 1.1 | 0.45 |
| Number of cycles per day | 12 | | 6 | | 6 | |
| Average volume skidded per cycle (m³) | 0.28 | 0.07 | 0.28 | 0.04 | 0.19 | 0.07 |
| Average volume skidded per hour (m³) | 0.43 | | 0.26 | | 0.13 | |
| Total volume skidded per day (m³) | 3.36 | | 1.68 | | 1.14 | |

[a]The time to rest the ox was counted as wasted time.

## Costs and Economic Analysis of the Proposed Forest Management System

The production costs were between US$33.5 and US$35.5/m³ of sawn planks at the roadside before transport to the market (table 8.7). Considering the costs of transportation, at around US$15/m³, the total costs would be around US$50/m³. The current market price for wood in Rio Branco varies between US$100 and 150/m³, according to species and the quality of the planks. Therefore, even with the low level of technology and experience available to the farmers for this activity, it was possible to achieve ratio of benefits to costs of around 2:1 (table 8.7). In a similar small-scale forest management system in Nicaragua, Castañeda et al. (1995) found a return of US$47 per work day and production costs around US$43 to US$65/m³.

*Table 8.7* Mean Cost of Each Phase of the Forest Management System per Cubic Meter of Harvested Timber

| Forest Management Phase | Cost (US$) |
|---|---|
| Trail opening | 4.2 |
| Prospective inventory | 1.4 |
| Silvicultural treatment | 0.8 |
| Felling and converting logs to planks | 19.9 |
| Skidding with animals | 7.1 |
| Transportation | 15.0 |
| Total | 48.4 |

# IMPLICATIONS FOR THE FOREST MANAGEMENT SYSTEM

## FOREST EXPLOITATION AND DYNAMICS AFTER LOGGING

Production is generally quite low in lightly exploited forests without silvicultural treatments (De Graaf 1986). The increased growth of the trees remaining after harvesting tends to disappear after only 3 to 4 years after the harvesting (Silva et al. 1989). Therefore, harvesting timber in a simple polycyclic system and leaving the forest to regenerate without further silvicultural assistance, such as enrichment plantings and refinement, is not a satisfactory approach for maintaining forest productivity (De Graaf 1986).

The implementation of liana cutting, directional felling, and planning the skid trails in this management system reduces the damage caused by logging and extraction and contributes to the maintenance of forest productivity (Pinard and Putz 1996). Additional silvicultural treatments should be considered, such as the elimination of badly formed trees, refinement of undesirable species, crown liberation (for commercial species), and gap liberation (*sensu* Kuusipalo et al. 1996). The goal of refinement should not be to eradicate undesirable species but to reduce their proportion and competitiveness in the stand (De Graaf 1986).

The proposed system will facilitate the application of silvicultural treatments, which are planned as part of the conventional system. Because of their high labor, demand and costs usually are not executed. Farmers regularly enter the forest management area on their properties during the work day for hunting, fishing, and rubber tree tapping. Therefore, it would be a simple matter to carry out the silvicultural treatments proposed here as part of the daily work schedule.

The use of the zorra over long distances reduces the productivity of the skidding phase. Alternatively, a small wagon pulled by one ox for the primary transport of the planks from the main skid trail to the edge of the secondary roads limits the skidding by zorra to the distance from the felled tree to the main skid trail, or a maximum journey of 200 m. This does not compromise the productivity of the overall operation.

Acquisition of more data from PSPs will allow the system to be fine-tuned by calculations of future harvest rates and the length of future felling cycles. This phase may be executed by a partnership between research and teaching institutes and the local people. The system also allows ongoing modifications of the basic model according to feedback provided through monitoring and data acquisition.

## ECONOMIC AND SOCIAL BENEFITS: LIMITATIONS AND STRENGTHS OF THE PROPOSED SYSTEM

It must be recognized that the system has a low profitability when compared with the yields obtained by mechanized forest management. A low profitability is to be expected for a system designed to be applied in communities with a shortage of investment capital. In this case, the social benefits obtained by returning low profits to the colonists rather than higher profits to forestry companies can be used to justify the application of the system. On the other hand, the other available land use options for small farmers and colonists (shifting cultivation, extractivism, and small-scale cattle ranching) also usually return low profits (Vosti et al. 2001).

The price of timber is likely to increase in the future because of the rise in the demand for tropical timber worldwide and the restriction in supply, especially of the more valuable timbers. The constant restrictions on the availability of the timber of certain highly valued species, combined with international pressure for preservation of some of these species, has created a strong incentive for introducing new species to the market. There is also a potential market for plywood species (e.g., *Ceiba* spp.), which was not considered because of the low prices in the local market for the wood sold in logs. The group of commercial species is changing quickly. Therefore the current standing stock of timber represents an investment rather like a savings account.

The small property, as a unit of production, does not prevent collective or cooperative agreements between neighboring proprietors. Indeed, the aggregation of producers into larger units may facilitate the acquisition of new technologies (e.g., one-person sawmills, oxen, and small tractors), result in increased prices in local markets, and reduce the cost of overheads such as transport. Collective working might generate a substantial increase in the yields from forest management, and within a short time the profits generated by the forest management as proposed here will increase significantly.

A potential problem with forest management is the effects it can have on the fauna, changing the abundance of individual species, their food availability, the distribution of microclimate or other environmental conditions and changes in competitive relationships. These changes also could affect pollination, seed production, and seed dispersal (e.g., mahogany in Budongo forest in Uganda; Plumptre 1995), which are usually correlated with logging intensity (e.g., seed predators in Gorupi Forest Reserve). These effects usually tend to decrease over time (e.g., number of species of understory birds in Kerala National Park in Uganda; Drauzoa 1998).

In the case of PC Peixoto, the impact of the management on the fauna probably will be minimized by the low harvesting intensity, the high number of commercial species (diluting the effect of reducing the density of a single species, such as the exploitation of mahogany in Pará State East Amazon; Verissimo et al. 1995), and the use of animal traction instead of mechanized log extraction. In addition, hunting throughout the year is a common practice among most of the farmers, which might have a much higher impact on the fauna and seed dispersal (Guariguata and Pinard 1998) than the forest management, which is restricted in space (the compartment) and time (the cycle length of 10 years).

## FUTURE PROSPECTS

Small-scale forest management provides an opportunity to fill a gap in land use in the Amazon by allowing small farmers to use the forest reserves on their properties in an economical and sustainable way. Forest management will help to maintain and preserve these reserves, which are currently under strong pressure to be converted to pastures and shifting cultivation.

It will be necessary to invest in farmer training to improve future yields. Additional time and work rationalization studies are needed and can be achieved by monitoring of the forest management activities involved in the forest management system. All forest management activities must be performed by the farmers themselves and, where possible, collectively. This avoids the costs of contracting the work to a third party.

To consolidate this proposal, some changes to forest legislation will be necessary, and policies must be implemented to enforce and promote these changes. A specific legislative framework covering inspection and implementation of management plans on small properties was approved in 1998. This legislation established the use of short cycles and animal traction by IBAMA agencies and provides promise for future sustained forest management by smallholders.

## ACKNOWLEDGMENTS

We wish to acknowledge the support of the ASB project and the Environment National Fund for equipment and field team funding.

## REFERENCES

Bráz, E.M., and M.V.N. d'Oliveira. 1995. Arraste em floresta tropical: Análise para a identificação dos parâmetros ideais. pp. 222–237. *In* II Simpósio Brasileiro sobre Colheita e Transporte Florestal. Salvador, Brazil. Soc. de Investigaçosa, Dep. de Engenharia Florestal, Univ. Fed. de Viçosa.

Bráz, E.M., and M.V.N. d'Oliveira. 1996. Planning to reduce damage. Trop. For. Update 6(3):13–14.

Bruce, R.W. 1989. Log supply in Amazonas state Brazil, availability and constraints to utilisation. Report to the Int. Tropical Timber Organization, Yokohama, Japan.

Castañeda, A., F. Carrera, and J. Flores. 1995. Extraccion con bueyes y aserrio con motosierra de marco: Una alternativa para el manejo florestal comunitario. Estudios de caso en el Adi "La Lupe," Rio San Juan, Nicaragua. Univ. Centro Americana–Proyecto Tropico Umido/ Sci. d'Anticipation Reconnaissance Evaluation Contrôle (UCA/SAREC).

Cavalcanti, T.J. da S. 1994. Colonização no Acre: Uma análise socio-econômica do projeto de assentamento dirigido Pedro Peixoto. Tese de Mestrado, não publicada. Univ. Federal do Ceará-Centro de Ciências Agrárias, Fortaleza, Brasil.

Chai, D.N.P., and M.P. Udarbe. 1977. The effectiveness of current silvicultural practice in Sabah. Malays. For. 40(1):27–35.

Chiew, K.Y., and A. Garcia. 1989. Growth and yield studies in the Yayasan Sabah forest concession area. pp. 192–205. *In* H.T. Chan and S. Appanah (eds.) Proceedings of the Seminar on Growth and Yield in Tropical Mixed/Moist Forest, Forest Res. Inst., Kuala Lumpur, Malaysia, 20–24 June 1988. For. Res. Inst., Malaysia.

Condit, R., S.P. Hubbell, J.V. Lafrankie, R. Sukumar, N. Manokaran, R.B.F. Foster, et al. 1996. Species–area and species–individual relationships for tropical trees: A comparison of three 50-ha plots. J. Ecol. 84:549–562.

Dawkins, H.C., and M.S. Philip. 1998. Tropical moist forest silviculture and management: A history of success and failure. CAB Int., Wallingford, UK.

De Graaf, N.R. 1986. A silvicultural system for natural regeneration of tropical rain forest in Suriname. Agric. Univ., Wageningen, The Netherlands.

Dickinson, B.M., J.C. Dickinson, and F.E. Putz. 1996. Natural forest management as a conservation tool in the tropics: Divergent views on possibilities and alternatives. Commonw. For. Rev. 75(4):309–315.

Drauzoa, C. 1998. The avifauna 23 years after logging in Kerala National Park, Uganda. Biodiversity Conserv. 7(6):777–797.

Dykstra, D.P., and R. Heinrich. 1992. Sustaining tropical forests through environmentally sound harvesting practices. Unasylva 43:9–15.

Embrapa–CPAF–Acre (Empresa Brasileira de Pesquisa Agropecuária–Centro de Pesquisa Agroflorestal–Acre). 1996a. Boletim Agro-metereológico 1990–1994 (no. 5). Rio Branco, Acre, n.p.

Embrapa–CPAF–Acre (Empresa Brasileira de Pesquisa Agropecuária–Centro de Pesquisa Agroflorestal–Acre). 1996b. Boletim Agro-metereológico 1995 (no. 6). Rio Branco, Acre, n.p.

Evans, J. 1986. Tropical forest plantations. pp. 37–50. *In* Proceedings of the Symposium of the Humid Tropic. Vol. 2. Embrapa–Centro de Pesquisas Agroflorestais da Amazonia Oriental, Belém, Brazil.

FAO (Food and Agriculture Organization). 1995. Uso de bueyes en operaciones de aprovechamiento forestal en areas rurales de Costa Rica. Estudios Monograficos de Exploitation Forestal 3. Rome.

Fox, J.E.D. 1968. Logging damage and the influence of climber cutting prior to logging in the lowland dipterocarp forest of Sabah. Malays. For. 31:326–347.

Guariguata, M.R., and M.A. Pinard. 1998. Ecological knowledge of regeneration from seed in neotropical forest trees: Implications for natural forest management. For. Ecol. Manage. 112:87–99.

Hendrison, J. 1990. Damage-controlled logging in managed rain forest in Suriname. Agricultural University, Wageningen, The Netherlands.

Howard, A.F. 1993. A linear programming model for predicting the sustainable yield of timber from community forest on the Osa Peninsula of Costa Rica. For. Ecol. Manage. 61:29–43.

Hummel, A.C. 1995. Aspectos gerais do controle da atividade madeireira na Amazonia brasileira. Univ. Fed. do Amazonas, Faculdade de Direito, Manaus. Monograph.

Johns, S.J., P. Barreto, and C. Uhl. 1996. Logging damage during planned and unplanned logging operations in the eastern Amazon. For. Ecol. Manage. 89:59–77.

Kent, M., and P. Coker. 1992. Vegetation description and analysis: A practical approach. Wiley, Chichester, UK.

Kuusipalo, J., S. Hadengganan, G. Adjers, and A.P. Sagala. 1996. Effect of gap liberation on the performance and growth of dipterocarp trees in a logged-over rainforest. For. Ecol. Manage. 92:209–219.

Leuschner, W.A. 1992. Introduction to forest resource management. Krieger, Malabar, FL.

Liew, T.C. 1973. The practicability of climber cutting and tree marking prior to logging as a silvicultural tool in Sabah. Malays. For. 36:5–19.

Miller, K.R. 1981. Growth and yield of a logged-over mixed dipterocarp forest in E. Kalimantan. Malays. For. 44(2):419–424.

Ocaña-Vidal, J. 1990. Natural forest management with strip clear-cutting. Unasylva 43:24–27.

Okali, D.U.U., and B.A. Ola-Adams. 1988. The population changes in treated rainforest at Omo Forest Reserve, south-western Nigeria. J. Trop. Ecol. 3:291–313.

Oliveira, M.V.N. d'. 1992. Exploração de madeira em várzea pelo método tradicional no paraná Abufari no médio rio Púrus. Boletim 7. Embrapa–CPAF–Acre, Brazil.

Oliveira, M.V.N. d'. 2000. Artificial regeneration in gaps and skidding trails after mechanised forest exploitation in Acre, Brazil. For. Ecol. Manage. 127:67–76.

Oliveira, M.V.N. d', and E.M. Bráz. 1995. Reduction of damage to tropical moist forest through planned harvesting. Commonw. For. Rev. 74(3):276–278.

Pinard, M.A., and F.E. Putz. 1996. Retaining forest biomass by reducing logging damage. Biotropica 28:278–295.

Plumptre, A.J. 1995. The importance of seed trees for the natural regeneration of selectively logged tropical forest. Commonw. For. Rev. 74(3):253–258.

Primack, R.B. 1995. Essentials of conservative biology. Sinauer, Sunderland, MA.

Rai, S.N. 1989. Rate of diameter growth of tree species in humid tropics of western Ghats, India. pp. 106–116. *In* W.R.W. Mohd, H.T. Chan, and S. Appanah (eds.) Proceedings of the Seminar on Growth and Yield in Tropical Mixed/Moist Forest, Forest Res. Inst., Kuala Lumpur, Malaysia, 20–24 June 1988. For. Res. Inst., Malaysia.

Ramos, J.M., and S. del Amo. 1992. Enrichment planting in tropical secondary forest in Vera Cruz, Mexico. For. Ecol. Manage. 54:289–304.

Santos, J. 1986. Situação da Indústria Madeireira no Município de Manaus (1981–1983) e das Serrarias no Estado do Amazonas (1981). Universidade Federal do Paraná. Tese de Mestrado, não publicada. Curitiba, Brasil.

Sheil, D., D.F.R.P. Burlem, and D. Alder. 1995. The interpretation and misinterpretation of mortality rate measures. J. Ecol. 83:331–333.

Silva, J.N.M., J.O.P. Carvalho, and J.C.A. Lopes. 1989. Growth of a logged-over tropical rain forest of the Brazilian Amazon. pp. 117–136. *In* W.R.W. Mohd, H.T. Chan, and S. Appanah (eds.) Proceedings of the Seminar on Growth and Yield in Tropical Mixed/Moist Forest, Forest Res. Inst., Kuala Lumpur, Malaysia, 20–24 June 1988. For. Res. Inst., Malaysia.

Silva, J.N.M., J.O.P. Carvalho, J.C.A. Lopes, R.P. Oliveira, and L.C. Oliveira. 1996. Growth and yield studies in the Tapajos region, central Brazilian Amazon. Comm. For. Rev. 75(4):325–329.

Silva, J.N.M., and T.C. Whitmore. 1990. Prospects of sustainable yield management in the Brazilian Amazon. *In* Anais de le "Atelier sur l'amenagement et la conservation de l'ecosystème forestier tropical humide." Centre de Coopération Int. en Recherche Agron. Pour le Dév. Forêt, Cayena, Guyana.

Swaine, M.D., D. Lieberman, and F.E. Putz. 1987. The dynamics of tree populations in tropical forest: A review. J. Trop. Ecol. 3:289–290.

Thang, H. 1980. Factors affecting regeneration methods for typical high forests in southeast Asia. Malaian For. 43(4):469–480.

Uhl, C., D. Nepstad, R.J. Buschbacher, K. Clark, B. Kauffman, and S. Subler. 1990. Studies of ecosystem response to natural and anthropogenic disturbances provide guidelines for designing sustainable land-use systems in Amazonia. pp. 25–42. *In* A. Anderson (ed.) Alternatives to deforestation in Amazonia. Columbia Univ. Press, New York.

Uhl, C., and I.C.G. Vieira. 1988. Extração seletiva de madeiras: Impactos ecologicos em Paragominas. Pará Desenvolvimento, IDESP (23):46–52.

Verissimo, A., P. Barreto, R. Tarifa, and C. Uhl. 1995. Extraction of a high-value natural resource in Amazonia: The case of mahogany. For. Ecol. Manage. 72:39–60.

Vosti, S.A., J. Witcover, C.L. Carpentier, S.J.M. de Oliveira, and J.C. dos Santos. 2001. Intensifying small-scale agriculture in the western Brazilian Amazon: Issues, implications and implementation. pp. 245–266. *In* D. Lee and C. Barrett (eds.) Tradeoffs or synergies? Agricultural intensification, economic development and the environment. CAB Int., Wallingford, UK.

Witcover, J., S.A. Vosti, F.R.A. Barbosa, J. Batista, G. Boklin, S.B. França, et al. 1994. Alternatives to Slash-and-Burn Agriculture (ASB): A characterisation of Brazilian benchmark sites of Pedro Peixoto and Theobroma August/September 1994. MP Working Pap. US 96-003. IFPRI, Washington, DC.

# 9 Permanent Smallholder Rubber Agroforestry Systems in Sumatra, Indonesia

Gede Wibawa and Sinung Hendratno
  *Indonesian Rubber Research Institute  Sungei Putih, Indonesia*
Meine van Noordwijk
  *ICRAF Southeast Asia  Nairobi, Kenya*

Although there is a long tradition in Southeast Asia of trading resins and latex collected from the natural forest or secondary forests that were part of shifting cultivation cycles, the introduction more than a century ago of Pára rubber (*Hevea brasilienses* [Willd. ex Adr. Juss.] Muell Arg.) from the Amazon to Southeast Asia formed the basis for the spontaneous and broad-based adoption of new agroforestry practices at a scale not matched elsewhere. "The history of agriculture probably has not seen any other case where the introduction of a single crop had such a dramatic effect on the economic condition of smallholders in vast areas, as the introduction of *Hevea brasiliensis* in Indonesia" (van Gelder 1950:428). The food crop–based shifting cultivation systems in which the fallow was of secondary importance were transformed into systems in which the food crop that could grow in between young rubber trees became a secondary aspect of a production system relying on rubber to generate income. Rubber agroforestry appears to have many of the attributes of a best-bet alternative to food crop–based slash-and-burn agriculture: They are profitable, produce easily marketed products, and generate environmental benefits. Therefore rubber agroforests of various management intensities have become one important focus of Alternatives to Slash and Burn's (ASB's) research program (Tomich et al. 1998, 2001; van Noordwijk et al. 1995, 1997). Yet the impact of this land use system—which helped attract migrants to the forest margins—on the rate of deforestation is still debated (van Noordwijk et al. 1995; Tomich et al. 2001).

Rubber is a major export commodity supporting the Indonesian economy. More than 1 million households now depend on rubber as their main source of income. Smallholder rubber constitutes 83 percent of the total Indonesian rubber area (3.5 million ha) and 68 percent of total rubber production. Smallholder rubber systems often are called jungle rubber (Gouyon et al. 1993; Williams et al. 2001), a complex agroforestry system based on production of an economically important commodity that maintains the structure, carbon stocks, and species richness of secondary forest vegetation (Foresta and Michon 1996). Typically, management by smallholders is extensive and uses very few external inputs. However, major opportunities may exist to increase the productivity of these systems by making use of improved rubber germplasm.

All rubber agroforestry systems in Indonesia start (or started) by clearing land: slashing, cutting, and felling the forest and burning it during the dry season. Rubber seedlings typically are planted into an upland rice crop (for 1 or 2 years) and left to grow along with those forest species that can regrow from stumps and the secondary forest species that come into the plot as seeds from neighboring areas. When the rubber trees have reached a girth of about 40 cm (after 5 to 10 years, depending on site conditions), tapping can begin and part of the vegetation is cleared to create a path for walking from tree to tree and to promote rubber seedling growth. When the first generation of trees becomes old and unproductive, two basic options exist for rejuvenation of the stand: cyclical and permanent agroforestry.

A cyclical rubber agroforestry system begins a new cycle with another round of land clearing: slashing, cutting, and felling the old jungle rubber and burning it during the dry season. Cleared land is replanted with seedlings or grafted clonal rubber trees, sometimes in combination with upland food crops (e.g., rice [*Oryza sativa* L.], maize [*Zea mays* L.], or mung bean [*Vigna radiata* L.]). Leguminous cover crops are used only in establishing a new rubber plantation on large estates. Technical, economic, and ecological aspects of these systems are well documented (Gouyon 1996; Penot and Wibawa 1997; Wibawa and Thomas 1997).

But the cyclical system can suffer from or pose financial, agronomic, and environmental problems. For example, replanting rubber after slash-and-burn land clearing in cyclical systems may reduce farmers' incomes from rubber during the immature period (5–7 years), and replanting with clonal varieties is expensive. Substantial risk of plant damage also exists throughout the establishment period from pests (wild pigs, monkeys), diseases (white root rot), and fire. Global environmental benefits of such agroforestry systems in terms of biodiversity conservation and carbon stocks (chapters 2 and 4, this volume) are limited by the recurrence of a burn after each cycle of 25 to 30 years.

An alternative method of rejuvenating old rubber agroforests in Sumatra is the sisipan system, which culminates in a permanent rubber agroforest that more closely resembles a natural forest in terms of the age and size distributions of trees. This permanent system is based on the management of small plots (about 1 ha in size) within which very small parcels (about 100 m² in size) are rejuvenated either by spontaneous regeneration from seeds or by rubber seedlings planted in forest gaps. This type of rejuvenation is common in Sumatra in damar (*Shorea javanica* Koord. & Valeton) and fruit tree agroforests and home gardens. With this type of management, a single field can contain rubber trees of all ages, with a subset always available for tapping. Decisions on gap replacement are made at the tree rather than field level, thereby providing more opportunities to introduce valuable nonrubber trees and to retain older, productive rubber trees. We hypothesize that the prospects for biodiversity conservation and time-averaged carbon stocks are higher in permanent rubber agroforestry systems than in cyclical systems and that the risks and investment associated with permanent systems are better suited to smallholders with little land, labor, and capital at their disposal.

As part of the ASB research activities in Indonesia, villages in and surrounding the benchmark areas in the lowland peneplain and piedmont zones (van Noordwijk et al. 1995) were surveyed to better understand farmers' interests in and constraints to adopting the sisipan permanent agroforestry system as an alternative to the cyclical system. Land use systems (LUSs) were characterized at the field, patch or gap, and tree levels. At the LUS level, the following issues were addressed: What farm and farmer characteristics (e.g., gender, age) are associated with sisipan system adoption; how does the economic performance of the sisipan system compare with the cyclical slash-and-burn alternative; and what are the scope for and obstacles to increasing the productivity of sisipan systems? This chapter presents the materials and methods, results, and conclusions from this study.

## MATERIALS AND METHODS

The survey was carried out in Jambi Province, Sumatra, in an area extending beyond the original ASB benchmark site (van Noordwijk et al. 1995, 1997; Murdiyarso et al. 2002). Jambi is one of the main rubber-producing provinces in Indonesia and represented approximately 17 percent of national smallholder rubber area (495,556 ha) in 1995 (DGE 1995). From this province, seven villages in the Bungo Tebo district were chosen to represent two main agroecological zones: the foothills (piedmont zone) and the lowland peneplain zone. Five of the villages are in the piedmont zone (Rantau Pandan site), and the other two are in the peneplain zone (Bungo Tebo site; see table 9.1). The survey was carried out between October 1998 and January 1999, so all financial information refers to the period after the monetary crisis that began in the second half of 1997.

In these villages, farmers who had implemented sisipan as part of their livelihood strategy were chosen for interviews. Thus the survey was of an exploratory nature and did not propose to identify the proportion of farmers who practiced sisipan or slash-and-burn–based systems. The objective was to improve our understanding of how sisipan systems were practiced and to explore why farmers chose sisipan for rejuvenating rubber agroforests. Insights for selecting larger, random samples for future studies can be gleaned from this research. Respondents selected were those available at the time of the interview and chosen from lists provided by village chiefs and farmer leaders. Seventy-six farmers were involved in the study.

The interview process had two stages. The first stage consisted of interviews with village chiefs and farm leaders. The aim was to collect secondary data on village char-

*Table 9.1* Villages Surveyed and Numbers of Respondents, by Agroecological Zone

| Agroecological Zone | Village | Number of Respondents |
|---|---|---|
| Piedmont zone | Sepungur | 9 |
| | Lubuk | 7 |
| | Muara Kuamang | 11 |
| | Pintas Tuo | 8 |
| | Embacang Gedang | 10 |
| Peneplain zone | Rantau Pandan | 14 |
| | Muara Buat | 17 |
| Total sample size | | 76 |

acteristics, the number of farmers who had implemented permanent systems, and general rubber-farming conditions. In the second stage, interviews were conducted at the household level to collect primary data on farmer, farm household, and farm characteristics and to obtain detailed information on the implementation of permanent systems. These structured interviews were supported by direct observation of the respondents' rubber agroforests.

To compare the necessary inputs and financial performance of sisipan and cyclical rubber agroforestry systems, five variations on these basic systems were identified and analyzed: cyclical systems using locally acquired seedlings, cyclical systems using high-productivity clonal rubber seedlings, sisipan systems using local seedlings and standard yields, sisipan systems using low-productivity seedlings (15 percent lower yields than those of local standard seedlings), and sisipan systems using local seedlings with standard yields but also benefiting from offtake from fruit trees.

The net present values (NPV), internal rates of return (IRR), and benefit:cost (BC) ratios were calculated for each of the five systems. In addition, for each system two cost scenarios were calculated, one (called fully costed) that used market prices to value all inputs used in production (land, family labor, hired labor, small farm equipment, and fertilizers) and a second (called partially costed) that used market prices to value inputs actually purchased in the market (i.e., land, family labor, and upland rice seeds were not included in this cost scenario because their true opportunity costs may have been below the market price).

## RESULTS AND DISCUSSION

### CHARACTERISTICS OF FARMERS INTERESTED IN PERMANENT RUBBER AGROFORESTS AND THEIR FARMS

In the study area, sisipan practices appeared to be widespread. Between one- and two-thirds of the farmers had adopted sisipan on at least part of their operational holdings. The seventy-six respondents who were managing permanent rubber agroforests at the time of the survey had the following characteristics.

The head of the family managing a permanent rubber agroforest was typically male (95 percent), was a local rather than migrant farmer (75 percent), and had completed primary school (71 percent). Twenty-eight percent of farmers were partially employed in off-farm, nonagricultural activities (e.g., teachers, carpenters, or traders), and 17 percent had official village roles, such as village officer or Muslim scholar (*ulama*).

The average respondent was 41 years old (the median age was 36 years), had long experience of rubber farming (18 years), and had known about the sisipan technique for about 7 years. Older farmers tended to be more recent adopters of the sisipan system, whereas younger farmers tended to have known about it for as long as they had had rubber agroforests. This result suggests that land availability, distance to forest plots, and establishment costs may affect sisipan adoption. For example, young farmers tended to have land further from the village than the older farmers, making it more difficult to control pest damage in a new plantation. And, as an alternative to rejuvenating old rubber agroforests, forest land could be opened, cleared, and planted using the cyclical system. But forest clearing is done by young farmers, who still have strength to do the hard work it entails, or by the rich, who can afford to hire such services. Most new rubber agroforest land is prepared using slash-and-burn. Of the land opened by slash-and-burn in our survey, most was forest and fallow (bush) land (88 percent), and only 12 percent was old (cyclical system) rubber.

The average operational holding was 6.4 ha and included several land uses (table 9.2). Most farmers (61 percent) had other farm land or forest, bush, or fallow land, suggesting that they could expand the area under production. Size of operational holding did not seem to influence sisipan adoption, which was practiced by some farmers with very large and others with very small farms.

Eighty four percent of farmers indicated that knowledge of sisipan was passed from father to son. The role of extension officers in influencing sisipan adoption decisions was very limited; only 4 percent of the sample reported learning about sisipan from extension workers.

Average household size was 5.7 people. Of these, the average number of potential family laborers (males and females between ages 15 and 55) was about 3, and the amount of family labor used on the farm was about 2.2 people (roughly equivalent to 660 person-days per year). Perhaps most importantly, the majority of farmers (68 percent) reported facing labor shortages. Sisipan is well adapted to labor shortages

*Table 9.2* Average Area Dedicated to Particular Land Uses and Total Operational Holding

| Land Uses | Average Areas (ha) | Number of Respondents Reporting a Given Land Use |
|---|---|---|
| Rubber garden | | |
|   Mature rubber | 2.2 | 71 |
|   Immature rubber | 1.8 | 60 |
| Rice fields and other farming operations | 0.7 | 50 |
| Housing | 0.1 | 42 |
| Other land (forest, bush, and fallow) | 1.6 | 46 |
| Total operational holding | 6.4 | |

because little time must be devoted specifically to it. For example, farmers manage emerging components of sisipan systems (planting or maintaining the saplings) after tapping mature trees, while performing other tasks in the field, or during rainy days when the opportunity cost of their time is low.

Regarding overall labor use, 54 percent of farmers depended exclusively on family labor in rubber production, and the remainder reported using family and hired labor. Most respondents (97 percent) agreed that hired labor was available in the village at a daily wage rate of Rp7000 to Rp17,000 (approximately US$1–2 at the late 1998 exchange rate of US$1 = Rp7500). Wage rates varied by task, location of task, and gender of laborer and were linked to the price of rice; the daily wage rate was generally equivalent to the market value of 2.5 kg of rice.

The average, continuously tapped rubber area was 2.2 ha and contained approximately 525 trees/ha. This average area produced an 82.4-kg slab of rubber per week. The dry rubber content of this slab was about 45 percent, so the average productivity of a rubber garden was about 880 kg of dry rubber/ha/yr, or approximately 12 g of dry rubber per tree per tapping-day. The productivity of rubber in the study areas was 35 percent higher than the national average for smallholders (Ditjenbun 1997) but much lower than the productivity of clonal rubber in plantations (1500 kg of dry rubber/ha/yr) (Hendratno et al. 1997).

Sixty-nine percent of the farmers' income was derived from rubber, with the remainder coming from off-farm employment, rice production, and the collection of wood and nontimber forest products (table 9.3). Because of the importance of rubber in generating income, most farmers could not afford to slash and burn and replant entire areas that contain low-productivity trees because doing so could interrupt income flows for up to 7 years. The sisipan system provides a continuous, though sometimes reduced, flow of revenues from rubber tapping by introducing seedlings while retaining older but still productive rubber and other trees. Income flows from

*Table 9.3* Average Annual Income and Expenditures by Source and Use

| | Income and Expenditures (thousands of 1998 Rp)[a] | Percentage of Total Income or Expenditures |
|---|---|---|
| **Income** | | |
| Rubber | 4819 | 69 |
| Other farm activities | 1424 | 20 |
| Off-farm activities | 768 | 11 |
| Subtotal | 7011 | 100 |
| **Expenditures** | | |
| Consumption (mainly food) | 4344 | 68 |
| Education | 46 | 1 |
| Others (clothes, socials, etc.) | 2028 | 31 |
| Subtotal | 6418 | 100 |

[a]US$1 — Rp7500 in late 1998.

agroforests were sustained during a sisipan phase by intensively tapping all remaining rubber trees (and accepting the consequent reduction in their lifespans) or by selling fruits and timber products. Farmers were aware that the growth of sisipan rubber seedlings was very slow, but by maintaining high plant density and planting low- or no-cost seedlings farmers could stabilize incomes at acceptable levels. As regards over-all family budgets, most farmers (76 percent) reported an annual income surplus after basic necessities were met, whereas the remaining 24 percent of farm households faced recurring deficits; for most farmers, then, the sisipan rubber system seemed to provide an adequate living.

Damage to seedlings by pests (mainly monkeys and wild pigs) could be substantial. To reduce these risks farmers could plant seedlings in fenced, large-diameter stumps or in bushy areas to hide seedlings from pests. In areas where risk of pest damage was very high, farmers generally used low-cost (and low-productivity) local seedlings as planting material, thereby reducing the value of unavoidable losses. Farmers wanting to boost productivity in these high-risk areas could plant clonal rubber and protect the seedlings with fences or live temporarily on the plot to guard seedlings.

Nonrubber trees in permanent systems also provided benefits to farm households, and the abundance of these trees depended on the growth stage of the patch and man-agement intensity. Farmers surveyed mentioned more than eighty valuable nonrub-ber tree species, forty of which could be exploited from permanent rubber agroforest systems, and others were of less value but still retained if they did not compete with valuable species. Three fruit species were identified by many farmers as sources of food or income: petai (also known as parkia; *Parkia speciosa* Hassk.), jengkol (also known as blackbead; *Pithecellobium jiringa* W. Jack]), and durian (*Durio zibethinus* Murray). The number and diversity of nonrubber plants in rubber agroforests were closely relat-ed to the management choices by the farmers who weeded intensively (two to three times per year) during the first 2 years while food crops were grown (*ladang* phase) and thereafter only minimally managed the agroforest (again, via weeding). During this period of less intensive weeding, forest regrowth from seedlings or resprouting from stumps emerged and valuable trees (timber, fruits, and, rattan) were selected for retention every 3 to 4 years as farmers slashed weeds and other less valuable vegetation. This management process continued selectively cutting trees to allow light to promote rubber seedling growth.

## FARMER CONCERNS, ECONOMIC PERFORMANCE OF ALTERNATIVE SYSTEMS, AND STRATEGIES FOR IMPROVING RUBBER AGROFOREST PRODUCTIVITY

The survey identified five main factors that jointly affected farmers' decisions to adopt permanent rubber agroforestry systems (table 9.4). Note that continuity of income flows and risk reduction were key farmer objectives met by the sisipan system.

*Table 9.4* Factors Influencing Farmers' Decisions to Practice Sisipan, in Descending Order of Positive Response Rates

| Factor | Percentage of Respondents Indicating a Positive Effect on Sisipan Adoption Decision |
|---|---|
| Sisipan increases land productivity and maintains income flows from existing rubber and other trees. | 99 |
| Sisipan reduces the risk of pest damage. | 74 |
| Sisipan can be practiced using family labor alone. | 58 |
| Sisipan is a simple, known management practice. | 56 |
| Sisipan can be practiced with little or no capital or cash. | 51 |

As indicated earlier, economic performance indicators were calculated for two versions of the cyclical system (the first using local seedlings and the second using more productive clonal planting material) and three versions of the permanent system (the first using local seedlings, the second using seedlings yielding 15 percent less than local seedlings, and the third using local seedlings and deriving income from nonrubber trees). The results of this analysis appear in table 9.5. All calculations were done on the basis of 1-ha parcels managed over a 30-year period and assumed a farmgate price of dry rubber of Rp3570 per kg and daily wage rates for men and women of Rp7000 and Rp5000, respectively. Prices were derived from survey data and were assumed to remain constant over the entire 30-year evaluation period. Three measures of eco-

*Table 9.5* Financial Performance Indicators for Cyclical and Permanent Agroforestry Systems, by Productivity and System Scenario and by Cost Accounting Method

| Systems and Scenarios | Measures of Financial Performance | | |
|---|---|---|---|
| | Net Present Value (20% discount rate; thousands of late-1998 Rp) | Internal Rate of Return (%) | Benefit:Cost Ratio |
| Fully costed | | | |
| Cyclical | | | |
|     Local seedlings | 80 | 22 | 1.02 |
|     Improved seedlings | 250 | 21 | 1.03 |
| Permanent | | | |
|     Local seedlings | 1,300 | 33 | 1.09 |
|     Low-productivity seedlings | 400 | 32 | 1.03 |
|     Local seedlings and fruit | 3,900 | >50 | 1.27 |
| Partially costed | | | |
| Cyclical | | | |
|     Local seedlings | 1,800 | 35 | 2.80 |
|     Improved seedlings | 1,500 | 24 | 1.29 |
| Permanent | | | |
|     Local seedlings | 13,800 | >50 | 8.72 |
|     Low-productivity seedlings | 11,400 | >50 | 7.41 |
|     Local seedlings and fruit | 13,800 | >50 | 8.72 |

nomic performance were calculated (NPV, IRR, and BC ratio) all of which presented consistent patterns; in what follows we focus on important NPV results.

First, all rubber agroforestry systems evaluated generated positive economic returns; that is, the discounted streams of benefits minus costs were positive for all systems. Simply put, it paid to invest in rubber agroforests of any kind.

Second, the permanent systems clearly dominate the cyclical systems in terms of NPV. The cyclical system using improved seedlings (NPV = Rp250,000) could not compete with even the permanent system using low-productivity seedlings (NPV = Rp400,000). This result is more significant when one considers the continuity of income emerging from the permanent systems but absent from the cyclical systems (important to the results presented in table 9.5 but not specifically addressed there).

Third, including income derived from timber, bark, and fruit trees such as jeng-kol, petai, and durian dramatically increased the economic performance of permanent systems (NPV increased from Rp1,300,000 to Rp3,900,000).

Fourth, not surprisingly, all measures of economic performance improved if farm land and family labor were not considered in calculating production costs. Differences were largest for the permanent systems that used family labor more intensively.

Finally, rubber yields may vary spatially and over time. Sensitivity analysis (not presented in table 9.5) suggested a BC ratio of 1 if rubber yields fell to 656 kg/ha/yr.

The productivity of both cyclical and permanent systems was low when local seedlings were the source of planting materials. To increase productivity, new planting material must be introduced. Smallholder rubber yields per tree could be more than doubled if improved clonal material were to replace local seedlings. The Indonesian Rubber Research Institute has recommended the planting of several rubber clones that increase rubber productivity and also provide useful timber products (Lasminingsih 1995). Economic analysis suggests that farmers would benefit from switching to improved seedlings, but obstacles to adoption exist (Williams et al. 2001; Joshi et al. 2002). For example, the economic returns to investing in improved seedlings depended on farmers' abilities to protect them from pest damage by fencing, round-the-clock vigilance, or village-level hunting. Although pest risks under cyclical and permanent systems cannot be compared yet, fencing individual trees in permanent systems with bamboo shafts appears to be effective (unpublished ICRAF report). In addition, improved seedlings (which are usually grafted) grow more slowly in heavily shaded permanent systems than in cyclical systems, but growth can be sped up if improved material is grafted directly onto well-established local seedlings.

Although initial farmer responses to seedling grafting have been quite positive, impediments to adoption exist. Currently, there are few reliable sources of improved planting material (district-level markets in Muara Bungo or Rimbo Bujang dominate the market for these seedlings), and grafting skills are not widespread. Expansion of the area dedicated to improved planting material (via grafting) could promote the development of local businesses such as rubber and other tree crop nurseries and increase job opportunities for those skilled in grafting.

# CONCLUSION

Permanent rubber agroforestry systems occupy significant proportions of agricultural systems in the lowland peneplain and lower piedmont zones of Sumatra, Indonesia, where they also make substantial contributions to smallholder income. Although these systems are becoming more broadly adopted, little is known about their economic performance or the environmental services they generate. One traditional method of establishing and maintaining permanent rubber agroforests is the sisipan system, which does not use slash-and-burn practices but rather selectively removes old and less valuable trees and replaces them with rubber seedlings. The economic performance of permanent systems was found to be superior to the alternative cyclical systems that do use slash-and-burn techniques. Sisipan was also found to be compatible with smallholder characteristics in the region, especially labor shortages and lack of capital for agricultural investments. As the extensive margin is reduced in Sumatra and forest resources become scarcer, the sisipan system will become even more widespread.

But the productivity of sisipan systems based on local planting material remains low, with consequences for smallholder welfare. Productivity can be improved by introducing clonal rubber germplasm or by expanding the number of products extracted from rubber agroforests. More and more focused research is needed. Policy action to develop more productive germplasm and facilitate its adoption by smallholders is also needed.

# ACKNOWLEDGMENTS

We acknowledge financial support provided by the Australian Centre for International Agricultural Research through the ASB Programme, and the assistance of the ICRAF Southeast Asia staff during field data collection.

## REFERENCES

DGE (Directorate General of Estate). 1995. Statistik karet. Direktorat Jendral Perkebunan, Jakarta.

Ditjenbun (Direktorat Jenderal Perkebunan). 1997. Statistik Perkebunan Indonesia 1995–1997. Karet, Jakarta.

Foresta, H. de, and G. Michon. 1996. Tree improvement research for agroforestry: A note of caution. Agrofor. Forum 7(3):8–11.

Gouyon, A. 1996. Smallholder production faced with the world rubber market. Plantation, Recherche, Develop. 3(5.):338–345.

Gouyon, A., H. de Foresta, and P. Levang. 1993. Does the jungle rubber deserve its name? An analysis of rubber agroforestry systems in Southeast Sumatra. Agrofor. Syst. 22:181–206.

Hendratno, S., G. Wibawa, and C. Anwar. 1997. Evaluasi dan analisis proyek proyek pengembangan karet rakyat di Jambi. Jurnal Penelitian Karet (J. Indonesian Rubber Res. Inst.) 15(1):42–56.

Joshi, L., G. Wibawa, H.J. Beukema, S.E. Williams, and M. van Noordwijk. 2002. Technological change and biodiversity in the rubber agroecosystem. Pp. 133–157. *In* J. Vandermeer (ed.) Tropical agroecosystems: New directions for research. CRC Press, Boca Raton, FL.

Lasminingsih, M. 1995. Klon klon karet harapan untuk program HTI. Paper presented on Lokakarya Nasional Pemuliaan Tanaman Karet. Medan, 28–30 November.

Murdiyarso D., M. van Noordwijk, U.R. Wasrin, T.P. Tomich, and A.N. Gillison. 2002. Environmental benefits and sustainable land-use options in the Jambi transect, Sumatra, Indonesia. J. Vegetation Sci. 13:429–438.

Penot, E., and G. Wibawa. 1997. Complex rubber agroforestry systems in Indonesia: An alternative to low productivity of jungle rubber conserving agroforestry practices and benefits. pp. 56–80. *In* Proceedings of the Symposium on Farming System Aspects of the Cultivation of Natural Rubber (*Hevea brasiliensis*), Beruwala, Sri Lanka, 5–8 Nov. 1996. Int. Rubber Res. and Develop. Board, London, UK.

Tomich, T.P., M. van Noordwijk, S. Budidarsono, A. Gillison, T. Kusumanto, D. Murdiyarso, et al. 1998. Alternatives to Slash-and-Burn in Indonesia. Summary report and synthesis of phase II. ASB, ICRAF, Nairobi.

Tomich, T.P., M. van Noordwijk, S. Budidarsono, A. Gillison, T. Kusumanto, D. Murdiyarso, et al. 2001. Agricultural intensification, deforestation and the environment: Assessing tradeoffs in Sumatra, Indonesia. Pp. 221–244. *In* D. Lee and C. Barrett (eds.) Tradeoffs or synergies? Agricultural intensification, economic development and the environment. CAB Int., Wallingford, UK.

van Gelder, A. 1950. Bevolkingsrubber. Pp. 427–475. *In* C.J. van Hall and A. Van de Koppel (eds.) De Landbouw in de Indische Archipel. Van Hoeve, the Hague, the Netherlands.

van Noordwijk, M., T.P. Tomich, D.P. Garrity, and A.M. Fagi (eds.). 1997. Alternatives to Slash-and-Burn Research in Indonesia. Proceedings of the workshop, Bogor, 6–9 June 1995. Agency for Agric. Res. and Develop., Jakarta.

van Noordwijk, M., T.P. Tomich, R. Winahyu, D. Murdiyarso, S. Suyanto, S. Partoharjono, et al. (eds.). 1995. Alternatives to Slash-and-Burn in Indonesia: Summary report of phase 1. ASB–Indonesia Rep. No. 4. ASB–Indonesia Consortium and ICRAF, Bogor, Indonesia.

Wibawa, G., and Thomas. 1997. Study of *Hevea* based intercropping system functioning. pp. 25–39. *In* Proceedings of the Symposium on Farming System Aspects of the Cultivation of Natural Rubber (*Hevea brasiliensis*), Beruwala, Sri Lanka, 5–8 Nov. 1996. Int. Rubber Res. and Develop. Board, United Kingdom.

Williams, S.E., M. van Noordwijk, E. Penot, J.R. Healey, F.L. Sinclair, and G. Wibawa. 2001. On-farm evaluation of the establishment of clonal rubber in multistrata agroforests in Jambi, Indonesia. Agrofor. Syst. 53:227–237.

# 10 Coffee, Pastures, and Deforestation in the Western Brazilian Amazon

## A FARM-LEVEL BIOECONOMIC MODEL

Chantal L. Carpentier
> *North American Commission for Environmental Cooperation  Quebec, Canada*

Stephen A. Vosti and Julie Witcover
> *University of California  Davis, California*

Tropical moist forests are disappearing every year, and much clearing is driven by the demand for agricultural land. This conversion of forest to agriculture carries with it costs and benefits. The costs include soil degradation, deterioration in water quality and availability, biodiversity loss, and conflict with traditional forest dwellers. The benefits, production of food and fiber for consumption and sale, can also be considerable for inhabitants of forest margin areas and populations depending on agricultural exports from these areas, but large gaps in assessments of environmental and poverty dimensions prevent an evaluation of the overall impact of forest conversion. Activities at many levels (e.g., the Biodiversity Convention, Kyoto Protocol, Amazon Treaty Organization, Pilot Program to Conserve the Brazilian Rain Forest, and national-level movement to protect extractive reserves in Brazil) that seek to mitigate further deforestation via some kind of government intervention respond to a scenario in which, at the private level, the benefits of clearing land outweigh the costs of land conversion, and social costs of deforestation are higher than the benefits.

In the past, economists paid attention mainly to external drivers of deforestation such as distorting macro policies and Amazon settlement subsidies (e.g., Hecht 1985; Binswanger 1987). Most of these policies have been stopped, yet deforestation continues. This suggests that external drivers apart from policies may be at work, but more importantly, that internal drivers—factors within the region—may play an important role. Recent analyses of these internal drivers failed to integrate production systems effectively into either a whole-farm view or into current socioeconomic conditions of small-scale farmers in the western Brazilian Amazon

(Vosti et al. 2002). In their review of economic models of deforestation, Kaimowitz and Angelsen (1998) found that national models failed to account for internal drivers.

Although some believe that improving yields on already cleared land in forest margin areas will take pressure off the remaining forest, and promoting perennial and agroforestry systems will alleviate some ecological damage caused by deforestation, responses by resource users to technology and policy changes are not necessarily straightforward. This chapter looks at those responses, which ultimately will determine the impacts of forests and rural inhabitants on policy and technology change.

In part to fill this gap, a Farm Level Bioeconomic Model (FaleBEM) was built to study how various policies and technology interventions affect land use decisions of small-scale farmers in the western Brazilian Amazon. The western Brazilian Amazon is home to much of the world's remaining tropical moist forests and to more than 500,000 small-scale farmers whose annual decisions to deforest (or not) will have a large influence on the ultimate fate of the forest. For instance, an average small-scale farmer in the settlement project of Pedro Peixoto, Acre, slashed and burned 2.46 ha of forest per year (Lewis et al. 2002), annually emitting 367 t of carbon contained in this forest (Palm et al. 2002; Lewis et al. 2002). Using linear programming to simulate consumption-maximizing behavior of farm households, the FaleBEM incorporates farm-level objectives and constraints to production; can be adjusted to fit the heterogeneity of land, labor, and farm household characteristics prevalent in the area; and tracks the income, soil productivity, carbon stock, and forest depletion impacts of current and proposed technology or policy experiments.

The FaleBEM helps structure thinking about these issues and replaces "I think" statements with "if–then" statements through policy experiments. It differs from purely economic models in that it simulates biophysical processes and economic activities based on optimization algorithms. What differentiates this BEM from most BEMs applied to developed countries, such as those of Shortle (1984), Ellis et al. (1991), Dosi and Moretto (1993), and Carpentier et al. (1998), is the feedback of soil fertility depletion and regeneration on agricultural production and deforestation. The FaleBEM effectively links deforestation decisions to production decisions on the cleared land. Also, FaleBEM overcomes criticisms of many linear programming models by approximating nonlinear production and damage functions with linear segments (Barbier and Bergeron 1998).

For this chapter, the model was used to predict the effect of changes in input and product prices, particularly that of coffee (*Coffea canephora* Pierre ex Fröhner L.), between 1994 and 1996 in the state of Acre. Model simulations of land use for the 1994 baseline for the settlement project of Pedro Peixoto in Acre are compared with simulations of 1996 with more favorable coffee prices.

# METHODS

## THE MODEL

The FaleBEM, a dynamic mathematical programming model written and solved in GAMS (Brooke et al. 1992), was developed to model the decisions of representative small-scale subsistence-oriented settlers in the Pedro Peixoto project in the western Brazilian state of Acre. It simulates the typical farmer's responses to a wide range of policy, technology, and project interventions. The model incorporates all the important biophysical and economic factors thought to affect farmers' decisions about land use and deforestation (see Lewis et al. 2002, for a more detailed description of the model).

The model assumes that farmers maximize the discounted value of their household consumption over a 15-year time horizon, but it is not a utility-maximizing model because it values consumption but not leisure time. However, this maximization is subject to serious labor constraints. Previous work has shown that labor availability is the major factor in slowing deforestation (Lewis et al. 2002).

Although the model has a 15-year planning horizon, it is solved recursively at 5-year intervals. If one updates all the constraint values for each solution, a series of moving 15-year farm plans are obtained that can be used to track much longer periods of time than the initial 15-year period. This is especially useful for exploring long-term changes in land use and the sustainability aspects of different farming practices. The results presented in this chapter are based on a 25-year period and were derived from five recursive runs of the model for each policy experiment.

There are also minimum consumption constraints that must be met each year for food, clothes, and farm implements. The model allocates farm income each year to consumption and on-farm investments. When income is invested it increases future production potential, and hence future consumption, but at the expense of current consumption. Income is generated in the model by the production of products for home consumption or sale. Production choices are subject to an array of resource and technology constraints, including seasonal land, labor, and cash flow constraints. For example, in keeping with local restrictions on markets, milk sales are constrained by quotas, and the maximum amount of hired labor that can be acquired in any given month is restricted to 15 worker-days. In addition to agricultural production, the household can engage in extractive activities in the forest (e.g., harvesting Brazil nuts [*Bertholletia excelsa* Humb. & Bonpl.]) and can sell household labor off farm. It can also hire nonfamily labor to work on the farm. Because the region is only a small producer of most products, all output prices are fixed in the model. This assumption is less defensible for nontimber tree products because these products have limited marketing outlets. But the model produces such small quantities that the impact on

consumption of any price effects can reasonably be ignored. Potential general equilibrium effects on the input side, especially labor and wages, were addressed through sensitivity analyses. Because the model does not include risk, and land cannot be rented,
purchased, or sold, results must be interpreted in light of these realities: Would risk
and land markets change the land use patterns shown here? These issues are addressed
in this chapter.

The model also tracks soil fertility and soil nutrient balances, and these influence future productivity levels within the planning period of the model. Soil fertility
can be improved by adding inorganic fertilizers, by changing the cropping pattern,
by putting land into fallow, or opening new areas to production (deforesting). Soil
nutrients in the forest, fallow, and cultivated areas are tracked and linked to crop
nutrient demands and yields; this provides a link between deforestation decisions and
production decisions on the cleared land. This link is modeled by allowing farmers
to choose between growing the crops with all the nutrients needed to achieve the
average yield for a given soil type and crop or using fewer nutrients and suffering
the yield consequences depicted in figure 10.1. Choosing to produce with nutrient
deficiency (*c*) has a yield reduction effect (*b*) calculated as $y-(b/c\,ND)$, where $y$ is the
yield when nutrient requirements are met, and ND is the level of deficiency chosen by
the model. The model approximates each land use's yield response function by dividing and linearizing the nutrient yield–response function into three sections (O 1–3
in figure 10.1) and measuring yield reductions based on the slope of the curve at the
chosen level of deficiency, ND. Agronomic and soil productivity decline and buildup,

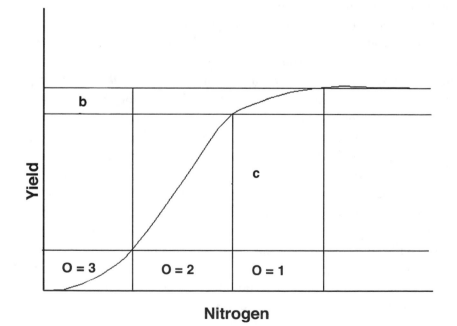

*Figure 10.1* Hypothetical crop yield response to varying soil nitrogen levels. Point *b* is the decrease in
crop yield expected for a given nitrogen deficiency in the soil of *c;* O = threshold levels of nutrients.

as well as crop yield responses, were modeled using local crop and soil expert opinion and published data.

The FaleBEM also keeps track of how many hectares of forest and of each cleared land use are on the farm in any year and the age of these land uses. Using this information, the farm's carbon stock in any year is determined. The FaleBEM can be used to perform carbon policy experiments, such as mandating a minimum amount of carbon that must be maintained in any year or allowing farmers to be paid for carbon stocks or flows (Carpentier et al. 2000). Estimates of carbon stocks by land use are from Lewis et al. (2002) and from chapter 2 of this volume.

Other agronomic constraints restrict land use dynamics and thus the long-term composition of the farm. Pasture is least restricted in that it can be planted after any land use and on all soil types. Annual and perennial crops can be planted only after other crops, burned forest, or fallow areas. In the absence of added inputs, the number of consecutive years crops can be planted on the same plot of land is limited by the decline in yields that accompanies the exhaustion of nutrients left after the burn and subsequent planting. In the model, farmers can choose to apply commercial fertilizer or to face smaller yields. Observed and reported yields declined over the years after the burn because most farmers do not use prohibitively expensive commercial fertilizers. After 2 years of annual cropping, farmers reported switching to pastures, fallow, or perennials because without adding fertilizers annual crop yields would be too low.

Economic activities and associated land uses affect soil productivity, which in turn affects future land uses and yields. The long-term effects of these interactions are taken into account in FaleBEM using a discretely dynamic modeling approach in which the state of the economic and environmental resources at the end of year $t = 1$ becomes the initial condition for decision-making in year $t = 2$.

More specifically, forest and other stocks are carried over from one production year to the next to become the initial natural resource stock for the next year. This discretely dynamic model is initiated in the first year of simulation with a set of initial conditions describing a farm and farmer's family characteristics in 1994 that were derived from field surveys for a group of farmers well situated vis-à-vis markets (see Witcover and Vosti 1996). These include characteristics such as hectares in different land uses, forest remaining, and on-farm labor (family composition). Basically, this model presents the farmer with the complete set of land use options and intensity levels available in the area, and some experimental ones, and then performs several "reality checks" that constrain farmer decisions, such as input availability, reversibility of land use decisions, and profitability. Financial returns for each activity are the product of the activity's yield and output prices minus input costs. With all this information in hand, the model selects, from all possible land use paths (over a 15-year period), the one that maximizes the discounted sum of consumption that results from yearly allocation of income to investment or consumption discounted to the present using a 9 percent discount rate.

Land use activities can be modeled at three levels of technology, V1, V2, and V3, each with associated input and output technical coefficients. V1 is the dominant traditional production system for small farmers in the area. It is land and labor intensive and uses limited external inputs. V3 is the recommended technology package of the state branch of the national agricultural research agency, Empresa Brasileira de Pesquisa Agropecuária (Embrapa). The intermediate technology level, V2, uses some improved management and commercial inputs but not necessarily at recommended levels. This level reflects the way small-scale farmers adopt new technology packages incrementally, instead of whole packages at once. As the level of technology intensifies from V1 to V3, management (controlled burning, increased weeding, spacing, control breeding, and herd rotation) generally improves, reliance on commercial inputs (seeds, fertilizers, pesticides, vaccines, feed supplements) increases, and the quality of these inputs (seeds, bulls, and cows) increases. Labor may decrease or increase depending on the activity. Generally, farmers using V3 technology apply commercial fertilizers and pesticides, whereas those using V1 and V2 do not. The V1 technology implies use of seeds kept from previous years, whereas V2 and V3 imply use of commercial seeds. Perennials are grown with technology V1 or V3; that is, farmers usually adopt the recommended technology package or keep their traditional practices. Perennials cannot be stored because they are highly perishable; they are sold in the month in which they are harvested (in Rondônia, 20 percent of output is consumed by the family or spoiled [Oliveira 1998]).

## Data

The model was built using economic parameters collected during fieldwork, such as input (including monthly labor) and output levels. Parameters for the model were generated through statistical analysis of detailed farm surveys conducted in Pedro Peixoto with eighty-one farmers in 1994 and sixty-two of the same farmers in 1996. Prices were drawn from secondary data supplemented by fieldwork. Our fieldwork revealed that farmers form their expectation of this year's prices based on last year's, mainly harvest, prices. Because the model tries to replicate the 1994 (1993–1994) and 1996 (1995–1996) land use decisions, 1992–1993 and 1994–1995 prices are used for all crops and livestock for the 1994 and 1996 simulations, respectively. Brazil nut prices are an exception to this rule; 1994 and 1996 prices were used because families can observe current prices before deciding whether to gather Brazil nuts. Together, these factors determine financial returns to activities undertaken at different scales. The preliminary results of the model were calibrated by groups of experts.

## BACKGROUND DATA AND MODELING RESULTS

### CHARACTERISTICS OF ACRE AND THE PEDRO PEIXOTO SETTLEMENT PROJECT

Nine percent of the state of Acre (15.25 million ha) has been deforested (chapter 12, this volume). Most of the deforested area is under pasture (900,000 ha), followed by annual crops (108,000 ha), fallow land (64,000 ha), and banana (*Musa* X *paradisiaca* L., 8000 ha) (IBGE 1996). Cattle herd size in 1996 was 794,307 head and has now reached 1.2 million (chapter 12, this volume). In 1996, 36 percent of these animals were on small farms of less than 100 ha, and this number is expected to have grown to 50 percent by 2000 (Valentim, pers. comm. 2002). Pests and insects are common and cause sporadic damage. Because of agronomic constraints coupled with economic viability, most cleared land eventually is planted to pasture. Most farmers use extensive pasture systems with minimum management and thus labor, which results in substantial amounts of pasture. Valentim (1989) reports that in 1989 an estimated 70 percent of the 600,000 ha of pasture in Acre was degraded or in the process of being degraded. Traditional pastures can degrade quickly. However, with better management (including past and present stocking rates, quality of the initial forest burn, frequency of pasture burning, and the quality and adaptability of the grass planted, as well as soil improvements), the decrease in pasture carrying capacity can be reduced.

Table 10.1 summarizes land uses of the farms surveyed in Pedro Peixoto in 1994 and 1996. In 1994, farm size averaged 91.1 ha, 70 percent of which was still forested, 58 percent of their cleared land was in pasture, and more than 90 percent of farmers had some pasture. The forest, annual crop, and fallow areas decreased between 1994 and 1996; pasture areas increased, as did mixed crops and perennials, with high growth rates but in extremely small areas. According to Fujisaka et al. (1996), after 2 years of annual crops, 64 percent of farmers in Pedro Peixoto in 1994 planted their land to pasture, 36 percent let it go into fallow, and none planted it to perennials or annuals.

Banana and coffee are the main perennial crops in Pedro Peixoto, although they are grown at very limited levels. Annuals and perennials are labor intensive, few herbicides are applied, and no animal traction or mechanical implements are used. On average, farmers had 0.37 ha of coffee in 1996 and a total of 1.3 ha of perennials, including banana. Bananas are integrated into agroforestry systems to shade young trees, planted in monoculture, or used in farm gardens. Although coffee is common

*Table 10.1* Area in Different Land Uses and Percentage Land Use Change for Farms Sampled in the Pedro Peixoto Project in 1994 and 1996

| Land Uses | 1994 (ha) | 1996 (ha) | Change (%) |
|---|---|---|---|
| Forest | 61.5 | 55.6 | −9.5 |
| Annuals | 4.6 | 2.5 | −45.7 |
| Perennials | 0.9 | 0.6 | −33.3 |
| Mixed annual and perennial crops | 0.1 | 0.7 | +600 |
| Fallow | 5.9 | 4.5 | −23.7 |
| Pasture | 17.8 | 19.5 | +9.5 |
| Total | 90.8 | 83.4 | −8.2 |
| Number of farms surveyed | 70 | 122 | |

*Source:* Field survey, 1994 and 1996.

in the neighboring state of Rondônia, it was just beginning to appear in Acre in 1994, when most coffee plants were too young to be productive. Coffee usually is planted in association with corn (*Zea mays* L.), followed by bean (*Phaseolus vulgaris* L.), and has a productive life of 5 to 9 years, depending on management practices.

The farm household modeled combines subsistence and market-oriented activities. Among the surveyed farmers, more than 90 percent keep their own seeds of annual crops from one year to the next instead of buying certified seeds. The model allows farm households to store grains for seeds and feed themselves. Seeds and grain for consumption can also be bought. Similarly, extra labor can be sold off farm, and labor can be hired on farm. Production systems were characterized by extensive land uses with low or nonexistent external inputs. For example, out of the 124 Acre farmers interviewed in 1996, 2 used chemical fertilizers, 15 insecticides, and 17 herbicides.

Among the major shifts in prices between the harvest years of 1994 and 1996 was an increase of 36 percent in common (V1) livestock prices, a milk price increase of 11 percent, and a decrease in animal care of 20 percent (table 10.2). Rice (*Oryza sativa* L.) prices decreased by 26 percent, whereas corn prices increased by 13 percent and bean prices by 2 percent. Coffee prices increased by 411 percent, and banana prices increased by 123 percent. Input prices such as pesticides and fertilizers decreased by 10 percent, and wages increased by 43 percent. Coffee yields in the model are the expected yields given average weather for each technology level and soil type. A medium-quality soil's peak coffee yield is 970 kg/ha with V1 technology and 3400 kg/ha with V3 technology.

From field data collected in 1994, farms were grouped on the basis of characteristics deemed to be exogenous to farmers' land use decisions as characterized by the model (e.g., soil type, distance to market, and age of settlement of land). Several groups emerged, each of which can be taken to represent a farm type. There were two main groups: smaller, well-situated farms, and bigger farms further from the market. The average farm and household characteristics for well-situated farms, in terms of access to markets, were used as the model's initial conditions. This group was dominated by soil types of medium quality, that is, with some fertility problems, mild slopes, or rockiness. The 60-ha farm's initial land uses are 2.5 ha of annuals, 1.5 ha of perennials, 4 ha of fallow, 9 ha of pasture, and 43 ha of forest. There are 10,067 t of total carbon stock over all land uses, 89 percent of it in the forest.

## BASELINE SIMULATION RESULTS

The baseline explicitly includes one forestry policy that prevents small-scale farmers from harvesting timber products from their forested land. Although technically permissible by law, the bureaucratic obstacles to obtaining official permission to sustainably harvest timber products in farmers' legal reserves have been insurmountable in practice and have made on-farm timber extraction difficult (see chapter 8, this volume). Another forestry law mandating that no more than half of any farm be cleared

*Table 10.2* Farmgate Prices in 1994 and 1996

| Prices | Farmgate Prices (in 1996 reais [R]) | | |
| --- | --- | --- | --- |
| | 1994 | 1996 | Change (%) |
| **Commodity Prices** | | | |
| Rice, kg | 0.27 | 0.20 | −26 |
| Corn, kg | 0.15 | 0.17 | +13 |
| Bean, kg | 0.51 | 0.52 | +2 |
| Coffee, kg | 0.28 | 1.43 | +411 |
| Banana, bunch | 0.87 | 1.94 | +123 |
| Brazil nut, 18 kg | 2.60 | 3.20 | +23 |
| Timber, m³ | 110 | 120 | +9 |
| Calf, per head (V1 tech.) | 102 | 134 | +31 |
| Cow, per head (V1 tech.) | 214 | 290 | +36 |
| Beef, per head (V1 tech.) | 350 | 364 | +4 |
| Milk, L (all technologies) | 0.36 | 0.40 | +11 |
| **Input Prices** | | | |
| Rice seeds, kg | 1.74 | 1.80 | +3 |
| Corn seeds, kg | 1.72 | 2.40 | +40 |
| Bean seeds, kg | 2.27 | 2.40 | +6 |
| Coffee seedlings, each | 1.00 | 0.30 | −70 |
| Grass seeds, kg (V2 tech.) | 2.36 | 2.36 | 0 |
| Kudzu seeds, kg (V2 tech.) | 11.60 | 10 | −14 |
| Sacks, each | 0.85 | 0.65 | −24 |
| Pesticides, kg | 24 | 21.60 | −10 |
| Nitrogen fertilizer, kg (V3 tech.) | 1.21 | 1.08 | −11 |
| Chainsaw (purchase price) | 1441 | 841 | −42 |
| Oxen + cart (purchase price) | 1525 | 1120 | −27 |
| Chainsaw + operator rental rate | 37 | 50 | +35 |
| Fence cost, km (V1 tech.) | 302 | 307 | +2 |
| Animal care (R/animal unit/m, V1 tech.) | 5.18 | 4.14 | −20 |
| Wage rate, June | 7 | 10 | +43 |
| Bull, purchase price (V1 tech.) | 823 | 823 | 0 |
| Timber transport (R/m³) | 15 | 10 | −33 |
| Truck rental (round trip to market) | 91 | 100 | +10 |

The price vectors labeled 1994 and 1996 are the vectors of prices judged to influence 1994 and 1996 land uses and reflect market prices for the agricultural years 1992–1993 and 1994–1995. All prices reflect values for average-quality products and inputs for that region; regional product quality is not high by national standards, especially for coffee.

*Source:* Banco da Amazonia, 1994, 1995, 1996, semester report and farming supply store survey.

for agricultural purposes (the 50 percent rule) was excluded because this law was not actively enforced in the 1994–1996 period.

Figure 10.2 depicts land uses (including forest, and therefore implicitly deforestation) generated by the model for a 25-year time span for this typical small-scale farm in the settlement project of Pedro Peixoto, Acre.

There are several results from this baseline simulation. The amount of forest retained declines over time, finally disappearing in about year 25, despite the small but positive revenue provided by the extraction of Brazil nuts (an activity undertaken by about 50 percent of sample farms in 1996). At the same time, cattle production eventually occupies about 85 percent of the farm. In addition, the survey results suggest that farmers do not plant V1 pasture, so the baseline results do not include any degraded pasture. The level of annual crop area is constant, and this activity occupies about 8 percent of the farm throughout the 25-year time horizon. Manioc (*Manihot esculenta* Crantz) takes up about 1 ha throughout the 25-year horizon (manioc is included in the perennial category for modeling purposes because it spans more than 1 year, although it is not a perennial). Young fallow up to 4 years in age weaves into and out of the baseline to support annual crop production, becoming more significant as the forest disappears completely. When baseline simulations are extended to 35 years, area in fallow continues to increase at approximately 0.2 ha every 2 years, to reach 5.5 ha in year 35. Finally, no coffee or bananas were grown under 1994 conditions (the only pseudo-perennial is manioc). Farm incomes plateau at about year 13, at a level of approximately R9000 per year (as all prices, in 1996 reais). The net present value of consumption over the 25-year period is R50,688. The other farm type is characterized

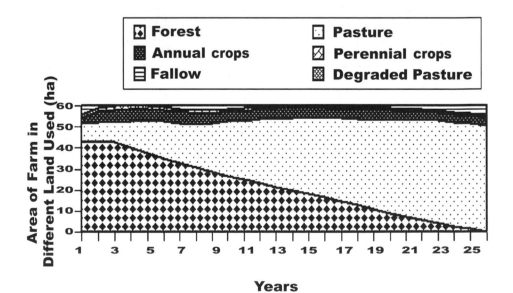

*Figure 10.2* Area (ha) of a typical farm in different land uses during the 25-yr time line of the baseline simulation using 1994 prices.

by farms further away from market, with 90 ha and less household labor. Vosti et al. (chapter 17, this volume) report that deforestation rate on these farms is lower, resulting in slightly less than half the area still forested after 25 years. For this farm type too, however, pasture is the dominant cleared land use.

## POLICY EXPERIMENT SIMULATION RESULTS

Some key product and input prices varied substantially between 1994 and 1996. A baseline simulation, using the medium-quality soils and 1996 prices, was run to assess the impact of some dramatic changes in relative prices since 1994, especially for coffee (a 411 percent increase) and labor (a 43 percent increase).

Figure 10.3 depicts land uses for a 25-year horizon using 1996 rather than 1994 prices (with adoption unaffected with risk factors such as price volatility). Comparing land use distributions on a farm with the baseline scenario (figure 10.2), the following results emerge. Deforestation rates slow somewhat, primarily because of the reallocation of labor (family and hired) to the establishment and especially the maintenance of coffee. Note that higher wages have a more significant impact on activities that depend on hired labor, such as coffee. The impact of increased labor needs for coffee (primarily during harvesting) is reflected in the rapid decline in deforestation after about year 7, when the substantial coffee area established during years 1 to 6 comes into full production and must be harvested in June, the time when new forest is usu-

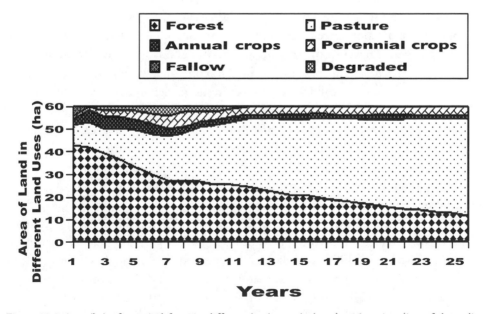

*Figure 10.3* Area (ha) of a typical farm in different land uses during the 25-yr time line of the policy experiment simulation using 1996 prices.

ally cleared. That said, at year 25, forest is 12 ha and still declining, whereas pasture increases and perennials remain stable. Land dedicated to annual crops declines, and area in secondary fallow drops to zero. Finally, family-discounted consumption for the 25-year period increases substantially under the 1996 price scenario to R71,305, R20,617 more than in the baseline and mostly from coffee.

Under current economic and policy conditions, simulation results suggest that a large tradeoff exists: Deforestation will continue until the forest is exhausted on small farms, but incomes will rise. Results suggest that changes in relative prices such as those occurring between 1994 and 1996 would substantially raise farm household income. The quadrupling of coffee prices, in particular, would have a braking effect on deforestation, delaying by about 5 years the total depletion of the forest. In the simulation, the use of cleared land is significantly affected, with more land dedicated to coffee and less to annuals and fallow. However, the amount of land in pasture remains constant with the baseline, and the typical farm is still dominated by pasture.

## CONCLUSION AND POLICY IMPLICATIONS

Four conclusions relevant for policy emerge from this modeling experiment. First, although farmers face constraints, these constraints do not shield farmers from major changes in product prices; therefore farmers are likely to respond to such large changes as occurred between 1994 and 1996, when input prices to establish coffee plummeted and the returns to this activity dramatically improved. Second, price changes between 1994 and 1996 led to substantial increases in farm income and a dramatic increase in the proportion of income coming from coffee. Third although overall deforestation was slowed by the shift in relative prices, it did not stop. In fact, if the time horizon for the 1996 simulation were extended by 5 years or so, forest retained on the farm would fall to zero. However, the gains in forest cover evaluated at year 25 are substantial when compared with the baseline, with 12 ha compared with none in the baseline, primarily because labor is reallocated from deforestation activities to coffee harvesting, activities that overlap in the annual agricultural calendar (although simulations suggest similar braking effects of total labor bottlenecks, even if in other seasons). Fourth, and perhaps most importantly for land use policy, area in pasture did not change much in the face of a dramatically changed set of relative prices for other commodities. Instead, adjustments in cleared area to establish coffee came at the expense of annual crops and fallow areas.

Two policy implications arise from these results. First, although major changes in input and product prices would be expected to affect land use practices and areas based on revised profitability, not all land uses necessarily will be significantly affected. For example, although increases in coffee prices would be expected to cause an increase in the area dedicated to coffee production, simulations show that this occurs at the expense of annual and fallow land rather than pasture. In this labor-scarce environment, farmers respond to favorable coffee prices initially by switching out of other labor-intensive activities rather than activities that use less labor per land unit (pasture, in this case). This also means that the price shift would not be expected to make a tremendous difference in deforestation rates. That livestock systems demand labor throughout the calendar year (rather than labor demand peaking, as it does for coffee, particularly at harvest time) only reinforces the propensity to stay with pasture if possible. Policymakers should not expect, then, that in the short to medium term (before the labor scarcity drew in more workers to the area), pricing policies aimed at establishing labor-intensive production systems would greatly affect the area dedicated to more extensive production systems. Because most agroforestry systems have a high overall labor demand and peak labor demands (as opposed to labor demands spread throughout the year), results obtained here for coffee are likely to apply for other perennial systems or simple or complex agroforests.

These results are so because the Linear Programming model sets out to capture a market setting in which farm households out to boost their consumption to the highest levels possible bump up against severe labor constraints, at least seasonally: They may have the money to buy more labor, but that labor is not available. This characterization of smallholder objectives and circumstances is one of several offered by Angelsen et al. (2001). Under these conditions, smallholders experiencing price changes are limited primarily by labor availability in the changes they can make to product mix or production technique. So, although price changes may greatly influence farm household incomes, changes in land and labor allocation across production activities in response to these prices can be concentrated among activities that compete seasonally for the most scarce factor: labor. This situation leaves pasture and deforestation unaffected. The good news is that the relationship is likely to be symmetric; as coffee prices fall, deforestation probably will not increase. Poorly functioning labor markets are an ingredient essential to both sides of this story; improvements in labor market performance will make the links between price changes and deforestation (via income) more direct and larger.

Second, some price changes, such as the shift in relative prices experienced between 1994 and 1996, simply cannot be managed by policymakers at any level. In this case, the supply and demand conditions of the international coffee market were chiefly responsible for the dramatic increase in coffee prices, and the private sector (with assistance for public sector research and extension) was responsible for much of the decrease in coffee establishment costs. Policymakers can influence the profitability of coffee production even though they cannot affect product prices by taking policy action focused on reducing costs, improving product quality, or discovering niche markets (e.g., organic coffee from the Amazon), but the effects (especially of the last option) probably will not be widespread.

Finally (these insights cannot be gleaned from the model in its current form), coffee is a perennial and as such can be managed more or less intensively—even to the point of abandonment—for a year or more while prices find their new low and begin to recover. A waiting period does not depend only on farmers' price expectations because converting land from coffee to pasture is not in itself costless: There are short-term constraints to herd expansion. Therefore it is unlikely that coffee will be converted to pasture immediately, although that will be the end result if return to profitability is delayed more than a couple of years. Also unlikely is any rush to convert more forest to pasture just because coffee prices have fallen because the seasonal nature of forest felling itself precludes hasty action, and the farmer still faces the short-term herd expansion constraints. That said, farmers might engage in other activities that require little investment and time commitment to cover livelihood needs and mitigate coffee losses; these could include off-farm employment or illegal logging.

## ACKNOWLEDGMENTS

The FaleBEM model was developed as part of the ASB consortium while the authors were at the International Food Policy Research Institute. The authors thank institute researchers Bruno Barbier, Hans Lofgren, Andrea Cattaneo, and Peter Hazell for their guidance in the writing of this model. We are also indebted to Tamara Gomes, Judson Valentim, Angelo Mansur Mendes, Claudenor Pinho de Sá, Alessandra Araujo, Dennys Russell, Samuel Oliveira, and many more colleagues at Embrapa Acre and Rondônia who provided valuable information and insight on key technical coefficients and biophysical parameters. Funding for research was provided by the Inter-American Development Bank, the Danish Agency for Development Assistance (via their contributions to the ASB Program), the government of Switzerland, and the government of Japan.

## REFERENCES

Angelsen, A., D. van Soest, D. Kaimowitz, and E. Bulte. 2001. Technological change and deforestation: A theoretical overview. pp. 19–34. *In* A. Angelsen and D. Kaimowitz (eds.) Agricultural technologies and tropical deforestation. CAB Int., Wallingford, UK.

Banco da Amazonia. 1994, 1995, and 1996. Informação trimestral sobre atividades agropecuarias. Rio Branco, Acre.

Barbier, B., and G. Bergeron. 1998. Natural resource management in the hillsides of Honduras: Bioeconomic modeling at the micro-watershed level. Environ. and Production Technol. Div. Discussion Paper 32. IFPRI, Washington, DC.

Binswanger, H. 1987. Fiscal and legal incentives with environmental effects on the Brazilian Amazon. Discussion Paper. Research Unit, Agric. and Rural Dev. Dep., Operational Policy Staff. World Bank, Washington, DC.

Brooke, A., D. Kendrick, and A. Meeraus. 1992. GAMS: A user's guide, Release 2.25. The Scientific Press Ser., Boyd & Fraser Publ. Co., Danvers, MA.

Carpentier, C.L., D.D. Bosch, and S.S. Batie. 1998. Using spatial information to reduce costs of controlling agricultural nonpoint source pollution. Agric. Resource Econ. Rev. (April):72–84.

Carpentier, C.L., S.A. Vosti, and J. Witcover. 2000. Small-scale farms in the western Brazilian Amazon: Can they benefit from carbon trade? Environ. and Production Technol. Div. Discussion Pap. no. 67. IFPRI, Washington, DC.

Dosi, C., and M. Moretto. 1993. Nonpoint-source pollution control, information asymmetry, and the choice of time profile for environmental fees. *In* C.S. Russell and J.F. Shogren (eds.) Theory, modeling and experience in the management of nonpoint-source pollution. Kluwer Academic Publ., Boston.

Ellis, J.K., D.W. Hugues, and W.R. Butcher. 1991. Economic modeling of farm production and conservation decision in response to alternative resource and environmental policies. Northeast. J. Agric. Resource Econ. 20 (April):198–208.

Fujisaka, S., W. Bell, N. Thomas, L. Hurtado, and E. Crawford. 1996. Slash-and-burn agriculture, conversion to pasture, and deforestation in two Brazilian Amazon colonies. Agric. Ecosyst. Environ. 59:115–130.

Hecht, S.B. 1985. Environment, development and politics: Capital accumulation and the livestock sector in eastern Amazonia. World Dev. 13(6):663–684.

IBGE (Instituto Brasileiro de Geografia e Estatistica). 1996. Anuário estatístico do Acre. IBGE, Rio de Janeiro.

Kaimowitz, D., and A. Angelsen. 1998. Economic models of tropical deforestation: A review. CIFOR, Bogor, Indonesia.

Lewis, J., S. Vosti, J. Witcover, P.J. Ericksen, R. Guevara, and T.P. Tomich (eds.). 2002. Alternatives to Slash-and-Burn (asb) in Brazil: Summary report and synthesis of phase II. November 2002. World Agroforestry Center (icraf), Nairobi.

Oliveira, S.J.M. 1998. Mercado de café no mundo, no Brasil e na Amazônia: Aspectos conjunturais. Circular Técnica, 38 nov. Porto Velho, Embrapa Rondônia, Brazil.

Palm, C.A., P.L. Woomer, J. Alegre, C. Castilla, K. Cordeiro, K. Hairiah, et al. 2002. Carbon sequestration and trace gas emissions in slash-and-burn and alternative land uses in the tropics. Alternatives to Slash-and-Burn Phase II Final Rep. ICRAF, Nairobi.

Shortle, J.S. 1984. The use of estimated pollution flows in agricultural pollution control policy: Implications for abatement and policy instrument. Northeast. J. Agric. Resource Econ. 13(October 1984):277–285.

Valentim, J.F. 1989. Impacto ambiental da pecuária no Acre. Documento Base do Curso de Avaliação do Impacto Ambiental da Pecuária no Acre. Embrapa–Unidade de Execução de Pessquisa de Âmbito Estadual Rio Branco/Inst. de Meio Ambiente do Acre, Acre, Brazil.

Vosti, S.A., J. Witcover, and C.L. Carpentier. 2002. Agricultural intensification by smallholders in the western Brazilian Amazon: From deforestation to sustainable use. IFPRI Res. Rep. 130. IFPRI, Washington, DC. Available at http://www.ifpri.org/pubs/pubs.htm#rreport (verified 7 Dec. 2003).

Witcover, J., and S.A. Vosti. 1996. Alternatives to slash-and-burn agriculture (asb): A characterization of Brazilian benchmark sites of Pedro Peixoto and Theobroma, August/September 1994. MP-8 Working Paper US96–003. IFPRI, Washington, DC.

# 11 Smallholder Options for Reclaiming and Using *Imperata cylindrica* L. (Alang-Alang) Grasslands in Indonesia

Pratiknyo Purnomosidhi
> *ICRAF Southeast Asia  Bogor, Indonesia*

Kurniatun Hairiah
> *Brawijaya University  Malang, Indonesia*

Subekti Rahayu
> *ICRAF Southeast Asia  Bogor, Indonesia*

Meine van Noordwijk
> *ICRAF Southeast Asia  Bogor, Indonesia*

The Alternatives to Slash and Burn (ASB) program in Indonesia aims to identify options for slowing down deforestation and promoting the rehabilitation of degraded (formerly forested) areas (van Noordwijk et al. 1997). Many previously forested areas have seen a trajectory of forest degradation similar to that shown in figure 1.1a, with a phase of low-use degraded land and a rehabilitation process. This macro process of degradation and rehabilitation may resemble the plot-level decline and restoration of productivity in a shifting cultivation cycle but is driven by more complex processes of migrating farmers, changing tenure and resource access of farmers, broader-scale landscape- or village-level control over free-ranging fires (Wibowo et al. 1997), and market-driven economic incentives. This chapter addresses technical issues associated with smallholder rehabilitation of grasslands derived from forest degradation at the ASB benchmark site in Pakuan Ratu (in the northern part of Lampung province) in Sumatra, Indonesia (see figure 13.1 later in this volume), which was chosen as representative of the vast area under *Imperata cylindrica* and related coarse grasses in Asia (approximately 35 million ha) and Indonesia (8.5 million ha) (Garrity et al. 1997). Although increasing the rate of rehabilitation of these grasslands does not necessarily slow down the rate of deforestation at the frontier, rehabilitated areas can offer an alternative attraction point for migrants.

Efforts to reclaim *Imperata* grassland areas and put them to intensive agricultural use where shifting cultivation is practiced have been debated in

Indonesia since at least the 1930s (Hagreis 1931; Danhof 1941). A common prescription was large-scale reforestation, possibly with international financial support via projects aiming to increase carbon sequestration (Drajat 1991; Tjitrosemito and Soerjani 1991). However, there is remarkably little evidence of economies of scale in reforestation (Tomich et al. 1997), and smallholder agroforestry may provide a socially, economically, and environmentally superior option.

From the history of past successful transitions of *Imperata* grasslands into densely inhabited agroforestry land use mosaics (Foresta and Michon 1997; Potter 1997), we can conclude that four conditions must be met for such reclamation to occur as a spontaneous, farmer-led process:

- A sense of security of tenure over the trees planted, if not the land itself
- Effective village-level institutions for controlling free-ranging fires
- Local farmer knowledge of agroforestry techniques and access to germplasm that can effectuate the transformation and address the often low fertility of the soils (Santoso et al. 1997)
- Physical and economic access to markets for the products of the land, leading to adequate profitability

The research results reported here focus on the third of these requirements and more specifically on technical requirements for shade-based control of *Imperata* in developing agroforestry systems.

## LAND USE PATTERNS IN THE RESEARCH SITE

One of the ASB benchmark sites in Indonesia is located in Pakuan Ratu subdistrict of northern Lampung, Sumatra, at the lower reaches of the Tulang Bawang River. This area was chosen to represent the rehabilitation phase of land use change and represents a situation in which conflicts over land did not (at the time of the survey) override other concerns because the area is not (or is no longer) considered to be state forest land. Three groups of farmers (Lampungese in villages along the rivers, transmigrants moved by the government from forest reserves in southern and central Lampung, and spontaneous migrant settlers) interact with large agroindustrial estates (sugar cane [*Saccharum officinarum* L.], cassava [*Manihot esculenta* Crantz], and fast-growing timber). However, after the "Reformasi" change in Indonesian government in 1998 serious conflicts emerged between Lampungese and the state sugar cane plantation, leading to a de facto closure of roads, loss of off-farm labor opportunity, and general hardship in the transmigration villages. Forest cover was lost rapidly after logging in the early 1970s, followed by government-sponsored conversion of the land to transmigration or plantation sites. Around the transmigration villages the landscape degraded rapidly as the initial soil fertility inherited from the forest was used, and large areas became dominated by *Imperata* fallows, alternating with cassava.

Transmigration programs started in 1905 in southern Lampung (Djojoprapto 1995) and—in combination with an influx of spontaneous migrants—have transformed Lampung into the most densely populated Indonesian province outside Java (174 people/km² in 1993), with the lowest remaining forest cover; hardly any state forest land outside national parks still had full forest cover in the late 1980s (van Noordwijk et al. 1995). Northern Lampung was the last frontier in the lowland peneplain and was used in the early 1980s to resettle spontaneous migrants from Java or Javanese born in transmigration settlements in Lampung from the fertile coffee belt in the hills, to protect the water supply to irrigation schemes (in the Way Sekampung, Way Seputih, and Tulang Bawang watersheds). These farmers were moved to Pakuan Ratu, the poorest subdistrict in Lampung and, in fact, in Sumatra as a whole (except for some of the adjacent islands), with thirty-nine of its forty-one villages classified as poor. The ASB benchmark area is largely in the Pakuan Ratu subdistrict, with Negeri Besar as the largest and oldest Lampungese settlement on the river. However, a traveler's report from 1920 had already commented on the degraded forests close to the Tulang Bawang River, linked partly to the demand for railway sleepers for the Bandar Lampung–Palembang railway construction (van Noordwijk et al. 1995).

The typical pattern in transmigration sites in the early 1980s was as follows: After clearing the forest by slash-and-burn, transmigrant farmers planted food crops in the first few years. When the fertility of the land declined by the fourth year, they shifted to off-farm activities such as daily wage labor or driving on the nearby sugar cane plantation (PG Bunga Mayang), in the remaining logging concession and forest timber company (Industrial Timber Plantation Company, or HTI), or in illegal logging operations. Only farmers who had land that could be transformed into paddy rice (*Oryza sativa* L.) could make a living from agriculture (Elmhirst 1996). The opening of cassava processing plants (PT Bumi Waras) made it worthwhile to continue farming on the acid upland soils, in what became an *Imperata*–cassava rotation, but cassava prices fluctuated, partly under the influence of European Union quotas for imports of tapioca as fodder. With declining fertility and more and more fires in the landscape, the area that was abandoned to *Imperata* increased.

By the late 1980s the sugar cane plantation started an "outgrowers" scheme, stimulating farmers to form groups (Petani Tebu Rakyat Intensifikasi) and providing credit for plowing, fertilizer, and cane planting, to be paid back through the cane harvest in the first 3 years. Although at some stage smallholder cane under this program almost equaled the area under sugar cane managed by the plantation company (and thus compensated for the overcapacity of the factory given the declining productivity of the plantation itself), relations between the plantation and farmers turned sour (Elmhirst et al. 1998) when the results for the farmers' fields were less than expected (for numerous reasons, including logistics of fertilizer delivery and transport at harvest time), and farmers could not pay back their credits. After this sugar cane phase, land was again abandoned to *Imperata* or reused for cassava, benefiting from good farmgate prices and possibly from the residual fertility of fertilizer used in the sugar cane.

The agility of the farmers' adaptations to changing income opportunities did not stop there. The transmigrant and spontaneous migrant farmers continued to struggle to transform the *Imperata* land into a productive resource, gradually clearing it manually (hoeing), plowing it by using draft animals (after a government program introduced cattle to the villages) or hired tractors, or applying herbicides, if they had the capital to do so. The farmers have tried to get tree crops started, with oil palm, fast-growing timber species (such as *Acacia mangium* Willd. and *Paraserianthes falcataria* [L.] Nielsen), and rubber as the main options. Doing so is risky because future markets for the timber are not clear, and marketing of oil palm to remote factories has been erratic because it depends on a reliable road network. Rubber became a serious option for farmers when road transport improved (especially that on the east–west axis, complementing the north–south access via the sugar cane plantation), and a new bridge provided contact with rubber-growing areas to the east of the benchmark area, around Manggala. In the ASB benchmark area, rubber planting gained importance in the villages of Panaragan, Karangsakti, and Karang Mulya, spreading from the village of Negeri Ujungkarang, where the Dinas Perkebunan (tree crop advisory service) established a nursery. Planting material is also bought from farmers in Madukoro, Negara Ratu, or Kotabumi, but village-level nurseries are now emerging. Farmers chose rubber because latex can give continuous income once the trees are tapped and can be marketed through various channels, wood of the rubber trees is valuable, and investment and maintenance costs are less than those for oil palm. Meanwhile, farmers in Batu Raja, Negara Batin, and villages further along the road to the Pakuan Ratu subdistrict office viewed oil palm as their main way out of poverty. They chose oil palm because it has a good market and can regrow after burning and drought, whereas rubber and timber trees are lost in *Imperata* fires.

Pepper and coffee have good prospects, too, and are the preferred option for the Lampungese farmers, who occupy the slightly better soils along the river (Van Noordwijk et al. 1996b). Transmigrant farmers chose this option only in the villages of Gedung Nyapah and Tulung Buyut. Coffee and black pepper have a good market, and their local price increased during the recent monetary crisis.

## PREVIOUS EXPERIMENTS ON SHADE-BASED CONTROL

In 1992, an on-farm experiment was begun by the Biological Management of Soil Fertility Project to plant trees in *Imperata* grassland as a low-cost method of shading out the grass (van Noordwijk et al. 1992, 1997). Two tree species—the fire-tolerant local *Peltophorum dasyrrachis* Kurz and a common legume *Gliricidia sepium* (Jacq.) Kunth ex Walp.—were planted in *Imperata* grasslands strips 4 m apart. After 1 year, the trees reduced the vigor of the *Imperata* but not sufficiently for reclamation. In the second year, tree canopy development continued, but it was still not enough to eliminate the *Imperata*. Tree growth showed wide variability, and only in the patches where *Peltophorum* grew best was *Imperata* controlled after 2 years. In the exceptionally dry season of the El Niño year 1994, fires (a perennial concern; see Bagnall-Oakeley et al., 1997) reached the plot from an adjacent area and provided a true test of fire tolerance. All trees of both species resprouted after the fire, and the experiment continued with food crops, pruned hedgerows, and spot applications of herbicides to control *Imperata*. The experiment thus showed that shade-based control of *Imperata* grass is not easily achieved and raised questions about the intensity and duration of shade needed to do so (MacDicken et al. 1997). Further work was clearly needed.

## RESEARCH QUESTIONS

Given that farmers in the ASB benchmark area had (at the time of the experiment, before the Reformasi period) reasonably secure access to land and were located near well-performing markets, and given the potential profitability of tree crops, we addressed the following specific issues:

- Which techniques are used by the farmers to convert the *Imperata* grasslands, and why?
- How can the developing agroforestry systems suppress *Imperata* regrowth and avoid the fire risks at an intermediate age (Bagnall-Oakeley et al. 1997); more specifically, how long and intense a shade is needed for adequate control (MacDicken et al. 1997).

The second research question was split into three parts: How much light can still penetrate to ground level in young rubber, oil palm, pepper–coffee, and timber production systems; for how many years can farmers still interplant food crops between the tree rows in these systems; and how does a well-established *Imperata* stand respond to shade of different intensities and duration.

## MATERIAL AND METHODS

Four research activities were undertaken to address these issues: a farm household survey of reclamation methods, field measurements of light intensity at ground level in selected agroforestry systems, an experiment aimed at defining the intensity and duration of shade needed for *Imperata* control, and in-depth interviews on the management practices in four smallholder agroforestry systems in the area.

### FARMER HOUSEHOLD SURVEY

A survey on farmer management options for converting and using *Imperata* grassland was conducted in an area extending beyond the ASB benchmark area and including villages in the Pakuan Ratu, North Sungkai, and South Sungkai subdistricts of North Lampung district (the district has since been subdivided and the study area now belongs partly to Way Kanan district). The survey was carried out in July 1997 and again in August 1998 and focused on the details of various management strategies and the costs associated with each. Total sample size was fifty intensive household interviews.

## FIELD MEASUREMENTS OF SUNLIGHT BELOW AGROFORESTRY SYSTEMS

On fifty farms, selected to cover the full spectrum of land use practices and a range of ages, light intensity and *Imperata* biomass were measured. On twenty locations per plot, relative light intensity (vis-à-vis full sunlight, measured using a photosynthetically active radiation sensor) was measured halfway between trees in the plant row and between rows. Tree diameter at 1.3 m above ground (diameter at breast height) was also measured. For oil palm plants, height was recorded instead of stem diameter. Biomass of *Imperata* grass was collected from 1-m$^2$ sampling areas. Results were averaged over the twenty sample points for each site for the current analysis.

## ARTIFICIAL SHADING EXPERIMENT

An experiment to quantify the response of well-established *Imperata* stands to shade of different intensities and duration was begun at the Biological Management of Soil Fertility Research Station (van Noordwijk et al. 1996a) in November 1995, with four levels of artificial shade in a randomized block design with four replicates. The experiment was monitored to measure (at monthly intervals) the decline of standing *Imperata* biomass under different shade conditions and to measure *Imperata*'s ability to regrow from rhizomes after a ground-level cut after 0 to 7 months at each level of shading.

## RESEARCH RESULTS

### FARMER HOUSEHOLD SURVEY

Farmers reported several techniques for clearing *Imperata* grasslands (figure 11.1) and selected one or more of the following depending on the availability of labor and cash and the crop to be planted after clearing.

The techniques range from manual slashing of the grass followed by hoeing, to application of systemic herbicides followed by plowing and sometimes preceded by burning, to plowing with animal or mechanical traction, usually after burning the

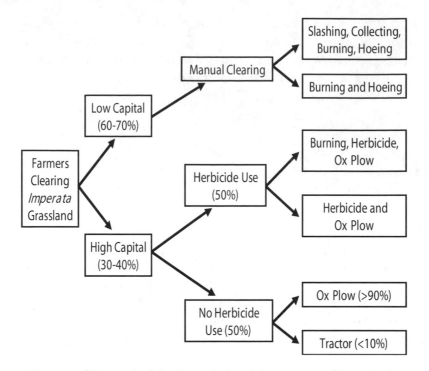

*Figure 11.1* Summary of *Imperata* land clearing methods and the percentage of farmers in the survey who used the various methods.

*Imperata* above-ground biomass to make work easier. Before clearing by almost any method, thatch can be manually collected from *Imperata* areas and used for roofing.

Cash-poor farmers (60–70 percent of respondents) rely on hoeing with family labor and can clear only a quarter to half a hectare per family per year, in the dry season (July–October). If labor were paid, this method would be very expensive. Land cleared in this way generally was used for planting food crops such as upland rice (*Oryza sativa* L.), maize (*Zea mays* L.), or soybean (*Glycine max* [L.] Merr.). Farmers mentioned that they prefer shallow soil tillage to deeper plowing because this keeps the dark top 15 to 20 cm of soil (the "soil meat") intact and avoids the iron-rich aggregates (locally called *crocos*) found below that depth and brought to the surface by plowing.

Farmers who can afford it prefer to use herbicides unless they have animal draft power available. Application rates ranged from 2 to 5 L/ha of one of the commercially available brands of glyphosate, often mixing more than one type. Herbicide normally was sprayed on young regrowth of *Imperata* 2 to 3 weeks after slashing or burning the standing biomass; 20 to 25 mL of herbicide is diluted in 15 L of water in a knapsack sprayer. According to the farmers, systemic herbicides remained effective for about 6 months, after which farmers commonly sprayed again, twice if the *Imperata* was not dense. The first spraying covered the entire area, and the second spraying covered only patches that remained green after 14 days; at least 5 L of herbicide was needed per hectare to achieve adequate control. Herbicide use without tillage was the preferred method of *Imperata* clearing before planting of rubber, oil palm, or timber trees; land dedicated to food crops needed plowing.

Farmers owning or having easy access to draft animals used them to convert *Imperata* grasslands. Plowing with draft animals normally is done in the dry season, when the *Imperata* rhizomes brought to the surface dry up easily, but sometimes (in 10 to 15 percent of interviewed cases) plowing extends into the early rainy season, when the soil is easier to work. Plowing in the early rains is preferred when the *Imperata* vegetation is not very dense and land is flat (on slopes manual hoeing is normal). Cattle were introduced into the area in about 1985 under a government loan scheme, benefiting transmigrants who were familiar with animal traction, rather than Lampungese farmers. Actually, farmers prefer animal drawn plows to tractors because the quality of work is good and no subsoil is brought to the surface, and they have seen what happens in tractor plowing at the sugar cane plantation. If the *Imperata* stand is dense, the early activities consist of a week of slashing, collecting, burning, and plowing per 0.25 ha or 3 to 4 days of burning and continued plowing per 0.25 ha. Normally a second tillage operation is needed once the rhizomes brought to the soil surface have dried off. Tractor-powered plows are used to clear *Imperata* land if the farmer intends to plant sugar cane or cassava; this technique became popular in the 1990s when the sugar cane factory started its outgrower scheme. In both Negara Jaya and Negara Tulang Bawang villages, a local (Lampungese) farmer has bought a tractor and started contract operations. Plowing mixes the soil to a depth of 50 cm, so most farmers perceive that soil fertility decreases because they see *crocos* appear on the top layer, to which they attribute in part the failure of the sugar cane outgrower scheme.

Of the several ways of converting *Imperata* grassland, which were the most cost effective? Table 11.1 reports the results of the farm household survey of conversion costs. The first column presents the main input used in conversion: labor, chemicals,

*Table 11.1* Costs of *Imperata* Grassland Clearing, by Clearing Method, 1998 and 1999

| Primary Input Used | Details of Clearing Method | Total Cost per Hectare (Rp000) | |
|---|---|---|---|
| | | 1998 | 1999 |
| Manual labor[a] | Burning–hoeing or slashing–collecting–burning–hoeing | 740–960 | 1500–1680 |
| Herbicide | Herbicide only | 104–260 | 90–225 |
| | Burning–herbicide–plowing or slashing–herbicide–plowing | 464–696 | 590–935 |
| Animal traction | Plowing, burning–plowing, or slashing–collecting–plowing | 360–540 | 500–800 |
| Tractor | Plowing | 160–200 | 350–400 |

[a]Mostly unpaid family labor. Average wage rate of labor in the survey area was Rp5200 in 1998 and Rp6400 in 1999.

animal traction, and tractors. The second column provides some details of the ranges of activities involved in clearing *Imperata* grassland. The final two columns of table 11.1 present ranges of cost estimates for each general type of grassland clearing practice; cost estimates are provided for 1998 and for 1999 separately to highlight the effects of changes in relative prices that occurred over that time period on conversion costs.

In 1998, clearing *Imperata* grassland using tractor-drawn plows was cheapest (costing Rp160,000 to Rp200,000 per hectare). Using herbicides alone to clear land was a bit more expensive, costing Rp104,000 to Rp260,000. Using animal traction to clear *Imperata* grassland cost more than twice the per-hectare rate of tractors, and manually clearing was by far the most expensive.

In 1999, however, changes in fuel and other prices dramatically increased the cost of tractor use (to a range of Rp350,000 to Rp400,000 per hectare), thereby making herbicide use alone the most cost-effective way of clearing *Imperata* grasslands. The cost advantage of tractors and herbicides over manual clearing techniques and those involving animal traction remained despite price changes over the 1998 to 1999 period.

## ARTIFICIAL SHADE CONTROL EXPERIMENT

The shade intensity experiment showed that even if light levels are reduced to about 10 percent of full sunlight, an established *Imperata* stand will only gradually decline; a 55 percent shade for up to 8 months had little effect (figure 11.2). Hence shade alone probably could not be relied on to reduce *Imperata* grasslands.

Regrowth after removing all above-ground biomass (figure 11.3) was more affected by shading than standing biomass, but a 55 percent shade, which would be considered problematic for most food crops, had no effect on the ability of *Imperata* rhizomes to resprout. Only when an 88 percent shade was applied for more than 2 months, did the ability of rhizomes to resprout decline to a negligible level. Further analysis of the physiological backgrounds of these effects is under way.

## LIGHT INTENSITIES BELOW AGROFORESTRY SYSTEMS

These results for artificial shade were compared with results of the survey of *Imperata* occurrence and light intensity under a range of agroforestry systems (figure 11.4). A statistically significant relationship was found between light levels below the tree canopy and *Imperata* biomass. *Imperata* biomass decreased drastically when a relative light intensity of 10 to 20 percent was reached (figure 11.4). When more than 20 percent of sunlight reaches the ground, *Imperata* still has a chance in these agroforestry systems.

The various tree and plantation crops differ in the age and tree basal area they need to achieve this control target of 10 to 20 percent. Light intensity reduces more

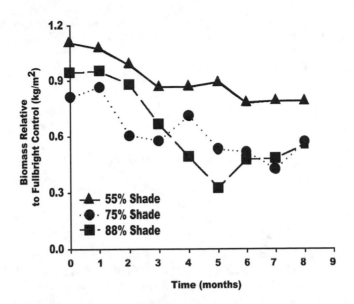

*Figure 11.2* Above-ground biomass of artificially shaded *Imperata* grassland plots relative to that of unshaded control plots in the same experiment.

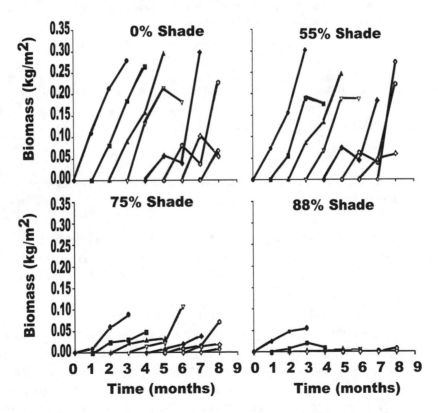

*Figure 11.3* Regrowth of *Imperata* plots after a ground-level cut, made after 0–7 mo of exposure to an artificial shade of 0–88%. The symbols distinguish the number of months of artificial shade received before cutting.

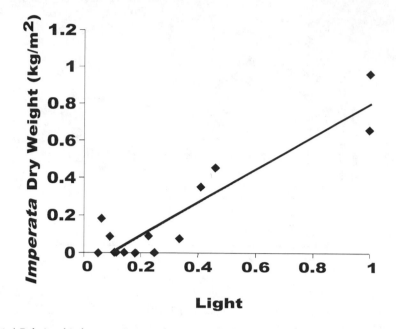

*Figure 11.4* Relationship between *Imperata* biomass and relative light intensity (taking full sunlight as 1) in a survey of smallholder agroforestry systems that include coffee and pepper systems, rubber, oil palm, *Paraserianthes falcataria,* and *Acacia mangium* Willd. block planting.

quickly for a given stem basal area in rubber and *Acacia mangium* systems than in pepper agroforestry (using *Gliricidia sepium* and other trees as support and shade trees) and *Paraserianthes falcataria* (sengon) (figure 11.5).

## Synthesis: Smallholder Agroforestry Options for Conversion of *Imperata* Grasslands

Because high degrees of shading were shown to reduce *Imperata* biomass and control regrowth, the next step was to identify agroforestry systems that could provide such shade and that would be attractive to smallholders. Four existing systems were evaluated in discussions with farmers.

The first system was based on fast-growing timber trees that became popular in the study area as a result of planting of *Acacia mangium* and *Paraserianthes falcataria* by the Industrial Timber Plantation Company in the early 1990s; both the technology and part of the seedlings became used outside their plantation area. Numerous farmers, stimulated by one of the village heads, started to spray the *Imperata* and plant *Paraserianthes falcataria* at a distance of $2 \times 2$ or $2 \times 2.5$ m² or at $2 \times 4$ m² when intended for intercropping with food crops (upland rice in year 1, cassava in years 2–4) for more than a year. Canopy closure of *Paraserianthes* is slow, so the farmers deemed weeding or plowing between rows after harvesting the food crops necessary.

In plantations that were 5 to 8 years old the light intensity at the soil surface still reached 18 to 28 percent of full sunlight, and *Imperata* remained a problem (Tjitrose-mito and Soerjani 1991). Some farmers abandoned the plantation, and secondary vegetation regenerated with tree species such as *Schima wallichii* (D.C.) Korth., *Dillenia* sp., *Peltophorum dassyrachys,* shrubs such as *Chromolaena odorata* (L.) R.M. King and H. Robinson, *Melastoma* sp. or *Mimosa* sp., and grasses such as *Setaria* sp. replacing the *Imperata.* The stands remain sensitive to fire, though, and tree performance was poorer than expected. The long dry season of 1997 showed that *Paraserianthes* is suited only for the wetter sites at the bottom of slopes. *Acacia mangium* planted at a spacing of $2 \times 4$ m$^2$ (1250 trees/ha) reduced light at ground level to 10 percent of full sunlight 4 years after planting at a stem basal area of 23 m$^2$/ha, which is adequate for *Imperata* control.

The second system was based on rubber trees planted at a spacing of $3.3 \times 6$ m$^2$ or $4 \times 5$ m$^2$ (500 trees/ha) and took an average of 7 years before stem basal area was 10 m$^2$/ha and light levels at ground level were reduced below 20 percent of full sunlight. Farmers usually plant maize or cassava between the rubber tree rows in years 1 to 3. Although cassava, which belongs to the Euphorbiaceae, the same family as rubber, is considered capable of transferring soilborne diseases to rubber trees, farmers preferred it as an intercrop because of its minimal maintenance needs and its ability to provide income. After year 3, however, the transition described by Bagnall-Oakeley et al. (1997) occurred; the system provided too much shade for food crop production and too little for *Imperata* control.

The third agroforestry system evaluated was smallholder oil palm, which was only recently introduced into the benchmark site. Farmers considered oil palm a good option because it regrew after burns and appeared less affected by drought than rubber or sengon. Oil palm agronomists emphasize negative drought impacts on palm fruit production up to a year after a drought, whereas rubber tapping can resume quickly if trees survive weather or fire shocks. Farmers in the survey planted oil palm at an $8 \times 9$ m$^2$ spacing (138 plants/ha), which leaves ample area for *Imperata* growth. Farmers generally cultivated maize or rice between oil palm rows during the first few years. In some instances, smallholders with little land were allowed to grow food crops between the oil palms of richer farmers because food crops are deemed less competitive with the oil palm than *Imperata* would have been. However, as is the case for rubber, the 2- to 5-year period between the time food crop production ceased and the palm canopy effectively cut off sunlight is long enough to allow *Imperata* to become reestablished. Indeed, a stand of oil palm 10 m high still allowed about 15 percent of full sunlight to penetrate to ground level; this is sufficient sunlight for *Imperata* growth.

Lastly, pepper (*Piper nigrum* L.) and coffee agroforestry systems are found on the better soils west of the ASB benchmark area in Pakuan Ratu. Farmers start these systems by planting *Gliricidia sepium* or *Erythrina orientalis* Murray as shade and support trees at a spacing of $2 \times 2$ m$^2$. Rice, maize, or other food crops are grown for 1 or 2 years, after which coffee is planted in the middle of the 4-m$^2$ spaces between shade trees, and pepper vines are planted at the stem base of the shade and support trees.

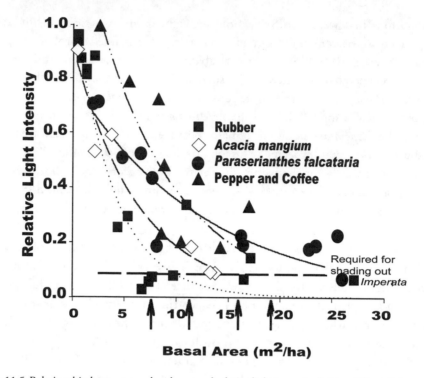

*Figure 11.5* Relationship between tree basal area and relative light intensity (taking full sunlight as 1) in a survey of smallholder agroforestry systems that include coffee and pepper systems, rubber, *Paraserianthes falcataria,* and *Acacia mangium* Willd. block planting; the line at a relative light intensity of 0.15 indicates the target for full control (compare figure 11.4).

Fruit trees such as *Parkia speciosa* Hassk, *Pithecellobium dulce* (Roxb.) Bentham, *Durio zibethinus* Murray, *Lansium domesticum* Corr., and *Ceiba pentandra* (L.) Gaertn. are mixed between the stands, often especially as boundary markers for the field. When these plantations are 4 years old (stem basal area 5 cm²/m²), light intensity at ground level may still be 45 to 50 percent because the shade trees are pruned for the benefit of the pepper and coffee. In an 8- to 10-year-old plantation (stem basal area of 10 cm²/m²) light intensity at ground level was 20 percent of full sunlight, again sufficient for *Imperata* growth.

## DISCUSSION AND CONCLUSION

*Imperata cylindrica* (alang-alang) grasslands occupy large areas of Southeast Asia and are viewed both as a consequence of failed rural development strategies and as an opportunity for expanding agricultural production in areas with diminished forest resources. However, reducing *Imperata* grassland area and controlling regrowth will not be easy and may be beyond the reach of cash-poor smallholders who need immediate returns to labor.

The first steps in controlling *Imperata* in the agroforestation of grasslands can be achieved by either mechanical or chemical control, and farmers use a range of techniques, depending on their resources and current prices. Food crops are used in the first few years of most tree crop or agroforestry systems to maintain income and provide a low-cost (from the tree crop perspective) *Imperata* control option. However, the gap between the last food crop interplanting and canopy closure leads to a major risk of *Imperata* regrowth and fire occurrence. Targets for shade duration and intensity as estimated in the experiment cannot be easily reached in practice. Farmers in the study area have been experimenting with a range of tree crops and agroforestry systems, but results during the El Niño drought of 1997 discouraged the use of trees such as *Paraserianthes falcataria*. A wider range of tree options is needed, and information on site-by-species matching can avoid (or reduce) disappointment.

In the broader picture, results for the ASB benchmark area are encouraging for the *Imperata* grasslands elsewhere, on state forest land. Farmers will explore and exploit a range of options once they have security of tenure and can develop village level rules and controls for the use of fire. For society to reap the benefits of additional carbon storage on these former grasslands, no specific subsidies are needed once tenure policies are right, although farmers welcome technical support in finding locally suited trees. In the benchmark area, the International Center for Research in Agroforestry and its partners are now engaged in this type of on-farm experimentation.

## REFERENCES

Bagnall-Oakeley, H., C. Conro, A. Faiz, A. Gunawan, A. Gouyon, E. Penot, et al. 1997. *Imperata* management strategies used in smallholder rubber-based farming systems. Agrofor. Syst. 36:83–104.

Danhof, G.N. 1941. Tweede bijdrage tot oplossing van het alang-alang vraagstuk in de Lampongse Districten [Second contribution to the solution of the *Imperata* problem in the Lampung Districts; in Dutch]. Tectona 34:67–85.

Djojoprapto, T. 1995. Perkembangan penyelenggaraan transmigrasi. pp. 51–66. *In* M. Utomo and R. Ahmad (eds.) 90 tahun Kolonisasi, 45 tahun Transmigrasi: Redistribusi penduduk di Indonesia. Penebar Swadaya, Jakarta.

Drajat, M. 1991. Alang-alang grassland and land management aspects. pp. 78–98. *In* M. Sambas Sabarnurdin, H. Iswantoro, and G. Adjers (eds.) Forestation of alang-alang (*Imperata cylindrica* Beauv. var Koenigii Benth) grassland: Lesson from South Kalimantan. Gadjah Mada Univ. Press, Yogyakarta, Indonesia.

Elmhirst, R.J. 1996. Soil fertility management in the context of livelihood systems among transmigrants in North Lampung. Agrivita 19:212–220.

Elmhirst, R., Hermalia, and Yulianti. 1998. "Krismon" and "Kemarau": A downward sustainability spiral in a north Lampung "Translok" settlement. pp. 106–121. *In* M. van Noordwijk and H. De Foresta (eds.) Agroforestry in landscapes under pressure: Lampung research planning trip, 17–21 June 1998. Rep. no. 6. ASB Indonesia, Bogor.

Foresta, H. de, and G. Michon. 1997. The agroforest alternative to *Imperata* grasslands: When smallholder agriculture and forestry reach sustainability. Agrofor. Syst. 36:105–120.

Garrity, D.P., M. Soekardi, M. van Noordwijk, R. de la Cruz, P.S. Pathak, H.P.M. Gunasena, et al. 1997. The *Imperata* grasslands of tropical Asia: Area, distribution and typology. Agrofor. Syst. 36:3–29.

Hagreis, B.J. 1931. Ladangbouw [Shifting cultivation; in Dutch]. Tectona 24:598–631.

MacDicken, K.G., K. Hairiah, A. Otsamo, B. Duguma, and N M. Majid. 1997. Shade-based control of *Imperata cylindrica:* Tree fallow and cover crops. Agrofor. Syst. 36:131–149.

Potter, L.M. 1997. The dynamics of *Imperata:* Historical overview and current farmer perspectives, with special reference to South Kalimantan, Indonesia. Agrofor. Syst. 36:31–51.

Santoso, D., S. Adiningsih, E. Mutert, T. Fairhurst, and M. van Noordwijk. 1997. Site improvement and soil fertility management for reclamation of *Imperata* grasslands by smallholder agroforestry. Agrofor. Syst. 36:181–202.

Tjitrosemito, S., and M. Soerjani. 1991. Alang-alang grassland and land management aspects. pp. 10–36. *In* M. Sambas, H. Iswantaro, and G. Adjers (eds.) Forestation of alang-alang (*Imperata cylindrica* Beauv. var Koenigii Benth) grassland: Lesson from south Kalimantan. Gadjah Mada Univ. Press, Yogyakarta, Indonesia.

Tomich, T.P., J. Kuusipalo, K. Menz, and B.N. Byron. 1997. *Imperata* economics and policy. Agrofor. Syst. 36(1–3):233–261.

van Noordwijk, M., K. Hairiah, B. Guritno, Y. Sugito, and S. Ismunandar. 1996a. Biological management of soil fertility for sustainable agriculture on acid upland soils in Lampung (Sumatra). Agrivita 19:131–136.

van Noordwijk, M., K. Hairiah, S. Partoharjono, R.V. Labios, and D.P. Garrity. 1997. Sustainable food-crop based production systems, as alternative to *Imperata* grasslands? Agrofor. Syst. 36:55–82.

van Noordwijk, M., K. Hairiah, S.M. Sitompul, and M. Syekhfani. 1992. Rotational hedgerow intercropping *Peltophorum pterocarpum* = new hope for weed infested soils. Agrofor. Today 4 (4):4–6.

van Noordwijk, M., B. Lusiana, S. Suyanto, and T.P. Tomich. 1996b. Soil and other constraints to agricultural production with or without trees in the North Lampung benchmark area of the "Alternatives to Slash and Burn" project. Agrivita 19:136–145.

van Noordwijk, M., T.P. Tomich, R. Winahyu, D. Murdiyarso, S. Suyanto, S. Partoharjono, et al. (eds.). 1995. Alternatives to Slash-and-Burn in Indonesia: Summary report of phase 1. ASB–Indonesia Rep. No. 4. ASB–Indonesia Consortium and ICRAF, Bogor, Indonesia.

Wibowo, A., M. Suharti, A.P.S. Sagala, H. Hibani, and M. van Noordwijk. 1997. Dealing with fire on *Imperata* grasslands as part of agroforestry development in Indonesia. Agrofor. Syst. 36:203–217.

# IV.  NATIONAL PERSPECTIVES

# 12   The Western Brazilian Amazon

Judson F. Valentim
*Embrapa  Rio Branco, Acre, Brazil*
Stephen A. Vosti
*University of California  Davis, California*

The Brazilian Amazon has long been viewed as empty space contributing little to overall national economic development (Government of Brazil 1969). Federal and state governments have taken action over the past several decades to address this issue, and partly as a consequence of those actions the Brazilian Amazon has been the focus of national and international debate on issues such as tropical deforestation, global climate change, biodiversity conservation, regional integration, the production and transportation of illegal drugs, national security, and the rights of indigenous populations. Although perhaps seemingly unrelated at first glance, these issues often are closely linked. For example, regional integration might increase the demand for agricultural land, which can come at a cost to forests, the biodiversity they contain, and the carbon they store. Therefore, these issues must be examined jointly to identify possible links. If links exist, policy action must consider them.

Moreover, these issues generate more than just debate. Indeed, deforestation and its environmental and social impacts have led to social conflict involving Amerindians and rubber tappers displaced from forested areas on one hand and agriculturalists and cattle ranchers on the other (Hecht 1984; Myers 1984; Denslow 1988; Valentim 1989; Lisboa et al. 1991; Homma 1993; Smith et al. 1995; ). Some of these displacements—and other encroachments into forested lands that do not spark social conflict—are directly linked to policy actions, and others result from more general economic trends that may themselves be beyond the reach of policymakers. Under both sets of circumstances policy action or policy reform may be needed. But what policy action is called for, and what should be the targeted agents or geographic areas? And—the question that is rarely asked—what will be the implications of corrective policy actions for broad development objectives (Vosti and Reardon 1997)? Finally, and most important for this chapter, do we have the knowledge needed to confidently respond to these policy questions? If not, has a process capable of identifying and filling knowledge gaps been initiated?

This chapter reviews past national priorities for the region, policy action taken to populate and integrate the Amazon into the national economy, and the environmental and social consequences of this action. Against this backdrop, we assess past and potential future contributions of the Alternatives to Slash and Burn (ASB) Program to promoting and guiding research and policy action in the region, with particular emphasis on the western Amazonian states of Acre and Rondônia, and ASB activities at the benchmark sites there (Ávila 1994).

We begin by examining national development priorities from the early 1960s to mid-1980s as they relate to the Amazon, including policies implemented by the Brazilian government to occupy and integrate this region into national and international markets. We then focus on the direct and indirect consequences of past regional and local policies on migration, deforestation, the expansion of agricultural activities, and their consequences for economic growth, human development, and environmental sustainability. We then look at future challenges stemming from past and ongoing widespread land degradation and the exhaustion of extensive agricultural frontier. These challenges are set alongside new opportunities provided by new and better-performing markets; new technology; some marked shifts in the political climate at the local, state, and international levels; and the emergence of a new vision of development that aims to reconcile economic growth, poverty alleviation, and natural resource conservation in the Amazon. The final section highlights the contributions of ASB's research and outreach activities in the western Brazilian Amazon and sets an agenda for future ASB-Brazil activities.

## DEVELOPMENT IN THE AMAZON (1960s–1990s)

The largest tracts of the world's remaining tropical moist rainforests are located in the Amazon Basin, which occupies about 7.86 million km$^2$ in nine countries and covers about 44 percent of the South American continent (Valente 1968). About half of the Amazon forest (3.87 million km$^2$) is located in northern Brazil. This forest covers more than 52 percent of Brazil's national territory (IBGE 1997), an area larger than the whole of Western Europe (INPE 2003) (figure 12.1).

Since the early 1960s, the Amazon region has been viewed by the federal government of Brazil as a source of natural resources (e.g., forests, agricultural land, minerals) that could be used to fuel regional and national economic growth. Low population density (about 0.9 inhabitants per square kilometer in 1970) was an obstacle to exploiting the region's resources and integrating it into the national economy. Labor needed to tap and transport resources was scarce, and the low population density was perceived as a threat to national security, particularly given the production and transportation of illicit drugs in neighboring countries (Fórum Sôbre a Amazônia 1968;

*Figure 12.1* Map of Brazil, with the North Region highlighted (INPE 2003).

Government of Brazil, 1969, 1981; SUDAM 1976; Smith et al. 1995; IBGE 1997; Santana et al. 1997; Homma 1998).

But two objectives, tapping the resources of the Amazon and developing the region, often became decoupled by policy action. There were several reasons, some of them known before the task began and others discovered after the processes had begun. First, huge distances separated the Amazon from major population and transportation centers, thereby making inputs needed in the Amazon more expensive and products from the region less valuable. Second, the Amazon was found to be a huge mosaic of different ecosystems rather than a homogenous forested area. This latter discovery had both positive and negative consequences. Biophysical scientists were introduced to the world's greatest cache of biodiversity, but development planners were faced with the unforeseen need for expensive niche-specific projects and support programs. Third, the biodiversity of the Amazon forest and the carbon stored in it were increasingly viewed as belonging to groups both larger and smaller than the Brazilian federal government, which held legal claim to much of this vast area. Indigenous communities were increasingly vocal about their claims to large tracts of land and the resources on and beneath them. Simultaneously, the international community, under the banners of greenhouse gas emissions and biodiversity conservation, provided much advice on what portions of the Amazon should be used and how (Myers 1984).

In the 1960s, the federal government decided to implement policies aimed at occupying the Amazon region and integrating it with the rest of the national economy. The development process was launched with policymakers hoping that research undertaken alongside development, and at times supported by the financiers of development activities, would provide answers needed for wise stewardship of the Amazon. We now know that knowledge was insufficient to appropriately guide development policy action at that time and that research could not close that gap in the dynamic decades of the 1960s, 1970s, and 1980s.

Operation Amazon, established in 1966, set out a broad geopolitical and economic plan for the region (Government of Brazil 1969; Mahar 1979; Santana et al. 1997). In support of Operation Amazon, new policy objectives and policy instruments were created that were to supply the legal and financial means, labor, transportation networks, and electrical power needed to establish migrants and industry in the Amazon. In addition, new regional development agencies such as the Amazon Development Agency (Superintendência de Desenvolvimento da Amazônia), the Amazonian Duty-Free Authority (Superintendência da Zona Franca de Manaus), and the Amazonian Regional Bank (Banco da Amazônia S.A.) were established to organize and support development activities, often via the provision of subsidized credit to agriculture, particularly extensive beef cattle ranching, and mining projects (Forum Sôbre a Amazônia 1968; Government of Brazil 1969, 1981; SUDAM 1976; Smith et al. 1995; IBGE 1997; Santana et al. 1997; Faminow 1998).

Since the establishment of federal subsidized credit in the late 1960s, thousands of agricultural and industrial projects have been approved and implemented in the Amazon. In the western Brazilian states of Acre and Rondônia alone, thirty-three projects were approved from 1965 to 1996 for agricultural and industrial activities. This was roughly 12 percent of the 392 projects implemented throughout the Amazon during that time (Santana et al. 1997).

To support these projects, large hydroelectric dams, such as the Tucuruí Dam in the state of Pará, were built. In addition, several highways were planned and partially constructed to provide access to the region. The Trans-Amazon highway, from the Atlantic Coast to the Peruvian border, was to comprise about 5000 km of all-weather roads but is yet to be finished. Other major highways were completed, such as the BR-364, linking Acre and Rondônia to São Paulo and southern Brazil, and the Belém–Brasília road, linking Pará with the rest of the country (SUDAM 1976; Santana et al. 1997).

In the early 1970s, world economic and oil crises led to a severe economic recession in Brazil. When combined with changes in agricultural technology and consequent changes in farm structure, this generated large increases in unemployment and landlessness in southern and southeastern Brazil, and consequent social conflicts in these regions. The Federal Government saw the opportunity to solve two problems simultaneously. Moving unemployed and especially landless people to the Amazon region and establishing them in settlement projects there would reduce social pressures in the southern regions of the country and increase the labor available for development in the Amazon (SUDAM 1976; Government of Brazil 1981; Bunker 1985).

The process of assisting migration and colonization of landless people to meet these dual objectives was rapid and intense. The federal government handed over millions of hectares of forested land to small- and large-scale migrants and local people with little knowledge of the potential for these areas to support agricultural activities of any kind. These small-scale farms (in the Brazilian context), ranging in size from 50 to 100 ha, came to be known as "dumb rectangles" because few soil, water, or watershed conditions were taken into consideration during their demarcation (Valentim 1989; Walker and Homma 1996; Wolstein et al. 1998).

## CONSEQUENCES OF THE DEVELOPMENT PROCESS

The policy-driven occupation of the Amazon has been under way for more than 30 years. Policy action, conditioned by economic forces and biophysical factors, has had direct and indirect consequences for economic growth, human welfare, environmental sustainability, and especially demographic change.

### MIGRATION

From about 1965 to 1995, more than 500,000 families settled in new colonization projects or spontaneously invaded forest areas along the highways that were opened throughout the Amazon. In the western Brazilian Amazon, population growth was substantial but uneven. In the state of Acre, the population grew from just over 100,000 in 1950 to nearly 500,000 by 1996. In the state of Rondônia, population grew from 36,000 in 1950 to more than 1.2 million in 1996, a staggering increase in 46 years. As a consequence, population density in Acre and Rondônia rose from 1.4 and 0.5 people per square kilometer in 1970 to 3.2 and 5.2 people per square kilometer in 1996. Although they were initially rural populations, by 1996 almost twice as many people lived in urban as in rural areas, as shown for Rondônia in figure 12.2 (IBGE 1997).

Starting in 1970, the western Brazilian Amazon also experienced a rapid process of urbanization. By 1996 more than 60 percent of the region's population was already in cities and towns, although rural–urban migration patterns differed by state. In Acre, rural population tended to be stable between 1970 and 1996, while the urban population grew. In Rondônia, rural population growth continued until about 1991.

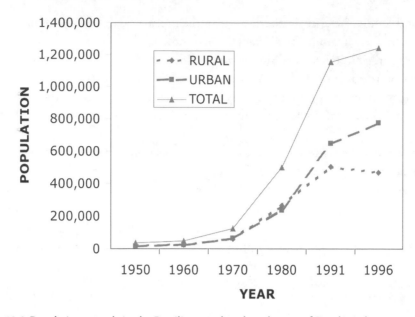

*Figure 12.2* Population growth in the Brazilian ASB benchmark state of Rondônia between 1950 and 1996 (IBGE 1996).

Upon arrival in these areas, settlers cut and burned primary forests, and the cleared areas were put under plow for a series of agricultural activities. But hardships awaited many settlers. Most of the newcomers were stricken by malaria, a disease that significantly reduced their capacity to work, generated medical expenses that further reduced already precariously low household financial resources, and was sometimes fatal (Bartolome and Vosti 1995). Promised social services generally were lacking in the early years of colonization: Health care facilities were built but not staffed, and schools often were constructed, but qualified teachers were hard to find and retain. By those measures, poverty probably increased for early settlers (Vosti et al. 1998).

## DEFORESTATION

The environmental consequences of the policies pursued in the Amazon were substantial and generally negative. In the past 30 years, forest cover in the Amazon has been substantially reduced, with consequent increases in emissions of $CO_2$ and other greenhouse gases, loss of biodiversity, nutrient leaching, soil erosion, and land degradation (Valentim 1989; Smith et al. 1995; Homma 1998; Wolstein et al. 1998; Embrapa 1999a; INPE 2003).

In some areas, forest conversion was particularly aggressive. For example, in Rondônia, accelerated settlement and agricultural programs have resulted in the conversion of approximately 23 percent of that state's forests to agriculture in the past 20 years, with annual deforestation rates reaching 2.8 percent of the total area of the state in 1995 (Fearnside 1991; Lisboa et al. 1991; INPE 2003). In Acre, migration and forest conversion to agriculture have been less rapid, resulting in the deforestation of approximately 9.3 percent of the total area of the state in the same period, with the peak annual deforestation rate also reached in 1995, about 0.8 percent of total state land, as shown in figure 12.3 (INPE 2003).

The predominant land use system in the area begins with the clearance of forests using slash-and-burn techniques for annual crops, which can be grown without the use of external nutrient inputs on a given plot of land for 2 to 3 years. The establishment of cultivated pastures for dual-purpose, extensive cattle ranching generally follows on plots that can no longer support annual crop production.

Most of the land clearing in the Brazilian Amazon, even in the large enterprises was done by slash-and-burn. There was only one case of a big international company that used herbicides to kill 10,000 ha of forests in Pará and then burned it. Bulldozers were not really used, with only a few exceptions, in the context of the Brazilian Amazon.

There is a tendency for farms of all sizes to decrease the area remaining of forest and increase the area under pasture over time. Other land uses (monoculture coffee [*Coffea canephora* Pierre ex Fröhner] or agroforestry systems) can contribute substantially to household income and absorb considerable amounts of family and hired labor, but the amount of land usually dedicated to these other uses remains small, relative to pasture, as shown in figure 12.4 (Dale et al. 1993; Browder 1994; Fujisaka et al. 1996; Vosti and Witcover 1996; Vosti et al. 2002).

## SOIL DEGRADATION

Lack of knowledge even among soil scientists of the degree of heterogeneity of Amazonian soils and their ability to support different agricultural activities, and failure on the part of planners and policymakers to put to effective use the partial knowledge that was available, led to the settling of thousands of farmers on land that could not support agriculture of almost any kind, certainly not the types of agriculture settlers were likely to pursue, given their experience in the south or northeast. As a result, soils became degraded and unproductive after just a few years, further fueling deforestation in the region as farmers sought to add to their stocks of usable soils. Moreover, and perhaps ironically, many farmers began to experience water scarcity in the world's largest and most productive watershed. The search for on-farm alternatives and supplements to annual cropping increased water needs, especially for livestock, and the deforestation needed to clear land for and to finance the establishment of alternative production systems may have decreased surface water supplies (Valentim 1989; Smith et al. 1995; Serrão et al. 1996; Wolstein et al. 1998; Amaral et al. 1999, 2000b).

It is estimated that by 1997, about 55 million ha of forests in the Brazilian Amazon (14 percent of the total area) had been converted to agriculture and that roughly one half of that deforested area (about 25 million ha) was already degraded (INPE

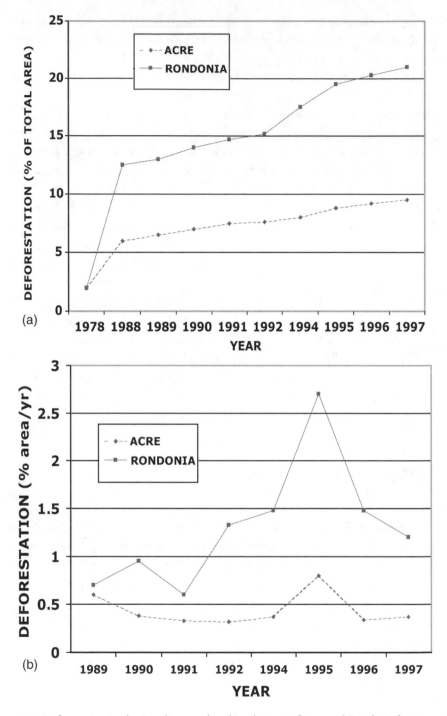

*Figure 12.3* Deforestation in the Brazilian ASB benchmark states of Acre and Rondônia between 1978 and 1997: (a) cumulative percentage of area and (b) annual rates (INPE 2003).

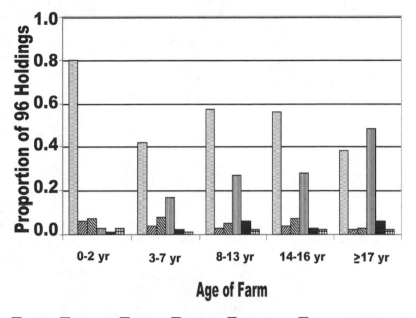

*Figure 12.4* Land uses, by farm age, in the Pedro Peixoto Settlement Project in the state of Acre, Brazil, in 1996 (Vosti et al. 2002).

2003). The states of Rondônia and Acre have an estimated 1.5 million and 450,000 ha of degraded pasture and 540,000 and 140,000 ha in secondary fallow (*capoeira*), respectively (Embrapa 1999a; INPE 2003).

## ECONOMIC GROWTH

Although the policies, economic forces, and biophysical factors guiding the occupation, use, and integration of the Brazilian Amazon have resulted in waves of migration and significant deforestation, progress in economic growth has been substantial over the past 30 years, with marked increases in gross domestic product and regional value added.

For example, Rondônia (with 5.4 million ha of forests converted to agriculture) became the third largest cocoa-producing and fifth largest coffee-producing state in Brazil by 1995. And, with 70 percent of the deforested area (3.8 million ha) planted to cultivated pastures, the state now has roughly 4 million head of cattle (IBGE 1997). Gross domestic product per capita in Rondônia rose from US$2025 in 1970 to US$6448 in 1996 (table 12.1), close to the national average for Brazil for that year (IBGE 1997; Faminow and Vosti 1998; UNDP 1999).

In Acre, economic progress over the past 25 years also has been substantial. Farmers have deforested only about 9.3 percent (1.4 million ha) of the total area, convert-

*Table 12.1* Changes in Indicators of Human Welfare for Acre, Rondônia, and All Brazil, 1970–1996

| Socioeconomic Indicator | Year | Acre | Rondônia | Brazil |
|---|---|---|---|---|
| Grammar school matriculation (% of school-aged children registered) | 1970 | 36.1 | 31.7 | 49.2 |
| | 1980 | 48.5 | 50.7 | 61.2 |
| | 1991 | 59.0 | 63.0 | 67.8 |
| | 1995 | 74.1 | 69.8 | 75.7 |
| | 1996 | 74.1 | 70.7 | 76.8 |
| Literacy rates (%) | 1970 | 47.3 | 64.7 | 67.0 |
| | 1980 | 55.2 | 68.5 | 74.7 |
| | 1991 | 65.7 | 80.4 | 80.6 |
| | 1995 | 70.2 | 84.3 | 84.4 |
| | 1996 | 70.2 | 85.8 | 85.3 |
| Per capita gross domestic product (us$ purchasing power parity) | 1970 | 1302 | 2025 | 2315 |
| | 1980 | 2343 | 3426 | 4882 |
| | 1991 | 3767 | 4185 | 5023 |
| | 1995 | 5499 | 5562 | 5986 |
| | 1996 | 5741 | 6448 | 6491 |
| United Nations Development Program human development index | 1970 | 0.376 | 0.474 | 0.494 |
| | 1980 | 0.506 | 0.611 | 0.734 |
| | 1991 | 0.662 | 0.725 | 0.787 |
| | 1995 | 0.752 | 0.782 | 0.814 |
| | 1996 | 0.754 | 0.820 | 0.830 |

The UNDP human development index is a summary index that incorporates life expectancy, literacy, and standard of living.
*Sources:* IBGE (1997a), UNDP (1999).

ing roughly 80 percent of the cleared areas to pastures (1.2 million ha), and now manage about 1 million head of cattle (Embrapa 1999a). Annual gross domestic product per capita in Acre (table 12.1) rose from us$1302 in 1970 to us$5741 in 1996 (IBGE 1997a; UNDP 1999).

## HUMAN WELFARE IMPROVEMENTS

There also have been large social benefits from the policies implemented in the last three decades in the western Brazilian Amazon. Poverty has been reduced, school matriculation rates have risen, incomes have increased, and nutritional status has improved. Total primary and secondary school matriculation in Acre and Rondônia more than doubled in 26 years, rising from 36 and 32 percent in 1970 to 74 and 71 percent in 1996, respectively. Over the same period, life expectancy at birth in both Acre and Rondônia rose from 53 years to more than 67 years, and illiteracy rates among adults decreased in Acre from 53 to 30 percent and in Rondônia from 35 to 14 percent. The UNDP human development indices for Acre and Rondônia rose from

0.38 and 0.47 in 1970 to 0.75 and 0.82 in 1996, respectively, although these are still below the value for Brazil as a whole, which was 0.83, as shown in table 12.1 (IBGE 1997a; UNDP 1999).

## NEED FOR A NEW DEVELOPMENT PARADIGM

It is clear that over the past three decades, the western Brazilian Amazon has experienced rapid socioeconomic and environmental change. But can, or should, this process continue? We argue that it cannot and need not continue for several reasons.

First, the forested land suitable and available for conversion to agriculture is becoming scarce. Most soils in Acre and Rondônia near roads and rivers with known and reasonable agricultural potential have already been used or soon will be. Remaining forested areas (some of which may have agricultural potential) are increasingly off-limits because of local, state, federal, or international agreements, especially concerning Amerindian and extractive reserves. Federal law since 1989 has prohibited public credit programs from extending loans to clear forests for agricultural purposes in the Brazilian Amazon. Rondônia, in particular, has almost exhausted its agricultural frontier and must now search for other means of increasing agricultural production. Productivity increases will be the primary source of future agricultural growth.

Second, soil degradation is pervasive in the western Brazilian Amazon, and this increasingly limits product choice and productivity. For example, 50 percent of the 532,000 ha of pasture land in Acre is located on soils now judged to be unsuitable for traditional braquiarão or brizantão (*Brachiaria brizantha* [Hochst. ex A. Rich.] Stapf) pastures. These pastures either already have suffered or will soon experience rapid decreases in carrying capacity (Valentim et al. 2000). With area for new pasture expansion increasingly limited, improved and more intensive pasture and cattle management systems will be needed, as will investments to establish them.

Third, water resources in this humid tropical region are becoming scarce in colonization projects and urban areas. Water pollution is also becoming a problem, especially in and around urban areas (Knight 1998).

Fourth, because of a shifting geographic focus and fiscal limitations, the federal agencies that played such broad and fundamental roles in opening up the western Brazilian Amazon and linking it to the rest of the country have substantially reduced their activities and shifted investments in established areas (Government of Brazil 1998). State and local governments, often working with other groups, are struggling to fill these gaps (Vosti et al. 1998).

Therefore, with new agricultural land becoming scarce, productivity on cleared land falling, water scarcities developing, and traditional funding sources eroding, a new regional development paradigm is needed. And the overall environment seems conducive to change; new economic circumstances, new technologies, and potential policy and organizational and institutional changes combine to offer development options that were not available even a decade ago (Almeida and Uhl 1995). The main reasons are as follows.

First, the western Brazilian Amazon is no longer the very distant outpost it was when development began 30 years ago. All-weather roads link most major urban centers, and recent investments in water transport have dramatically altered the potential for regional and international trade. So markets exist today that did not 20 years ago, and general market performance seems to be improving with economic integration and increased competition.

Second, new and better technology is now available to support agriculture, from production to harvesting, processing, and marketing. New technologies made available by the private and public sectors expand the product mix available to farmers and can improve profitability, too.

Third, and perhaps most important, some areas in the western Brazilian Amazon are experiencing broadening local support to better manage agricultural growth and integrate it with modern, sustainable forest stewardship. In Acre, for example, a state government of the forest was recently elected, with sustainable development driven by both forestry and agriculture as a fundamental part of its party platform.

What specific solutions might spur sustainable development in the face of the challenges and opportunities noted in this chapter? What can policymakers do to promote these solutions? What role remains for research? We briefly address these

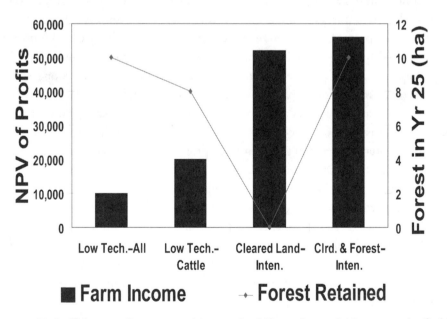

*Figure 12.5* Tradeoffs between forest area and income for different farm activities as a result of a bioeconomic simulation model in a small farm holding in the Pedro Peixoto Settlement Project in 1996 (Carpentier et al. 1998). Low Tech–All, traditional practices; Low Tech–Cattle, intensified cropping but traditional cattle pasture management; Cleared Land–Inten., intensification of all crop and cattle activities; Clrd. & Forest–Inten., intensification of all crop and cattle activities and forest management; NPV, net present value.

issues in the context of one promising land and forest use system: small-scale managed forestry (see also chapter 8, this volume).

Past policies failed to add value to the forest and usually achieved just the opposite, generally by design. As a result, even short-term gains from low-productivity agriculture were, and often continue to be, greater than the private financial returns to the types of forest extraction activities that would be practiced given policy and price conditions. Forests will continue to be cleared for agriculture until this broad profitability gap is closed. One way of doing so is to permit small-scale managed forestry, a best-bet alternative to slash-and-burn developed by Empresa Brasileira de Pesquisa Agropecuária (Embrapa) as part of the ASB program, which has been demonstrated under experimental conditions to be profitable, to reduce but not eliminate deforestation, and to be capable of retaining the resiliency and productivity of forest ecosystems (figures 12.5 and 12.6).

This managed forestry technology has not been easy or cheap to develop. Years of research on the response of forest systems to different types and intensities of logging were needed to identify a small subset of sustainable forest management techniques.

*Figure 12.6* Aspects of the Low Impact Sustainable Forest Management in Legal Reserves of the Pedro Peixoto Colonization Project: (**a**) the legal reserve areas being managed, (**b**) wood planks extracted from this forest area, (**c**) the house made with wood extracted from the managed area where the family of the small farmer lives, and (**d**) a field day demonstrating the research and development results to other farmers and extension agents.

Research was also needed to determine the farmer and market conditions under which it was profitable to pursue these techniques when alternative uses of farmers' time, land, and financial resources were considered (Homma 1993; Araújo 1998; Oliveira et al. 1998; Vosti et al. 2002; Vosti and Valentim 1998; Embrapa 1999b; Santos et al. 1999; Carpentier et al. 2000a, 2000b).

But experimental techniques are not easy to promote, refine, or replicate without enabling policies. Promoting these managed forestry systems beyond their experimental stages will entail policy action, such as changes in legal and practical impediments to timber management and credit programs to support investments in small-scale implements, as well as institutional change, such as the formation of groups of smallholders that can manage and monitor forest extraction activities. Refining systems in response to changes in farming and forest circumstances will entail new and continuing research and scientific monitoring. Replication on a broad scale will necessitate research into the effects of doing so on market and ecosystem conditions. If broad adoption is recommended, extension services will have to be retooled.

## THE MULTIPLE IMPACTS OF ASB

As indicated earlier, scientific and technical knowledge to support and guide development in the western Brazilian Amazon in the 1960s was insufficient. Although some measures were taken at that time to augment it, they were generally too small in scale or too narrowly focused to deliver new knowledge at the necessary pace. We know much more today about Amazonian ecosystems and the agents occupying these lands. However, we still do not have the knowledge we need for economically and ecologically sound planning on a regional or subregional basis (Valentim 1989; Smith et al. 1995; Homma 1998), but progress in filling knowledge gaps has quickened over the past 10 years. Multi-institutional, interdisciplinary research teams have been largely responsible for this broader knowledge base, and ASB is a leader among these teams, especially in Acre. Of course, there were other multidisciplinary groups of researchers working on development problems in the region, such as the Grupo de Pesquisa e Extensão em Sistemas Agroflorestais do Acre (PESACRE, a local research consortium) and the Universidade Federal do Acre. The ASB provided strong scientific and institutional leadership. In what follows, we focus on ASB impacts on Embrapa, but there were substantial spillovers to other research- and service-oriented organizations (especially PESACRE and Empresa de Assistência Técnica e Extensão Rural, the agricultural extension service).

From the outset, ASB's mandate, research methods, and research partners have had profound effects on Embrapa and the potential for Embrapa to effectively contribute to changing development objectives and policies in the western Brazilian Amazon. The ASB's research mandate was to better understand biophysical and socioeconomic processes and outcomes and the links between them and—based on new knowledge—to identify entry points for policy actions needed to achieve broad development objectives in the region. The specific outcomes of research on these issues are reported elsewhere in this publication. Here, we highlight the impacts of ASB in Brazil on the focus and nature of research, on the search for and development of new technologies, and on policy change in Embrapa Acre and Rondônia.

## THE FOCUS AND NATURE OF RESEARCH

With the arrival of ASB, its new research paradigm, collaborators, and financial resources, there was a substantial shift in the focus and nature of Embrapa's biophysical and social science and policy research at the two benchmark states (Ávila 1994).

First, biophysical research that traditionally examined single food production activities over short periods of time was expanded to include multiproduct land use systems practiced over much longer periods of time. And because the biophysical consequences of agricultural and other changes are not restricted to the boundaries of the farm, transects of land including but not restricted to farm land were studied. It was clear that these land use systems should not be examined in isolation but needed to be jointly analyzed at the landscape level and in the context of important on- and off-farm variables.

Second, the ways in which much of Embrapa's biophysical research is carried out have also changed, in part because of collaboration with ASB. In the past, most Embrapa research was carried out in plots located on experiment stations. The degree of farmer involvement in determining research topics or methods was limited, and the biophysical and socioeconomic contexts in which farmers made product, technology, and resource allocation decisions were not part of researcher-led experimental designs. For some scientific problems, such as fertilizer response trials, this de-linking of experiments from smallholder situations is effective and efficient. For many other problems, such as the potential for establishing legume-based pastures in farmers' fields, it is not.

Most of ASB's biophysical research was carried out on farmers' fields, often with the direct participation of farmers in developing, monitoring, and managing experiments.

Where scientifically appropriate, this emphasis on farmer participation and farm-based experimentation continues at Embrapa today. For example, research conducted in farmers' fields rose from less than 10 percent in 1994 to approximately 60 percent in 1998 in Embrapa Acre, with consequent increases in the use of participatory research methods and the validation of research products by farmers in their own socioeconomic and environmental situations.

Third, Embrapa's research traditionally focused on agronomic factors of immediate or short-term relevance to farmers. Links with ASB and its national and especially international network of research institutions expanded the geographic and temporal foci of Embrapa research. For example, the long-term consequences of particular land use patterns are now of central concern. In addition, identifying the impacts of land use and land cover change on local, regional, and even international communities is now very important in Embrapa research. The ASB is chiefly responsible for Embrapa's new focus on international environmental externalities (e.g., $CO_2$ emissions, changes in above- and below-ground biodiversity).

## SOCIOECONOMIC RESEARCH

Like biophysical researchers, social science researchers had spent little time on farmers' fields or in farm households collecting data. The ASB brought a substantial shift toward socioeconomic field research, especially the collection and use of field data. Efforts to develop and use secondary data, such as those containing comprehensive product and input price series, were also expanded with ASB guidance.

Perhaps the most important contribution of ASB to Embrapa's socioeconomic and policy research was the increased priority given to predicting the impacts of different price and technology changes and to developing the analytical tools to generate these predictions (Vosti et al. 2001a). For example, ASB and Embrapa collaborated to develop, test, and use a farm-level bioeconomic model capable of predicting the impact of changes in policy on land use patterns, deforestation, and household income (see also chapter 10, this volume). Simulated land uses over a 25-year period produced by this model and based on conditions for a typical small-scale farmer whose characteristics were derived from field research in Acre. Model simulations, under socioeconomic and policy conditions prevalent in 1994 to 1996 and subject to the biophysical and especially farm household labor constraints, show that forest will continue to fall in the western Brazilian Amazon and cleared land will be allocated predominantly to pasture (Carpentier et al. 2000a; chapter 10, this volume).

Combining information generated by model simulations can be much more informative. Figure 12.5 summarizes results of several simulations based on different policy and technology scenarios. Tradeoffs can be examined as we move from one scenario to another between household income (measured in terms of net present value of profit streams and represented by bars in figure 12.5) and the amount of forest retained on farms (measured in terms of hectares of forest remaining in year 25 of the scenario and represented by diamonds connected by lines in figure 12.5). In the scenarios examined here, increasing the scope of agricultural intensification (moving from left to right, beginning with no intensification on cleared or forested land to a scenario that permitted intensification of all activities on cleared lands, the third scenario) increases household income and decreases forest cover. Note that only when agricultural *and* forestry activities are intensified (final scenario in figure 12.5) do both income *and* forest cover increase (Carpentier et al. 2000b). Absolute levels of farm household income may seem high at first glance. Readers are reminded that figures reported represent the present discounted values of income streams earned over the 25-year time horizon of the farm household model. General equilibrium effects are not taken into consideration, nor is risk included explicitly into the model, except in the case of edible bean (*Phaseolus vulgaris* L.) production.

At a much higher level of spatial and economic aggregation, ASB also developed an economy-wide model capable of predicting the impact of changes in macroeconomic policy and region-wide changes in agricultural technology on deforestation in the Amazon. This model, the only one of its kind in Brazil, predicts, for example, that in response to a major devaluation of the Brazilian currency, in the Amazon region taken as a whole the area dedicated to coffee would double, extractive activities would experience a boom, production of consumer staples would decrease substantially, but logging would only be slightly affected (Cattaneo 1999; chapter 7, this volume).

## BIOPHYSICAL RESEARCH

The ASB collaboration has also modified the focus of and methods for Embrapa's technology development activities. Historically, Embrapa's research had focused on economic practices undertaken on cleared land and on traditional agricultural activities. Under the economic premise that adding value to the forest is fundamental to saving it, the search for new technologies has been expanded to include those that can be practiced on forested lands.

In addition, research has shifted somewhat from agricultural practices imported to the region from other areas in Brazil, such as upland rice (*Oryza sativa* L.) and bean production, to those involving native species, primarily woody perennials. Examples of these are agroforestry systems such as that of the Projeto Reca with mixtures of tree species such as peach palm (*Bactris gasipaes* Kunth), cupuaçú or theobroma (*Theobroma grandiflorum* [Willd. ex Spreng. K. Schum.]), and Brazil nut (*Bertholetia excelsa* Humb. & Bonpl.) (figure 12.7). Another is the cultivation of pimenta longa (*Piper hispidinervum* C.DC.), a native bush containing an essential oil (Safrol) that is used in cosmetics production (as a fixing agent of fragrances) and as a synergistic agent in the production of domestic insecticides. Embrapa has domesticated this species and developed the agricultural and agroindustrial production systems. Research on these emerging products focuses not only on their sustainable cultivation but also on post-harvest processing and marketing issues.

Finally, given the demonstrated attractiveness of dual-purpose (milk, beef) cattle ranching to local smallholders, special efforts are under way to make these systems more agronomically sustainable and to limit the need for and incentives to expanding new pasture lands. For example, in the Ramal da Enco farmers' association in Acre, research on the use of solar-charged, battery-powered electric fences for managing pastures and cattle herds is under way. Preliminary results suggest that pasture carrying capacity can be increased and pasture life extended by using these fences, which are inexpensive to establish and maintain (Vaz and Valentim 2001). To take another example, new legumes such as perennial peanut (*Arachis pintoi* Krap. & Greg.) and tropical kudzu (*Pueraria phaseoloides* [Roxb.] Benth.) are being recommended for the establishment of grass–legume pastures to increase the profitability and sustainability of cattle production systems in the western Brazilian Amazon (Valentim and Carneiro 2001; Valentim et al. 2001), as shown in figure 12.8.

*Figure 12.7* The simple agroforestry system of the Projeto Reca in Rondônia, which includes peach palm, cupuaçú, and Brazil nut trees.

## EMBRAPA'S ROLE IN REGIONAL POLICY DIALOGUE

In part as a result of ASB research, Embrapa's position in local, state, regional, and national policy debates has been strengthened, allowing it to offer more concrete policy advice on a broader array of issues and to help avoid costly policy mistakes. In most cases, the mechanisms for Embrapa input into policymaking predate ASB, but it was the ASB program that brought policy implications to the forefront in research design and also sought to extract policy-relevant lessons from all research projects. Moreover, the predictive power of the household and economy-wide models developed by ASB has provided Embrapa with greater voice and credibility in policy debates. The following are examples of the types of policy debates to which Embrapa is contributing:

Land use zoning was undertaken during the early period of modern occupation in Acre, and the resulting land use potential recommendations are 87 percent of the area for crops, 12 percent for pastures, and less than 1 percent for forest plantations. Less than 0.5 percent of the land was considered to have no agricultural potential. At that time, much of the state's land was deemed suitable for nearly any type of agricultural pursuit, at any scale. An Embrapa reevaluation of land use potential (carried out in part with ASB assistance) revealed a very different suggested set of land use options, this time highlighting the limits to traditional large-scale agricultural activities and the major role that small-scale agriculturalists, agroforestry, and forestry activities should

*Figure 12.8* Photographs *(clockwise)* of dairy cattle grazing a protein bank of perennial peanut (cv. Belmonte); dairy cattle grazing guineagrass (*Panicum maximum* Jacq.) cv. Massai, a new grass developed by Embrapa based on selection of ecotypes introduced from Africa; beef cattle grazing guineagrass cv. Tanzania, also a new grass developed by Embrapa based on selection of ecotypes introduced from Africa; and grass–legume pastures consisting of Tanzania grass and tropical kudzu.

play (Amaral et al. 2000a) (figure 12.9). This updated land use assessment is one of the cornerstones of state development planning and policy today.

A separate set of Embrapa-led land use zoning exercises has helped identify where subsoil impediments to drainage are causing the death of brizantão-based pastures over very broad areas (Valentim et al. 2000). Research is under way to identify replacement grasses.

Embrapa is routinely asked to provide suggestions for targeting subsidized agricultural credit in the region. Based on the results of collaborative forest ecology and farm household economic research, Embrapa has proposed that farmers or farmer cooperatives preparing plans to implement small-scale managed forestry schemes be eligible for special credit from a fund managed by the Amazonian Regional Bank.

In May 1999, the federal government of Brazil and the state government of Acre organized a workshop involving government and nongovernment organizations and representatives of the private sector to discuss a positive agenda for the Brazilian Amazon aimed at addressing growth, poverty, and environmental issues together. Embrapa was asked to provide the scientific and technical basis on which regional and state-level

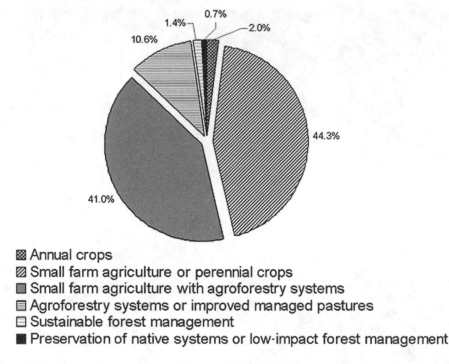

*Figure 12.9* Land use recommendations for Acre in 1999, focusing on small-scale agriculture, agroforestry, and small-scale forestry, based on work of Embrapa and ASB (Amaral et al. 2000a).

policies would be developed. Research results, methods, and experiences provided by ASB collaboration greatly assisted Embrapa in this task. The most important proposals to emerge from this workshop were to

• Gradually decrease deforestation rates in Acre.
• Establish a targeted amount of cleared land, initially set at 14 percent of total state area, to be reached by the year 2020.
• Establish policy disincentives to forest conversion for agricultural purposes and policy incentives to reclaim degraded land and increase the efficient and sustainable use of forests.

Although it attracts less attention now than in the past, the formal colonization process in the region is still ongoing, though at a much slower rate than in earlier decades. So the problems of where and how to settle smallholders and what sorts of support are needed to increase the chances of success remain. Embrapa (supported by ASB research results and research tools) is changing the way colonization projects are conceived and implemented.

For example, a settlement project recently approved for joint implementation in the Seringal São Salvador by Embrapa Acre, Instituto Nacional de Colonização e Reforma Agrária Acre (National Colonization Institute), PESACRE, the municipality of Mancio Lima, SOS Amazonia (an environmental organization), and the Brazilian Institute for the Environment and Natural Resources envisions land distribution and land and forest use patterns quite different from those implemented under traditional colonization schemes. In traditional colonization schemes, land allocation to farmers was done without much thought given to the potential and limits of the natural resource base (forests, soils, water) or to the socioeconomic circumstances of migrant families, and the legal reserve areas were established within individual plots and left to farmers to manage.

The current approach to settling smallholders pays much more attention to assessments of the natural resources done beforehand to determine land use potential and constraints, the possibility that some lands may not be suitable for settlement purposes and therefore should be set aside for conservation, the socioeconomic circumstances of candidate families, farmer participation in colonization planning and implementation phases, the potential for locating legal reserves to ensure that continuous blocks of forest remain in or around colonization projects, and the management of these legal reserves to sustainably produce timber and nontimber forest products. This new approach reduces settlement costs and limits deforestation to no more than 30 percent of the total colonization project area (as opposed to the 50 percent allowed in the traditional schemes).

Embrapa also played an important role in providing scientific and technical support to the federal government's decision in November 1999 to prohibit establishment of new settlement projects in forest areas of the Brazilian Amazon.

Finally, Embrapa input, some of which was based directly on ASB research results and research tools, has provided a sounder basis for establishing price policy at state and regional levels. For example, policymakers in Acre were contemplating a subsidy for upland rice and bean production, alleging that it would reduce deforestation. The ASB–Embrapa research results based specifically on simulations of the bioeconomic model demonstrated that such a price policy would not reduce deforestation, although it would improve smallholder incomes. The choice was left to policymakers, but with the predicted impacts of the proposed policy change more clearly articulated.

## ORGANIZATIONAL AND INSTITUTIONAL IMPACTS OF ASB

Collaborative Embrapa and ASB research provided and promoted the establishment of links with the international research community and consequently provided access to new individuals and institutions, new views, and new tools. In part as a result of Embrapa's support to ASB, there was a marked change in the profile and training of Embrapa's research staff. New specialists in the fields of forestry, economics, soil classification, and soil fertility were recruited and retained, and the level of research staff training rose considerably: The proportion of staff holding Ph.D. degrees rose from 6 to 19 percent between 1995 and 1999.

At the same time, laboratory infrastructure was significantly increased and improved. Soil fertility and physics laboratories that before 1995 had limited capacity and low levels of reliability are now certified by a national quality control program and analyzed more than 20,000 soil samples in 1999. Laboratories for food technology, seed analysis, seed certification and processing, animal nutrition, and plant analysis were recently constructed, and technical staff to run them were hired and trained. although these and other efforts to expand and improve laboratory capacity were only partially funded by ASB, ASB was central in helping identify them as priorities.

Improving and increasing computer services within Embrapa was also a high priority, to which ASB contributed significantly. In 1994, Embrapa Acre had only six microcomputers and one specialist in this field. By 1999, there were seventy-four microcomputers and a large staff to support them. Training in computer and software use (some of which was undertaken or financed directly by ASB) has resulted in the presence of a cadre of research and support staff that is highly computer literate and consequently much more productive.

## FUTURE COLLABORATIVE RESEARCH WITH ASB

Future collaborative research involving Embrapa, ASB, and other organizations will focus on plot-level, farm-level, and landscape-level issues, always overlaying biophysical and socioeconomic factors in generating scientific contributions to help promote sustainable economic growth, increase incomes, and improve living conditions of small-scale farmers and conserve the natural resource base. At all levels, the search for new combinations of policies, technologies, and institutional arrangements to meet development objectives will continue.

Plot-level research will focus on identifying the links between land use and changes in above- and below-ground biodiversity. Establishing these links will help researchers identify the private benefits of biodiversity (i.e., those affecting farm profits) and develop policies to use these benefits as entry points for enhancing biodiversity conservation.

At farm level, research will expand the set of products and land use activities for which complete biophysical and socioeconomic information is available and incorporate this new information into predictive models. In addition, the focus of research will expand beyond settlement project areas to include extractive reserves, where small numbers of households are responsible for the stewardship of very large tracts of forest land, and large-scale farms, where small numbers of economic agents make decisions on large tracts of cleared and forested land.

At landscape level, land use mosaics within and across farms that are financially attractive and have beneficial environmental characteristics will be identified, and policies for promoting their establishment and maintenance will be explored.

Finally, at all levels research will endeavor to generate predictive capacity by developing models that will allow researchers and policymakers to assess a priori the impacts on environmental sustainability, economic growth, and poverty alleviation of alternative policy interventions or combinations of them.

## References

Almeida, O.T. de, and C. Uhl. 1995. Developing a quantitative framework for sustainable resource-use planning in the Brazilian Amazon. World Dev. 23(10):1745–1764.

Amaral, E.F. do, E.A. de Araújo, A.W.F. de Melo, M.A. Ribeiro Neto, J.R.T. da Silva, and A.N. de Souza. 2000a. Solos e aptidão agroflorestal. pp. 37–49. *In* Acre. Governo do estado do Acre. Programa Estadual de Zoneamento Ecológico-Econômico do Estado do Acre: Indicativos para gestão territorial do Acre. Documento final da fase 1. Vol. 1. Secretaria de Ciência, Tecnologia e Meio Ambiente do Acre/Embrapa Acre, Rio Branco, Acre, Brazil.

Amaral, E.F. do, E.A. de Araújo, J.R.T. da Silva, A.W.F. de Melo, and A.N. de Souza. 1999. Os solos do Acre: Potencialidades e restrições. Secretaria de Ciência, Tecnologia e Meio Ambiete do Acre/Embrapa Acre, Rio Branco, Acre, Brazil. Relatório Técnico do Zoneamento Ecológico Econômico.

Amaral, E.F. do, E.A. de Araújo, J.F. Valentim, and J.F. do Rêgo. 2000b. Indicativos para agricultural familiar e empreendimentos agropecuários de médio e grande porte. pp. 78–97. *In* Programa Estadual de Zoneamento Ecológico-Econômico do Estado do Acre: Indicativos para gestão territorial do Acre. Documento final da fase 1. Vol. 3. Secretaria de Ciência, Tecnologia e Meio Ambiente do Acre /Embrapa Acre, Rio Branco, Acre, Brazil.

Araújo, H.J.B. de. 1998. Índices técnicos da exploração e transformação madeireira em pequenas areas sob manejo florestal no PC. Pedro Peixoto: Acre. Circular Técnica 23. Embrapa Acre, Rio Branco, Acre, Brazil.

Ávila, M. 1994. Alternatives to slash-and-burn in South America: Report of research site selection in Acre and Rondônia states of Amazon Region of Brazil. Alternatives to Slash-and-Burn Agriculture Programme. Conducted from 31 Aug. to 15 Sept. 1992. ICRAF, Nairobi.

Bartolome, C.A.M. de, and S.A. Vosti. 1995. Choosing between public and private health-care: A case study of malaria treatment in Brazil. J. Health Econ. 14:191–205.

Browder, J.O. 1994. Surviving in Rondônia: The dynamics of colonist farming strategies in Brazil's northwest frontier. Studies Comp. Int. Dev. 29(3):45–69.

Bunker, S.G. 1985. Underdeveloping the Amazon: Extraction, unequal exchange, and the failure of the modern state. Univ. of Illinois, Chicago.

Carpentier, C.L., D.D. Bosch, and S.S. Batie. 1998. Using spatial information to reduce costs of controlling agricultural nonpoint source pollution. Agric. Resource Econ. Rev. (April):72–84.

Carpentier, C.L., S. Vosti, and J. Witcover. 2000a. FaleBEM: A farm-level bioeconomic model for the western Amazonian forest margin. Environment and Production Technology Div. Discussion Paper. IFPRI, Washington, DC.

Carpentier, C.L., S. Vosti, and J. Witcover. 2000b. Intensified production systems on western Brazilian Amazon settlement farms: Could they save the forest? Agric. Ecosyst. Environ. 1635:1–16.

Cattaneo, A. 1999. Brazil: Economic crisis and deforestation in the Amazon. Final Report to ICRAF. Markets and Structural Studies Div. IFPRI, Washington, DC.

Dale, V.H., R.V. O'Neill, M. Pedlowski, and F. Southworth. 1993. Causes and effects of land-use change in central Rondônia, Brazil. Photogramm. Eng. Remote Sens. 59(6):997–1005.

Denslow, J.S. 1988. The tropical rain-forest setting. pp. 25–36. *In* J.S. Denslow and C. Padoch (eds.) People of the tropical rain forest. Univ. of California Press, Berkeley.

Embrapa (Empresa Brasileira de Pesquisa Agropecuária). 1999a. Centro de Pesquisa Agroflorestal do Acre (Rio Branco, AC). Redução dos impactos ambientais da pecuária de corte no Acre. Rio Branco, Acre, Brazil. (Embrapa–Centro de Pesquisa Agroforestal do Acre. Impactos 1999).

Embrapa (Empresa Brasileira de Pesquisa Agropecuária). 1999b. Manejo florestal sustentável para projetos de assentamento. Embrapa–CPAF/AC. Impactos 1999. Embrapa Acre, Rio Branco, Acre, Brazil.

Faminow, M.D. 1998. Cattle, deforestation and development in the Amazon: An economic, agronomic and environmental perspective. CAB Int., Wallingford, UK.

Faminow, M.D., and S.A. Vosti. 1998. Livestock–deforestation links: Policy issues in the western Brazilian Amazon. pp. 88–103. *In* A.J. Nell (ed.) Livestock and the environment international conference, Wageningen, The Netherlands. 16–20 June 1997. World Bank, FAO, and the Int. Agric. Centre, Wageningen.

Fearnside, P.M. 1991. Rondônia: Estradas que levam à devastação. Ciencia Hoje Spec. ed. Dec.:116–122.

Forum Sobre a Amazônia, 2. 1968. Rio de Janeiro, RJ. Problematica da Amazônia. CEB, Rio de Janeiro.

Fujisaka, S., W. Bell, N. Thomas, L. Hurtado, and E. Crawford. 1996. Slash-and-burn agriculture, conversion to pasture, and deforestation in two Brazilian Amazon colonies. Agric. Ecosyst. Environ. 59:115–130.

Government of Brazil. 1969. Amazônia: Instrumentos para o desenvolvimento. Ministerio do Interior, Banco da Amazonia, Belem, Pará, Brazil.

Government of Brazil. 1981. III Plano nacional de desenvolvimento, 1980/85. Presidencia da Republica e Secretaria de Planejamento, Brasília, Brazil.

Government of Brazil. 1998. Programa Brasil em Ação: Dois anos. Presidência da República, Brasília, DF, Brazil.

Hecht, S.B. 1984. Cattle ranching in Amazonia: Political and ecological considerations. Pp. 366–398. *In* M. Schmink and C.H. Wood (eds.) Frontier expansion in Amazonia. Univ. of Florida Press, Gainesville.

Homma, A.K.O. 1993. Extrativismo vegetal na Amazônia: Limites e oportunidades. Empresa Brasileira de Pesquisa Agropecuária. Centro de Pesquisa Agroflorestal da Amazonia Ocidental. Embrapa–Serviço de Produção de Informação, Brasília.

Homma, A.K.O. (ed.). 1998. Amazônia: Meio ambiente e desenvolvimento agrícola. Embrapa Centro de Pesquisa Agroflorestal da Amazonia Oriental. Belem, Pará, Brazil.

IBGE (Instituto Brasileiro de Geografia e Estatistica). 1996. Anuário estatístico do Acre. IBGE, Rio de Janeiro.

IBGE (Instituto Brasileiro de Geografia e Estatística). 1997a. Anuário estatístico do Brasil. IBGE, Rio de Janeiro.

INPE (Instituto Nacional de Pesquisas Espaciais). 2003. Monitoramento da floresta amazônica brasileira por satellite: Projeto PRODES. Available at www.obt.inpe.br/prodes.html.

Knight, D. 1998. Environment bulletin—Water: Worldwide water shortage to worsen. Available at http://www.ips.org//Critical/Enviroment/Environ/env1209006.htm (verified 7 Dec. 2003).

Lisboa, P.L.B., U.N. Maciel, and G.T. Prance. 1991. Perdendo Rondônia. Ciência Hoje (Vol. Especial Amazonia, Dez.):74–82.

Mahar, D. 1979. Frontier policy in Brazil: A study of the Amazonia. Praeger, New York.

Myers, N. 1984. The primary source: Tropical forests and our future. W.W. Norton, New York.

Oliveira, M.V.N. d', E.M. Bráz, D.F.R.P. Burslem, and M.D. Swaine. 1998. Small-scale natural forest management: A new model for small farmers in the Brazilian Amazon. Trop. For. Update 8(1):5–7.

Santana, A.C. de, M.I.R. de Alencar, P.N. Mattar, R.M.Q. da Costa, J.L. d'Ávila, and R.F. Souza. 1997. Reestruturação produtiva e desenvolvimento na Amazônia: Condicionantes e perspectivas. Banco da Amazônia S.A., Belem, Pará, Brazil.

Santos, J.C. dos, C.P. de Sá, and H.J.B. de Araújo. 1999. Aspectos financeiros e institucionais do manejo florestal madeireiro de baixo impacto em áreas de reserva legal de pequenas propriedades, na Amazônia. *In* Congresso Brasileiro de Economia e Sociologia Rural, 37, 1999, Foz do Iguacú. Anais. 1999, CD, Seção Trabalhos Científicos. Soc. Brasileira de Econ. Rural, Brasília DF, Brazil.

Serrão, E.A.S., D. Nepstad, and R. Walker. 1996. Upland agricultural and forestry development in the Amazon: Sustainability, criticality and resilience. Ecol. Econ. 18:3–13.

Smith, N.J.H., E.A.S. Serrão, P.T. Alvim, and I.C. Falesi. 1995. Amazônia: Resiliency and dynamism of the people. United Nations Univ., New York.

SUDAM (Superintendência de Desenvolvimento da Amazônia). 1976. II Plano de Desenvolvimento da Amazônia: Detalhamento do II Plano Nacional de Desenvolvimento (1975–79). Belem, Pará, Brazil.

UNDP (United Nations Development Program). 1999. Human development report. Oxford Univ. Press, New York.

Valente, M.G. 1968. A Amazônia brasileira e as outras amazônias. pp. 277–295. *In* Forum sobre a Amazônia, 2. Problemática da Amazônia. CEB, Rio de Janeiro.

Valentim, J.F. 1989. Impacto ambiental da pecuária no Acre. Documento Base do Curso de Avaliação do Impacto Ambiental da Pecuária no Acre. Embrapa–Unidade de Execução de Pessquisa de Âmbito Estadual Rio Branco/Inst. de Meio Ambiente do Acre, Acre, Brazil.

Valentim, J.F., E.F. do Amaral, and A.W.F. de Melo. 2000. Zoneamento de risco atual e potencial de morte de pastagens de *Brachiara brizantha* no Acre. Embrapa Acre. Boletim de Pesquisa, 29. Embrapa–Acre, Rio Branco, Acre, Brazil.

Valentim, J.F., and J. da C. Carneiro. 2001. Pueraria phaseoloides e *Calopogonium mucunoides*. pp. 427–458. *In* A.M. Peixoto, C.G.S. Pereira, J.C. de Moura, and V.P. Faria (eds.) Anais do 18th Simpósio Sobre Manejo de Pastagens: A Planta Forrageira No Sistema de Produção. Fundação de Estudos Agrários "Luiz de Queiroz," Piracicaba, Brazil.

Valentim, J.F., J. da C. Carneiro, and M.F.L. Sales. 2001. Amendoim forrageira cv. Belmonte: Leguminosa para a diversificação das pastagens e conservação do solo no Acre. Rio Branco. Embrapa, Acre, 2001. Circ. Técnica 43. Embrapa, Acre, Brazil.

Vaz, F.A., and J.F. Valentim. 2001. Utilização de energia solar e cercas eletrificadas no manejo das pastagens no Acre. Circ. Técnica 40. Embrapa–Acre, Rio Branco, Acre, Brazil.

Vosti, S.A., C.L. Carpentier, J. Witcover, and J.F. Valentim. 2001a. Intensified small-scale livestock systems in the western Brazilian Amazon. pp. 113–133. *In* A. Angelsen and D. Kaimowitz (eds.) Agricultural technologies and tropical deforestation. CAB Int., Wallingford, UK.

Vosti, S.A., and T. Reardon (eds.). 1997. Agricultural sustainability, growth, and poverty alleviation: A policy and agroecological perspective. Johns Hopkins Univ. Press, Baltimore.

Vosti, S.A., and J. Valentim. 1998. Foreword. *In* M.D. Faminow (ed.) Cattle, deforestation and development in the Amazon: An economic, agronomic and environmental perspective. CAB Int., Wallingford, UK.

Vosti, S.A., and J. Witcover. 1996. Slash-and-burn agriculture: household perspectives. Agric. Ecosyst. Environ. 58:23–38.

Vosti, S.A., J. Witcover, and C.L. Carpentier. 1998. Final report: Convenio de Cooperación Técnica Regional No Reembolsable no. ATN/SF-4827-RG: Programa 1994 de Tecnología Agropecuaria Regional en América Latina y El Caribe of the Inter-American Development Bank. Environ. and Production Technol. Div. IFPRI, Washington, DC.

Vosti, S.A., J. Witcover, and C.L. Carpentier. 2002. Agricultural intensification by smallholders in the western Brazilian Amazon: From deforestation to sustainable use. IFPRI Res. Rep. 130. IFPRI, Washington, DC. Available at http://www.ifpri.org/pubs/pubs.htm#rreport (verified 7 Dec. 2003).

Walker, R., and A.K.O. Homma. 1996. Land use and land cover dynamics in the Brazilian Amazon: An overview. Ecol. Econ. 18:67–80.

Wolstein, A.R.P., E.M. Lima, E.F. do Amaral, E.M. Bráz, F.L.N. Pinheiro, I.L. Franke, et al. 1998. Metodologia para o planejamento, implantação e monitoramento de projetos de assentamentos sustentaveis na Amazonia. Embrapa–CPAF/AC/INCRA/FUNTAC, Rio Branco, Brazil.

# 13   The Forest Margins of Sumatra, Indonesia

Soetjipto Partohardjono, Djuber Pasaribu, and Achmad M. Fagi
*Center for Research in Food Crops  Agency for Agricultural Research
and Development  Bogor, Indonesia*

Indonesia still has large forest areas, but they are rapidly being converted to other land uses. Transformation from primary to secondary forest is caused largely by timber extraction, and traditional shifting cultivation systems play a smaller role. Subsequent transformation of secondary and logged-over forest types generally is based on slash-and-burn practices by large-scale farmers and smallholders for a variety of reasons. Migrants convert part of the forest to temporary cropland either in government-sponsored schemes or spontaneously. Such land can evolve into alang-alang (*Imperata cylindrica* [L.]) grasslands or into permanent tree-based production systems (agroforests).

Slash-and-burn is both a land-clearing technique and a land use system. It is inaccurate to equate slash-and-burn agriculture only with permanent forest conversion and unsustainable land use. The technique is attractive because fire is the cheapest, most effective way to clear land (Ketterings et al. 1999). The Alternatives to Slash and Burn (ASB) characterization data (van Noordwijk et al. 1995, 1998; Tomich et al. 1998) suggest that in Jambi (Sumatra), most slash-and-burn is used for replacing old jungle rubber, rather than for conversion of primary forest. Traditional shifting cultivation of food crops, practiced for generations by local people in Sumatra, was sustainable as long as population densities were low enough to allow long fallow rotations. Traditional shifting cultivation has been disappearing as rural population densities increase, but slash-and-burn is used for land clearing by almost all those (public and private, large- and small-scale) who contribute to forest conversion, sometimes in systems that are unsustainable but often in systems that apparently are sustainable for the foreseeable future.

Agroforests begin with slash-and-burn clearing and intercropping of upland food crops, but the primary objective is the establishment of tree crops such as rubber and various fruit and timber species. This system accommodates natural regeneration. As a result, agroforests replicate some elements of natural forest structure and ecology (Michon and de Foresta 1995). In the ASB global project, the island of Sumatra was chosen to represent the lowland humid tropical forest zone in Southeast Asia.

In this chapter we give an overview of the results in phase 1 and 2 of the ASB Project in Indonesia, with a brief historical background of the forest conversion process, discussing the categorization of forest lands in Indonesia and describing the benchmark areas in Jambi and Lampung, before we discuss the main ASB hypothesis on the relationships between intensification of land use and the developmental and environmental consequences this may have.

## HISTORICAL BACKGROUND

Since the beginning of the twentieth century, population density in Sumatra has increased by migration from Java, both spontaneous and government sponsored. A clear gradient in population density occurs from the south (Lampung province) to the middle (Jambi, Riau provinces) of the island. Although most land in Sumatra is considered to be government "forest land," a substantial part of this land is no longer under forest cover, and the amount of "forest damage" is correlated with population density at the provincial level, with Riau and Jambi provinces at the lower end of the spectrum and Lampung at the higher end. Because many smallholder farmers practicing slash-and-burn appear to do so because they lack feasible livelihood options, the development of sustainable, labor-intensive land use practices that are viable alternatives to slash-and-burn could discourage deforestation.

The major part of the island of Sumatra was still under forest cover in 1932 (Van Steenis 1935). Forest conversion by that time had taken place mainly in coastal zones (especially in Aceh, West Sumatra, Bengkulu and Lampung provinces), close to the major rivers in the eastern peneplain (especially the Musi River in south Sumatra and the Batanghari River in Jambi), and areas involved in the tobacco (*Nicotiana tabacum* L.) and rubber (*Hevea brasiliensis* [Willd. Ex A. Juss.] Muell.-Arg.) plantation booms in the late nineteenth and early twentieth centuries in north Sumatra. Forest conversion by 1982 had affected most of the remaining forest in Lampung and south Sumatra but not in Jambi (MacKinnon 1982).

This changed with the completion of the Trans-Sumatra highway and associated transmigration projects in the early 1980s. The ASB benchmark areas in Jambi are thus located in an area where forest conversion along the major rivers took place before the 1930s but that otherwise remained mostly under forest cover at least until the early 1980s. The north Lampung benchmark area abuts one of the few forest patches left in the Lampung–south Sumatra part of the eastern peneplain.

## INDONESIAN FOREST LANDS

In the 1980s, "Agreed Forest Use Categories" were established on all state forest land in Indonesia. Under this system, forest land is categorized as follows:

- National parks and conservation forests: These are areas in which nature conservation gets priority.
- Protection forests: This class is defined mainly on the basis of slope and protects water supplies for downstream sites.
- Limited production forests: Only collection of nontimber forest products is allowed in this category, which is intended to provide a buffer zone around conservation or protection forests.
- Production forests: Here the Indonesian Selective Logging System is supposed to be followed. Under this system, only a few large-diameter trees are harvested per hectare, followed by a 30-year regrowth period before the next logging operation, to secure sustained harvest with little loss of biodiversity. In practice few (if any) logging concessions have met this target. Forest damage in the concessions is much larger than anticipated because of a combination of logging of more trees than allowed (using inefficient techniques that unnecessarily damage the remaining forest) and the use of forest land for other purposes by large-scale forest squatters following the logging roads. Production forest can be divided into limited production forests with stricter regulation on timber use and nonconvertible production forests.
- Convertible production forests: These are forests officially targeted for conversion to other land use, including industrial timber estates (*hutan tanaman industri*, HTI), transmigration projects, and plantations of oil palm (*Elaeis guineensis* Jacq.), sugar cane (*Saccharum officinarum* L.), and other crops. The total areas in the different categories are shown in table 13.1.

Because any conversion of primary forest entails a significant decline in biodiversity, conservation reserves always have an important potential role in biodiversity conservation. In Sumatra, efforts to conserve large national parks tend to concentrate on mountain areas (such as Kerinci Seblat National Park and the Gunung Leuser Park), while little of the rich lowland forests has been protected effectively. Allowing some use of highland park areas while protecting more of the lowlands probably would increase conservation efficiency while allowing the same number of people to achieve a similar level of livelihood (van Noordwijk et al. 1995). For Sumatra as a whole, 6.6 percent of the original forest is protected in reserves; this equates to 16 percent of the forest that remained in 1982 (MacKinnon 1982). The montane or submontane forests have a better protection status than average, and the mangrove and swamp forest are most endangered.

*Table 13.1* Areas in the Different Categories of Forest Land[a] in Indonesia, April 1999

| Category | Area (million ha) | Percentage |
|---|---|---|
| Park and reservation forests | 20.62 | 17.02 |
| Protection forests | 33.92 | 28.01 |
| Limited production forests | 23.17 | 19.13 |
| Nonconvertible production forests | 35.32 | 29.16 |
| Convertible production forests | 8.08 | 6.67 |
| Total | 121.11 | 100 |

[a]This refers to state forest land rather than to the actual vegetation.
*Source:* Santoso (1999).

Forest classification may have little bearing on the situation on the ground because there is often confusion over the exact location of boundaries. Both protection and production forest categories show the same relationship between forest damage and population density in Sumatra (van Noordwijk et al. 1995). Only the national parks are well protected.

## LAND USE IN THE ASB BENCHMARK SITES

The ASB Indonesia consortium has focused on benchmark areas in the forest margins of Jambi in the central part of Sumatra and the deforested and degraded lands with higher population densities found in the southern part of the island, close to Java, with its high population densities. Figure 13.1 shows the main ecological zones of Sumatra and the benchmark areas.

### JAMBI

Two sites in Jambi province were chosen for detailed characterization by the ASB Project. The Bungo Tebo site is a dissected peneplain of acid tuffaceous sediments, and the elevation is generally less than 100 m above sea level. The Rantau Pandan site is 100 to 500 m above sea level and represents the piedmont zone, which was formed mainly by granite and andesitic lava. Soils in Bungo Tebo are predominantly ultisols, deep, well drained, very acid, and of low fertility. Soils in Rantau Pandan are more varied and complex—ranging from shallow to very deep, moderate to fine texture, and well to moderately excessive drained—but they are also very acid and have low soil fertility. Both Jambi sites average seven to nine wet months (more than 200 mm rainfall) and less than 2 dry months (100 mm rainfall) per year, with annual rainfall of 2100 to 3000 mm. Forestry and the rubber-processing industry (crumb rubber) contributed 99 percent of the exports from the province in 1993. In the rubber industry, small-

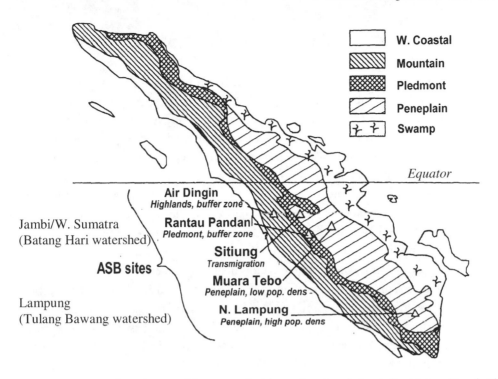

Figure 13.1 Agroecological zones of Sumatra and with ASB benchmark sites indicated (van Noordwijk et al. 1995).

holder rubber plays a crucial role. The total area of rubber cultivation in Jambi in 1993 was 502,642 ha, of which only 3447 ha was planted with high-yielding varieties under intensive management; the rest was jungle rubber (rubber agroforests). About 64 percent of the land in Jambi is categorized as state forest land. However, forest status often was declared long after local communities had settled there. In practice, a large part of the forest land is used for rubber agroforests and other forms of agriculture.

After the completion of the Trans-Sumatra highway in the 1980s, Jambi became a popular migrant destination. The ASB studies indicate that more than 25 percent of spontaneous migrants came between 5 and 15 years ago, and almost 40 percent came less than 5 years ago; more than 80 percent of spontaneous migrants came from Java, and less than 20 percent came from other parts of Sumatra.

Almost every smallholder household interviewed in the ASB surveys in Jambi is engaged in agriculture. Less than 10 percent of households and spontaneous migrants engage in nonagricultural activities. This is in strong contrast to transmigrants. Although agricultural activities are the main occupation of transmigrants, 75 percent of these households reported nonagricultural work (in trading, services, and paid labor). Most household heads did not complete primary school; the figure exceeded 70 percent for each site and was as high as 95 percent for the sample of local people in Bungo Tebo.

## LAMPUNG

The peneplain of northern Lampung, Sumatra, was chosen to represent the landscape degradation that can follow forest conversion if intensive food crop production is pursued on these soils. Of the benchmark sites, only the Pakuan Ratu subdistrict in north Lampung has no forest left, except for an industrial timber plantation or HTI (production forest). All other forest remnants have been converted into agricultural areas or are too small to be included in the statistics.

The spontaneous movement of people between Java and Lampung, and additional efforts by the government during various periods in the twentieth century, are key to understanding its landscape dynamics. Government-sponsored transmigrants generally have found the lowland peneplain soils unsuitable for their crop-based systems. Only in depression and valleys, where paddy fields could be created, has agriculture become a major source of their livelihood. Otherwise off-farm labor has had to provide the income that the remaining population of the area had; a substantial number of transmigrants left the area in the first few years. This exodus may have accelerated as conditions worsened because of drought and the national financial crisis; eleven out of thirty households interviewed in 1993 had left the village when a repeat survey was done in 1998 (Elmhirst et al. 1998).

Some migrants settled of their own accord, despite the hardships in the area, including the second generation of the government-sponsored transmigrants, for whom there is no land in the village. Spontaneous migrants tend to use agricultural systems intermediate between the local system and the Javanese food crop–based system, with a greater emphasis on tree crops.

The indigenous Lampung people, who live along the rivers, still have their semipermanent food crop production on flooded riverbanks, but two decades ago they stopped the extensive shifting cultivation of the lowland peneplain. Along the rivers, they still have old jungle rubber gardens on the margin of Sumatra's rubber domain. Recently there has been renewed interest in rubber production, but as a whole the indigenous Lampungese now aim to secure their livelihoods outside agriculture (Elmhirst 1997; Elmhirst et al. 1998).

The research site of Krui is on the west coast of Lampung province (across the mountainous Bukit Barisan range), where a narrow coastal strip has had a long history of settlement but little immigration over the last century. Here an extraordinary form of agroforestry was developed by local farmers about a century ago, the *Shorea javanica*–based damar agroforests (De Foresta et al. 2000). International organizations and national partners led by ASB formed the Krui team' that helped in obtaining government recognition for the value of this land use system as property rights (Fay et al. 1998). This work culminated in 1998 in the signing by the minister of forestry of a decree creating a special class within state forest land, Kawasan Dengan Tijuana Istimewa ("Zone with Distinct Purpose") granting the local community tree tenure in perpetuity and the right to fully manage state forest land, preventing outsiders from gaining access to that land.

## ASB Hypotheses for Indonesia

The key hypothesis underlying phases I and II of the ASB project in Indonesia is that intensifying land use as an alternative to slash-and-burn can simultaneously reduce deforestation and poverty (van Noordwijk et al. 2001). In phase I, the research program was designed to characterize selected benchmark sites and identify and prioritize research following the ASB global guidelines. In phase II, the research program was designed to better understand how the Indonesian government and donor agencies could balance global environmental objectives with economic development and poverty reduction. Although conversion of primary forest has the major effect on biodiversity and carbon stocks, the resulting land uses also matter a great deal for the supply of these global public goods. Measurements of differences in environmental consequences of the various land uses provide the basis for quantifying major tradeoffs involved in land use change.

The ASB surveyed the five main agricultural land uses in the Jambi benchmark areas:

• Wet rice fields (*sawah*). Except for local farmers in Bungo Tebo (who reported none), households typically have one wet rice (*Oryza sativa* L.) or paddy field. The average size of wet rice plots is 0.31 ha for the sample of transmigrants and 0.68 ha for spontaneous migrants in Bungo Tebo, compared with 0.84 ha for the sample of local people in Rantau Pandan.

• Upland fields (*ladang*). This category includes both the shifting cultivation rotation of food crops followed by fallow, and upland fields that will be—or already have been—planted with perennials such as rubber. Local people and transmigrants both average about one plot per household. Spontaneous migrants have more upland plots (1.6 per household), and their upland fields are bigger (1.6 ha on average, compared to less than 1 ha for other groups).

• Perennial plots including agroforests (*kebun*). As just noted, perennial plots also begin with intercropping of upland food crops, but the primary objective is establishment of tree crops such as rubber agroforests (the main land use for these sites), various fruit species, and (recently, in Rantau Pandan) cinnamon (*Cinnamomum burmanii* [Nees] Bl.). Local people in Bungo Tebo typically have two perennial plots (mainly rubber) per household, with plots averaging 3.6 ha each. Spontaneous migrants at this site have somewhat fewer plots (1.8 per household), but their plots are bigger on average (4.3 ha per plot). Transmigrants reported an average of 1.4 plots per household and an average size of only 1.8 ha per plot. Surprisingly, data from the sample of local people in Rantau Pandan yielded averages similar to those of the transmigrants in Bungo Tebo. This probably reflects underreporting of plots located on state forest land.

•  Bush fallow (*belukar*). Bush fallow comprises two categories. *Semak*—land covered by grasses, shrubs, and small trees—is the first fallow stage. The second stage, *belukar tua,* often resembles secondary forest; land is covered by larger trees and may even include old rubber trees that no longer are productive. In Rantau Pandan, sample households reported an average of 1.7 bush fallow plots with an average size of 1.5 ha, whereas in Bungo Tebo the number of plots per household is somewhat lower (1.2–1.3 plots) but the average plot size is larger (1.6–2.8 ha).

•  Home gardens (*pekarangan*). Home gardens, comprising a variety of annuals and perennials used for many purposes, are cultivated intensively by transmigrants and spontaneous migrants but are less used by local people.

The ASB study of land use change in the 1982 to 1996 period showed that jungle rubber is the predominant farming system in the Jambi area. In a 1982 vegetation map, large areas were indicated as "mosaics of rubber and shrub" or "mosaics of rubber and forest." On 1992 and 1994 satellite maps, however, the major part of the rubber complex is indicated as "old secondary forest." Whether this change is a true maturation of the jungle rubber system or a result of the coarser scale of the 1986 map is not clear. Farmers said that jungle rubber is inherited from generation to generation and seldom rejuvenated because of limited access to better planting material, loss of potential income while waiting for the new plantation to become productive, and wild pigs disturbing plants (Hadi et al. 1997). Farmers replace jungle rubber only after production has become very low and when they need land for their food crops. Plots of rubber, cinnamon (traded as *cassiavera*), or both range from 0.5 to 4 ha per household.

Since 1999, a pilot project from the Department of Forestry, Hutan Rakyat ("community forest"), has been carried out in the community's bush fallow. About 50 ha of this *belukar* was given to families to be cultivated with durian (*Durio zibethinus* Murr.), cinnamon, surian (*Toona sinensis* [A. Juss.] Roem), and sengon (*Paraserianthes falcataria* [L.] I. Nielsen) as agroforests. Planting material also came from the project, which recommended a slash-and-mulch system without burning. It is a first step in the government's recognition of the role of local people in managing the forest. If this project succeeds, it may be a good basis for future programs.

No agricultural land use consistently harvests products without putting management efforts into maintenance of the system, so all judgments of sustainability depend on a specified management regime and on farmers' efforts to overcome obstacles. Land-clearing techniques play an important role. The effects of improper land-clearing methods are observed even 8 to 10 years after the land has been cleared, and especially when the overall soil fertility has drastically declined. Improved understanding of people's interactions with forests is fundamental to development of effective options for sustainable management for forested lands. The ASB's research project in Indonesia has assessed which land use options are agronomically sustainable (Weise 1998a, 1998b; chapter 6, this volume).

A set of field-level criteria and indicators was used to evaluate the sustainability of a range of land use systems that can follow forest conversion (van Noordwijk et al. 2001). Natural forest can be used as a starting point for all land use types. Synthesis of sustainability indicators showed that most land use systems considered have one or more aspects that need attention, but most of these stay within the range of solvable problems at the farm level. The various tree crop systems appear to be freely convertible to each other, but extensive rubber agroforests will change in character once the seedbank of original natural vegetation is depleted and the site is out of reach of seed dispersal. The cassava–*Imperata* cycle has a number of associated issues, such as maintaining a nutrient balance, which are so serious that they probably cannot be resolved at the farm level within the current constraints (Weise 1998a, 1998b; chapter 6, this volume).

## ASB's Research Activities and Major Research Findings

Major findings in phases I and II of ASB activities are as follows:

• No surveyed households practiced shifting cultivation in the classic sense (van Noordwijk et al. 1995).

• All households, whether local farmers, government-sponsored transmigrants, or spontaneous migrants, use slash-and-burn methods for land clearing (van Noordwijk et al. 1995).

• The most common land use system in the Jambi benchmark site is clearance of logged-over or secondary forest or old jungle rubber to plant upland rice mixed with rubber trees; in the second year upland rice or other food crops may be grown, but the emphasis is on the tree crops.

• Most of the existing rubber agroforests in Jambi are old and have low productivity. To get sufficient income, a large area is needed. Currently, land for rubber expansion is very limited; most of the forested land that is seen as potential areas for rubber expansion by local people is already distributed by the government to projects and therefore is off limits.

• The most common land use system in the north Lampung benchmark site is clearance of secondary (or logged-over) forest or shrub fallow vegetation to plant food crops or sugar cane. Recently, however, interest is growing in converting the land to better-adapted and more profitable tree crops in the form of rubber, oil palm, or fast-growing timber species. Such tree-based systems can accommodate short-term needs for food production.

• Vertebrate pests (wild pigs and monkeys in the forest margins, rats on the degraded lands) are perceived as major constraints in cultivating food crops. Wild pigs are also a threat to young rubber plants and deter farmers from investing in more expensive higher-yielding rubber planting material.

• Soil fertility constraints are most obvious on the peneplain sites where transmigrant farmers have attempted continuous food crop production. Aluminum toxicity, phosphorus deficiency, and rapid depletion of soil organic matter means that continuous food crop production is not possible without substantial inputs of fertilizers. Many of the current high-yielding crop varieties also need lime.

• North Lampung has more frequent, more pronounced dry seasons than the rest of Sumatra. These are a limitation for several tree crops, including hybrid coconut (*Cocos nucifera* L.) and various fruit trees. These dry periods also entail a fire risk and tend to maintain *Imperata* grasslands.

• Logging concessions in Jambi have affected large areas of primary forest in the piedmont and the peneplain zone; logging roads encourage an inflow of spontaneous migrants who usually plant rubber. Thus, rubber expansion may prevent the regeneration of logged-over forests and speed up permanent forest conversion.

• The transmigration program can have two results: Where villages are successful, they attract a spontaneous influx of people from Java. Where they do not succeed, they became a source of spontaneous migrants, who either search for more fertile land in the forest margins or go to urban areas.

• Land tenure in the transmigration areas is recognized officially, whereas that in the local villages is based mainly on customary law (*adat*); land disputes are common where the two tenure systems overlap.

• Conflict over forest land use occurs when current regulations and policies are declared after settlers have occupied the forest or when new settlers occupy forest land where such regulations are not effectively implemented.

• As much as 59 percent of the above-ground carbon stocks were removed by forest fire, and about 97 percent of unburned trees were removed from the plots. Changes in soil carbon stocks were small (Murdiyarso et al. 1997).

• The methane oxidation capacity of upland soils under trees (which partly offsets methane emissions in other land uses, such as paddy rice fields) declines with soil compaction (Murdiyarso et al. 1997; chapter 3, this volume).

• Nitrous oxide emissions appear to be related to the temporary abundance of soil mineral nitrogen or the amount of nitrogen cycling through the system (Davidson et al. 2000). At certain times during the year and during the land use cycle fluxes from forests are higher than those from other land uses and vice versa. No consistent relationship between land use and net emissions of nitrous oxide over a system's lifespan has yet been found (Tomich et al. 1998; Davidson et al. 2000).

• Alternative land uses at the forest margins differ in their potential for conservation of above-ground biodiversity, with a range of alternatives falling between the extremes of the smallholder's complex agroforests and large-scale plantation monoculture.

• All tree-based alternatives appear to be agronomically sustainable.

• Because of the currency collapse in 1997, profitability of many tree-based systems has increased substantially, which boosts incentives for forest conversion by smallholders and large-scale operators alike.

• There may be tradeoffs between potential profitability and above-ground biodiversity in tree-based production systems, but this must be verified.

• Potential profitability of some tree-based alternatives for smallholders (such as rubber agroforestry with higher-yielding rubber varieties) appears to be comparable to large-scale oil palm estates, but this also must be verified.

• Smallholders must address some important institutional questions to enable widespread adoption of profitable agroforestry alternatives.


## LESSONS LEARNED

Forest-derived land uses differ significantly in their ability to substitute for specific functions of natural forests (De Jong et al. 2001). Because of the multiple objectives of production and environmental services of forests, deforestation must be viewed as a multidimensional phenomenon. Sometimes this policy problem can be simplified with tradeoff analysis.

The Sumatra case shows that agroforestry solutions help alleviate poverty but that they may speed up rather than slow down forest conversion as their profitability attracts migrant farmers and thus reduces biodiversity (Tomich et al. 2001).

The rapid spread of rubber as a smallholder crop in Sumatra since the beginning of the twentieth century and of smallholder oil palm in the late 1990s have contributed to large-scale forest conversion, to the point that there is very little lowland primary forest left. The logging concessions, especially those of the 1960s to 1980s, followed by an inflow of spontaneous settlers with rubber-based agriculture, have completed the conversion. Murdiyarso et al. (2002) show that the labor absorption of rubber agroforests can be high (providing a decent living to population densities of the order of sixty people per square kilometer), similar to that of oil palm, indicating that rubber agroforests so far are our best bet for integrating biodiversity and profitability of land use. If possible, however, segregating land into full protection status with more intensive agriculture in the remaining land might be superior (Van Schaik and van Noordwijk 2002). The returns to labor for logging in the presence of roads are so high that labor-intensive agroforestry as such can never compete with forest destruction, and a combination of social or government-based rules for protecting forests and labor-intensive, profitable land use systems is a prerequisite for forest protection (van Noordwijk et al. 1995; Tomich et al. 2001). Efforts to develop land use alternatives and policy options to pursue global environmental objectives (biodiversity conservation and carbon sequestration) are futile without consideration of agronomic sustainability and environmental services at other scales, objectives of farmers and policymakers at various levels, and weaknesses in markets and other institutions that influence the adoptability of land use alternatives by smallholders.

Tenure, institutions, trade policies, and macroeconomic shocks affect a household's livelihood options and thereby either reduce or intensify further deforestation.

This policy and institutional environment also has a powerful effect on the natural resource management decisions made by people at the forest margins.

Ongoing collaboration, contact, and presence of national and international members of the research team are essential for real impact on policy and technology options. Building effective multidisciplinary teams to study complexities of land use change is feasible but involves high costs.

## FUTURE RESEARCH NEEDS

Scientists active in the ASB Indonesia team identified future research needs:

- Examine a wider range of tree-based best bets regarding their environmental, agronomic, and economic impacts and feasibility of adoption (Williams et al. 2001).
- Gain a better understanding about the relationships between above-ground and below-ground biodiversity, production sustainability, and potential profitability (Murdiyarso et al. 2002).
- Expand the assessments of sustainability from plot-level agronomic issues to include environmental externalities at the landscape level, including watershed functions.
- Complete the landscape transect by expanding the present focus on the peneplains and piedmont agroecological zones to include the montane zone and coastal swamps.
- Study more intensively the underlying causes of fires, policy issues, and technological alternatives to alleviate such catastrophic fires and smoke problems as happened in 1997 and 1998.
- Analyze how macroeconomic shocks affect land use change, environmental services, poverty, and household food security.
- Verify the potential environmental, social, and economic benefits of a smallholder-based development strategy as an alternative to large-scale plantation monoculture.

## CONCLUSION

Indonesia still has large forest areas, and conversion to other land uses is rapid. The transformation from primary to secondary forest is caused largely by timber extraction, with traditional shifting cultivation playing a smaller role.

Although a part of the deforestation resulting from slash-and-burn is linked to the poverty of people living at the forest margins, the conditions necessary for increased productivity of agroforestry and other land use systems to reduce poverty and reduce deforestation are not sufficiently well understood.

The ASB's study of the present land use systems has revealed that all tree-based alternatives to slash-and-burn appear to be agronomically sustainable.

In developing alternative land uses and policy options that address global environmental objectives (biodiversity conservation and carbon sequestration), agronomic sustainability, and other environmental services, we must continue to consider the objectives of farmers and policymakers at various levels and weaknesses in markets and other institutions that influence the adoptability of land use alternatives by smallholders.

## REFERENCES

Davidson, E.A., M. Keller, H.E. Erickson, L.V. Verchot, and F. Veldkamp. 2000. Testing a conceptual model of soil emissions of nitrous and nitric oxide. BioScience 50:667–680.

De Foresta, H., A. Kusworo, G. Michon, and W.A. Djatmiko. 2000. Ketika Kebun Berupa Hutan—Agroforest Khas Indonesia—Sebuah Sumbangan Masyarakat. ICRAF, Bogor, Indonesia.

De Jong, W., M. van Noordwijk, M. Sirait, N. Liswanti, and S. Suyanto. 2001. Farming secondary forests in Indonesia. J. Trop. For. Sci. 13:705–726.

Elmhirst, R. 1997. Gender, environmental and culture: A political ecology of transmigration in Indonesia. Ph.D. diss. Environment Dep., Wye College, UK.

Elmhirst, R., Hermalia, and Yulianti. 1998. "Krismon" and "Kemarau": A downward sustainability spiral in a north Lampung "Translok" settlement. pp. 106–121. *In* M. van Noordwijk and H. De Foresta (eds.) Agroforestry in landscapes under pressure: Lampung research planning trip, 17–21 June 1998. Rep. no. 6. ASB Indonesia, Bogor.

Fay, C., H. de Foresta, M. Sarait, and T.P. Tomich. 1998. A policy breakthrough for Indonesian farmers in the Krui damar agroforests. Agrofor. Today 10 (2):25–26.

Hadi, P.U., V.T. Manurung, and B.M. Purnama. 1997. General socio-economic features of the slash-and-burn cultivator in north Lampung and Bungo Tebo. pp. 191–229. *In* M. Van Noordwijk, T.P. Tomich, D.P. Garrity, and A.M. Fagi (eds.) Alternatives to Slash-and-Burn research in Indonesia, Rep. no 6. ASB–Indonesia.

Ketterings, Q.M., T. Wibowo, M. Van Noordwijk, and E. Penot. 1999. Farmers' perceptions on slash-and-burn as land clearing method for small-scale rubber producers in Sepunggur, Jambi province, Sumatra, Indonesia. For. Ecol. Manage. 120:157–169.

MacKinnon, J. 1982. National conservation plan for Indonesia, Vol. II. Sumatra. FAO, Bogor, Indonesia.

Michon, G., and H. de Foresta. 1995. The Indonesian agroforest model: Forest resource management and biodiversity conservation. pp. 90–106. *In* P. Halladay and D.A. Gilmour (eds.) Conserving biodiversity outside protected areas: The role of traditional agroecosystems. IUCN, Gland, Switzerland.

Murdiyarso, D., K. Hairiah, Y.A. Husin, and U.R. Wasrin. 1997. Greenhouse gas emission and carbon balance in slash-and-burn practices. pp. 35–58. *In* M. Van Noordwijk, T.P. Tomich, D.P. Garrity, and A.M. Fagi (eds.) Alternatives to Slash-and-Burn Research in Indonesia. Rep. no. 6. ASB–Indonesia, Bogor.

Murdiyarso, D., M. van Noordwijk, U.R. Wasrin, T.P. Tomich, and A.N. Gillison. 2002. Environmental benefits and sustainable land-use options in the Jambi transect, Sumatra, Indonesia. J. Vegetation Sci. 13:429–438.

Santoso, H. 1999. Pengelolaan sumber daya hutan, hutan tanaman dan hutan rakyat. Disajikan pada Seminar Pencapaian Pengelolaan Hutan Berkelanjutan Diambang Abad 21, Departemen Kehutanan dan Perkebunan, Bogor, Indonesia.

Tomich, T.P., M. van Noordwijk, S. Budidarsono, A. Gillison, T. Kusumanto, D. Murdiyarso, et al. 1998. Alternatives to Slash-and-Burn in Indonesia. Summary report and synthesis of phase II. ASB, ICRAF, Nairobi.

Tomich, T.P., M. van Noordwijk, S. Budidarsono, A. Gillison, T. Kusumanto, D. Murdiyarso, et al. 2001. Agricultural intensification, deforestation and the environment: Assessing tradeoffs in Sumatra, Indonesia. pp. 221–244. *In* D. Lee and C. Barrett (eds.) Tradeoffs or synergies? Agricultural intensification, economic development and the environment. CAB Int., Wallingford, UK.

van Noordwijk, M., D. Murdiyarso, K. Hairiah, U.R. Wasrin, A. Rachman, and T.P. Tomich. 1998. Forest soils under alternatives to slash-and-burn agriculture in Sumatra, Indonesia. pp. 175–185. *In* A. Schulte and D. Ruhiyat (eds.) Soils of tropical forest ecosystems: Characteristics, ecology and management. Springer-Verlag, Berlin.

van Noordwijk, M., T.P. Tomich, R. Winahyu, D. Murdiyarso, S. Suyanto, S. Partoharjono, et al. (eds.). 1995. Alternatives to Slash-and-Burn in Indonesia: Summary report of phase 1. ASB–Indonesia Rep. No. 4. ASB–Indonesia Consortium and ICRAF, Bogor, Indonesia.

van Noordwijk, M., S.E. Williams, and B. Verbist (eds.). 2001. Toward integrated natural resource management in forest margins of the humid tropics: Local action and global concerns. ASB Lecture Notes 1–12. ICRAF, Bogor, Indonesia. Available at http://www.icraf.cgiar.org/sea/Training/Materials/ASB-TM/ASB-ICRAFSEA-LN.htm.

Van Schaik, C.P., and M. van Noordwijk. 2002. Agroforestry and biodiversity: Are they compatible? pp. 37–48. *In* S.M. Sitompul and S.R. Utami (eds.) Akar Pertanian Sehat: Konsep dan Pemikiran. Biol. Manage. of Soil Fert., Brawijaya Univ., Malang, Indonesia.

Van Steenis, C.G.F.J. 1935. Maleische vegetatieschetsen. Tijd. Kon. Ned. Aard. Gen. 52:25–67, 171–203, 363–390.

Weise, S. 1998a. Agronomic sustainability: ASB Phase II working group report: A first attempt at cross-site comparisons. Int. Inst. of Trop. Agric. Yaoundé, Cameroon. Available at http://www.asb.cgiar.org/sust_SLUM.shtm.

Weise, S. 1998b. Agronomic sustainability: ASB Phase II working group report on methodology. Int. Inst. of Trop. Agric., Yaoundé, Cameroon. Available at http://www.asb.cgiar.org/sust_SLUM.shtm.

Williams, S.E., M. van Noordwijk, E. Penot, J.R. Healey, F.L. Sinclair, and G. Wibawa. 2001. On-farm evaluation of the establishment of clonal rubber in multistrata agroforests in Jambi, Indonesia. Agrofor. Syst. 53:227–237.

# 14　The Forest Margins of Cameroon

James Gockowski
> *IITA  Humid Forest Research Station  M'Balmayo, Cameroon*

Jean Tonyé
> *IRAD  Yaoundé, Cameroon*

Chimere Diaw
> *CIFOR  Humid Forest Research Station  M'Balmayo, Cameroon*

Stefan Hauser
> *IITA  Humid Forest Research Station  M'Balmayo, Cameroon*

Jean Kotto-Same and Rosaline Njomgang
> *IRAD  Yaoundé, Cameroon*

Appolinaire Moukam
> *IRAD  Deceased*

Dieudonné Nwaga
> *Université de Yaoundé I  Yaoundé, Cameroon*

Téophile Tiki-Manga
> *IRAD  Yaoundé, Cameroon*

Jerome Tondoh
> *Université d'Abobo-Adjame  Cameroon*

Zac Tschondeau
> *World Agroforestry Centre-Cameroon  Yaoundé, Cameroon*

Stephan Weise
> *IITA  Humid Forest Research Station  M'Balmayo, Cameroon*

Louis Zapfack
> *Université de Yaoundé I  Yaoundé, Cameroon*

The Congo Basin encompasses the world's second largest contiguous rainforest after the Amazon and includes six countries: Congo–Brazzaville, Congo–Kinshasa, Gabon, Central African Republic, Equatorial Guinea, and Cameroon. Deforestation rates for the Congo Basin were estimated to be 1.14 million ha/yr (0.6 percent/yr) (FAO 1997), compared with 1.08 million ha/yr (1.0 percent/yr) for Indonesia and 2.55 million ha/yr (0.5 percent/

yr) for Brazil. Unlike Brazil and Indonesia, where large-scale agricultural operations play an important role, much of the deforestation in the Congo Basin is attributed to smallholder agriculturalists using extensive slash-and-burn techniques. Thus rural population density plays a significant role in determining the extent of closed-canopy forest and the stock of woody biomass in a given area, but the relationship is far from linear and depends on a complex assortment of factors. The low productivity of slash-and-burn agriculture, in combination with rapid population growth, results in the continual extension of the forest margins, with a highly fragmented boundary in the Congo Basin, as shown in figure 14.1.

An Alternatives to Slash and Burn (ASB) benchmark site in Cameroon was chosen to represent the Congo Basin (figure 14.2). Cameroon's forest resources, one of the country's greatest riches, have played and continue to play a significant role in its economic growth and development. In the 1950s, 1960s, and 1970s, conversion

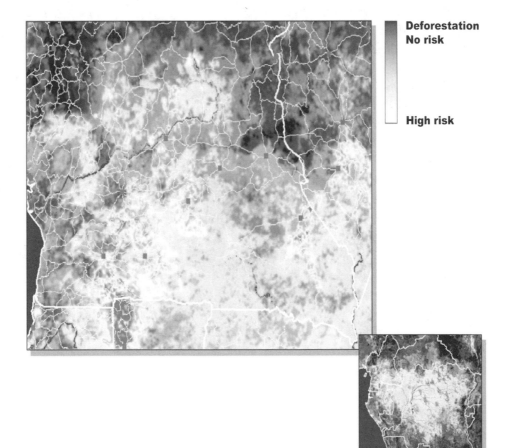

*Figure 14.1* Satellite photo of the Congo rainforest region showing the risk of deforestation (the lighter the color, the higher the risk), with a close-up of the Cameroon benchmark site. Note the fragmentation of the forest margins (Ericksen and Fernandes 1998).

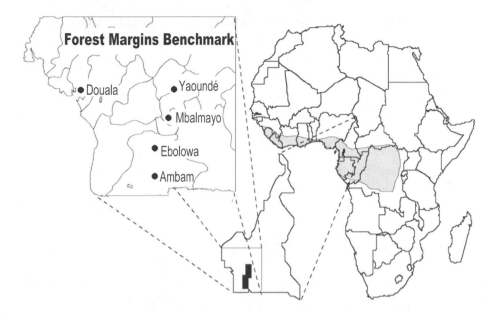

*Figure 14.2* The ASB forest margin benchmark area in southern Cameroon showing the Yaoundé, M'Balmayo, and Ebolowa blocks. Shaded area is the humid tropical zone of West and Central Africa. Most of the West African zone is deforested.

of approximately 500,000 ha of moist forests to smallholder coffee (*Coffea* spp.) and cocoa (*Theobroma cacao* L.) agroforests resulted in equitable economic growth, averaging 3 to 4 percent. In more recent years, timber exploitation has overtaken coffee and cocoa production as the most important economic activity in the moist forests. Cameroon is now the leading African exporter of tropical timber, with more than $270 million in annual export sales.

One of the most rapid changes affecting the agricultural sector throughout the Congo Basin has been the tremendous growth in urban populations. Both Douala and Yaoundé have grown at annual rates of more than 6 percent in the years since independence, which means that the number of urban consumers is doubling roughly every 12 years. The most important single market in the benchmark site is Yaoundé, with more than a million inhabitants. The largest food commodity markets in terms of value are plantain (*Musa paradisiaca* L.), cassava (*Manihot esculenta*), and cocoyam (*Xanthosoma sagittifolium* [L.] Schott). Approximately 80 percent of the total tonnage sold in Cameroon of these three crops is produced in the humid forest zone (Ministry of Agriculture [MINAGRI] survey statistics, 1984–1990).

The rate of deforestation in Cameroon is estimated by FAO (1997) at 0.6 percent, with about 108,000 ha of closed-canopy forest lost annually. About half of the annual clearing is for agricultural purposes, the remaining largely for logging (Ekoko 1995), although shifting cultivators follow logging roads, making this distinction hard to quantify. Across the benchmark site, 25 percent of the total land area was estimated to be in some agricultural use (including fallow fields) in 1994 (Gockowski et al. 1998).

A poor nation, Cameroon has little choice but to develop its forest resources. From the standpoint of government policy, the critical question is whether Cameroon's tropical forests will be turned into sustainable agricultural and forestry production systems or "mined" into a state of degraded vegetation. The benchmark site in Cameroon spans a resource use and population density gradient and also encompasses significant variation in market access, soils, and climate. This site allowed the ASB Project to explore the opportunities for and constraints to income generation, sustainable land use, and environmental protection in the area and in the end to assess which land use systems are the most promising and what policies must be in place to ensure their adoption.

## BENCHMARK SITE CHARACTERIZATION

The benchmark site in southern Cameroon was divided into three blocks that were distinguished according to intensity of resource use and population density as follows: the Yaoundé block, with 30 to 90 people per square kilometer; the M'Balmayo block, with 10 to 30 people per square kilometer; and the Ebolowa block, with up to 10 people per square kilometer (figure 14.2). At the southern end is the Ebolowa block, with low population density and large tracts of intact primary forest (59 percent of land cover). Cocoa is the primary source of farm income, with food crops grown mainly to meet subsistence needs. There is still significant reliance on natural resource–based activities, such as bushmeat hunting and gathering of nontimber forest products. Local agricultural markets are comparatively small, agricultural input markets are underdeveloped, and road infrastructure is poor and not maintained. At the northern end is the Yaoundé block, with most of the land in some phase of an agricultural cycle; only 4 percent of land remains covered by primary forest. Proximity to the Yaoundé market, better-developed market institutions, and rural infrastructure has led to a process of agricultural intensification, diversification, and commercialization.

### Natural Ecosystems

The dense, humid forests comprising the benchmark area are classified as Guineo-Congolian forests (IUCN 1992), which are subdivided into four categories (table 14.1). This distinction is important in terms of biodiversity richness. The climax vegetation in the benchmark site is the dense semideciduous forests characteristic of the Yaoundé block, extending south into the M'Balmayo block, and the dense, humid Congolese forest in the southern reaches of the M'Balmayo block, extending to the Ebolowa block. In addition, there are small pockets along the western border of the Ebolowa and M'Balmayo blocks that are characterized by the biologically diverse, moist, evergreen Atlantic forest. The highest biodiversity is found in the Barren forests of these

*Table 14.1* Extent of Humid Forest Ecosystems in Cameroon and Their Main Characteristics

| Guineo-Congolian Forests | Area (million ha) | Main Characteristics |
| --- | --- | --- |
| Submontane forest | 0.377 | Lies between 800 and 2200 m in elevation, increasing diversity of epiphytic flora with elevation, *Prunus africana* found at higher elevations. Biology of ecosystem not well known compared with lowland and Afromontane forest systems. |
| Dense, humid evergreen Atlantic forest, including Barren forests | 5.400 | Very high floristic diversity with marked endemism, with affinities to Atlantic South American forests. Center of diversity of genera *Cola, Diospyros, Garcinia,* and *Dorstenia.* Gregarious associations of Caesalpinaceae characterize the Barren forest subtype. |
| Dense, humid Cameroon–Congo forest | 8.100 | Intermediate in floristic diversity between the Atlantic forest and the semideciduous forest, flora affinities with Congo basin forests. Important ecosystem for large primates and elephants. |
| Dense, humid semideciduous forest | 4.000 | Often fragmented, subject to fire during the dry season, particularly rich in commercial timber species although less biologically diverse than other tropical forest types. Close to the savanna zone. |
| Total | 17.877 | |

*Source:* IUCN (1992).

Atlantic forests, with many of the plants being endemic. More than 200 plant species have been counted in a 1000-m$^2$ transect, which purportedly represents higher plant diversity than any other forest in Africa or Southeast Asia and is greater than that of most South American forests (Garland 1989). The Barren forest is a center of genetic diversity for important genera such as *Cola* spp., *Diospyros* spp. (ebony), and *Garcinia* spp. (which includes the bitter cola). The Cameroon–Congo and the semideciduous forests, which are widespread in the southeast of the country, have a much lower rate of plant endemism than Barren forests.

## CLIMATE AND SOILS

Rainfall in the benchmark site is typical of equatorial rainforest climates with no pronounced dry season. Annual precipitation ranges from 1350 to 1900 mm and has a bimodal rainfall distribution. There is increasing precipitation from the north to the south.

The red and red-yellow soils in the benchmark area fall mainly into the broad soil classes of acrisols (ultisols) and ferrasols (oxisols). Three soil profile classes—Yaoundé (Rhodic Kandiudults, pH 5.2, 35 percent clay), M'Balmayo (Typic Kandiudults, pH 6.5, 25 percent clay), and Ebolowa (Epiaquic Kandiudults, pH 4.8, 42 percent clay)—form a north–south fertility gradient, with lower fertility in the southern part of the benchmark area (Gockowski et al. 1998). Though generally acidic and infertile, these soils are suitable for cocoa, coffee, oil palm (*Elaeis guineensis* Jacq.), and rubber (*Hevea brasiliensis* [A. Juss.] Muell.-Arg.) production if clay content is high enough (more than 20 percent).

## LAND USE SYSTEMS

Farms in the benchmark site are small and fragmented (Gockowski and Baker 1996) The average number of annual crop fields per household is slightly more than four; 62 percent of the households in the Yaoundé block had five to eight distinct field types, compared with only 28 and 44 percent in the M'Balmayo and Ebolowa blocks, respectively (Gockowski et al. 1998). The mean annual land cover in productive agricultural land use, not including the fallow vegetation, was 2.6 ha per household in the Yaoundé block, 2.4 ha in the M'Balmayo block, and 3.6 ha in the Ebolowa block.

Nine land use systems were evaluated by the ASB Cameroon team (table 14.2). These systems included two food crop systems, four variants of the widespread cocoa agroforests, two variants of hybrid oil palm plantations, and community-managed forests. With the exception of community-based forest management, all systems began with slash-and-burn of the primary forest, secondary forest fallows (10–15 years), or short-duration *Chromolaena odorata* (L.) RM King and H. Robinson fallows (2–4 years). The environmental parameters measured were carbon stocks, plant diversity,

*Table 14.2* The Nine Predominant Land Use Systems in the Cameroon Benchmark Site

| Meta–Land Use System (Cameroon land use system) | Fallow Type and Duration (yr) |
| --- | --- |
| **Crop–Fallow Rotations** | |
| Mixed peanut–cassava | Chromolaena (4) |
| Mixed melon–plantain–cassava | Secondary (9–23) |
| **Complex Cacao Agroforests** | |
| Extensive cacao and tree fruits | Secondary (9–23) |
| Extensive cacao, no fruit harvests | Secondary (9–23) |
| Intensive cacao and tree fruits | Chromolaena (4) |
| Intensive cacao, no fruit harvests | Chromolaena (4) |
| **Simple Agroforests** | |
| Extensive oil palm | Secondary (9–23) |
| Intensive oil palm | Chromolaena (4) |
| **Forest** | |
| Community-managed forest | |

and soil fauna diversity; the results are detailed in chapters 2, 4, and 5, respectively, and in Gillison (2000). Agronomic sustainability issues are presented in chapter 6 and the socioeconomic aspects and farmer concerns in chapter 17.

## FOOD CROP–FALLOW ROTATIONS

Mixed peanut (*Arachis hypogea* L.)–cassava production is the most important food crop system in the benchmark site. It largely guarantees household food security and in areas with market access generates marketable surpluses. The two dominant crops are peanut and cassava. Other crops interplanted in lower densities include cocoyam, maize (*Zea mays* L.), leafy vegetables (*Solanum scabrum* Miller, *Corchorus olitorius* L.), and plantain. The crops are normally planted after slashing and burning a 4-year *Chromolaena odorata* fallow and are grown for 2 years before reverting back to the *Chromolaena* fallow. Women manage this system, which is typically planted twice: in March–April and again in August–September, given the bimodal rainfall distribution. Surplus revenues tend to be controlled by women.

The mixed melon (*Cucumeropsis mannii* Naudin)–plantain (*Musa* × *paradisiaca*)–cassava cropping system that follows long fallows is the third most common land use system (70 percent of households) after the peanut–cassava and cocoa agroforests. Melon, plantains, maize, and cocoyams are planted after slashing and burning of 9- to 23-year-old secondary forest fallows and grown for 2 years, after which they are put back into another secondary forest fallow. Although both male and female labor is used, the cash income from this field tends to be controlled by men. This land use system became a major commercial alternative for cocoa farmers when cocoa prices collapsed in 1989. Together these systems account for an estimated 75 percent of all cropland in the benchmark area (Gockowski et al. 1998).

## COCOA AGROFORESTS

The second most important system and the largest source of household agricultural revenues are the cocoa complex agroforests, or jungle cocoa. Men mainly manage these systems, although in certain instances widows also manage such systems. They cover 3.8 percent of total land area in the benchmark site and represent 48 percent of total agricultural land use. An estimated 75 percent of households in the benchmark site have these systems, with the mean area per household estimated at 1.3 ha (Gockowski et al. 1998).

Cocoa is established after slashing and burning of a primary forest, a long-term secondary forest fallow, or even a short-term *Chromolaena* fallow. There are four variations on this land use system, based on the level of crop intensification and the duration of the preceding fallow. It begins with a food intercropping of plantain, cocoyam, and melon in the first 3 years. Cocoa is grown for about 25 years. Sometimes jungle cocoa is established through gap and understory plantings in forests without the food cropping stage. Descriptions of cocoa agroforests can be found in Duguma et al. (2001) and Gockowski and Dury (1999).

## EXTENSIVE COCOA SYSTEMS

Extensive cocoa systems, jungle cocoa, are characteristic of the less populated areas and usually are established in primary forest or old secondary fallows. Cocoa is grown under the shade of taller trees that include fruit trees such as avocado (*Persea americana* Miller), mango (*Mangifera indica* L.), African plum (*Dacryodes edulis* [G. Don f.] H.J. Lam), and mandarin oranges (*Citrus* spp.). These fruit trees provide substantial income in areas that have good market access. The two major pest constraints for cocoa production in southern Cameroon are cocoa blackpod disease (caused by *Phytophthora megakarya* Brasier and Griffin) and capsids (plant-sucking insects belonging to Miradeae family). Without pesticides these pathogens typically reduce yields by more than 50 percent. Fungicide use is about half of that used of the intensive cocoa systems, and there is no insect control. Many producers with more intensive systems shifted to these more extensive types when cocoa prices collapsed in 1989.

## INTENSIVE COCOA SYSTEMS

Intensive cocoa systems are characterized by higher levels of management, fungicides, and insecticides. They tend to be in areas of more pronounced land pressures and are associated with good market access. The system often is established after 4 years of a *Chromolaena* fallow and intercropped with peanut, maize, leafy vegetables, plantains, and cocoyams during the first 3 years of establishment. Although fruit trees are almost always a component of cocoa agroforests, it is only in areas with easy market access that they assume commercial importance because of their bulky nature and low value-to-weight ratio.

## OIL PALM PLANTATIONS

Palm oil has always been the most consumed edible oil in Cameroon. In rural areas of the humid forest zone, most households are self-sufficient, relying on production from the semidomesticated Dura variety of oil palm. The bulk of production for the urban market comes from large-scale parastatal plantations (Cameroon Development Corporation, Palmol, and Société Camerounaise de Palmeraies) producing the *tenera* hybrid (a cross between the Dura and Piscifera varieties). However, as urban populations have increased, small-scale producers have also adopted industrial-type plantation monoculture of the hybrid tenera variety in recent years. Oil palm trailed cocoa, coffee, plantains, cassava, cocoyams, and dessert bananas, as measured by total producer revenues (MINAGRI, unpublished survey data, 1984–1990). The tenera oil palm plantations are grown as a monoculture at a planting density of 143 trees per hectare. Forested land or *Chromolaena* fallow is converted with intercropping of plantain, cocoyam, and melon during the first 2 years of oil palm establishment. There is a 7-year establishment phase and a 25-year rotation.

## COMMUNITY-BASED FORESTS

It is currently illegal for a farmer to cut down and sell timber growing on his land even if he has legal title to the land; however, he may harvest it for his own construction purposes.

Commercial rights to timber belong to the state, with the exception of timber cut for the landholder's own use. The minimal economic incentives faced by farmers for maintaining timber species on the landscape do not provide a competitive alternative to slash-and-burn agricultural use. The 1994 forestry law has established a statutory framework through which a village can gain communal commercial rights to timber in community forests of 5000 ha. This tenure permits a community to legally harvest and sell timber. Another concept of the community forest is found in the community's dependence on the common property resources in forested land. The forest and local institutions governing the exploitation of its natural resources (wild fruits, honey, building materials, rattan, fish, game, and medicinal plants) are the defining parameters of this alternative concept.

## OTHER SYSTEMS

There are several other important land use systems that were not evaluated. These include livestock, shaded robusta coffee (*Coffea canephora* Pierre ex. Fröhner) systems, large-scale industrial plantations of oil palm and rubber, horticultural cropping systems, and various inland valley systems. The livestock sector is not well developed in the benchmark site. Cattle grazing is practically nonexistent because of tsetse fly (*Glossina* spp.) infestation, so there are essentially no planted pastures. Goats (*Capra hircus* L.), tropical sheep (*Ovis aries* L.), swine, and poultry are raised in a free-range, extensive fashion. Although robusta coffee systems are important in the Congo Basin, this system is very limited in extent in the Cameroon benchmark area. Industrial-scale plantations of rubber and oil palm are found around Mount Cameroon in the Southwest Province and along the coast in the South Province but were not included in the study largely because they are not expanding their operations and are no longer a driving force of deforestation. Input-intensive monocultures of horticultural crops and maize for the fresh market are encountered in the Yaoundé block. The horticultural commodities tend to be high value compared with staple food crops and have replaced cocoa as the most important source of revenues in many villages close to Yaoundé.

## MARKETS AND INSTITUTIONS

Institutions and infrastructure are in general much better developed in the Yaoundé block, where population densities are higher. Remote sensing estimates indicate a rural road density in Yaoundé that is three times the density in the Ambam area of the Ebolowa block. Institutional development is also more evolved in the Yaoundé block, where traditional customary land tenure systems are evolving gradually toward individualistic, legally recognized land ownership characterized by cadastral surveys and an increased incidence of land titling (IITA, unpublished data, 1997).

Among the important institutional differences is the development in the Yaoundé block of a fairly competitive marketing system for both outputs and inputs. Farmers in this area generally have easy access to purchased inputs, which are heavily applied to cocoa agroforests (fungicides and insecticides) and horticultural fields (fungicides, insecticides, and fertilizers). In the rest of the benchmark site, farmers can spend more than a full day in acquiring inputs.

## MACROECONOMICS

Sectoral and macroeconomic policy reforms since the late 1980s have had important impacts on slash-and-burn agricultural systems. Most of these reforms occurred in the cocoa and coffee sectors, with the state disengaging and liquidating the national marketing boards for these crops during this period. At the same time, fertilizer and pesticide subsidies (ranging from 60 to 100 percent) were removed. Most of these reforms were driven through as part of a structural adjustment package with the World Bank and the International Monetary Fund in an effort to help the Cameroon government diminish internal and external deficits. Unfortunately, these reforms took place in the context of and, indeed, were necessitated by an overvalued Central African franc (FCFA) and depressed world commodity markets. As a result, cocoa and coffee producers in Cameroon faced historically low producer prices and, in response, neglected their agroforests and shifted resources into the production of plantain, cocoyams, and horticultural crops to make up for the declining profitability of coffee and cocoa. This put significant additional pressure on the forest margins as new forest lands were cleared and brought into annual food crop production (Gockowski et al. 2001).

## TRADEOFFS BETWEEN GLOBAL ENVIRONMENTAL BENEFITS, AGRONOMIC SUSTAINABILITY, AND PROFITABILITY

From an environmental perspective only the community forest system retains the bulk of the biodiversity and carbon stocks, whereas the tree-based systems lose about 60 percent of the carbon and the crop–short fallow systems lose 95 percent of the carbon (chapter 2, this volume). The tree-based systems, including both intensive and extensive cacao systems, and long-term fallows retain high levels of biodiversity, although the high values in the intensive cacao system include many weedy species (chapter 4, this volume). Given the mosaic of fallow fields on the landscape needed to support the long rotation, biodiversity probably is not greatly threatened by this system. The tree-based systems still serve as a rich form of nontimber forest products, including game, fuel, and medicines (Kotto-Same et al. 2000). The short-term fallow systems and oil palm plantations are depauperate in comparison.

In summary, the cacao and long fallow systems have the highest global environmental benefits. Likewise the agronomic sustainability of these systems is high, although pest concerns can threaten the cacao production (chapter 6, this volume). Although negative environmental concerns are associated with most land use systems in the forest margins because they have much less biodiversity and carbon storage than the forest, the starting point of a particular land conversion process has enormous importance in whether there will be gains or losses in terms of global environmental benefits. The rehabilitation of degraded short fallow–crop rotation systems with perennial systems will increase the current carbon stocks and biodiversity levels and is a clear objective of the ASB Program.

## ADOPTION

No matter how positive the parameters for agronomic sustainability or the environment may be, small-scale farmers are likely to adopt such systems only if they improve farmer livelihoods without entailing an extraordinary amount of risk. Endeavors to promote the systems with environmental benefits and sustainability must specifically consider the profitability, labor needs, food security, and equity biases. Additionally, livelihoods in the forest margins of Cameroon are sustained by a complex set of productive and social activities conducted in the context of a risk-reducing kinship network of social relationships. Some land use systems entail high institutional costs and support services, which can limit adoption. Some of these issues and constraints to adoption are discussed later in this chapter (table 14.3); details are provided in Kotto-Same et al. (2000), Gockowski et al. (2001), and chapter 17.

## PROFITABILITY

Profitability is arguably the most important criterion for adoption in a commercialized agricultural economy. In land surplus economies, adoption potential is more appropriately measured by the financial returns to labor than by returns to land. On this basis, intensive cocoa with fruit and oil palm from forest fallow were considered as high profit, the extensive and intensive cocoa systems with fruit as medium profit, and

*Table 14.3* Ordinal Ranking of Land Use Systems by Adoption Criteria

| Rank | Adoption Criteria | | | |
|------|-------------------|---|---|---|
| | Social Profitability (return/ha) | Financial Profitability (return to labor, $/d) | Labor Intensity (lowest to highest) | Household Food Security (kcal/ha) |
| 1 | Intensive cocoa with fruit | Oil palm in forest fallow | Extensive cocoa without fruit | Intercropped food in short fallow rotation |
| 2 | Oil palm in forest fallow | Intensive cocoa with fruit | Intercropped food in long fallow | Intercropped food in long fallow rotation |
| 3 | Intensive cocoa without fruit | Extensive cocoa with fruit | Extensive cocoa with fruit | Intensive cocoa with fruit |
| 4 | Extensive cocoa with fruit | Intensive cocoa without fruit | Oil palm in short fallow | Extensive cocoa with fruit |
| 5 | Oil palm in short fallow | Oil palm in short fallow | Oil palm in long fallow | Oil palm in short fallow |
| 6 | Intercropped food in short fallow | Intercropped food in short fallow | Intensive cocoa without fruit | Intensive cocoa without fruit |
| 7 | Extensive cocoa without fruit | Intercropped food in long fallow | Intensive cocoa with fruit | Oil palm in long fallow |
| 8 | Intercropped food in long fallow | Extensive cocoa without fruit | Intercropped food in short fallow | Extensive cocoa without fruit |

*Source:* Kotto-Same et al. (2000).

the mixed groundnut, oil palm from short fallow, melon and plantain, and extensive cocoa without fruit systems as low profit. However, this static view of profitability masks the volatility that characterizes agricultural and world commodity markets. The recent episode of low cocoa prices (1988–1996) had a significant impact on the profitability of the sector, with prices received being halved.

## LABOR

Labor intensity is an important determinant of adoption in areas with labor scarcity and poorly developed labor markets. The most labor-extensive systems are the *Cucumeropsis*–plantain field and the extensive cocoa systems, whereas the mixed groundnut field and the intensive cocoa systems used two to three times the labor (table 14.4). The oil palm systems were intermediate between the two types of cocoa systems.

## FOOD SECURITY

The capacity of land use systems to contribute to food security is a concern of both household and national decision makers. In areas where rural food markets do not

*Table 14.4* Labor Needs and Food Entitlements for the Alternative Land Use Systems

| System | Scale (ha) | Labor | | Food Entitlements During Productive Stage | | |
|---|---|---|---|---|---|---|
| | | Establishment Phase (d/ha/yr) | Operating Phase (d/ha/yr) | Calories (000 kcal/ ha/yr) | Protein (kg/ha/yr) | Micronutrients |
| SF, food intercrop | 0.25 | NA | 115 | 3803 | 54.8 | Yes |
| LF, food intercrop | 0.25 | NA | 44 | 780 | 10.9 | Yes |
| SF, intensive cocoa with fruit | 1.3 | 148 | 97 | 1463 | 19.8 | Yes |
| SF, intensive cocoa without fruit | 1.3 | 135 | 95 | 762 | 11 | Yes |
| FOR, extensive cocoa with fruit | 1.3 | 136 | 46 | 1143 | 15 | Yes |
| FOR, extensive cocoa without fruit | 1.3 | 123 | 43 | 442 | 6.2 | No |
| SF, oil palm | 1 | 209 | 71 | 762 | 11 | Yes |
| FOR, oil palm | 1 | 196 | 73 | 442 | 6.2 | Yes |
| Community-based forest | 5000 | | | | | |

SF, short fallow; LF, long fallow; FOR, agroforest.
*Source:* Adapted from Kotto-Same et al. (2000).

exist or function properly, most households rely on their own production. The mixed food crop field is the household granary and is planted throughout the benchmark area. This is also true for the *Cucumeropsis*–plantain field, although in some areas this system is planted for commercial reasons. In terms of calorie and protein supply, the mixed groundnut field was the highest of all the systems and the cocoa system with fruits was high largely because of the significant contribution of avocado and African plum, with high fat contents (table 14.4). Palm oil is an important component of the diet in Cameroon, a fact that is recognized by government trade policy prohibiting oil palm exports during the dry season, when production declines, to ensure urban supply at low prices. Oil palm is also the major source of cooking oil in the Congo Basin, and many producers cite meeting household oil demand as a factor in their adoption decision.

## MARKETS

In a liberalized economy, the functioning of market institutions is a key determinant to adoption of intensive production systems. Cameroon producers are still adapting to the new economic reality of liberalized input markets that came about in the early 1990s. In the densely populated areas of the benchmark area and the Congo Basin, markets and communication infrastructure tend to be better developed, resulting in more commercially oriented and diversified agriculture. Better functioning, more competitive markets in conjunction with better infrastructure result in significantly lower marketing margins and, consequently, higher producer prices and lower input prices. Still a major handicap for producers throughout the benchmark area is the near nonexistence of capital markets in rural areas. When an unexpected financial crisis arrives (e.g., illness, death), liquid assets that might have been set aside for purchasing agrochemicals are spent, and production suffers.

The market institutional needs (inputs, outputs, labor, and capital) of the intensive cocoa systems are the most dependent on the reliable supply of agrochemicals. Intensive cocoa systems with fruit trees also presume good access to urban fruit markets. The oil palm systems depend on fertilizer inputs and the multiplication and distribution of hybrid palm varieties. Oil palm production also entails further transformation, ranging from artisanal methods necessitating almost no capital investment, small-scale oil presses with intermediate levels of capital investment, and large-scale industrial processing with high capital needs.

## Land Tenure

Land tenure is still largely by customary right, although there has been an evolution toward more individualistic ownership patterns and away from communal control of land in the high population areas. There is a much higher incidence of official land disputes in these areas. However, there is little official titling of land, in part because of the high transaction costs of doing so (estimated at more than $500 at current prices). Land tenure and property rights raise issues for systems requiring access to new forest lands for planting perennial tree crops. In certain parts of the benchmark area, this land remains in the domain of the larger family clan, and use is negotiated within the clan unit. These issues do not affect the planting of perennial systems on existing fallow lands for which customary tenure rights at the household level are robust.

## Extension Services

The move toward intensification necessitates a viable and dynamic research and extension system capable of responding to farmers' demands and generating appropriate solutions. Intensive knowledge generation and diffusion is perhaps most critical for the oil palm systems because the production of commercial hybrid oil palm is just being introduced at the household level. A World Bank–sponsored training and visit extension program in Cameroon (and in many other African countries) is intended to reinvigorate a moribund extension service, although there are serious questions about the success of this type of extension system. The encouraging development of local farmer groups, farmer federations, and grassroots nongovernment organizations

(NGOs) throughout southern Cameroon offers an additional avenue for combining the knowledge generated by agricultural research and rural development.

## EQUITY

There are two major types of equity issues surrounding these alternative land use systems. The first is that of an increasing concentration of wealth and land holding. This is a concern mainly for oil palm systems, where economies of scale in both production and transformation seem to exist. In the long run, there is a question as to whether smallholder production, which typically relies on family labor, can remain competitive with large-scale plantations. To the extent that these systems are also meeting subsistence needs, the issue of economies of scale is less likely to impede the continued adoption of these systems.

The other equity issue is the intrahousehold distribution of returns. Women manage only mixed groundnut fields, and there is significant risk that women might not receive their share if an expansion of the other land use systems were to occur. Any strategy therefore should focus attention on improving cropping systems and crops that are traditionally grown and marketed by women. Such improvements could deflect the pressure to clear more forested land as populations grow and would increase women's revenues and social prestige. In the perennial tree crop systems, the labor divisions must be further studied and, if possible, innovations developed to ensure that women also benefit. Indications are that women receive a more equitable share of fruit tree revenues than is the case for the cocoa component in the fruit–cocoa agroforests found in the Yaoundé block (Dury 1999).

## EXPECTED TRENDS IN LAND USE, IMPACTS, AND RESEARCH NEEDS

### FOOD CROP AND FALLOW SYSTEMS

Despite the negative environmental aspects and lack of agronomic sustainability of the short-fallow, mixed food cropping system, efforts to replace this slash-and-burn system are likely to fail given its central role in the social fabric of village life and the underdeveloped rural food markets of the Congo Basin. A significant proportion of the food crops in the urban markets comes from this field system and generates an important portion of women's income. Increased demand for food from the urban areas indicates that this system will increase in the future; therefore efforts should focus on improving the productivity and sustainability of this system. To do so, soil degradation and crop protection urgently need to be addressed. Crop breeding should focus on increasing varietal tolerance to pests, diseases, and the many mineral deficiencies that characterize the soils of the basin. The introduction of improved varieties should be combined with integrated soil fertility management that combines the use of organic materials, including improved fallow species, with the strategic use of fertilizers, particularly in areas with developed input markets and good rural roads.

The long fallow food cropping system, although higher in carbon and biodiversity, requires land-abundant households, which limits its extent and adoption in areas where population pressures are high. In areas where land is still abundant and populations are low, market infrastructure and institutional development are poor and hence profitability is low. Low profitability could be ameliorated by an increase in agricultural research targeting the three principal crops—melon, cocoyam, and plantain—which have been largely neglected by agricultural research to date. Given the current population growth rate of 2.9 percent and the fact that plantains are the most important commercial food crop in the humid forest zone, this system probably will continue to increase in area. However, increasing population in rural areas and demand for food from the urban sector are likely to lead to a decline in the fallow period of this system and the eventual shift to the short-fallow food system. This shift would have high environmental costs, with increased loss of biodiversity and carbon.

There is the Pandora's box issue of increasing land and labor productivity in the two food crop systems and whether this would lead to an expansion in this land use type and increase deforestation (Angelsen and Kaimowitz 2001). This valid concern may be assuaged by broad-based productivity increases in land use systems. Achieving this difficult task will entail a balanced agenda involving multi-institutional collaboration on the research and development of the major components of the Congo Basin farming systems. The Pandora's box issue also is a function of the size of output markets and the elasticity of demand. If they were small, as is likely, then an increase in productivity of these systems probably would deflect pressure to clear new forest. Both of the crop–fallow rotational systems are likely to remain important across the Congo Basin and should be the focus of land-saving and labor-neutral or labor-saving interventions. Abating the environmental loss associated with extensive slash-and-burn systems will entail both alternative perennial systems capable of sustaining rural livelihoods and more productive slash-and-burn systems. The latter would permit farmers to convert land currently in these crop–fallow systems to what are arguably more agronomically sustainable perennial tree crop systems.

## CACAO-BASED SYSTEMS

The intensive cocoa system with fruit trees planted to short fallow is among the most profitable of the systems; in addition, its high carbon stocks and biodiversity make it a desirable land use alternative at the forest margins. Elevated productivity of this system will depend on an increase in labor and pesticide input. Institutional constraints in many areas of the Congo Basin, such as the unavailability of inputs and scarce labor availability, are likely to limit the extent of this particular land use system. The fruit tree component contributes significantly to the profitability of this system, but because of the low value-to-weight ratio of fruit, it results in increasing transportation costs with distance to market. The underdeveloped road infrastructure of the Congo Basin will also constrain the development of this multistrata complex agroforestry system. The most extensive extrapolation domains for this particular system are likely to lie in the more densely populated, humid forest areas of West Africa (Ghana, Côte d'Ivoire, Nigeria, and Togo), where cocoa is already a significant cash crop and market institutions are more robust. Extensive cocoa systems with fruit trees planted in forest land are moderately profitable, but the institutional and labor constraints attached to cocoa production are less than those of the intensive cocoa systems. However, urban market access will limit the extent of this system.

Rather than the preferred expansion of these cocoa systems at the expense of degraded lands, the area in cocoa probably declined between 1990 and 1996 as farmers abandoned production in the face of low world and national prices. Most of these plantations were old and had low productivity. Labor was reduced in both extensive and intensive cocoa systems and was largely reallocated to long fallow–intercrop rotations focused on the production of melon, plantain, and cocoyams. There was a negative environmental impact (loss of biodiversity and carbon stocks) as this annual cropping system replaced secondary forest. The decline in cocoa profitability and the reduced foreign exchange earnings during this period had major repercussions on economic growth and probably led to a higher incidence of poverty in the humid forest zone. Despite the decline, cocoa still remains the dominant land use system and the major source of household revenues.

An overvalued fCFA also can affect farmer returns. If the fCFA is overvalued by 50 percent, the producer's return to labor would be lower in the cocoa system than the slash-and-burn systems. Before the devaluation in 1994, the overvalued fCFA was a source of heavy implicit taxation for producers of tradable commodities such as oil palm and cocoa. Overall, the effect of the overvalued fCFA was to favor food production systems over export crops such as coffee, cocoa, and oil palm.

Given current and expected supply and demand conditions in world cocoa markets, it is likely that cocoa prices will remain robust in the foreseeable future, which should ease the negative trend seen in recent years. The higher prices of 1997 and 1998 (550–650 fCFA vs. 350 fCFA in 1996) increased farmer incentives and, subsequently, input use in cocoa systems. Input markets, which have been liberalized since 1992, are better developed today than they were 5 years ago, reinforcing the trend toward more intensive cocoa systems. A large proportion of this increase probably will come from a shift from extensive to intensive production systems. Whether there will be significant new conversion to either extensive or intensive cocoa production is difficult to predict. Indications from the robusta coffee sector in Cameroon and the cocoa sector of Côte d'Ivoire are that there is likely to be some expansion in new planting area (Akiyami 1988; Gockowski 1994).

The impact on the environment of an increase in new plantings will depend on whether these systems are targeted to degraded short-fallow land or forested land. Given the choice, the producer normally will choose the latter in an effort to capture the forest rent (Ruf 1998). Policy incentives should be targeted toward the creation of perennial crop systems in degraded lands. This strategy should be accompanied by an increase in the productivity of food cropping systems to compensate for a reduction in the area of the food crop fallow system. To encourage the intensification of cocoa production, policies to promote the agricultural input supply sector should be considered.

One of the major problems in the Cameroon cocoa sector is the low level of plant resistance to cocoa blackpod disease, caused by *Phytophthora* spp. The efforts under way at Institut de Recherche Agricole pour le Développement (IRAD) to evaluate, test, and disseminate resistant varieties, working with the increasingly vital grassroots farmer organizations, must be strongly supported. The ecological relationships between biodiversity, management practices, and productivity are an area for future research, especially in the species-rich cocoa agroforests. Specifically, interactions between entomopathogenic fungi, plant functional attributes, ant and termite mosaics, applications of copper fungicides, and the population dynamics of *Phytoptera* spp. are important for strategic research.

## OIL PALM

The oil palm system planted on forest land is the most profitable of all land use systems; carbon stocks are similar to those of the other tree-based systems, but there is little doubt about the lack of plant and faunal diversity in these monoculture systems. The overall contribution to the rural economy of smallholder oil palm production from 1986 to 1990 was still minor, with the exception of the area around Edea-Eseka-Makak in the westernmost portion of the benchmark area. Whether the small producer movement, which has been fairly robust in recent years, continues will depend on several critical institutional issues. Postharvest processing must normally occur within 48 hours of harvest. There are likely to be scale economies in both time and space, which will warrant some type of collective action in the processing phase. If smallholder systems are to expand significantly, improvements in the distribution and supply of these hybrid plants will also be needed. Currently there are only two suppliers: the national research institute and parastatal industrial oil palm plantations charging 200 to 250 fCFA per germinated seed and wielding significant market power. The ability of small producers to compete with large-scale producers in the face of economies of scale in production and processing is questionable in the long run. Economies of scale could outweigh the advantage of the lower opportunity cost of family labor, driving producer prices and profits too low. Mitigating in favor of the expansion of the smallholder sector is the perception by producers that unlike cocoa, palm oil and its multiple products (oil, wine, and building materials) can also be used to meet direct household needs in consumption. As for cocoa and coffee, the net environmental impact of an expansion of oil palm systems will depend on whether they are planted in short fallow or forest land. The most likely candidate is for farmers to choose the latter, again because of the fertility rent they capture. When planted to forested land, these systems tend to decrease the total carbon and biodiversity in the landscape.

## COMMUNITY-BASED FORESTS

Communal management of forest lands for commercial timber production and other purposes received positive scores on all environmental and sustainability accounts, although the sustainable commercial harvest of tropical timbers has proved to be an elusive goal for many timber companies. The impact of sustainable logging practices on biodiversity also remains a question. The financial incentives attached to the commercial harvest of timber could deter the practice of slash-and-burn agriculture. However, there are numerous institutional and regulatory issues that a community must resolve before it can obtain legal community tenure to timber. As currently written, the state-imposed regulatory framework requires more than twenty procedures to obtain community tenure. There are also many collective action problems associated with distribution of benefits, sanctions, and free-ridership. Overcoming these obstacles is a necessary condition if slash-and-burn farming communities are to limit their agricultural activities to areas outside the community forest.

## LAND USE SHIFTS, POLICY, AND ACTION

The framework developed for promoting alternative land use systems that are best bets in terms of minimizing the tradeoffs between the environment and livelihoods is based on existing systems. It encompasses the notion that households' needs in the humid forest zone typically are met through the integration of multiple crops and tree-based systems, complemented by an array of activities including monocropping, hunting, and gathering of nontimber forest products, providing a food, cash, and social basket (figure 14.3). Current land use is shaped by household structure and preferences, land and natural resource configurations, and the institutional makeup of property and access rights in the rural landscape. It is unlikely that policy or technological innovation, however radical, would drastically alter those patterns and trends. To improve the performance of expanding land uses and lift the obstacles to the development of other promising systems, our best option is to mimic farmers' integrative strategies while improving individual components of the system. We have called this approach an improved mosaic within a strategy of integrated landscape management. It is within that realm that technological innovation and improvements can be targeted for research, development, and policy efforts. A summary of the anticipated benefits and losses associated with expected land use shifts is provided in table 14.5.

In areas of low population density, policies and practices should be geared toward sustainable use and conservation of forested land to improve rural livelihoods and environmental values. Policy-led intensification at the household level should focus on

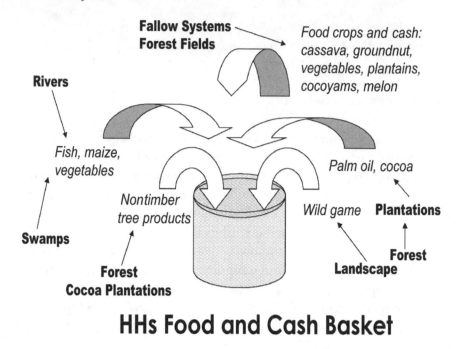

**Fallow Systems Forest Fields**

*Food crops and cash: cassava, groundnut, vegetables, plantains, cocoyams, melon*

**Rivers**

*Fish, maize, vegetables*

*Palm oil, cocoa*

*Nontimber tree products*

*Wild game*   **Plantations**

**Swamps**

**Forest Cocoa Plantations**

**Forest Landscape**

# HHs Food and Cash Basket

*Figure 14.3* Household (HH) food, cash, and social basket as provided by the landscape mosaic of forest and land use systems (Kotto-Same et al. 2000).

the two major components of farming systems: perennial crop agroforests and slash-and-burn food crop production systems. Policies to encourage agricultural intensification are needed to overcome the divergence between the farmer's valuation of forest woody biomass resource as a fertility input and the societal value of a forest (timber revenues, environmental values, and intrinsic value). For primary production alternatives to develop their full potential and create positive spinoffs for the overall development–conservation nexus in the forest, a host of interconnected initiatives must be taken simultaneously or at least in a close sequence. Research indicates that revenue increase for nontimber forest products is not consistent with resource preservation unless the pace of species domestication is accelerated and information is adequately disseminated to farmers (Ndoye and Kaimowitz 2000). Cocoa plantations would fit naturally with endeavors related to the marketing and domestication of nontimber forest products . Market mechanisms such as ECO-OK labeling and the fair trade movement are attempting market corrections for coffee and cocoa produced in an environmentally benign fashion, albeit on a small scale and largely without the support of large donors. These efforts should be expanded for increasing revenues in these systems.

The development of postharvest systems and periurban enterprises is also necessary to reduce postharvest losses and to benefit from the added value of small-scale rural businesses and the proximity of expanding urban markets. Such enterprises could generate rural wealth while deflecting some of the anthropic pressure on land

*Table 14.5* Summary of Beneficiaries, Benefits, and Risks or Losses Associated with the Expansion of Different Land Use Alternatives

## Oil Palm Systems

Context and assumptions:

Strong spread of oil palm systems in the benchmark area.

Dominant smallholder monocrop system based on the industrial Société Camerounaise de Palmeraies model (oil palm associated with food crops in the first 3 yr, followed by monocropping).

| Beneficiaries | Benefits | Risks and Losses |
|---|---|---|
| Farm H H s<br>Social elites<br>Palm oil industry<br>Government<br>Urban consumers<br>Regional consumers | Increased revenues from sales (men mainly) and artisanal processing (women included)<br>Increased revenues, prestige, and money<br>Greater profits (privatization in process), steady supply at favorable prices<br>Increased tax revenues<br>Mitigation of the monocrop Soca model<br>Better supply of oil palm products and byproducts<br>Urban bias through seasonal quotas on exports (hidden tax) | Reduced women's influence on H H decisions.<br>Loss of common property forest lands.<br>Concentration risk against capital-poor H H s.<br>Producers' dependency on the industry (tied loans for inputs).<br>Rural producers' loss of market advantages and revenues during low season.<br>Some loss in environmental benefits. |

Options: Develop and promote improved varieties; mitigate environmental, concentration, and gender biases through mosaic. Develop small-scale processing. Maintain seasonal quotas for resource preservation.

## Cocoa Systems

Context and assumptions:

Likely to remain stable in present conditions, following structural adjustment programs that cut subsidies and state services. Recent increase in world and producer market prices for cocoa might result in a renewal of the activity but not in its dramatic upscaling throughout the landscape. Increase in the quantity and quality of cocoa production could result from appropriate policies and the availability of affordable technologies to control pests, particularly blackpod fungal disease.

| Beneficiaries | Benefits | Risks and Losses |
|---|---|---|
| Farm H H s<br>Farmer organizations<br>Government<br>International cocoa sector and chocolate industry<br>Global consumers | Increased revenues<br>New occupational niche in marketing sector<br>Fiscal benefits and rents<br>Biggest profit from the sector's growth | No control on world prices; producer is mainly a price-taker.<br>Intensification might induce bias against poor farmers.<br>Information and position in regulatory bodies still weak.<br>Lower benefits than desirable under present international terms of trade. |

Further conditions: Fair international share of the cost of environmental conservation. Internal policies supporting plantation renewal and the strengthening of farmer organizations. Increased representation of farmers in regulatory bodies.

*Table 14.5* (Continued)

**Community Forestry: Scenario 1**

Context and assumptions:

No change in present policy orientations.

Weak implication of traditional tenure institutions.

1994 Forestry Reform includes provisions for granting C F concessions to communities represented by legal entities taken from a pool of farmer organizations, which acquired legal status through the 1990, 1992, and 1993 laws on associations, common interest groups, and economic interest groups. These organizations can play a strong proactive role in conservation and development. However, they do not have the community mandates required in matters of tenure and devolution. Anthropological institutions, such as lineages, clans, and village councils, which are not considered by the reform, retain these functions.

| Beneficiaries | Position and Power | Benefits | Potential Risks and Losses |
|---|---|---|---|
| Communities | Medium: little information, can participate but only through legal entities | Small tax and logging-related revenues | Loss of forest and forest-related revenues; risks of social destructuration. |
| Local elites | Strong: main beneficiary of information asymmetries | Rent capture of logging-related revenues and taxes | Conflicts harmful to influence in community. |
| Farmer organizations | Intermediate: can be recognized as legal entity; low information and legal limits to economic benefits | | Common initiative groups as a potential vehicle of vested interests. |
| Farm H H s and lineages | Weak: family institutions not recognized as legitimate stakeholders | | Low returns from forest exploitation, loss of agricultural lands, weakening of traditional authority. |
| National and international logging interests | Strong bargaining position; have the technical and financial capacity to fulfill inventory and logging requirements in C F S | Quick profit Low-cost logging in C F S | Nonsustainable logging, small size of C F s (5000 ha). Loss of environmental and economic benefits. |
| National public interests | Intermediate: limited influence through N G O s and other private and public bodies | | |
| Government | Strong: retain main decision-making power for recognition, design, and monitoring of C F S | | Loss of long-run fiscal revenues, negotiation failure. |
| Global consumers | | | Loss of global environment benefits, nonsustainable consumer benefits. |

*Table 14.5* (Continued)

**Community Forestry: Scenario 2**

Context and assumptions:
Adoption of reform at implementation stage.
Empowerment of customary tenure institutions.
Flexible adaptation of criteria related to size of C F s.
Adaptive management plan that takes into account the relationship between forest and agricultural cycles.

| Beneficiaries | Position and Power | Benefits | Potential Risks and Losses |
|---|---|---|---|
| Communities | Strong: can participate through all institutions and organizations | Balanced revenues from agriculture, small-scale logging, gathering and domestication of nontimber forest products, use of other natural resources; tax revenues from logging | |
| Local elites | Intermediate: benefit from information but not institutional asymmetries | | |
| Farmer organizations | Strong: can participate and play a proactive role | Reinforced collective action for poverty alleviation and forest-related alternatives | |
| Farm H H s and lineages | Strong: family institutions recognized as stakeholders | Increased H H welfare | |
| National and international logging interests | Intermediate: have the technical and financial capacity to invest C F s, but this influence is subordinated to larger community interests | More local accountability and economic discipline of logging; sustainable logging based on genuine stakeholder negotiation | Higher short-term transaction costs. |
| National public interests | Intermediate: some influence through N G O s and other civil interests | Forest conservation and increased availability of forest-related products | |
| Government | Strong: main supervision power in recognition, design, and monitoring of C F S | Long-term economic and environmental benefits and fiscal revenues | Loss of short-term tax revenues. |
| Global consumers | Intermediate: through donors and international agencies | Gain of global environment benefits at sustainable consumer prices | |

*Table 14.5* (Continued)

**Improved Food Crop and Long Fallow or Forest Fields**

Context and assumptions:
Significant labor constraints restrict the possibility of a large portfolio of food crops and forest fields per H H. Under present technological conditions, a large-scale spread of these systems is likely to happen only with the multiplication of farm H H s, as a consequence of demographic growth. These two types of fields are complementary within H H agricultural cycles.
Their improvement depends on research and technological innovation (e.g., short-fallow and multistrata systems, integrated pest management, plant health management).

| Beneficiaries | Benefits | Risks and Losses |
|---|---|---|
| Women for food crops<br>Men for forest fields<br>Farm H H s in general<br>National and regional consumers | Increased revenues from increase in marketed surplus<br>Increase in farm H H food security<br>Increased food supplies and improved regional food security | Lack of marketing infrastructure and difficult market access limit farmer incentives to intensify.<br>Small market size and inelastic demand lead to decrease in farm prices and fall in farm revenues.<br>Increased profitability of extensive long-fallow systems leads to an increase in resources allocated to this land use system, increasing its relative extent and depleting forest resources.<br>Enhanced rural technologies and increased profitability of slash-and-burn farming along forest margins lead to influx of rural migrants.<br>Marketing infrastructure remains underdeveloped. |

HH, household; CF, community forest; NGO, nongovernment organization.
*Source:* Kotto-Same et al. (2000).

and forest. Oil palm systems are a natural candidate for these postharvest enterprises because small-scale palm oil processing technology can be readily made available to farmers at a large scale. The deflection feature of these off-farm alternatives cannot be neglected as we try to mitigate the negative environmental impacts of any single technological option.

In areas of high population pressure, annual crop systems must be made more productive and sustainable. If this can be achieved, then it may be possible to put aside land for specialized perennial systems (e.g., cocoa–fruit agroforests) and to protect pockets of forest to increase carbon stocks and maintain biodiversity across the landscape. One policy instrument that the Cameroon government could consider is to target new planting subsidies of both cocoa and oil palm systems to degraded short fallow–crop rotational systems. Under these conditions, carbon would be sequestered, and, at least in the case of shaded cocoa, biodiversity in the landscape would increase. Farmers normally will choose to establish their plantations in long bush and forest fallows when this type of land is disposable, to capture the fertility rent (Ruf 1998). Since the Kyoto conference on global warming, discussion of carbon emissions trading between nations has focused some attention on perennial tree crop systems in the tropics as a possible sink for carbon sequestration. A strong economic argument for subsidizing production from agroforests can be made on the basis of the range of out-puts that are not valued by markets (biodiversity, carbon sequestration, and watershed functions). There is, of course, a major caveat: Perennial tree crop systems generate net environmental benefits only when they replace degraded short-fallow lands.

A necessary element for policy-led intensification is strong local and national institutions. A viable and dynamic research and extension system capable of respond-ing to farmers' demands and generating and disseminating appropriate solutions is paramount. The overall capacity of the public sector in Cameroon was significantly weakened by the across-the-board salary reduction that the government implemented as part of its structural adjustment program. Without support for institutional devel-opment, the significant gains achieved in environmental and forestry policies since the mid-1990s will remain little more than paper policies. Public sector capacity to pro-vide a continuous stream of technology consistent with resource endowments gener-ally is most effective when the political environment has encouraged the development of farmer organizations (Binswanger and Ruttan 1978).

Changes in the institutional makeup of the research, development, and conserva-tion sectors in Cameroon and Central Africa offer a great opportunity for the emergence of a broad-based alliance. The decentralization reforms of the early 1990s have created a favorable environment for community-based collective action. Thousands of grass-roots organizations have acquired legal status and have formed large federations and confederations of farmers. These organizations have started numerous initiatives and are seeking collaboration with research institutions and NGOs. These grassroots initia-tives are a potentially important vehicle for accomplishing the bottom-up institutional change so desperately needed to effect agricultural intensification in the Congo Basin. In collaboration with the Consultive Group on International Agricultural Research NGO committee, International Institute for Tropical Agriculture, IRAD, International Center for Research in Agroforestry, and Center for International Forestry Research have initiated talks with two dozen NGOs and farmer federations about a platform of action on common research and development priorities. This alliance could shape the orientation of land use systems in a manner coherent with ASB's objectives and results and develop an influence at both the community and state levels of decision making. Given the global environmental services that would result from the adoption of best bets, it must be stressed that the level of policy action or lobbying needed goes beyond national states to include the contribution of global interests to the environmental, economic, and social alternatives inherent to the ASB program. This also will require appropriate intervention at the appropriate level.

## SUMMARY AND CONCLUSION

In Cameroon, smallholder slash-and-burn agriculture is the major source of defores-tation. Any proposed approach for addressing deforestation must start with agricul-ture. We argue for a proactive, policy-led effort to intensify both perennial and food crop systems to deflect further advance of the forest margin at the household level. Any technology or policy innovation that increases the productivity of farming in the humid forest region runs the risk that additional land and labor resources will be allocated to that particular activity, increasing deforestation. Therefore, at the regional and national level, policies should strive to limit rural migration to the forest frontier. So far, in the Cameroon benchmark area, customary tenure institutions have been sufficiently robust to prevent large-scale in-migration (Diaw 1997).

Such has not been universally the case, as in the large-scale rural-to-rural migration to the forested lowlands of the Littoral and Southwest Province from the densely populated western highlands (Dongmo 1981). More research is needed to understand the factors affecting migration so that better-informed policies can be devised.

At the national level, policymakers are concerned about food security issues and maintaining adequate food supplies in urban areas. Interregional trade liberalization should be encouraged, particularly across agroecological zones, to address these concerns. The countries of West and Central Africa might be better off concentrating food production in savanna areas, which potentially have higher production at fewer environmental costs than the humid zone, while promoting diversified perennial tree crop systems to generate foreign exchange in the humid forest zone. The areas in the world agronomically able to successfully produce cocoa, coffee, rubber, oil palm, and other tree crops are limited compared with the areas that can grow maize (*Zea mays* L.), wheat (*Triticum aestivum* L.), rice (*Oryza sativa* L.), and other staple grains. However, a large portion of the population of the Congo Basin lives in urban centers with extremely poor links to these potentially productive savanna areas. Developing transport corridors could significantly reduce the intensification pressures around urban centers in the humid forest zone and increase urban food supply.

## REFERENCES

Akiyami, T. 1988. Cocoa and coffee pricing policies in Côte d'Ivoire. International Economics Department WPS 164, Washington, DC, the World Bank.

Angelsen, A., and D. Kaimowitz. 2001. Introduction: The role of agricultural technologies in tropical deforestation. pp. 1–17. *In* A. Angelsen and D. Kaimowitz (eds.) Agricultural technologies and tropical deforestation. CAB Int., Wallingford, UK.

Binswanger, H.P., and V. Ruttan. 1978. Induced innovation: Technology, institutions and development. Johns Hopkins Univ. Press, Baltimore.

Diaw, C. 1997. Si, Nda bot and Ayong. Shifting cultivation, land uses and property rights in southern Cameroon. Mimeograph. IITA Humid Forest Station, Yaoundé.

Dongmo, J.-L. 1981. Le Dynamisme Bamiléké (Cameroun). Vol. I: La maitrise de l'espace agraire. Univ. de Yaoundé, Yaoundé, Cameroon.

Duguma, B., J. Gockowski, and J. Bekala. 2001. Smallholder cacao (*Theobroma cacao* Linn.) cultivation in agroforestry systems of West and Central Africa: Challenges and opportunities. Agrofor. Syst. 51 (3):177–188.

Dury, S. 1999. Les conditions économiques d'adoption d'innovations agro-forestières: Le cas de l'arboriculture fruitière au centre du Cameroun. Rapport AUPELF-UREF, IITA, Univ. de Dschang, IRAD, INRA-ESR, CIRAD-FLHOR.

Ekoko, F. 1995. Deforestation in Cameroon. Ministry of Environment and Forest, Yaoundé, Cameroon.

Ericksen, P., and E.C.M. Fernandes (eds.). 1998. Alternatives to slash and burn systemwide program. Final report of phase II. ICRAF, Nairobi.

FAO (Food and Agriculture Organization). 1997. State of the world's forests. FAO, Rome.

Garland S. 1989. La conservation des ecosystèmes forestiers du Cameroun. UICN, Alliance mondiale pour la nature. Commission des Communautés Européennes.

Gillison, A.N. (compiler). 2000. Phase II Above-Ground Biodiversity Assessment Working Group summary report 1996–99, Part E: Biodiversity and Productivity Assessment for Sustainable Agroforest Ecosystems. Alternatives to Slash-and-Burn Project, ICRAF, Nairobi.

Gockowski, J. 1994. Supply responses among smallholder producers of arabica and robusta coffee in Cameroon. Ph.D. diss. Univ. of Florida, Gainesville.

Gockowski, J., and D. Baker. 1996. An ecoregional methodology for targeting resource and crop management research in the humid forest of Central and West Africa. Paper presented at 1996 Biennial Meeting of Rockefeller Social Science Research Fellows, 15–17 Aug. 1996. Nairobi.

Gockowski, J., D. Baker, J. Tonye, S. Weise, M. Ndoumbé, T. Tiki-Manga, et al. 1998. Characterization and diagnosis of farming systems in the ASB Forest Margins Benchmark of southern Cameroon. IITA Humid Forest Ecoregional Center, Yaoundé. Resource and crop management research monograph. IITA, Ibadan, Nigeria.

Gockowski, J., and S. Dury. 1999. The economics of cocoa–fruit agroforests in southern Cameroon. Paper present to International Workshop on Multi-strata Systems with Perennial Tree Crops. CATIE, Costa Rica, 22–25 Feb. Organized by the International Union of Forestry Research Organisations.

Gockowski, J., B. Nkamleu, and J. Wendt. 2001. Implications of resource use intensification for the environment and sustainable technology systems in the central African rainforest. pp. 197–217. In D. Lee and C. Barrett (eds.) Tradeoffs or synergies? Agricultural intensification, economic development and the environment. CAB Int., Wallingford, UK.

IUCN (International Union for Conservation of Nature and Natural Resources). 1992. The conservation atlas of tropical forest in Africa. IUCN, Gland, Switzerland.

Kotto-Same, J., A. Moukam, R. Njomgang, T. Tiki-Manga, J. Tonye, C. Diaw, et al. (eds.). 2000. Alternatives to Slash-and-Burn in Cameroon. Summary report and synthesis of phase II. ASB Programme, ICRAF, Nairobi.

Ndoye, O., and D. Kaimowitz. 2000. Macro-economics, markets, and the humid forests of Cameroon, 1967–1997. J. Modern Afr. Studies 38:225–253.

Ruf, F. 1998. Cocoa: From deforestation to reforestation. Paper presented at the First International Sustainable Cocoa Workshop, Smithsonian Tropical Research Inst., 29 Mar.–3 Apr. 1998. Panama City, Panama. Available at http://natzoo.si.edu/ConservationAndScience/MigratoryBirds/Research/Cacao/ruf.cfm (verified 7 Dec. 2003).

# 15 The Peruvian Amazon

## DEVELOPMENT IMPERATIVES AND CHALLENGES

Douglas White
   *CIAT  Pucallpa, Peru*
Manuel Arca
   *INIA  Lima, Peru*
Julio Alegre
   *World Agroforestry Centre  Lima, Peru*
David Yanggen
   *Centro Internacional de la Papa  Quito, Ecuador*
Ricardo Labarta
   *World Agroforestry Centre  Pucallpa–Ucayali, Peru*
John C. Weber
   *Corvallis, Oregon*
Carmen Sotelo-Montes
   *World Agroforestry Centre  Lima, Peru*
Héctor Vidaurre
   *World Agroforestry Centre  Lima, Peru*

The Amazon region occupies parts of seven sovereign nations and is highly heterogeneous both biophysically and socioeconomically. The Amazon of Peru is especially heterogeneous. For example, the forests in the tropical Andes, a region in the western section of the Amazon, by virtue of the nearby mountains, contain more biodiversity than those in other Amazon regions. Exceptionally large numbers of endemic plants (up to 20,000) have been identified in these forests, which are now considered a strong hotspot candidate for conservation support (Myers et al. 2000). The varied topography (200–2000 m above sea level) and the wide range of annual rainfall (1100–5000 mm/yr) provide conditions for very large numbers of different species to thrive.

Alongside this biophysical heterogeneity is a broad array of socioeconomic and policy contexts. Multiple decision-making domains coexist in the region and sometimes overlap. For example, national administrative divisions (e.g., municipalities) exist alongside the domains occupied and managed by indigenous populations that have their own decision-making processes. The combined biophysical, socioeconomic, and policy heterogeneity lead not only to very different resource use strategies and patterns by economic agents but also to a wide range of environmental consequences. Therefore predicting the effects of policy changes on land use patterns is complicated, and foreseeing related effects on the environment is even more so.

Despite this multidimensional and interrelated context, developing the Peruvian Amazon is imperative to the long-term growth of the country. Indeed, the region is undergoing rapid change from increasing economic activity such as timber extraction, slash-and-burn agriculture, livestock production, mineral extraction, and fishing. Although a small human population now lives in the Peruvian Amazon (only about 2.2 million people, or 9 percent of the country's population), typical economic activities are predictably land-extensive and may have severe consequences for plant and animal biodiversity and the environment in general.

Nearly 60 percent of Peru's national territory is in the Amazon region. Since the 1980s, government policies such as tax breaks, subsidies, and road building have attempted to speed development in this region as part of a national response to general economic malaise and a growing population (Bedoya Garland 1987). By some accounts, the economic gains associated with these policy actions have been meager (Hecht 1993); by other accounts the gains have been more significant. There is general agreement that the environmental effects have been large and negative.

Yet systematic empirical assessments of the effects of land use change on economic growth and the environment are largely absent. As a result, huge gaps in knowledge limit the efficacy of policy initiatives. To fill some of these knowledge gaps, the Alternatives to Slash and Burn (ASB) consortium in Peru undertakes, coordinates, and integrates many research activities in the region. National and international partners conduct both biophysical and socioeconomic research to understand why and how the region is being transformed. Most importantly, lessons are distilled from this research to guide and promote future development activities in the region.

Specific research themes of scientists in the ASB consortium in Peru focus on soil and nutrient management, farmer participatory research, environmental–economic tradeoffs, tree genetic resource management, and improved germplasm of tree and agricultural crops. Research also seeks to improve our understanding of the magnitudes and mechanics of pressing local and global environmental issues, including soil degradation, greenhouse gas emissions, and biodiversity loss.

The two central objectives of ASB research are to have impact at field level and to generate knowledge, management strategies, and policy options that can be useful outside the Peruvian Amazon. A mix of scientific and other research products, including capacity strengthening, are produced to meet these two objectives.

# UNDERSTANDING THE AMAZON: HETEROGENEITY AND CHANGING PATTERNS OF RESOURCE USE

With the hope of earning a better living, settlers migrate to and about the Amazon (Townsend 1983; Aramburú 1984; Barham and Coomes 1995). Yet after forested land is cleared for agricultural use, soil fertility and associated bountiful harvests are short-lived (Nye and Greenland 1960). To maintain production levels, farmers are compelled to cut more forest (Ruthenberg 1976). Therefore there is an apparent tradeoff between preserving the environment and providing basic human needs. At the crux of the environment–economic tradeoff is the fallow period, where vegetative regrowth of 2 to 15 years becomes the nutrient supply for the next agricultural cycle. Although purchased inputs, especially fertilizers, can increase and sustain yields, they are prohibitively expensive for small-scale farmers. Moreover, extensive production techniques are more cost-effective because a hectare of land can cost less than a 50-kg bag of fertilizer (Holland 1999; White et al. 2001). Therefore land use options must be developed with special regard to their financial feasibility and the resource constraints (land, labor, and capital) farmers face.

The Amazon region of Peru is markedly different from the rest of the country. Cooler sierra (mountain) and drier coastal regions are distinct agroecosystems to the hot and humid tropical forests of the Amazon. National policies must be tailored to specific regions of the country. The Peruvian Amazon poses the greatest challenges to policymakers. First, a majority of the national policymakers have little knowledge of this isolated region. Second, the Amazon remains disconnected from the rest of the country, especially the seat of political power and decision making in Lima. Therefore effective policy implementation is difficult and costly in the Amazon. In part because of complexity and costs associated with promoting development, the overall development objectives associated with the region have been pared back.

Despite the lackluster performance of organized settlement programs undertaken when the region was envisioned as a breadbasket (Nelson 1973), Peru continues to formally promote development in the Amazon. In the 1990s, the Peruvian government instituted a series of regional tax relief measures and fuel subsidies. The government also began permitting large tracts of Amazon forest to be logged by national and foreign companies. Other natural resources, such as oil and gas, are being prospected and extracted. Unofficial settlements commonly follow logging or mineral access roads and often encroach into national forests and indigenous community lands. More generally, though, the potential effects of such national policies and settlements on long-term forest cover, the well-being of indigenous communities, or the economic welfare of the region are not known.

The physical characteristics of the Amazon region are diverse, much like its famed plant communities and animal populations. Topography and soils differ throughout the region, ranging from fertile alluvial soils on riverbanks to nutrient-deficient, acidic soils in the upland areas (Sanchez 1976; Denevan 1984; Padoch and de Jong 1992). Therefore broad generalizations regarding resource endowments or the suitability of agriculture cannot be made. To adequately capture a broad array of biophysical characteristics and understand their roles in determining land use, ASB activities take place at two sites: a main benchmark area near Pucallpa and a second smaller site near Yurimaguas.

Pucallpa is located in the Department of Ucayali (figure 15.1), which borders Acre, Brazil, to the east. The department corresponds to an area 80 percent the size of El Salvador but has about 5 percent of that country's population. Settlement of the Pucallpa area began in the 1940s after construction of a road linking the Ucayali River, a major Amazon tributary, and the capital city of Lima. The current cropping and ranching activity on any given piece of land typically is associated with the number of years since the forest was originally cleared (Fujisaka and White 1998; Labarta 1998; Smith et al. 1999). For example, the amount of area remaining in forest on farms is inversely related to the time since it was first settled. In the more recently settled areas, 59 percent of the rural holdings remain forested, whereas in more mature settlements, forest coverage decreases to 40 percent. Cattle ranches, which tend to dominate the oldest settlements, have an average of 19 percent of their land in forest. Conversely, the land area dedicated to pastures generally increases according to the age of the settlement. The recent settlers have about 10 percent of their holdings in pasture, compared with 19 percent on older farms. Cattle ranches have 66 percent of their land in pasture (Smith et al. 1999). The stocking rate on traditional pastures is approximately 0.6 animal units (AUs) per hectare. Land values are low, ranging from US$10 to US$200/ha depending on the quality of road access (Fujisaka and White 1998). Political instability in the region in the 1990s caused cattle herds to decrease markedly. More than a third of the regional cattle herd was sold or stolen between 1990 and 1995 (Fujisaka and White 1998). The ensuing situation of low stocking rates in the region has led to an oversupply of pasture plant biomass given the size of the regional cattle herd. In some cases, pastures are so overgrown that they become flammable and often permit fire to spread into the surrounding forest (White et al. 2001).

The Pucallpa region has bimodal rainfall pattern, with wet months of February to May and September to November and dry months of June to August and December to January. As in many humid tropical regions, soil infertility is a major factor affecting the production potential of agricultural systems (Nye and Greenland 1960; Ruthenberg 1976). The basic soil constraints are low cation exchange capacity, soil acidity, high aluminum saturation, and low nutrient stocks (particularly phosphorus, nitrogen, and calcium). Soils include more favorable alluvial but less common riverine areas, where pH is about 7.7 and available phosphorus is 15 ppm, and the more common well-drained upland areas of acidic (pH 4.4), low-phosphorus (2 ppm) soils (Loker 1993). Invasive weeds are another factor influencing land use decisions, as discussed later in this chapter.

The Pucallpa site offers two important research advantages. First, the ranges of some key characteristics (e.g., rainfall amounts and patterns, and soil types) are quite similar to those of other broad regions in the Amazon, including the ASB research site in Acre, Brazil (IICA 1995). Thus, research outcomes can be compared with, and may

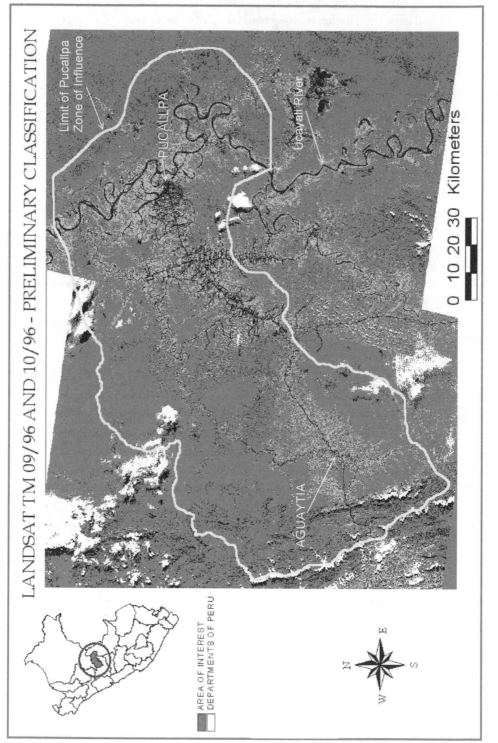

LANDSAT TM 09/96 AND 10/96 - PRELIMINARY CLASSIFICATION

Limit of Pucallpa
Zone of Influence

PUCALLPA

Ucayali River

AGUAYTIA

0 10 20 30   Kilometers

AREA OF INTEREST

DEPARTMENTS OF PERU

N
W    E
S

*Figure 15.1* Landsat image showing the boundaries of the Pucallpa research site.

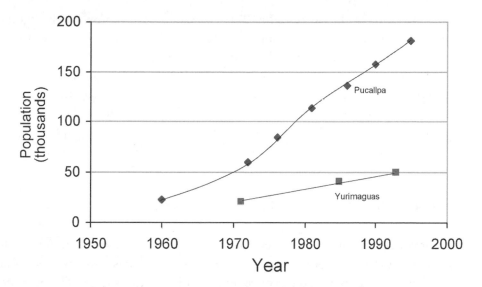

*Figure 15.2* Population growth in Yurimaguas and Pucallpa from 1960 to 1995 (INEI 1997).

be applicable to, larger swaths of the Amazon basin. Second, approximately 50 years of occupation by a steadily growing human population has led to a wide range of deforestation patterns and land uses in this small area (17,000 km², or 2 percent of the Peruvian Amazon). Although only about 10 percent of the Peruvian Amazon was estimated to be deforested as of 1995, approximately 25 percent of forests in the Pucallpa region had been cleared by then (IIAP 1999). Therefore the Pucallpa experience may offer an important window through which to view, understand, and help manage future deforestation and land use patterns in other areas of the Peruvian Amazon.

The second site, Yurimaguas, adds geographic breadth and a longer-term research context. The Yurimaguas site was home to the North Carolina State/TropSoils Collaborative Research Support Program, where experimental agronomic data have been collected for nearly 30 years. It also provides an interesting comparison with Pucallpa

*Table 15.1* Area in Different Land Use Systems, Length of Fallow Period, and Residence Time of Migrants on Farms in Two ASB Peru Research Sites

|  | Yurimaguas | Pucallpa |
| --- | --- | --- |
| Average farm size, ha | 23.6 | 28.7 |
| Primary forest, ha | 8.5 | 9.5 |
| Fallow, ha | 9.4 | 8.2 |
| Annual crops, ha | 1.9 | 1.6 |
| Perennials, ha | 0.8 | 2.3 |
| Pasture, ha | 3.1 | 7.1 |
| Average fallow period | 3.6 yr | 3.2 yr |
| Migrants who arrived before 1960 | 45% | 25% |

*Source:* ASB site characterization survey (Labarta 1998).

regarding migration in the Amazon. In 1971, Yurimaguas had approximately 20,000 residents, and within 14 years the population doubled. As of 2000, there were about 55,000 inhabitants in Yurimaguas, half of whom were living in rural areas. In contrast, Pucallpa has grown at a much faster rate since 1971 (figure 15.2), and the population has doubled in less than 10 years. Implications of the growing population are seen in the rapidly changing land uses around urban centers. In part because of better market access, land use systems in Pucallpa have shorter fallow periods, and larger areas of cleared land are dedicated to perennial crops and pasture (table 15.1).

## BIOPHYSICAL RESEARCH

The biophysical component examines how different land uses are associated with changes in biodiversity, carbon stocks, and greenhouse gas emissions. The ASB also seeks to identify geographic patterns of genetic variation in tree species. The ultimate objective is to provide practical policy guidance for improved land management.

### ABOVE-GROUND AND BELOW-GROUND BIODIVERSITY

Slash-and-burn creates spatially diverse sets of land uses that can complicate traditional methods of vegetation classification and limit their usefulness for characterizing above-ground plant biodiversity. Two different approaches were used to assess the effects of land use on above-ground biodiversity. Gillison and Alegre (2000) used a plant functional attributes approach to measure the diversity of plants (chapter 4, this volume). Fujisaka et al. (2000) used an ecological approach, combined with an ethnographic component that addressed farmers' understanding of and preferences for different plants, including weeds. A third study of below-ground animal biodiversity examined soil macrofauna in different land uses and their links to soil quality.

For the species richness and plant functional types approach, twenty-one 40- by 5-m transects were used to sample a range of land use types and chronosequences in Yurimaguas. The highest species and functional type richness were recorded in a forest logged 40 years previously, 20-year abandoned gardens, and 2-year successional fallows dominated by plants from the Asteraceae or the daisy family. Multistrata agroforests showed moderate degrees of species and plant functional attribute richness, and improved pastures were least rich, with only four plant species and functional types (Gillison and Alegre 2000). Initial analysis of the data revealed close associations between plant-based classifications, land use type, and vegetation succession but generally weak correlations between these same classifications and soil physical and chemical characteristics. The most significant correlations of soil attributes arose between vegetation structure, plant functional attributes, and ratios of richness of plant species to functional types.

Fujisaka et al. (2000) examined the sequence of interactions between farmers and ecosystems to examine how farmers manage biodiversity. In samples taken across a chronosequence in Pucallpa, 235 plant species were recorded in the forest, of which 143 were not found in any successive land use. Plants not existing in the forest colonized both cropland fields and fallow areas. In total, 595 species were identified across the land uses. Changes in plant communities generally reflected the replacement of shade-tolerant plants and plants for which seeds are dispersed by bats, other mammals, ants, and larger birds. Pioneer plants were those adapted to conditions of more direct sunlight and produced larger numbers of small seeds dispersed by smaller birds or the wind. Each form of land use contained 7 to 25 percent of the original forest species plus thirteen to sixty-six new plant species adapted to that land use.

As field conditions changed over time, different sets of more competitive weeds emerged. In response, farmers adapted agricultural product mix and management strategies, relegated weed-infested plots to fallow, and cleared more forest. Farmers were most concerned about *Rottboellia cochinchinensis* (Lour.) Clayton in fields after fallow and *Imperata brasiliensis* Trin., both of which serve as indicators of soil degradation. Farmers identified useful species across treatments, but counts of these species were very low, suggesting high levels of human intervention in the forest and heavy pressure on such species in all land uses. Although fallowed areas regained some of the original forest-like plant species, valuable shade-tolerant, slow-growing hardwood trees did not reappear in fallow areas, perhaps because of their short duration. Perhaps because many settlers were new to the region, they did not use indicator species to identify fertile forest areas or signal decreased soil productivity after cropping (Fujisaka et al. 2000).

The below-ground soil macrofauna diversity was significantly affected by land use in Yurimaguas (table 15.2). As intensity of land use increased, macrofauna numbers decreased significantly. The number of taxonomic units identified in a traditional tree-based fallow area (thirty) was nearly twice that of low-input annual cropping system with a legume-based cover crop fallow (sixteen). By this measure, the multistrata agroforestry system contained the most biodiversity. However, more detailed analysis revealed that 95 percent of the total biomass of the multistrata system (55.7 g/m$^2$) corresponded to the exotic earthworm species *Pontoscolex corethrurus* Muller (Alegre et al. 2001). Thus even though this agroforestry system helped conserve (or rebuild) below-ground biodiversity, the emerging composition was quite different from that of the original forest. Research into the functional consequences for agricultural productivity and other ecosystem functions of this shift in the composition of below-ground biodiversity is under way.

## CARBON STOCKS

Scientists from the Instituto Nacional de Investigación Agraria (INIA), Universidad Nacional del Ucayali (UNU), Tropical Soil Biology and Fertility Programme (TSBF),

*Table 15.2* Taxonomic Richness, Mean Abundance, and Biomass of Macroinvertebrates in Different Land Use Systems in Yurimaguas, Peru

| Land Use System | Shifting Agriculture | High-Input Cropping | Low-Input Cropping | Multistrata Agroforestry | Peach Palm Plantation | Secondary Forest Fallow |
|---|---|---|---|---|---|---|
| Number of taxonomic units[a] | 22 | 16 | 16 | 31 | 22 | 30 |
| Population density/m$^{2a}$ | 151 | 171 | 175 | 557 | 115 | 806 |
| Biomass (g/m$^2$)[a,b] | 21.8 | 22.4 | 23.3 | 55.9 | 35.5 | 42.9 |

Land use systems are defined as follows:

Shifting agriculture: 1-yr annual cropping alternated with a 7-yr fallow.

High-input cropping: mechanized maize–soybean continuous rotational cropping over 7 yr with high nutrient input from fertilizers and lime.

Low-input cropping: 2-yr rotational cycle of annual crops with fallow of tropical kudzu (*Pueraria phaseoloides*).

Multistrata agroforestry: a diversified production system with timber, pole, and fruit trees (tornillo, *Cedrelinga catenaeformis* D. Ducke; coffee, *Coffea canephora* Pierre ex Fröhner; bolaina blanca, *Colubrina glandulosa;* peach palm, *Bactris gasipaes* Kunth; araza, *Eugenia stipitata* McVaugh; and *Inga edulis* Mart.), annual crops in the first 2 yr, followed by a *Centrosema macrocarpum* Benth. understory, forming different strata in the system.

Peach palm plantation: peach palm planted at 5 by 5 m with a *Centrosema macrocarpum* Benth. understory.

Secondary forest fallow: maintenance of a secondary forest fallow, 7 yr old in 1985.

[a]Includes earthworms, termites, ants, Coleoptera, Arachnida, Myriapodes, and others.

[b]Fresh weight.

*Source:* Alegre et al (2001).

and International Centre for Research in Agroforestry (ICRAF) evaluated the above- and below-ground carbon stocks in land use chronosequences near Pucallpa and Yurimaguas. The evaluation was accomplished using the procedural guidelines developed by the TSBF for ASB (chapter 2, this volume). This report includes only the above-ground carbon stocks, not the time-averaged carbon stocks for the entire rotation as reported in chapter 2.

The above-ground carbon stocks for natural forests in the Yurimaguas area were almost twice those of the forests in Pucallpa (table 15.3). This difference in forest biomass could be a result of the higher rainfall and less disturbance of the forest from a lower population density in Yurimaguas. Not surprisingly, when forest is converted to agricultural uses, above-ground carbon is reduced; in fact, the 15-year-old fallows in each location attained about 70 percent of the biomass of the primary forest. The natural fallows had carbon accumulation rates as high as 10 t C/ha/yr (table 15.3), as high as or higher than those reported in chapter 2. Among the managed, tree-based systems, the carbon content ranged from 41 t C/ha for oil palm (*Elaeis guineenisis* Jacq.) plantations to 74 t C/ha for rubber (*Hevea brasiliensis* [A. Juss.]) plantations (Pucallpa), whereas that of multistrata agroforestry system in Yurimaguas was intermediate at 59 t C/ha. Rubber plantations and multistrata systems have a permanent understory of tropical kudzu (*Pueraria phaseoloides* [Roxb.]), which increased the carbon stocks by 2 to 5 t C/ha (Alegre et al. 2002; Palm et al. 2002).

*Table 15.3* Above-Ground Carbon Stocks of Different Land Use Systems in Yurimaguas and Pucallpa, Peru

| Site and Land Use | Above-Ground Carbon (t/ha)[a] |
|---|---|
| **Yurimaguas** | |
| Forest | |
| Moderately logged (>40 yr) | 294 |
| Fallow | |
| 15 yr | 185 |
| 5 yr | 44 |
| 3 yr | 19 |
| Agricultural crops | |
| Rice | 17 |
| Pasture | |
| Degraded (30 yr) | 2 |
| Improved (w/ *Brachiaria*) | 5 |
| Agroforestry | |
| Multistrata[b] | 59 |
| **Pucallpa** | |
| Forest | |
| Primary (untouched) | 162 |
| Residual (logged) | 123 |
| Fallow | |
| 15 yr | 126 |
| 3 yr | 21 |
| Agricultural crops | |
| Maize | 8 |
| Cassava | 3 |
| Plantain | 16 |
| Pasture | |
| Degraded | 3 |
| Perennial crops | |
| Rubber (30 yr) with kudzu | 74 |
| Oil palm with grasses | 41 |

[a]Includes standing trees and dead and fallen logs.

[b]Peach palm (*Bactris gasipaes* Kunth), tornillo (*Cedrelinga catenaeformis* D. Ducke), Inga edulis Mart., bolaina blanca (*Colubrina glandulosa* Perkins), and coffee (*Coffea arabica* L.) with cover crop of *Centrosema macrocarpum* Benth.

*Source:* Alegre et al. (2002).

The amount of carbon in annual cropping systems is very low (3–17 t C/ha). The upland rice (*Oryza sativa* L.) system in Yurimaguas showed carbon stocks similar to those of the biennial plantain system in Pucallpa, but much of that was the carbon still held in the remaining unburned logs from the clearing. Pastures contained the lowest quantities of carbon. Of note, as with the forests, carbon stocks were greater in similar land use systems in Yurimaguas than in Pucallpa. This is probably a result of the lower levels of agricultural intensification and higher rainfall in Yurimaguas (Fujisaka et al. 1998; Alegre et al. 2002).

## GREENHOUSE GAS EMISSIONS

In addition to net carbon emissions, deforestation and resulting land use can lead to the release of other greenhouse gases, including methane ($CH_4$) and nitrous oxide ($N_2O$). Although tropical soils can provide sinks for atmospheric $CH_4$, they are also reputed to be a major source of $N_2O$ gases (Keller et al. 1997). Evidence suggests that the $CH_4$ sink strength of well-drained upland tropical soils diminishes as the intensity of land use increases. Early analyses of tropical forest conversion to pasture indicated a large positive flux (4.18 µg/cm²/h) of $N_2O$ into the atmosphere (Luizao et al. 1989). More recent studies suggest that such emission increases are temporary and that the rates may eventually decrease to less than those of the nearby undisturbed forest (Keller and Reiners 1994; Erickson and Keller 1997). Because few studies on trace gas emissions in the tropics have been undertaken in areas other than natural forests and pastures, a goal of ASB was to sample and compare fluxes from the full spectrum of land uses ranging from natural forests to degraded pastures (see chapter 3, this volume).

A strategy of intensive sampling of $N_2O$ and $CH_4$ fluxes in fewer, well-characterized locations was adopted for sites in Peru and Indonesia. Similar land use categories were and continue to be monitored in both Pucallpa and Yurimaguas, representing the entire range of land uses from forest to pasture.

In Yurimaguas, monthly measurements were taken over the course of 2 years, 1997 to 1999, in a long-term experiment comparing different land uses (Palm et al. 2002). Five of the six land use systems were established 13 years previously by slashing and burning of a 10-year-old shifting cultivation forest fallow. In 1985, a portion of the 10-year fallow was slashed and burned and the following five treatments were installed: traditional shifting agriculture system, high-input cropping with fertilization and liming, low-input cropping, a multistrata agroforestry system, and a peach palm (*Bactris gasipaes* Kunth) plantation (table 15.2). These five treatments were all compared with the original forest fallow that was 23 years old at the time gas measurements were taken.

Average monthly $N_2O$ fluxes ranged from 0.6 to 0.9 kg N/ha/yr in the tree-based systems, were almost twice as high in the low-input cropping system, and reached 2.3 kg N/ha/yr in the high-input cropping system. The fluxes in the nonfertilized systems (tree-based and low-input cropping) are similar to those on the acid, infertile soils in the Indonesia ASB site in Jambi (chapter 3, this volume)

Methane fluxes also showed differences across treatments, with the high-input cropping system actually switching to a net source of $CH_4$ of +1.3 kg C/ha/yr (Palm et al. 2002). All of the other systems maintained a net $CH_4$ sink, showing decreasing sink strength with increasing land use intensity (e.g., –2.6 kg C/ha/yr in the 23-year-old forest fallow and –1.6 kg C/ha/yr in the low-input cropping). The differences in $CH_4$ flux are related primarily to increased soil bulk density and corresponding increased water-filled pore space. These methane consumption rates are similar to those reported from the Jambi site in Indonesia (chapter 3, this volume).

These preliminary results demonstrate that agroforestry systems maintain $CH_4$ sink and have low $N_2O$ emissions, and as land use intensification increases, $CH_4$ sink strength decreases and $N_2O$ emissions increase if nitrogen fertilization and tillage are practiced.

An analysis of the net global warming potential (GWP), which includes the net radiative forcing effects of $CO_2$, $N_2O$, and $CH_4$, of the different land use systems in Yurimaguas indicated that the $CO_2$ released from the vegetation as a result of biomass burning from deforestation (75 mol C/m²/yr; dashed line in figure 15.3; Palm et al. 2004) exceeded any subsequent emissions of $CO_2$, $N_2O$, and $CH_4$ from the soils. Carbon dioxide emissions from the decomposition of soil organic matter after deforestation, 0 to 8 mol C/m²/yr, were as high as or higher than the combined GWP of $N_2O$ and $CH_4$ fluxes, despite the higher net radiative forcing values for the latter two gases, 21 for $CH_4$ and 310 for $N_2O$ (Watson et al. 2000). The GWP from $CH_4$ production in

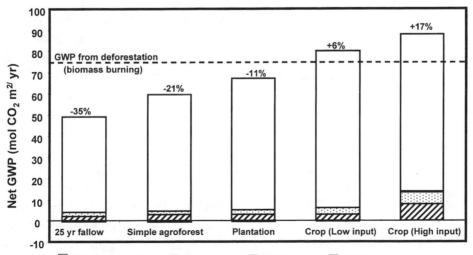

*Figure 15.3* Sources of the net global warming potential (GWP) over a 25-yr period for the different land use systems in Yurimaguas in the Peruvian Amazon. The dashed line represents the GWP resulting from deforestation and biomass burning (adapted from Palm et al. 2004).

the high-input cropping system or consumption in the other systems were undetectable in comparison to the GWP from $CO_2$.

The establishment of tree-based systems reduced the initial GWP as a result of deforestation by 11 to 35 percent (figure 15.3); this decrease resulted from carbon sequestered in the vegetation. In contrast, establishment of the two cropping systems increased the initial GWP by more than 20 percent through losses of soil carbon and, in the case of the high-input cropping system, higher $N_2O$ losses and net $CH_4$ production. Efforts to mitigate this dominating effect of the release of $CO_2$ from the slash-and-burn process should focus on reducing rates of deforestation or establishing tree-based land use systems that sequester more carbon in the vegetation and soil than annual cropping systems and pasture.

## GENETIC VARIATION IN TREE SPECIES AND ITS ROLE IN PROMOTING SUSTAINABLE LAND USE

The ASB research program on tree domestication takes discoveries regarding spatial and temporal variation within tree species and uses them to promote on-farm productive diversity and improved tree germplasm. Farmers in the lowland jungle of the Peruvian Amazon depend on more than 250 agroforestry tree species for construction material, fenceposts, firewood, charcoal, fibers, resins, fruits, medicines, and service functions such as soil conservation and shade (Sotelo Montes and Weber 1997). These trees contribute significantly to the income and food security of resource-poor farmers (Labarta and Weber 1998) and provide environmental services at local, national, and global levels.

It is widely known that deforestation and logging decrease the abundance of tree species around many rural communities in the tropics (Pearce and Brown 1994). As a result, these communities have fewer natural resource options for economic development in the future. Less widely recognized but equally important is that genetic variation within tree species may also be decreasing around rural communities (Ledig 1992). If this continues unchecked, communities may have even fewer opportunities for sustainable economic development in the future because reduced variation within tree populations is likely to decrease production stability and yield over time. Therefore it is imperative that domestication projects focus not only on increasing the number of valuable tree species on farm but also on managing the genetic resources of these species (O'Neill et al. 2001).

Intraspecific genetic variation in tree species is fundamental for the improvement of agroforestry systems. Through appropriate selection strategies, significant improvements can be made in timber tree form, fruit quality, and other commercially important traits (Simons et al. 1994). The presence of intraspecific genetic variation not only creates opportunities for selection but also provides an adaptive buffering capacity to changing user needs and environmental pressures.

One challenge for ASB was to quickly and cheaply identify the most productive germplasm for different agroforestry systems. Farmers consistently cite the lack of high-quality tree germplasm as a major obstacle to diversifying and expanding their agroforestry practices, and traditional tree improvement methods are too slow and expensive to meet their needs (Simons 1996). Nontraditional approaches involving farmers as collaborators in the research and development process are needed (Weber et al. 2001), and ASB has taken steps to develop and implement them. An example follows.

In the Pucallpa region, farmers want more productive germplasm of bolaina blanca (*Guazuma crinita* Mart.), capirona (*Calycophyllum spruceanum* Benth.), and other timber trees (Sotelo Montes and Weber 1997). In 1996, researchers and farming communities worked together to collect seed from eleven natural populations of bolaina blanca and capirona and established on-farm provenance trials in 1998. These were the first genetics trials of native tree species in the Peruvian Amazon. The principal objective of the trials was to identify the most promising provenances as seed sources for reforestation in different environmental conditions in the Peruvian Amazon. The trials were established on farms in the Aguaytía watershed (near Pucallpa), which is representative of many watersheds in the western Amazon Basin. Farmers participate in the evaluation of growth and other characteristics and provide useful information about their selection criteria for tree germplasm.

Preliminary results of the on-farm provenance trials illustrate the potential gains in productivity that farmers can realize from an early selection of provenances of fast-growing timber trees (Sotelo Montes et al. 2000). In both bolaina blanca and capirona there was significant variation in average height between provenances in the nursery and after 6 and 12 months in the field ($p < .001$). In the case of bolaina blanca, after 12 months in the field the local provenance from the Aguaytía watershed (Von Humboldt) was 13 percent taller than the average height of the other provenances combined ($p < .05$). Capirona did not grow as rapidly as bolaina blanca during the first few years.

Traditional studies of variation in provenance trials provide essential information about the adaptive and commercial value of germplasm from different regions (Morgenstern 1996), but they cannot fully quantify the underlying diversity and genetic constitution of tree populations. Molecular methods can provide this information and are being used to complement traditional approaches. Molecular methods provide insights into the origin of tree populations, and the relationships between these populations—essential information for management of tree genetic resources. For example, molecular techniques were used to identify diverse populations of capirona for cultivation and for in-situ and on-farm conservation in the Peruvian Amazon (Russell et al. 1999).

Accelerating the delivery of high-quality tree germplasm to farmers is the second principal objective of participatory tree domestication. A traditional forestry approach involves many steps: species selection trials, provenance trials to identify the best seed sources of each species, progeny tests to identify the best mother trees within each selected site, collection of seeds or vegetative material from the best mother trees to establish seedling or clonal seed orchards, and finally the production of high-quality seed for dissemination. Using this slow and costly process, government and nongovernment organizations cannot meet the growing demand for high-quality germplasm, particularly when formal institutions and networks break down.

Involving farmers in germplasm selection, production, and dissemination can accelerate delivery of high-quality germplasm. On-farm genetics trials, like the provenance trials just mentioned, can be transformed directly into seed orchards. Farmers with on-farm genetics trials are being organized into networks for the production and commercialization of high-quality seed, seedlings, and timber. These seed orchards are a new form of small business enterprise in Peru and also serve as ex situ conservation sites.

Provisional guidelines were determined for seed transfer within the region based on geographic patterns of genetic similarity between populations. In general, one should try to match the environment conditions of the seed source with those of the plantation. This entails characterizing the environmental conditions of potential plantation sites and seed sources. In the absence of such characterization data, seeds should be collected from trees that grow near the plantation site and have desirable phenotypic characteristics. Using seeds from geographically distant regions should be avoided unless there is evidence from genetic trials that such seedlots are adapted to local environmental conditions.

## SOCIOECONOMIC RESEARCH

Farmers in the Amazon, like their counterparts worldwide, face many agronomic and marketing challenges: Yields are uncertain, market prices typically are low and can fluctuate wildly, and transportation to major markets is expensive. In the case of the Peruvian Amazon, however, transportation costs are much higher than those faced by agriculturalists in other areas; to reach international markets, products must be transported down one of the longest rivers or over some of the highest mountains in the world. Such conditions make farming (and hence farmers) uncompetitive in all but local markets for most of their products, and these markets suffer from severe seasonal gluts. Political and social instability also complicate production and marketing activities, putting farmers in the region at a further competitive disadvantage even compared with their Amazonian counterparts in Brazil and Bolivia. For example, unrest in the late 1980s led to a severe decline in livestock herd sizes in the Pucallpa region (Fujisaka and White 1998). Contributing to the slow and ongoing recovery is the drastic reduction of agricultural support programs (e.g., product price subsidies and subsidized credit) in the 1990s (Hopkins 1998; Yanggen 2000a).

In an effort to improve smallholder welfare in the region, numerous land use alternatives have been developed, ranging from improved traditional annual cropping systems to new multistrata agroforestry systems. Though agronomically suited to the region, improvements in income and food security based on these new systems have been limited by several factors, some of which are beyond the reach of any policymaker. For example, in 1999 perennial crops such as coffee (*Coffea* spp.), palm oil, and cocoa

(*Theobroma cacao* L.) suffered price declines ranging from 25 to 50 percent. Despite a large set of well-funded activities to promote exotic Amazonian fruits and forest products (Clay and Clement 1993; Toledo 1994), citrus and achiote (*Bixa orellana* L.) have failed commercially. Consequently, farmers near Pucallpa continue to sell citrus and other perennial tree crops at low prices in local markets. Despite these failures, new projects that encourage the production of other Amazonian agricultural goods, such as camu-camu (*Myrciaria dubia* [Kunth] McVaugh) and uña de gato (*Uncaria tomentosa* [Willd.] DC), are under way. Although these products provide an opportunity to diversify production, demand for these specialty products is uncertain.

The ASB socioeconomic research also addressed the issue of how government policies could best promote sustainable production systems, improve smallholder welfare, and reduce the impact of agriculture on deforestation (Yanggen 2000b). More specifically, the research analyzed how changes in Peruvian agricultural policies, including those of structural adjustment in the 1990s, affected use of cleared land and forest cover. Analysis based on a 1998 household survey revealed that upon provision of subsidized agricultural credit and guaranteed minimum prices for agricultural products in the latter half of the 1980s, 94 percent of farmers increased production (predominantly of rice and maize [*Zea mays* L.]), 90 percent of farmers hired more labor, but only 11 percent of farmers increased capital input use. These government policies led farmers to increase output by hiring more labor for slash-and-burn production of annual crops. A sharp increase in forest clearing resulted; 75 percent of farmers reported clearing more primary forest for agricultural use. When subsidized credit and guaranteed prices were eliminated in the context of structural adjustment, production levels and deforestation sharply declined in the region around Pucallpa (Yanggen 2000a). Satellite images confirmed this decrease in deforestation rates over a broader area (IIAP 1999).

The econometric component of this research analyzed the dynamics of agriculture's impact on deforestation at three levels: how economic and policy incentives and other factors (e.g., biophysical conditions) affect farmer decisions concerning choice of production technology, product mix, and the amount of land cultivated and how these decisions, in turn, affect rates of deforestation. (figure 15.4).

The regression model results showed a clear evolution of land use patterns. Annual crop production was most strongly associated with early frontier development and led to deforestation at the forest margin. Pasture and cattle tended to occupy land previously used for annual cropping, and also displaced secondary forest fallows. These results confirm those of Fujisaka and White (1998) and Smith et al. (1999). Area dedicated to perennial tree crops stagnated over the period covered by the sample, primarily because the profitability of these activities was undermined by steep declines in product prices.

Regression results also confirm the key role of labor as a constraining factor of production. Farmers with above-average amounts of family labor produced more of all the principal outputs: annual crops, perennial tree crop products, and livestock products. Greater overall labor availability (both hired labor and family labor) led to

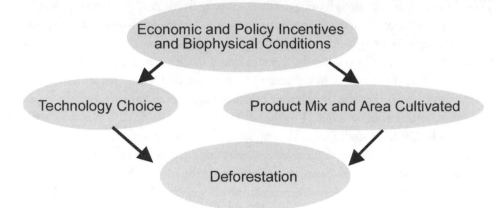

*Figure 15.4* Causal relationships between socioeconomics and technology leading to deforestation.

greater amounts of primary and secondary forest clearing. Farm households engaged in above-average amounts of off-farm employment activities reported significantly lower annual and perennial crop production. Clearly, reducing labor availability can reduce the pressure on forests.

These models also capture the key role of financial capital in determining product mix, technology choice, and deforestation. The use of credit was positively correlated with the use of purchased inputs and hired labor. Credit was negatively correlated with labor- and capital-saving technologies, such as kudzu-improved fallows and *Brachiaria*-improved pastures. Although the impacts of these specific inputs and technologies on deforestation were not uniform, it is clear that access to credit played a key role in determining the farmers' decisions regarding scale of operation and product mix, and these decisions did affect deforestation.

This research distinguished between the clearing of primary and secondary forests. Primary forests are areas that have never been felled (but often selectively logged); vegetative regrowth on fallow land becomes secondary forests. A common perception is that once primary forest deforestation has occurred, the forest (and all the services it provides) is lost forever. However, research by the Food and Agriculture Organization (FAO 1996) estimated that in 1990 there existed 165 million ha of secondary forest in Latin America; hence, the potential exists for recouping at least some of the forest services via increases in area in secondary fallow. In the Pucallpa area, farmers maintain nearly equivalent areas of secondary and primary forest, 30 and 31 percent of the average operational holding, respectively (Yanggen 2000a). Econometric analysis showed that use of kudzu-improved fallows, purchased inputs (e.g., fertilizer, improved seed, and herbicides), and alluvial soils increased the amount of secondary forest cleared on farms but decreased the amount of primary forest cleared. Increases in land productivity in these cases seemed to mitigate declines in soil fertility linked to annual crop production, thereby enabling farmers to reuse secondary forest fallows, which decreased the need to clear primary forest (Yanggen and Reardon 2001).

A central conclusion of this research is that the production of annual crops using shifting slash-and-burn agriculture is a key driver of deforestation in the Pucallpa research area. Greater labor availability increased these extensive production systems and deforestation. One general policy objective, then, is to reduce the labor available for shifting annual crop production. One option is to promote off-farm income opportunities that siphon labor away from annual cropping and other agricultural activities. Development of a nonagricultural economic sector therefore may be key to removing pressures on forests. This implies the need for a broad-based development strategy including other sectors such as industry, tourism, and other services. In addition, research and policy initiatives must promote more sustainable annual cropping practices. The use of productivity-enhancing inputs such as improved seeds, fertilizer, and pesticides intensified land use and reduced clearing of primary and secondary forests in our sample of farmers from the Pucallpa area. However, given low product prices and poor transportation infrastructure, agricultural research must redouble efforts to identify product and technology packages that are affordable to and profitable for smallholders.

One option is to intensify pasture production systems. Indeed, kudzu-improved fallows and *Brachiaria*-improved pastures have been widely adopted by farmers because they increase returns to the labor. However, these systems use less labor per hectare, thereby freeing labor for deforestation and other uses; analysis revealed that the adoption of kudzu-improved fallows increased secondary forest clearing, and the adoption of *Brachiaria*-improved pastures increased clearing of all types of forests (Yanggen 2000b). The challenge is to identify production practices that both increase returns to labor and decrease pressure on primary and secondary forests. Labor-intensive production of high-value perennial crops can do this by absorbing labor while still providing high returns to labor. Agroforestry techniques that incorporate trees with high-value products into pastures and fallow areas have the potential to do this. Therefore, integrating perennial tree crops into production systems should be a research priority. In addition, on-farm processing of agricultural products into oils, preserves, flour, and other products can dramatically lower the transportation costs relative to unit value of output, and refined products also tend to suffer less price turbulence than do primary products. Finally, policies that promote forest-based processing can help promote sustainable production of nontimber forest products.

This research proposed a series of strategies to encourage more intensive and sustainable agricultural production practices. However, this research also pointed out that if new practices or crops were sufficiently profitable, farmers would invest in labor-saving equipment or simply hire more labor to expand production and would do so at the expense of forests. Thus more intensive forms of cultivation may promote deforestation. Therefore there is a need to complement the promotion of intensive cropping systems with policies that restrict access to forests. Options such as reductions in new road construction and enforceable regulations limiting the clearing of primary forest merit consideration.

Recent geographic information system analysis by the International Center for Tropical Agriculture (CIAT) used high-detail images to identify the ASB Pucallpa benchmark area of the Aguaytía watershed while identifying and coding land uses. Complementary research by the Instituto de Investigacion de la Amazonia Peruana (IIAP) delineated and estimated the rates of deforestation from 1955 to 1995. This work has served as an input to policy planning (e.g., road construction and agricultural development projects) according to environmental and economic criteria (IIAP 1999).

## CAPACITY STRENGTHENING, ASB IMPACT, AND FUTURE RESEARCH PRIORITIES

In 1998, national and international organizations working in Pucallpa held a workshop on participatory planning by objective to define research priorities. Using the logical framework method, participating organizations selected biodiversity research, research on and development of markets for Amazonian products, and the refinement and application of farmer participatory research methods as priority issues. The establishment of a Training and Information Center also was deemed necessary.

The 1998 workshop yielded quick results for ASB and its collaborators. National research partners and universities began to include agroforestry in their research portfolios and curricula and also began to refine and replicate research methods, such as tree domestication processes and the measuring of carbon stocks in production systems. Training in tree domestication and genetic resource management has motivated INIA, the Instituto Nacional de los Recursos Naturales, and the Reforestation Committees to include similar projects in their research portfolios, thereby expanding the overall impact of ASB research in Peru. In addition, the government of Peru is incorporating recommendations regarding tree genetic resource management in its new national forestry laws.

The ASB collaborators are involved in participatory, farm-based research on the management of pastures and secondary forests. Tropileche, a research consortium involving CIAT, IIAP, and the Instituto Veterinario de Investigaciones Tropicales y de Altura (IVITA) aims to improve pasture quality and productivity for milk and beef (dual-purpose) cattle production systems (Holmann 1999; White et al. 2001). The Secondary Forest Project collaborates with institutions in Peru (Centre for International Forestry Research [CIFOR], INIA, Universidad Nacional Agraria la Molina), Brazil (Empresa Brasileira de Pesquisa Agropecuária), and Nicaragua to characterize secondary forest use, examine the biophysical dynamics of secondary fallow systems, and identify management options for enriching and otherwise improving secondary fallows (Smith et al. 2001).

Planned future research and outreach efforts include expanding efforts to distill practical policy messages from field-based research results, with special attention paid to policies likely to affect smallholder land use decisions and welfare. Examples include more careful assessments of the affects of policy changes on smallholders; help in prioritizing spending on agricultural research and extension, and greater efforts to identify and transfer to Peru relevant policy lessons learned from other ASB sites, especially Brazil.

## ACKNOWLEDGMENTS

We are indebted to the three international centers involved in ASB activities in Latin America—CIAT, CIFOR, and the World Agroforestry Center (ICRAF)—and for pioneering research on tropical soils and agronomy begun by North Carolina State University.

We are also indebted to our ASB partner organizations: INIA, Cámara Nacional Forestal, Comité de Reforestación de Ucayali, Instituto Nacional de los Recursos Naturales, IIAP, IVITA, Dirección Regional de Agricultura–Ucayali, Universidad Nacional Agraria la Molina, Universidad Nacional de la Amazonía Peruana, UNU, Consorcio de Desarrollo Sostenible del Ucayali, and Desarrollo Participativo Amazónico.

The authors are grateful for the helpful comments from Polly Ericksen, Sam Fujisaka, Jessa Lewis, and an anonymous reviewer. The ASB Peru team appreciates the financial support from the governments of Spain (Agencia Española de Cooperación Internacional), Canada (International Development Research Centre), the Netherlands (DML/BD), Norway, the United States (Agency for International Development), England (Department for International Development), Denmark (Danish International Development Agency), the European Union, the Interamerican Development Bank, and the International Tropical Timber Organization.

REFERENCES

Alegre, J.C., L.A. Arévalo, A. Ricse, D. Callo-Concha, and C. Palm. 2002. Secuestramiento de carbono con sistemas alternativos en el Perú. Memorias del IV Congreso Brasilero de Sistemas Agroflorestais, Ilhéus, Bahia, October 21–26, 2002.

Alegre J.C., B. Pashanasi, L. Arévalo, C. Palm, and R. Ferrera. 2001. Efecto del manejo del suelo sobre las propiedades biológicas del suelo en los trópicos húmedos del Perú. Memorias del XV Congreso Latinoamericano de la Ciencia del Suelo y V Cubano, Varadero, Cuba.

Aramburú, C.E. 1984. Expansion of the agrarian and demographic frontier in the Peruvian Selva. pp. 155–179. In M. Schmink and C. Wood (eds.) Frontier expansion in Amazonia. Univ. of Florida Press, Gainesville.

Barham, B.L., and O.T. Coomes. 1995. Prosperity's promise: The Amazon rubber boom and distorted economic development. Westview Press, Boulder, CO.

Bedoya Garland, E. 1987. Intensification and degradation in the agricultural systems of the Peruvian upper jungle: The upper Huallaga case. pp. 290–315. In P. Little and M. Horowitz (eds.) Land at risk in the third world: Local level perspectives. Westview Press, Boulder, CO.

Clay, J.W., and C.R. Clement. 1993. Selected species and strategies to enhance income generation from Amazonian forests. FAO: Misc/93/6 Working Paper: FAO of the United Nations, Rome. Available at http://www.fao.org/docrep/V0784E/V0784E00.htm (verified 7 Dec. 2003).

Denevan, W.M. 1984. Ecological heterogeneity and horizontal zonation of agriculture in the Amazon floodplain. Pp. 311–336. *In* M. Schmink and C.H. Wood (eds.) Frontier expansion in Amazonia. Univ. of Florida Press, Gainesville.

Erickson, H.E., and M. Keller. 1997. Tropical land use change and soil emissions of nitrogen oxides. Soil Use Manage. 13:278–287.

FAO (Food and Agriculture Organization). 1996. Forest resource assessment 1990. FAO Forestry Paper 130. FAO, Rome.

Fujisaka, S., C. Castilla, G. Escobar, V. Rodrigues, E.J. Veneklaas, R.J. Thomas, et al. 1998. The effects of forest conversion on annual crops and pastures: Estimates of carbon emissions and plant species loss in a Brazilian Amazon colony. Agric. Ecosyst. Environ. 69:17–26.

Fujisaka, S., G. Escobar, and E. Veneklaas. 2000. Weedy forest and fields: Interaction of colonists' land use and plant community and diversity in the Peruvian Amazon. Agric. Ecosyst. Environ. 78:175–186.

Fujisaka, S., and D. White. 1998. Pasture or permanent crops after slash-and-burn cultivation? Land use choice in three Amazon colonies. Agrofor. Syst. 42:45–59.

Gillison, A.N., and J.C. Alegre. 2000. The use of plant functional attributes in characterising plant biodiversity and land use impact in a forested land use mosaic in the Peruvian Amazon basin. CIFOR-ICRAF-ASB Working paper.

Hecht, S.B. 1993. The logic of livestock and deforestation in Amazonia. Considering land markets, value of ancillaries, the larger macroeconomic context, and individual economic strategies. BioScience 43 (10):687–695.

Holland, D. 1999. Causes of human migration in the Pucallpa region of Peru. *In* Sustainable systems for smallholders (Project PE-5) annual report. CIAT, Cali, Colombia.

Holmann, F. 1999. Análisis ex-ante de nuevas alternativas forrajeras en fincas con ganado de doble propósito en Perú, Costa Rica y Nicaragua. Pasturas Trop. 21(2):2–17.

Hopkins, R. 1998. The impact of structural adjustment on agricultural performance. pp. 88–105. *In* J. Crabtree and J. Thomas (eds.) Fujimori's Peru: The political economy. Inst. of Latin Am. Studies, Univ. of London, London.

IIAP (Instituto de Investigacion de la Amazonia Peruana). 1999. Zonification ecologica economica de la cuenca del rio aguaytia. Convenio IIAP–CTAR–Ucayali.

IICA (Instituto Interamericano de Cooperación para la Agricultura). 1995. Preservación del bosque Amazónico: Una estrategia común en base a la estabilización de la agricultura migratoria y al manejo sostenible del bosque. Programa Cooperativo de Investigación y Transferencia de Tecnología para los Trópicos Suramericanos (PROCITROPICOS). Proceedings of the Regional Seminar in Pucallpa, Peru. IICA, San Jose, Costa Rica.

INEI (Instituto Nacional de Esatadistica e Informatica). 1997. Estadistica del medio ambiente. INEI, Lima, Peru.

Keller, M., J. Mellilo, and W.A. de Mello. 1997. Trace gas emissions from ecosystems of the Amazon Basin. Cienc. Cult. 49:87–97.

Keller, M., and W.A. Reiners. 1994. Soil–atmosphere exchange of nitrous oxide, nitric oxide and methane under secondary succession of pasture to forest in the Atlantic lowlands of Costa Rica. Global Biogeochem. Cycles 8(4):399–409.

Labarta, R.A. 1998. Los productores de la cuenca amazónica del Perú y la dinámica de uso de la tierra: Resultados de la caracterización de Pucallpa y Yurimaguas. ICRAF Res. Rep., Pucallpa, Peru.

Labarta, R.A., and J.C. Weber. 1998. Valorización económica de bienes tangibles de cinco especies arbóreas agroforestales en la cuenca amazónica peruana. Rev. For. Centroam. 23:12–21.

Ledig, F.T. 1992. Human impacts on genetic diversity in forest ecosystems. Oikos 63:87–108.

Loker, W.M. 1993. Medio ambiente y agricultura en la Amazonia Peruana: Un experimento metodológico. pp. 13–25. In W.M. Loker and S. Vosti (eds.) Desarrollo rural en la Amazonia Peruana. CIAT/IFPRI, Cali, Colombia.

Luizao, F., P. Matson, G. Livingston, R. Luizao, and P. Vitousek. 1989. Nitrous oxide flux following tropical land clearing. Global Biogeochem. Cycles 3(3):281–285.

Morgenstern, E.K. 1996. Geographic variation in forest trees: Genetic basis and application of knowledge in silviculture. Univ. of British Columbia Press, Vancouver, BC.

Myers, N., R.A. Mittermeier, C.G. Mittermeier, G.A.B. da Fonseca, and J. Kent. 2000. Biodiversity hotspots for conservation priorities. Nature (London) 403:853–858.

Nelson, M. 1973. The development of tropical lands: Policy issues in Latin America. Johns Hopkins Univ., Baltimore.

Nye, P.H., and D.J. Greenland. 1960. The soil under shifting cultivation. Technical Communications 51. Commonw. Bureau of Soils, Harpenden, UK.

O'Neill, G.A., I.K. Dawson, C. Sotelo Montes, L. Guarino, D. Current, M. Guariguata, et al. 2001. Strategies for genetic conservation of trees in the Peruvian Amazon basin. Biodiversity Conserv. 10(6):837–850.

Padoch, C., and W. de Jong. 1992. Diversity, variation, and change in Ribereno agriculture. pp. 158–174. In K.H. Redford and C. Padoch (eds.) Conservation of neotropical forests working from traditional resource use. Columbia Univ. Press, New York.

Palm, C.A., J.C. Alegre, L. Arevalo, P.K. Mutuo, A.R. Mosier, and R. Coe. 2002. Nitrous oxide and methane fluxes in six different land use systems in the Peruvian Amazon. Global Biogeochem. Cycles 16:1073.

Palm, C.A., T. Tomich, M. van Noordwijk, S. Vosti, J. Gockowski, J. Alegre, and L. Verchot. 2004. Mitigating GHG emissions in the humid tropics: Case studies from the Alternatives to Slash and Burn Program (ASB). Environment, Development and Sustainability 6:145–162.

Pearce, D., and K. Brown. 1994. Saving the world's tropical forests. pp. 2–26. In D. Pearce and K. Brown (eds.). The causes of tropical deforestation: The economic and statistical analysis of factors giving rise to the loss of the tropical forests. Univ. of British Columbia Press, Vancouver.

Russell, J.R., J.C. Weber, A. Booth, W. Powell, C. Sotelo Montes, and I.K. Dawson. 1999. Genetic variation of *Calycophyllum spruceanum* in the Peruvian Amazon Basin, revealed by amplified fragment length polymorphism (AFLP) analysis. Mol. Ecol. 8:199–204.

Ruthenberg, H. 1976. Farming systems in the tropics. Oxford Univ. Press, Oxford.

Sanchez, P.A. 1976. Properties and management of soils in the tropics. Wiley, New York.

Simons, A.J. 1996. Delivery of improvement for agroforestry trees. pp. 391–400. In M.J. Dieters, A.C. Matheson, D.G. Nikles, C.E. Harwood, and S.M. Walker (eds.) Tree improvement for sustainable tropical forestry. Proceedings of the QFRI-IUFRO Conference, Caloundra, Queensland, Australia, 27 Oct.–1 Nov. 1996. Queensland for. Res. Inst., Gympie, Australia.

Simons, A.J., D.J. MacQueen, and J.L. Stewart. 1994. Strategic concepts in the domestication of non-industrial trees. pp. 91–102. In R.R.B. Leakey and A.C. Newton (eds.) Tropical trees: The potential for domestication and the rebuilding of forest resources. Proceedings of a Conference, Heriot-Watt Univ., Edinburgh, Scotland, 23–28 Aug. 1992. HMSO, London.

Smith, J., B. Finegan, C. Sabogal, M.S.G. Ferreira, G. Siles, P. van de Kop, et al. 2001. Management of secondary forests in colonist swidden agriculture in Peru, Brazil and Nicaragua. pp. 263–278. *In* M. Palo, J. Uusivuori, and G. Mery (eds.) World forests, markets and policies. World forests, Vol. III. Kluwer Academic Publ., Boston.

Smith, J., P. van de Kop, K. Reategui, I. Lombardi, C. Sabogal, and A. Diaz. 1999. Dynamics of secondary forests in slash-and-burn farming: Interactions among land use types in the Peruvian Amazon. Agric. Ecosyst. Environ. 76:85–98.

Sotelo Montes, C., H. Vidaurre, J.C. Weber, A.J. Simons, and I.K. Dawson. 2000. Producción de semillas a partir de la domesticación participativa de árboles agroforestales en la amazonía peruana. pp. 65–72. *In* R. Salazar (ed.) Memorias del segundo symposio sobre avances en la producción de semillas forestales en América Latina, Santo Domingo, República Dominica. 18–22 Oct. 1999. Proyecto de Semillas Forestales (PROSEFOR)— Centro de Agricultura Tropical y de Enseñanza (CATIE)—International Union of Forest Research Organizations (IUFRO), Turrialba, Costa Rica.

Sotelo Montes, C., and J.C. Weber. 1997. Priorización de especies arbóreas para sistemas agroforestales en la selva baja del Perú. Agrofor. Am. 4(14):12–17.

Toledo, J.M. (ed.). 1994. Biodiversidad y desarrollo sostenible de la Amazonia en una economia de mercado. Stansa SA, Lima, Peru.

Townsend, J. 1983. Seasonality and capitalist penetration in the Amazon Basin. pp. 140–157. *In* E. Moran (ed.) The dilemma of Amazon development. Westview Press, Boulder, CO.

Watson, R.T., I.R. Noble, B. Bolin, N.H. Ravindranath, D.J. Verardo, and D.J. Doken (eds.). 2000. Land use, land-use change and forestry. Intergovernmental Panel on Climate Change. Cambridge Univ. Press, Cambridge.

Weber, J.C., C. Sotelo Montes, H. Vidaurre, I.K. Dawson, and A.J. Simons. 2001. Participatory domestication of agroforestry trees: An example from the Peruvian Amazon. Dev. Practice 11(4):425–433.

White, D.S., F. Holmann, S. Fujisaka, K. Reategui, and C.E. Lascano. 2001. Will intensifying pasture management in tropical Latin America protect forests (or is it the other way around)? pp. 91–111. *In* A. Angelsen and D. Kaimowitz (eds.) Agricultural technologies and tropical deforestation. CABI, Cambridge.

Yanggen, D. 2000a. Deforestación en la selva peruana: Un análisis del impacto de los diversos productos agropecuarios y tecnologías de producción. *In* I. Hurtado, C. Trivelli, and A. Brack (eds.) Peru: El problema agrario en debate, VIII Conf. Seminario Permanente de Investigacion Agraria (SEPIA), Lima, Peru.

Yanggen, D. 2000b. Sustainable agriculture and deforestation in the Peruvian Amazon. Ph.D. diss. Michigan State Univ., East Lansing (Diss. Abstr. 134 929 ths).

Yanggen, D.R., and T. Reardon. 2001. Kudzu-improved fallows in the Peruvian Amazon. pp. 213–230. *In* A. Angelsen and D. Kaimowitz (eds.) Agricultural technologies and tropical deforestation. CABI, Cambridge.

# 16 Northern Thailand

## CHANGING SMALLHOLDER LAND USE PATTERNS

Plodprasop Suraswadi
  *Ministry of Agriculture and Cooperatives  Bangkok, Thailand*
David E. Thomas
  *World Agroforestry Centre  Chiang Mai, Thailand*
Komon Pragtong
  *Ministry of Agriculture and Cooperatives  Bangkok, Thailand*
Pornchai Preechapanya
  *Ministry of Agriculture and Cooperatives  Chiang Mai, Thailand*
Horst Weyerhaeuser
  *World Agroforestry Centre  Kunming, Yunnan, China*

The Alternatives to Slash and Burn (ASB) research program in northern Thailand seeks to understand land use change in the mountainous mainland Southeast Asia (MMSEA) ccorcgion and to develop technologies and policies that can improve land use management and human welfare in the region. The MMSEA includes the large region of hill and mountain terrain that joins the Himalayan mountains in southwestern China and extends through northern portions of Myanmar, Thailand, and Laos, to Vietnam in the east (figure 16.1). Several major river systems flow through or have headwaters in this region, also long known for its diverse ethnic composition and complex mosaic patterns of traditional land use that include shifting cultivation. Because this region also includes most of what remains of mainland Southeast Asia's rapidly dwindling forest resources, it is the focus of increasing environmental concern related to the use and management of surface water and biodiversity and to global climate change.

Improving natural resource management, reducing rural poverty, and understanding the important role of socioeconomic context in which resource use decisions are made are key ASB objectives. More specifically, given strong and growing concern over watersheds and river systems that support major lowland populations, their rice bowl production areas, and urban and industrial centers, ASB chose watersheds as its unit of observation in establishing

*Figure 16.1* Mountainous mainland Southeast Asia and the ASB Thailand benchmark site.

an analytical framework. Moreover, special focus is given to land use in upper tributaries, where many poor minority communities have benefited least from the rapid economic development that has characterized Thailand and the region. We also seek to incorporate into our analysis relevant lessons from the Asian economic crisis and constitutional and governance issues emerging in Thai society and the wider region.

This chapter focuses on changes in patterns of land use in mountainous landscapes of northern Thailand, with particular attention to changing land uses of mountain minority communities and the effects of these changes on environmental services emerging from watersheds. The next two sections describe changes in land use in the study area, discuss some of the factors influencing land use change, and identify some of the environmental consequences of these changes. Then we examine selected project-specific responses to factors influencing changes in forest and land use, describe promising technological and institutional innovations, and provide details of ASB's research, capacity strengthening, and outreach agendas in Thailand.

# CHANGING LAND USE PATTERNS IN MOUNTAIN WATERSHEDS

The ASB Thailand research strategy began with a review of policy concerns and issues associated with changing patterns of land use in northern Thailand, with emphasis on upper watershed areas (Thomas 1996). We also reviewed the literature and ongoing research to identify strategic knowledge gaps and to guide the selection of an appropriate benchmark site and program development. Based on these reviews, the 4000-km$^2$ Mae Chaem watershed was selected as the primary ASB benchmark site. The ASB's secondary focus in Thailand has been on one ridge of the Mae Tacng watershed where the Sam Mun Highland Development Project was conducted over the period 1987 to 1994.

Because most land in upper watershed areas is officially classified as reserved or protected forest, our first task was to identify types of forest resource user groups and examine their uses of forested land for timber and other purposes and then to assess the effects of user practices on watershed degradation.

## DEFORESTATION

Thailand entered its era of rapid economic growth in 1960 with the launching of its first national 5-year economic and social development plan. Although much economic development has been achieved, one cost has been the loss of more than half of Thailand's natural forest resources, resulting in growing concern about loss of biodiversity and contributions to global climate change. Table 16.1 summarizes changes in proportions of land under forest, agriculture, and other uses over the period 1960 to 1998, for the nation as a whole and for northern Thailand.

*Table 16.1* Changes in Percentage Land Cover in Thailand and Northern Thailand, 1960–1998

| Land Cover | | Proportion of Total Area (%) | | | | |
|---|---|---|---|---|---|---|
| | | 1960 | 1970 | 1980 | 1990 | 1998 |
| Forest cover | National | 54.0 | 46.0 | 32.0 | 27.3 | 25.3 |
| | Northern Thailand | 68.8 | 67.3 | 53.9 | 46.4 | 43.1 |
| Farm land | National | 20.0 | 29.0 | 37.1 | 41.2 | 41.5 |
| | Northern Thailand | 11.0 | 17.0 | 24.5 | 28.0 | 27.5 |
| Other nonforest | National | 26.0 | 25.0 | 30.9 | 31.5 | 33.2 |
| | Northern Thailand | 20.2 | 15.7 | 21.6 | 25.6 | 29.4 |

*Sources:* Adapted from Charuppat (1998) (Royal Forest Department), Center for Agricultural Statistics (1994), and Center for Agricultural Information (1998).

Although dramatic decreases in forest cover began later in northern Thailand than in much of the rest of the country, major losses occurred at both levels in the 1970s. Rates of loss appear to have begun to decline recently, but percentage losses in forest cover are still above the national average. Moreover, although most remaining forest is in the north, losses there are already greater than in other areas of the MMSEA. There are three principal proximate causes of deforestation in northern Thailand: conversion of forests to agriculture, logging, and traditional farming practiced in forested areas.

- **Conversion of Forests to Agriculture.** Conversion of forest after 1960 throughout Thailand was associated primarily with expansion of land for agriculture, as seen in table 16.1, both to feed the growing population and to produce export crops to provide foreign exchange for the rapidly growing economy. Conversion to agriculture was facilitated by heavy logging and, in the late 1970s, by policies promoting agricultural expansion. Policies to address political and national security issues further encouraged forest clearing (Pragtong and Thomas 1990). As agriculture began to expand into increasingly marginal sites, overall population growth rates began to decline, the economy underwent structural adjustments that favored the industrial and service sectors, and urban and suburban growth began to accelerate. Forest conversion then became increasingly associated with cities, industry, housing, resorts, and, more recently, land speculation (Thomas 1996, 1997).
- **Logging of Natural Forest.** Logging helped fuel economic growth initially, but the combination of huge concession areas overlapping with protected forest areas and local communities, high official and unofficial harvest rates, low replanting rates, settlement and cultivation of logged areas, and slow expansion of plantation forests made such contributions to economic growth unsustainable (Pragtong and Thomas 1990). Although logging concessions were stopped in 1989, illegal logging is still a problem in reserved forest and protected areas. Forest department policy now emphasizes forest conservation rather than timber production and the strict enforcement of established rules.
- **Traditional Agriculture within the Forest.** In the mountains of northern Thailand, various ethnic minorities have long lived as farmers in the forest (Kunstadter et al. 1978). A web of interrelated issues is associated with their land use practices, including opium production, shifting cultivation, rural poverty, and the impact of land use practices on protected forest areas and on the environmental services these forests provide (Rerkasem and Rerkasem 1994; TDRI 1994; Thomas 1996; Kaosa-ard 2000). The 1997 distribution of mountain ethnic minority populations living in the midlands and highlands (above 600 m a.s.l.) is presented in table 16.2 for the nation as a whole, the northern region, Chiang Mai province, and the ASB benchmark site (Mae Chaem). Although national proportions of mountain ethnic minorities are quite low, they often make up more than half of the population in northern upper watershed areas.

The grouping of communities into highland, midland, and lowland categories corresponds to the altitude zones in which they have been most prevalent and the

*Table 16.2* Distribution of Mountain Ethnic Populations, by Ethnic Group and Geographic Area, 1997

| Groups | Nation | Northern Thailand | Chiang Mai | Mae Chaem |
|---|---|---|---|---|
| **With Highland Agricultural Traditions** | | | | |
| H'mong | 126,300 | 119,768 | 19,011 | 4,814 |
| Lahu | 85,845 | 84,262 | 32,583 | — |
| Akha | 56,616 | 56,157 | 5,486 | — |
| Yao | 48,357 | 42,561 | 353 | — |
| Lisu | 33,365 | 31,040 | 13,201 | 431 |
| Subtotal | 350,483 | 333,788 | 70,634 | 5,245 |
| **With Midland Agricultural Traditions** | | | | |
| Karen | 353,574 | 310,909 | 111,667 | 29,197 |
| Htin | 38,823 | 40,302 | — | — |
| Lua | 17,637 | 16,225 | 5,473 | 1,451 |
| Khamu | 13,674 | 10,567 | 21 | — |
| Mlabri | 125 | 125 | — | — |
| Subtotal | 423,833 | 378,128 | 117,161 | 30,648 |
| Mountain minorities[a] | 774,316 | 711,916 | 187,795 | 35,893 |
| Proportion of total | 100% | 92% | 24% | 5% |
| Total population | 60,816,227 | 12,091,337 | 1,573,757 | 67,912 |
| Mountain minorities | 1% | 6% | 12% | 53% |

[a]Mountain minorities are defined as members of the ethnic groups listed in this table.
*Source:* Adapted from Hilltribe Welfare Division (1998).

types of agroecosystem management practices they have traditionally used (Preechapanya 2001). (Highland peak areas, a strategically important but small altitude zone not densely inhabited by humans, are excluded from the analysis presented here.) Although such groupings are based on traditional distinctions widely applicable across the MMSEA ecoregion, altitude zones are approximate, geographic domains of ethnic groups' overlap, and conditions change and traditions adapt over time. Table 16.3 presents estimates for the ASB benchmark site of the distribution of ethnic groups across altitude zones (top portion of table 16.3; rows sum to 100 percent) and ethnic distributions within each zone (bottom portion of table 16.3, columns sum to 100 percent) as of 1997. Note that 27 percent of highland tradition populations (H'mong and Lisu) are now located in midland and lowland zones, whereas 42 percent of midland tradition populations (Karen and Lua) are located in the highland zone (usually near its lower boundary), where they outnumber traditional highland groups by a factor of four.

From an environmental viewpoint, the most important distinction between traditional groups is their agroecosystem management (Thomas 1996). Attention usually has focused on shifting cultivation, or swidden components of their systems: Highland groups are associated with pioneer swidden agriculture, midland groups with

*Table 16.3* Distribution of Ethnic Groups in the A S B site, by Altitude Zone, 1997

|  | Population | Distribution of Ethnic Groups Across Zones (%) | | |
|---|---|---|---|---|
|  |  | Highlands | Midlands | Lowlands |
| H'mong and Lisu | 6,192 | 73 | 12 | 15 |
| Karen and Lua | 42,900 | 42 | 47 | 11 |
| Thai | 18,820 | — | 3 | 97 |
| Total | 67,912 | 33 | 32 | 35 |
|  | Population | Ethnic Composition of Altitude Zones (%) | | |
|  |  | Highlands | Midlands | Lowlands |
| H'mong and Lisu | 6,192 | 20 | 3 | 4 |
| Karen and Lua | 42,900 | 80 | 94 | 19 |
| Thai | 18,820 | — | 3 | 77 |
| Total | 67,912 |  |  |  |

*Source:* Unpublished International Center for Research in Agroforestry and Ministry of Interior data.

established swidden agriculture, and lowland groups with northern Thai swidden agriculture (Sheng 1979). There has never been a basis for official recognition of forest fallow fields as a component of agricultural land holdings, and clearing of fields in a shifting cultivation system is officially viewed as forest destruction. Critics of these official views claim that when a new field is cleared—especially under established or rotational swidden agriculture—an old field is returned to fallow, resulting in no net deforestation. Although remote sensing can provide estimates of the proportion of an area that is cleared of forest at a given time, little is known about the impact on forest ecosystems of changing swidden agriculture practices.

## WATERSHED DEGRADATION

Many believe that groups practicing agriculture of different types in different altitude zones are damaging the watersheds they cultivate (Rerkasem and Rerkasem 1994; TDRI 1994; Thomas 1996; Tangtham 1999; Kaosa-ard 2000). Two primary concerns are reductions in the quantity and quality of watershed services and increased conflict over watershed services. Although these concerns are most urgent in northern Thailand, they are relevant throughout MMSEA, including portions of the Hong (Red), Mekong, Salween, Irawaddy, Yangtze, and Xi Jiang (Pearl) river systems (Kaosa-ard et al. 1995; CMU 1996; Revenga et al. 1998; Tangtham 1999).

### Reductions in the Quality and Quantity of Watershed Services

The mountains of northern Thailand are the headlands of the Chao Phraya river system, which nourishes Thailand's key rice (*Oryza sativa* L.) production areas in the central plains and the vast urban–industrial complex around Bangkok. Concern about deterioration of watershed services began in the 1960s when a group from the Kasetsart University Faculty of Forestry began research at three small highland subcatchments at Doi Pui. Findings through 1980 from a detailed set of studies suggest that the effects of swidden agriculture on stream flow, soil erosion, and water pollution were negative but modest, especially when compared with the effects on the same environmental parameters of more intensive forms of agriculture and the road construction and other activities associated with the human settlements that accompanied agricultural intensification (Chunkao et al. 1974, 1981; Lapudomlert et al. 1974; Prachoom et al. 1974; Aksornkoae et al. 1977; Chunkao 1983). Several follow-up studies have been undertaken (e.g., Royal Forest Department 1993; Vincent et al. 1995; Kaosa-ard 2000), but there is still insufficient socioeconomic and environmental information for comprehensive land use planning (Kaosa-ard 1996; Tangtham 1999). In particular, almost nothing is known about the effects of changes in product mix or production technology in mountain mosaic land use patterns on the quantity or quality of watershed services on-site or downstream or of the effects of such changes on the human welfare; both are key research questions for ASB.

### Conflict Between Resource User Groups

Growing environmental awareness combined with increasing demands for water by agriculture, cities, and industry are focusing attention on land use in upper watersheds (Hirsch 1997). Increasing competition for water resources among a growing range of stakeholders, combined with shortages of key data and limited access to existing knowledge, are fueling debate, conflict, and confrontation (Kaosa-ard 2000). Various schools of thought are developing, some of which appear to reject most scientific analysis, whereas others seem unable to integrate local knowledge regarding watershed management practices, water rights, and water use into policy debates. In order for water scarcity to prompt innovation, conservation, and efficiency, established and agreed-upon criteria for measuring and valuing resource stocks and flows are needed (Kaosa-ard 1996). Valuation and other measures should be developed using both traditional and contemporary tools and concepts. Organizations and institutions to manage disputes at various levels also must be strengthened. Meanwhile, because action programs must proceed with less-than-ideal knowledge, tools, and institutions, mechanisms must be developed to systematically distill lessons learned from ongoing successes and failures into future action programs.

## DETERMINANTS, EFFECTS, AND SPATIAL PATTERNS OF LAND USE

Three sets of factors contribute to land use and land cover change in northern Thailand: incentives and pressures for land use change, responses to these incentives and pressures by traditional mountain land use systems, and the spatial distribution of these responses.

## INCENTIVES AND PRESSURES FOR LAND USE CHANGE

Six interrelated factors influence incentives and pressures for land use change.

### Demographic Change

High population growth rates of mountain ethnic minority communities combined with migration to these areas from neighboring countries have increased the pressure of population on land (Rerkasem and Rerkasem 1994). In recent decades Thailand has been a safe haven and an economic magnet for many people in neighboring countries. Because many ethnic minority communities in the midlands and highlands are still being integrated into the formal Thai administration system, they are included only in recent demographic data. Table 16.2 presents estimates from the Hilltribe Welfare Division (1998) of mountain minority populations living above 600 m a.s.l. in 1997 at the benchmark, provincial, regional, and national levels. Although the mountain minority population represents only about 1 percent of the national population, almost all (92 percent) mountain minority members live in the northern region, and in the Mae Chaem site ethnic minorities represent more than half (64 percent) of the resident population.

Moreover, some mountain minority populations are the fastest-growing segment of the Thai population. Compared with estimates from the same source in 1972 (Kunstadter et al. 1978), highland groups have experienced population increases of nearly 10 percent per year, whereas midland groups have experienced growth rates of only about 2 and 3 percent in the north and in Chiang Mai province, respectively. This compares with an average annual growth rate of total population of approximately 2 percent in Chiang Mai and northern Thailand since 1972.

### Agricultural Change

Expansion of area dedicated to agriculture and changes in product mix have been brought about by opium crop replacement projects in the highlands and by the expansion of now–land-constrained lowland agroindustry (TDRI 1994). Work in northern Thailand on replacement of opium with intensive commercial crops was pioneered largely by projects under the king's patronage, followed by a set of public and private projects in various northern areas. Although some highland production activities (e.g., cabbages [*Brassica* spp.], barley [*Hordeum vulgare* L.], ginger [*Zingiber officinale* Roscoe], and some fruit crops) are now conducted through private channels, Royal

Project centers specializing in fruits, vegetables, or ornamental plants are under the umbrella of the Royal Project Foundation, and some products are marketed under their own Doi Kham brand name (for details see Royal Project Foundation 2002).

In addition to these project-motivated changes in product mix, expanding Thai agroindustry is being displaced in urbanizing lowland areas and is pushing field crop and horticultural production onto hillsides and into mountain valleys in the midland zone. Examples of products produced in these new areas include soybean (*Glycine max* [L.] Merr.), maize (*Zea mays* L.), potato (*Solanum tuberosum* L.), longan (*Dimocarpus longan* Lour.), mango (*Mangifera indica* L.), and lychee (*Litchi chinensis* Sonn.). Although these efforts often have the blessing of rural development and poverty reduction programs, success in achieving these program objectives has varied substantially spatially and over time and has been hampered generally by the high investment requirements, higher agricultural risk, and lower profitability characteristic of agriculture in marginal areas, especially when pursued under highly fluctuating economic conditions.

## Government Policy Incentives

Forest policy has resulted in the establishment of forest reserves, national parks, wildlife sanctuaries, and protected watershed forests that preclude formal recognition of private land ownership claims in most mountain areas. The importance of reserved and protected areas to populations living above 600 m a.s.l. is suggested in table 16.4. In some areas, land has been degazetted from reserved or protected status when local communities have demonstrated long-term residency and met other requirements. In all midland and highland areas, though, the absence of property rights may affect incentives to invest in more sustainable land management and agricultural activities. Note that the ASB benchmark site (Mae Chaem) is well placed to study issues asso-

*Table 16.4* Spatial Distribution of Populations Living Above 600 m Above Sea Level, by Geographic Area and Land Status, 1997

| Land Category | National | Northern Thailand | Chiang Mai | Mae Chaem |
|---|---|---|---|---|
| Reserved forest | 611,400 | 589,279 | 174,224 | 30,794 |
| National parks | 39,421 | 37,877 | 15,742 | 311 |
| Wildlife sanctuaries | 40,600 | 30,900 | 6,755 | — |
| No-hunting areas | 2,001 | 1,957 | 1,895 | — |
| Degazetted areas | 283,878 | 250,104 | 46,689 | 3,309 |
| Planned reserves | 8,322 | 8,322 | 8,322 | 4,615 |
| Military lands | 5,500 | — | — | — |
| Total | 991,122 | 918,439 | 253,672 | 39,029 |

*Source:* Adapted from Hilltribe Welfare Division (1998).

ciated with communities living in reserved forest, planned reserves and parks, and degazetted areas.

The perceived importance of watershed issues has prompted another set of policies directly related to land use in the mountainous areas of northern Thailand. A watershed classification system was developed and implemented throughout the country, initially under the aegis of the National Research Council and subsequently under the Ministry of Science, Technology, and Environment. Five watershed classes were identified using 1:50,000 scale topographic maps, and land use regulations were developed for each class; land use was most restricted in Class 1 areas and least restricted in Class 5 areas (Chunkao 1996).

Table 16.5 presents the spatial distribution of watershed classes nationally, for the northern region, for the Ping Basin, and for the ASB site located in the Ping Basin. Although proportions of land in classes with severe restrictions appear modest at national level, this proportion increases rapidly as one moves upstream. For example, although only 26 percent of the nation's land falls into Class 1 and Class 2 (the most limiting land use restriction categories), the proportion in these classes is twice that for the northern region and the Ping and climbs to about 90 percent in the Mae Chaem watershed, a major tributary of the Ping River.

But hydrologic services are not the only concern in mountainous areas. Illegal logging, production, and processing of narcotics and national security all contribute to the felt need for government policy action in midland and highland areas, and the sources of policy action are becoming more diverse. For example, whereas in the past rural poverty programs in the mountains have been conducted largely through the Public Welfare Department, in the contexts of special projects, or by missionaries (Renard et al. 1988), since constitutional reform was enacted in 1997 rural development decision making has been shifting to elected local governments. Various new provisions that shift responsibility and authority for watershed management from national to local policymakers, including a community forestry law, are now being considered by Parliament.

*Table 16.5* Distribution of Land by Watershed Class at National and Subnational Levels

| Geographic Area | Distribution of Land by Watershed Classification (%) | | | | |
|---|---|---|---|---|---|
| | Class 1 | Class 2 | Class 3 | Class 4 | Class 5 |
| Thailand | 18.1 | 8.3 | 7.7 | 15.8 | 49.0 |
| North | 32.6 | 15.0 | 10.8 | 9.5 | 31.8 |
| Ping Basin | 38.3 | 14.2 | 9.6 | 8.9 | 28.3 |
| Mae Chaem (ASB site) | | | | | |
| Overall | 63.9 | 25.0 | 8.7 | 1.8 | 0.7 |
| Highlands | 82.6 | 14.5 | 2.9 | 0.0 | — |
| Midlands | 54.7 | 32.4 | 10.2 | 2.7 | — |
| Lowlands | 17.7 | 41.9 | 28.2 | 6.0 | 6.1 |

Area covered by water are not included in this table, so rows do not sum to 100%.

*Sources:* Chunkao (1996), International Center for Research in Agroforestry unpublished data.

## Infrastructure Development, Market Access, and Public Services

Programs to eradicate opium production and to promote national security have increased efforts to expand road infrastructure in mountain regions. Expanded road networks have had direct and indirect negative environmental effects; road construction and roads themselves disrupt ecosystems, and improved access to forests can fuel illicit logging and forest extraction operations. On the other hand, roads have brought market access for alternative cash crop production to many remote areas. Expansion of public services is another public policy objective, including registration of minority communities, the provision of improved education and health services, and increased access to electricity and mass media, all of which increase opportunities to integrate these communities into national society.

## Urbanization, Industrialization, and Tourism

Tourism, resorts, and recreational facilities are bringing new claims, pressures, and opportunities to mountain areas (Dearden 1996). Urbanization and industrialization have also begun affecting various aspects of life and decision making in mountainous areas. For example, land in these areas is coming to be valued as a tradable commodity and a store of wealth rather than simply an input into an agricultural production process (Thomas 1996). The consequences of this shift for land values, land use, poverty, and environmental services are not known.

## Environmentalism

Rapid growth of environmental awareness has been associated with both a populist element calling for more local control over natural resource management and a more ecocentric element that believes local communities should be excluded from protected areas for the longer-term benefit of larger society. Although these two factions were allies during the early emergence of the environmental movement into the national public policy arena, they have since split into camps that often oppose each other (Thomas 1997). Tension between these elements is substantial and growing and occasionally breaks out into open conflict.

## EFFECTS OF INCENTIVES AND PRESSURES ON TRADITIONAL MOUNTAIN LAND USE SYSTEMS

The effects of these incentives and pressures on the natural resource base and on human welfare are conditioned by the traditional land use systems developed for specific altitude zones and by ethnic groups that practice them. Three general categories of traditional systems have evolved in the mountain ecosystems of northern Thailand: highland, midland, and lowland. These systems reflect the natural forest types that exist in the area—which are strongly associated with altitude, as modified by geology, aspect, fire, and other factors—and the cultural diversity of the region (Grandstaff 1976; Kunstadter et al. 1978; Schmidt-Vogt 1999). Table 16.6 presents some of the basic features of these three altitude-specific zones, as of about 1960, that are important for understanding the distribution of resources, people, and activities in northern Thailand and other parts of the MMSEA.

Traditional highland land use systems are generally characterized as pioneer systems and are practiced by mobile villages using long cropping cycles and very long "abandoned" forest fallow cycles that are viable only in areas with small populations with access to extensive areas (Grandstaff 1976; Kunstadter et al. 1978; Sheng 1979).

Traditional midland land use systems are associated with more established villages and systematic, short cropping cycles, long rotational forest fallow systems that often include paddy rice land where topography and water allow, and systematic management of landscape components including areas kept under permanent forest cover (Grandstaff 1976; Kunstadter et al. 1978; Chammarik and Santasombat 1993; Thomas et al. 2000). Some of these managed forest parcels include miang or jungle tea production, where *Camellia sinensis* L. is planted as an understory tree in hill evergreen forest. Leaves are steamed and sold with or without fermentation for chewing as a traditional stimulant. Livestock also grazes in these midland systems (Preechapanya 1996, 2001).

Traditional lowland land use systems have focused largely on irrigated paddy rice production and home gardens (Preechapanya 2001), sometimes with supplemental short-fallow cropping practiced on nearby slopes.

*Table 16.6* General Features of Traditional Land Use Systems, by Altitude Zone and Natural Forest Type

| Zone Label | Altitude Range (m a.s.l.) | Natural Forest | Ethnic Groups | Traditional Agricultural Practices |
|---|---|---|---|---|
| Highlands | 1000–1800 | Hill evergreen and coniferous | H'mong, Lisu, Akha, other | Pioneer shifting cultivation (perhaps with opium) |
| | 1000–1200 | | Thai, Karen | Jungle tea (in some areas) |
| Midlands | 600–1000 | Mixed deciduous | Lua, Karen | Paddy (limited) and rotational long-fallow shifting cultivation |
| Lowlands | <600 | Dry deciduous and swamp | Thai | Paddy, gardens (perhaps with short-fallow shifting cultivation) |

*Source:* Adapted from International Center for Research in Agroforestry and Royal Forest Department unpublished data.

As indicated earlier, over the past 30 years or more, the incentives and pressures for change have altered product mix and production technology within and across the traditional altitude zones, with consequences for producers, consumers, and the environment (Chammarik and Santasombat 1993; Rerkasem and Rerkasem 1994; TDRI 1994; Thong-ngam et al. 1996; Kaosa-ard 2000; Thomas et al. 2000, 2002; Thomas 2001). Table 16.7 (and the following text) summarizes these changes.

• **Highlands.** Pioneer shifting cultivation and opium production have been largely replaced by commercial vegetable production that is now pushing from the highlands down into the midlands (TDRI 1994). There is growing downstream concern about impacts on stream flow, erosion, and pesticide water pollution.

• **Midlands.** Pressures from population growth, expanding lowland and highland systems, and government policy have reduced land availability, often resulting in much shorter forest fallow cycles and some conversion to permanent fields. In some cases, sacred tree groves are being threatened.

• **Lowlands.** Field crop production systems, and in some cases orchards, have moved from lowland areas into forested watersheds above rice paddies and are pushing up into the midland zone.

## SPATIAL DISTRIBUTION OF LAND USE CHANGE

Neither the factors influencing land use change nor the changes themselves are distributed uniformly within or between altitude zones. Estimates of the proportions of

*Table 16.7* Changes in Land Use and Their Consequences, by Altitude Zone

| Zone Label | Altitude Range (m.a.s.l.) | New Land Uses | Producer and Consumer Issues | Environmental Issues |
|---|---|---|---|---|
| Highland | 1000–1800 | Commercial horticulture, grasslands, forest plantations | Crop markets, land security | Deforestation, reduced stream flow, water pollution |
| | 1000–1200 | Jungle tea (in some areas) | Crop markets, land security | Less forest buffer |
| Midlands | 600–1000 | Paddy (limited) and short-rotation shifting cultivation, permanent upland fields | Food security, land security, crop markets | Deforestation, reduced stream flow, water pollution |
| Lowlands | <600 | Paddy, gardens, upland field crops, orchards | Crop markets, irrigation water, land security | Deforestation, reduced stream flow, water pollution |

*Source:* Adapted from International Center for Research in Agroforestry and Royal Forest Department unpublished data.

*Table 16.8* Distribution of Land Cover Type, by Geographic Area, 1990

| Geographic Area | Proportion of Total Area (%) | | |
| --- | --- | --- | --- |
| | Forest | Agriculture | Nonforest |
| Thailand | 27.3 | 41.2 | 31.5 |
| Northern Thailand | 46.4 | 28.0 | 25.6 |
| Mae Chaem (A S B) | 79.4 | 1.5 | 19.0 |
| Highlands | 81.5 | 0.4 | 18.1 |
| Midlands | 74.8 | 1.6 | 23.7 |
| Lowlands | 85.4 | 7.5 | 7.1 |

*Sources:* Adapted from Charuppat (1998) (Royal Forest Department) and unpublished International Center for Research in Agroforestry data.

land in forest, agriculture, and other nonforest categories at national, regional, and site levels are presented in table 16.8. As one moves from the nation to the watershed level, forest cover increases (e.g., from 27 to 46 to 79 percent) and area dedicated to agriculture decreases (e.g., from 41 to 28 to 1.5 percent). Within Mae Chaem, roughly similar patterns occur among altitude zones that comprise the site. One must be cautious in interpreting such data, however, because issues of measurement error loom large, especially for midland and highland land systems; boundaries of components of these systems are located using remote sensing techniques that have difficulty distinguishing between some system components, such as between fallow and forest cover.

*Table 16.9* Subdistricts of the Mae Chaem Benchmark Watershed, by Altitude Zone

| Subdistrict Labels | Total Area (ha) | Altitude Zones (percentage of total land) | | | Land Use Features |
| --- | --- | --- | --- | --- | --- |
| | | Highlands | Midlands | Lowlands | |
| Ban Chan | 18,504 | 92 | 8 | — | High-value horticulture |
| Chaem Luang | 24,851 | 84 | 15 | — | Med-SC, veg., park |
| Pang Hin Fon | 24,167 | 75 | 25 | — | Short-SC, veg., park |
| Mae Daet | 16,453 | 70 | 31 | — | Med-SC, veg., park |
| Mae Suk | 68,200 | 60 | 38 | 3 | Med-SC, veg. |
| Mae Na Chon | 72,545 | 45 | 51 | 3 | Short-SC, veg., park |
| Ban Tub | 40,647 | 36 | 53 | 11 | Short-SC, veg., park |
| Kong Khaek | 36,918 | 18 | 61 | 21 | Fixed fields, park |
| Ta Pha | 10,672 | 25 | 45 | 30 | Fixed fields, park |
| Chang Koeng | 19,961 | 22 | 52 | 26 | Town, fixed fields, park |
| Total | 332,918 | 51 | 41 | 7 | |

Med-SC, medium-cycle, shifting cultivation; veg., vegetable crop production; park, parkland; short-SC, short-cycle shifting cultivation.
*Sources:* Adapted from unpublished Royal Forest Department, International Center for Research in Agroforestry, and Care-Thailand data and unpublished Ministry of Interior data.

Policy domains can also influence spatial patterns of land use. For example, the 4000-km$^2$ Mae Chaem watershed can be disaggregated into administrative subdistricts, or tambons, ten of which make up about 90 percent of the watershed. These subdistricts are increasingly important decision-making units for natural resource management, especially since the 1997 constitution changes that delegated power and responsibility for many such decisions to local authorities. Table 16.9 indicates the relative size of these subdistricts, how their land is distributed between altitude zones, and a few major features of land use within their domains. Differences within altitude ranges across subdistricts are explained by natural factors such as geology and geography and by policy decisions related to road access, current and past project activities, and government programs.

## EFFORTS TO ADAPT TO CHANGING CONDITIONS

In response to these incentives, pressures, and resulting patterns of change, innovative farmers and pilot projects have been seeking ways to improve livelihoods while reducing pressure on forests and protected watersheds. Some of these are local efforts by individual households or local leaders, and others are facilitated or promoted by projects executed at various scales by government agencies or nongovernment organizations (NGOS) (TDRI 1994; Thomas 1996; Kaosa-ard 2000). ASB Thailand seeks to learn from, build on, and support such efforts. In addition to the continuing efforts of the Royal Project Foundation, several projects are providing useful insights regarding organized efforts to influence land use change.

### SAM MUN PROJECT

One particularly noteworthy project is the 1987 to 1994 Sam Mun Highland Development Project (hereafter called the Sam Mun Project), an interagency project led by the Royal Forest Department in collaboration with the Office of the Narcotics Control Board, with funding assistance from the United Nations Drug Control Program and the Ford Foundation (Limchoowong 1994; Thomas 1997). The 2000-km$^2$ project area is located in the midland and highland zones of a ridge of mountains beginning northwest of Chiang Mai City and extends to the Myanmar border. This area, like some of the ridges in the ASB Thailand benchmark watershed, was once an important opium production area; opium poppies occupied more than 800 ha in 1989. Although one of the last internationally supported projects focusing on opium crop substitution, it is generally recognized as the most effective and the most integrated in its approach. Its Thai leaders made serious efforts to learn from previous projects, and even academics usually very critical of forestry policies and projects have recognized the value of their approach (Ganjanapan 1997:208).

To paraphrase a former project director, the Sam Mun Project focused on strengthening the capacity of community organizations so they could be self-reliant in managing their communities, food supplies, and natural resources (soil, water, and forest) in a manner that was appropriate to their lifestyles and values, ensured community stability, and developed their community and environment in response to local needs and government policies, including reductions in opium production (Limchoowong 1994:11). The project assumed that people and forests could live in harmony and emphasized food self-sufficiency, income generation, reduced use of chemicals in agriculture, reduced swidden agriculture, increased forest protection, initiation of watershed management networks, and the development of tools for local land use planning. Many of the methods and tools pioneered by this project, such as participatory land use planning (PLP, explained later in this chapter) (Tan-kim-yong et al. 1994) and three-dimensional village land use models, are now being used and further adapted by projects in Thailand and neighboring countries. In addition to promoting important changes in land use in the project area (e.g., area under shifting cultivation was reduced by more than 80 percent and forest cover more than doubled; Tan-kim-yong et al. 1994), the project also helped communities gain access to health and education services, citizenship, and infrastructure improvements needed to implement their development plans. Finally, as regards opium production, the project was highly successful; area dedicated to opium decreased by about 90 percent from 1989 to 1994 (figure 16.2).

## QUEEN SIRIKIT FOREST DEVELOPMENT PROJECT (*SUAN PAH SIRIKIT*)

Building on previous smaller-scale efforts, this interagency project in the Mae Chaem watershed has been conducted under the patronage of H.M. the Queen of

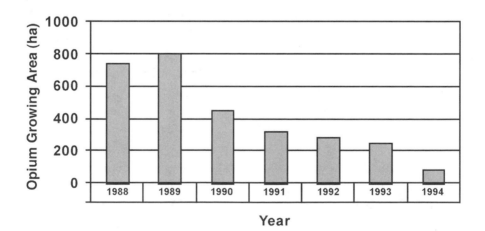

*Figure 16.2* Opium-growing area in the Sam Mun Highland Development Project, by year (Limchoowong 1994).

Thailand since 1996 (Suan Pah Sirikit Project 2000). The Royal Forest Department has a leading role in implementation through its ten watershed management units in the area. The project philosophy is that people can live in harmony with the forest through community participation in conservation and forest resource development. Collaboration between villagers and government agencies in developing and implementing local land use plans is viewed as essential to improving livelihoods in ways that protect watershed headlands. Initial work began in response to rapid deforestation after the end of a foreign-funded project in the late 1980s that, despite major reductions in opium production and some useful innovations, had no lasting positive impact on watershed management. The Suan Pah Sirikit project has built on promising innovations and adapted several participatory methods and tools used in the Sam Mun Project, along with experience from various Royal Projects and other sources.

## CARE-THAILAND INTEGRATED NATURAL RESOURCES CONSERVATION PROJECT

The Integrated Natural Resources Conservation Project sought to conserve watersheds in the northern provinces of Chiang Mai (Mae Chaem district) and Mae Hong Son that had been degraded by illegal logging, forest fires, and agricultural expansion. From 1994 to 1999 the project worked with local communities to promote sustainable agriculture and the improved management of fragile watershed forests. Project components included agroforestry, soil and water conservation, paddy rice and fish pond development, and nonfarm income-generating activities. Project partners included the Royal Forest Department, agencies of the Ministry of Agriculture and Cooperatives, and the local governments. They also worked closely with Chiang Mai University to study and implement approaches for promoting community participation in sustainable land use. The project provided valuable assistance during establishment of the ASB Thailand benchmark site, and ASB is a partner in the implementation of their follow-on project focusing on strengthening local institutions associated with natural resource management launched in 2000.

## OTHER DEVELOPMENT AND CONSERVATION PROJECTS

The ASB Thailand is also seeking to learn from the experience of previous projects, including the Thai–German Highland Development Project, the Thai–Australian Highland Development Project, and the Thai–U.S. Agency for International Development Mae Chaem Development Project, and from other current efforts being conducted by Thai NGOs, local groups, and government agencies.

# PROMISING AGRICULTURAL INNOVATIONS

Drawing on experience of these projects, including numerous examples of ideas and adaptations that came directly from farmers, among the most promising technical approaches to improving livelihoods while reducing pressure on forest or watersheds are those that focused on decreasing the area dedicated to upland rice production and those that increased trees on the landscape.

## MEETING FOOD SECURITY NEEDS WITH LESS AREA DEDICATED TO RICE PRODUCTION

Three approaches have been proposed for meeting food needs while decreasing the total area dedicated to food production, all of which presume that agricultural intensification will reduce pressure on forests.

### Expanding Paddy Rice Production

Preliminary findings suggest that expansion of irrigated paddy rice land, in the small niches where terrain and water resources allow, can greatly reduce land dedicated to upland rice production. Given the higher productivity per hectare of paddy rice compared with upland rice, every hectare of paddy rice added can reduce by 10–20 ha the amount of upland rice area needed to meet food needs, depending on paddy yields and the length of the swidden fallow cycle. The response by farmers to paddy rice incentives provided by the Sam Mun Project was substantial (Limchoowong 1994), especially during the initial phase of the project (figure 16.3).

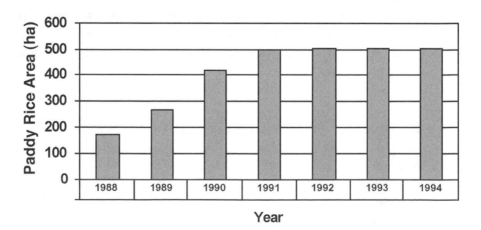

*Figure 16.3* Paddy rice area in the Sam Mun Highland Development Project, by year (Limchoowong 1994).

Preliminary data from a range of sites in the ASB benchmark watershed (Thomas et al. 2002) indicate that paddy rice production is much more profitable than upland rice production (in short fallow or permanent field systems), primarily because of high labor needs for weeding, the cost of chemical inputs, and the low productivity and higher variability of upland fields. Experiments have also been launched under ASB using new rice varieties to explore the possibility and potential impacts of double-cropping of rice in midland paddies.

## Permanent Field Upland Rice Production

In areas in the Suan Pah Sirikit Project where terrain or water availability does not allow sufficient expansion of paddy to meet local food needs, some farmers have developed a crop rotation system for permanent upland fields in which upland rice is rotated with soybean every third year. This has allowed farmers to reduce substantially the total area needed for upland rice production and has also provided a new source of income from the sale of soybeans. Land taken out of upland rice is converted to permanent community-protected forest. Farmers who have used this system for up to 10 years report no decline in yields. Because of the need for purchased inputs (at least fertilizer and herbicides), however, profitability is lower than in medium- to long-cycle forest fallow systems. Although forest fallows as short as 5 years can be sustainable without chemical inputs (Wangpakapattanawong 2001), yields are much lower than those in 10-year cycles (Thomas et al. 2002), which are now increasingly rare. Moreover, low soybean prices have caused many farmers to switch to maize as their main cash crop; it is not yet clear whether or how this substitution will affect sustainability or farmer incomes. The ASB Thailand is conducting agronomic and economic studies of this system.

## Permanent Fields of High-Value Commercial Vegetables

This approach involves meeting food security needs by generating cash income and is particularly suited to highland areas where the climate supports production of temperate zone vegetables. One example of this approach is the Ban Chan subdistrict of Mae Chaem, where a project of the Royal Project Foundation has been operating for many years (Royal Project Staff 1999). There, many villagers are producing high-value specialty vegetables that are marketed largely through the Royal Project. These intensive systems use much less land than shifting cultivation, and although profits can be quite high, crops suffer from periodic severe damage caused by pests and weather shocks. Drastic price fluctuations also affect profits. Many villagers are responding to these factors by diversifying their production into two or more crops (B. Ekasingh, unpublished data 1999), in some cases including fruit trees. Land use change in this area is being studied in depth (Peters 2000), where traditional forms of shifting cultivation are now quite rare and land ownership has largely been privatized. These and other cash crop systems with various degrees of diversification are also components of land use patterns found in other areas of the watershed (Thomas et al. 2002).

But vegetable production can damage the environment. For example, highland cabbage production has come under strong criticism because of planting on steep slopes (and consequent soil erosion) and the heavy application of pesticides (and consequent water pollution) (Tangtham 1999). Projects are trying to introduce soil conservation practices and alternative pest management strategies, but with little success so far (Royal Project Foundation 2002).

## IMPROVING LIVELIHOODS THROUGH AGROFORESTRY

There have been three major approaches to increasing the number of trees on midland and highland landscapes.

### Simple Agroforestry

This approach has centered on inducing farmers to plant fruit trees in fields, following approaches pioneered by the Royal Project. In the highlands, temperate zone fruits such as Japanese apricot (*Prunus mume* Siebold & Zuccarini), Japanese plum (*Prunus salicina* Lindley), Asian pear (*Pyrus pyrifolia* [N.L. Burman]), and persimmon (*Diospyros* spp.) were introduced. In the midlands, subtropical fruits such as lychee were introduced. Results of efforts to encourage fruit tree production in the Sam Mun Project are presented in figure 16.4. These data probably understate the full impact of agroforestry inducement efforts because many trees were also planted in areas that

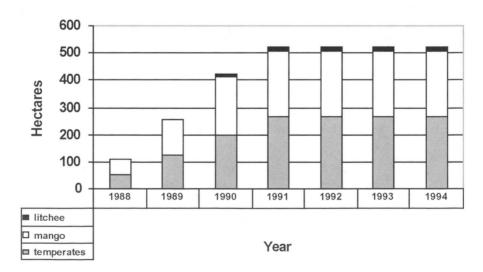

*Figure 16.4* Area in fruit trees in the Sam Mun Highland Project, by year (Limchoowong 1994). *Temperates* refers to temperate zone fruits (e.g., plums, apricots, pears).

were not included in agroforestry area tallies, such as around houses and along field boundaries. Note that the gains were largest during the initial phase of the project; further planting has continued after the end of the project. A preliminary ASB study of fruit tree agroforestry in Sam Mun Project areas reports a substantial range of strategies and planting configurations (Withrow-Robinson et al. 1998; Withrow-Robinson 2000).

## Complex Agroforests

The primary example of an indigenous complex agroforest in northern Thailand is the miang or jungle tea plantations embedded in hill evergreen forest (described in Preechapanya 1996, 2001). Although changing consumption patterns especially among young consumers have decreased demand, prices for miang tea appear to have recovered from the low levels of the early 1990s, and many producers now claim that their biggest problems are finding hired labor and fuelwood needed to process the tea. The Sam Mun Project had some success in helping Karen producers manage debt and obtain higher product prices.

An interesting variant of this system with potentially large implications for development projects has been observed among farmers in an area adjacent to the Sam Mun Project area (Castillo 1990). There, farmers have gradually transformed miang complex agroforests by substituting fruit trees and seed crops for many or most of the forest and tea trees. During this process farmers are careful to maintain a very complex structure that mimics the complexity of the original tea forest system (Tanpanich 1997).

## Community-Managed Forests

This approach seeks to expand the area of permanent forest that local communities protect and manage as components of their overall mosaic agroforestry landscapes (Thomas et al. 2000, 2002; Thomas 2001). Efforts build on traditional concepts and beliefs of midland groups (in particular) to find ways to maintain traditionally conserved forest areas (Chammarik and Santasombat 1993), convert forest fallow in fragile areas to permanent forest, or reforest degraded areas by planting trees or protecting areas where natural regeneration is occurring. In the context of the Sam Mun Project, the forest department reforested 4855 ha using standard planting techniques. Villagers responded by using these techniques to recover 242 ha but chose to protect the natural regeneration of nearly 60,000 additional hectares (Limchoowong 1994). The keys to the success of this approach were reaching a clear mutual agreement on land use plans and establishing active community participation in controlling access, use, fires, and other factors. Although the project was initially successful, researchers and others are concerned that communities that switch from shifting cultivation to permanent forest cover will lose access to important natural products they obtained from forest fallow fields during intermediate stages of regeneration (Thomas et al. 2002). Natural products are a strategically important livelihood component for many mountain households (Nawichai 2000; Preechapanya 2001).

A fourth type of innovation quietly developed primarily by local farmers themselves is just beginning to emerge. Various examples of reduced-fallow upland rice systems that use improved fallow management to maintain higher yields are being documented and explored (Rerkasem et al. 2002).

## PROMISING INSTITUTIONAL INNOVATIONS

Although technological advances can help induce land use change, institutional changes are also needed. Three important examples follow.

### Land Use Planning

Pilot experiments have shown that it is possible to reach mutually acceptable land use agreements between villagers and agency officials using participatory methods (Kaosa-ard 2000). Pioneering efforts under the Sam Mun Project developed the now widely accepted approach known as participatory land use planning (PLP). In the words of its chief architect, "PLP can be defined as an operational tool or process which creates conditions of frequent communication and analytical discussions, hence strengthening local organizations by generating common understandings and shared rights and responsibilities among project partners, who carry out activities that lead to the solving of local forest management problems and other related community problems" (Tan-kim-yong et al. 1994:6). The conceptual framework of PLP focuses on identifying and resolving conflicts associated with natural resource management and development. Establishing a broad set of objectives and setting in place institutions to achieve them entails changes in the roles and responsibilities of stakeholders, both of which can emerge as parties come to understand each others' positions. Open access to information for all participants, involvement of a third party as moderator or facilitator, and the presence of long-term community workers were all essential ingredients to success. One overarching objective was to help upland villagers become active participants in watershed forest protection rather than unwilling subjects of government control.

Once basic agreements were reached, villagers articulated their own sets of rules, penalties for violation, and mechanisms for enforcement. Local penalties often included fines substantially higher than those imposed by lowland law, and communities subsequently proved their willingness and ability to enforce their rules. When outsiders challenged village rules and their right to enforce them, local leaders sought assistance from project staff or local authorities.

Various tools were used to help facilitate this process and to document mutual agreements that were reached. Particularly useful tools include scale contour maps and scale three-dimensional models of the local landscape, which served as a centerpiece for discussions and negotiations and as a clear and accessible record of changes in land use zones and forest use rights that were established through mutual agreement. This approach and its tools are being adapted and refined by various projects, including those conducted by ASB pilot project partners in Mae Chaem (Thomas et al. 2000, 2002).

## Watershed Management Networks

With increased levels of upstream–downstream conflict over water use and quality being encountered in many areas, projects and organizations are promoting watershed management networks. Projects have experimented with local, multivillage and multi–ethnic group watershed management networks to coordinate land use management across areas that sometimes comprise several subwatersheds. Building on earlier work, the Sam Mun Project facilitated the establishment of watershed networks and encouraged groups to formulate their own rules, penalties, and enforcement mechanisms (Limchoowong 1994). The approach was basically an application of the PLP process at a broader scale and involved communities already familiar with PLP at village level. A recent study suggests that watershed management networks can be institutionally sustainable even after project establishment funds and guidance are withdrawn (Kaosa-ard 2000).

## Constitutional and Legal Reform

Under the 1997 constitution and related legal reforms, opportunities are emerging that may allow arrangements such as those being formulated and mapped using PLP to gain formal recognition. Examples include the constitutional provision for local participation in natural resource management, a set of laws and programs to strengthen elected local governments, and community forestry legislation now under consideration by Parliament. Yet practical issues of implementation remain unresolved. For example, it is not clear how to strengthen embryonic subdistrict governments often found in poor mountain ethnic minority areas, nor have effective and efficient methods been discovered for agencies such as the forest department to interact with the thousands of local government entities in these areas.

## ASB IN THAILAND

As we have seen, land use in northern Thailand is in transition. Although this transition has had some negative environmental consequences and conflicts between stakeholders are becoming more numerous and intense, a growing body of experience suggests that the ongoing land use transition can generate environmental and welfare benefits and that policy has a role in managing the direction and pace of change. However, effective and efficient natural resource management is hampered by gaps in knowledge and insufficient methods and tools. The Royal Forest Department has given a mandate to ASB Thailand to assist in addressing these issues.

To facilitate ASB collaboration, the Royal Forest Department has officially established the Northern Mountain Area Agroforestry Systems Research and Development Project, an open-ended project with a national steering committee and administrative support. The project facilitates interdisciplinary, multi-institutional research by the ASB Thailand Consortium in subject areas of mutual interest in Thailand, collaboration with international researchers, and information exchange (Thomas 2002). The ASB Thailand seeks to build on existing knowledge and experience, to strengthen ongoing research and development efforts by identifying and filling strategic gaps in knowledge, and to undertake pilot project testing to improve policies and expand adoption of promising approaches. Particular emphasis is on landscape agroforestry in upper tributary watershed areas (Thomas 2001). Key partners in the Mae Chaem watershed include the Suan Pah Sirikit Project and the Collaborative Natural Resources Management Project launched by Care-Thailand and the Raks Thai Foundation. The ASB Thailand consortium expects to make major contributions in five areas.

## Measuring and Predicting the Costs, Benefits, and Tradeoffs of Land Use Change

One of the key weaknesses of pilot efforts to improve land use technologies has been the lack of data on their effects on local livelihoods or environmental services (watershed services, biodiversity, and climate change). These data are essential for measuring the tradeoffs between these societal objectives and for assessing the prospects for longer-term sustainability. Moreover, this information is critical for formulating and justifying changes in land use and forestry policies. Therefore, the first stage of ASB Thailand's research activities has focused on providing such data by completing the ASB matrix for important and emerging land use systems in northern Thailand (Buddhaboon 2000; Gillison and Liswanti 2000; Thomas et al. 2002).

## Addressing Policy Issues at the Landscape Scale

The second major ASB research activity focuses on scaling up these analyses to levels that are ecologically, economically, and politically relevant for mountain areas of northern Thailand. At this more aggregate level, broader land use mosaic patterns become relevant, and the socioeconomic and biophysical interactions that occur at that level become parts of the research agenda. One study of two villages in the Sam Mun Project found that although villagers perceived substantial improvement in forest components of their landscape over the past decade, water and wild animals have become more scarce, prompting farmer concerns regarding future food and economic security (Kao-sa-ard 2000). Access to natural products was a factor that interacted with various forms of social capital in shaping the response to and impact of the Asian economic crisis on mountain households and communities in Mae Chaem (Geran 2001).

Expanding on pioneering work (Ekasingh et al. 1996), studies in several subwatersheds of the ASB site with different land use mosaics are being conducted. One of the next major tasks will be to identify suitable criteria for assessing livelihood and environmental impacts and potential carrying capacities of major types of land use mosaics. These criteria must be associated with standards that accurately reflect management goals and indicators that can be used to assess current status and progress toward meeting those goals. We also seek to understand the socioeconomic, biophysical, and political factors that influence the establishment and maintenance of major land use mosaics (Thomas et al. 2002). A geographic information system (GIS) for the ASB Thailand benchmark watershed is in place (Thomas et al. 2000). Future work will use this system to develop and validate analytical models capable of predicting the effects of policy and technology changes on the adoption and performance of alternative land use mosaics in agroforestry landscapes.

## INFORMATION SYSTEMS TO SUPPORT LAND USE PLANNING, WATERSHED NETWORKS, AND LOCAL GOVERNANCE

The third major area of activity is to develop and test methods to support local institutions, government agencies, and NGOs involved in the development and implementation of land use plans and watershed management networks (Kaosa-ard 2000). Particular emphasis is placed on establishing criteria for use in negotiating, establishing, and monitoring local land use agreements developed using PLP; developing and disseminating simple tools based on science and local knowledge to measure effects of land use change on watershed functions at local level for use in resolving local disputes and documenting local conditions; and developing information systems to monitor compliance and provide transparency and accountability in enforcing land use agreements and to monitor welfare and environmental conditions. Pilot efforts have developed a simplified GIS node in Mae Chaem to link PLP land use maps with ASB's GIS system in Chiang Mai to support ongoing local planning activities and to monitor compliance with existing local land use agreements in upper watershed areas. An expanding number of local pilot watershed management networks in Mae Chaem are also using basic tools to monitor watershed functions (Thomas et al. 2000, 2002).

## MOVING BEYOND THE BENCHMARK SITE

In collaboration with the Royal Forest Department and other organizations and agencies, ASB Thailand will provide technical support for the formulation and implementation of larger-scale pilot activities beyond the benchmark site. The primary objective of this activity is to improve the capacity of the forest department and related natural resource management groups and institutions to design, implement, and assess the impacts of programs throughout Thailand.

## INTERNATIONAL RESEARCH COLLABORATION AND INFORMATION EXCHANGE

The final major area of ASB activity aims to facilitate information exchange and collaboration with groups conducting related work in neighboring countries of MMSEA and at other ASB sites (Thomas 2001, 2002). Our vision is to help strengthen Thailand's ability to function as a peer-to-peer node, both contributing to and benefiting from the emerging global web of scientific infrastructure aimed at addressing rural poverty, land use, and environmental issues. The Royal Forest Department is working closely with the International Center for Research in Agroforestry and ASB Thailand to further develop and strengthen specific partnerships and activities to accomplish this goal.

## CONCLUSION

Land use in upper tributary watersheds in northern Thailand is in transition. Ecological and cultural diversity in these mountainous areas have led to the development over many years of altitude zone–specific traditional land use systems that comprise both permanent and shifting agriculture practices alongside and within forests. An array of local, regional, national, and international factors have combined recently to put pressure on these traditional systems and landscapes. In response, land uses are changing, and the poor in these areas may not be prepared to manage or benefit from these changes. Indeed, little is known about how to improve traditional systems and practices in the zones for which they were developed, and perhaps more important, we cannot predict the environmental and human welfare consequences of agricultural activities suited for one zone but being practiced in another. In addition, there is growing concern about the downstream environmental and other consequences of land use change in upland landscapes. Although some pilot development projects are demonstrating the effectiveness of participatory approaches to improved land use management in these areas and the environmental and welfare benefits of certain types of land use change that can emerge, there is still inadequate knowledge to assess the feasibility and implications of efforts to replicate or scale up these approaches. Mechanisms to monitor and assess their longer-term impacts and effectiveness over large areas are not in place. Finally, the role of government and civil society at all levels in managing land use transitions in the mountainous areas must be reviewed and refined. The ASB's research, capacity strengthening, and outreach activities in Thailand address these issues.

# REFERENCES

Aksornkoae, S., S. Boonyawat, and P. Dhanmanonda. 1977. Plant succession in relation to sediment in different areas after shifting cultivation at Doi Pui, Chiangmai. (In Thai.) Kog-ma Watershed Res. Bull. 31. Faculty of For., Kasetsart Univ., Bangkok, Thailand.

Buddhaboon, C. 2000. Methane emission from various land use types in Mae Chaem watershed. M.S. thesis. Chiang Mai Univ., Chiang Mai, Thailand.

Castillo, D. 1990. Analysis of the sustainability of a forest-tea production system: A case study in Ban Kui Tui, Tambon Pa Pae, Mae Taeng District, Chiang Mai Province. M.S. thesis. Chiang Mai Univ., Chiang Mai, Thailand.

Center for Agricultural Information. 1998. Agricultural statistics of Thailand, crop year 1996/97. Agric. Statistics Publ. 18/1998. Office of Agric. Econ., Ministry of Agric. and Coop., Bangkok, Thailand.

Center for Agricultural Statistics. 1994. Land use for agriculture. (In Thai.) Agric. Statistics Publ. 449. Office of Agric. Econ., Ministry of Agric. and Coop., Bangkok, Thailand.

Chammarik, S., and Y. Santasombat (eds.). 1993. Community forestry in Thailand: Development perspectives. 3 vol. (In Thai.) Local Dev. Inst., Bangkok, Thailand.

Charuppat, T. 1998. Forest situation of Thailand in the past 37 years (1961–1998). (In Thai.) Forest Resources Assessment Division, Forest Research Office, Royal Forest Department, Bangkok.

Chunkao, K. 1983. Final report: Research on hydrological evaluation of land use factors related to water yields in the highlands as a basis for selecting substitute crops for opium poppy, 1980–83. Highland Agric. Project. Kasetsart Univ., Bangkok, Thailand.

Chunkao, K. 1996. Principles of watershed management. (In Thai.) Kasetsart Univ., Bangkok, Thailand.

Chunkao, K., P. Santudgarn, and N. Tangtham. 1974. Effects of shifting cultivation on some physical properties of hill evergreen forest soils. (In Thai.) Kog-ma Watershed Res. Stn. Bull. 19. Faculty of For., Kasetsart Univ., Bangkok, Thailand.

Chunkao, K., N. Tangtham, S. Boonyawat, and W. Niyom. 1981. Watershed management research on mountainous land, 15-year tentative rep., 1966–80. (In Thai.) Dep. of Conserv., Faculty of For. Kasetsart Univ., Bangkok, Thailand.

CMU (Chiang Mai University) Forest Research Office, Royal Forestry Department, Bangkok, Thailand. 1996. Montane mainland Southeast Asia in transition. Proceedings of an International Symposium, 12–16 Nov. 1995. Chiang Mai Univ., Chiang Mai, Thailand.

Dearden, P. 1996. Trekking in northern Thailand: Impact distribution and evolution over time. pp. 204–225. *In* M. Parnwell. (ed.) Uneven development in Thailand. Avebury, Ashgate Publ. Ltd., Aldershot, England.

Ekasingh, M., B. Shinawatra, T. Onpraphai, P. Promburom, and C. Sangchyoswat. 1996. Role of spatial information in assessing resources of highland communities in northern Thailand. pp. 402–425. *In* CMU. 1996. Montane mainland southeast Asia in transition. Chiang Mai Univ., Chiang Mai, Thailand.

Ganjanapan, A. 1997. The politics of environment in northern Thailand: Ethnicity and highland development programs. pp. 202–222. *In* P. Hirsch (ed.) Seeing forests for trees: Environment and environmentalism in Thailand. Silkworm Books, Chiang Mai, Thailand.

Geran, J. 2001. Coping with crisis: Social capital and the resilience of rural livelihoods in northern Thailand. Ph.D. diss. Univ. of Wisconsin, Madison. (Diss. Abstr. AAT 3012508).

Gillison, A.N., and N. Liswanti. 2000. Biodiversity and productivity assessment for sustainable agroforest ecosystems: Mae Chaem, Northern Thailand Preliminary Report. Alternatives to Slash and Burn Project Above-Ground Biodiversity Assessment Working Group summary report 1996–99. ASB Coordination Office, ICRAF, Nairobi.

Grandstaff, T. 1976. Swidden society in north Thailand: A diachronic perspective emphasizing resource relationships. Ph.D. diss. Univ. of Hawaii, Honolulu. (Diss. Abstr. AAI 0326236).

Hilltribe Welfare Division. 1998. Highland communities within 20 provinces of Thailand, 1997. (In Thai.) Tech. Rep. Vol. 536:101/1998. Public Welfare Dep., Ministry of Labor and Social Welfare, Bangkok, Thailand.

Hirsch, P. (ed.). 1997. Seeing forests for trees: Environment and environmentalism in Thailand. Silkworm Books, Chiang Mai, Thailand.

Kaosa-ard, M. 1996. Valuation of natural resources and environmental degradation: A first step toward conflict resolution. pp. 290–297. *In* CMU. Montane mainland southeast Asia in transition. Chiang Mai Univ., Chiang Mai, Thailand.

Kaosa-ard, M. 2000. Ecosystem management in northern Thailand. Resources Policy Brief. Resources Policy Initiative, Institutions and Governance Program. WRI, Washington, DC.

Kaosa-ard, M., S. Pednekar, S. Christensen, K. Aksornwong, and A. Rala. 1995. Natural resources management in mainland southeast Asia. Thailand Dev. Res. Inst., Bangkok, Thailand.

Kunstadter, P., E. Chapman, and S. Sabhasri (eds.). 1978. Farmers in the forest: Economic development and marginal agriculture in northern Thailand. East–West Center Press, Honolulu, Hawaii.

Lapudomlert, P., P. Santadkarn, and K. Chunkao. 1974. Changes in organic matter after different period of clearing at Doi Pui Hill Evergreen Forest, Chiangmai. (In Thai.) Kog-ma Watershed Res. Bull. 18. Faculty of For., Kasetsart Univ., Bangkok, Thailand.

Limchoowong. S. 1994. Final report of the Sam Mun Highland Development Project, 1987–1994. Project AD/THAI 86/334–335. United Nations Int. Drug Control Program, Bangkok, Thailand.

Nawichai, P. 2000. Use of wild plants in Karen Women's livelihood systems. M.S. thesis. Chiang Mai Univ., Chiang Mai, Thailand.

Peters, J. 2000. Trends in land use systems in the Wat Chan area of northern Thailand in the 20th century: Development from the inside out. Proceedings of the International Symposium II on Montane Mainland Southeast Asia (MMSEA): Governance in the natural and cultural landscape, 1–5 July 2000 (CD-ROM). ICRAF, Chiang Mai, Thailand.

Prachoom, S., K. Chunkao, and N. Tangtham. 1974. Deterioration of some chemical properties of soils after clearing of hill evergreen forest. (In Thai.) Kog-ma Watershed Res. Bull. 20. Faculty of For., Kasetsart Univ., Bangkok, Thailand.

Pragtong, K., and D. Thomas. 1990. Evolving systems in Thailand. *In* M. Poffenberger (ed.) Keepers of the forest: Land management alternatives in southeast Asia. Kumarian Press, West Hartford, CT.

Preechapanya, P. 1996. Indigenous ecological knowledge about the sustainability of tea gardens in the hill evergreen forest of northern Thailand. Ph.D. diss. Univ. of Wales, Bangor.

Preechapanya, P. 2001. Folk knowledge about agroforestry ecosystems in watershed areas of northern Thailand. (In Thai.) Royal For. Dep., Bangkok and ICRAF, Chiang Mai, Thailand.

Renard, R., P. Bhandhachat, G. Robert, M. Roongruangsee, S. Sarobol, and N. Prachadetsu-wat. 1988. Changes in the northern Thai hills: An examination of the impact of hill tribe development work, 1957–1987. Res. Rep. no. 42. Res. and Dev. Center, Payap Univ., Chiang Mai, Thailand.

Rerkasem, K., and B. Rerkasem. 1994. Shifting cultivation in Thailand: Its current situation and dynamics in the context of highland development. IIED and Land Use Ser. no. 4. IIED, London.

Rerkasem, K., N. Yimyam, C. Korsamphan, C. Thong-ngam, and B. Rerkasem. 2002. Agro-diversity lessons in mountain land management. Mountain Res. Dev. 22 (1):4–9.

Revenga, C., S. Murray, J. Abramovitz, and A. Hammond. 1998. Watersheds of the world: Ecological value and vulnerability. The World Resources Inst. and WorldWatch Inst., Washington, DC.

Royal Forest Department. 1993. Thai Forestry Sector Master Plan, Vol. 5: Subsectoral plan for people and forestry environment. Royal For. Dep., Bangkok, Thailand.

Royal Project Foundation. 2002. GMS 2000: Proceedings of the International Conference on Sustainable Development by Science and Technology in Greater Mekong Subregion and Related Developing Countries. The Royal Project Foundation, Bangkok, Thailand.

Royal Project Staff. 1999. Annual Implementation Report, 1999. (In Thai.) Wat Chan Development Center of the Royal Project. Royal Project Foundation, Chiang Mai, Thailand.

Schmidt-Vogt, D. 1999. Swidden farming and fallow vegetation in northern Thailand. Geo-ecological Res. Vol. 8. Franz Steiner Verlag, Stuttgart, Germany.

Sheng, T. 1979. Watershed management and conservation farming in northern Thailand. Mae Sa integrated watershed and forest land use project, Chiangmai, Thailand. Working Pap. 11. FAO-FO-THA/76/001. FAO, Rome.

Suan Pah Sirikit Project. 2000. Summary of results of project implementation during fiscal year 1999. (In Thai.) Suan Pah Sirikit Project, Watershed Conserv. Div., Royal For. Dep., Chiang Mai, Thailand.

Tangtham, N. 1999. Hydrological roles of highland watersheds in Thailand. pp. 25–51. *In* B. Thaiutsa, C. Traynor, and S. Thammincha (eds.) Highland ecosystem management: Proceedings of the International Symposium on Highland Ecosystem Management, 26–31 May 1998. The Royal Project Foundation, Chiang Mai, Thailand.

Tan-kim-yong, U., S. Limchoowong, and K. Gillogly. 1994. Participatory land use planning: A method of implementing natural resource management. Sam Mun Highland Dev. Project. Watershed Conserv. Div., Royal For. Dep., Bangkok, Thailand.

Tanpanich S. 1997. Canopy structure and root architecture in Miang-based agroforestry systems. M.S. thesis. Chiang Mai Univ., Chiang Mai, Thailand.

TDRI (Thailand Development Research Institute). 1994. Assessment of sustainable highland agricultural systems. TDRI Natural Resources and Environment Program. TDRI, Bangkok, Thailand.

Thomas, D. 1996. Opportunities and limitations for agroforestry systems in the highlands of north Thailand. pp. 126–160. *In* Highland farming: Soil and the future? Proceedings of a forum, 21–22 Dec. 1995. MJU–K. U. Leuven Soil Fertil. Conserv. Project. Mae Jo Univ., Chiang Mai, Thailand.

Thomas, D. 1997. Forests for a dynamic kingdom: Support for the emergence of social forestry in Thailand. A report to the Ford Foundation. Ford Foundation, Hanoi and Bangkok, Thailand.

Thomas, D. 2001. Agroforestry systems research: Evolving concepts and approaches. pp. 277–303. *In* A. Patanothai (ed.) Rabobkaset pua kanjodkan sapayakorn lae pattana ongkornchumchon yang yangyuen (Agricultural systems for sustainable resource management and development of community institutions). Report of the First Thailand National Agricultural Systems Seminar, 15–17 Nov. 2000. Dep. of Agric. Res., Ministry of Agric. and Coop., Bangkok, Thailand.

Thomas, D. 2002. Managing agroforestry landscapes in mountain watershed regions. pp. 56–62. *In* GMS 2000: Proceedings of the International Conference on Sustainable Development by Science and Technology in Greater Mekong Subregion and Related Developing Countries. The Royal Project Foundation, Bangkok, Thailand.

Thomas, D., P. Preechapanya, and P. Saipothong. 2002. Landscape agroforestry in upper tributary watersheds of northern Thailand. J. Agric. (Thailand) 18(Suppl. 1):S255–S302.

Thomas, D., H. Weyerhaeuser, P. Saipothong, and T. Onpraphai. 2000. Negotiated land use patterns to meet local and societal needs. pp. 414–433. *In* X. Jianchu (ed.) Links between cultures and biodiversity: Proceedings of the Cultures and Biodiversity Congress 2000. Yunnan Sci. and Technol. Press, Yunnan, China.

Thong-ngam, C., B. Shinawatra, S. Healy, and G. Trebuil. 1996. Farmer's resource management and decision-making in the context of changes in the Thai highlands. pp. 462–487. *In* CMU. 1996. Montane mainland southeast Asia in transition. Chiang Mai Univ., Chiang Mai, Thailand.

Vincent, J., M. Kaosa-ard, and L. Worachai. 1995. The economics of watershed management: A case study of Mae Taeng. TDRI, Bangkok, Thailand.

Wangpakapattanawong, P. 2001. Ecological studies of reduced forest fallow shifting cultivation of Karen People in Mae Chaem Watershed, Northern Thailand, and implications for sustainability. Ph.D. diss. Univ. of British Columbia, Vancouver, BC, Canada.

Withrow-Robinson, B. 2000. The role and function of fruit trees and fruit tree-based agroforestry systems in a highland watershed in northern Thailand. Ph.D. diss. Oregon State Univ., Corvallis. (Diss. Abstr. AAT 3005538).

Withrow-Robinson, B., D. Hibbs, P. Gypmantasiri, and D. Thomas. 1998. A preliminary classification of fruit-based agro-forestry in a highland area of northern Thailand. Agrofor. Syst. 42 (2):195–205.

# V. CROSS-SITE COMPARISONS AND CONCLUSIONS

# 17 Land Use Systems at the Margins of Tropical Moist Forest

## ADDRESSING SMALLHOLDER CONCERNS IN CAMEROON, INDONESIA, AND BRAZIL

Stephen A. Vosti
*University of California  Davis, California*
James Gockowski
*International Institute for Tropical Agriculture  Yaoundé, Cameroon*
Thomas P. Tomich
*World Agroforestry Centre  Nairobi, Kenya*

A primary objective of Alternatives to Slash and Burn (ASB) research is to identify new combinations of policies, technologies, and institutions capable of simultaneously promoting three fundamental development objectives: poverty reduction, economic growth, and environmental sustainability (Vosti and Reardon 1997; Tomich et al. 1998b; World Bank 2001). To be successful in this effort, we must first understand why the currently predominant land use systems (LUSS) are more attractive to smallholders than existing alternatives. We must then measure the environmental and other consequences of each LUS. Then, if currently predominant LUSS are judged to be unsatisfactory with respect to one or more of the three objectives, alternative LUSS must be identified or developed. Finally, policymakers will need guidance regarding how to promote alternative LUSS: which policy instruments and institutional mechanisms should be used, how much policy action probably will be needed, and for how long this action will be needed to achieve and sustain desired changes.

Research aiming to address these issues must focus on the concerns of resource users, that is, farmers or farm managers charged with allocating scarce resources to best achieve household or firm objectives (Vosti and Witcover 1996; Reardon and Vosti 1997). Therefore, for a subset of the ASB meta-LUS, this chapter shifts the focus from environmental and agronomic issues to economic issues and the incentives and constraints faced by agriculturalists who manage and depend on the LUS for household food security, livelihoods, and profit.

The next section defines farmers' concerns more precisely and describes how the performance of specific LUSS with respect to farmers' concerns was systematically measured across all ASB sites. We then report assessments of LUS performance and labor needs and examine market-related impediments to the adoption of existing and alternative LUSs at ASB benchmark sites in Cameroon, Indonesia, and Brazil. The next section makes cross-site comparisons of LUSs and broader issues that influence LUS choice. The final section forecasts LUS adoption trends for each benchmark site.

# METHODS

## DEFINING LAND USE SYSTEMS

### Ranges of Land Use Systems

Deforestation is a primary concern at all benchmark sites, so for analytical purposes natural forest was considered the point of departure for all land uses. Grasslands, short fallow–cultivation systems, and pastures were included as reference points at the opposite ecological extreme. In between, a range of LUSs representative of systems at each site were selected: extraction of forest products; complex multistrata agroforestry; simple tree crop systems, including but not limited to monoculture; fallow–cultivation systems, which include the textbook version of shifting cultivation or slash-and-burn agriculture; continuous annual cropping systems, which may be monocultures or mixed cropping; and cattle production systems. This array of LUSs covers a gradient of meta–land uses often used by biophysical scientists to describe varying levels of disturbance of forest for purposes of agriculture (NRC 1993; Ruthenberg 1980; Angelsen and Kaimowitz 2001).

### Spatial Issues

The spatial scale at which LUSs are practiced can vary across systems and, for given systems, over time and across farmers or firms. To deal with this important issue, for each system at each site the observed (or projected) scale of general operation was identified and used in evaluating system performance and resource needs. For example, at one extreme, the short-fallow food cropping system in Cameroon was evaluated at an operational scale of 0.25 ha, whereas community-based managed forestry in Indonesia was evaluated at an operational scale of 35,000 ha. However, to allow for cross-system and cross-site comparisons, all reporting is done on a per hectare basis.

### Temporal Issues

Finally, LUSs vary in terms of their active growing periods, the number of times particular components of LUSs can be repeated on a given piece of land, and the necessary fallow periods. In order to correctly compare the performances and requirements of different LUSs, these temporal issues had to be considered explicitly and adjustments made to ensure that performances were measured over the same time horizons. For example, to compare a coffee production system with a 20-year cycle to a swidden agricultural system with a 10-year cycle, the latter's performance must be measured and appropriately discounted because given the choice between volumetrically identical harvests at two different points in time, farmers will always choose the earlier of the two cycles.

## MEASURING FARMERS' CONCERNS

A set of three socioeconomic parameters were used to assess LUSs from the smallholders' perspective: financial profitability, labor needs, and household food security (Tomich et al. 1998a, 1998b; Vosti et al. 2000). The results in this chapter rely heavily on Gockowski et al. (2001), Tomich et al. (2001), and Vosti et al. (2001b).

### Financial Profitability

Land use systems that generate inadequate profits will not be attractive to farmers. Financial profitability considers all establishment costs, and all cost and benefit streams associated with the production activities of each LUS, over the lifetime of each system. It then discounts these cost and benefit streams to arrive at summary measures (e.g., net present value [NPV], used in this analysis) that can be used to compare LUSs across and especially within benchmark sites. Private prices, those actually faced by farm households, are used in most NPV calculations presented here. Summary measures of financial profitability can be expressed in many ways; we express them in terms of two inputs critical to small-scale agriculturalists: returns to land and labor, reported in 1996 U.S. dollars. Returns to land represent the present discounted value of the net profits from land dedicated to a specific LUS, that is, the per hectare return a farmer would expect to earn from land allocated to a particular LUS, taking into account the stream of costs and benefits over time and valuing family labor used in that system at the market wage. Returns to labor represent the daily wage for family labor input to a system, that is, the average, daily wage that each family member involved in a given LUS could expect to earn from participating in it if all profits were distributed to family members as wages. Returns to labor that exceed the market wage suggest that an LUS will be attractive to family members or would justify hiring labor to operate it.

　　For these ASB sites it is important to point out that the costs and benefits of commercial logging operations that clear forest for agriculture are not included in the calculations of the returns to the LUS at some sites because the one-time value of timber extracted as a byproduct of land clearing often exceeds the value of the derived land use and would obscure differences in profitability between the derived land uses. Moreover, in most cases smallholders do not reap the full benefits of timber extraction.

## Labor Needs

In labor-scarce rural economies or where labor markets are underdeveloped, labor needs are an important determinant of LUS attractiveness. The LUSs that continually entail more labor input than a typical rural household can provide or hire may not be attractive, especially if these systems provide low returns to labor. Of primary concern for ASB was the labor input needed to maintain a given LUS once established, so the adopted measure of LUS labor needs was the time-averaged labor input (measured in person-days) during the operational phase. Moreover, competition for family labor between traditional cropping systems and alternative LUSs can exist; if this competition was likely to be substantial, labor need numbers appearing in the tables in this chapter were set in boldface type. Labor needs for establishing some LUSs can also be very high and therefore reduce system overall attractiveness; data on labor needed for LUS establishment are available but are not presented here.

## Household Food Security

Even if an LUS is financially profitable and feasible given household labor constraints and labor market conditions, it may be too risky either in terms of variability in food yields or as a source of income to exchange for food. To identify LUSs for which increased food security risk might be an issue, we adopted an indicator based on Sen's (1982) concept of risk of food entitlement failure that encompasses trade-based and production-based entitlements to food. A system of indicators identifies the key paths households adopting a particular LUS would use to gain access to food: Is food derived from one's own production, is food purchased with the proceeds of the production and sale of nonfood commodities or wage labor, or is access to food accomplished via some combination of the two paths? Once paths are identified, cross-LUS comparisons of food access can be made.

## POLICY DISTORTIONS, INSTITUTIONAL ISSUES, AND MARKET IMPERFECTIONS

Although the aforementioned measures of the farmer concerns capture a great deal of the relative attractiveness of the different LUSs, they must be supplemented by assessments of distortions of incentives arising from national policies and assessments of the institutional setting, especially as regards markets for land, labor, capital, and commodities. For all these cases, trade and marketing policies affect prices received and paid by smallholders (often negatively) compared with what they would receive under free trade. These policy distortions of incentives are examined in detail in Gockowski et al. (2001) for Cameroon and Tomich et al. (1998b) for Indonesia. Assessment of the institutional setting is critical in developing countries for two reasons. First, markets are notoriously imperfect in rural areas and therefore can limit the robustness of standard quantitative assessments; for example, if capital markets routinely fail and credit is needed to establish some LUSs, our estimates of returns to land and labor for these LUSs may be overstated. Second, because of structural adjustment policies and changing world trade regulations, national policymakers are less able to use blunt trade policies and therefore must rely increasingly on investments in institutions and organizations to promote development objectives (World Bank 2001). Consequently, cash-poor policymakers need guidance in setting institutional or organizational investment priorities, which can include support to fledgling organizations created to compensate for market failures.

As a first step in identifying LUSs that were likely to suffer from market imperfections, experts familiar with rural institutions at each benchmark site evaluated LUSs in regard to their dependence on input supply, output, labor, and capital markets and the ability of local and regional markets to meet the challenges posed by the potential expansion of given LUSs. What emerged was a series of market-specific flags (linked, respectively, to the markets just listed and abbreviated as *I, O, LB,* and *K* in tables 7.1 through 7.3) indicating that large problems with particular markets were likely to exist. Less important but still significant market-related problems are identified using lowercase letters.

## Cross-LUS Comparisons Using Policy Analysis Matrix

The policy analysis matrix (PAM) technique, originally developed by Monke and Pearson (1989), is the basis for calculating LUS financial profitability and comparing multiyear LUS budgets. We augment the PAM with LUS-specific labor needs, indicators for food security, and institutional concerns. The matrix framework used here to evaluate LUSs specifies LUS trajectories, including technology, land area, and time line associated with each system (matrix rows); defines indicators corresponding to different farmer concerns (matrix columns); and presents measurements of how well each selected LUS addressed each of the farmers' concerns (matrix cells). It should be noted that the matrices for each site take as given the agricultural and other policies in place at the time the analysis was performed and the socioeconomic conditions prevalent at the time and place of analysis (Vosti et al. 2000).

## RESULTS FROM ASB BENCHMARK SITES

In this section we present evidence on the financial profitability, labor needs, and market-related obstacles to adoption of selected LUSs at the three benchmark sites. For each site, we begin with a brief description of LUSs, present research results in PAM form, and discuss the implications of these results.

## CAMEROON

## Land Use Systems

Eight LUSs were evaluated and compared in the Cameroon benchmark area; two dominant slash-and-burn systems (listed first) involving crop–fallow rotations that together account for approximately 75 percent of all annual and biennial cropland (Gockowski et al. 1998) and six alternative perennial-based systems practiced at different levels of intensity and frequency and are described more thoroughly in chapter 14.

- Intercropped food field planted after a short (4-year) *Chromolaena odorata* (L.) R.M. King and H. Robinson fallow (abbreviated as "SF–annual food crop"). This semicommercial system is the most common LUS in the forest zone of Cameroon, is agronomically and commercially managed by women, and provides the bulk of the food consumed by households practicing it.
- Intercropped food field planted in a long fallow ("LF–forest crop field"). This LUS, comprising melonseed (*Cucumeropsis mannii* Naudin), plantain (*Musa* spp.), maize (*Zea mays* L.), and cocoyam (*Xanthosoma sagittifolium* Schott), all cultivated in a 15-year fallow field, became a major commercial alternative for cocoa farmers when cocoa prices collapsed in 1989.
- Intensive cocoa with mixed fruit tree shade canopy planted after a short (4-year) *Chromolaena* fallow ("SF–intensive cacao w/fruit"). This cacao-based system includes avocado (*Persea americana* Miller), mango (*Mangifera indica* L.), African plum (*Dacryodes edulis* [G. Don] H.J. Lam), and mandarin orange (*Citrus reticulata* Blanco), all of which can provide significant secondary revenues when location permits access to urban markets (Duguma et al. 2001).
- Intensive cocoa with shade canopy planted after a short (4-year) *Chromolaena* fallow ("SF–intensive cocoa w/o fruit"). This is essentially the same LUS as the short-fallow intensive cacao with fruit, except that fruit trees are not a commercial component because of limited market access.
- Extensive cocoa with mixed fruit tree shade canopy planted to forest land or long fallow ("FOR–extensive cocoa w/fruit"). This system represents the extensive cocoa production systems more characteristic of the less populated areas of the benchmark site that enjoy good market access.
- Extensive cocoa with shade canopy planted to forest land or long fallow ("FOR–extensive cocoa w/o fruit"). This is essentially the same LUS as extensive cocoa with fruit except that fruit trees are not a commercial component.
- Improved Tenera hybrid oil palm (*Elaeis guineensis* Jacq.) system planted after a short (4-year) *Chromolaena* fallow ("SF–oil palm"). In this LUS, oil palm is established in a 4-year *Chromolaena odorata* fallow with intercropped groundnuts, maize, leafy vegetables, and cocoyams during the first year; after the food crops are harvested a monoculture oil palm of the hybrid Tenera remains.

• Improved Tenera hybrid oil palm system planted to forested land or long fallow ("FOR–oil palm"). As in the case of short-fallow –oil palm, hybrid Tenera oil palm is produced in a monoculture. In this case, however, forested land is converted.

## Land Use System Evaluation and Performance

### Financial Profitability: Returns to Land

The more lucrative perennial crop systems tended to strongly dominate the two slash-and-burn systems (table 17.1, column 3). The NPVs per hectare were $283 and $623 for the traditional long- and short-fallow intercropped food systems, respectively, compared with $1409 and $1471 for the intensive cocoa and mixed fruit tree system and the hybrid oil palm system in forested land, respectively. Among the perennial crop systems, the extensive cocoa system was least profitable at $424 per hectare. Because per hectare profitability is measured on an annual basis and includes the fallow period, annual profitability of the slash-and-burn systems is significantly lower.

### Financial Profitability: Returns to Labor

The highest returns to labor were found in the oil palm system planted in forested land ($2.44 per person-day) and in the intensive cocoa system with fruit trees ($2.36 per person-day). (See table 17.1). Returns to labor in intensive cocoa with no fruit ($1.95 per person-day) and in the extensive cocoa with fruit ($2.13 per person-day) were similar to the official minimum wage ($2.17 per person-day for unskilled manual labor). Returns tended to lie below the official minimum wage for the short-fallow annual food crop system ($1.79 per person-day), the long-fallow forest crop field system ($1.70 per person-day), the extensive cocoa system without fruit ($1.63 per person-day), and the short-fallow oil palm system ($1.81 per person-day). Although the absolute differences in labor returns do not seem to be very substantial, the difference between the highest and the lowest return is about 40 percent.

This static view of financial profitability masks price volatility that characterizes agricultural and world commodity markets. For example, in 1997 the average farm-gate price per kilogram of cacao in southern Cameroon varied from 600 to 700 Central African francs (fCFA), whereas in 1996 producers received 350 to 400 fCFA per ton. At 400 fCFA per ton of cocoa, the return to labor for the short-fallow intensive cocoa system with fruit fell to $1.58 from $2.36 per person-day.

### Labor Needs

Person-days of labor needed to operate a hectare of each selected LUS, once they are established, are presented in table 17.1. The systems using the least labor are the extensive cocoa without fruit (43 person-days/ha/yr) and the long-fallow forest crop field (44 person-days/ha/yr). The labor needs of the crop–fallow system are averaged over the entire rotation and therefore are artificially low in table 17.1. If one were to consider only the cropping phase, it would take 731 person-days of labor per hectare

*Table 17.1* Land Use System Performance and Resource Inputs at the Cameroon Site

| Land Use System | | Financial Profitability[a] | | Labor Needs | Household Food Security | Institutional Issues |
|---|---|---|---|---|---|---|
| | Scale of Operation (ha) | Returns to Land (US $/ha) | Returns to Labor (wage setting NPV = 0) (US $/person-day) | Operational Phase (person-day/ ha/yr) | Food Entitlement Paths[b] | Market Imperfections[c] |
| SF–annual food crop | 0.25 | 623 | 1.79 | 115 | op, ex | lb |
| LF–forest crop field | 0.25 | 283 | 1.70 | 44 | op, ex | o, lb |
| SF–intensive cocoa w/fruit | 1.30 | 1409 | 2.36 | 97 | op, ex | I, o, lb, K |
| SF–intensive cocoa w/o fruit | 1.30 | 889 | 1.95 | 95 | op, ex | I, o, lb, K |
| FOR–extensive cocoa w/fruit | 1.30 | 943 | 2.13 | 46 | op, ex | i, o, k |
| FOR–extensive cocoa w/o fruit | 1.30 | 424 | 1.63 | 43 | ex only | i, o, k |
| SF–oil palm | 1.00 | 736 | 1.81 | 71 | op, ex | I, O, lb, K |
| FOR–oil palm | 1.00 | 1471 | 2.44 | 73 | op, ex | I, O, lb, K |

[a]A discount rate of 10% was used, and the opportunity cost of household labor was set at $1.21 per day. The local currency unit (fcFA) was converted at rate of 1 US $ = 577 fcFA. Each proposed system's socioeconomic indicators are based on optimistic yield parameters. Sensitivity analyses to establish lower ranges of profitability figures and to check robustness of results to observed swings in relative output prices and a range of discount rates are ongoing.

[b]For food security, "own production (op)" and "exchange (ex)" reflect whether the system generates food for own consumption or income that could be used to buy food; combined food entitlement paths are common.

[c]For institutional issues, letters indicate market imperfections judged to constrain LUS adoption (with uppercase indicating a serious problem and lowercase indicating a more minor difficulty), as follows: i, input markets; o, output markets; lb, labor markets; k, capital markets.

*Source:* Data derived from Gockowski et al. (2001).

to cultivate the long-fallow field crop, which helps to explain the small size (2500 m²) of the cultivated plots. The short-fallow annual food crop system and the intensive cocoa with fruit made the most intensive use of labor (115, which includes the 6 years of fallow, and 97 person-days/ha/yr, respectively). The extensive cocoa systems were the least labor demanding, at roughly half the labor needs of the intensive systems, and the oil palm systems were intermediate between the two types of cocoa-based LUS.

### Household Food and Health Security

In many areas of the Congo basin, rural food markets either do not exist or, if they do, are often periodic, and access is limited by transportation costs. As a consequence, most households at this site rely on own production to meet food needs. Household food security usually is not a major concern because of stable rainfall patterns and the safety net provided by extended kinship groups. In essence, the short-fallow annual food crop LUS provides the bulk of food consumed in the household and usually is planted with subsistence objectives paramount and commercial objectives only secondary (Gockowski and Ndoumbé 1999). The same subsistence objective is largely true of the long-fallow forest crop field. With one exception, that of extensive cocoa without fruit, all LUSs at the Cameroon benchmark site contributed directly (via own production) and indirectly (via production sales) to meeting food needs.

### Institutional Issues: Market Imperfections

The performance of input, output, labor, and credit markets exhibit wide geographic variation within the benchmark site, and LUSs vary in terms of purchased input intensity. That said, some consistent patterns regarding institutional obstacles to adoption emerged (table 17.1). The intensive cocoa systems are the most dependent on the reliable supply of agrochemicals. Intensive cocoa systems with fruit trees presume good access to urban fruit markets. In areas where access to market is difficult, the profitability of these systems will consequently decline. Labor market imperfections affected all intensive cropping systems.

Of note is that the oil palm systems face several market-related obstacles to broad adoption. First, the performance of these LUSs depends on the multiplication and distribution of hybrid palm varieties. Current capacity in Cameroon for producing pregerminated hybrid oil palm seed is low and in the hands of only a few suppliers, so prices are high ($0.42 per seed). By the time the seedling has spent a year in the nursery, farmers can expect to spend up to $400/ha on planting material alone. Second, three levels of postharvest processing technologies are commonly used: artisanal methods requiring almost no capital investment, small-scale manual and motorized turnscrew presses with some capital investment, and large-scale industrial processing with high capital investment. As operational scale increases, market development and market access become more critical. Third, export restrictions on palm oil during the dry season period drive down producer prices.

An additional constraint is that poorly maintained rural road networks in Central Africa contribute to high marketing margins that can lower farmgate prices in areas distant from markets (e.g., low-value, bulky fruits from cocoa agroforests) to the point that these enterprises are no longer commercially viable. The high costs of marketing in Central Africa reduce its competitiveness in world markets, with negative implications for consumer and producer welfare and the adoption of agroforest-based LUSs.

## INDONESIA

### Land Use Systems Evaluated

The eight Sumatran land use systems examined in this section are presented here. For an overview of LUSs, the driving forces that promote and sustain them, and their environmental consequences, see van Noordwijk et al. (1995), Tomich et al. (1998b), and Tomich et al. (2001).

- Natural forest. These forests, though generally not pristine, have been undisturbed for at least 100 years and are not currently used for economic purposes. They serve as the reference point for assessing alternative LUSs, although they no longer are common in the benchmark sites in Sumatra.
- Community-based forest management. This LUS is practiced on 10,000- to 35,000-ha blocks of common forest land managed by indigenous smallholders.
- Commercial logging. Concessions of 35,000 ha or more are logged for timber using a system based on a 20- to 25-year cycle that is generally practiced but probably does not meet sustainable logging criteria.
- Rubber agroforests. This is the dominant smallholder LUS and is an integral part of an indigenous landscape mosaic. One- to five-hectare plots of forest or existing rubber (*Hevea brasiliensis*) agroforest are cleared, and the land is planted to upland rice (*Oryza sativa* L.) and unselected rubber seedlings, with natural regeneration of forest species.
- Rubber agroforests with improved planting material. This is an experimental LUS based on traditional rubber agroforests but with the introduction of rubber clones with higher yield potential. One- to five-hectare plots were planted to upland rice and rubber clones, with regeneration of natural forest species.
- Oil palm monoculture. Practiced on estates of 35,000 ha or more, plantation oil palm is grown with substantial use of purchased inputs and wage labor, in close association with processing plants.
- Upland rice–bush fallow rotation. This shifting cultivation LUS was once practiced by most smallholders on 1- to 2-ha plots on community land as part of an indigenous landscape mosaic but is now almost nonexistent. The version of this LUS examined here consists of 1 year of upland rice followed by a short bush fallow of 5 years.
- Continuous cassava degrading to *Imperata* grasslands. Aside from irrigated rice production, continuous annual cropping is rare in Sumatra except in transmigration settlement sites. Estimates for continuous cassava (*Manihot esculenta* Crantz) mono-

culture degrading to *Imperata cylindrica* L. are reported here for comparison with other ASB sites. Smallholders cultivated 1- to 2-ha plots of monocrop cassava with little use of purchased inputs.

## Land Use System Evaluation and Performance

### Financial Profitability: Returns to Land and Labor

For the food crop systems, the upland rice and bush fallow rotation stands out as being unprofitable (negative US$62/ha), which helps explain its disappearance in most of Sumatra's peneplains. Cassava, on the other hand, may be among the most profitable of the technically feasible continuous food crop alternatives for the peneplains (US$60/ha), but its longer-run sustainability warrants further study (van Noordwijk et al. 1997b; chapter 6, this volume).

Returns to labor are highest for community-based forest management (extraction of nontimber forest products (NTFPs; US$4.77/d), but these high returns depend on the ability of existing local communities to regulate access and exclude outsiders. The low returns to land, US$5/ha, suggest that NTFP extraction is not a feasible alternative for large numbers of people because there is not enough land for everyone to practice this extensive livelihood strategy. These results should be interpreted with care because not all extractive activities were accounted for, which may bias profitability estimates downward. In particular, timber extraction (currently illegal and hence not reported) is likely to be significant, and tenure insecurity on State Land might have biased reported offtake of NTFPs. On the other hand, long-run profitability may be overstated because of unsustainable harvesting.

Several profitability estimates for commercial logging can be calculated, depending on the degree of compliance with government regulations. However, companies circumvent regulations on timber extraction, and most typically are vertically integrated firms producing products such as plywood for the export market. Therefore, the best profitability estimate for commercial logging is $1080/ha, valued at social prices that reflect world prices of forestry products.

Oil palm is widely viewed as the most profitable alternative for Sumatra's peneplains, and Indonesia's oil palm producers have the lowest unit costs in the world. Thus, it is no surprise that large-scale oil palm monoculture is among the most profitable alternatives in terms of returns to land and returns to labor, both of which are indicators of firm-level profitability, because the official wages for plantation workers are well below our estimates of returns to labor.

The two contrasting rubber agroforest systems produce a wide range of results. It is encouraging that returns to labor are almost identical to the market wage ($1.67 per person-day) for rubber agroforests planted with seedlings. Although these smallholders are the lowest-cost producers of natural rubber in the world (Barlow et al. 1994), returns to land at private prices are not much higher than for upland rice with a long bush fallow rotation and are well below those of oil palm monoculture.

Perhaps the most striking result in table 17.2 is the returns to land for rubber agroforests planted with PB 260 clones, which exceed those of large-scale oil palm monoculture (US$878 vs. US$114/ha). This system also produces attractive returns to labor. These are based on projections from farmer-managed trials and therefore should be interpreted with caution. However, these results support the idea that potential profitability of rubber agroforests planted with clonal material (and other smallholder agroforests planted with appropriate, higher-yielding germplasm) may be comparable to large-scale oil palm plantation monoculture.

### Labor Requirements

For the rubber and oil palm systems evaluated, total time-averaged labor needs are similar, ranging between 108 and 150 person-days/ha/yr. Harvesting labor is the biggest component in these systems. Because of lack of pronounced seasonality in much of Sumatra, harvesting of rubber and oil palm can go on roughly 10 months a year. The two extractive activities—community-based forest management and commercial logging—fall at the opposite extreme, with less than 1 person-day per hectare per year. Neither of these extractive activities nor the upland rice–bush fallow rotations, using 31 person-days/ha/yr, can provide many employment opportunities.

### Household Food Security

A wide range of household food entitlement paths were identified for Sumatra, from complete dependence on wage labor (commercial logging) to complete self-sufficiency in food production (upland rice production). The norm for Sumatran smallholders falls between these extremes, with some production for household food consumption supplementing income earned from sale of export commodities such as rubber.

### Institutional Issues: Market Imperfections

#### INPUT SUPPLY MARKETS

Markets for planting material are the greatest barrier to adoption of profitable alternatives by smallholders, as indicated by *I* in the final column of table 17.2 for clonal rubber and oil palm. For example, the Treecrops Advisory Service, almost the sole provider of rubber budwood, has focused its efforts on supplying planting materials to settlement project participants in the past and has largely ignored the much larger number of nonparticipants (Tomich 1991). The private nursery industry has only begun to develop in a few areas of Sumatra. For public and private sources alike, there are serious problems of reliability of quality of planting material, which is difficult to assess until several years after planting. Current delivery pathways for improved planting material and the information needed to use it seem inadequate, but direct government intervention to supply germplasm may be neither feasible nor desirable.

Table 17.2 Land Use System Performance and Resource Inputs at the Sumatra Site

| Land Use System | Scale of Operation (ha) | Profitability[a] Returns to Land (US $/ha, at private prices) | Returns to Labor (US $/d, at private prices) | Labor Requirements Time-Averaged Labor Input (person-day/ha/yr) | Household Food Security Food Entitlement Paths[b] | Institutional Issues Market Imperfections[c] |
|---|---|---|---|---|---|---|
| Natural forest | 25-ha fragment | 0 | 0 | 0 | NA | NA |
| Community-based forest management | 35,000-ha common forest | 5 | 4.77 | 0.2–0.4 | op, ex | o |
| Commercial logging | 35,000-ha concession | 1080[d] | 0.78 | 31 | Wages | O, K |
| Rubber agroforest | 1- to 5-ha plots | 0.70 | 1.67 | 111 | ex | — |
| Rubber agroforest w/ clonal planting material | 1- to 5-ha plots | 878 | 2.25 | 150 | ex | I, k |
| Oil palm monoculture | 35,000-ha estate | 114 | 4.74 | 108 | ex | I, o, K |
| Upland rice–long bush fallow rotation | 1- to 2-ha plots | (62) | 1.47 | 15–25 | op | — |
| Continuous cassava degrading to *Imperata* | 1- to 2-ha plots within settlement project/1 ha | 60 | 1.78 | 98–104 | op, ex | o, K |

NA, not applicable.

[a]A discount rate of 15% was used, and the opportunity cost of household labor was set at $1.67 per day. The local currency unit (Indonesian rupiah) was converted at rate of 1 US $ = Rp2400 (June 1997). Sensitivity analyses to establish lower ranges of profitability figures and to check robustness of results to observed swings in relative output prices and a range of discount rates are ongoing.

[b]For food security, "own production (op)" and "exchange (ex)" reflect whether the LUS generates food for own consumption or income that could be used to buy food; combined food entitlement paths are common.

[c]For institutional issues, letters indicate market imperfections judged to constrain LUS adoption (with uppercase indicating a serious problem and lowercase indicating a more minor difficulty), as follows: i, input markets; o, output markets; lb, labor markets; k, capital markets.

[d]Social prices were used in the case of commercial logging (see text).

Source: Data are derived from Tomich et al. (1998b, 2001).

## OUTPUT MARKETS

Government restrictions on marketing and international trade are the greatest barriers to development of smallholder timber-based alternatives and also hinder community-based forest management. Export promotion and job creation were the official rationale for these restrictions, but the main results were rent seeking and inefficiency. In 1998, the Indonesian government agreed to begin deregulation of timber exports, to abolish joint marketing associations that functioned as cartels, and to end export quotas and numerous other restrictive marketing arrangements. As export taxes are gradually reduced, private firms should be free to trade timber, but local restrictions on timber trade continue to be significant barriers.

Previous restrictive marketing practices also damaged most timber companies' marketing capacity by inhibiting development of marketing networks that could respond to buyers' needs. The situation is particularly bad for rattan because the export ban on raw rattan destroyed overseas markets and induced importers to seek alternate supplies.

In a largely ineffective quest to stabilize cooking oil prices, oil palm also has been subject to export taxes (set at 60 percent through the end of 1998) and at times to export bans that seriously depressed farmgate prices (Tomich and Mawardi 1995). For oil palm and cassava there also are some concerns about the structure and performance of local markets that are needed to link smallholders with processors. However, competitive market links seem to be emerging.

Local markets for natural rubber have functioned for a century or more. Although there are some imperfections affecting quality (e.g., difficulty of assessing dry rubber content), these markets transmit world price changes to the farmgate rapidly, and marketing margins reflect transport and other costs. Markets for natural rubber have been subject to few distortions from national policy, but at times the international buffer stock has depressed prices.

## LABOR MARKETS

Although the complete analysis also included skilled labor, the summary analysis presented here focuses on unskilled labor. Instead of hiring permanent skilled workers, smallholders may be more likely to develop certain technical skills themselves. So the relevant barrier is the acquisition of technical information rather than the market for skilled labor. Although labor markets in Sumatra fall short of the theoretical ideal, recent empirical studies (Suyanto et al. 1998a, 1998b) indicate that labor markets work reasonably well. It is worth noting that casual markets for skilled labor (e.g., chainsaw operators) also are emerging.

## CAPITAL MARKETS

Capital market problems are second only to planting material supply as a barrier to adoption resulting from market imperfections. Although no long-term institutional credit is available in rural Sumatra, household savings, which financed investments in existing smallholder agroforestry systems such as rubber agroforests, often are underestimated, and farmers are able to receive credit from informal sources (relatives, moneylenders). However, recent economic hardships may be straining these resources. Capital market imperfections may constrain smallholders' fertilizer purchases for cassava production and use of clonal rubber planting material and certainly are a barrier to the establishment of smallholder oil palm. Whether smallholder timber extraction is constrained by capital market imperfections depends in part on development of contract markets for chainsaw services and log transport.

# BRAZIL

## Land Use Systems Evaluated

Eight LUSs were evaluated at the ASB benchmark site in the western Brazilian Amazon (Souza and Homma 1993; Ávila 1994). Details of the LUSs can be found in Vosti et al. (2002), Fujisaka et al. (1996), Lewis et al. (2002), and Witcover et al. (1996b).

- Natural forest. Limited stocks of marketable products and limited smallholder knowledge regarding forest products generally combine to dramatically limit the number of sustainably harvested products extracted by smallholders from forests in this region. Currently, Brazil nut (*Bertholletia excelsa* Humb. & Bonpl.) extraction is the only major NTFP activity undertaken sustainably in forested areas.
- Managed forestry. This experimental LUS permits low-impact extraction of up to 13 m³ of timber from selected tree species per hectare per year, a rate and method judged by local foresters as conservatively sustainable over a 10-year cycle for a 40-ha tract; a different 4-ha plot is used for extraction each year (chapter 8, this volume). This LUS involves labor for felling, on-farm transport, and sawing of planks, explicitly accounted for here.
- Coffee–bandarra. This is a smallholder coffee (*Coffea canephora* Pierre ex Fröhner) production system averaging about 2 ha in which native bandarra (*Schizolobium amazonica* Huber ex Ducke), a quick-growing, native tree valued for its timber, is allowed to emerge, with some thinning to avoid excess shade. This LUS and the following are in initial stages of on-farm experimentation.
- Coffee–rubber. Similar to coffee and bandarra in scale, this LUS contains rubber trees planted among coffee trees; regeneration of native species is suppressed.
- Traditional pasture. Low-productivity, mixed cattle production systems, and the pastures needed to support them are the dominant LUS at the Brazil benchmark site. Traditional cattle breeds and grass-based pastures are most prominent, and the use of purchased inputs generally is limited to those needed to allow the marketing of beef and milk. Scale of operation can vary between 20 and 250 ha for smallholders. Large farm enterprises can practice this LUS on large scales, sometimes exceeding 50,000 ha.

• Improved pasture. Similar in scale to the traditional cattle–pasture system, the improved cattle–pasture LUS comprises more productive breeds of cattle, uses substantial amounts of fencing for pasture management, and makes much more intensive use of purchased inputs for livestock management. Beef and milk offtake increase substantially (Faminow et al. 1997; Vosti et al. 2001a).

• Annual–fallow. This LUS, constructed to provide a cross-site comparison, represents a swidden agriculture system that is rarely found in settlement areas at the benchmark site. Approximately 2 ha of forest is felled and burned, followed by 3 years of crop production (2 years of rice, bean (*Phaseolus vulgaris* L.), and maize (*Zea mays* L.) production followed by 1 year of maize and cassava production), after which the land is put to fallow for about 7 years. This cycle is repeated twice to fit into the 20-year time horizon to allow cross-LUS comparisons.

• Improved fallow. This system models that of experimental sites in the region and begins by felling approximately 2 ha of forest, followed by 2 years of annual crop production (rice, bean, and maize) after which land is place in a legume-based fallow for 2 years. The production cycle is repeated for LUS comparability.

## Land Use System Evaluation and Performance

### Financial Profitability: Returns to Land
The returns to land range from a low of –$17/ha for the annual crop–fallow system to a high of $2056/ha for the experimental improved fallow system. The least profitable LUSs (forest, –$2/ha and annual–fallow, –$17/ha) no longer exist in isolation from other LUSs. Indeed, the former is practiced only if the opportunity cost of labor is far below the market wage. The most common land use (traditional cattle and pasture) generated only $2/ha, but the more intensive version of this LUS (improved cattle and pasture) boosted returns to land to $710/ha. The small-scale managed forest scheme dramatically increased returns to land over the forest-based alternative (Brazil nut extraction, forest) to $416/ha. The coffee-based LUSs generated impressive returns to land: $1955/ha for coffee–bandarra and $872/ha for coffee–rubber. Finally, the highest returns to land (but not to labor) were found in the improved fallow system.

### Returns to Labor
In this labor-scarce environment, returns to labor would outweigh returns to land in farmers' decisions to adopt. Returns to labor estimates: ranged from $1 per person-day in the extractive forest activities to $22 in the improved livestock–pasture system (table 17.3). Systems at or below the average rural daily wage for unskilled labor of approximately $6.25 probably would not attract farmers, although imperfections in the labor market, seasonality of labor demand, and heterogeneity of labor type within a household make this less than a hard-and-fast rule. Indeed, the annual–fallow system that is no longer practiced yields slightly lower returns than working for wages. Traditional pasture–livestock production systems, the most prevalent in the study area,

yield slightly better returns than working for wages; the more labor-intensive systems yielded even more, with the higher of the two coffee-based systems (coffee–bandarra) bringing in about twice the wage and the improved pasture–livestock and managed forestry bringing in nearly three times as much as the traditional livestock system. Farmers more interested in returns to labor than to land would select improved pasture–livestock systems, whereas those more concerned with per hectare asset value (including improvements in the form of established production systems) might prefer systems scoring high on both counts, such as managed forest, improved fallow, and coffee–bandarra.

### Labor Requirements

An LUS with high returns to labor may simply be out of reach of small farmers in the area, given current labor scarcity and imperfectly functioning labor markets. The coffee–rubber system demands the most labor by far to operate, nearly 60 person-days/ha/yr. At the other end of the spectrum sits the low-level forest extraction systems in Acre, which take only about 1 person-day/ha/yr to manage. The system currently forming the end of the land use trajectory, traditional pasture, uses the least labor of any system other than the forest systems, approximately 11 person-days/ha, but its intensified version (improved pasture) needs just slightly more than this. Clustered at one-and-a-half to just over two times the labor needs of these systems are two other intensified systems (coffee–bandarra and improved fallow) and the annual–fallow LUS.

### Household Food Security

Forest extraction, small-scale managed forestry, and the two coffee-based systems share the characteristic that once established, they produce no food (table 17.3). To meet food needs, households adopting these LUSs will depend on markets for food and on product markets for Brazil nuts, timber, coffee, or rubber. The two cattle-based systems and the two food crop–based systems produce food and provide cash to exchange for food; the proportion of exchange to own production probably will be greater for cattle-based systems.

### Institutional Issues: Market Imperfections

The market for Brazil nuts has been functioning reasonably well for decades, and collecting nuts takes almost no skill or capital investment, so there are no flags in the market imperfections column for the forest LUS (table 17.3). All other LUSs presented obstacles to adoption linked to market imperfections.

#### OUTPUT MARKETS

Although markets for sawn timber have existed in the region for more than two decades, small-scale agriculturalists generally have not participated in it, either individually or in groups. Therefore, product quality and volume issues loom large for these new market entrants. Coffee markets have also existed for some time and continue to develop thanks to policy-induced expansion of area in coffee, especially in Rondônia (e.g., free

*Table 17.3* Land Use System Performance and Resource Inputs at the Brazil Benchmark Site

| Land Use System | Scale of Operation (ha) | Financial Profitability[a] | | Labor Needs[b] | Household Food Security[c] | Institutional Issues[d] |
|---|---|---|---|---|---|---|
| | | Returns to Land (us $/ha) | Returns to Labor (us $/ person-day) | Time-Averaged Labor Input (person-day/ ha/yr) | Food Entitlement Path (operational phase) | Market Imperfections |
| Forest (AC)[e] | 30 | −2 | 1 | 1 | ex | — |
| Managed forestry (AC) | 40 | 416 | 20 | 1.22 | ex | i, lb, k, o |
| Coffee–bandarra (RO) | 2 | 1955 | 13 | 27 | ex | i, o, lb, k |
| Coffee–rubber (RO) | 2 | 872 | 9 | 59 | ex | i, o, LB, k |
| Traditional pasture (AC) | 40 | 2 | 7 | 11 | ex, op | i, o |
| Improved pasture (AC) | 40 | 710 | 22 | 13 | ex, op | i, lb, k |
| Annual–fallow (AC) | 2.5 | −17 | 6 | 23 | ex, op | lb |
| Improved fallow (AC) | 2.5 | 2056 | 17 | 21 | ex, op | LB |

[a]A discount rate of 9% was used, and the opportunity cost of household labor was set at $6.25 per day. Prices are based on 1996 averages and expressed in December 1996 us $: us $1 = R1.04. Each proposed system's socioeconomic indicators are based on optimistic yield parameters. Sensitivity analyses to establish lower ranges of profitability figures and to check robustness of results to observed swings in relative output prices and a range of discount rates are ongoing. For example, for managed forestry, a less optimistic offtake of 10 m³/ha/ yr would mean returns to land and labor of R252/ha and R13.50, respectively, and only slightly less labor (1.2 person-day/ha/yr).

[b]For labor needs, a boldface number indicates competition for labor with other agricultural activities for a typical household.

[c]For food security, "own production (op)" and "exchange (ex)" reflect whether the lus generates food for own consumption or income that could be used to buy food; combined food entitlement paths are common.

[d]For institutional issues, letters indicate market imperfections judged to constrain lus adoption (with up-percase indicating a serious problem and lowercase indicating a more minor difficulty), as follows: i, input markets; o, output markets; lb, labor markets; k, capital markets.

[e]"AC" and "RO" refer, respectively, to the Brazilian states of Acre and Rondônia, where measurements on specific luss were taken.

*Sources:* Data derived from Vosti et al. (2001b) and Oliveira (2000b).

technical assistance and subsidized planting materials). Sufficient processing capacity for fluid milk exists in the region, but membership in a dairy cooperative (not available to all) is generally necessary to access this capacity.

## LABOR MARKETS

Imperfections in the labor market were considered a factor in adoption in all intensified systems, particularly the improved fallow. Seasonal shortages in unskilled labor especially hampered coffee-based production systems, and shortages of skilled labor probably would occur if more intensive LUSS were adopted.

## INPUT MARKETS

All of the more intensive systems also relied more heavily on purchased inputs, especially the improved cattle–pasture system. While markets for these inputs are developing, the private sector continues to focus on medium- and large-scale producers. Most systems needed at least periodic soil nutrient enhancements (e.g., chemical fertilizers); markets for these inputs are just emerging, and suppliers face staggering transportation costs. It is noteworthy that the market prices of purchased inputs generally do not include the costs of training to effectively use them; for example, cattle vaccines are readily available, but many smallholders do not know how and when to use them. Therefore returns to LUSS that depend heavily on such inputs may be overstated.

## CAPITAL MARKETS AND RISK

All nonforest LUSS entailed greater capital input (with the exception of the improved fallow system) and hence dependence on capital markets. In this frontier area, no informal systems of production credit are locally available; there are no established private banks or money lenders that provide investment capital for agriculture. The only formal sources of credit are the regional and federal banks that provide smallholder credit at subsidized rates, but nonprice rationing (allocation of credit based on something other than the cost of credit, that is, the interest rate paid by farmers) of capital effectively excludes most smallholders from routine borrowing. Moreover, all LUSS entail some production and price risk. To date, there are few institutional mechanisms for managing these risks. Therefore, LUSS that entail large outlays for establishment or purchased inputs for operation (e.g., improved pasture–cattle) may be perceived as more risky to smallholders and therefore less likely to be adopted by them (Vosti et al. 2002; Faminow et al. 1999).

All this said, as in the Cameroon case, market performance in the Brazilian benchmark site varies with distance to main roads and major cities. In hinterland areas transportation costs are high and vary enormously seasonally, so food, information, inputs, and products are much more expensive than in closer-lying areas, especially during the rainy season. More important for market performance, intermediaries capable of reducing overall costs and seasonal swings in costs generally are not in place in remote areas. Finally, small-scale farmers are much more likely to suffer from market imperfections than are their larger-scale counterparts because the latter can invest in private forms of transportation and communication.

# CROSS-SITE COMPARISONS OF LAND USE SYSTEMS AND BROADER ISSUES

In this section, we briefly examine the socioeconomic and policy elements of the ASB matrices for Cameroon, Indonesia, and Brazil side by side and then highlight cross-site similarities and differences in a set of broader issues that lie behind the matrices but affect land use choices.

## COMPARING ASB MATRICES

Comparing the LUS evaluation matrices for the three ASB benchmark sites reveals some interesting parallels and some differences. First, at the benchmark sites in Brazil and Cameroon, tapping the forest for anything but timber products generated very low returns to labor. This was not the case in Indonesia, where people involved in the sustainable offtake of NTFPS could expect to earn well above the market wage. The long-term success of this LUS makes it worthy of attention and support, but the sustainability of this LUS requires that extraction *not* be intensified. Moreover, spatially expanding this LUS within Indonesia is questionable, and the mechanism for replicating this LUS in other sites is unexplored. Second, using the market wage (at each site) as our guide, swidden agriculture is at best marginally profitable and will continue to exist only in areas where food markets fail or the cultural significance surrounding its practice is strong (e.g., Cameroon). Third, certain smallholder tree-based LUSs can increase returns to land and labor, but market-related impediments to adoption exist at all sites. Fourth, large agricultural enterprises (in Brazil and Indonesia today, perhaps in Cameroon in the future) may have comparative advantages in some aspects of production or (more likely) processing, but room for smallholder participation in many aspects of production surely exists; policy action should promote, not constrain, this participation.

## BROAD SOCIOECONOMIC ISSUES

### Market Imperfections

There was wide variation in the performance of markets across ASB sites: Indonesian labor and commodity markets and customary land tenure institutions worked well, but capital markets did not; even food markets, usually the first set of markets to develop, failed at certain locations in the Cameroon site, and the Brazil site occupied an intermediate position, with some markets functioning well (e.g., food from southern Brazil was commonly consumed in rural areas of the Amazon) and others (e.g., formal credit markets) performing poorly.

At all benchmark sites, institutions and infrastructure tend to be much better where population densities are higher. In these areas, farmers have better access to competitive markets system for purchased outputs and inputs, including hired labor. Moreover, traditional land tenure institutions in Cameroon and Indonesia seem to be evolving gradually toward individualistic land ownership, which in Cameroon is characterized by cadastral surveys and an increased incidence of land titling (IITA, unpublished data 1997). This trend can facilitate the development of land markets, which may be fundamental to LUS change in these areas.

However, several important caveats to this general trend in market development should be noted. First, better functioning capital markets do not generally spontaneously emerge alongside improved markets for products or other agricultural inputs, and informal credit systems that have developed (in Cameroon and Indonesia) often are not able to finance major changes in LUSs. Government action to date has failed to fill this important gap in investment capital; smallholder investments favoring noncapital inputs have been the result. Second, market development is never geographically uniform: Periurban areas generally benefit first, and some outlying areas may never benefit at all. Governments have a role in improving and extending the benefits of market development to all. Finally, the existence of well-performing markets is a necessary but not sufficient condition for market access; some socioeconomic groups clearly have preferential access to certain markets in each of the ASB benchmark sites (e.g., large-scale ranching operations in Brazil). Governments have a clear role in making market access more uniform across socioeconomic groups, too.

## Food Markets and Cultural Roles

When food markets fail to develop, smallholder households can become locked into LUSs that generate very low returns to labor (e.g., less than the market wage in Brazil and Cameroon). Policy action such as rice price stabilization in Indonesia reduced risks of specialization in export commodities and permitted households the flexibility to invest in more lucrative LUSs. At the same time, underdeveloped food markets only partially explain the persistence of the subsistence mixed food crop field in southern Cameroon, where gender plays fundamental roles in food security.

## Poverty

Poverty continues to persist widely at the Cameroon site but has been substantially reduced at the Brazil and Indonesia sites, in part because of the success of the LUSs that remaining smallholders have chosen to practice and the abandonment of agriculture by those who could not establish such systems. At all sites, however, although some farmers may have risen above abject poverty, many may still be unable to meet high establishment costs associated with some LUSs; that is, although they may have escaped welfare poverty, they still may be investment poor (Reardon and Vosti 1995).

## Scope for Policy Action

Dramatic differences were identified across the benchmark sites in the power and responsibilities of policymakers and the policy instruments and resources available to carry out their mandated tasks. For example, at the Brazil benchmark site a complicated patchwork (with gaps and overlaps) of responsibilities for maintaining rural roads has emerged, and no clear system of resource generation and disbursement has developed to match these responsibilities. Consequently, even vital transportation arteries can fall into disrepair. In Cameroon, the downturn in primary commodity markets for coffee, cocoa, cotton, and oil in the late 1980s plunged the country into a deep recession during which per capita incomes declined by more than 50 percent from 1986 to 1993. Accompanying the downturn was a shift in policy objectives and a drastic fall in public investments in vital sectors such as transportation, public health, education, and agricultural research and extension, all of which can influence LUS choice at the forest margin. Another factor influencing land use change in Cameroon and most of West Africa has been the rapid urbanization since the 1970s that has increased demand for staple food crops relative to the demand for perennial export crops. This switch has consequent environmental impacts because the LUSs associated with the tree-based systems provide many more environmental services than those associated with food crop systems.

As regards the management of forests, in all three benchmark sites management of public forests (e.g., parks, preservation areas, indigenous areas) is extremely difficult, primarily because of the vast areas involved and the lack of resources to do the job and also because local communities surrounding these areas often exploit the natural resources of the forest to invest and to survive. Under these circumstances, curtailing access to forests is expensive and can increase poverty.

Finally, and perhaps most important as regards policy action, at all benchmark sites, most of the fundamental economic factors driving LUS adoption were beyond the scope of local, regional, and sometimes even national policymakers. For example, in Cameroon the prices of coffee, cocoa, oil, and timber are of fundamental importance and are set in international markets. A similar situation exists in Indonesia for rubber, timber, and palm oil. In Brazil, farmgate prices of cattle products and food are set thousands of miles from the ASB benchmark site. All these prices, and the incentives and disincentives they pose to the adoption of particular LUSs, are largely beyond the reach of national and subnational policymakers (chapter 7, this volume), so the scope for policy action is narrowed.

## Forests and Economic Growth

The relative importance of forests in meeting national growth objectives varied widely across ASB countries. Cameroon's forest resources, one of the country's greatest riches, have played and continue to play a significant role in its economic growth and development. In the 1950s, 1960s, and 1970s conversion of approximately 500,000 ha of moist forests to smallholder coffee and cocoa agroforests resulted in equitable broad-based economic growth averaging 3 to 4 percent. In more recent years, timber exploitation has overtaken coffee and cocoa production as the most important economic activity in the moist forests. Cameroon is now the leading African exporter of tropical timbers, with more than $270 million in annual export sales. It is a poor nation, and at this stage in its economic development Cameroon has little choice but to develop its forest resources. From the standpoint of government policy, the critical question is whether Cameroon's tropical forests will be converted into sustainable agricultural and forestry production systems or mined into a state of degraded vegetation.

By contrast, Brazil is an industrialized country with a highly diversified economy. It is also in the globally unique situation of having two remaining agricultural frontiers: large savanna areas and huge forest areas. Is converting the Amazon to agriculture necessary to achieve national growth objectives? Probably not. Would converting the Amazon to agriculture contribute to national growth objectives? Probably so, but not without large environmental costs. Perhaps the more relevant question is whether converting the Amazon to agricultural is necessary to meet regional (i.e., Amazonian) growth objectives (Soares 1997). To this question the answer probably is "yes," although this objective probably would be better achieved by promoting intensive non–forest-based LUSs in areas with low rainfall and more pronounced and extended dry periods within the Amazon basin.

Indonesia probably occupies an intermediate position on this issue, despite macroeconomic upheaval in the late 1990s. Indonesia had experienced rapid economic growth, poverty reduction, and structural transformation from the early 1970s through the mid-1990s. The financial and monetary crisis of the late 1990s probably will be a temporary setback to absolute declines since the early 1990s in the labor force dependent on agriculture and the resulting decline in pressure on the natural resource base. However, as in Brazil (which crossed this turning point much earlier), there is great regional variation in these patterns, and although agriculture and forestry will play a declining role in the overall economy, they loom large in many regions.

## CONCLUSION

### LAND USE SYSTEM TRENDS

Against this backdrop of LUS performance and inputs and the institutional and other issues that underlie LUS choice and guide policy action, we now look forward at each benchmark site and predict trends in land use.

What will be the likely paths of LUS adoption in the three benchmark sites over the next two decades? Although changes in policy and economic factors could alter LUS adoption patterns, the following scenarios are likely to play out.

At all ASB sites, traditional swidden agriculture has or will soon disappear because of population pressure and low rates of return to labor. What replaces swidden agriculture varies across sites.

In Cameroon, the slash-and-burn annual cropping short fallow system is likely to increase in area in rough proportion to the increase in rural and urban population. However, in the absence of productivity-enhancing technical change, this system is increasingly unsustainable because of its shortened fallow. In locales with good market access, opportunities for commercial surplus production would be expected to lead to a proportionally greater expansion of these short-fallow systems than in areas with poor market access. Under current and foreseeable market conditions, the cocoa and oil palm perennial crop systems are the most profitable of the systems examined. Currently cocoa is not widely produced in the Congo basin but could be an important LUS, especially when the economies of Southeast Asian competitors such as Indonesia and Malaysia resume rapid economic growth and structural transformation. Moreover, input markets, liberalized since 1992, are better developed today. These factors will combine to increase the financial profitability of cocoa and increase the amount of land dedicated to intensive cocoa systems, a large proportion of which probably will come from a shift from extensive to intensive production systems. Whether there will be significant new land conversion to either extensive or intensive cocoa production is difficult to predict. Evidence indicates that West African smallholder producers of perennial export crops are price responsive, suggesting that some expansion in new planting area will occur if currently high world cocoa prices are maintained (Akiyami 1988; Gockowski 1994). If new plantings substitute for short-fallow land uses, net environmental gains are expected. On the other hand, if new planting occurs at the expense of secondary and primary forest, environmental losses will result. Given the choice, the producer normally will choose the latter in an effort to capture forest rents (Ruf 1995).

In Indonesia, large-scale oil palm plantations probably will continue to expand if government development strategies continue to discriminate against the emergence of independent smallholder oil palm producers. These strategies emphasized Nucleus Estate/Smallholder schemes that required marketing of tree products through project channels to repay credit. In addition, in some areas local authorities have attempted to prevent development of free markets in palm oil, which has retarded development of market outlets for independent smallholders.

In Brazil, several trends are likely. First, given labor scarcity, seasonality in production activities, and market imperfections (especially for capital and emerging cultivated tropical products), cattle production will continue to dominate the landscape (Faminow 1998; Faminow and Vosti 1998; chapter 10, this volume). Cattle production systems, especially pasture management, will become more intensive, primarily in response to increasing pressure on soils and market access needs. Technological change in pasture management (e.g., solar-charged, battery-powered electric fences; see Melado 2003) are expected to facilitate this trend. Coffee and other tree-based systems will continue to be adopted and will occupy small amounts of farm land but large amounts of household labor. With sufficient technical assistance and capital, and with effective and efficient monitoring, small-scale managed forestry could become an important LUS (chapter 8, this volume), with very broad environmental impact. Finally, given scale economies in managing some existing LUSS (e.g., cattle production) and some emerging LUSS (e.g., managed forestry), it is likely that small-scale agricultural holdings will be consolidated.

Estimates of returns to land and labor presented in this chapter indicate that from a purely private perspective, returns to forest conversion are high at all benchmark sites. If no action is taken to identify workable options either to shift incentives for conversion or restrict access to the remaining natural forests, these rainforests will continue to disappear. Small-scale managed forestry (in Brazil), improved rubber agroforests (in Indonesia), and forest-based cocoa agroforests with fruit (in Cameroon) are all good candidates for increasing the returns to environmentally benign activities at these sites (and perhaps more broadly). But among these, only managed forestry shifts incentives for conversion.

## ACKNOWLEDGMENTS

We are indebted to collaborators at all three ASB benchmark sites for suggestions, insights, and clarifications and to the InterAmerican Development Bank, Asian Development Bank, Ford Foundation, Danish Agency for Development Assistance, United Nations Development Program Global Environment Facility, Australian Centre for International Agricultural Research, U.S. Agency for International Development, Rockefeller Foundation, and Center for Natural Resources Policy Analysis, University of California at Davis, for financial support.

REFERENCES

Akiyami, T. 1988. Cocoa and coffee pricing policies in Côte d'Ivoire. International Economics Department WPS 164, Washington, DC, the World Bank.
Angelsen, A., and D. Kaimowitz. 2001. Conclusions. In A. Angelsen and D. Kaimowitz (eds.) Agricultural technologies and tropical deforestation. CAB Int., Wallingford, UK.
Ávila, M. 1994. Alternatives to slash-and-burn in South America: Report of research site selection in Acre and Rondônia states of Amazon Region of Brazil. Alternatives to Slash-and-Burn Agriculture Programme. Conducted from 31 Aug. to 15 Sept. 1992. ICRAF, Nairobi.
Barlow, C., S.K. Jayasuriya, and C.S. Tan. 1994. The world rubber industry. Routledge, London.
Duguma, B., J. Gockowski, and J. Bekala. 2001. Smallholder cacao (Theobroma cacao Linn.) cultivation in agroforestry systems of West and Central Africa: Challenges and opportunities. Agrofor. Syst. 51 (3):177–188.
Faminow, M.D. 1998. Cattle, deforestation and development in the Amazon: An economic, agronomic and environmental perspective. CAB Int., Wallingford, UK.

Faminow, M., C. Dahl, S. Vosti, J. Witcover, and S. Oliveira. 1999. Smallholder risk, cattle, and deforestation in the western Brazilian Amazon. World animal review. J. FAO 93(1999/2):16–23.

Faminow, M.D., C.P. de Sá, and S. Oliveira. 1997. Development of an investment model for the smallholder cattle sector in the Western Amazon: I. Preliminaries. IFPRI, Washington, DC. Mimeo.

Faminow, M.D., and S.A. Vosti. 1998. Livestock–deforestation links: Policy issues in the western Brazilian Amazon. pp. 88–103. *In* A.J. Nell (ed.) Livestock and the environment international conference, Wageningen, The Netherlands. 16–20 June 1997. World Bank, FAO, and the Int. Agric. Centre, Wageningen.

Fujisaka, S., W. Bell, N. Thomas, L. Hurtado, and E. Crawford. 1996. Slash-and-burn agriculture, conversion to pasture, and deforestation in two Brazilian Amazon colonies. Agric. Ecosyst. Environ. 59:115–130.

Gockowski, J. 1994. Supply responses among smallholder producers of arabica and robusta coffee in Cameroon. Ph.D. diss. Univ. of Florida, Gainesville.

Gockowski, J., D. Baker, J. Tonye, S. Weise, M. Ndoumbé, T. Tiki-Manga, et al. 1998. Characterization and diagnosis of farming systems in the ASB Forest Margins Benchmark of southern Cameroon. IITA Humid Forest Ecoregional Center, Yaoundé. Resource and crop management research monograph. IITA, Ibadan, Nigeria.

Gockowski, J., and M. Ndoumbé. 1999. The economic analysis of horticultural production and marketing in the farming systems of the forest margins benchmark of southern Cameroon. Resource and Crop Management Research Monograph No. 27. IITA, Ibadan, Nigeria.

Gockowski, J., B. Nkamleu, and J. Wendt. 2001. Implications of resource use intensification for the environment and sustainable technology systems in the central African rainforest. pp. 197–217. *In* D. Lee and C. Barrett (eds.) Tradeoffs or synergies? Agricultural intensification, economic development and the environment. CAB Int., Wallingford, UK.

Lewis, J., S. Vosti, J. Witcover, P.J. Ericksen, R. Guevara, and T.P. Tomich (eds.). 2002. Alternatives to Slash-and-Burn (ASB) in Brazil: Summary report and synthesis of phase II. November 2002. World Agroforestry Center (ICRAF), Nairobi.

Melado, J. 2003. Pastagem ecológica: Sistema voisin silvipastoril. Agroecologia Hoje, Editora Agroecológica, Brazil.

Monke, E., and S.R. Pearson. 1989. The policy analysis matrix for agricultural development. Cornell Univ. Press, Ithaca, NY.

NRC (National Research Council). 1993b. Sustainable land use options. pp. 265–351. *In* National Research Council (ed.) Sustainable agriculture and the environment in the humid tropics. National Academy Press, Washington, DC.

Oliveira, M.V.N. d'. 2000b. Sustainable forest management for small farmers in Acre State in the Brazilian Amazon. Unpublished Ph.D. diss. Aberdeen Univ., Scotland.

Reardon, T., and S.A. Vosti. 1995. Links between rural poverty and the environment in developing countries: Asset categories and investment poverty. World Develop. 23 (9):1495–1506.

Reardon, T., and S.A. Vosti. 1997. Policy analysis of conservation investments: Extensions of traditional technology adoption research. *In* S.A. Vosti and T. Reardon (eds.) Sustainability, growth, and poverty alleviation: A policy and agroecological perspective. Johns Hopkins Univ. Press, Baltimore.

Ruf, F. 1995. Booms et crises du cacao. Les vertiges de l'or brun. Karthala, Paris.

Ruthenberg, H. 1980. Farming systems in the tropics. Clarendon Press, Oxford.

Sen, A. 1982. Poverty and famines: An essay on entitlement and deprivation. Oxford Univ. Press, New York.

Soares, O. 1997. Rondônia produz. Senado Federal PTB, Brasília, Brazil.

Souza Serrao, E.A., and A.K.O. Homma. 1993. Brazil. Country profile. *In* ed. National Research Council (ed.) Sustainable agriculture and the environment in the humid tropics. National Academy Press, Washington, DC.

Suyanto, S., K. Otsuka, and T.P. Tomich. 1998a. Land tenure and farm management efficiency: The case of smallholder rubber production in customary land areas of Sumatra. Agrofor. Syst. 52 (2001):145–160.

Suyanto, S., T.P. Tomich, and K. Otsuka. 1998b. Land tenure and farm management efficiency: The case of paddy and cinnamon production in customary land areas of Sumatra. Aust. J. Agric. Resource Econ. 45 (3):411–436.

Tomich, T.P. 1991. Smallholder rubber development in Indonesia. pp. 249–270. *In* D.H. Perkins and M. Roemer (eds.) Reforming economic systems in developing countries. Harvard Univ. Press, Cambridge, MA.

Tomich, T.P. and M.S. Mawardi. 1995. Evolution of palm oil trade policy in Indonesia, 1978–1991. Elaeis: J. Palm Oil Res. Inst. Malaysia 7(1):87–102.

Tomich, T.P., M. van Noordwijk, S. Budidarsono, A. Gillison, T. Kusumanto, D. Murdiyarso, et al. 1998b. Alternatives to Slash-and-Burn in Indonesia. Summary report and synthesis of phase II. ASB, ICRAF, Nairobi.

Tomich, T.P., M. van Noordwijk, S. Budidarsono, A. Gillison, T. Kusumanto, D. Murdiyarso, et al. 2001. Agricultural intensification, deforestation and the environment: Assessing tradeoffs in Sumatra, Indonesia. pp. 221–244. *In* D. Lee and C. Barrett (eds.) Tradeoffs or synergies? Agricultural intensification, economic development and the environment. CAB Int., Wallingford, UK.

Tomich, T.P., M. van Noordwijk, S.A. Vosti, and J. Witcover. 1998b. Agricultural development with rainforest conservation: Methods for seeking best bet alternatives to slash-and-burn, with applications to Brazil and Indonesia. Agric. Econ. 19(1–2):159–174.

van Noordwijk, M., K. Hairiah, S. Partoharjono, R.V. Labios, and D.P. Garrity. 1997b. Sustainable food-crop based production systems, as alternative to *Imperata* grasslands? Agrofor. Syst. 36:55–82.

van Noordwijk, M., T.P. Tomich, R. Winahyu, D. Murdiyarso, S. Suyanto, S. Partoharjono, et al. (eds.). 1995. Alternatives to Slash-and-Burn in Indonesia: Summary report of phase 1. ASB–Indonesia Rep. No. 4. ASB–Indonesia Consortium and ICRAF, Bogor, Indonesia.

Vosti, S.A., C.L. Carpentier, J. Witcover, and J.F. Valentim. 2001a. Intensified small-scale livestock systems in the western Brazilian Amazon. pp. 113–133. *In* A. Angelsen and D. Kaimowitz (eds.) Agricultural technologies and tropical deforestation. CAB Int., Wallingford, UK.

Vosti, S.A., and T. Reardon (eds.). 1997. Agricultural sustainability, growth, and poverty alleviation: A policy and agroecological perspective. Johns Hopkins Univ. Press, Baltimore.

Vosti, S.A., and J. Witcover. 1996. Slash-and-burn agriculture: household perspectives. Agric. Ecosyst. Environ. 58:23–38.

Vosti, S.A., J. Witcover, and C.L. Carpentier. 2002. Agricultural intensification by smallholders in the western Brazilian Amazon: From deforestation to sustainable use. IFPRI Res. Rep.

130. IFPRI, Washington, DC. Available at http://www.ifpri.org/pubs/pubs.htm#rreport (verified 7 Dec. 2003).

Vosti, S.A., J. Witcover, C.L. Carpentier, S.J.M. de Oliveira, and J.C. dos Santos. 2001b. Intensifying small-scale agriculture in the western Brazilian Amazon: Issues, implications and implementation. pp. 245–266. *In* D. Lee and C. Barrett (eds.) Tradeoffs or synergies? Agricultural intensification, economic development and the environment. CAB Int., Wallingford, UK.

Vosti, S.A., J. Witcover, J. Gockowski, T.P. Tomich, C.L. Carpentier, M.D. Faminow, et al. 2000. Working Group on Economic and Social Indicators: Report on methods for the ASB matrix. Alternatives to Slash-and-Burn Agriculture Research Programme, August 2000. World Agroforestry Center (ICRAF), Nairobi.

Witcover, J., S.A. Vosti, F.R. de Almedia Barbosa, J. Batista, V. Beatriz, G. Böklin, et al. 1996b. Alternatives to Slash-and-Burn Agriculture (ASB): A characterization of Brazilian benchmark sites of Pedro Peixoto and Theobroma. August–September 1994. MP-8 Working Paper No. 3. Environ. and Production Technol. Div. IFPRI, Washington, DC.

World Bank. 2001. World development report 2001/2002. Published for the World Bank by Oxford Univ. Press, New York.

# 18 Balancing Agricultural Development and Environmental Objectives

## ASSESSING TRADEOFFS IN THE HUMID TROPICS

Thomas P. Tomich
   *World Agroforestry Centre  Nairobi, Kenya*
Andrea Cattaneo
   *Economic Research Service, USDA  Washington, DC*
Simon Chater
   *Green Ink Publishing Services Ltd.  Buckfastleigh, Devon, United Kingdom*
Helmut J. Geist
   *Université Catholique Louvain  Louvain-la-Neuve, Belgium*
James Gockowski
   *IITA Humid Forest Station  Yaoundé, Cameroon*
David Kaimowitz
   *Center for International Forestry Research  Bogor, Indonesia*
Eric F. Lambin
   *Université Catholique Louvain  Louvain-la-Neuve, Belgium*
Jessa Lewis
   *Consultant  La Jolla, California*
Ousseynou Ndoye
   *Center for International Forestry Research  Yaoundé, Cameroon*
Cheryl A. Palm
   *The Earth Institute of Columbia University  New York*
Fred Stolle
   *Université Catholique Louvain  Louvain-la-Neuve, Belgium*
William D. Sunderlin
   *Center for International Forestry Research  Bogor, Indonesia*
Judson F. Valentim
   *Embrapa Acre  Rio Branco, Brazil*
Meine van Noordwijk
   *World Agroforestry Centre Indonesia  Bogor, Indonesia*
Stephen A. Vosti
   *University of California  Davis*

## MANY CONCERNS, CONFLICTING INTERESTS

This volume so far has presented numerous issues, opportunities, and concerns from specific national and thematic perspectives on tropical forests and deforestation. This chapter attempts to pull these together through analysis of tradeoffs across those various perspectives. And, indeed, everyone in the world seems to want something from tropical forests. Forest dwellers want to continue aspects of their traditional way of life based on hunting and gathering while improving the welfare of themselves and their families. They are losing their land to migrant smallholders, who clear small amounts of forest to earn a living by raising crops and livestock. Both these groups tend to lose out to larger, more powerful interests—ranchers, plantation owners, large-scale farmers, or logging concerns—whose aim is to convert large areas of forest into big money. Outside the forests is the international community, who want to see forests preserved for the carbon they store, which would otherwise contribute to global warming, for the wealth of biological diversity they harbor, and for the many other ecosystem services they provide.

Deforestation continues because converting forests to other uses is almost always profitable for the individual, household, or firm that engages in it. However, society as a whole bears the costs of lost biodiversity, global warming, smoke pollution, and the degradation of water resources. Every year the world loses about 13 million ha of tropical forest, an area more than three times the size of Belgium. None of the land use systems that replace this natural forest can match it in terms of biodiversity richness and carbon storage. However, the land use systems that replace the forest vary greatly in the degree to which they combine at least some environmental benefits with their contributions to economic growth and poor peoples' livelihoods. Therefore it is always worth asking what will replace forest (and for how long), both under the current mix of policies, institutions, and technologies and compared with possible alternatives, some of which may leave forests largely intact. In other words, what can and should be done to secure the best balance between the conflicting interests of different groups, including some who are poor and experience chronic hunger?

## FORCES DRIVING TROPICAL DEFORESTATION

Most often, blame for tropical deforestation falls exclusively on specific groups, such as smallholders practicing shifting cultivation or large companies growing plantation crops or raising cattle. Few studies have attempted to gain an overall picture of forest uses and users by evaluating and comparing the evidence from a large set of locations.

A review by Geist and Lambin (2002) has provided a framework for analyzing and classifying the causes of deforestation. They examined and compared the factors at work in 152 cases of tropical deforestation in Africa, Asia, and Latin America. They distinguish between the proximate causes of deforestation—human activities on the ground at local level—and the larger driving forces that underlie these activities. This is an improvement on previous thinking because it recognizes that the people in the front line of deforestation—those wielding the chainsaws or driving the bulldozers—do not make their decisions in a vacuum but are strongly influenced by macroeconomic and social factors operating at the national, regional, or global levels, factors over which they have little control.

In their analytical framework, four broad clusters of proximate causes (agricultural expansion, wood extraction, infrastructure development, and other factors) are linked to five clusters of underlying causes (demographic, economic, technological, policy and institutional, and cultural). In each case, the clusters are subdivided into more specific factors (figure 18.1). For example, agricultural expansion may take the form of permanent cultivation, shifting cultivation, cattle ranching, or colonization.

A mix of causes normally is at work when deforestation occurs. The review goes on to identify what it calls causal synergies: associations of proximate and underlying causes that help to explain deforestation more convincingly than previous single-factor explanations. Together with other recent research, the review by Geist and Lambin tells us much about the real causes of tropical deforestation.

Although agricultural expansion was found to be at least one of the factors in 96 percent of the cases, shifting cultivation of food crops by smallholders, so often thought to be a major cause, was in fact a minor contributor to deforestation. Other forms of agricultural expansion, such as permanent cropping and cattle ranching, appear equally or more significant in most regions, although the agroecological and policy factors influencing this cause of forest loss vary widely across regions—with very different pathways identified for the Amazon, the Congo Basin, and Southeast Asia—and even within regions across countries.

Far more influential than shifting cultivation, or indeed any of the proximate causes of deforestation, are the macroeconomic forces that create the incentives to which individuals respond. Often, these forces manifest themselves as shocks that destabilize the lives of poor people; for example, an increase in urban unemployment may trigger reverse migration into the countryside. These shocks punctuate longer periods in which social and economic trends bring about more gradual changes in the opportunities available to poor rural people, such as the steady growth of the international timber trade or of demand for livestock products and the steadily expanding ecological and economic footprint of distant city markets. The economic integration of forest margins and the continual development of product and labor markets that accompany this process are factors at work in almost all cases.

Strongly associated with the influence of macroeconomic forces is the building of roads. Often paid for by logging companies or through international aid, new roads open up forest areas first for wood extraction and then for the expansion of agriculture. New migrants colonize roadsides and use roads to obtain inputs and deliver their produce to markets. By linking forested areas to the broader economy, roads lower costs and increase returns of conversion and thereby heighten the sensitivity of these areas to changes in macroeconomic conditions.

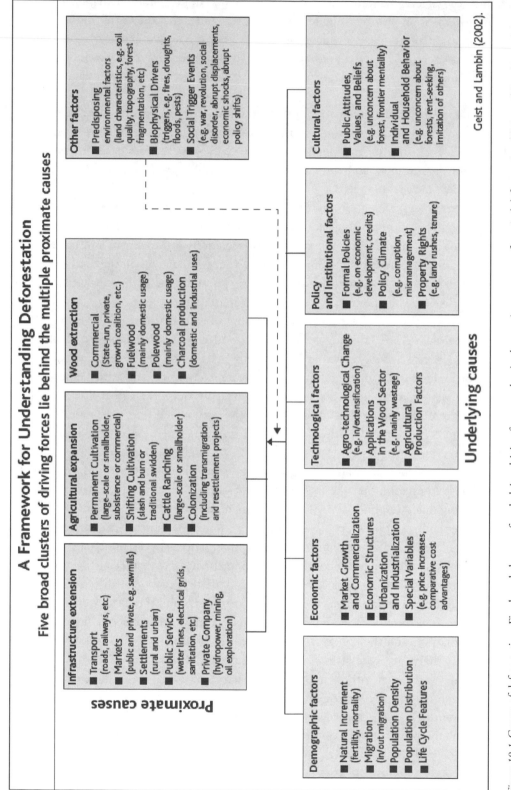

*Figure 18.1* Causes of deforestation: Five broad clusters of underlying driving forces underpin the proximate causes of tropical deforestation (Geist and Lambin 2002).

The findings of Geist and Lambin confirm those of the location-specific studies conducted by Alternatives to Slash and Burn (ASB) and by colleagues at the Center for International Forestry Research (CIFOR) in tropical forests of Southeast Asia, the western Amazon, and the Congo Basin, as shown in the following examples.

## BRAZIL: HOW MACROECONOMIC FACTORS AND ROADS COMBINE TO INFLUENCE DEFORESTATION

Logging, cropping, and ranching (not necessarily in that order) often are identified as the proximate causes of deforestation in the Brazilian Amazon. However, the underlying macroeconomic factors influencing these land uses, some of which can be addressed by policy change, are not often explored and have become more important as new roads have linked activities in the Amazon with other parts of the Brazilian economy.

For example, ASB researchers modeled the effects of various macroeconomic changes on the region's development (chapter 7, this volume; Cattaneo 2003). They found that a 40 percent devaluation of the Brazilian real against the U.S. dollar would lead to increases in deforestation of 6 percent in the short term and 20 percent in the long term, with an increase in logging of 16 to 20 percent. The production of annual crops and livestock would expand rapidly to fill the shortfall in national demand for foodstuffs as other regions switched to export crops. Building more roads—planned under a government development strategy for the region—would reduce transport costs by 20 percent, driving an increase in deforestation of 15 to 40 percent as the returns to cultivating arable land rose.

## CAMEROON: HOW MACROECONOMIC SHOCKS AFFECT FARMERS' ACTIONS

Cameroon is the only ASB case study country in which shifting cultivation appears as a significant proximate cause of deforestation (chapter 14, this volume). Yet even here, macroeconomic policies and economic shocks drive change. Cameroon provides a textbook case of how economic signals alter the attractiveness of different cropping systems to small-scale farmers, with major implications for deforestation rates (Mertens et al. 2000; Ndoye and Kaimowitz 2000; Sunderlin et al. 2000; Gockowski et al. 2001). From 1977 to 1985 Cameroon enjoyed an export-led boom based on oil, coffee, and cocoa. Migrants from the countryside flocked to take up jobs in the cities, while the rural population switched from subsistence farming to growing tree crops for cash. This boom period was followed by an abrupt decline in the second half of the 1980s as the country's oil ran out and the international prices of all three of its export commodities slumped. In 1989 shrinking export revenues forced the government to stop subsidizing agricultural inputs and to halve the prices of coffee and cocoa offered to farmers. These measures were followed, in the early 1990s, by imposed structural adjustment measures that resulted in draconian cuts in public sector employment and wages. Finally, Cameroon's currency was devalued in 1994.

The crisis had a dramatic effect on Cameroon's rural areas. Satellite imagery shows that in 1986 to 1996, annual deforestation had doubled over its 1973 to 1986 level in areas close to the capital city and quadrupled in more remote, thickly forested areas (Sunderlin et al. 2000). As the crisis deepened, rural–urban migration first slowed and then went into reverse as impoverished city dwellers returned to the countryside to take up farming. The population of rural villages grew by only 1.6 percent in the 1976 to 1987 period, but by 24 percent in 1987 to 1997 (Sunderlin and Pokam 2002). Most of the returnees put their efforts into growing food crops to ensure family food security and also produced some food for the market.

Existing farmers also grew more food crops while maintaining or expanding their area in tree crops in the hope that high prices would return. The switch to food crops, which was more pronounced in remote, thickly forested areas, greatly accelerated deforestation because food crops tended to be established on newly cleared land rather than on old plantations (Sunderlin et al. 2000).

Four other factors in the larger economy drove the expansion of food cropping: Demand for food crops rose as food imports declined during the crisis, the phasing out of subsidies for inputs forced farmers to cultivate larger areas to meet production goals, some flexibility in gender division of labor allowed an increase in labor inputs, and logging, which clears the way for food and cash crops, accelerated after the 1993 currency devaluation.

The Cameroon case reveals how the effects of macroeconomic forces are mediated by the responses of thousands of small-scale farmers. But it also shows that these forces affect the pace, location, and proximate causes of deforestation rather than whether it happens at all. In other words, changes in macroeconomic conditions can replace one cause of deforestation with another.

## INDONESIA: HOW MULTIPLE ACTORS JOSTLE FOR PROFITABLE OPPORTUNITIES

Forest conversion in Sumatra, Kalimantan (Indonesian Borneo), Sulawesi, and other "Outer Islands" of Indonesia involves a range of actors and objectives. Local smallholders, migrants, loggers, large-scale tree crop estates (including industrial timber plantations), and government-sponsored resettlement schemes (called transmigration) all play a role in forest conversion. A large volume of literature exists documenting aspects of land use, cover change, and forest conversion in Indonesia, but much of the data in these documents is unreliable or extremely difficult to interpret beyond the scale of case studies. So although smallholders often receive much of the blame for forest conversion, it is very difficult to place accurate numbers on areas converted by the various agents responsible for deforestation in Indonesia.

The island of Sumatra was chosen to represent the lowland humid forest zone of Asia for the global ASB project (Tomich and van Noordwijk 1996; Tomich et al. 1998b; Murdiyarso et al. 2002; chapter 13, this volume). Most of the ASB work in Sumatra has concentrated on benchmark sites in Jambi and Lampung provinces, both of which are located in Sumatra's broad peneplain agroecological zone. The peneplains have been the focus of government-sponsored transmigration schemes, large-scale logging, and various large-scale public and private land development projects since the 1970s.

As with Indonesia as a whole, there are too many holes and inconsistencies in the data to distinguish with any precision the impacts of the various actors, large and small, on deforestation in Sumatra. However, three broad conclusions can be inferred from an overview of the literature (Lewis and Tomich 2002), drawing particularly on extensive reviews of available evidence conducted by Dick (1991) and Holmes (2000) and cross-checked by ASB researchers using a geographic information system. Specifically, for the period 1980 to 1998, approximately one-quarter of total deforestation in Sumatra can be attributed to large-scale estates, and a roughly equal share can be attributed with some confidence to smallholder activity, although the available statistics probably skew this overall percentage downward. However, about half of Sumatran deforestation remains largely unattributable for that period, representing the actions and interactions of smallholders (both local and migrant), large-scale tree crop and industrial timber estates, medium-scale absentee investors in tree crop plantations, illegal encroachment on "protected" forest and clear-cutting of large-scale timber concessions, and periodic fires.

Dick (1991) and Holmes (2000) both concluded that deforestation resulting from individual actions of small-scale farmers was the most difficult category to assess for large areas. Moreover, the term *shifting cultivator* has been consistently criticized as being both misleading and inaccurate as a category of smallholder activity. This is particularly true in the case of Sumatra, where the textbook version of traditional shifting cultivation (annual crop rotations with bush fallow) had nearly disappeared by the 1990s (Tomich and van Noordwijk 1996). This is consistent with ASB researchers' estimate of very low returns to labor in shifting cultivation and attractive returns to tree crop–based systems (table 18.3 later in this chapter).

Three groups of smallholders were studied in detail in ASB research in Sumatra: local people, spontaneous migrants, and government-sponsored transmigrants. The general features of the livelihood strategies of these three groups are remarkably similar. Although food crops are produced after initial forest conversion, food production per se does not appear to be the primary objective. Hence, food production insecurity was not a major driving force in Sumatra in the 1990s. And although poverty clearly plays a role as a driving force, for reasons elaborated in this chapter, it is clear that certain measures to raise income run the risk of increasing deforestation. Thus, poverty alone is too simplistic an explanation, and numerous push and pull factors affecting migration must be considered.

Although shifting cultivation has largely disappeared in Sumatra, all households, whether local farmers, government-sponsored transmigrants, or spontaneous migrants, use slash-and-burn for land clearing. When slash-and-burn is used by smallholders in Sumatra's peneplains, it often is to clear and replant old rubber agroforests ("jungle rubber"). With increasing pressure on land, however, a method of "internal rejuvenation" by gap replanting appears to have become an attractive alternative to the slash-and-burn of rotational rubber systems (chapter 9, this volume). Migrants (mainly from Java) have been quick to adopt rubber-based systems similar to those developed and used by the indigenous Sumatran population since early in the twentieth century. The rapid spread of rubber as a smallholder crop in Sumatra since the beginning of the twentieth century has been a major force behind forest conversion.

Thus, deforestation caused by slash-and-burn by Sumatran smallholders has been driven in large part by profitable income-generating opportunities, specifically production of tree crops. Some of main lessons from Sumatra for the global ASB project are that some tree crop–based systems are economically attractive alternatives to extensive food crop–based systems, and these alternatives to slash-and-burn help to alleviate poverty. But, as pointed out by Angelsen (1999), these profitable alternatives also can speed up rather than slow down the rate of natural forest conversion because they attract an inflow of migrants seeking a share of the economic benefits of these systems.

It is revealing that Lampung Province is sometimes described as "North Java," indicating its role as a focal point for migration from densely populated Java. The movement of people between Java and Lampung, and additional efforts by government during various periods in the twentieth century, are key to understanding the landscape dynamics. Only a minority of residents of Lampung can claim Lampungese decent.

Macroeconomic forces fundamentally affect households' livelihood options and thereby reduce (or intensify) forces that push migrants to forest margins; macroeconomic, trade, and sectoral policies also affect resource management decisions once they get there. In times of rapid economic growth and industrialization, migration to urban and industrial areas has been a major escape route from rural poverty. A number of these migratory forces reversed during the Southeast Asian monetary crisis in the late 1990s. Beginning in August 1997, Indonesia had one of the greatest real exchange rate depreciations experienced by any country in the last half century. Simulations by ASB researchers using partial equilibrium models of financial returns to various land uses suggest that profitability of many tree-based systems (which produce commodities for export) increased substantially because of that exchange rate collapse, which would boost incentives for conversion of forests to tree crops by both smallholders and large-scale operators (Tomich et al. 1998b:101–102). A survey of more than 1000 households in the "Outer Islands" (Sunderlin et al. 2001) found that these farmers did significantly increase conversion of forest to tree crops during the monetary crisis. (Nevertheless, sample households felt worse off during the crisis, despite income from export crops.)

Jambi Province became a popular destination for migrants (more than 80 percent of whom are from Java) later than Lampung and only after completion of the

Trans-Sumatra Highway in the 1980s. Secondary roads built by logging companies, transmigration projects, and other large-scale actors contributed to forest conversion by making forest access easier for migrants. But construction of main roads such as the Trans-Sumatra Highway and other infrastructure investments probably had even more powerful effects on people's access to forest resources and the marketing links that condition land use choices. To examine the complex issue of the two-stage deforestation process in which smallholders "encroach" on logged-over forest, a sample of 9477 data points was drawn from lowland forest logged in Jambi in the 1980s using a 1-km grid and, following Chomitz and Gray (1996), a multivariate econometric model was used to control for biophysical differences and estimate effects of distances to main roads and rivers on probability of conversion to rubber agroforests and other uses. Site characteristics (soil and topography) were highly significant, indicating that smallholders are selective in their choice of sites. This model indicated that conversion of logged forest was much more likely within 10 km of main (asphalted) roads (Chomitz et al. 1999).

Deforestation by Sumatran smallholders also is driven by their desire to establish claims over land. Planting tree crops such as rubber is a well-established mechanism for securing informal land tenure in Sumatra. Where communal forest land has to be cleared before it can be claimed by individual families, this tenure arrangement accelerates forest conversion. Within smallholder communities, slash-and-burn followed by tree planting is the chief means to establish private claims over (formerly) communal land (Otsuka et al. 2001; Suyanto et al. 2001). This is one reason for the existence of extensively managed jungle rubber. In addition to direct effects on conversion, appropriation of large tracts of land for public and private projects can have important effects on smallholders' perception of their tenure security. Even the expectation of new projects can accelerate forest conversion as a preemptive strategy to retain control of land.

As emphasized earlier, smallholders are not the only actors converting forest, nor are they the only group using slash-and-burn in Sumatra. Forest concessionaires, industrial timber estates, tree crop plantations, and transmigration projects all have played a role too. Large-scale operators also use slash-and-burn because it is the cheapest method to clear land. Logging concessions, especially of the 1960s to 1980s, followed by an inflow of spontaneous settlers attracted by opportunities in rubber and other perennial-based agriculture, have completed the process to the point that there is hardly any lowland primary forest left.

## POPULATION PRESSURE FROM WITHIN AND OUTSIDE THE FOREST MARGINS

Deforestation has often been attributed to population growth per se—the growth resulting from location-specific human fertility. But the Geist and Lambin review, like the Cameroon and Indonesia case studies, shows that migration is a far more important factor: People move, as they have always done, to where the opportunities exist. But institutional and policy-related factors also can be significant underlying causes of deforestation via their effects on population movements. This category of policy-induced causes of deforestation includes colonization in Brazil, transmigration in Indonesia, and other government-sponsored resettlement schemes as well as public investment in transportation infrastructure, subsidies for farming, and policies and institutions affecting property rights, resource access, and land tenure.

At all ASB benchmark sites, managing interregional migration will be key to future land use patterns. Any technology or policy innovation that increases the productivity and profitability of farming in the humid forest region runs the risk that additional land and labor resources will be attracted to that particular activity and bring increasing deforestation. So far, in Cameroon, customary tenure institutions have been sufficiently robust to prevent large-scale interregional migration (Diaw 1997). However, traditional institutions are changing (rapidly in some cases) and cannot be relied on to solely (and peacefully) manage future population movements. Policy action to address these issues is exceptionally difficult.

## THE ASB MATRIX: LINING UP THE FACTS IN WAYS USEFUL TO POLICYMAKERS

Policymakers need accurate, objective information regarding the private and social costs and benefits of alternative land use systems on which to base their inevitably controversial decisions. To help them weigh the difficult choices they must make, ASB researchers developed a tool known as the ASB matrix (Tomich et al. 1998b; see also chapter 1).

In the ASB matrix, natural forest and the land use systems that replace it are scored against different criteria reflecting the objectives of different interest groups. To enable results to be compared across sites, the systems specific to each site are grouped according to broad categories, ranging from agroforests to grasslands and pastures. The criteria may be fine-tuned for specific locations, but the matrix always comprises indicators for the following:

- Two major global environmental concerns: carbon storage and biodiversity
- Agronomic sustainability, assessed according to a range of soil, nutrient, and pest trends
- Policy objectives: economic growth and employment opportunities
- Smallholders' concerns: returns to their labor and land, their workload, food security for their family, and startup costs of new systems or techniques
- Policy and institutional barriers to adoption by smallholders, including the availability of credit and improved technology, and access to and the performance of input and product markets

Over the past 10 years, ASB researchers filled in this matrix for representative benchmark sites across the humid tropics. (See tables 18.1, 18.2, and 18.3 for simplified matrices emphasizing quantitative indictors for ASB study sites in three countries; full sets of quantitative and qualitative indicators and complete explanations are available for Brazil in Vosti et al. 2001b and Lewis et al. 2002, for Cameroon in Kotto-Same et al. 2000 and Gockowski et al. 2001; and for Indonesia in Tomich et al. 1998b, 2001.) The social, political, and economic factors at work at these sites vary greatly, as does their current resource endowment, from the densely populated lowlands of the Indonesian island of Sumatra, through a region of varying population density and access to markets south of Yaoundé in Cameroon, to the remote forests of Acre state in the far west of the Brazilian Amazon, where settlement by small-scale farmers is recent and forest is still plentiful. At each site, ASB researchers have evaluated land use systems both as they are currently practiced and in the alternative forms that could be possible through policy, institutional, and technological innovations. A key question addressed was whether the intensification of land use through technological innovation could reduce both poverty and deforestation.

## UNDERSTANDING THE TRADEOFFS

The ASB matrix allows researchers, policymakers, environmentalists, and others to identify and discuss tradeoffs between the various objectives of different interest groups and to discuss ways of promoting land use systems that seem likely to benefit all groups but were not broadly adopted. The studies in Indonesia and Cameroon have revealed the feasibility of a middle path of development involving smallholder agroforests and community forest management for timber and other products. In Brazil, small-scale managed forestry poses the same potential benefits. Such a path could deliver an attractive balance between environmental benefits and equitable economic growth. *Could* is the operative word, however, because whether this balance is struck in practice depends on the ability of these countries to deliver the necessary policy and institutional innovations (see Tomich and Lewis 2001a, 2001b; Vosti et al. 2002, 2003).

Take the examples of Sumatran rubber agroforests and their cocoa and fruit counterparts in Cameroon. These systems offer levels of biodiversity that, though not as high as those found in natural forest, are nevertheless far higher than those in monocrop tree plantations or annual cropping systems (chapter 4, this volume). Like any tree-based system, they also offer substantial levels of carbon storage (chapter 2, this volume). It is also interesting to note that there are several tree-based systems in Cameroon with similar levels of carbon storage but drastically different profitability and hence attractiveness to farmers (table 18.2 and figure 18.2); this example clearly illustrates the value of the ASB matrix. Crucially, technological innovations have the potential to increase the yields of the key commodities in these systems, thereby raising farmers' incomes substantially, to levels that either outperform or at least compete well with almost all other systems. However, to realize this potential it will be vital to find

*Table 18.1* The ASB Summary Matrix for the Brazil Benchmark Site

| Land Use System | Global Environmental Concerns | | Agronomic Sustainability[a] | | | National Policymakers' Concerns | | Smallholders' Concerns and Adoptability by Smallholders | |
| | Carbon Storage | Biodiversity | Plot-Level Production Sustainability | | | Potential Profitability[b] | | Returns to Labor[b] | Household Food Security[c] |
| | Above-Ground t C/ha (time-averaged)[d] | Above-Ground Plants (no. species per standard plot) | Soil Structure | Nutrient Export | Crop Protection | Returns to Land (private prices, R/ha) | Labor Inputs (person-day/ ha/yr) | $/Person-Day (private prices) | Entitlement Path (operational phase) |
|---|---|---|---|---|---|---|---|---|---|
| Forests | 148 | 80 | 0 | 0 | 0 | −2 | 1 | 1 | NA |
| Managed forestry | ~148 | NM | 0 | 0 | 0 | 416 | 1.22 | 20 | $ |
| Coffee–bandarra | 56 | 27 | 0.5 | −0.5 | −0.5 | 1955 | 27 | 13 | $ |
| Coffee–rubber | 56 | 16 | −0.5 | −0.5 | −0.5 | 872 | 59 | 9 | $ |
| Traditional pasture | 3 | 10 | 0 to −1 | −0.5 | −0.5 to −1 | 2 | 11 | 7 | $, consumption |
| Improved pasture | 3 | NM | 0 to −1 | −0.5 | −0.5 to −1 | 710 | 13 | 22 | $, consumption |
| Annual–fallow | 7 | 34 | 0 to −0.5 | 0 to −0.5 | −0.5 to −1 | !17 | 23 | 6 | $, consumption |
| Improved fallow | ~3–6 | 26 | 0 to −0.5 | 0 to !0.5 | −0.5 to −1 | 2056 | 21 | 17 | $, consumption |

NA, not applicable; NM, not measured.

[a] For agronomic sustainability, 0 indicates no difficulty, −0.5 indicates some difficulty, −1 indicates major difficulty.

[b] Prices are based on 1996 averages and expressed in December 1996 reais (US $ = R1.04), discounted at 9% per annum.

[c] For food security, "consumption" and "$" reflect whether the technology generates food for own consumption or income that can be used to buy food, respectively.

[d] Indicates time-averaged above-ground carbon (see chapter 2, this volume).

*Sources:* Adapted from Vosti et al. (2001b), Gillison (2000a), and chapters 2, 6, and 17, this volume.

Table 18.2 The ASB Summary Matrix for the Cameroon Benchmark Site

| Land Use System | Global Environmental Concerns | | Agronomic Sustainability[a] Plot-Level Production Sustainability | | | National Policymakers' Concerns | | Smallholders' Concerns and Adoptability by Smallholders | |
| | Carbon Storage | Biodiversity | | | | Potential Profitability[b] | Labor Inputs | Returns to Labor[b] | Household Food Security[c] |
| | Above-Ground t C/ha (time-averaged)[d] | Above-Ground Plants (no. species per standard plot) | Soil Structure | Nutrient Export | Crop Protection | Returns to Land (private prices, $/ha) | Labor (person-days/ha/yr) | $/Person-Day (private prices) | Entitlement Path (operational phase) |
|---|---|---|---|---|---|---|---|---|---|
| Forest | 211 | 76 | 0 | 0 | 0 | NM | NM | — | $ |
| Oil palm | 61 | NM | -0.5 to -1 | -0.5 | -0.5 | 722–1458 | 93 | 1.81–2.44 | $, consumption |
| Extensive cocoa | 61 | 63 | -0.5 | -0.5 | -1 | 424–943 | 65 | 1.63–2.13 | $, consumption |
| Intensive cocoa | 61 | 63 | 0 | -1 | -1 | 889–1409 | 107 | 1.95–2.36 | $, consumption |
| Food crop–long fallow | 63 | 53 | -0.5 | 0 | 0 | 283 | 44 | 1.70 | $, consumption |
| Food crop–short fallow | 4 | 63 | -1 | -1 | -1 | 623 | 115 | 1.79 | $, consumption |

NM, not measured.

[a]For agronomic sustainability, 0 indicates no difficulty, −0.5 indicates some difficulty, −1 indicates major difficulty.

[b]Prices are based on the averages of the different establishment systems, from forest or fallow, for oil palm and whether fruits are sold in the cocoa systems and are expressed in Central African francs (US$ = 577 FCFA), discounted at 10% per annum.

[c]For food security, "consumption" and "$" reflect whether the technology generates food for own consumption or income that can be used to buy food, respectively.

[d]Indicates time-averaged above-ground carbon (see chapter 2, this volume).

Sources: Adapted from Gockowski et al. (2001), Kotto-Same et al. (2000), Gillison (2000a), and chapters 2, 6, and 17, this volume.

Table 18.3 The ASB Summary Matrix for the Indonesian Benchmark Sites

| Land Use System | Global Environmental Concerns | | Agronomic Sustainability[a] | | | National Policymakers' Concerns | | Smallholders' Concerns and Adoptability by Smallholders | |
| | Carbon Storage | Biodiversity | Plot-Level Production Sustainability | | | Potential Profitability[b] | Labor Inputs | Returns to Labor[b] | Household Food Security[c] |
| | Above-Ground t C/ha (time-averaged)[d] | Above-Ground Plants (no. species per standard plot) | Soil Structure | Nutrient Export | Crop Protection | Returns to Land (private prices, $/ha) | Labor (person-d/ha/yr) | $/Person-Day (private prices) | Entitlement Path (operational phase) |
|---|---|---|---|---|---|---|---|---|---|
| Forest | 306 | 120 | 0 | 0 | 0 | 0 | 0 | 0 | NA |
| Community-based forest management | 120 | 100 | 0 | 0 | 0 | 5 | 0.2–0.4 | 4.77 | $, consumption |
| Commercial logging | 94 | 90 | −0.5 | 0 | 0 | 1080[e] | 31 | 0.78 | $ |
| Rubber agroforest | 79 | 90 | 0 | 0 | −0.5 | 0.70 | 111 | 1.67 | $ |
| Rubber agroforest with clonal planting material | 66 | 60 | −0.5 | −0.5 | −0.5 | 878 | 150 | 2.25 | $ |
| Oil palm | 62 | 25 | 0 | −0.5 | 0 | 114 | 108 | 4.74 | $ |
| Upland rice–bush fallow | 37 | 45 | 0 | −0.5 | −0.5 | −62 | 15–25 | 1.47 | Consumption |
| Continuous cassava–Imperata | 2 | 15 | −0.5 | −1.0 | −0.5 | 60 | 98–104 | 1.78 | $, consumption |

NA, not applicable.

[a] For agronomic sustainability, 0 indicates no difficulty, −0.5 indicates some difficulty, −1 indicates major difficulty.

[b] Output prices are based on 10-yr (1988–1997) averages and expressed in U.S. dollars in 1997 (US $ = Rp2400 in 1997), discounted at 20% per annum.

[c] For food security, "consumption" and "$" reflect whether the technology generates food for own consumption or income that can be used to buy food, respectively.

[d] Time-averaged carbon from Tomich et al. (1998b) and chapter 2.

[e] Social prices, rather than private prices, were used for logging (see chapter 17, this volume).

Sources: Adapted from Tomich et al. (1998b, 2001), Gillison (2000a), and chapters 2, 6, and 17, this volume.

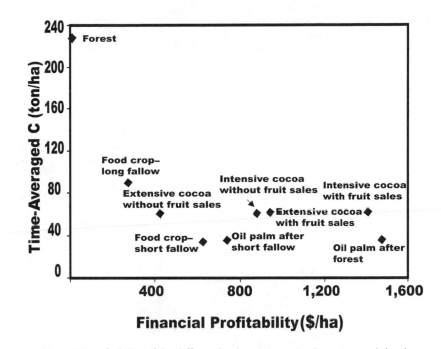

*Figure 18.2* Financial profitability of the different land use systems in Cameroon and the above-ground time-averaged carbon stocks. Adapted from table 2.2 and chapter 17.

ways of delivering improved planting material, the key input needed. Other obstacles to more widespread adoption of these agroforestry systems are the higher labor inputs compared with other systems (tables 18.1, 18.2, 18.3), the costs of establishment, and the number of years farmers must wait for positive cash flow (table 18.4).

In contrast, the Brazilian Amazon presents much starker tradeoffs between global environmental benefits and the returns to smallholders' labor. Here the most commonly practiced pasture–livestock system, which occupies most converted forest land, is reasonably profitable and provides the best fit for the situations and needs of smallholders but entails huge carbon emissions and biodiversity loss. Systems that are preferable to this one from an environmental point of view, such as coffee combined with bandarra (*Schizolobium amazonicum* Huber ex Ducke), a fast-growing timber tree, can pay better but have prohibitively high labor costs and are riskier for farmers. An alternative, "improved" pasture–livestock system, in which farmers are expressing interest, offers even higher returns to land and labor but only slightly improves biodiversity and carbon storage. In other words, the land use alternatives that are attractive privately are those most at odds with global environmental interests. Only a radical overhaul of the incentives (or disincentives) facing land users—including smallholders—is likely to change land use patterns.

Just how radical would the overhaul have to be? Depending on the policy instrument chosen, it would have to be very radical—even for a small effect—according to ASB research (Vosti et al. 2002). Consider, for example, the gathering of Brazil nuts

*Table 18.4* Establishment Costs and Years to Positive Cash Flow for the Different Land Use Systems for the A S B Benchmark Sites in Indonesia and Cameroon

| Meta–Land Use | Establishment Costs[a] ($/ha) | | Years to Positive Cash Flow | |
|---|---|---|---|---|
| | Sumatra | Cameroon | Sumatra | Cameroon |
| **Forest** | | | | |
| Managed | NA | NA | NA | NA |
| Logged | 352 | NA | 2 | NA |
| **Tree Crop–Based** | | | | |
| Complex | 117–1119 | 1188–1304 | 7–10 | 7–8 |
| Simple | 869–3350 | 1200 | 10 | 5 |
| **Crops–Fallow** | | | | |
| Short fallow | NA | NA | Never | NA |
| Annual crops | NA | NA | 2 | NA |

NA, not applicable.

[a] A calculated using private (financial) prices and discount rates of 10% for Cameroon and 20% for Indonesia.

*Sources:* Tomich et al. (1998b) and Kotto-Same et al. (2000).

(*Bertholletia excelsa* Humb. & Bonpl.) from the natural forest, one of the most environmentally benign uses of the Amazon's forests. Settlers in Brazil's Acre state clear forest gradually over the years, with pasture for cattle becoming the dominant land use. In addition, approximately 50 percent of farm families in the ASB study sample harvested nuts from the part of their farms that remained forested. Using a specially developed bioeconomic model, ASB researchers explored how labor, capital, and land would be allocated to different on-farm activities over a 25-year period under different price and market scenarios. When the model was used to examine the effects of changes in the farmgate price of Brazil nuts, researchers found that doubling the farmgate price of nuts would not decrease and might even increase the rate of deforestation because farmers probably would reinvest the extra cash they earned in clearing forest faster. This would be a sensible response from the farmers' perspective because, even at the higher Brazil nut price, cattle production would remain by far the more profitable activity. Only in the unlikely event that prices quadrupled over their current level might the rate of deforestation slow, but even then the braking effect would be slight and the modest saving in forest probably would be short-lived. At current prices offered to smallholders, Brazil nut harvesting pays well below the going rate for wage labor. The researchers concluded that subsidizing the price of Brazil nuts would not, by itself, be an effective policy measure for conserving forests, and even if it were effective, the highly charged political issue of paying for the subsidy looms large. Carpentier et al. (chapter 10) found a similar result with coffee systems in the Brazilian Amazon; policy-induced expansion of smallholder coffee production slowed but did not halt deforestation.

Research by ASB scientists of the Empresa Brasileira de Pesquisa Agropecuária (Embrapa) on the pasture–livestock system in the western Amazon of Brazil shows that, with a combination of legumes to enrich pastures and solar-powered electric fences to control the pattern of grazing by their cattle, smallholders could double milk production per cow, triple the carrying capacity of their land, and earn substantially higher profits. And because this pasture system is sustainable without annual burning to control weeds, seasonal smoke pollution would be reduced (see Tomich and Lewis 2002).

So why have these practices not been widely adopted already? First, most small-holders cannot get access to the necessary credit, seeds, or hired labor and are too far from markets to be able to sell the increased milk supplies. Second, aiming for these higher profits entails increased risk, in part because of the higher initial investment costs and the increased dependence on product and input markets. But even if these barriers were eliminated, widespread adoption of such improvements probably would increase—not decrease—the pressure on neighboring forests for two reasons. First, established smallholders probably would use increased profits to clear more forest for agriculture. Second, the greater profitability of the improved system would make the agricultural frontier more attractive to new settlers. Thus under the present mix of policies and institutions, and the incentives they create, the forests in Brazil's western Amazon will continue to fall whether the smallholder succeeds or fails, although the pace of forest conversion and the prevalence of poverty will vary depending on which of the two scenarios plays out.

A case in Lampung Province in southwest Sumatra provides a more encouraging example in which policy action has ensured the continuation of productive and sustainable agroforestry. The Krui people of the area grow rice (*Oryza sativa* L.) in permanent irrigated plots as their staple crop, whereas in the uplands they cultivate a succession of crops, building to a climax that mimics mature natural forest. The tall-growing timber species they plant include the damar tree (*Shorea javanica* Koord. & Valeton), a source of valuable resin that provides a steady flow of income over the long term. The Krui system is able to deliver broad-based growth in which the poor can participate. Combining environmental and economic benefits, the Krui system offers advantages over many other systems that replace or exploit natural forest.

In 1991 the Krui system came under threat. The Suharto government, which had a long history of appropriating traditionally managed land and reallocating it to public or private ownership, declared large areas of the Krui agroforests to be State Forest Land, a classification that would allow logging followed by conversion to oil palm plantations. A forestry company was awarded the right to harvest an estimated 3 million trees—trees that had been planted by the local people.

The Krui stopped planting damar and other tree species, saying that they would not resume until they were certain they would be able to reap the benefits of their work. A consortium of research institutions, nongovernment organization (NGOS), and universities was able to provide support to these local communities through convincing scientific evidence on the social and environmental benefits of the Krui system precisely when it was needed. The scientific evidence helped to legitimize the Krui system in the eyes of professional foresters and refute arguments by vested interests intent on taking the land. The consortium conveyed requests to the government from village leaders for dialogue on the status of their land, arranged field visits for key government officials, and organized a workshop to present research results and discuss the tenure issue. The activities of the consortium were reported in detail to the Minister for Forestry, who signed a new decree in 1998 reversing the official position. This historic decree declared the Krui system to be a unique form of forest use, recognized the legitimacy of community-managed agroforests in Lampung Province, and restored the rights of the Krui to harvest and market timber and other products from the trees they plant. The decree is a powerful instrument for restoring social justice and promoting sustainable development. In the short term it benefits at least 7000 families in the 32,000 ha of reclassified Krui lands. This principle of local management could be extended to benefit hundreds of thousands of rural Indonesians in similar areas. Although it would not work everywhere, Indonesian NGOs have identified at least fifty other communities across the archipelago that have developed production systems comparable to the Krui case that would be ripe for replication of this approach to reform.

## The Balancing Act

Based on these results and others presented in this publication, what can be done to balance the objectives of forest conservation and poverty reduction in these tricky settings? Some assert that the best opportunities for meeting both objectives lie in the harvest of various products from community-managed forests. In practice, such extensive systems require low population densities plus effective mechanisms for keeping other groups out if they are to prove sustainable. Where forests are converted, agroforests often represent the next best option for conserving biodiversity and storing carbon while also providing attractive livelihood opportunities for smallholders. However, for both economic and ecological reasons, no single land use system should predominate at the expense of all others. Mixes of land uses increase biodiversity at a landscape level, if not within individual systems, and also can enhance economic and ecological resilience. A mixed landscape mosaic is an especially attractive option in cases such as Brazil, where no single system (with the exception of the experimental small-scale managed forestry system) offers a reasonable compromise between profitability and environmental objectives.

   Where the productivity of the natural resource base has already sunk to very low levels, concentrating development efforts on the simultaneous environmental and economic restoration of degraded landscapes is an option well worth exploring. The precise mix of interventions needed—hence the benefits and costs of restoration— varies from place to place. In Cameroon, improved cocoa (*Theobroma cacao* L.) and fruit tree systems could be a win–win proposition in place of unsustainably short-fallow rotations (chapter 14, this volume). In Indonesia, millions of hectares of *Imperata* grasslands are the obvious starting point (chapter 11, this volume; Garrity 1997), as are the millions of hectares of degraded pastures in Brazil. The direction of change in land use systems determines the environmental consequences. For example, if farmers replace unsustainable cassava production with an improved rubber agroforest, they help restore habitats and carbon stocks. But if such a system replaces natural forest, the environment loses.

Intensification of land use through technological change is a two-edged sword. It has great potential to increase the productivity and sustainability of existing forest-derived systems, thereby raising incomes. By the same token, however, these higher incomes attract more landless people to the agricultural frontier in search of a better living. Therefore technological innovation to intensify land use may not be enough to stop deforestation. Indeed, it often can accelerate it (see Angelsen 1999; Angelsen and Kaimowitz 2001a). If both objectives are to be met, policy measures intended to encourage intensification must be accompanied by measures to protect those forest areas that harbor globally significant biodiversity.

# RESEARCH INNOVATIONS AND NEW DIRECTIONS FOR ASB

Numerous methodological and organizational innovations were necessary to analyze these tradeoffs between the concerns of poor households, national development objectives, and global environmental concerns. In its early phases, ASB focused on understanding and ultimately quantifying these contrasting perspectives. Standardized methods were used across sites to assess the environmental and agronomic sustainability of the various land use alternatives found on farms in each benchmark site, and participatory methods were used in the same sites to understand household problems, opportunities, and constraints. Similarly, consultations with local and national policymakers provided insights about their perceptions of problems, opportunities, and constraints. In this way, participatory research and policy consultations guided the iterative process necessary to identify and develop policy, institutional, and technological options that are workable and relevant. The ASB's multidisciplinary thematic working groups—on biodiversity, climate change, agronomic sustainability, and global synthesis of implications for policy, institutional, and technological options—developed new methods as needed and ensured that data were comparable across sites. They share a commitment to measurement techniques that are reliable, cost-effective, and therefore readily adoptable by national partners. The ASB researchers have developed and tested innovative indicators of above- and below-ground biodiversity, carbon stocks and greenhouse gas emissions, agronomic sustainability, returns to labor and other determinants of adoptability by smallholders, and national policymakers' concerns. These methods have been applied to a range of land use systems at ASB benchmark sites, and these integrated results enabled the analysts to the link global environmental benefits to sustainable land use alternatives. The basic concepts and methods were made available for education systems at postgraduate level (van Noordwijk et al. 2001b; Wunder and Verbist 2003).

Instead of supporting the simple sustainable–unsustainable dichotomy, ASB results indicate that a remarkably wide range of smallholder land use options can be agronomically sustainable and profitable, depending on the larger environmental and economic context. A key policy insight from this work is that these (locally) sustainable options differ significantly in their environmental impacts and their profitability and adoptability by poor households.

Much of the institutional innovation and reorientation necessary to produce this integrated assessment of tradeoffs and alternatives occurs at the national level as ASB scientists work with partners in national research systems to develop research strategies that combine environmental and development concerns. In Brazil, for example, scientists from Embrapa have taken the lead in incorporating the environmental insights derived from their collaborative work with ASB into Embrapa's agricultural research agenda. In addition, Embrapa scientists are achieving impact at the national level by assisting government officials as they set national priorities for sustainable agricultural and silvopastoral development in the Amazon. With the support of ASB research, Embrapa scientists also collaborated with Brazil's Ministry of Environment in designing a new Forest Code that will have large and widespread implications for Brazil's land use and deforestation policies.

Although no forest-derived system is a perfect substitute for the global environmental benefits of rainforest conservation, ASB results suggest that a middle path of development exists—involving smallholder tree-based systems and community-based and private forest resource management—that could attain an attractive balance between the environment and development. Whether this balance can be achieved depends on a range of policy and institutional innovations, including means to effectively protect natural forests and compensate households for foregone opportunities.

The ASB does not claim to have all the answers to these challenges in hand. However, by building on what is known about participatory research and development and by simultaneously considering the workings of coupled biophysical and socioeconomic systems, we feel that the various ASB consortiums can become vehicles for participation by diverse interests in the countries concerned. Examples include local community associations and conservation groups, local government and civic organizations, local and national NGOs, and policymakers and other officials at various levels.

Looking ahead, the ASB consortium plans to stick to its basic goals: to identify and articulate combinations of policy, institutional, and technological options that can raise productivity and income of rural households without increasing deforestation or undermining essential environmental services. However, the consortium recognizes it is both feasible and desirable to shift its emphasis as follows:

**From plot to landscape:** The ASB has made important contributions to clarification of tradeoffs between the welfare of poor rural households and global environmental concerns. However, hydrologic, ecological, and other more localized environmental services are a significant gap in this analysis in terms of impacts on local people, priorities of key policymakers, and their potential complementarity with global environmental objectives. The ASB will work to help fill this gap by developing replicable assessment techniques and policy-relevant databases on local environmental services that underpin the sustainability, resilience, and stability of rural production systems at various scales. These methods and databases will build on and extend ASB's repertoire of data and techniques to assess global environmental concerns, agronomic sustainability, household socioeconomic concerns, institutional options, and opportunities for policy reform. A working group on sustainable mosaics of land uses focuses and implements ASB's work in a broader landscape context.

**From prescription to dynamic adaptation:** The ASB works in a broader context of social, political, economic, and environmental change. Natural resource problems in the tropics are compounded by population growth, climatic shocks such as El Niño, and social, economic, and political turmoil. Clearly no single prescription can deliver a sustainable balance between human needs and environmental services under these shifting circumstances over time and space. The ASB will seek replicable ways to better meet the needs of various stakeholders for methods they can use to monitor and understand the impacts of ongoing change and develop workable responses under dynamic and uncertain conditions. A range of flexible tools—including participatory approaches, formal models, and practical methods to assess impact—will be identified and developed for communities, local government agencies, NGO activists, research managers, and policymakers and other officials. These diverse stakeholders can then better explore their options to influence the individual choices that ultimately determine the rate and pattern of land use change.

**From assessment of tradeoffs to management of inevitable conflicts:** The ASB's work to clarify tradeoffs between global, national, and local objectives is just the beginning, because achieving impact on natural resource problems depends on effective means to disseminate information to myriad stakeholders in forms they can use. But even more and better information is not enough because social and political mechanisms also are needed to address the inevitable conflicts between the interests of these stakeholders, who range from extractivists and farmers, to national research managers and policymakers, to environmental advocacy groups, multinational corporations, and international development agencies. Unless workable interventions can be identified and disseminated, the future in much of the tropics will include intensifying social conflicts over natural resources and environmental services. The ability to strengthen or create mechanisms for conflict management—between neighboring communities, upstream and downstream populations, and local, national, international, and global concerns—depends on a better understanding of collective processes of governance, including negotiation, identification, and implementation of incentive schemes and sanctions and monitoring and enforcement of agreements (van Noordwijk et al. 2001a). The ASB will seek to identify means and build capacities to manage inevitable conflicts between stakeholders at various scales, including mechanisms to compensate local people for foregone opportunities.

## CONCLUSION

The challenge of preventing deforestation is complicated by two facts: In some cases halting deforestation would increase poverty, and in most cases deforestation has no single cause that can be easily identified and tackled. Regarding poverty in forest margins areas, knowing how and how much the forest can help reduce poverty is an essential factor in policy decisions. Regarding the causes of deforestation, it generally results from a combination of different factors, so a mix of policies, rather than a single measure, will be needed. Careful identification of the factors at work in a given location will be a prerequisite for getting the mix right while minimizing the cost to other legitimate development objectives. However, a common and dominant theme for all ASB sites, despite the variability of their socioeconomic and biophysical conditions, is that small-scale farmers cut down tropical forests because current national and international policies, market conditions, and institutional arrangements either provide them with incentives for doing so or do not provide them with alternatives.

If the development community is serious about preventing deforestation, it must pay more attention to powerful macroeconomic forces that drive people to clear land for other uses. At present, these forces can swamp local conservation efforts: The area of forest cleared by successive waves of migrants, facilitated by the building of roads and driven by the lack of opportunities elsewhere in the economy, vastly exceeds the area "saved" by projects focusing on sustainable forest use by individual farms or villages. A major weakness of past conservation efforts is that they have routinely limited their activities to technical interventions at the local level while failing to tackle the larger policy and institutional issues that also determine success or failure. Changing the economic incentives to clear forest into incentives to conserve it will be extremely costly, not only in terms of the direct costs of changing incentives at the local level but also perhaps in terms of the opportunity costs of forgone economic growth. Indeed, the developing countries that still have large areas of natural forest are unlikely to design their macroeconomic policies solely to protect these forests, because they face other pressing development imperatives.

But without tangible incentives linked to the supply of global environmental benefits, people will continue to cut down tropical rainforests. Results from ASB research at all the benchmark sites show that it is futile to attempt to conserve forests in developing countries without addressing the needs and objectives of local people, poor or not. But how can the necessary incentives to conserve be put in place? Only a limited number of policy instruments have been tried, and there is still much to learn about what does and does not work. Part of the answer lies in the developing countries themselves, which can take measures such as securing land tenure and use rights. But should these countries have to shoulder the entire financial burden of forest conservation when all face urgent development imperatives, such as educating and vaccinating rural children?

If the international community wants the global benefits of rainforest preservation, it is going to have to pay some of the costs. Opportunities for changing tropical land use patterns through the Clean Development Mechanism of the Kyoto Protocol are being explored as one of many possible approaches to environmental service payments. In Latin America, pilot carbon sequestration projects implemented after the Earth Summit in Rio de Janeiro have demonstrated the economic feasibility of carbon storage by smallholders at costs likely to be attractive in a global carbon market (CIFOR 2000; also see Smith and Scherr 2002). The ASB research provides evidence of the potential responsiveness of Brazilian smallholders to payments for carbon storage and forest conservation (Carpentier et al. 2000). If an institutional framework can be designed to efficiently deal with the significant transactions costs and monitoring issues associated with such pilot projects, there is the promising possibility of internalizing some of the environmental costs and benefits of various agricultural land uses along the forest margins. This could help shift incentives toward more environmentally benign land uses and provide resources for addressing the many constraints to the adoption of these systems. Moreover, ASB research has already provided some guidance to the international community regarding where forests might be most cheaply preserved via these mechanisms and where the greatest amount of poverty alleviation might be achieved per conservation dollar spent.

## ACKNOWLEDGMENTS

We have benefited particularly from discussions with Arild Angelsen, Kenneth Chomitz, Polly Ericksen, Merle Faminow, Erick Fernandes, Dennis Garrity, Andy Gillison, Anne-Marie Izac, Stewart Maginnis, Pedro Sanchez, Mike Swift, Stephan Weise, Julie Witcover, and participants in the ASB "Synthesis and Linkages" working group. Support for elements of this work has been provided by the Global Environmental Facility, the Danish International Development Agency, the Ford Foundation, the Asian Development Bank, the Interamerican Development Bank, the Australian Centre for International Agricultural Research, Embrapa, and the governments of Indonesia, Japan, the Netherlands, and the United States. Portions of the text draw on ASB Policybrief no. 5 and no. 6 (Tomich and Lewis 2003a, 2003b).

REFERENCES

Angelsen, A. 1999. Agricultural expansion and deforestation: Modeling the impact of populations, market forces and property rights. J. Develop. Econ. 58:185–218.

Angelsen, A., and D. Kaimowitz (eds.). 2001a. Agricultural technologies and tropical deforestation. CAB Int., Wallingford, UK.

Carpentier, C.L., S.A. Vosti, and J. Witcover. 2000. Small-scale farms in the western Brazilian Amazon: Can they benefit from carbon trade? Environ. and Production Technol. Div. Discussion Pap. no. 67. IFPRI, Washington, DC.

Cattaneo, A. 2003. Balancing agricultural development and deforestation in the Brazilian Amazon. IFPRI Res. Rep. 129. IFPRI, Washington, DC.

Chomitz, K.M., D. Deborah, D. Hadi, F. Stolle, T.P. Tomich, and U.R. Wasrin. 1999. Dynamics of land use change in Jambi, Indonesia: Issues, data, and methods. Selected poster presented at ASA Annual Meetings, Salt Lake City, UT, November 1999. ASA, Madison, WI.

Chomitz, K.M., and D.A. Gray. 1996. Roads, land use, and deforestation: A spatial model applied to Belize. World Bank Econ. Rev. 10 (3):487–512.

CIFOR (Center for International Forestry Research). 2000. Forest carbon for local livelihoods. CIFOR, Bogor, Indonesia.

Diaw, C. 1997. Si, Nda bot and Ayong. Shifting cultivation, land uses and property rights in southern Cameroon. Mimeograph. IITA Humid Forest Station, Yaoundé.

Dick, J. 1991. Forest land use, forest use zonation, and deforestation in Indonesia: A summary and interpretation of existing information. Project Publ. EMDI, Jakarta.

Garrity, D.P. (ed.). 1997. Agroforestry innovations for Imperata grassland rehabilitation. Kluwer Academic Publ., Dordrecht, The Netherlands.

Geist, H.J., and E.F. Lambin. 2002. Proximate causes and underlying driving forces of tropical deforestation. BioScience 52(2):143–149.

Gillison, A.N. (coord.). 2000a. Above-ground biodiversity assessment working group summary report 1996–98. Impact of different land uses on biodiversity and social indicators. Alternatives to Slash and Burn Project, ICRAF, Nairobi.

Gockowski, J., B. Nkamleu, and J. Wendt. 2001. Implications of resource use intensification for the environment and sustainable technology systems in the central African rainforest. pp. 197–217. *In* D. Lee and C. Barrett (eds.) Tradeoffs or synergies? Agricultural intensification, economic development and the environment. CAB Int., Wallingford, UK.

Holmes, D. 2000. Deforestation in Indonesia: A review of the situation in Sumatra, Kalimantan, and Sulawesi. Unpublished draft report, the World Bank, Jakarta.

Kotto-Same, J., A. Moukam, R. Njomgang, T. Tiki-Manga, J. Tonye, C. Diaw, et al. (eds.). 2000. Alternatives to Slash-and-Burn in Cameroon. Summary report and synthesis of phase II. ASB Programme, ICRAF, Nairobi.

Lewis, J., and T.P. Tomich. 2002. Agents of deforestation in Sumatra: The big, the small, and the unaccounted (miscounted). Unpublished technical review. ASB Programme, Nairobi.

Lewis, J., S. Vosti, J. Witcover, P.J. Ericksen, R. Guevara, and T.P. Tomich (eds.). 2002. Alternatives to Slash-and-Burn (ASB) in Brazil: Summary report and synthesis of phase II. November 2002. World Agroforestry Center (ICRAF), Nairobi.

Mertens, B., W.D. Sunderlin, O. Ndoye, and E.F. Lambin. 2000. Impact of macro-economic change on deforestation in south Cameroon: Integration of household survey and remotely sensed data. World Develop. 28 (6):983–999.

Murdiyarso, D., M. van Noordwijk, U.R. Wasrin, T.P. Tomich, and A.N. Gillison. 2002. Environmental benefits and sustainable land-use options in the Jambi transect, Sumatra, Indonesia. J. Vegetation Sci. 13:429–438.

Ndoye, O., and D. Kaimowitz. 2000. Macro-economics, markets, and the humid forests of Cameroon, 1967–1997. J. Modern Afr. Studies 38:225–253.

Otsuka, K., S. Suyanto, T. Sonobe, and T.P. Tomich. 2001. Evolution of land tenure institutions and development of agroforestry: Evidence from customary land areas of Sumatra. Agric. Econ. 25:85–101.

Smith, J., and S.J. Scherr. 2002. Forest carbon and local livelihoods: Assessment of opportunities and policy recommendations. Occasional Paper no. 37. CIFOR, Bogor, Indonesia.

Sunderlin, W.D., A. Angelsen, I.A.P. Resosudarmo, A. Dermawan, and E. Rianto. 2001. Economic crisis, small farmer well-being, and forest cover change in Indonesia. World Develop. 29 (5):767–782.

Sunderlin, W.D., O. Ndoye, H. Bikié, N. Laporte, B. Mertens, and J. Pokam. 2000. Economic crisis, small-scale agriculture and forest cover change in southern Cameroon. Environ.
Conserv. 27 (3):284–290.

Sunderlin, W.D., and J. Pokam. 2002. Economic crisis and forest cover change in Cameroon:
The roles of migration, crop diversification, and gender division of labor. Econ. Develop.
Cultural Change 50(3):581–606.

Suyanto, S., T.P. Tomich, and K. Otsuka. 2001. Agroforestry management in Sumatra. pp.
97–143. In K. Otsuka and F. Place (eds.) Land tenure and natural resource management:
A comparative study of agrarian communities in Asia and Africa. Johns Hopkins Univ.
Press, Baltimore.

Tomich, T.P., and J. Lewis. (eds.). 2001a. Deregulating agroforestry timber to fight poverty
and protect the environment. ASB Policybriefs no. 3. ASB Programme, Nairobi.

Tomich, T.P., and J. Lewis. (eds.). 2001b. Putting community-based forest management on the
map. ASB Policybriefs no. 2. ASB Programme, Nairobi.

Tomich, T.P., and J. Lewis. (eds.). 2002. Reducing smoke pollution from tropical fires. ASB
Policybriefs no. 4. ASB Programme, Nairobi.

Tomich, T.P., and J. Lewis. (eds.). 2003a. Balancing rainforest conservation and poverty reduction. ASB Policybriefs no. 5. ASB Programme, Nairobi.

Tomich, T.P., and J. Lewis. (eds.). 2003b. Forces driving tropical deforestation. ASB Policybriefs no. 6. ASB Programme, Nairobi.

Tomich, T.P., and M. van Noordwijk. 1996. What drives deforestation in Sumatra? pp. 120–
149. In B. Rerkasem (ed.) Proceedings of the International Symposium on Montane
Mainland Southeast Asia in Transition. Chiang Mai Univ., Chiang Mai, Thailand.

Tomich, T.P., M. van Noordwijk, S. Budidarsono, A. Gillison, T. Kusumanto, D. Murdiyarso,
et al. 1998a. Alternatives to Slash-and-Burn in Indonesia. Summary report and synthesis
of phase II. ASB, ICRAF, Nairobi.

Tomich, T.P., M. van Noordwijk, S. Budidarsono, A. Gillison, T. Kusumanto, D. Murdiyarso,
et al. 2001. Agricultural intensification, deforestation and the environment: Assessing
tradeoffs in Sumatra, Indonesia. pp. 221–244. In D. Lee and C. Barrett (eds.) Tradeoffs
or synergies? Agricultural intensification, economic development and the environment.
CAB Int., Wallingford, UK.

Tomich, T.P., M. van Noordwijk, S.A. Vosti, and J. Witcover. 1998b. Agricultural development with rainforest conservation: Methods for seeking best bet alternatives to slash-and-
burn, with applications to Brazil and Indonesia. Agric. Econ. 19(1–2):159–174.

van Noordwijk, M., T.P. Tomich, and B. Verbist. 2001a. Negotiation support models for integrated natural resource management in tropical forest margins. Conserv. Ecol. 5(2).
Available at http://www.consecol.org/vol5/iss2/art21.

van Noordwijk, M., S.E. Williams, and B. Verbist (eds.). 2001b. Toward integrated natural
resource management in forest margins of the humid tropics: Local action and global
concerns. ASB Lecture Notes 1–12. ICRAF, Bogor, Indonesia. Available at http://www.
icraf.cgiar.org/sea/Training/Materials/ASB-TM/ASB-ICRAFSEA-LN.htm.

Vosti, S.A., E.M. Bráz, C.L. Carpentier, M.V.N. d'Oliveira, and J. Witcover. 2003. Small-scale managed forestry at the Brazilian agricultural frontier: Adoption, effects and policy issues. Paper presented at the CIFOR-sponsored workshop Forests and Livelihoods, Bonn, Germany, 19–23 May.

Vosti, S.A., J. Witcover, and C.L. Carpentier. 2002. Agricultural intensification by smallholders in the western Brazilian Amazon: From deforestation to sustainable use. IFPRI Res. Rep. 130. IFPRI, Washington, DC. Available at http://www.ifpri.org/pubs/pubs.htm#rreport (verified 7 Dec. 2003).

Vosti, S.A., J. Witcover, C.L. Carpentier, S.J.M. de Oliveira, and J.C. dos Santos. 2001. Intensifying small-scale agriculture in the western Brazilian Amazon: Issues, implications and implementation. pp. 245–266. *In* D. Lee and C. Barrett (eds.) Tradeoffs or synergies? Agricultural intensification, economic development and the environment. CAB Int., Wallingford, UK.

Wunder, S., and B. Verbist. 2003. The impact of trade and macroeconomic policies on frontier deforestation. ASB Lecture Note 13. ICRAF, Bogor, Indonesia. Available at http://www.icraf.cgiar.org/sea/Training/Materials/ASB-TM/ASB-ICRAFSEA-LN.htm.

# Index